Tibet

Bradley Mayhew
Robert Kelly
John Vincent Bellezza

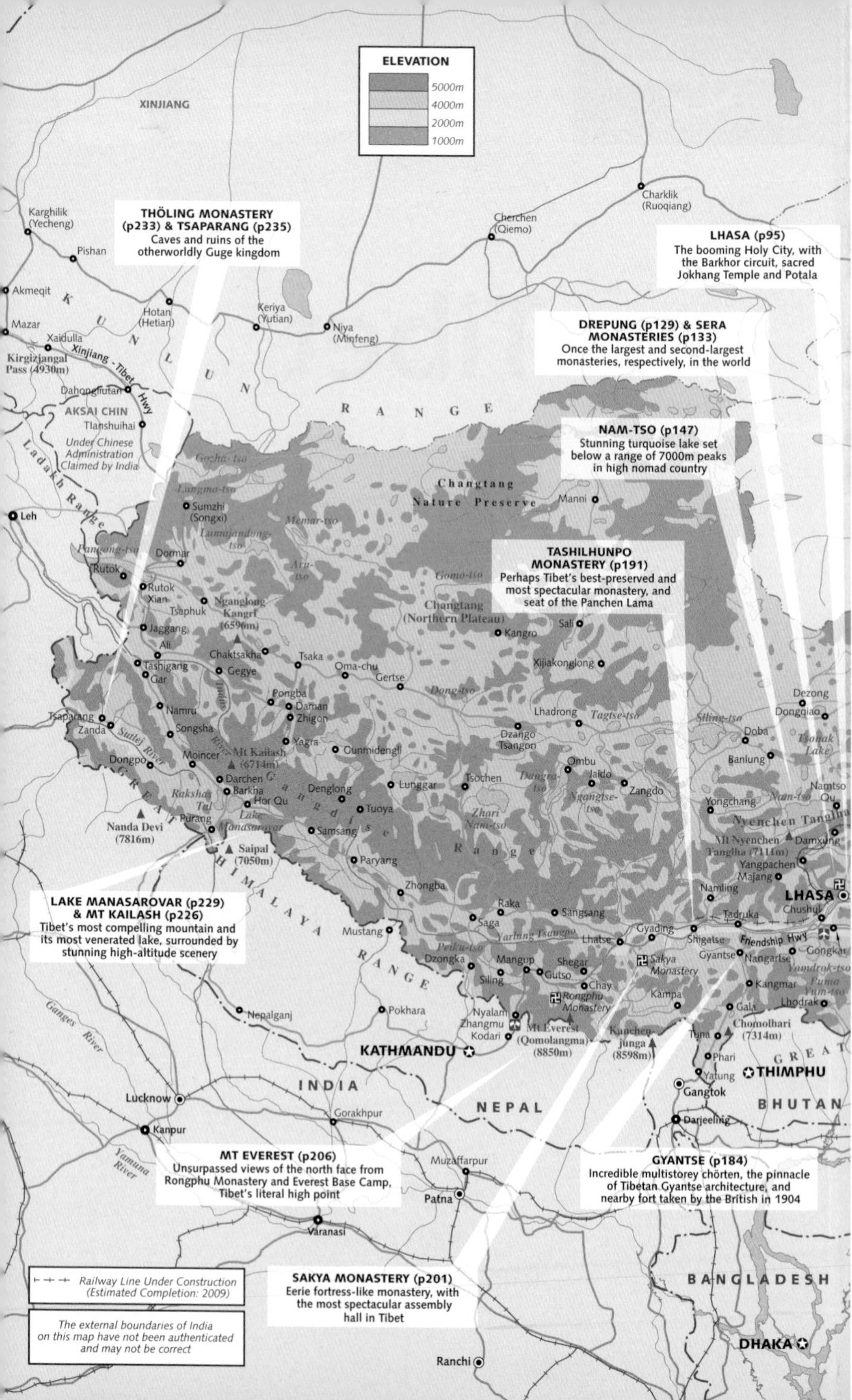

ELEVATION
5000m
4000m
2000m
1000m
THÖLING MONASTERY (p233) & TSAPARANG (p235)
Caves and ruins of the otherworldly Guge kingdom
LHASA (p95)
The booming Holy City, with the Barkhor circuit, sacred Jokhang Temple and Potala
DREPUNG (p129) & SERA MONASTERIES (p133)
Once the largest and second-largest monasteries, respectively, in the world
NAM-TSO (p147)
Stunning turquoise lake set below a range of 7000m peaks in high nomad country
TASHILHUNPO MONASTERY (p191)
Perhaps Tibet's best-preserved and most spectacular monastery, and seat of the Panchen Lama
LAKE MANASAROVAR (p229) & MT KAILASH (p226)
Tibet's most compelling mountain and its most venerated lake, surrounded by stunning high-altitude scenery
MT EVEREST (p206)
Unsurpassed views of the north face from Rongphu Monastery and Everest Base Camp, Tibet's literal high point
GYANTSE (p184)
Incredible multistorey chörten, the pinnacle of Tibetan Gyantse architecture, and nearby fort taken by the British in 1904
SAKYA MONASTERY (p201)
Eerie fortress-like monastery, with the most spectacular assembly hall in Tibet
Railway Line Under Construction (Estimated Completion: 2009)
The external boundaries of India on this map have not been authenticated and may not be correct
XINJIANG
KUNLUN RANGE
AKSAI CHIN
Under Chinese Administration Claimed by India
Changtang Nature Preserve
Changtang (Northern Plateau)
GREAT HIMALAYA RANGE
INDIA
NEPAL
BHUTAN
BANGLADESH
LHASA
KATHMANDU
THIMPHU
DHAKA
Mt Kailash (6714m)
Mt Everest (Qomolangma) (8850m)
Kanchenjunga (8598m)
Chomolhari (7314m)
Nanda Devi (7816m)
Saipal (7050m)
Mt Nyenchen Tangiha (7111m)
Shigatse
Gyantse
Sakya Monastery
Rongphu Monastery
Friendship Hwy
Xinjiang - Tibet Hwy

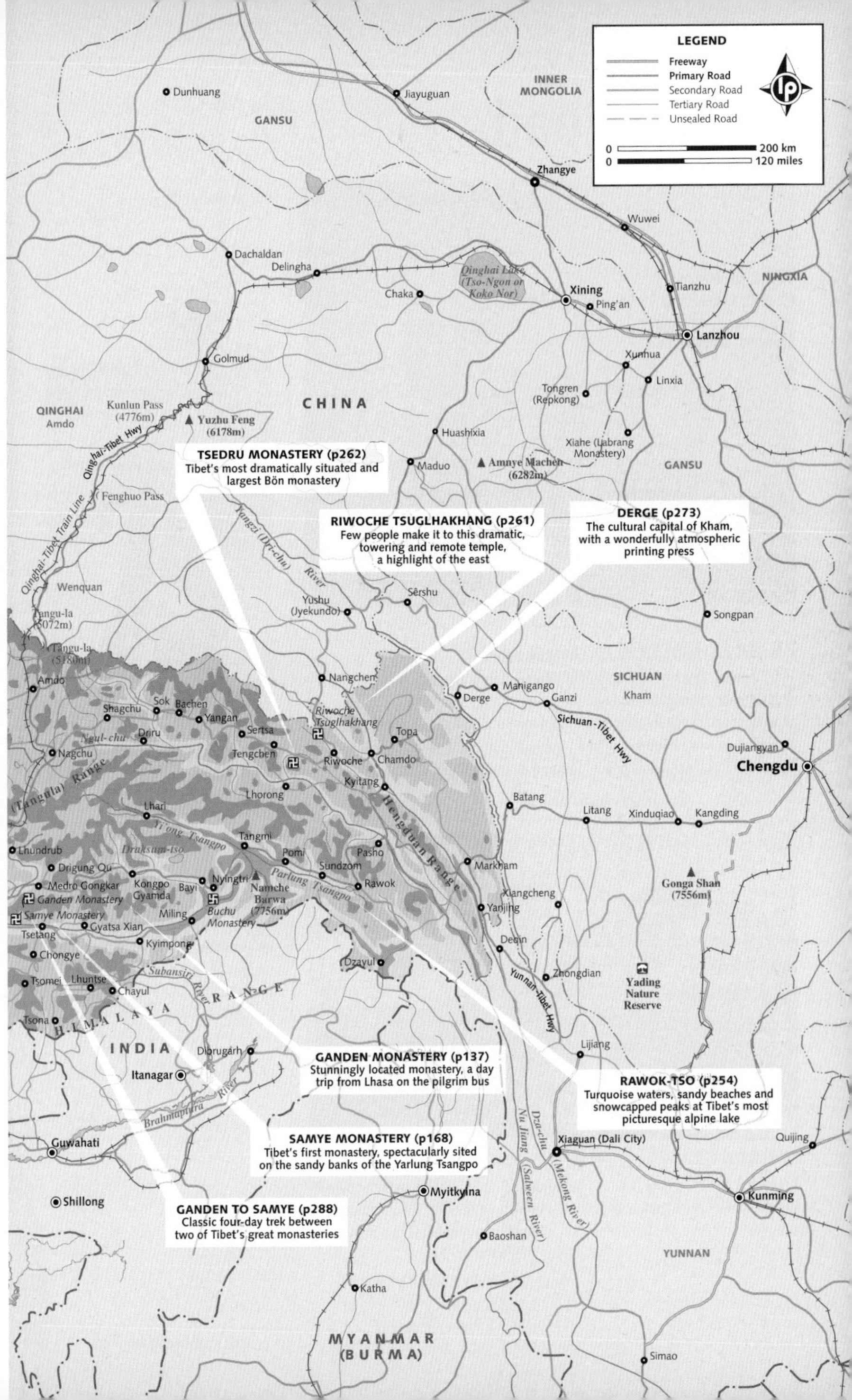
LEGEND
Freeway
Primary Road
Secondary Road
Tertiary Road
Unsealed Road
0 200 km
0 120 miles
TSEDRU MONASTERY (p262)
Tibet's most dramatically situated and largest Bön monastery
RIWOCHE TSUGLHAKHANG (p261)
Few people make it to this dramatic, towering and remote temple, a highlight of the east
DERGE (p273)
The cultural capital of Kham, with a wonderfully atmospheric printing press
GANDEN MONASTERY (p137)
Stunningly located monastery, a day trip from Lhasa on the pilgrim bus
RAWOK-TSO (p254)
Turquoise waters, sandy beaches and snowcapped peaks at Tibet's most picturesque alpine lake
SAMYE MONASTERY (p168)
Tibet's first monastery, spectacularly sited on the sandy banks of the Yarlung Tsangpo
GANDEN TO SAMYE (p288)
Classic four-day trek between two of Tibet's great monasteries
Dunhuang
GANSU
Jiayuguan
INNER MONGOLIA
Zhangye
Wuwei
Dachaldan
Delingha
Qinghai Lake (Tso-Ngon or Koko Nor)
Chaka
Xining
Ping'an
Tianzhu
NINGXIA
Lanzhou
Golmud
Xunhua
Linxia
Tongren (Repkong)
QINGHAI
Amdo
Kunlun Pass (4776m)
Yuzhu Feng (6178m)
CHINA
Qinghai-Tibet Hwy
Huashixia
Maduo
Amnye Machen (6282m)
Xiahe (Labrang Monastery)
GANSU
Fenghuo Pass
Qinghai-Tibet Train Line
Yangzi (Dri-chu) River
Wenquan
Yushu (Jyekundo)
Sêrshu
Songpan
Tangu-la (5072m)
Tangu-la (5180m)
Amdo
Nangchen
SICHUAN
Kham
Manigango
Derge
Ganzi
Sichuan-Tibet Hwy
Shagchu
Sok
Bachen
Yangan
Sertsa
Driru
Riwoche Tsuglhakhang
Topa
Nagchu
Tengchen
Riwoche
Chamdo
Dujiangyan
Chengdu
(Tangula) Range
Kyitang
Lhorong
Hengduan Range
Batang
Lhari
Litang
Xinduqiao
Kangding
Yi'ong Tsangpo
Tangmi
Lhundrub
Draksum-tso
Pomi
Pasho
Drigung Qu
Sundzom
Markham
Medro Gongkar
Kongpo Gyamda
Bayi
Nyingtri
Namche Barwa (7756m)
Parlung Tsangpo
Rawok
Gonga Shan (7556m)
Ganden Monastery
Xiangcheng
Samye Monastery
Miling
Buchu Monastery
Yanjing
Tsetang
Gyatsa Xian
Deqin
Kyimpong
Chongye
Dzayul
Zhongdian
Yading Nature Reserve
Subansiri River
Tsomei
Lhuntse
Chayul
Yunnan-Tibet Hwy
HIMALAYA RANGE
Tsona
INDIA
Dibrugarh
Lijiang
Itanagar
Brahmaputra River
Guwahati
Nu Jiang (Salween River)
Dza-chu (Mekong River)
Xiaguan (Dali City)
Quijing
Shillong
Myitkyina
Kunming
Baoshan
YUNNAN
Katha
MYANMAR (BURMA)
Simao

On the Road

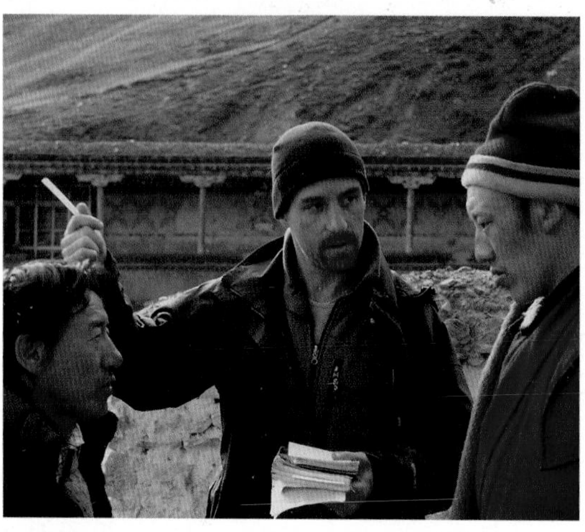

BRADLEY MAYHEW Coordinating Author
The hardest part of researching Tibet is tracking down the names of obscure monasteries. Five attempts at transliterating the name of one monastery in eastern Tibet (Djraa? Zha? Jar? Drayab? Traa?) had this monk laughing and shaking his head. Eventually we settled on Tra'e but I never was able to pronounce it properly.

JOHN VINCENT BELLEZZA
A day hike on the Changtang. There were fierce winds and snow that morning but I was still on my feet and ready to go. Nothing like being in untrammelled spaces for one's peace of mind and physical health.

ROBERT KELLY I'm just giddy up here at Everest Base Camp (p209). I didn't expect to be: it's just a mountain. But what a mesmerising chunk of ice and rock. I've called my dad to let him know where I am. He's more excited than I am. I have to climb this one day.

For author bios see p371.

Tibet Highlights

For many, the highlights of Tibet will be of a spiritual nature – magnificent monasteries, remote retreats and pilgrim paths; for others it will be the inspiring and raw high-altitude valleys, lakes and mountains of this unique plateau. Almost everyone, though, comes away with admiration and an affinity for the Tibetan people, whose openness of heart makes travelling in Tibet such a joy.

GARRY WEARE

1 MT KAILASH

Worshipped by both Buddhists and Hindus, Asia's most sacred mountain (p226) rises like a gigantic 6714m chörten. The three-day ritual circumambulation takes you along a 52km kora. Prostrate to the holy ground at the *shapjes* (rock cairns) that mark the four footprints of the Buddha. One circuit erases the sins of a lifetime. Consider it a bargain!

luppy2, Bluelist contributor

RICHARD I'ANSON

EVEREST BASE CAMP

Undoubtedly more magnificent than any of her Himalayan neighbours (and they're no shrimps in the mountain world). Viewed from Tibet, unobscured by other mountains, it's hard not to feel awed by one of nature's boldest achievements (p209).

jakki_b, Bluelist contributor

3

GARRY WEARE

2

POTALA PALACE

There are instances in your life that are completely unforgettable: pulling aside the faded hotel curtain on my first night in Tibet was one of these. In the crisp, Himalayan air sat the iconic Potala Palace (p108) above the town of Lhasa: quiet and stately, tremendous in its grandeur. The visit to the hallowed halls extended that excitement; here, on a grand scale, are sights that characterise the country: rich reds and warm golds, devoted rural pilgrims, turning prayer wheels, the flickering light of yak-butter candles. It's impossible for a romantic not to fall for such a place, or to stand on the upper levels, looking out over surrounding hills, with growing anticipation about the journey ahead.

Suzannah Shwer, Lonely Planet staff

JANE SWEENEY

4

GANDEN MONASTERY

We walked to the top of a 'hill' that rose some 300m above Ganden Monastery (p137). This was not by any means a stroll as it was quite steep and the effect of the altitude of over 4500m could be strongly felt. It was all worth it – the view was sublime, looking down over the monastery, the river flood plain far below and the mountains stretching into the distance in every direction. Prayer flags flapped wildly in the omnipresent breeze.

Mike Lee-Ack, traveller

BRADLEY MAYHEW

5 DEBATING WITH THE MONKS OF SERA MONASTERY

Home of the 'debating monks', Sera Monastery (p133) introduces debating as a spectator sport. Fantastic, friendly monks who will try as hard as they can to communicate with you. Just don't mention the Dalai Lama – you don't know who could be listening!

Songbird1979, Bluelist contributor

THE JOKHANG

Dark, throbbing medieval passages full of pilgrims and yak-butter candles, incense and murmuring, shuffling in and out of shrines and alcoves, up and down stairways. Lhasa's true heart – untouched by Chinese or tourist; indifferent to both (p103).

Steve Waters, Lonely Planet staff

6

JULIET COOMBE

FESTIVAL OF SAGA DAWA

The chanting, fingering of prayer beads, and spinning of prayer wheels along the 8km Lingkhor circuit in Lhasa stops only long enough to throw juniper and roasted barley offerings into the ceremonial burners (p119).

bvoegele, Bluelist contributor

7

BILL WASSMAN

BOTTOMLESS CUP OF YAK-BUTTER TEA

At Pabonka Monastery several friendly monks invited me to join them for a cup of 'tea'. I watched as a monk scooped us each a cup of the yellow broth out of a medieval-like cauldron. I reluctantly sipped away, struggling with its thick, rich, salty taste, determined to finish it and not offend my kind hosts. With a sense of accomplishment I finished off my last mouthful of yak-butter tea (p78). Much to my dismay my empty cup was eagerly picked up by one of the monks and refilled to the top. While not necessarily my cup of tea, there is no better display of Tibetan generosity and warmth than an invitation to share their favourite brew.

Trent Holden, Lonely Planet staff

JULIET COOMBE

9

BRADLEY MAYHEW

8

THÖLING & TSAPARANG

The spectacular ruined kingdom of Guge (p232) is quite unlike anything in central Tibet and has more in common with Ladakh than Lhasa.

Bradley Mayhew, Coordinating Author

BRADLEY MAYHEW

10

RIWOCHE TSUGLHAKHANG

Tibet is large enough to hold some hidden wonders. You'll have to overland for days to reach it, but the dramatic, towering and remote Riwoche Tsuglhakhang (p261) in eastern Tibet feels like it's marooned in an earlier age.

Bradley Mayhew, Coordinating Author

Contents

Regional Map Contents

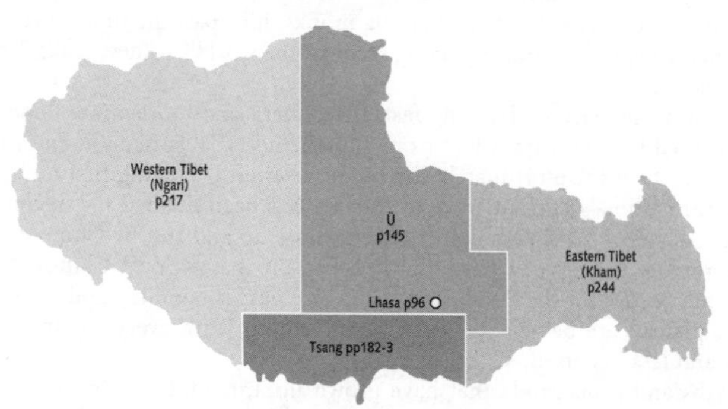

Destination Tibet

Go to Tibet and see many places, as much as you can; then tell the world.
His Holiness the Dalai Lama

Tibet: the Land of Snows, the roof of the world. For centuries this mysterious Buddhist kingdom, locked away in its mountain fastness of the Himalaya, has exercised a unique hold on the imagination of the West. For explorers, imperialists and traders it was a forbidden land of treasure and riches. Dreamers on a spiritual quest have long whispered of a lost Shangri-la, steeped in magic and mystery.

When the doors were finally flung open in the mid-1980s, Tibet lay in ruins. Between 1950 and 1970, the Chinese wrested control of the plateau, drove the Tibetans' spiritual leader, the Dalai Lama, and some 100,000 of Tibet's finest into exile and systematically dismantled most of the Tibetan cultural and historical heritage, all in the name of revolution. For a while images of the Buddha were replaced by icons of Chairman Mao.

Today, Tibetan pilgrims across the country are once again mumbling mantras and swinging their prayer wheels in temples that are heavy with the thick intoxicating aroma of juniper incense and yak butter. Monasteries have been restored across the country, along with limited religious freedoms. A walk around Lhasa's lively Barkhor pilgrimage circuit is proof enough that the efforts of the communist Chinese to build a brave new (roof of the) world have foundered on the remarkable and inspiring faith of the Tibetan people.

For many people, Tibet is a uniquely spiritual place. Those moments of peace, fleeting and precious, when everything seems to be in its proper place, seem to come more frequently in Tibet, whether inspired by the devotion apparent in the face of a pilgrim or the dwarfing scale of a beautiful landscape. Tibet can truly claim to be on a higher plain.

Tibet is without doubt one of the most remarkable places to visit in Asia. It offers fabulous monastery sights, breathtaking high-altitude treks, stunning views of the world's highest mountains and one of the most likeable peoples you will ever meet. Your trip will take you past glittering mountain turquoise lakes and over high passes draped with prayer flags. Find a quiet spot in a prayer hall full of chanting monks, hike past the ruins of remote hermitages or make an epic overland trip along some of the world's wildest roads. The scope for adventure is limitless.

This remarkable place is changing fast. Investment and tourism are flooding into the region, inspired by a new train line from China, and GDP is rising even faster than the train tracks to Lhasa. Unfortunately the modernisation is coming first and foremost on China's terms. China's current wave of tourists has been dubbed the 'second invasion', with a slew of new hotels, restaurants and bars set up and run by Chinese for Chinese. Once the remote preserve of hardy backpackers, it is now local Chinese tourists who dominate the queues for the Potala and Jokhang. Lhasa is booming and even small towns across the plateau are being modernised and rebuilt. With every passing month Tibet looks less and less like itself.

The myths and propaganda that have grown up around Tibet can be so enticing, so pervasive and so entrenched that it's hard to see the place through balanced eyes. The reality is that Tibet is no fragile Shangri-la but a resilient land underpinned by a unique culture and faith. But you are never far from the reality of politics here. For anyone who travels with their eyes open, a visit to Tibet will be memorable and fascinating, but also a sobering experience. It's a place that's likely to change the way you see the world and that will remain with you for years to come. And that's surely the definition of the very best kind of travel.

Preface

THE DALAI LAMA

The issue of Tibet is not nearly as simple as is sometimes made out. I believe that there are still widespread misunderstandings about Tibetan culture and what is happening inside and outside Tibet. Therefore, I welcome every opportunity for open-minded people to discover what is the reality in Tibet for themselves.

In the context of the growing tourist industry in Tibet, the Lonely Planet travel guide has an invaluable contribution to make in providing reliable and authoritative background information about places to visit, how to get there, where to stay, where to eat and so forth. Presenting the basic facts allows visitors to prepare themselves for what they will encounter and enables individuals to use their own intelligence to evaluate the evidence before them.

We live in times of rapid change throughout the world, but particularly at present in Asia and China. I remain confident that not very far in the future some mutually agreeable solution may be found to the Tibetan problem. I believe that my strictly non-violent approach, entailing constructive dialogue and negotiation, will ultimately attract effective support and sympathy from within the Chinese community. In the meantime, I am also convinced that as more people visit Tibet, the numbers of those who support the justice of a peaceful solution will grow.

I am grateful to everyone involved in the preparation of this seventh edition of the Lonely Planet guide to Tibet for the care and concern they have put into it. I trust that those who rely on it as a companion to their travels in Tibet will enjoy themselves in what, despite all that has happened, remains for me one of the most beautiful places on earth.

HH signed

September 15, 2004

Getting Started

Travelling in Tibet is not as difficult as you'd think – at least once you've worked your way around the latest permit situation (see p323) and have acclimatised to the altitude. Most travellers hire Land Cruisers (p343) to explore the country these days, but an adventurous combination of buses, hitching and hiking can get you to many places cheaply. (For information on the risks associated with hitching, see p344.)

On a practical level, Chinese modernisation has hit the Tibetan plateau big time and even small towns now offer everything from internet connections to cans of Budweiser. Out in the countryside traditional Tibetan life continues without much interruption.

WHEN TO GO

See Climate Charts (p316) for more information.

Climate is not such a major consideration when visiting Tibet as many people might imagine. For a place nicknamed 'The Land of Snows', there's a surprising lack of snow. The boom in domestic tourism means that Lhasa swells with Chinese tourists in the summer and particularly in the week-long holidays around 1 May and 1 October. Finding accommodation can be trickier during these weeks, so try to have something nailed down by lunch time. Winter is very cold, many restaurants are shut and snow can close mountain passes, but some travellers swear by the winter months. There are few travellers about at this time and Lhasa is crowded with *drokpas* (nomads). The average temperature in January is -2°C.

Spring, early summer and late autumn are probably the best times to visit Tibet. March is a politically sensitive month in the country (see p320) and there is occasional tightening of restrictions on travellers heading into Tibet at this time, but the weather's pretty good. April brings reliable weather in eastern Tibet and discounts on accommodation and vehicle rental in Lhasa. Mt Everest is particularly clear during April and May.

From mid-July through to the end of September the monsoon starts to affect parts of Tibet. (The months of July and August bring half of Tibet's annual rainfall.) Travel to western Tibet becomes slightly more difficult, the roads to the east are temporarily washed out and the Friendship Hwy sometimes becomes impassable on the Nepal side or on the border itself.

Trips to Mt Kailash can be undertaken from April to October, although September and October are considered the best months. October is also the best time to make a trip out to the east. Lhasa and its environs don't get *really* cold until the end of November.

It's worth trying to time your trip with one of Tibet's festivals. New Year (Losar) in January or February is an excellent time to be in Lhasa, as is the Saga Dawa festival in April or May (see p318).

COSTS & MONEY

Accommodation and food are both very economical in Tibet. The major expense – unless you have plenty of time and enjoy rough travelling – is getting around. If you really want to see a lot in a short space of time, you will probably have to consider hiring a vehicle and driver. Shared hired transport tends to work out at around US$30 per person per day. The per-person cost for a group of six travelling with stops from Lhasa to the Nepali border is around US$200.

FOUR THINGS YOU NEED TO KNOW ABOUT GETTING INTO TIBET

- You need a Tibet Tourism Bureau (TTB) permit to be able to board a plane to Lhasa, and in theory at least to take the train or bus – see p323. For this you need to go through a travel agent.
- You need an Alien Travel Permit to travel outside Lhasa Prefecture and you can currently only get one of these by booking a tour, either from outside Tibet, or more cheaply in Lhasa – see p324.
- If you plan to enter Tibet from Nepal, you will have to travel on a short-term group visa, which is hard to extend – see p327.
- All these rules have exceptions and by the time you have finished reading this list, all these rules have probably changed.

HOW MUCH?

Land Cruiser hire per day, split between four around Y250 per person.

Chinese meat dish Y15-25

Monastery entry fee Y20-50

Internet connection per hour Y3-5

Prayer flags from Y4

For additional price information see inside front cover.

Getting into Tibet is also relatively expensive. Train packages from Xining start at around US$170 (including permits), while the cheapest package by air costs around US$245 from Chengdu.

If you don't hire transport (and it is still perfectly possible to see most of the places covered in this guide if you don't), costs are very reasonable. If you are staying in Lhasa and visiting the surrounding sights you can do it comfortably on US$20 per day, staying in a dorm room or sharing a double. Outside the cities, daily costs drop drastically, especially if you're hitching or hiking out to remote monasteries. Keep in mind that entry tickets can really add up: visit Lhasa's main sights and you'll end up shelling out around US$60 in entry fees.

At the other end of the scale there's a lot more scope to go top end these days, at least in the cities. New five-star hotels, paved roads and a luxury train look set to take out much of the rigour of a visit to the Roof of the World.

TRAVEL LITERATURE

Literature on Tibet is abundant. Quite a bit of it is of the woolly 'how to find enlightenment in the mysterious Land of Snows' variety, but there is still a lot of very good stuff about.

Seven Years in Tibet by Heinrich Harrer, translated from the German in 1952 and made into a film in 1997, is an engaging account of Harrer's sojourn in Tibet in the final years before the Chinese takeover.

Magic and Mystery in Tibet by the French Tibetologist Alexandra David-Neel has the lot for the starry-eyed dreamer – flying nuns, enchanted daggers, ghosts and demons, and also some interesting background information on the mystic side of Tibet. Another good David-Neel title to look out for is *My Journey to Lhasa*.

A Mountain in Tibet by Charles Allen is a superbly crafted book that centres on the holy Mt Kailash and the attempts of early European explorers to reach it and to determine its geographical significance. It's a must for anyone heading out to western Tibet. Allen builds on this work with his *Search for Shangri-La* in which he returns to western Tibet to examine the region's pre-Buddhist history and mythology, focusing on Bön. For other books on Mt Kailash, see p230.

The Heart of the World by Ian Baker is an account of several explorations into the physical and spiritual landscapes of the Pemako region of southeastern Tibet, and the Tsangpo gorges in particular. Part-scholar, part-mystic and part-nutcase (Baker's trekking supplies included alchemical foods and magic Tantric pills), Baker makes for a fascinating and erudite literary companion for the journey into one of Tibet's remotest regions.

TOP PICKS

TIBET
Lhasa •

GREAT READS

Stuff your rucksack with a couple of these insightful looks into the Tibetan experience:

- *Tears of Blood: A Cry for Tibet* by Mary Craig is a riveting and distressing account of the Tibetan experience since the Chinese takeover and should be read by every visitor to Tibet.
- *A Stranger in Tibet* by Scott Berry tells the fascinating story of Ekai Kawaguchi, a young Japanese monk who was one of the first foreigners to reach Lhasa in 1900 and who managed to stay over a year in the capital before his identity was discovered and he was forced to flee the country.
- *Trespassers on the Roof of the World* by Peter Hopkirk is a superb read primarily concerned with European explorers' early attempts to enter forbidden Tibet.
- *Fire Under the Snow: Testimony of a Tibetan Prisoner* by Palden Gyatso is a moving autobiography that recounts Gyatso's life as a Buddhist monk imprisoned for 33 years for refusing to denounce the Dalai Lama.
- *Tibet Tibet* by Patrick French is an attempt to look beyond the propaganda and myth surrounding Tibet (what he terms 'the mind's Tibet') to portray a more complex and unsettling reality.

MUST-SEE FILMS

Get inspired down at the video shop with these big- and low-budget flicks:

- *Kundun* (Martin Scorsese) tells the story of the Dalai Lama ('Kundun'), through an all-Tibetan and Chinese cast, many of them descendants of the figures they portray (the Dalai Lama's mother, for example, is played by the Dalai Lama's niece). The cinematography in particular is gorgeous.
- *Himalaya* (Eric Valli) tells a community of Tibetan herders' epic story of succession on the salt caravan from Nepal to Tibet. The cinematography is also gorgeous (it was filmed largely in Dolpo in Nepal) and the entire cast is Tibetan.
- *Seven Years in Tibet* (Jean-Jacques Annaud) is a US$70-million film that tells the story of the daring escape of Heinrich Harrer (Brad Pitt) and Peter Aufschnaiter (David Thewlis) from a prisoner-of-war camp in northern India, their epic trek across Tibet and their seven-year sojourn in Lhasa as aides to the young Dalai Lama.
- *Tibet: Cry of the Snow Lion* (Tom Peosay) is a powerful pro-Tibetan documentary with narration by Martin Sheen and voiceovers by Ed Harris, Tim Robbins and Susan Sarandon.
- *The Saltmen of Tibet* (Ulrike Koch) is a Swiss-German documentary (hold on, don't turn off yet!) that follows four Tibetan traders and 160 yaks on their annual trek to carry salt from northern Tibet to Nepal. The scenery is stunning; equally intriguing is the secret language the saltmen speak to each other.

OUR FAVOURITE TIBETAN CULTURAL EXPERIENCES

Don't overlook these simple joys of being in Tibet when planning your itinerary:

- The smell of juniper incense, the low murmur of Tibetan chanting and the warm glow of butter lamps in monasteries everywhere.
- Following a kora (a pilgrimage circuit) with a band of happy pilgrims or scoring a lift in the back of a pilgrim truck.
- Overnighting in a small monastery such as Mindroling (p167), Dorje Drak (p165) or Drigung Til (p162).
- Repeatedly wandering the Barkhor (p102), different every time.
- A post-hike thermos of sweet milky tea in a crowded Tibetan teahouse.

DON'T LEAVE HOME WITHOUT...

- A good pair of sunglasses, high-factor sunscreen lotion and lip balm to block out the strong high-altitude light.
- A sleeping bag, if heading off the beaten track or travelling outside of high summer (see p314).
- A water bottle for cooling boiled water (thus doubling as a hot-water bottle!), an alarm clock for early morning transport and a strong torch (flashlight) for viewing the inside of monasteries (and midnight trips to the toilet).
- Warm clothing – a polar fleece will do in the summer months unless you're planning to be trekking at high altitudes or heading out to western Tibet. A waterproof jacket is useful if you are heading out to eastern Tibet in summer.
- Hard-to-find toiletries like shaving cream, razor blades, hand sanitiser, deodorant, dental floss and tampons. Cold medicines and throat pastilles are useful as many travellers develop a cold and cough as a result of altitude.
- The latest word on permit regulations from the Lonely Planet Thorn Tree (www.lonelyplanet.com). Also, read the information on p323 and throughout the Transport chapter.

The Siege of Shangri-La by travel journalist Michael McRae takes a wider (and sometimes testosterone-drenched) look at the explorations, recent and historical, of the Tsangpo gorges, with good sections on early botanists Frank Kingdon-Ward and FM 'Hatter' Bailey.

Travelers' Tales Tibet is an entertaining compendium of travel writing on Tibet by such authors as Pico Iyer, Peter Hessler and Alexandra David-Neel.

INTERNET RESOURCES

Australia Tibet Council (www.atc.org.au) Excellent travel information, including the latest travel restrictions.

Canada Tibet Committee (www.tibet.ca) Click on World Tibet Archive for a useful, free news-gathering service on issues relating to Tibet.

China Tibet Information Center (http://en.tibet.cn/) News, background and tourism information from the Chinese perspective. The travel site www.tibettour.com.cn is connected.

Kham Aid (www.khamaid.org) Excellent organisation with good travel information for Tibetan areas of Western Sichuan.

Office of the Dalai Lama in London (www.tibet.com) Provides lots of background information on Tibet.

Tibet Information Network (www.tibetinfonet.net) Another news-gathering service with a good but dated rundown of tourist regulations in Tibet.

Tibet Map Institute (www.tibetmap.com) Highly detailed downloadable maps of almost every region of Tibet, with an overview of other commercial map sources.

Shanghai Odyssey Travel (www.tibet-tour.com) Travel agency site with lots of background information on Tibet. See also www.tibettrip.com and www.tibettravel.info.

Itineraries

CLASSIC ROUTES

LHASA & AROUND **Two weeks**

The chief goal of travellers is Lhasa itself, the spiritual heart of Tibet, and there's no better way to get here than the 26-hour **train ride** (p339) from Xining or other cities in China.

There's enough to see in and around Lhasa to occupy at least a week. Highlights include the **Potala** (p108), a Unesco World Heritage Site, the **Jokhang Temple** (p103) and the **Barkhor** pilgrimage circuit (p101). The huge monastic institutions of **Drepung** (p129) and **Sera** (p133) lie on the edge of town, and **Ganden Monastery** (p137) is a fantastic day trip away.

There are plenty of excursions to be made from Lhasa. An overnight return trip to stunning lake **Nam-tso** (p147) offers a break from peering at Buddhist deities, though you should allow at least a few days in Lhasa to acclimatise before heading out here. Add a day or two and return via the timeless and little-visited **Reting Monastery** (p151) to avoid backtracking.

With another couple of days, visit atmospheric **Drigung Til Monastery** (p162) and **Tidrum Nunnery** (p163), both east of Lhasa. You can visit these directly from Reting or on a two- or three-day excursion from Lhasa.

The area around Lhasa offers an excellent range of monasteries, both popular and remote, and no travel permits are required. Nam-tso offers a glimpse of the nomad life of the north. This route gives a good look at Tibet in a short time.

LHASA TO KATHMANDU

Seven to 10 days

The Friendship Hwy between Lhasa and Kathmandu in Nepal is the main travellers' route through Tibet and allows a number of excellent detours. Combine it with the train route into Tibet for an epic overland tour.

With a hired Land Cruiser (see p343) you can head straight from Lhasa to the coiling scorpion-lake of **Yamdrok-tso** (p181) and take in the views from **Samding Monastery** (p183) before heading over the glacier-draped Karo-la pass to **Gyantse** (p184). This town is well worth a full day: the *kumbum* (literally '100,000 images') chörten is a must-see and there are several adventurous excursions in the nearby area. A 90-minute drive away is Shigatse, with its impressive **Tashilhunpo Monastery** (p191). **Shalu Monastery** (p199) is a worthwhile half-day trip from Shigatse, especially if you have an interest in Tibetan art.

A popular side trip en route to Kathmandu is to recently renovated **Sakya** (p201), a small monastery town located just 25km off the Friendship Hwy. Stay the night here and investigate the northern ruins or stay in the nearby town of Lhatse.

The most popular excursion from the road is to **Rongphu Monastery** (p207) and **Everest Base Camp** (p209). A new paved road has cut down driving time to just a few hours. If you are hitchhiking, allow at least three days to get to Rongphu and back from the Friendship Hwy. (See p344 for information on risks associated with hitchhiking in Tibet.)

After Everest most people take the opportunity to stay the night in old **Tingri** (p210), with its wonderful views of Mt Cho Oyu, before the scenic rollercoaster ride to **Nyalam** (p211), **Zhangmu** (p212) and the Nepali border.

A classic overland route of around 1300km that can be done in a week on an organised Land Cruiser trip or in twice this time by bus and hitch-hiking. It's also a classic mountain-biking route. It takes in central Tibet's most important monasteries, plus views of the world's highest peak.

ROADS LESS TRAVELLED

MOUNT KAILASH PILGRIMAGE 15 to 23 days

Much talked about but little visited, **Mt Kailash** (p226) sits out in remote western Tibet. Most foreigners get here in a rented Land Cruiser (p343), though a few hardy souls hitch (p344). If you just want to visit Mt Kailash and Lake Manasarovar, the most direct route is the southern road (870km), a four-day drive from Lhasa along the northern spine of the Himalayas. A kora (pilgrimage circuit) of the mountain will take three days and you should allow a day afterwards to relax at **Lake Manasarovar** (p229), probably at Chiu Monastery. Pilgrims traditionally then visit the sacred hot springs at **Tirthapuri** (p231).

An ambitious but rewarding alternative is to travel out from Lhasa along the longer (1700km) northern route to **Ali** (p224) and back along the southern route, a loop that will take three weeks. The six-day drive from Lhasa to Ali is brilliantly scenic but the rapidly expanding towns en route are charmless, so consider camping somewhere such as **Tagyel-tso** (p222). From Ali you can make an overnight visit to **Pangong-tso** (p238) and **Rutok Monastery** (p238), before heading down to Zanda and **Thöling Monastery** (p233). Allow at least two days here, with a day to explore the otherworldly Guge kingdom ruins at **Tsaparang** (p235). From Thöling it's a day's drive to Mt Kailash, though most groups stop overnight at Tirthapuri en route.

If you are heading to Nepal from Mt Kailash, it's well worth taking the short cut south via stunning **Peiku-tso** (p219) and its views of Shishapangma to join the Friendship Hwy near Nyalam.

A rugged mini-expedition to one of the remotest and most sacred corners of Asia, best undertaken with a Land Cruiser. You can just about get to many of these sights by public transport or hitching but you'll need a month or more and plenty of patience.

EASTERN TIBET LOOP

18 to 21 days

Equally remote, but different scenically, are the routes through eastern Tibet. Road conditions mean that the trip is best attempted from late March to late April, or late September to early November. It's possible to leave Tibet this way but you can't beat the comprehensiveness of the loop route.

From Lhasa the southern route heads eastwards over a high pass to the beautiful but touristed lake of **Draksum-tso** (p247) and the fascinating Kongpo region, with its lovingly restored **Lamaling Temple** (p250). From here the road climbs to the **Serkhym-la** (p251), for excellent views in good weather of 7756m Namche Barwa, before dropping down into the dramatic misty gorges that lie north of the Yarlung Tsangpo. Camping is excellent near Barkhor Monastery and by the shores of the turquoise lake **Rawok-tso** (p254), where you can overnight after a half-day trip to the nearby Lhegu Glacier. Swing north over the high passes into the deep parallel red-hued gorges of the Salween and Mekong Rivers. Reach the modern town of **Chamdo** (p257) after five or six days and rest for a day, visiting the large Galden Jampaling Monastery.

This three-week Land Cruiser loop takes you through dramatic scenery to some rarely visited corners of Tibet. It's perhaps best suited to a second trip to Tibet.

From Chamdo the northern route continues three or four days westwards to **Nagchu** (p264), gradually climbing to the high-altitude pasturelands of Amdo. The route passes the impressive temple of the **Riwoche Tsuglhakhang** (p261) and the remote and incredibly sited **Tsedru Monastery** (p262), the largest Bön monastery in Tibet.

From Nagchu visit **Nam-tso** (p147) and **Reting Monastery** (p151) en route to Lhasa (allow three to four days), though the road can be completed in a day.

A shorter and cheaper five- to seven-day loop itinerary from Lhasa to Kongpo could take in Draksum-tso and Lamaling Temple before returning via Tsetang, Samye and possibly the remote oracle lake of **Lhamo La-tso** (p178).

OVERLAND ROUTES TO LHASA

Two to three weeks

There are three main overland routes from the east: the **northern route** (p270) and **southern route** (p275) through Sichuan and the shorter **Yunnan route** (p337). The Tibetan areas of western Sichuan and northwestern Yunnan do not require travel permits; the eastern Tibetan Autonomous Region does.

The northern route through Sichuan starts from Kangding and passes the grasslands and monastery of **Tagong** (p270) and several large monasteries around **Ganzi** (p271). The timeless printing press of **Derge** (p273) is a day's bus ride further but there are plenty of exciting excursions en route, including to the remote **Dzogchen Monastery** (p273) and the pretty **Yilhun La-tso** (p273). From Derge you cross into Tibet proper over some wild passes to **Chamdo** (p257), the biggest town in eastern Tibet. For the route west of Chamdo, see the second half of the Eastern Tibet loop; alternatively travel south to join the southern route.

The southern route through Sichuan runs west from Kangding past the Khampa town and monastery of **Litang** (p275), home to an epic horse festival in August, and then low-lying **Batang** (p278) before climbing up into Tibet at Markham and continuing over concertina passes to Pomda. For the route west, reverse the first half of the Eastern Tibet loop itinerary (opposite).

A popular alternative option is to start in Yunnan at the Tibetan town of Zhongdian (Gyeltang), from where it's a day's bus ride to Deqin. From here you cross into the Tibet Autonomous Region (TAR) near the salt pans of Yanjing; then it's 111km to Markham on the Sichuan southern route.

From Zhongdian to Lhasa, allow a week in a Land Cruiser. From Chengdu it takes 10 days to two weeks along either the northern or southern route. Figure on three weeks if hitchhiking (see p344).

A wild overland adventure through spectacular alpine scenery. The route is officially open only to organised Land Cruiser tours, but a small number of hitchhikers and cyclists are making their way through.

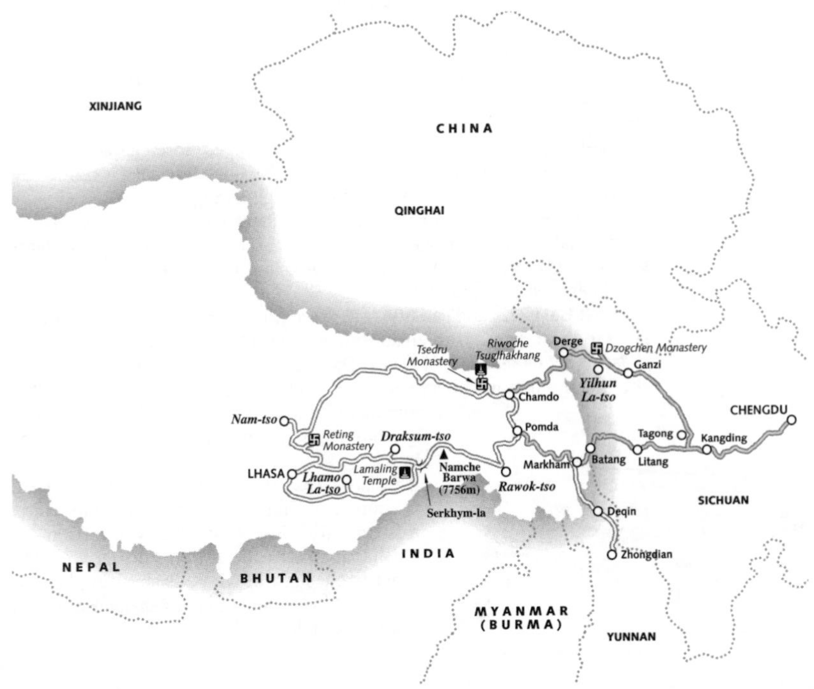

TAILORED TRIPS

MONASTERIES OFF THE BEATEN TRACK

A visit to one of Tibet's smaller monasteries could well be a highlight of your trip. The monasteries are more intimate, the monks tend to be friendlier, and it's often possible to spend the night and attend prayer meetings after all the tourists have melted away.

Between Lhasa and Samye, **Mindroling Monastery** (p167) is a friendly place that's easily accessible. The surroundings offer some enjoyable walks and it's possible to stay the night.

A short and scenic ferry ride across the Yarlung Tsangpo is **Dorje Drak Monastery** (p165). The monastery guesthouse and dramatic desert kora feel a million miles away from bustling Lhasa, though a planned road looks set to change this soon.

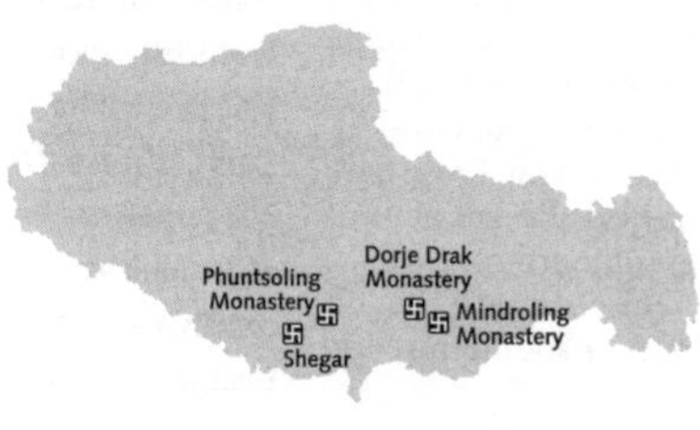

En route between Shigatse and Lhatse is the remote and little-visited **Phuntsoling Monastery** (p200). The monastery has a superb location and there are lots of ruins to explore, both at the site and a couple of hours' walk away at the ruined Jonang chörten. Permits are required here.

Along the Friendship Hwy, **Shegar** (p205) is just 7km off the main road, not far from the turn-off to Mt Everest, and has a charming monastery at the base of the impressive ruined 'Crystal Fort'.

NATURAL HIGHS

Almost everywhere in Tibet offers superb scenery, but let's start at the top: **Mt Everest** (p206). Views of the north face from Rongphu Monastery are simply unsurpassed.

Nam-tso (p147) offers a very different landscape, more characteristic of northern Changtang than of central Tibet. The huge tidal lake is framed by the jagged white peaks of the Nyenchen Tanglha range.

The scenery of the east is different again. **Rawok-tso** (p254) is possibly the prettiest lake in Tibet, fringed by both sandy beaches and snowy peaks. **Draksum-tso** (p247), further west, is another gorgeous alpine lake, with a superbly photogenic island monastery.

Tagyel-tso (p222) and **Dawa-tso** (p223) are two of the most impressive of the lakes in the far west, with great camping en route to Mt Kailash.

Yading Nature Reserve (p277) near Daocheng in southwestern Sichuan offers sublime mountain scenery without the need for pesky travel permits. Stay overnight in tourist tents and then hike up to meadows and glacial lakes or do the full mountain kora.

Peiku-tso (p219), near the border with Nepal, is another of Tibet's awesome mountain lakes, this time with impressive views of 8012m Mt Shishapangma to the south. Further west the remarkable sight of Mt Kailash rising behind the deep blue waters of **Lake Manasarovar** (p229) is unforgettable.

PILGRIM PATHS

Mt Kailash (p226) is the most sacred pilgrimage path in Tibet. The 53km trek (p302) is generally done in three days by foreign trekkers and takes you over the 5600m Drölma-la and past several monasteries and sacred sights.

Lake Manasarovar (p229) is another sacred kora, but is less popular with foreigners. Still, it's possible to just walk a section, such as the day hike from Chiu Monastery to Hor Qu.

Ganden Monastery (p137) has one of Tibet's most interesting monastery koras and the views of the Kyi-chu Valley below are just wonderful. The **Tsurphu kora** (p144) is also worth walking for its meditation retreats and valley views.

Tashilhunpo Kora (p191) in Shigatse is always full of pilgrims. The trail passes chörtens and rock paintings, and offers the best views of the old town and Shigatse *dzong* (fort). **Sakya Monastery** (p201) also has an interesting kora around the ruins of its northern monastery complex.

Tirthapuri kora (p231) is another short kora, but is full of interesting medicinal sites, hot springs and pilgrim action.

Perhaps shortest of all is the **Barkhor** (p102), the fascinating circuit that surrounds the Jokhang in Lhasa.

FESTIVALS

Tibet's traditional festivals offer everything from horse racing to monk dances, plus the opportunity to mingle with a Tibetan crowd picnicking and partying in their finest garb. For details on festivals and dates, see p318.

The annual **Saga Dawa** (p318) festival in April/May brings thousands of pilgrims onto the streets of **Lhasa** (p119) to walk the city's Lingkhor pilgrim circuit. Pilgrims and tourists also flock to **Mt Kailash** (p226) at this time to watch the auspicious raising of a prayer pole at Tarboche and then trek around the mountain (p302).

Tsurphu Monastery (p144) has a colourful three-day festival just before Saga Dawa, featuring monk processions, *cham* dancing and the unveiling of a large thangka.

Summer horse-racing festivals are a centuries-old tradition on the grasslands of Amdo and Kham. The best ones take place in August at **Nagchu** (p264) and **Litang** (p275), where tens of thousands of visiting nomads set up a veritable tent city in the surrounding countryside. There's more equestrian fun and games around the time of Saga Dawa at the **Gyantse Horse-Racing Festival** (p184), which also features archery competitions and musical performances.

Other colourful monastery festivals include *cham* dancing at **Samye** (p168) and the unveiling of a multistorey sacred thangka during three days of festivities at Shigatse's **Tashilhunpo Monastery** (p191), both in June/July.

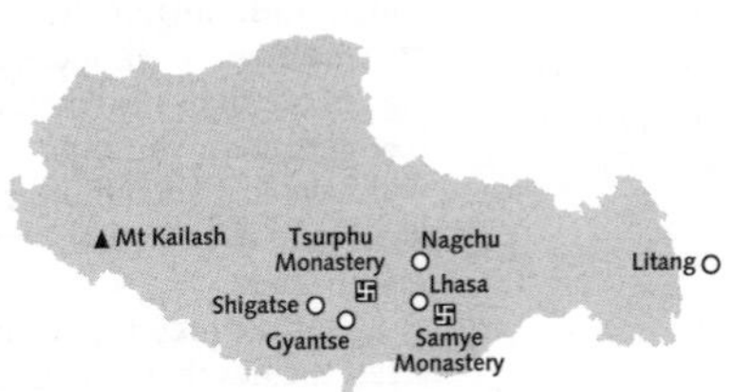

Snapshot

Change is afoot in Tibet. The economy is booming, new train links, airports and roads are revolutionising transport on the plateau and Tibet's urban areas are expanding at an unprecedented rate. As part of its 'great leap west', the Chinese government has poured over US$10 billion into Tibet's infrastructure. A domestic tourist boom is fuelling hotel construction across the plateau. You can now take the train to Lhasa and a paved road all the way up to Everest Base Camp.

In most parts of the world this would all be good news, but here lies Tibet's conundrum. Alongside the short-term tourists has come a flood of Chinese immigrants, who Tibetans claim are the real beneficiaries of Tibet's economic boom. Many Tibetans feel they are becoming increasingly marginalised in their own land; the Chinese counter that they are just trying to bring economic prosperity to Tibet.

FAST FACTS

Tibetan Autonomous Region (TAR) population: 2.81 million (2006)

Global Tibetan population: 5.5 million

Area of TAR: 1.23 million sq km, or one-eighth of China's landmass

Local drink: yak-butter tea

Average number of cups of tea drunk by a nomad per day: 40

Funeral custom: sky burial

Economic growth: 13.4% in 2006

Number of functioning monasteries in Tibet: 1700

World's highest railway line: 5072m Tangula Pass on Qinghai–Tibet Railway

Average per capita net income for a Tibetan herder: US$300

As the face of Tibet changes, it's looking more and more Chinese. And as Tibetan culture becomes diluted, there is a fear that Tibetans will become a minority in their own country, a situation the Dalai Lama has described as 'cultural genocide'. Ironically, Tibet is now seriously cool among Chinese backpackers from Beijing to Guangzhou, many of whom are as enamoured with Tibet as their Western counterparts.

Yet the more things change, the more they stay the same. Talks between the Chinese and the Dharamsala-based Tibetan government in exile remain stalled, with the Chinese taking every opportunity to accuse the Nobel-peace prize winning Dalai Lama of 'political splittism'. The Dalai Lama himself has abandoned any hope of nationhood, opting to push for genuine cultural, religious and linguistic autonomy within the Chinese state. Fearful of upsetting their trade balance with China, foreign governments continue to be careful not to receive the Dalai Lama in any way that recognises his political status as the head of an exiled government.

Politically speaking, Tibet remains a place lacking basic religious and political freedoms, where political propaganda reigns and torture is commonplace. Religious institutions are repeatedly the focus of 'patriotic education' and 'civilising atheism' campaigns, and strict quotas are still imposed on the numbers of resident monks and nuns, who are often forced to sign documents denouncing the Dalai Lama. The carefully hidden brutality was brought into sharp focus in 2007 when a Romanian mountaineer filmed Chinese border guards shooting unarmed Tibetan refugees in the Everest region. In 2007 the Dharamsala-backed 11th Panchen Lama turned 18 in his 12th year of house arrest (see p196).

Disputes between Dharamsala and Beijing over the selection of various lamas, most notably the Panchen Lama, have spotlighted the tricky politics of reincarnation, an increasingly hot topic as the Dalai Lama heads into his 70s. More than just 'a simple monk' or even a god-king, the Dalai Lama has become a shining symbol of Tibetan identity. When he dies, Tibet will have lost something essential to its modern identity. The Dalai Lama has made it clear that he will only be reborn in Tibet if he is allowed to return there.

As for the present, the longest-lasting result of Tibet's economic boom is clear; the ties that bind China and Tibet are stronger than ever.

History

by Bradley Mayhew, with Timeline by Tsering Shakya

YARLUNG VALLEY DYNASTY

As early myths of the origin of the Tibetan people suggest, the Yarlung Valley was the cradle of the civilisation of central Tibet. The early Yarlung kings, although glorified in legend, were probably no more than chieftains whose domains extended not much further than the Yarlung Valley (p175) itself. A reconstruction of Tibet's first fortress, Yumbulagang, can still be seen in the Yarlung Valley, and it is here that the 28th king of Tibet is said to have received Tibet's first Buddhist scriptures in the 5th century AD. According to legend, they fell on the roof of Yumbulagang.

Neolithic artefacts discovered in Karo village are displayed in the Tibet Museum in Lhasa (p116).

Credible historical records regarding the Yarlung Valley dynasty date only from the time when the fledgling kingdom entered the international arena in the 6th century. By this time the Yarlung kings, through conquest and alliances, had made significant headway in unifying much of central Tibet. Namri Songtsen (c 570–619), the 32nd Tibetan king, continued this trend and extended Tibetan influence into inner Asia, defeating the Qiang tribes on China's borders. But the true flowering of Tibet as an important regional power came about with the accession to rule of Namri Songtsen's son, Songtsen Gampo (r 630–49).

Under Songtsen Gampo, central Tibet entered a new era. Tibetan expansion continued unabated. The armies of Tibet ranged as far afield as northern India and emerged as a threat to the Tang dynasty in China. Both Nepal and China reacted to the Tibetan incursions by reluctantly agreeing to alliances through marriage. Princess Wencheng, Songtsen Gampo's Chinese bride, and Princess Bhrikuti, his Nepali bride, became important historical figures for the Tibetans, as it was through their influence that Buddhism first gained royal patronage and a foothold on the Tibetan plateau.

Contact with the Chinese led to the introduction of the sciences of astronomy and medicine, and a Tibetan script was developed from Indian sources. It was used in the first translations of Buddhist scriptures, in drafting a code of law and in writing the first histories of Tibet.

For two centuries after the reign of Songtsen Gampo, Tibet continued to grow in power and influence. By the time of King Trisong Detsen's reign (r 755–97), Tibetan influence extended over Turkestan, northern Pakistan, Nepal and India. In China, Tibetan armies conquered Gansu and Sichuan, and controlled the great Buddhist cave complex of Dunhuang.

A Sino-Tibetan treaty was signed in 822 during the reign of King Tritsug Detsen Ralpachen (r 817–36). It was immortalised in stone on three steles: one in Lhasa, outside the Jokhang; one in the Chinese capital of Chang'an; and one on the border of Tibet and China. Only the Lhasa stele still stands (see p102).

TIMELINE

28, 000 BC

The Tibetan plateau is covered in ice. It's cold. Very cold. But there are people are living there. Tools, stone blades and hunting instruments are in use in Chupsang, 85km from Lhasa.

300 BC

Throughout the plateau people are building stone dwellings and fine potteries; petroglyphs indicate that Buddhism may have started to spread by this time.

c 600

Nyatri Tsenpo, the first king of Tibet, founds the Yarlung dynasty and unifies the people and the land; according to legend he is responsible for the first building in Tibet.

ORIGINS OF THE TIBETAN PEOPLE *Tsering Shakya*

The origins of the Tibetan people are not clearly known. Today Chinese historians claim that there was a westward migration and the Tibetan people originally migrated from the present-day areas of Qinghai-Gansu plains and were descended from people known as Qiang. Although there is evidence of westward migration, it is not possible to trace a single origin of the Tibetan people. Modern genetic studies may be able to show different traces and complex ties with people from the neighbouring areas. The settlement of Tibetan people in Western Tibet and areas of Ladakh shows other connections with Central Asia. Matthew Kapstein, one of the leading Western Tibetologists writes, 'the people of Tibetan plateau became Tibetan primarily owing to cultural developments during the past two millennia, rather than to common genetic origins'.

The Tibetan people have mythic stories of their origin and, according to legend, the earth was covered in a vast sea and eventfully the water receded and land appeared in the present-day Tsetang area in central Tibet. A monkey and an ogress first inhabited the land and were later identified as the emanations of Avalokiteshvara (the Buddha of Compassion) and the goddess Tara. The first people were descendents of the union between the monkey and ogress (see p173). The children of the monkey and ogress gave rise to the Tibetan people and as the number of children increased, the people evolved into six families known as Se, Mu, Dong, Tong, Wra and Dru. They became the six clans of the Tibetan people.

Signatories to the treaty swore that '…the whole region to the east…being the country of Great China and the whole region to the west being assuredly that of the country of Great Tibet, from either side of that frontier there shall be no warfare, no hostile invasions, and no seizure of territory…'.

Songtsen Gampo went as far as passing a law making it illegal *not* to be a Buddhist.

The Sino-Tibetan treaty heralds an era in which 'Tibetans shall be happy in Tibet and Chinese shall be happy in China'.

INTRODUCTION OF BUDDHISM

By the time Buddhism first arrived in Tibet during the reign of Songtsen Gampo, it had already flourished for around 1100 years and had become the principal faith of all Tibet's neighbouring countries. But it was slow to take hold in Tibet.

Early missionaries, such as Shantarakshita from the Indian Buddhist centre of Nalanda (in modern-day Bihar), faced great hostility from the Bön-dominated court. The influence of Songtsen Gampo's Chinese and Nepali wives was almost certainly limited to the royal court, and priests of the time were probably Indian and Chinese, not Tibetan.

It was not until King Trisong Detsen's reign that Buddhism began to take root. Trisong Detsen was responsible for founding Samye Monastery (p168), the first institution to carry out the systematic translation of Buddhist scriptures and the training of Tibetan monks.

Contention over the path that Buddhism was to take in Tibet culminated in the Great Debate of Samye, in which King Trisong Detsen is said to have

608

The first mission is sent to the court of Chinese Emperor Yang-ti. This brings Tibet in direct contact with China and sees increasing Tibetan interest in the frontier of China

629

Namri Songtsen is assassinated and his son, Songtsen Gampo, aged 13, inherits the throne. He comes to be regarded as the founder of the Tibetan empire and remains an important cultural hero for the Tibetan people.

640s

Songtsen Gampo marries Chinese Princess Wencheng and Nepalese Princess Bhrikuti. They both contribute to Tibetan cultural formation; they are credited with bringing Buddhism, silk weaving and new methods of agriculture to Tibet.

adjudicated in favour of Indian teachers who advocated a gradual approach to enlightenment, founded in scholastic study and moral precepts. There was, however, much opposition to this institutionalised, clerical Buddhism, largely from supporters of the Bön faith. The next Tibetan king, Tritsug Detsen Ralpachen, fell victim to this opposition and was assassinated by his brother, Langdharma, who launched an attack on Buddhism. In 842, Langdharma was himself assassinated – by a Buddhist monk disguised as a Black Hat dancer, during a festival – and the Tibetan state soon collapsed into a number of warring principalities. In the confusion that followed, support for Buddhism dwindled and clerical monastic Buddhism experienced a 150-year hiatus.

Langdharma is described as possessing two horns on the side of his head; he tied his hair in a knotted fashion to hide his evil origin.

SECOND DIFFUSION OF BUDDHISM

The collapse of the Tibetan state in 842 put a stop to Tibetan expansion in Asia; Tibet was never again to rise to arms. Overwhelmed initially by local power struggles, Buddhism gradually began to exert its influence again, giving the Tibetan mind a spiritual bent and turning it inward on itself. As the tide of Buddhist faith receded in India, Nepal and China, Tibet slowly emerged as the most devoutly Buddhist nation in the world.

The so-called second diffusion of Buddhism corresponded with two developments. First, Tibetan teachers who had taken refuge in Kham, to the east, returned to central Tibet in the late 10th century and established new monasteries. Second, the kingdom of Guge in western Tibet invited the Bengali scholar Atisha (Jowo-je; 982–1054) to Tibet in the mid-11th century. Disciples of Atisha (Jowo-je), chiefly Dromtönpa, were instrumental in establishing the Kadampa order and monasteries such as Reting (see p151).

GURU RINPOCHE

Padmasambhava is one of the most important Buddhist saints in Tibet and his statues can be found in most temples and households. He is more widely known by Tibetans as Guru Rinpoche. Guru Rinpoche was a Tantric master from Uddiyana, in modern-day Swat valley in Pakistan. His journey to Tibet was obstructed by evil forces, but through his magical powers he subdued evil sprits and converted them as protectors of Buddhism. Guru Rinpoche arrived in Samye and dispelled the obstructed forces, transforming it into a tranquil and holy site. While in Samye, Padmasambhava took Yeshe Tsogyal, one of the ladies of Trisong Detsen's court, as his consort. She is deified as a form of goddess today and regarded as one of the spiritual mothers of Tibet.

Guru Rinpoche is said to have stayed in Tibet for 55 years and have travelled to every corner of the empire quelling demonic forces and hiding secret objects and texts that are to be revealed at an appropriate time. These objects and texts are known as Terma (Hidden Treasures). The discoverers of these texts are called Terton.

730

King Tri Ditskuktsen requests translations of Chinese classics; one Tang court minister opposes, arguing that the secrets of the classic could not be revealed as they contained information on governance and military strategy.

765-80

Samye, the first monastery in Tibet, is built on the north bank of the Tsangpo River. Its construction is hampered by demonic forces, which are eventually overcome by Tantric master Padmasambhava, who possesses magical powers.

815-35

King Tri Ralpachen champions Buddhism, providing strong state support for the clergy, the construction of temples and translation of Buddhist texts. Ralpachen is murdered by his brother, Langdharma, in 835.

TANGTONG GYELPO

Tangtong Gyelpo (1385–1464) was Tibet's Renaissance man *par excellence*. Nyingmapa yogi, treasure finder, engineer, medic and inventor of Tibetan opera, Tangtong formed a song-and-dance troupe of seven sisters to raise money for his other passion, bridge building. He eventually built 108 bridges in Tibet, the most famous of which was over the Yarlung Tsangpo near modern-day Chushul. Tangtong is often depicted in monastery murals with long white hair and a beard, and is usually holding a section of chain links from one of his bridges.

SAKYAPA ORDER ASCENDANCY & MONGOL OVERLORDSHIP

With the collapse of a central Tibetan state, Tibet's contacts with China dwindled. By the time the Tang dynasty reached the end of its days in 907, China had already recovered almost all the territory it had previously lost to the Tibetans. Throughout the Song dynasty (960–1276) the two nations had virtually no contact with each other, and Tibet's sole foreign contacts were with its southern Buddhist neighbours.

This was all to change when Genghis Khan launched a series of conquests in 1206 that led to a vast Mongol empire that straddled Central Asia and China. Preoccupied with other matters, the Mongols did not give Tibet serious attention until 1239, when they sent a number of raiding parties into the country. Numerous monasteries were razed and the Mongols almost reached Lhasa before turning back.

Tibetan accounts have it that returning Mongol troops related the spiritual eminence of the Tibetan lamas to Godan Khan, grandson of Genghis Khan and ruler of the Kokonor region (modern-day Qinghai). In response Godan summoned Sakya Pandita, the head of Sakya Monastery, to his court. The outcome of this meeting was the beginning of a priest-patron relationship between the deeply religious Tibetans and the militarily adventurous Mongols. Tibetan Buddhism became the state religion of the Mongol empire in east Asia, and the head Sakya lama became its spiritual leader, a position that also entailed temporal authority over Tibet. Many monasteries converted (or were converted) to the Sakya school. For more on the Sakyapa reign, see p203.

The Sakyapa ascendancy lasted less than 100 years. It was strife-torn from the start. The Sakyapa relationship with the Mongol court and its rule of Tibet aroused the jealousy of other religious orders. Political intrigue, power struggles and violence were the order of the day. By 1350, Changchub Gyaltsen, a monk who had first trained in Sakya and then returned to his home district in the Yarlung Valley as a local official, contrived, through alliances and outright confrontation, to overturn the Sakya hegemony. Just 18 years later, the Mongol Yuan dynasty in China lost its grip on power and the Chinese Ming dynasty was established.

822

The Sino-Tibetan treaty is signed, confirming Tibet's right to rule all the conquered territories. The bilingual inscription of the treaty is erected outside the Jokhang.

842

A monk paints his face black, conceals a bow and arrow beneath a long-sleeved robe, and assassinates Langdharma. The event is still commemorated by the Black Hat Dance performed during monastic festivals.

c 900-1600

The Tibetan Empire fragments into smaller kingdoms, the most notable being Guge in Western Tibet. The kings of Guge send students to Kashmir and bring skilled craftsmen from Nepal and Kashmir to build temples and shrines

TIBETAN INDEPENDENCE

Certain Chinese claims on Tibet have looked to the Mongol Yuan dynasty overlordship of the high plateau, and the priest-patron relationship existing at the time, as setting a precedent for Chinese sovereignty over Tibet. Pro-independence supporters state that this is like India claiming sovereignty over Myanmar (Burma) because both were ruled by the British.

In fact, Tibetan submission was offered to the Mongols before they conquered China and it ended when the Mongols fell from power in that country. When the Mongol empire disintegrated, both China and Tibet regained their independence. Sino-Tibetan relations took on the form of exchanges of diplomatic courtesies by two independent governments.

After defeating the Sakyapas, Changchub Gyaltsen undertook to remove all traces of the Mongol administration. In doing this, he drew on the tradition of the former Yarlung kings: officials were required to dress in the manner of the former royal court, a revised version of King Songtsen Gampo's code of law was enacted, a new taxation system was enforced, and scrolls depicting the glories of the Yarlung dynasty were commissioned (although Changchub Gyaltsen claimed they were 'discovered'). The movement was a declaration of Tibet's independence from foreign interference and a search for national identity.

Changchub Gyaltsen and his successors ruled Tibet from Nedong, near the Yarlung Valley, until 1435. Their rule was succeeded by the princes of Rinphug, an area southwest of Lhasa. In 1565, the kings of Tsang became secular rulers of Tibet from Shigatse. Spiritual authority at this time was vested in the Karmapa, head of a Kagyupa suborder at Tsurphu Monastery (p144).

Tibet and its History (1962) by Hugh Richardson offers an excellent, nonpoliticised view of Tibetan history, concentrating on the years from the Gelugpa ascendancy to the Chinese takeover. Richardson headed Britain's trade missions in Gyantse and Lhasa in the 1930s and 1940s.

RISE OF THE GELUGPA & THE DALAI LAMAS

In 1374, a young man named Tsongkhapa set out from his home near Kokonor in eastern Tibet to central Tibet, where he undertook training with all the major schools of Tibetan Buddhism. By the time he was 25, he had already gained a reputation as a teacher and a writer, although he continued to study under eminent lamas of the day.

Tsongkhapa established a monastery at Ganden, near Lhasa, and it was here that he had a vision of Atisha (Jowo-je), the 11th-century Bengali scholar who had been instrumental in the second diffusion of Buddhism in Tibet. At Ganden, Tsongkhapa maintained a course of expounding his thinking, steering clear of political intrigue, and espousing doctrinal purity and monastic discipline. Although it seems unlikely that Tsongkhapa intended to found another school of Buddhism, his teachings attracted many disciples, who found his return to the original teachings of Atisha (Jowo-je) an exciting alternative to the politically tainted Sakyapa and Kagyupa orders.

996

The important monastery of Thöling (p233) is founded and becomes the main centre of Buddhist activities in Tibet. It is there that a massive number of translations of Buddhist texts began.

1042

Atisha, the abbot of the Buddhist Monastic University of Vikramasila, arrives in Tibet. With his disciple Drömtonpa (1004–64) he is credited with founding Kadampa, the first distinctive Tibetan Buddhist School.

1073

The Khon family, which traces its lineage from the nobility of the Yarlung dynasty, founds the Sakya school of Tibetan Buddhism. The family remains the hereditary head of Sakya tradition to this day

REINCARNATION LINEAGES

It is not unusual for an important Tibetan lama to be a *trulku* (also spelt *tulku*), or 'incarnate lama'. There are thought to be several thousand of these lamas in contemporary Tibet. The abbots of many monasteries are *trulku*, and thus abbotship can be traced back through a lineage of rebirths to the original founder of a monastery, or at least to an important figure associated with the founding of the monastery.

Strictly speaking, however, this investiture of power through rebirth is known as *yangsid*, and a *trulku* is a manifestation of a Bodhisattva that repeatedly expresses itself through a series of rebirths. The honorific title *rinpoche*, meaning 'very precious', is a mark of respect and does not necessarily imply that the holder is a *trulku*.

The most famous manifestation of a deity is, of course, the Dalai Lama lineage. The Dalai Lamas are manifestations of Chenresig (Avalokiteshvara), the Bodhisattva of Compassion. The Panchen Lama is a manifestation of Jampelyang (Manjushri), the Bodhisattva of Insight. There is no exclusivity in such a manifestation: Tsongkhapa, founder of the Gelugpa order, was also a manifestation of Jampelyang (Manjushri), as traditionally were the abbots of the Sakya Monastery.

Lamas approaching death often leave behind clues pointing to the location of their reincarnation. The Panchen Lamas have their reincarnation confirmed by lots drawn from a golden urn. Potential candidates are tested by being required to pick out the former lama's possessions from a collection of objects. Disputes over *trulku* status are not uncommon (see The Karmapa

Disciples of Tsongkhapa, determined to propagate their master's teachings, established monasteries at Drepung, Sera and Tashilhunpo, and the movement came to be known as the Gelugpa (Virtuous) order.

By the time of the third reincarnated head of the Gelugpa, Sonam Gyatso (1543–88), the Mongols began to take an interest in Tibet's new and increasingly powerful order. In a move that mirrored the 13th-century Sakyapa entrance into the political arena, Sonam Gyatso accepted an invitation to meet with Altyn Khan near Kokonor in 1578. At the meeting, Sonam Gyatso received the title of *dalai*, meaning 'ocean', and implying 'ocean of wisdom'. The title was retrospectively bestowed on his previous two reincarnations, and Sonam Gyatso became the third Dalai Lama.

The Gelugpa-Mongol relationship marked the Gelugpa's entry into the turbulent waters of worldly affairs. Ties with the Mongols deepened when, at the third Dalai Lama's death in 1588, his next reincarnation was found in a great-grandson of the Mongolian Altyn Khan. The boy was brought to Lhasa with great ceremony under the escort of armed Mongol troops.

It is no surprise that the Tsang kings and the Karmapa of Tsurphu Monastery saw this Gelugpa-Mongol alliance as a direct threat to their power. Bickering ensued, and in 1611 the Tsang king attacked Drepung and Sera Monasteries. The fourth Dalai Lama fled central Tibet and died at the age of 25 in 1616.

1201

Sakya Pandita (1182–1251) travels to India for his education, studying under great Indian gurus. He becomes a religious figure but also a great cultural figure, creating a Tibetan literary tradition drawing on inspiration from Sanskrit poetry.

1206

Genghis Khan launches a series of conquests that lead to a vast Mongol empire that straddles Central Asia and China. Tibetan chiefs submit to the Mongols to avoid invasion.

1240

The grandson of Genghis Khan, Godan, invades central Tibet with 30,000 troops. They ransack the monastery of Reting and put a number of monks to death.

Connection, p146). A family's fortunes are likely to improve if an incarnate lama is discovered among the children; this creates an incentive for fraud.

Most Dalai Lamas comes from poor or well-to-do peasant families; only one Dalai Lama was born in an aristocratic family. The reason is that if a child from wealthy or aristocratic family was chosen there would be dispute and questions of corruption. Therefore, a boy chosen from a poor family is less likely to lead to dispute. The family becomes noble or aristocratic after the son has been chosen as the Dalai Lama. The family of the present Dalai Lama, for example, was by no means aristocratic but his elder brother had already been identified as a *trulku* and his younger brother was also later recognised as a *trulku*.

It is possible to see in the *trulku* system a substitute for the system of hereditary power (as in Western royal lineages) in a society where, historically, many of the major players were celibate and unable to produce their own heirs. Not that celibacy was overwhelmingly the case. The abbots of Sakya took wives to produce their own *trulku* reincarnations, and it is not uncommon for rural *trulkus* to do the same.

The major flaw with the system is the time needed for the reincarnation to reach adulthood. Regents have traditionally been appointed to run the country but this tradition takes on an added dimension under modern political circumstances. The Dalai Lama has made it clear that he will not be reincarnated in Chinese-occupied Tibet and may even be the last Dalai Lama.

THE GREAT FIFTH DALAI LAMA

A successor to the fourth Dalai Lama was soon discovered, and the boy was brought to Lhasa, again under Mongol escort. In the meantime, Mongol intervention in Tibetan affairs continued in the guise of support for the embattled Gelugpa order.

In 1640, Mongol forces intervened on behalf of the Gelugpas, defeating the Tsang forces. The Tsang king was taken captive and later executed, probably at the instigation of Tashilhunpo monks.

Unlike the Sakya-Mongol domination of Tibet, under which the head Sakya lama was required to reside in the Mongol court, the fifth Dalai Lama was able to rule from within Tibet. With Mongol backing, all of Tibet was pacified by 1656, and the Dalai Lama's control ranged from Mt Kailash in the west to Kham in the east. The fifth Dalai Lama had become both the spiritual and temporal sovereign of a unified Tibet.

The fifth Dalai Lama is remembered as having ushered in a great new age for Tibet. He made a tour of Tibet's monasteries, and although he stripped most Kadampa monasteries – his chief rivals for power – of their riches, he allowed them to re-establish. A new flurry of monastic construction began, the major achievement being Labrang Monastery (in what is now Gansu province). In Lhasa, work began on a fitting residence for the head of the Tibetan state: the Potala. The Dalai Lama, with Mongol

1249

Sakya Pandita becomes the preceptor to Godon and converts the Mongols to Buddhism. Godon invests Sakya Pandita as the secular ruler of Tibet, giving him the right to govern 13 myriarchies of central Tibet, Amdo and Kham.

1260

Kublai Khan (1215–94) appoints Phagpa as an imperial preceptor. This ushers in what the Tibetans call the Priest and Preceptor relationship between Mongol Khans, later Chinese Emperors and Tibetan lamas.

1268

The first census of central Tibet is carried out measuring household, land holding and livestock. The census counts some 40,000 households. Basic taxation and a new administrative system is established in Tibet.

financial support, saw to the renovation and expansion of many temples and monasteries.

MANCHUS, MONGOLS & MURDER

Reincarnation lineages were probably first adopted as a means of maintaining the illusion of a continuous spiritual authority within the various monastic orders of Tibet. With the death of the fifth Dalai Lama in 1682, however, the weakness of such a system became apparent. The Tibetan government was confronted with the prospect of finding his reincarnation and then waiting 18 years until the boy came of age. The great personal prestige and authority of the fifth Dalai Lama had played no small part in holding together a newly unified Tibet. The Dalai Lama's regent decided to shroud the Dalai Lama's death in secrecy, announcing that the fifth lama had entered a long period of meditation (over 10 years!).

The fifth Dalai Lama wrote a detailed history of Tibet and his autobiography is regarded as a literary treasure of Tibet.

In 1695 the secret was leaked and the regent was forced to hastily enthrone the sixth Dalai Lama, a boy of his own choosing. The choice was an unfortunate one (see boxed text, below) and could not have come at a worse time.

In China, the Ming dynasty had fallen in 1644 and the Manchus from the north had swiftly moved in to fill the power vacuum, establishing the Manchu Qing dynasty (1644–1912). The events that followed were complicated. Basically, Tibet's ineffectual head of state, the Qing perception of the threat of Tibetan relations with the Mongols, disunity within the ranks of Tibet's Mongol allies and Qing ambitions to extend its power into Tibet led to a Qing intervention that was to have lasting consequences for Tibet.

Tibet's dealings with the new Qing government went awry from the start. Kangxi, the second Qing emperor, took offence when the death of the fifth Dalai Lama was concealed from him. At the same time, an ambitious Mongol prince named Lhabzang Khan came to the conclusion that earlier Mongol leaders had taken too much of a back-seat position in their relations with the Tibetans and appealed to Emperor Kangxi for support. It was granted and, in 1705, Mongol forces descended on Lhasa, killing the Tibetan regent and deposing the sixth Dalai Lama. Depending on your source, he was either captured, with the intention of delivering him to Kangxi in Beijing, dying en

THE SIXTH DALAI LAMA

Tsangyang Gyatso was, shall we say, an unconventional Dalai Lama. A sensual youth with long hair and a penchant for erotic verse, he soon proved himself to be far more interested in wine and women than meditation and study. He refused to take his final vows as a monk and he would often sneak out of the Potala at night to raise hell in the bawdy brothels of Shöl. A resident Jesuit monk described him as a 'dissolute youth' and 'quite depraved', noting that 'no good-looking person of either sex was safe from his unbridled licentiousness'.

1290

Kublai Khan's army supports the Sakya and destroys the main centres of Kagyu. With the death of Kublai Khan in 1294, the power of Sakya also begins to wane in Tibet.

1350-54

Phagmodrupa Jangchuk Gyaltsen overthrows the rule of Sakya, and the Phagmodru Myriarchy establishes its power over central Tibet.

1357-1419

During his lifetime Tsongkhapa establishes himself as a reformer, and is responsible for introducing strict monastic discipline. It was also during Tsongkhapa's time that his disciples founded the strict monastic order.

route at Litang (where he was probably murdered), or he lived to a ripe old age in Amdo. Whatever the sixth Dalai Lama's fate, Lhabzang Khan installed a new Dalai Lama in Lhasa.

Lhabzang Khan's machinations backfired. The Mongol removal, possible murder and replacement of the sixth Dalai Lama, aroused intense hostility in Tibet. Worse still, it created enemies among other Mongol tribes, who saw the Dalai Lama as their spiritual leader.

The Dalai Lamas are depicted in wall paintings holding the Wheel of Law (Wheel of Dharma) as a symbol of the political power gained under the Great Fifth Dalai Lama.

In 1717 the Dzungar Mongols from Central Asia attacked Lhasa, killing Lhabzang Khan and deposing the new Dalai Lama. The resulting confusion in Tibet was the opportunity for which Emperor Kangxi had been waiting. He responded by sending a military expedition to Lhasa in 1720. The Chinese troops drove out the Dzungar Mongols and were received by the Tibetans as liberators. They were unlikely to have been received any other way: with them, they brought the seventh Dalai Lama, who had been languishing in Kumbum Monastery under Chinese 'protection'.

Emperor Kangxi wasted no time in declaring Tibet a protectorate of China. Two Chinese representatives, known as Ambans, were installed at Lhasa, along with a garrison of Chinese troops. It was just a beginning, leading to two centuries of Manchu overlordship and serving as a convenient historical precedent for the communist takeover nearly 250 years later.

MANCHU OVERLORDSHIP

In the 120 years between the death of the seventh Dalai Lama and the majority of the 13th, actual power was wielded by the Dalai Lamas for only seven years.

The seventh Dalai Lama ruled until his death in 1757. However, at this point it became clear that another ruler would have to be appointed until the next Dalai Lama reached adulthood. The post of regent was created, and it was decided that it should be held by a lama.

It is perhaps a poor reflection on the spiritual attainment of the lamas appointed as regents that few were willing to relinquish the reins once they were in the saddle. In the 120 years between the death of the seventh Dalai Lama and the adulthood of the 13th, actual power was wielded by the Dalai Lamas for only seven years. Three of them died very young and under suspicious circumstances. Only the eighth Dalai Lama survived into his adulthood, living a quiet, contemplative life until the age of 45.

BARBARIANS AT THE DOORSTEP

Early contact between Britain and Tibet commenced with a mission to Shigatse headed by a Scotsman, George Bogle, in 1774. Bogle soon ingratiated himself with the Panchen Lama – to the extent of marrying one of his sisters. With the death of the third Panchen Lama in 1780 and the ban on foreign contact that came after the Gurkha invasion of Tibet in 1788, Britain lost all official contact with Tibet.

Meanwhile, Britain watched nervously as the Russian empire swallowed up Central Asia, pushing its borders 1000km further towards India. The reported

c 1300-1500

Peace allows for a renewed flourishing of Buddhism in Tibet, and some of the major monasteries in Tibet are established.

1368

The Mongol Yuan dynasty in China ends, and the Ming dynasty begins. This coincides with the final demise of Sakya rule in Tibet

1391

Gedundrup is born in Tibet; he is later recognized as the first Dalai Lama.

arrival of Russian 'adviser' Agvan Dorjieff in Lhasa exacerbated fears that Russia had military designs on Britain's 'jewel in the crown'.

Dorjieff was a Buryat Buddhist monk from near Lake Baikal who had studied at Drepung Monastery for 15 years before finally becoming a debating partner of the 13th Dalai Lama. Dorjieff seems to have convinced both himself and the Dalai Lama that the Russian empire was the home of Shambhala, the mythical kingdom from the north whose king (or tsar) would come to save Tibet from its enemies.

The concept of reincarnation was first introduced by the Karmapa and later adopted by the Dalai Lamas.

When Dorjieff led an envoy from the Dalai Lama to Tsar Nicholas II in 1898, 1900 and 1901, and when British intelligence confirmed that Lhasa had received Russian missions (while similar British advances had been refused), the Raj broke into a cold sweat. There was even wild conjecture that the tsar was poised to convert to Buddhism.

It was against this background that Lord Curzon, viceroy of India, decided to nip Russian designs in the bud. In late 1903, a British military expedition led by Colonel Francis Younghusband entered Tibet via Sikkim. After several months waiting for a Tibetan delegation, the British moved on to Lhasa, where it was discovered that the Dalai Lama had fled to Mongolia with Dorjieff. However, an Anglo-Tibetan convention was signed following negotiations with Tri Rinpoche, the abbot of Ganden whom the Dalai Lama had appointed as regent in his absence. British forces withdrew after spending just two months in Lhasa. For more on the story of the British invasion, see p186.

The missing link in the Anglo-Tibetan accord was a Manchu signature. In effect, the accord implied that Tibet was a sovereign power and therefore had the right to make treaties of its own. The Manchus objected and, in 1906, the British signed a second accord with the Manchus, one that recognised China's suzerainty over Tibet. In 1910, with the Manchu Qing dynasty teetering on collapse, the Manchus made good on the accord and invaded Tibet, forcing the Dalai Lama once again into flight – this time into the arms of the British in India.

TIBETAN INDEPENDENCE REVISITED

In 1911 a revolution finally toppled the decadent Qing dynasty in China, and by the end of 1912 the last of the occupying Manchu forces were escorted out of Tibet. In January 1913 the 13th Dalai Lama returned to Lhasa from Sikkim.

The government of the new Chinese republic, anxious to maintain control of former Qing territories, sent a telegram to the Dalai Lama expressing regret at the actions of the Manchu oppressors and announcing that the Dalai Lama was being formally restored to his former rank. The Dalai Lama replied that he was uninterested in ranks bestowed by the Chinese and that he was assuming temporal and spiritual leadership of his country.

1409

Tsongkhapa introduces the Mönlam festival, marking Buddha's attainment of enlightenment. The festival is celebrated continuously until the 1960s, revived in 1985 and later banned because it became the focus of Tibetan protest.

1481

The power of the Phagmodurpa is challenged by rulers of Tsang who emerge as a powerful force in Tibet. Powerful local rulers establish alliances with religious orders.

1578

Altan Khan converts to Buddhism and invested Sonam Gyatso as spiritual master. Khan bestows the title 'Dalai Lama', signifying the depth of Sonam Gyatso's knowledge and wisdom.

Tibetans have since read this reply as a formal declaration of independence. As for the Chinese, they chose to ignore it, reporting that the Dalai Lama had responded with a letter expressing his great love for the motherland. Whatever the case, Tibet was to enjoy 30 years free of interference from China. What is more, Tibet was suddenly presented with an opportunity to create a state that was ready to rise to the challenge of the modern world and, if need be, protect itself from the territorial ambitions of China. The opportunity foundered on Tibet's entrenched theocratic institutions, and Tibetan independence was a short-lived affair.

ATTEMPTS TO MODERNISE

During the period of his flight to India, the 13th Dalai Lama had become intimate friends with Sir Charles Bell, a Tibetan scholar and political officer in Sikkim. The relationship was to initiate a warming in Anglo-Tibetan affairs and to see the British playing an increasingly important role as mediators in problems between Tibet and China.

The Snow Lion and the Dragon by Melvyn Goldstein is worth wading through if you want an unsentimental analysis of the historically complex issue of China's claims to Tibet, and the Dalai Lama's options in dealing with the current Chinese leadership.

In 1920 Bell was dispatched on a mission to Lhasa, where he renewed his friendship with the Dalai Lama. It was agreed that the British would supply the Tibetans with modern arms, providing they agreed to use them only for self-defence. Tibetan military officers were trained in Gyantse and India, and a telegraph line was set up linking Lhasa and Shigatse. Other developments included the construction of a small hydroelectric station near Lhasa and the establishment of an English school at Gyantse. Four Tibetan boys were even sent to public school at Rugby in England. At the invitation of the Dalai Lama, British experts conducted geological surveys of parts of Tibet with a view to gauging mining potential.

It is highly likely that the 13th Dalai Lama's trips away from his country had made him realise that it was imperative that Tibet begin to modernise. At the same time he must also have been aware that the road to modernisation was fraught with difficulties. The biggest problem was the Tibetan social system.

Since the rise of the Gelugpa order, Tibet had been ruled as a theocracy. Monks, particularly those in the huge monastic complexes of Drepung and Sera in Lhasa, were accustomed to a high degree of influence in the Tibetan government. And for the monks of Tibet, the principal focus of government was the maintenance of the religious state. Attempts to modernise were seen as inimical to this aim, and they began to meet intense opposition.

Before too long, the 13th Dalai Lama's innovations fell victim to a conservative backlash. Newly trained Tibetan officers were reassigned to nonmilitary jobs, causing a rapid deterioration of military discipline; a newly established police force was left to its own devices and soon became ineffective; the English school at Gyantse was closed down; and a mail service set up by the British was stopped.

1601

A Mongol child, the grandson of Atan Khan, is recognised by the Panchen Lama as the fourth Dalai Lama. This establishes the tradition of the Dalai Lamas being recognized by the Panchen.

1642

Gushri Khan of the Khoshot Mongols subdues the King of Gtsang, and then hands over religious and secular power to the fifth Dalai Lama. Gaden Potrang is established at this time.

1652

The fifth Dalai Lama is invited to China by the Manchu Emperor Shunzhi; to mark the occasion the Yellow Temple (Huangsi) is built on the outskirts of Beijing.

The definitive (but weighty) account of Tibetan history since 1947 is *The Dragon in the Land of Snows* by Tsering Shakya.

However, Tibet's brief period of independence was troubled by more than just an inability to modernise. Conflict sprang up between the Panchen Lama and the Dalai Lama over the autonomy of Tashilhunpo Monastery and its estates. The Panchen Lama, after appealing to the British to mediate, fled to China, where he stayed for 14 years until his death.

In 1933 the 13th Dalai Lama died, leaving the running of the country to the regent of Reting. The present (14th) Dalai Lama was discovered at the village of Pari Takster, near Xining in Amdo, but was brought to Lhasa only after the local Chinese commander had been paid off with a huge 'fee' of 300,000 Chinese dollars. The boy was renamed Tenzin Gyatso and he was installed as the Dalai Lama on 22 February 1940, aged 4½.

In 1947 an attempted coup d'état, known as the Reting Conspiracy, rocked Lhasa. (Reting Rinpoche was thrown into jail for his part in the rebellion, though it remains unclear whether he was set up or not.) And in 1949 the Chinese Nationalist government, against all odds, fell to Mao Zedong and his communist 'bandits'.

LIBERATION

Unknown to the Tibetans, the communist takeover of China was to open what is probably the saddest chapter in Tibetan history. The Chinese 'liberation' of Tibet was eventually to lead to 1.2 million Tibetan deaths, a full-on assault on the Tibetan traditional way of life, the flight of the Dalai Lama to India and the large-scale destruction of almost every historical structure on the plateau. The chief culprits were Chinese ethnic chauvinism and an epidemic of social madness known as the Cultural Revolution.

The Younghusband invasion of Tibet included 10,091 porters, 7096 mules, 2668 ponies, 4466 yaks and six camels!

On 7 October 1950, just a year after the communist takeover of China, 40,000 battle-hardened Chinese troops attacked central Tibet from six different directions. The Tibetan army, a poorly equipped force of around 4000 men, stood little chance of resisting, and any attempt at defence soon collapsed before the onslaught. In Lhasa, the Tibetan government reacted by enthroning the 15-year-old 14th Dalai Lama, an action that brought jubilation and dancing on the streets but did little to protect Tibet from advancing Chinese troops.

An appeal to the UN was equally ineffective. To the shame of all involved, only El Salvador sponsored a motion to condemn Chinese aggression, and Britain and India, traditional friends of Tibet, actually managed to convince the UN not to debate the issue for fear of Chinese disapproval.

Presented with this seemingly hopeless situation, the Dalai Lama dispatched a mission to Beijing with orders that it refer all decisions to Lhasa. As it turned out, there were no decisions to be made. The Chinese had already drafted an agreement. The Tibetans had two choices: sign on the dotted line or face further Chinese aggression.

1706

Lhabzang Khan's army marched into Lhasa and deposes (then executes) the sixth Dalai Lama and installs Yeshi Gyatso, who is not accepted by Tibetans as a Dalai Lama.

1720

The Manchu have conquered the Mongols, and the Tibetans, under the leadership of Pholhana and Khangchennas, organise resistance to Lhabzang Khan. The Manchu army, supported by the Tibetans, overthrow Lhabzang Khan.

1757

The seventh Dalai Lama dies, and a regent rules Tibet; from now until the 1950s regents are appointed from monastic ranks. Regency is seen as a chance for ambitious politicians to make their mark.

The 17-point *Agreement on Measures for the Peaceful Liberation of Tibet* promised a one-country-two-systems structure much like that offered later to Hong Kong and Macau, but provided little in the way of guarantees that such a promise would be honoured. The Tibetan delegates protested that they were unauthorised to sign such an agreement and anyway lacked the seal of the Dalai Lama. Thoughtfully, the Chinese had already prepared a forged Dalai Lama seal, and the agreement was ratified.

Initially, the Chinese occupation of central Tibet was carried out in an orderly way, but tensions inevitably mounted. The presence of large numbers of Chinese troops in the Lhasa region soon depleted food stores and gave rise to massive inflation. Rumours of massacres and forced political indoctrination in Kham (eastern Tibet) began to filter through to Lhasa.

In 1956 uprisings broke out in eastern Tibet (see p243), and in 1957 and 1958 protests and armed revolt spread to central Tibet (with covert CIA assistance). With a heavy heart, the Dalai Lama returned to Lhasa in March 1957 from a trip to India to celebrate the 2500th anniversary of the birth of the Buddha. It seemed inevitable that Tibet would explode in revolt and equally inevitable that it would be ruthlessly suppressed by the Chinese.

An excellent scholarly account of modern Tibet is Melvyn Goldstein's *A History of Modern Tibet 1913–1959: The Demise of the Lamaist State,* which pulls no punches in showing the intrigues, superstitions and governmental ineptitude that led to the demise of the Lhasa government.

1959 UPRISING

The Tibetan New Year of 1959, like all the New Year celebrations before it, attracted huge crowds to Lhasa, doubling the city's usual population. In addition to the standard festival activities, the Chinese had added a highlight of their own – a performance by a Chinese dance group at the Lhasa military base. The invitation to the Dalai Lama came in the form of a thinly veiled command. The Dalai Lama, wishing to avoid offence, accepted.

As preparations for the performance drew near, however, the Dalai Lama's security chief was surprised to hear that the Dalai Lama was expected to attend in secrecy and without his customary contingent of 25 bodyguards. Despite the Dalai Lama's agreement to these conditions, news of them soon leaked, and in no time simmering frustration at Chinese rule came to the boil among the crowds on the streets. It seemed obvious to the Tibetans that the Chinese were about to kidnap the Dalai Lama. Large numbers of people gathered around the Norbulingka (the Dalai Lama's summer palace) and swore to protect him with their lives.

The Dalai Lama had no choice but to cancel his appointment at the military base. In the meantime, the crowds on the streets were swollen by Tibetan soldiers, who changed out of their People's Liberation Army (PLA) uniforms and started to hand out weapons. A group of government ministers announced that the 17-point agreement was null and void, and that Tibet renounced the authority of China.

The Dalai Lama was powerless to intervene, managing only to pen some conciliatory letters to the Chinese as his people prepared for battle on Lhasa's

John Avedon's *In Exile from the Land of Snows* is largely an account of the Tibetan community in Dharamsala, but is an excellent and informative read.

1879

The 13th Dalai Lama is enthroned. In 1895 he takes his final ordination and becomes the secular and spiritual ruler of Tibet, uniting the country with the same authority exercised by the fifth Dalai Lama.

1904

The British mobilise over 8000 soldiers and launch an invasion of Tibet from the Sikkim frontier. The ill-equipped Tibetan army is no match. The 13th Dalai Lama escapes to Mongolia

1909

The 13th Dalai Lama returns to Lhasa; at the ceremony handing over power the Dalai Lama is presented with a new gold seal that described his authority over Tibet as 'indestructible as a diamond'.

TIBET IN EXILE

Modern political boundaries and history have led to the fracture of the Tibetan nation. Large areas of historical and ethnic Tibet are now incorporated into the Chinese provinces of Qinghai and Gansu (traditionally known as Amdo), and Sichuan and Yunnan (traditionally known as Kham). More Tibetans now live outside the Tibetan Autonomous Region than inside it.

Then figure on the 120,000 Tibetans in exile. Refugees continue to brave high passes and rapacious border guards to get to Kathmandu, paying as much as Y800 for a guide to help them across. The trek can take up to 25 days, with no supplies other than all the dried yak meat and *tsampa* (roasted-barley flour) they can carry, and no equipment except canvas shoes to help them get over the 6000m passes. Dharamsala and McLeod Ganj (see www.tibet.net) in India's Himachal Pradesh have become de facto Tibetan towns, although the Dalai Lama, after personally meeting each refugee, actively encourages many of them to return to Tibet.

The great monasteries of Tibet have also relocated, many to the sweltering heat of South India, where you can find replicas of Sera, Ganden and Drepung Monasteries. There are also large communities of Tibetans in mountainous Switzerland and the USA.

With exile has come an unexpected flowering of Tibetan Buddhism abroad; you can now find prayer flags gracing the Scottish glens of Samye Ling Monastery in Dumfrieshire and huge chörtens decorating the countryside of California.

streets. In a last-ditch effort to prevent bloodshed, the Dalai Lama even offered himself to the Chinese. The reply came in the sound of two mortar shells exploding in the gardens of the Norbulingka. The attack made it obvious that the only option remaining to the Dalai Lama was flight. On 17 March, he left the Norbulingka disguised as a soldier. Fourteen days later he was in India.

BLOODSHED IN LHASA

With both the Chinese and the Tibetans unaware of the Dalai Lama's departure, tensions continued to mount in Lhasa. On 20 March, Chinese troops began to shell the Norbulingka and the crowds surrounding it, killing hundreds of people. Later, as the corpses were searched, it became obvious that the Dalai Lama had escaped – 'abducted by a reactionary clique' went the Chinese reports.

Still the bloodshed continued. Artillery bombed the Potala, Sera Monastery and the medical college on Chagpo Ri. Tibetans armed with petrol bombs were picked off by Chinese snipers, and when a crowd of 10,000 Tibetans retreated into the sacred precincts of the Jokhang, that too was bombed. It is thought that after three days of violence, hundreds of Tibetans lay dead in Lhasa's streets. Some estimates put the numbers of those killed far higher.

SOCIALIST PARADISE ON THE ROOF OF THE WORLD

The Chinese quickly consolidated their quelling of the Lhasa uprising by taking control of all the high passes between Tibet and India. Freedom

1910

Imperial Resident for Tibet Zhao Erfeng attempts to re-establish Qing authority and storms Lhasa. The Dalai Lama once again escapes. On his return to Tibet from India, he declares Tibet independent.

1913

The Simla Convention between Britain, China and Tibet is held in India. The main agenda for the conference is to delimit and define the boundary between Tibet and China.

1923

A clash with Lhasa sends the Panchen Lama into exile in China. This is to have disastrous consequences for Tibet: he comes under Chinese influence and never returns.

fighters were disarmed by superior Chinese troops, and able-bodied young men were rounded up, shot, incarcerated or forced to join Chinese work teams. As the Chinese themselves put it, they were liberating Tibet from reactionary forces and ushering in a new socialist society, whether the Tibetans liked it or not.

The Chinese abolished the Tibetan government and set about reordering Tibetan society in accordance with their Marxist principles. The monks and the aristocratic were put to work on menial jobs and subjected to struggle sessions, known as *thamzing*, which sometimes resulted in death. A ferment of class struggle was whipped up and former feudal exploiters – some of whom Tibet's poor may have harboured genuine resentment towards – were subjected to punishments of awful cruelty.

The Chinese also turned their attention to Tibet's 6000-plus 'feudal' monasteries. Tibetans were refused permission to donate food to the monasteries, and monks were compelled to join struggle sessions, discard their robes and marry. Monasteries were stripped of their riches, Buddhist scriptures were burnt and used as toilet paper, and the wholesale destruction of Tibet's monastic heritage began in earnest.

Notable in this litany of disasters was the Chinese decision to alter Tibetan farming practices. Instead of barley, the Tibetan staple, farmers were instructed to grow wheat and rice. Tibetans protested that these crops were unsuited to Tibet's high altitude. They were right, and mass starvation resulted. It is estimated that by late 1961, 70,000 Tibetans had died or were dying of starvation.

By September 1961, even the Chinese-groomed Panchen Lama began to have a change of heart. He presented Mao Zedong with a 70,000-character report on the hardships his people were suffering and also requested, among other things, religious freedom and an end to the sacking of Tibetan monasteries. Four years later he was to disappear into a high-security prison for a 10-year stay. More would soon join him.

THE CULTURAL REVOLUTION

Among the writings of Mao Zedong is a piece entitled 'On Going Too Far'. It is a subject on which he was particularly well qualified to write. What started as a power struggle between Mao and Liu Shaoqi in 1965 had become by August 1966 the Great Proletarian Cultural Revolution, a movement that was to shake China to its core, trample its traditions underfoot, cause countless deaths and give the running of the country over to mobs of Red Guards. All of China suffered in Mao's bold experiment in creating a new socialist paradise, but it was Tibet that suffered most.

The first Red Guards arrived in Lhasa in July 1966. Two months later, the first rally was organised and Chinese-educated Tibetan youths raided the Jokhang, desecrating whatever religious objects they could get their

1933

The 13th Dalai Lama dies, and secular authority is passed to Reting Rinpoche. He is an eminent Gelugpa Lama, but young and totally inexperienced in state affairs. (He is also rather fond of women.)

1935

Birth of the present 14th Dalai Lama; his younger and older brothers are also *trulkus.*

1950

China attacks central Tibet; the Tibetan army is greatly outnumbered and defeat is inevitable. The Tibetan government in Lhasa reacts by enthroning the 15-year-old 14th Dalai Lama. There is jubilation and dancing in the streets.

It's estimated that by late 1961, 70,000 Tibetans had died or were dying from starvation.

hands on. It was the beginning of the large-scale destruction of virtually every religious monument in Tibet, and was carried out in the spirit of destroying the 'Four Olds': old thinking, old culture, old habits and old customs. The Buddhist *'om mani padme hum'* ('hail to the jewel in the lotus') was replaced by the communist mantra, 'long live Chairman Mao'. The Buddha himself was accused of being a 'reactionary'.

For more than three years the Cultural Revolution went about its destructive business of turning the Tibetan world on its head. Tibetan farmers were forced to collectivise into communes and were told what to grow and when to grow it. Anyone who objected was arrested and subjected to *thamzing*. The Dalai Lama became public enemy number one and Tibetans were forced to denounce him as a parasite and traitor. The list goes on, a harrowing catalogue of crimes against a people whose only fault was to hold aspirations that differed from those of their Chinese masters.

By late 1969 the PLA had the Red Guards under control but Tibet continued to be the site of outbreaks of violence. Tibetan uprisings were brief and subdued brutally. In 1972 restrictions on Tibetans' freedom of worship were lifted with much fanfare but little in the way of results. In 1975 a group of foreign journalists sympathetic to the Chinese cause were invited to Tibet. The reports they filed gave a sad picture of a land whose people had been battered by Chinese-imposed policies and atrocities that amounted to nothing less than cultural genocide. In the same year the last CIA-funded Tibetan guerrilla bases, in Mustang, northern Nepal, were closed down.

THE POST-MAO YEARS

By the time of Mao's death in 1976 even the Chinese must have begun to realise that their rule in Tibet had taken a wrong turn. Mao's chosen successor, Hua Guofeng, decided to soften the government's line on Tibet and called for a revival of Tibetan customs. In mid-1977 China announced that it would welcome the return of the Dalai Lama and other Tibetan refugees, and shortly afterwards the Panchen Lama was released from more than 10 years of imprisonment.

Sorrow Mountain: The Journey of a Tibetan Warrior Nun by Ani Pachen and Adelaide Donnelly is the story of a nun who became a resistance leader and was imprisoned by the Chinese for 21 years before escaping to India.

The Tibetan government-in-exile received cautiously the invitation to return to Tibet, and the Dalai Lama suggested that he be allowed to send a fact-finding mission to Tibet first. To the surprise of all involved, the Chinese agreed. As the Dalai Lama remarked in his autobiography, *Freedom in Exile*, it seemed that the Chinese were of the opinion that the mission members would find such happiness in their homeland that 'they would see no point in remaining in exile'. In fact, the results of the mission were so damning that the Dalai Lama decided not to publish them.

Nevertheless, two more missions followed. Their conclusions were despairing. The missions catalogued up to 1.2 million deaths, the destruction

1951

The 17 Point Agreement is signed. It is the first document that formally acknowledges Tibet as a part of the People's Republic of China (PRC). At the signing ceremony Chairman Mao's first remark is 'Welcome Back to the Motherland'.

1954

In 1954 the Dalai Lama is invited to Beijing, where, amid cordial discussions with Mao Zedong, he is told that religion is 'poison'.

late 1950s

The Khampas found the resistance group known as Four Rivers, Six Ranges. The Tibetan exile groups in India make contact with the Americans, securing the CIA's aid and Tibetans were sent for training to the Pacific island of Saipan.

of 6254 monasteries and nunneries, the absorption of two-thirds of Tibet into China, 100,000 Tibetans in labour camps and extensive deforestation. In a mere 30 years, the Chinese had turned Tibet into a land of nearly unrecognisable desolation.

In China, Hua Guofeng's short-lived political ascendancy had been eclipsed by Deng Xiaoping's rise to power. In 1980 Deng sent Hu Yaobang on a Chinese fact-finding mission that coincided with the visits of those sent by the Tibetan government-in-exile.

Hu's conclusions, while not as damning as those of the Tibetans, painted a grim picture of life on the roof of the world. A six-point plan to improve the living conditions and freedoms of the Tibetans was drawn up, taxes were dropped for two years and limited private enterprise was allowed. The Jokhang was reopened for two days a month in 1978; the Potala opened in 1980. As in the rest of China, the government embarked on a programme of extended personal freedoms in concert with authoritarian one-party rule.

The journalist Harrison Salisbury referred to Tibet in the mid-1980s as a 'dark and sorrowing land'.

THE DENG YEARS

The early 1980s saw the return of limited religious freedoms. Monasteries that had not been reduced to piles of rubble began to reopen and some religious artefacts were returned to Tibet from China.

Importantly, there was also a relaxation of the Chinese proscription on pilgrimage. Pictures of the Dalai Lama began to reappear on the streets of Lhasa. Not that any of this pointed to a significant reversal in Chinese thinking on the question of religion, which remained an 'opiate of the masses'. Those who exercised their religious freedoms did so at considerable risk.

Talks aimed at bringing the Dalai Lama back into the ambit of Chinese influence continued, but with little result. A three-person team sent to Beijing from Dharamsala in 1982 heard lectures on how Tibet was part of China, and was told in no uncertain terms that the Dalai Lama would be given a desk job in Beijing if he were to return. By 1983 talks had broken down and the Chinese had decided that they did not want the Dalai Lama to return after all. Tibet, according to the Chinese government, became the 'front line of the struggle against splittism'.

Education was once under the exclusive control of the monasteries, and the introduction of a secular education system has been a major goal of the communist government.

Perhaps most dismaying for Tibetans, however, was the emergence of a Chinese policy of Han immigration to the high plateau. Sinicisation had already been successfully carried out in Xinjiang, Inner Mongolia and Qinghai, and now Tibet was targeted for mass immigration. Attractive salaries and interest-free loans were made available to Chinese willing to emigrate to Tibet, and, in 1984 alone, more than 100,000 Han Chinese took advantage of the incentives to 'modernise' the backward province of Tibet.

In 1986 a new influx of foreigners arrived in Tibet, with the Chinese beginning to loosen restrictions on tourism. The trickle of tour groups and individual travellers soon became a flood. For the first time since the Chinese

1959

Chinese shells explode in the Norbulingka. Amid mounting violence the 14th Dalai Lama flees to exile in India dressed as a soldier.

1964

The Panchen Rinpoche writes the 70,000 Characters Petition, accusing China of committing genocide. It states the policy was creating 'death to a nationality'. Arrested, he is charged with instigating rebellion and planning to flee to India.

1965

On 1 September 1965 the Tibetan Autonomous Region was formally brought into being with much fanfare and Chinese talk of happy Tibetans fighting back tears of gratitude at becoming one with the great motherland.

takeover, visitors from the West were given the opportunity to see the results of Chinese rule in Tibet.

For the Chinese, the foreigners were a mixed blessing. The tourist dollars were appreciated, but foreigners had an annoying habit of sympathising with the Tibetans. They also got to see things that the Chinese would rather they did not see.

When in September 1987 a group of 30 monks from Sera Monastery began circumambulating the Jokhang and crying out 'Independence for Tibet' and 'Long live his Holiness the Dalai Lama', their ranks were swollen by bystanders and arrests followed. Four days later, another group of monks repeated their actions, this time brandishing Tibetan flags.

The monks were beaten and arrested. With Western tourists looking on, a crowd of 2000 to 3000 angry Tibetans gathered. Police vehicles were overturned and Chinese police began firing on the crowd.

The Chinese response was swift. Communications with the outside world were broken and foreigners were evicted from Lhasa. It was still too late, however, to prevent eyewitness accounts from reaching newspapers around the world. A crackdown followed in Lhasa, but it failed to prevent further protests in the following months.

The Mönlam festival of March 1988 saw shooting in the streets of Lhasa, and that December a Dutch traveller was shot in the shoulder; 18 Tibetans died and 150 were wounded in the disturbances.

THE DALAI LAMA & THE SEARCH FOR SETTLEMENT

By the mid-1970s, the Dalai Lama had become a prominent international figure, working tirelessly from his government-in-exile in Dharamsala to make the world more aware of his people's plight. His visits to the USA led to official condemnation of the Chinese occupation of Tibet. In 1987 he addressed the US Congress and outlined a five-point peace plan.

An illuminating glimpse of the Tibetan experience is provided by *Freedom in Exile: The Autobiography of the Dalai Lama*. With great humility the Dalai Lama outlines his personal philosophy, his hope to be reunited with his homeland and the story of his life. *Kundun* by Mary Craig is a biography of the Dalai Lama's family.

The plan called for Tibet to be established as a 'zone of peace'; for the policy of Han immigration to Tibet to be abandoned; for a return to basic human rights and democratic freedoms; for the protection of Tibet's natural heritage and an end to the dumping of nuclear waste on the high plateau; and for joint discussions between the Chinese and the Tibetans on the future of Tibet. The Chinese denounced the plan as an example of 'splittism'. They gave the same response when, a year later, the Dalai Lama elaborated on the speech before the European parliament at Strasbourg in France, conceding any demands for full independence and offering the Chinese the right to govern Tibet's foreign and military affairs.

Protests and crackdowns continued in Tibet through 1989, and despairing elements in the exiled Tibetan community began to talk of the need to take up arms. It was an option that the Dalai Lama had consist-

1967-76

The Cultural Revolution sweeps China and Tibet. The Bhuddist *'om mani padme hum'* ('hail to the jewel in the lotus') is replaced by the Communist mantra 'long live Chairman Mao'.

1979-85

Tibet, under the rule of China, enters a period of liberalisation and reform; limited religious freedoms are restored.

1987-89

Pro-independence demonstrations take place in Lhasa; the response is violent, and martial law is declared.

ently opposed. His efforts to achieve peace and freedom for his people were recognised on 4 October 1989, when he was awarded the Nobel peace prize.

On 5 March 1989 Lhasa erupted in the largest anti-Chinese demonstration since 1959. Beijing reacted strongly, declaring martial law in Tibet, which lasted for more than a year. Hu Jintao was appointed Party Secretary in Tibet. Under his leadership some cultural and religious freedoms were tolerated, but control was strict. The issue of religious practices remained one of the main sources of friction between the government and the Tibetan people.

In January 1989 while visiting Tashilhunpo. the traditional seat of all the Panchen Lamas, the 10th Panchen Lama died, triggering a succession crisis that remains unresolved (see p196). The Dalai Lama identified the 11th Panchen Lama in 1995, whereupon the Chinese authorities detained the boy and his family (who have not been seen since) and orchestrated the choice of their own preferred candidate.

The Chinese began to toughen their policy towards the Dalai Lama and launched the anti-Dalai Lama campaign inside Tibet, compelling all government officials to denounce the Dalai Lama. Even in the monasteries the monks had to sign statements opposing the Dalai Lama. On 5 September 2007, the Chinese government passed a new law requiring all incarnate lamas to be approved by the government.

The Chinese authorities believe that one of the reasons for continuing separatist sentiments and opposition is Tibet's lack of integration with China. Since the 1990s the chief aim of the government has been to fully integrate Tibet with China. This has meant the opening of Tibet, allowing (and actively encouraging) Chinese migration into the region. In June 2006 President Hu Jintao formally inaugurated the controversial train that directly links Beijing and Lhasa for the first time (see p340).

Neither Mao Zedong nor Deng Xiaoping ever visited Tibet.

1989

The 14th Dalai Lama's efforts to achieve peace and freedom for his people are recognised when he is awarded the Nobel Peace Prize.

1995

The Dalai Lama recognises Gedhun Choekyi Nyima as the 11th Panchen Lama. The Chinese government appoints Choekyi Gyaltsen as the 11th Panchen Lama; Choekyi Nyima and family are not seen or heard in public since.

2007

The railway linking Beijing to Lhasa opens, bringing with it a huge number of Chinese travellers – more than two million in the first year.

The Culture

TIBETAN IDENTITY

Tibetans are such a deeply religious people that a basic knowledge of Buddhism is essential in understanding their world. Buddhism permeates most facets of Tibetan daily life and shapes aspirations in ways that are often quite alien to the Western frame of mind. The ideas of accumulating merit, of sending sons to be monks, of undertaking pilgrimages, and of devotion to the sanctity and power of natural places are all elements of the unique fusion between Buddhism and the older shamanistic Bön faith.

www.tibetanculture.org offers bite-sized overviews of many aspects of Tibetan culture.

For travellers, the easy smile of most Tibetans is infectious and it is rare for major cultural differences to get in the way of communication. Tibetans are among the loveliest people in Asia and very easy to get along with: open, joyful, sincere, tolerant and good-humoured. This combination is all the more remarkable in view of the anger and long-harboured resentment that must lie under the surface in Tibet.

TRADITIONAL LIFESTYLE

Traditionally there have been at least three distinct segments of Tibetan society: the *drokpa* (nomads; p148); the *rongpa* (farmers of the Tibetan valleys); and the *sangha* (community of monks and nuns). Each lead very different lives but share a deep faith in Buddhism.

These communities have also shared a remarkable resistance to change. Until the early 20th century Tibet was a land in which virtually the only use for the wheel was as a device for activating mantras. Tibet has changed more in the past 50 years than in the previous 500, although many traditional social structures have endured Chinese attempts at iconoclasm.

Farming communities usually comprise a cluster of homes surrounded by agricultural lands that were once owned by the nearest large monastery and protected by a *dzong* (fort). The farming itself is carried out with the assistance of a *dzo*, a breed of cattle where bulls have been crossbred with yaks. Some wealthier farmers own a small 'walking tractor' (a very simple tractor engine that can pull a plough or a trailer). Harvested grain is carried by donkeys to a threshing ground where it is trampled by cattle or threshed with poles. The grain is then cast into the air from a basket and the task of winnowing carried out by the breeze. Animal husbandry is still extremely important in Tibet, and there are around 21 million head of livestock in the country.

Until recently such communities were effectively self-sufficient in their needs and, although theirs was a hard life, it could not be described as abject poverty. Village families pulled together in times of need. Plots of land were usually graded in terms of quality and then distributed so that the land of any one family included both better- and poorer-quality land. This is changing rapidly as many regions become more economically developed.

Imports such as tea, porcelain, copper and iron from China were traditionally compensated by exports of wool and skins. Trading was usually carried out in combination with pilgrimage or by nomads. Most villages now have at least one entrepreneur who has set up a shop and begun to ship in Chinese goods from the nearest urban centre.

Individual households normally have a shrine in the home or in a small building in the family compound. There might also be several religious texts, held in a place of honour, which are reserved for occasions when a monk or holy man visits the village. Ceremonies for blessing yaks and other livestock to ensure a productive year are still held. One of the highlights of the year for rural Tibetans is visiting nearby monasteries at festival times or making a pilgrimage to a holy site. As traditional life reasserts itself after 50 years of communist dogma and the disastrous Cultural Revolution, many of these traditions are slowly making a comeback. A burgeoning economy is starting to fuel a growth in traditional crafts, at least in Lhasa, though this is partially for the tourism market.

Pilgrimage

Pilgrimage is practised throughout the world, although as a devotional exercise it has been raised to a level of particular importance in Tibet. This may be because of the nomadic element in Tibetan society; it may also be that in a mountainous country with no roads and no wheeled vehicles, walking long distances became a fact of life, and by visiting sacred places en route pilgrims could combine walking with accumulating merit. To most Tibetans their natural landscape is imbued with a series of sacred visions and holy 'power places': mountains can be perceived as mandala images, rocks assume spiritual dimensions, and the earth is imbued with healing powers.

RESPONSIBLE TOURISM

Tourism has already affected many areas in Tibet. Most children will automatically stick their hand out for a sweet, a pen or anything. In some regions, eg around Mt Everest, Tibetans have become frustrated at seeing a stream of rich tourist groups but few tangible economic results. Please try to bear the following in mind as you travel through Tibet:

- Try to patronise as many small local Tibetan businesses, restaurants and guesthouses as possible. Revenues created by organised group tourism go largely into the pockets of the Chinese authorities.
- Doling out medicines can encourage people not to seek proper medical advice, while handing out sweets or pens to children encourages begging. If you wish to contribute something constructive, it's better to give pens directly to schools and medicines to rural clinics, or make a donation to an established charity. See p327.
- Monastery admission fees go largely to local authorities, so if you want to donate to the monastery, leave your offering on the altar.
- Don't buy skins or hats made from endangered animals such as snow leopards.
- Don't pay to take a photograph of someone, and don't photograph someone if they don't want you to. If you agree to send a photograph of someone, please follow through on this.
- If you have any pro-Tibetan sympathies, be very careful with whom you discuss them. Don't put Tibetans in a politically difficult or even potentially dangerous situation. This includes handing out photos of the Dalai Lama (these are illegal in Tibet) and politically sensitive materials.
- Act respectfully when visiting temples and monasteries. Always circle a monastery building, statue or *chörten* (stupa) in a clockwise direction (unless it is a Bön monastery)
- If you have a guide, try to ensure that he or she is a Tibetan, as Chinese guides invariably know little about Tibetan Buddhism or monastery history.
- Dress responsibly. Short skirts and shorts are not a suitable option, especially at religious sites. Wearing shorts in Tibet (even when trekking) is akin to walking around with 'TOURIST!' tattooed on your forehead.
- For more on the ethical issues involved in visiting Tibet, see www.savetibet.org.

For more on the etiquette of visiting monasteries, see p102. For information on responsible trekking, see p286.

TOURISTS & SKY BURIAL

Sky burials are funeral services and, naturally, Tibetans are often very unhappy about camera-toting foreigners heading up to sky-burial sites. The Chinese authorities do not like it either and may fine foreigners who attend a burial. You should never pay to see a sky burial and you should *never* take photos. Even if Tibetans offer to take you up to a sky-burial site, it is unlikely that other Tibetans present will be very happy about it. If nobody invited you, don't go.

The motivations for pilgrimage are many, but for the ordinary Tibetan it amounts to a means of accumulating *sonam* (merit) or *tashi* (good fortune). The lay practitioner might go on pilgrimage in the hope of winning a better rebirth, to cure an illness, end a spate of bad luck or as thanks for an answered prayer.

Death

Although the early kings of Tibet were buried with complex funerary rites, ordinary Tibetans have not traditionally been buried. The bodies of the very poor were usually dumped in a river when they died and the bodies of the very holy were cremated and their ashes enshrined in a chörten (or their bodies dried in salt). But in a land where soil is at a premium and wood for cremation is scarcer still, most bodies were, and still are, disposed of by sky burial.

Older country folk may stick out their tongue when they meet you, a very traditional form of respect that greeted the very first travellers to Tibet centuries ago. Some sources say that this is done to prove that the person is not a devil, since devils have green tongues, even when they take human form.

After death, the body is kept for 24 hours in a sitting position while a lama recites prayers from *The Tibetan Book of the Dead* to help the soul on its journey through the 49 levels of Bardo, the state between death and rebirth. Three days after death, the body is blessed and early-morning prayers and offerings are made to the monastery. The body is folded up (the spine is broken and the body itself is folded into a surprisingly small package) and carried on the back of a close friend to the *dürtro* (burial site). Here, special body-breakers known as *rogyapas* cut off the deceased's hair, chop up the body and pound the bones together with tsampa (roasted-barley flour) for vultures to eat.

There is little overt sadness at a sky burial; the soul is considered to have already departed and the burial itself is considered to be mere disposal, or rather a final act of compassion to the birds. Sky burial is, however, very much a time to reflect on the impermanence of life. Death is seen as a powerful agent of transformation and spiritual progress. Tibetans are encouraged to witness the disposal of the body and to confront death openly and without fear. This is one reason that Tantric ritual objects such as trumpets and bowls are often made from human bone.

Dress

Many Tibetans in Lhasa now wear modern clothes imported from China but traditional dress is still the norm in the countryside. The Tibetan national dress is a *chuba* (long-sleeved sheepskin cloak), tied around the waist with a sash and worn off the shoulder with great bravado by nomads and Khampas (people from Kham). *Chubas* from eastern Tibet in particular have super-long sleeves, which are tied around the waist. An inner pouch is often used to store money belts, amulets, lunch and even small livestock. Most women wear a long dress, topped with a colourful striped apron known as a *pangden*. Traditional Tibetan boots have turned-up toes, so as to kill fewer bugs when walking (or so it is said).

Women generally set great store in jewellery, and their personal wealth and dowry are often invested in it. Coral is particularly valued (as Tibet is so far from the sea), as are amber, turquoise and silver. The Tibetan *zee*, a unique elongated agate stone with black and white markings, is highly prized for its protective qualities and can fetch tens of thousands of US dollars. Earrings are common in both men and women and they are normally tied on with a piece of cord. You can see all these goodies for sale around the Barkhor in Lhasa.

Tibetan women, especially those from Amdo (northeastern Tibet and Qinghai), wear their hair in 108 braids, an auspicious number in Buddhism. Khampa men plait their hair with red or black tassels and wind the lot around their head. Cowboy hats are popular in summer and fur hats are common in winter. Most pilgrims carry a *gau* (amulet), with perhaps a picture of the owner's personal deity or the Dalai Lama inside.

TRADITIONAL CULTURE UNDER THREAT

The greatest threat to Tibetan cultural life comes from development and Chinese migration, as government subsidies and huge infrastructure projects change the face and ethnic make-up of cities across the breadth of Tibet.

Investment from Beijing has brought with it a surge in Han immigrants hungry for jobs or just filled with idealism about life on the roof of the world. Although no figures are available, it is obvious that many Chinese people, attracted by preferential loans and tax rates, a less strictly enforced one-child policy, stipends for a hardship posting and easy business opportunities, are setting up shop in urban centres all over Tibet. An education system that exclusively uses the (Mandarin) Chinese language at higher levels reinforces the fact that only Sinicised Tibetans are able to actively participate in Tibet's economic advances.

Religious freedoms have increased in recent years, though any form of political dissent is quickly crushed. Monks and nuns, who are often the focus of protests and Tibetan aspirations for independence, are regarded with suspicion by the authorities. Nuns, in particular, considering their small numbers, have been very politically active and accounted for 55 of the 126 independence protests in the mid-1990s. Regulations make it impossible for nuns, once arrested and imprisoned, to return to their nunneries.

And yet for all the new roads, karaoke joints, brothels, Chinese TV, internet bars and mobile phones that have swept across Tibet, traditional and religious life remain at the core of most Tibetans' identities. Pepsi and Budweiser may now rival Buddhist deities as the most popular icons in Tibet, but the quintessence of Tibet remains remarkably intact.

Tibetans are often named after the day of week they were born on; thus you'll meet Nyima (Sunday), Dawa (Monday), Mingmar (Tuesday), Lhagpa (Wednesday), Phurba (Thursday), Pasang (Friday) and Pemba (Saturday). Popular names such as Sonam (merit) and Tashi (good fortune) carry religious connotations.

ECONOMY

China's epic drive to develop its western hinterland has had a considerable impact on Tibet, and its economy is booming. Growth over the last six years has averaged an impressive 12%, trade is growing at 50% and GDP hit

GUCCI GUCHI

Being a devout Buddhist region, Tibet has a long tradition of begging for alms. Generally, beggars will approach you with thumbs up and mumble *'guchi, guchi'* – 'please, please' (not a request for Italian designer clothes).

Tibetans tend to be generous with beggars and usually hand out a couple of mao to anyone deserving. Banks and monasteries will swap a Y10 note for a wad of one-mao notes, which go a long way.

If you do give (and the choice is entirely yours), give the same amount Tibetans do; don't encourage the beggars to make foreigners a special target by handing out large denominations. It's worth keeping all your small change in one pocket – there's nothing worse than pulling out a Y100!

PILGRIMAGE

In Tibet there are countless sacred destinations that act as pilgrim magnets, ranging from lakes and mountains to monasteries and caves that once served as meditation retreats for important yogis. Specific pilgrimages are often prescribed for specific ills; certain mountains, for example, expiate certain sins. A circumambulation of Mt Kailash offers the possibility of liberation within three lifetimes, while a circuit of Lake Manasarovar can result in spontaneous buddhahood. A circuit of Tsari in southeastern Tibet can improve a pilgrim's chances of being reborn with special powers, such as the ability to fly.

Pilgrimage is also more powerful in certain auspicious months; at certain times, circumambulations of Bönri are reckoned to be 700 million times more auspicious than those of other mountains.

The three foremost pilgrimage destinations of Tibet are all mountains: Mt Kailash, in western Tibet; Tapka Shelri and the Tsari Valley in southeastern Tibet; and Mt Labchi, east of Nyalam, in Tsang. Only the first is open to foreigners. Lakes such as Manasarovar, Yamdrok-tso, Nam-tso and Lhamo La-tso attract pilgrims, partly because their sacred water is thought to hold great healing qualities. The cave hermitages of Drak Yerpa, Chim-puk and Sheldrak are particularly venerated by pilgrims for their associations with Guru Rinpoche.

Pilgrims often organise themselves into large groups, hire a truck and travel around the country visiting all the major sacred places in one go. Pilgrim guidebooks have existed for centuries to help travellers interpret the 24 'power places' of Tibet. Such guides even specify locations where you can urinate or fart without offending local spirits (and probably your fellow pilgrims).

Making a pilgrimage is not just a matter of walking to a sacred place and then going home. There are a number of activities that help focus the concentration of the pilgrim. The act of kora (circumambulating the object of devotion) is chief among these. Circuits of three, 13 or 108 koras are especially auspicious, with sunrise and sunset the most auspicious hours. The particularly devout prostrate their way along entire pilgrimages, stepping forward the length of their body after each prostration (often marking the spot with a small conch shell) and starting all over again. The hardcore even do their koras sideways, advancing one side step at a time!

Most pilgrims make offerings during the course of a pilgrimage. *Kathaks* (white ceremonial scarves) are offered to lamas or holy statues as a token of respect (and then often returned by the lama as a blessing). Offerings of yak butter or oil, fruit, tsampa (dough made with roasted-barley flour), seeds and money are all left at altars, and bowls of water and *chang* (barley beer) are replenished. Monks often act as moneychangers, converting Y10 notes into wads of one-mao notes, which helps stretch limited funds.

Outside chapels, at holy mountain peaks, passes and bridges, you will see pilgrims throwing offerings of tsampa or printed prayers into the air (often with the cry *'sou, sou, sou*!'). Pilgrims also collect sacred rocks, herbs, earth and water from a holy site to take back home to those who couldn't make the pilgrimage, and leave behind personal items as a break from the past, often leaving them hanging in a tree. Other activities in this spiritual assault course include adding stones to cairns, rubbing special healing rocks, and squeezing through narrow gaps in rocks as a method of sin detection. Many of these actions are accompanied by the visualisation of various deities and practices.

Koras usually include stops of particular spiritual significance, such as rock-carved syllables or painted buddha images. Many of these carvings are said to be 'self-arising', ie not having been carved by a human hand. The Mt Kailash kora is a treasure trove of these, encompassing sky-burial sites, stones that have 'flown' from India, monasteries, bodhisattva footprints and even a lingam (phallic image).

Other pilgrimages are carried out to visit a renowned holy man or teacher. Blessings from lamas, *trulkus* (reincarnated lamas) or *rinpoche*s (highly esteemed lamas) are particularly valued, as are the possessions of famous holy men. According to Keith Dowman in his book *The Sacred Life of Tibet,* the underpants of one revered lama were cut up and then distributed among his eager followers!

$3.7 billion in 2006. New businesses and hotels are popping up everywhere, spurred on by investment from China's eastern provinces.

Not all Chinese are here to earn money, though. Wealthy urban Chinese tourists are flocking to Tibet in droves to spend it, and tourism is an increasingly important source of revenue. Tibet currently receives three million tourists in a year, a rate growing by an amazing 40% annually. This influx bring in US$300 million each year. More than 93% of tourists to Tibet are Chinese. Over 30,000 tourists arrived at Lhasa airport during the May 1 national holiday.

Tibetans still use the lunar calendar for traditional events. Years are calculated on a 60-year cycle and divided into five elements and 12 zodiac animals. Thus 2007/8 is the Tibetan year of the Fire Pig.

The 2006 opening of the train line between Tibet and Qinghai Province (see p339) has had a huge effect on both tourism and economic growth, cutting transport costs by US$23 million in the first year alone. The train also transported over 1.5 million additional people to Tibet during the same period

The Tibetan plateau has rich deposits of gold, zinc, chromium, silver, boron, uranium and other metals. The plateau is home to most of China's huge copper reserves. A single mine in northern Tibet is said to hold over half the world's total deposits of lithium. Chinese scientists announced the discovery of five billion tonnes of oil and gas in the Changtang region in 2001. Reports indicate mining now accounts for one-third of Tibet's industrial output. Mining has long been traditionally inimical to Tibetans, who believe it disturbs the sacred essence of the soil. Many fear that the train will speed up mining. The Chinese name for Tibet, Xizang – the Western Treasure House – now has a ring of prophetic irony.

A Cultural History of Tibet by David Snellgrove and Hugh Richardson is a good introduction to the history and culture of Tibet, but is marred by the use of a scholarly and at times indecipherable transliteration system of Tibetan, eg Samye Monastery is rendered 'bSam-yas'.

There is an increasing economic and social divide in Tibet. Per capita disposable income currently stands at over US$1000 in the towns and only $260 in the countryside.

Many Tibetans maintain that Chinese immigrants are the real winners in the race to get rich in Tibet, while China protests that it is simply developing and integrating one of its most backward provinces, at a large financial loss.

POPULATION

Modern political boundaries and history have led to the fracture of the Tibetan nation. Large areas of historical and ethnic Tibet are now incorporated into the Chinese provinces of Qinghai and Gansu (traditionally known as

ON THE ROAD

'The hardest thing?' Phurba asked, clacking his crude wooden hand covers in front of his forehead and chest and dropping to the ground in full prostration.

'The hardest thing is definitely crossing the passes, especially when it's snowing. It'll take us three months to get from Pasho to Lhasa; we do about 7km a day. Yes, we have support – we take turns pushing that cart with our supplies.' He pointed to a decrepit-looking wheelbarrow loaded with duvets, a blackened kettle and a huge bag of tsampa.

All over eastern and northern Tibet, in the run-up to the Saga Dawa festival, you'll see similar bands of pilgrims hiking, prostrating and inching their way like caterpillars along the highways. Each prostration takes them a body length closer to their goal; the holy city of Lhasa. Dressed in aprons and hair nets, equipped with basic rucksacks of cloth and sticks, the pilgrims burn with a devotion that's hard to fathom.

'Why don't you take the bus?' I asked foolishly.

'The bus isn't interesting – you can't see anything travelling that fast.'

Looking guiltily back at my waiting Land Cruiser, I nodded in agreement. To me, at least, their pilgrimage seemed part-devotion, part-workout, part-camping expedition. It was a kind of spiritual road trip, a chance to see the country and earn a higher rebirth. And maybe lose a few pounds.

Tibetan babies are considered to be one year old at the time of birth, since reincarnation took place nine months previously upon conception.

Tibetans show respect to an honoured guest or a lama by placing a *kathak* (prayer scarf) around their neck. When reciprocating, hold the scarf out in both hands with palms turned upwards.

Amdo), and Sichuan and Yunnan (traditionally known as Kham). More Tibetans now live outside the Tibetan Autonomous Region (TAR) than inside it. Over 120,000 Tibetans live in exile abroad, mostly in India, and over 3000 make the dangerous illegal crossing over the high mountain passes via Nepal every year.

Population Control

Population control is a cornerstone of Chinese government policy, but the regulations are generally less strictly enforced in Tibet. 'Minority nationalities' such as the Tibetans are allowed two children before they lose certain stipends and housing allowances. Ironically, the most effective form of birth control in modern Tibet still seems to be to join a monastery.

Ethnic Groups

Although local mythology has the Tibetan people descended from the union of a monkey and ogress, the Tibetan people probably descended from nomadic tribes who migrated from the north and settled to sedentary cultivation of Tibet's river valleys. About a quarter of Tibetans are still nomadic. There are considerable variations between regional groups of Tibetans. The most recognisable are the Khampas of eastern Tibet, who are generally larger and a bit more rough-and-ready than other Tibetans and who wear red or black tassels in their long hair. Women from Amdo are especially conspicuous because of their elaborate braided hairstyles and jewellery.

There are pockets of other minority groups, such as the Lhopa (Lhoba) and Monpa in the southeast of Tibet, but these make up less than 1% of the total population and only very remote pockets remain. A more visible ethnic group

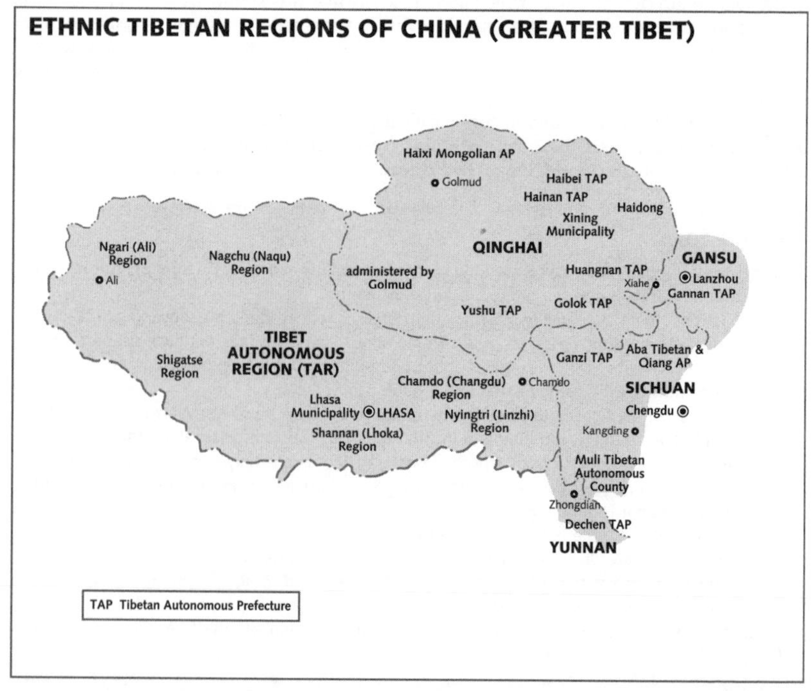

TIBET & THIS GUIDEBOOK

This book covers the areas of the Tibetan cultural region that fit best with travel patterns of the majority of travellers to Tibet – the Tibetan Autonomous Region (TAR) and Western Sichuan province (as well as Kathmandu, a prominent travel gateway to Tibet). Other parts of the Tibetan region (in Sichuan, Gansu and Qinghai provinces) are covered in Lonely Planet's *China* and *China's Southwest* guides.

are the Hui Muslims. Tibet's original Muslim inhabitants were largely traders or butchers (a profession that most Buddhists abhor), although the majority of recent migrants are traders and restaurant owners from southern Gansu province. Tibetans are also closely related to the Qiang people of northern Sichuan, the Sherpas of Nepal and the Ladakhis of India.

MULTICULTURALISM

Official statistics claim 93% of the TAR's population is Tibetan, a figure that is hotly contested by almost everyone except the government. Chinese figures for the population of Lhasa, for example, suggest it is just over 87% Tibetan and just under 12% Han Chinese, a ratio that stretches the credulity of anyone who has visited the city in recent years. It is more likely that somewhere in the vicinity of 50% of Lhasa's population is Han Chinese.

Tibetans often gesture with their lips to indicate a particular direction, so if a member of the opposite sex pouts at you, they are just showing you where to go. Also if a road worker looks like he's blowing you kisses, he probably just wants a cigarette. Then again, maybe he's just blowing you kisses…

The current flood of Chinese immigrants into Tibet has been termed China's 'second invasion'. The Chinese government is very coy about releasing figures that would make it clear just how many Chinese there are in Tibet, but for visitors who have made repeated trips to Tibet the increased numbers of Han Chinese are undeniable.

Perhaps unsurprisingly, there's an endemic mistrust between the Tibetans and Chinese and ethnic tensions bubble just under the surface. Many Tibetans see the Han Chinese as land-hungry outsiders, while the Chinese often complain that the Tibetans are ungrateful and slow to adjust to economic opportunities. The Han Chinese word for Tibetan, *zàng* (藏), is a homonym for 'dirty' (*zāng*; 脏), which easily lends itself to racist slurs. Actual violence between the two communities is rare, but it's quickly apparent to visitors that most towns have quite separate Chinese and Tibetan (and in some cases also Hui Muslim) quarters.

WOMEN IN TIBET

Women have traditionally occupied a strong position in Tibetan society, often holding the family purse strings. Several of Tibet's most famous Buddhist practitioners, such as Yeshe Tsogyel and Machik Labdronma, were women, and Tibet's nuns remain at the vanguard of political dissent. Most of the road workers you see across the plateau are women!

Up until the Chinese invasion many Tibetan farming villages practised polyandry. When a woman married the eldest son of a family she also married his younger brothers (providing they did not become monks). The children of such marriages referred to all the brothers as their father. The practice was aimed at easing the inheritance of family property (mainly the farming land) and avoiding the break-up of small plots.

Torma are small offerings made of yak butter and tsampa (roasted-barley flour) adorned with coloured medallions of butter. They probably developed as a substitute for animal sacrifice. Most are made during the Shötun festival and remain on display throughout the year.

ARTS

Almost all Tibetan art, with perhaps the exception of some folk crafts, is inspired by Buddhism. Wall hangings, paintings, architecture, literature, even dance: all in some way or another attest to the influence of the Indian religion that found its most secure resting place in Tibet.

TIBET CHIC

Hollywood's flirtation with Tibet started way back in 1937 with the film version of James Hilton's classic *Lost Horizon*. The pseudo-Tibet theme underwent a bit of a revival with such films as *The Golden Child* (1986), apparently inspired by the young Karmapa of Tsurphu Monastery, and Bernardo Bertolucci's *Little Buddha* (1993), merging the life story of the Buddha (Keanu Reeves, dude!) with the tale of a young Seattle boy who is discovered to be a reincarnated lama. But it was the release in 1997 of *Seven Years in Tibet* and *Kundun,* two films detailing the Chinese invasion of Tibet, that really made Tibet chic.

Richard Gere remains the most outspoken advocate of Tibetan independence in Tinseltown, using the Academy Awards ceremony in 1992 as a platform to publicise the cause. But the Hollywood connection doesn't end there. Robert Thurman, the father of actress Uma Thurman, is the Tsongkhapa Professor of Indo-Tibetan Studies at Columbia University. Other celebrities with an active interest in Tibetan Buddhism include Harrison Ford, Goldie Hawn and Oliver Stone. There is even talk that *Star Wars* creator George Lucas got the name for the character Luke Skywalker from the Tibetan *Khandroma* (or Dakini), which is generally translated as a 'sky walker'. Perhaps most surprising of all was the announcement that Steven Seagal, the ponytailed, kick-boxing movie star, was discovered to be a reincarnated *trulku* (incarnate lama) of the Nyingma order of Tibetan Buddhism!

Whether all this media fuss actually helped the Tibetan cause is up for debate. Some argue that the hype has merely helped to perpetuate a media myth of Tibet that doesn't serve the interests of the Tibetan people. Back in Hollywood they grin knowingly: 'There's no such thing as bad press.'

At the same time, the arts of Tibet represent the synthesis of many influences. The Buddhist art and architecture of the Pala and Newari kingdoms of India and Nepal were an important early influence in central Tibet, and the Buddhist cultures of Khotan and Kashmir were dominant in western Tibet. Newari influence is clearly visible in the early woodcarvings of the Jokhang, and Kashmiri influence is particularly strong in the murals of Tsaparang in western Tibet. As China came to play an increasingly major role in Tibetan affairs, Chinese influences, too, were assimilated, as is clear at Shalu Monastery near Shigatse and in the Karma Gadri style prevalent in eastern Kham. A later, clearly Tibetan style known as Menri was perfected in the monasteries of Drepung, Ganden and Sera.

Tibetan art is deeply conservative and conventional. Personal expression and innovation are not valued. Individual interpretation is actually seen as an obstacle to Tibetan art's main purpose, which is to represent the path to enlightenment. The creation of religious art in particular is an act of merit and is generally anonymous. The use of colour is decided purely by convention and rigid symbolism.

If you are interested in actually creating, not just understanding, Tibetan art, look for the master work on the subject, *Tibetan Thangka Painting: Methods & Materials* by David P Jackson and Janice A Jackson.

Much of Tibet's artistic heritage fell victim to the Cultural Revolution. What was not destroyed was, in many cases, ferreted away to China or onto the Hong Kong art market. In recent years over 13,500 images have been returned to Tibet, still just a fraction of the number stolen. Many of Tibet's traditional artisans were persecuted or fled Tibet. It is only in recent years that remaining artists have again been able to return to their work and start to train young Tibetans in skills that faced the threat of extinction.

Dance & Drama

Anyone who is lucky enough to attend a Tibetan festival should have the opportunity to see performances of *cham*, a ritual dance performed over several days by monks and lamas. Although every movement and gesture of *cham* has significance, it is no doubt the spectacle of the colourful masked dancers that awes the average pilgrim.

Cham is about the suppression of malevolent spirits and is a throwback to the pre-Buddhist Bön faith. It is a solemn masked dance accompanied by long trumpets, drums and cymbals. The chief officiant is an unmasked Black Hat lama who is surrounded by a mandalic grouping of masked monks representing manifestations of various protective deities. The act of exorcism – it might be considered as such – is focused on a human effigy made of dough or perhaps wax or paper in which the evil spirits are thought to reside.

The proceedings of *cham* can be interpreted on a number of levels. The Black Hat lama is sometimes identified with the monk who slew Langdharma, the anti-Buddhist king of the Yarlung era, and the dance is seen as echoing the suppression of malevolent forces inimical to the establishment of Buddhism in Tibet. Some anthropologists, on the other hand, have seen in *cham* a metaphor for the gradual conquering of the ego, which is the ultimate aim of Buddhism. The ultimate destruction of the effigy that ends the dance might represent the destruction of the ego itself. Whatever the case, *cham* is a splendid, dramatic performance and is well worth going out of your way to see. For details of the major festivals in Tibet, see p318.

To see some contemporary Tibetan art visit the Gedun Cheophul Gallery in Lhasa (p103) or go online to www.mechakgallery.com.

Performances of *cham* are usually accompanied by other, less significant performances that seem to have evolved as entertainment in festivals. *Lhamo*, not to be confused with *cham*, is Tibetan opera. A largely secular art form, it portrays the heroics of kings and the villainy of demons, and recounts events in the lives of historical figures. *Lhamo* was developed in the 14th century by Tangtong Gyelpo, known as Tibet's Leonardo da Vinci because he was also an engineer, a major bridge builder and a physician. Authentic performances still include a statue of Tangtong on the otherwise bare stage. After the stage has been purified, the narrator gives a plot summary in verse and the performers enter, each with his or her distinct step and dressed in the bright and colourful silks of the aristocracy.

Other festival dances might depict the slaying of Langdharma or the arrival of the Indian teachers in Tibet at the time of the second diffusion of Buddhism. Light relief is provided by masked clowns or children.

www.asianart.com is an online journal with articles and galleries of Tibetan art.

Music

Music is one aspect of Tibetan cultural life in which there is a strong secular heritage. In the urban centres, songs were an important vent for social criticism, news and political lampooning. In Tibetan social life, both work and play are seen as occasions for singing. Even today it is not uncommon to see the monastery reconstruction squads pounding on the roofs of buildings and singing in unison. Where there are groups of men and women, the singing alternates between the two groups in the form of rhythmic refrains. Festivals and picnics are also opportunities for singing.

Tibet also has a secular tradition of wandering minstrels. It's still possible to see minstrels performing in Lhasa and Shigatse, where they play on the streets and occasionally (when they are not chased out by the owners) in restaurants.

When going over a pass, Tibetans say '*La la so, lha gyelo!*' – 'May the gods be victorious!'

Generally, groups of two or three singers perform heroic epics and short songs to the accompaniment of a four-stringed guitar and a nifty little shuffle. In times past, groups of such performers travelled around Tibet, providing entertainment for villagers who had few distractions from the constant round of daily chores. These performers were sometimes accompanied by dancers and acrobats.

While the secular music of Tibet has an instant appeal for foreign listeners, the liturgical chants of Buddhist monks and the music that accompanies *cham* dances is a lot less accessible. Buddhist chanting creates an eerie haunting effect, but soon becomes very monotonous. The music of *cham* is a discordant

THE TWO FACES OF TIBET

'Why did I come to Tibet? For the money, of course!' taxi driver Li grinned, his cigarette dropping ash over the dashboard. 'It's much easier to earn money here than in Mianyang, where my family lives.'

It's not that easy, though. After paying the taxi company Y260 a day rental and shelling out the ever-increasing petrol costs, Li reckons that he has to make between 30 and 50 fares a day just to turn a profit. Still, he likes it in Tibet: 'The people are friendly, the weather's good and there's hardly any traffic! Anyway, why shouldn't I come here? This is a province of China!'

Other Chinese immigrants are not so enamoured. 'I've been here three months and I'm leaving already', said Mr Wang, the owner of a Xinjiang-style restaurant in the southeast of town.

'We have health problems because of the high altitude, plus the cold winters are hard to face and the Tibetans aren't friendly to us.'

'I came on the train,' Wang continued, 'and I'll go back on the train. Without the train I wouldn't have come here.'

The flood of Chinese immigrants into Tibet is a major bone of contention between the Chinese and Tibetans in Lhasa, as is government interference in religious affairs.

After showing us a banned photograph of the Dalai Lama, one monk at a monastery in Lhasa told us in characteristically compassionate tones, 'A Tibetan plain-clothed policeman keeps tabs on the monks here, but I don't really blame him. He's got two kids, a wife and parents to support... What is he supposed to do?'

He pauses as someone moves outside the closed door of the chapel, then starts again in a low voice. 'The Tibetans and Chinese are different people. Different clothes, different ways of thinking. We are tsampa eaters,' he grinned, 'They are rice eaters.'

His eyes grew heavy, 'But there are so many, what can we do?'

He raised the photo to his forehead in a gesture of respect, placed it back in the cabinet, locked the door and smiled... 'But our hearts are in India.'

cacophony of trumpet blasts and boom-crash drums – atmospheric as an accompaniment to the dancing but not exactly the kind of thing you would want to slip into the iPod.

Chö by Choying Drolma and Steve Tibbets (Hannibal Music Label) is a deeply beautiful and highly recommended recording of chants and songs by Tibetan nuns. The follow-up, *Selwa* (Six Degrees Records), is also recommended.

Tibetan religious rituals use *rolmo* and *silnyen* (cymbals), *nga* (suspended drums), *damaru* (hand drums), *drilbu* (bells), *dungchen* (long trumpets), *kangling* (conical oboes; formerly made from human thighbones) and *dungkar* (conch shells). Secular instruments include the *dramnyen* (a six-stringed lute), *piwang* (two-stringed fiddle), *lingbu* (flute) and *gyumang* (Chinese-style zither).

Most recordings of traditional Tibetan music have been made in Dharamsala or Dalhousie in India. The country's biggest musical export (or rather exile) is Yungchen Lhamo, who fled Tibet in 1989 and has since released several excellent world-music recordings. She also appeared on Natalie Merchant's *Ophelia* album. Other Tibetan singers based abroad include Dadon Dawa Dolma and Kelsang Chukie Tethong (whose recent release *Voice from Tara* is worth checking out).

For world music with modern production try *Coming Home* (Real World, 1998) by Yungchen Lhamo, or her recent *Ama* (2006), which features a duet with Annie Lennox.

Even the monks of Sherab Ling Monastery in northern India were surprised when they won the 2003 Grammy for Best Traditional World Music Recording for their *Sacred Tibetan Chant*. The album is an unadorned recording of traditional monk chanting: deep and guttural, and similar to what you'll hear in prayer halls across Tibet.

Literature

The development of a Tibetan written script is credited to a monk by the name of Tonmi Sambhota and corresponded with the early introduction of Buddhism during the reign of King Songtsen Gampo. Accordingly, pre-

Buddhist traditions were passed down as oral histories that told of the exploits of early kings and the origins of the Tibetan people. Some of these oral traditions were later recorded using the Tibetan script.

But for the most part, literature in Tibet was dominated by Buddhism, first as a means of translating Buddhist scriptures from Sanskrit into Tibetan and second, as time went by, in association with the development of Tibetan Buddhist thought. There is nothing in the nature of a secular literary tradition – least of all novels – such as can be found in China or Japan.

Tales of Tibet – Sky Burials, Prayer Wheels & Wind Horses, edited by Herbert J Batt, gathers contemporary fiction by Tibetan and Chinese writers. The scholarly introduction explains how the nationality of the authors influences this sometimes elegiac, sometimes confronting collection.

One of the great achievements of Tibetan culture was the development of a literary language that could, with remarkable faithfulness, reproduce the concepts of Sanskrit Buddhist texts. The compilation of Tibetan-Sanskrit dictionaries in the early 9th century ensured consistency in all subsequent translations.

Alongside Buddhist scriptures exists an ancient tradition of storytelling, usually concerning the taming of Tibet's malevolent spirits to allow the introduction of Buddhism. Many of these stories were passed from generation to generation orally, but some were recorded. Examples include the epic *Gesar of Ling* and the story of Guru Rinpoche, who is said to have been born in a lotus in the ancient kingdom of Swat before coming to Tibet and performing countless miracles to prepare the land for the diffusion of Buddhism. The oral poetry of the Gesar epic is particularly popular in eastern Tibet, where a tiny number of ageing bards just keep alive a tradition that dates back to the 10th century.

Through the 12th and 13th centuries, Tibetan literary endeavour was almost entirely consumed by the monumental task of translating the complete Buddhist canon into Tibetan. The result was the 108 volumes of canonical texts (Kangyur), which record the words of the Historical Buddha, Sakyamuni, and 208 volumes of commentary (Tengyur) on the Kangyur by Indian masters that make up the basic Buddhist scriptures shared by all Tibetan religious orders. What time remained was used in the compilation of biographies and the collection of songs of revered lamas. Perhaps most famous among these is the *Hundred Thousand Songs of Milarepa*. Milarepa was an ascetic to whom many songs and poems concerning the quest for buddhahood are attributed.

The Tibetan epic *Gesar of Ling* is the world's longest epic poem, 25 times as long as *The Iliad*, and takes years to recite in full!

Wood-block printing has been in use for centuries and is still the most common form of printing in monasteries. Blocks are carved in mirror image; printers then work in pairs putting strips of paper over the inky block and shuttling an ink roll over it. The pages of the text are kept loose, wrapped in cloth and stored along the walls of monasteries. Tibet's most famous printing presses were in Derge in modern-day Sichuan, at Nartang Monastery and at the Potala.

Very little of the Tibetan literary tradition has been translated into English. Translations that may be of interest include *The Tibetan Book of the Dead*, a mysterious but fascinating account of the stages and visions that occur between death and rebirth; *The Jewel Ornament of Liberation*, which describes the path to enlightenment as seen by the chief disciple of Milarepa and founder of the Kagyupa order; and *The Life of Milarepa*, the autobiography of the country's most famous ascetic.

Architecture

Most early religious architecture – the Jokhang in Lhasa for example – owed much to Pala (Indian) and especially Newari (Nepali) influences. Still, a distinctively Tibetan style of architectural design emerged, and found its greatest expression in the Kumbum of Gyantse, the monasteries of Samye and Tashilhunpo, and the Potala. The great American architect Frank Lloyd Wright is said to have had a picture of the Potala on the wall of his office.

CHÖRTENS

Probably the most prominent Tibetan architectural motif is the chörten (stupa). Chörtens were originally built to house the cremated relics of the Historical Buddha and as such have become a powerful symbol of the Buddha and his teachings. Later, chörtens also served as reliquaries for lamas and holy men. Monumental versions would often encase whole mummified bodies, as is the case with the tombs of the Dalai Lamas in the Potala. And the tradition is very much alive: a stunning gold reliquary chörten was constructed in 1989 at Tashilhunpo Monastery to hold the body of the 10th Panchen Lama.

For an in-depth look at Lhasa's traditional Tibetan architecture and interactive maps of Lhasa, check out www.tibetheritagefund.org

In the early stages of Buddhism, images of the Buddha did not exist and chörtens became the major symbol of the new faith. Over the next two millennia, chörtens took many different forms across the Buddhist world, from the sensuous stupas of Burma to the pagodas of China and Japan. Most elaborate of all are the *kumbums* (100,000 Buddha images), of which the best remaining example in Tibet is at Gyantse. Many chörtens were built to hold ancient relics and sacred texts and have been plundered over the years by treasure seekers and vandals.

Chörtens are highly symbolic. The five levels represent the four elements, plus eternal space: the square base symbolises earth, the dome is water, the spire is fire, and the top moon and sun are air and space. The 13 discs of the

MONASTERY LAYOUT

Tibetan monasteries are based on a conservative design and share a remarkable continuity of layout. Many are built in spectacular high locations above villages. Most were originally surrounded by an outer wall, built to defend the treasures of the monastery from bands of brigands, Mongolian hordes or even attacks from rival monasteries. Most monasteries have a kora (pilgrimage path) around the complex, replete with holy rocks and meditation retreats high on the hillside behind. A few monasteries have a sky-burial site and most are still surrounded by ruins dating from the Cultural Revolution.

Inside the gates there is usually a central courtyard used for special ceremonies and festivals and a *darchen* (flag pole). Surrounding buildings usually include a *dukhang* (main assembly or prayer hall) with *gönkhang* (protector chapels) and *lhakhang* (subsidiary chapels), as well as monks' quarters, a *kangyur lhakhang* (library) and, in the case of larger monasteries, *tratsang* (colleges), *kangtsang* (halls of residence), kitchens and a *barkhang* (printing press).

The main prayer hall consists of rows of low seats and tables, often strewn with cloaks, hats, ritual instruments, drums and huge telescopic horns. There is a small altar with seven bowls of water, butter lamps and offerings of mandalas made from seeds. The main altar houses the most significant statues, often Sakyamuni, Jampa (Maitreya) or a trinity of the Past, Present and Future Buddhas and perhaps the founder of the monastery or past lamas. Larger monasteries contain funeral chörtens of important lamas. There may be an *tsangkhang* (inner sanctum) behind the main hall, the entrance of which is flanked by protector gods, often one blue, Chana Dorje (Vajrapani) and the other red, Tamdrin (Hayagriva). There may well be an inner kora of prayer wheels. At the entrance to most buildings are murals of the Four Guardian Kings and perhaps a Wheel of Life or a mandala mural. Side stairs lead up from here to higher floors.

Gönkhang are dark and spooky halls that hold wrathful manifestations of deities, frequently covered with a cloth because of their terrible appearance. Murals are often traced against a black background and walls are decorated with Tantric deities, grinning skeletons or even dismembered bodies. The altars often have grain dice or mirrors, used for divination, and the pillars are decorated with festival masks, weapons and sometimes stuffed snakes and wolves. Women are often not allowed into protector chapels.

The monastery roof usually has excellent views as well as vases of immortality, victory banners, dragons and copper symbols of the Wheel of Law flanked by two deer, recalling the Buddha's first sermon at the deer park of Sarnath.

ceremonial umbrella can represent the branches of the tree of life or the 10 powers and three mindfulnesses of the Buddha. The top seed-shaped pinnacle symbolises enlightenment. The chörten as a whole can be seen as a representation of the path to enlightenment. The construction can also physically represent the Buddha, with the base as his seat and the dome as his body.

SECULAR ARCHITECTURE

Typical features of Tibetan secular architecture, which are also used to a certain extent in religious architecture, are buildings with inward-sloping walls made of large, tightly fitting stones or sun-baked bricks. Below the roof is a layer of twigs, squashed tight by the roof and painted to give Tibetan houses their characteristic brown band. Roofs are flat, as there is little rain or snow, made from pounded earth and edged with walls. You may well see singing bands of men and women pounding a new roof with sticks weighted with large stones. In the larger structures, the roof is supported inside by wooden pillars. The exteriors are generally whitewashed brick, although in some areas, such as Sakya in Tsang, other colours may be used. In rural Tibet, homes are often surrounded by walled compounds, and in some areas entrances are protected by painted scorpions and swastikas.

Nomads, who take their homes with them, live in *bar* (yak-hair tents), which are normally roomy and can accommodate a whole family. An opening at the top of the tent lets out smoke from the fire.

Painting

As with other types of Tibetan art, painting is very symbolic and can be interpreted on many different levels. It is almost exclusively devotional in nature.

STYLES

The strongest influence came from India. Paintings usually followed stereotyped forms with a central Buddhist deity surrounded by smaller, lesser deities. Poised above the central figure was often a supreme buddha figure of which the one below it was an emanation. Later came depictions of revered Tibetan lamas or Indian spiritual teachers, often surrounded by lineage lines or incidents from the lama's life.

Chinese influence began to manifest itself more frequently in Tibetan painting from around the 15th century. The freer approach of Chinese landscape painting allowed some Tibetan artists to break free from some of the more formalised aspects of Tibetan religious art and employ landscape as a decorative motif in the context of a painting that celebrated a particular religious figure. This is not to say that Chinese art initiated a new movement in Tibetan art. The new, Chinese-influenced forms coexisted with older forms, largely because painting in Tibet was passed on from artisan to apprentice in much the same way that monastic communities maintained lineages of teaching.

www.tibetart.org has online examples of Tibetan art from dozens of collections.

THANGKAS

Religious paintings mounted on brocade and rolled up between two sticks are called thangkas. Their eminent portability was essential in a land of nomads, and they were often used by mendicant preachers and doctors as a visual learning aid. Not so portable are the huge thangkas known as *gheku* or *koku,* the size of large buildings, that are unfurled every year during festivals. Traditionally, thangkas were never bought or sold.

The production of a thangka is an act of devotion and the process is carefully formalised. Linen (or now more commonly cotton) is stretched

MANDALAS

The mandala (*kyilkhor,* literally 'circle') is more than a beautiful artistic creation, it's also a three-dimensional meditational map. What on the surface appears to be a plain two-dimensional design emerges, with the right visual approach, as a three-dimensional picture. Mandalas can take the form of paintings, patterns of sand, three-dimensional models or even whole monastic structures, as at Samye. In the case of the two-dimensional mandala, the correct visual approach can be achieved only through meditation. The painstakingly created sand mandalas also perform the duty of illustrating the impermanence of life (they are generally swept away after a few days).

A typical mandala features a central deity surrounded by four or eight other deities who are aspects of the central figure. These surrounding deities are often accompanied by a consort. There may be several circles of these deities, totalling several hundred deities. These deities and all other elements of the mandala have to be visualised as the three-dimensional world of the central deity and even as a representation of the universe.

The mandala is associated with Tantric Buddhism and is chiefly used in a ritual known as *sadhana* (means for attainment). According to this ritual, the adept meditates on, invokes and identifies with a specific deity, before dissolving into emptiness and re-emerging as the deity itself. The process, in so far as it uses the mandala as an aid, involves a remarkable feat of imaginative concentration. One ritual calls for the adept to visualise 722 deities with enough clarity to be able to see the whites of their eyes and hold this visualisation for four hours.

on a wooden frame, stiffened with glue and coated with a mix of chalk and lime called *gesso*. Iconography is bound by strict mathematical measurements. A grid is drawn onto the thangka before outlines are sketched in charcoal, starting with the main central deity and moving outwards.

Colours are added one at a time, starting with the background and ending with shading. Pigments were traditionally natural: blue from lapis, red from cinnabar and yellow from sulphur. Most thangkas are burnished with at least a little gold. The last part of the thangka to be painted is the eyes, which are filled in during a special 'opening the eyes' celebration. Finally a brocade backing of three colours and a protective 'curtain' are added, the latter to protect the thangka.

Statuary & Sculpture

Tibetan statuary, like Tibetan painting, is almost exclusively religious in nature. Ranging in height from several centimetres to several metres, statues usually depict deities and revered lamas. Most of the smaller statues are hollow and are stuffed with paper prayers and relics when consecrated.

Metal statues are traditionally sculpted in wax and then covered in clay. When the clay is dry it is heated. The wax melts and is removed, leaving a mould that can be filled with molten metal. Statues are generally then gilded and painted.

Sculptures are most commonly made from bronze or stucco mixed with straw, but can even be made out of butter and tsampa. Butter sculptures are normally made on wooden frames and symbolise the impermanence of all things.

You can see traditional craftsmen at work at the Ancient Art Restoration Centre (AARC) in Lhasa, next to Dropenling – see p125. The AARC managed the restoration of the Potala and Sera and Drepung monasteries, and craftsmen here include thangka painters, metal workers, woodcarvers and dyemakers.

Handicrafts

Tibet has a 1000-year history of carpet making; the carpets are mostly used as seat covers, bed covers and saddle blankets. Knots are double tied (the best carpets have 100 knots per square inch), which results in a particularly thick pile. Tibet's secret carpet ingredient is its particularly high-quality sheep wool, which is hand spun and coloured with natural dyes such as indigo, walnut, madder and rhubarb. Gyantse and Shigatse were the traditional centres of carpet production, although the modern industry is based almost exclusively in Tibetan exile communities in Nepal.

Inlaid handicrafts are common, particularly in the form of prayer wheels, daggers, butter lamps and bowls, although most of what you see these days in Lhasa is made by Tibetan communities in Nepal. Nomads in particular wear stunning silver jewellery; you may also see silver flints, amulets known as *gau,* and ornate chopstick and knife sets.

Tibetan singing bowls, made from a secret mix of seven different metals, are a meditation device that originated from pre-Buddhist Bön practices. The bowls produce a 'disassociated' mystic hum when a playing stick is rotated around the outer edge of the bowl.

Woodcarving is another valued handicraft, used in the production of brightly coloured Tibetan furniture and window panels, not to mention wood-print blocks.

The Art of Tibet by Robert Fisher is a portable colour guide to all the arts of Tibet, from the iconography of thangkas (Tibetan religious paintings usually framed by silk brocade) to statuary.

Tibetan Buddhism

A basic understanding of Buddhism is essential to getting beneath the skin of things in Tibet. Buddhism's values and goals permeate almost everything Tibetan. Exploring the monasteries and temples of Tibet and mixing with its people, yet knowing nothing of Buddhism, is like visiting the Vatican and knowing nothing of Roman Catholicism. To be sure, it might still seem an awe-inspiring experience, but much will remain hidden and indecipherable.

www.buddhanet.net is a good online resource for anyone interested in Buddhism.

For those who already do know something of Buddhism, who have read something of Zen, for example, Tibet can be baffling on another level. The grandeur of the temples, the worship of images and the fierce protective deities that stand in doorways all seem to belie the basic tenets of an ascetic faith that is basically about renouncing the self and following a path of moderation.

On a purely superficial level, Buddhism has historically encompassed the moral precepts and devotional practices of lay followers, the scholastic tradition of the Indian Buddhist universities and a body of mystic Tantric teachings that had a particular appeal to followers of the shamanistic Bön faith.

Tibetan Buddhism's reaction with existing Bön spirit worship and the Hindu pantheon created a huge range of deities, both wrathful and benign (although these are technically all merely aspects of the human ego). Apart from a whole range of different buddha aspects there are also general protector gods called *dharmapalas* and personal meditational deities called *yidams,* which Tantric students adopt early in their spiritual training. Yet for all its confusing iconography the basic tenets of Buddhism are very much rooted in daily experience. Even high lamas and monks come across as surprisingly down-to-earth.

Nagas (*lu* in Tibetan) are serpent spirits that occur in wells, springs, rivers and lakes, and control the weather and disease.

Buddhism is perhaps the most tolerant of the world's religions. Wherever it has gone it has adapted to local conditions, like a dividing cell, creating countless new schools of thought. Its basic tenets have remained very much the same and all schools are bound together in their faith in the value of the original teachings of Sakyamuni (Sakya Thukpa), the Historical Buddha. The Chinese invasion has ironically caused a flowering of Tibetan Buddhism abroad and you can now find Tibetan monasteries around the world.

Closely linked to both Bön and Buddhism is the folk religion of Tibet, known as *mi chös* (the dharma of man), which is primarily concerned with spirits. These spirits include *nyen,* which reside in rocks and trees; *lu* or *naga,* snake-bodied spirits, which live at the bottom of lakes, rivers and wells; *sadok,* lords of the earth, which are connected with agriculture; *tsen,* air or mountain spirits, which shoot arrows of illness and death at humans; and *dud,* demons linked to the Buddhist demon Mara. Spirits of the hearth, roof and kitchen inhabit every Tibetan house. The religious beliefs of the average Tibetan are a fascinating melange of Buddhism, Bön and folk religion.

Chaktsal (prostration) is a powerful way for pilgrims to show their devotion: practitioners place their hands in a *namaste* (prayer-like) position, touch their forehead, throat and heart, get down into a half-prostration (as for Muslim prayer) and then lie full on the ground with their hands stretched out, before repeating the exercise, often for hours.

HISTORY

Buddhism originated in the northeast of India around the 5th century BC, at a time when the local religion was Brahmanism. Some brahman, in preparation for presiding over offerings to their gods, partook of an asceticism that transported them to remote places where they fasted, meditated and practised yogic techniques.

Many of the fundamental concepts of Buddhism find their origin in the brahman society of this time. The Buddha (c 480–400 BC), born Siddhartha

Gautama, was one of many wandering ascetics whose teachings led to the establishment of rival religious schools. Jainism was one of these schools, Buddhism was another.

Little is known about the life of Siddhartha. It was probably not until some 200 years after his death that biographies were compiled, and by that time many of the circumstances of his life had merged with legend. It is known that he was born in Lumbini (modern-day Nepal) of a noble family and that he married and had a son before renouncing a life of privilege and embarking on a quest to make sense of the suffering in the world.

After studying with many of the masters of his day he embarked on a course of intense ascetism, before concluding that such a path was too extreme. Finally, in the place that is now known as Bodhgaya in India, Siddhartha meditated beneath a *bo* (pipal) tree. At the break of dawn at the end of his third night of meditation he became a buddha (awakened one).

Tibetan rosary beads are made of 108 dried seeds. Prayers are marked off by each bead; a second string marks off higher multiples. Spies working for the British adapted rosaries to record distances as they secretly mapped large areas of Tibet during the 19th century.

BUDDHIST CONCEPTS

Buddhism's early teachings are based on the insights of the Buddha, known in Mahayana tradition as Sakyamuni (Sakya Thukpa in Tibetan), and form the basis of all further Buddhist thought. Buddhism is not based on a revealed prophecy or divine revelation but rather is rooted in human experience. The later Mahayana school (to which Tibetan Buddhism belongs) diverged from these early teachings in some respects, but not in its fundamentals.

The Buddha commenced his teachings by explaining that there was a Middle Way that steered a course between sensual indulgence and ascetic self-torment – a way of moderation rather than renunciation. This Middle Way could be pursued by following the Noble Eightfold Path. The philosophical underpinnings of this path were the Four Noble Truths, which addressed the problems of karma and rebirth. These basic concepts are the kernel of early Buddhist thought.

In a modern sense, Buddhist thought stresses nonviolence, compassion, equanimity (evenness of mind) and mindfulness (awareness of the present moment).

The lotus (*padma* in Sanskrit, *metok* in Tibetan) is an important Buddhist symbol and the thrones of many deities are made from a lotus leaf. The leaf symbolises purity and transcendence, in the world but not of it, rising as it does from muddy waters to become a flower of great beauty.

Rebirth

Life is a cycle of rebirths. The common assumption is that there are many rebirths, but in Buddhist thought they are innumerable. The Sanskrit word 'samsara' (Tibetan: *khorwa*), literally 'wandering on', is used to describe this cycle, and life is seen as wandering on limitlessly through time, and through the birth, extinction and rebirth of galaxies and worlds. There are six levels of rebirth or realms of existence. It is important to accumulate enough merit to avoid the three lower realms, although in the long cycle of rebirth, all beings pass through them at some point. These six levels are depicted on the Wheel of Life (p64). All beings are fated to tread this wheel continuously until they make a commitment to enlightenment.

Karma

All beings pass through the same cycle of rebirths. Their enemy may once have been their mother, and like all beings they have lived as an insect and as a god, and suffered in one of the hell realms. Movement within this cycle, though, is not haphazard. It is governed by karma.

Karma (*las* in Tibetan) is a slippery concept. It is sometimes translated simply as 'action', but it also implies the consequences of action. Karma might be thought of as an overarching condition of life. Every action in life leaves a psychic trace that carries over into the next rebirth. It should not be thought of as a reward or punishment, but simply as a result. In Buddhist thought

Keith Dowman's *Sacred Life of Tibet* builds on his earlier *Power Places of Central Tibet* to provide an excellent insight into how Tibetans see the spiritual landscape of their land. It also offers a pilgrim's perspective on travelling in Tibet.

WHEEL OF LIFE

The Wheel of Life (Sipa Khorlo in Tibetan), depicted in the entryway to most monasteries, is an aid to realising the delusion of the mind; a complex pictorial representation of how desire chains us to samsara, the endless cycle of birth, death and rebirth.

The wheel is held in the mouth of Yama, the Lord of Death. The inner circle of interdependent desire shows a cockerel (representing desire or attachment) biting a pig (ignorance or delusion) biting a snake (hatred or anger). A second ring is divided into figures ascending through the realms on the left and descending on the right.

The six inner sectors of the wheel symbolise the six realms of rebirth: gods, battling demigods and humans (the upper realms); and hungry ghosts, hell and animals (the lower realms). All beings are reborn through this cycle dependent upon their karma. The Buddha is depicted outside the wheel, symbolising his release into a state of nirvana.

At the bottom of the wheel are hot and cold hells, where Yama holds a mirror that reflects one's lifetime. A demon to the side holds a scale with black and white pebbles, weighing up the good and bad deeds of one's lifetime.

The *pretas,* or hungry spirits, are recognisable by their huge stomachs, thin needle-like necks and tiny mouths, which cause them insatiable hunger and thirst. In each realm the Buddha attempts to convey his teachings (the dharma), offering hope to each realm.

The 12 outer segments depict the so-called '12 links of dependent origination', and the 12 interlinked, codependent and causal experiences of life that perpetuate the cycle of samsara. The 12 images (whose order may vary) are of a blind woman (representing ignorance), a potter (unconscious will), a monkey (consciousness), men in a boat (self-consciousness), a house (the five senses), lovers (contact), a man with an arrow in his eye (feeling), a drinking scene (desire), a figure grasping fruit from a tree (attachment), pregnancy, birth and death (a man carrying a corpse to a sky burial).

karma is frequently likened to a seed that ripens into a fruit: thus a human reborn as an insect is harvesting the fruits of a previous immoral existence.

Mani (prayer) stones are carved with sutras as an act of merit and placed in long walls, often hundreds of metres long, at holy sites.

Merit

Given that karma is a kind of accumulated psychic baggage that we must lug through countless rebirths, it is the aim of all practising Buddhists to try to accumulate as much 'good karma' – merit – as possible. Merit is best achieved through the act of rejoicing in giving, although merit can even be achieved through giving that is purely motivated by a desire for merit. The giving of alms to the needy and to monks, the relinquishing of a son to monkhood, and acts of compassion and understanding are all meritorious and have a positive karmic outcome.

The Four Noble Truths

The dharma wheel symbolises the Buddha's first sermon at Sarnath. The eight spokes recall the Eightfold Path. The wheel was the earliest symbol of Buddhism, used long before images of the Buddha became popular.

If belief in rebirth, karma and merit are the basis of lay-followers' faith in Buddhism, the Four Noble Truths (Tibetan: *phakpay denpa shi*) might be thought of as the deep structure of the faith, or its philosophical underpinning. The Buddha systematised the truths in the manner of the medical practice of his time: (1) diagnose the illness, (2) identify its cause, (3) establish a cure and (4) map a course for the cure. Their equivalents in Buddhism's diagnosis of the human condition are: (1) *dukkha* (suffering), caused by (2) *tanha* (desire), which may be cured by (3) *nibbana,* nirvana (cessation of desire), which can be achieved by means of (4) the Noble Eightfold Path, or the Middle Way.

The first of the Four Noble Truths, then, is that life is suffering. This suffering extends through all the countless rebirths of beings, and finds its origin in the imperfection of life. Every rebirth brings with it the pain of birth, the pain of ageing, the pain of death, the pain of association with unpleasant things, the loss of things we are attached to and the failure to achieve the things we desire.

The reason for this suffering is the second Noble Truth, and lies in our dissatisfaction with imperfection, in our desire for things to be other than they are. What is more, this dissatisfaction leads to actions and karmic consequences that prolong the cycle of rebirths and may lead to even more suffering, much like a mouse running endlessly in a wheel.

Prayer flags are strung up to purify the air and pacify the gods. All feature the *longta,* or windhorse, which carries the prayers up into the heavens. The colours are highly symbolic – red, green, yellow, blue and white represent fire, wood, earth, water and iron.

The third Noble Truth was indicated by the Buddha as *nibbana (namtrol),* which is known in English as nirvana. It is the cessation of all desire, an end to attachment. With the cessation of desire comes an end to suffering, the achievement of complete nonattachment and an end to the cycle of rebirth. Nirvana is the ultimate goal of Buddhism. Nit-pickers might point out that the will to achieve nirvana is a desire in itself. Buddhists answer that this desire is tolerated as a useful means to an end, but it is only when this desire, too, is extinguished that nirvana is truly achieved.

The Noble Eightfold Path is the fourth of the Noble Truths. It prescribes a course that for the lay practitioner will lead to the accumulation of merit, and for the serious devotee may lead to nirvana. The components of this path are (1) right understanding, (2) right thought, (3) right speech, (4) right action, (5) right livelihood, (6) right effort, (7) right mindfulness and (8) right concentration. Needless to say, each of these has a 'wrong' corollary.

The 10 Meritorious Deeds

The 10 meritorious deeds are to refrain from killing, stealing, inappropriate sexual activity, lying, gossiping, cursing, sowing discord, envy, malice and opinionatedness.

Prayer wheels are filled with up to a mile of prayers; the prayers are 'recited' with each revolution of the wheel. Pilgrims spin the wheels to gain merit and to concentrate the mind on the mantras and prayers they are reciting.

SCHOOLS OF BUDDHISM

Not long after the death of Sakyamuni, disagreements began to arise among his followers – as they tend to do in all religious movements – over whose interpretations best captured the true spirit of his teachings. The result was the development of numerous schools of thought and, eventually, a schism that saw the emergence of two principal schools: Hinayana and Mahayana.

Hinayana, also known as Theravada, might be seen as the more conservative of the two, a school that encouraged scholasticism and close attention to what were considered the original teachings of Sakyamuni. Mahayana, on the other hand, with its elevation of compassion *(nyingje)* as an all-important idea, took Buddhism in a new direction. It was the Mahayana school that made its way up to the high plateau and took root there, at the same time travelling to China, Korea and Japan. Hinayana retreated into southern India and took root in Sri Lanka and Thailand.

Full moon days see an intensification of prayers and activity in most monasteries. On the 10th day of the lunar month there are prayers dedicated to Guru Rinpoche, on the 15th day to Öpagme (Amitayus), on the eighth day to the medicine Buddha, and at the new moon prayers are dedicated to Sakyamuni (Sakya Thukpa).

Mahayana

The claims that Mahayanists made for their faith were many, but the central issue was a change in orientation from individual pursuit of enlightenment to bodhisattvahood. The bodhisattva, rather than striving for complete nonattachment, aims, through compassion and self-sacrifice, to achieve enlightenment for the sake of all beings.

In another development, Sakyamuni began to take on another form altogether. Mahayanists maintained that Sakyamuni had already attained buddhahood many aeons ago and that he was a manifestation of a long-enlightened transcendent being who sent such manifestations to many worlds to assist all beings on the road to enlightenment. There were many such transcendent beings, the Mahayanists argued, living in heavens or 'pure lands', and all were able to project themselves into the innumerable worlds of the cosmos for the sake of sentient life there.

The philosophical reasoning behind the Mahayana transformation of Buddhism is extremely complex, but it had the effect of producing a pantheon of bodhisattvas, a feature that made Mahayana more palatable to cultures that already had gods of their own. In Tibet, China, Korea and Japan, the Mahayana pantheon came to be identified with local gods as their Mahayana equivalents replaced them.

The Buddhist parable of the Four Harmonious Brothers is painted on walls at the entrance to many monasteries. The image is of a bird picking a tree-top fruit, while standing atop a hare, who is atop a monkey, who is atop an elephant. On its most basic level the image symbolises cooperation and harmony with the environment.

Tantrism (Vajrayana)

A further Mahayana development that is particularly relevant is Tantrism. The words of Sakyamuni were recorded in sutras and studied by students of both Hinayana and Mahayana but, according to the followers of Tantrism, a school that emerged from around AD 600, Sakyamuni left a corpus of esoteric instructions to a select few of his disciples. These were known as Tantra (Gyü).

Tantric adepts claimed that through the use of unconventional techniques they could jolt themselves towards enlightenment, and shorten the long road to bodhisattvahood. The process involved identification with a tutelary deity invoked through deep meditation and recitation of the deity's mantra. The most famous of these mantras is the '*om mani padme hum*' ('hail to the jewel in the lotus') mantra of Chenresig (Avalokiteshvara). Tantric practice employs Indian yogic techniques to channel energy towards the transformation to enlightenment. Such yogic techniques might even include sexual practices. Tantric techniques are rarely written down, but rather are passed down verbally from tutor to student.

The Eight Auspicious Symbols *(tashi targyel)* are associated with gifts made to Sakyamuni upon his enlightenment and appear as protective motifs across Tibet. They are the knot of eternity, wheel of law, lotus flower, pair of golden fishes, victory banner, precious umbrella, white conch shell and vase of treasure.

Most of the ritual objects and images of deities in Tibetan monasteries and temples are Tantric in nature. Together they show the many facets of enlightenment – at times kindly, at times wrathful.

BUDDHISM IN TIBET

The story of the introduction of Buddhism to Tibet is attended by legends of the taming of local gods and spirits and their conversion to Buddhism as protective deities. This magnificent array of buddhas, bodhisattvas and sages occupies a mythical world in the Tibetan imagination. Chenresig is perhaps chief among them, manifesting himself in early Tibetan kings and later the Dalai Lamas. Guru Rinpoche, the Indian sage who bound the native spirits and gods of Tibet into the service of Buddhism, is another. And there are countless others worshipped in images throughout the land: Drölma (Tara), Jampelyang (Manjushri), Milarepa, Marpa and Tsongkhapa, among others. While the clerical side of Buddhism concerns itself largely with textual study and analysis, the Tantric shamanistic-based side seeks revelation through identification with these deified beings and through their *terma* ('revealed' words or writings).

The *dorje* (thunderbolt) and *drilbu* (bell) are ritual objects symbolising male and female aspects used in Tantric rites. They are held in the right and left hands respectively. The indestructible thunderbolt cuts through ignorance.

It is useful to consider the various schools of Tibetan Buddhism as revealing something of a struggle between these two orientations: shamanism and clericalism. Each school finds its own resolution to the problem. In the case of the last major school to arise, the Gelugpa order, there was a search for a return to the doctrinal purity of clerical Buddhism. But even here, the Tantric forms were not completely discarded; it was merely felt that many years of scholarly work and preparation should precede the more esoteric Tantric practices.

The clerical and shamanistic orientations can also be explained as the difference between state-sponsored and popular Buddhism respectively. There was always a tendency for the state to emphasise monastic Buddhism, with its communities of rule-abiding monks. Popular Buddhism, on the other hand, with its long-haired, wild-eyed ascetic recluses capable of performing great feats of magic, had a great appeal to the ordinary people of Tibet, for whom ghosts and demons and sorcerers were a daily reality.

The Dalai Lama is a one-man publishing empire! Many books attributed to the Dalai Lama are actually transcripts of public lectures. The most popular titles are *The Art of Happiness, Ethics for the New Millennium, The Meaning of Life* and *The Power of Compassion.*

Nyingmapa Order

The Nyingmapa order is the Old School, and traces its origins back to the teachings and practices of Guru Rinpoche, who came to Tibet from India and lived in the country in the 8th and 9th centuries. As Buddhism fell into decline until the second diffusion of the faith in the 11th century (see p29), the Nyingmapa failed to develop as a powerful, centralised school, and for the most part prospered in villages throughout rural Tibet, where it was administered by local shamanlike figures.

With the second diffusion of Buddhism in Tibet and the emergence of rival schools, the Nyingmapa order experienced something of a revival through the 'discovery' of hidden texts in the 'power places' of Tibet visited by Guru Rinpoche. In many cases these *terma* (revealed texts) were discovered through yogic-inspired visions by spiritually advanced Nyingmapa practitioners, rather than found under a pile of rocks or in a cave. Whatever their origins, these *terma* gave the Nyingmapa a new lease of life.

The *terma* gave rise to the Dzogchen (Great Perfection) teachings. Much maligned by other Tibetan schools, Dzogchen postulates a primordial state of purity that pre-existed the duality of enlightenment and samsara, and offered a Tantric short cut to nirvana. Dzogchen teaches that enlightenment can come in one lifetime. Such ideas were to influence other orders of Buddhism in the 19th century. For more on the Dzogchen school see www.dzogchen.org.

The Nyingmapa never enjoyed the political power of other major Tibetan schools of Buddhism. Its fortunes improved somewhat with the accession of the fifth Dalai Lama, who was born into a Nyingmapa family. He personally saw to the expansion of Mindroling and Dorje Drak Monasteries, which became the head Nyingmapa monasteries of Ü and all Tibet. In particular,

There are many modern guides to practising Tibetan Buddhism – Western authors such as Lama Surya Das and Pema Chodron have written a selection of books dealing with Tibetan Buddhist concepts in a modern context.

THE WORLD OF A MONK

The Western term 'monk' is slightly misleading when used in the context of Tibetan Buddhism. The Tibetan equivalent would probably be *trapa,* which means literally 'scholar' or 'student', and is an inclusive term that covers the three main categories of monastic inmates. Monks in these categories should also be distinguished from lamas who, as spiritual luminaries, have a privileged position in the monastic hierarchy, may have considerable wealth and, outside the Gelugpa order, are not necessarily celibate.

The first step for a monk, usually after completing some prior study, is to take one of two lesser vows, the *genyen* or *getsul* ordination – a renunciation of secular life that includes a vow of celibacy. This marks the beginning of a long course of study that is expected to lead to the full *gelong* vows of ordination. While most major monasteries have a number of *gelong* monks, not all monks achieve *gelong* status.

These three categories do not encompass all the monks in a monastery. There are usually specific monastic posts associated with administrative duties, with ritual and with teaching. *Gelong* vows are also supplemented by higher courses of study, which are rewarded in the Gelugpa order by the title *geshe.* In premodern Tibet the larger monasteries also had divisions of so-called 'fighting monks', or monastic militias. To a large extent they served as a kind of police force within a particular monastery, but there were also times when their services were used to hammer home a doctrinal dispute with a rival monastery. In 1950, on the eve of the Chinese invasion, it was estimated that 30% of Tibet's male population were monks.

Butter lamps, or *chömay*, are kept lit continuously in all monasteries and many private homes, and are topped up continuously by visiting pilgrims equipped with a tub of butter and a spoon.

he is supposed to have overcome and taught mountain goddesses with the use of Tantric sexual techniques.

Kagyupa Order

This resurgence of Buddhist influence in the 11th century led to many Tibetans travelling to India to study. The new ideas they brought back with them had a revitalising effect on Tibetan thought and produced other new schools of Tibetan Buddhism. Among them was the Kagyupa order, established by Milarepa (1040–1123), who was the disciple of Marpa the translator (1012–93).

The influence of one of Milarepa's disciples, Gampopa (1079–1153), led to the establishment of numerous monasteries that became major teaching centres, eventually overshadowing the ascetic-yogi origins of the Kagyupa. The yogi tradition did not die out completely, however, and Kagyupa monasteries also became important centres for synthesising the clerical and shamanistic orientations of Tibetan Buddhism.

Found on all altars and replenished twice a day, the seven bowls of water refer to the 'Seven Examined Men' – the first seven monks in Tibet, or the seven first steps of Buddha.

Several suborders of the Kagyupa sprung up with time, the most prominent of which was the Karma Kagyupa, also known as the Karmapa. The practice of renowned lamas reincarnating after death probably originated with this suborder, when the abbot of Tsurphu Monastery, Dusum Khyenpa (1110–93),

THE HISTORY OF BÖN

As a result of the historical predominance of Buddhism in Tibet, the Bön religion has been suppressed for centuries and has only recently started to attract the attention of scholars. Many Tibetans remain quite ignorant of Bön beliefs and your guide might refuse to even set foot in a Bön monastery. Yet Bön and Buddhism have influenced and interacted with each other for centuries, exchanging texts, traditions and rituals. In the words of Tibet scholar David Snellgrove, 'every Tibetan is a Bönpo at heart'.

The word 'Bön' has three main connotations. The first relates to the pre-Buddhist religion of Tibet, suppressed and supplanted by Buddhism in the 8th and 9th centuries. The second is the form of 'organised' Bön (Gyur Bön) systematised along Buddhist lines, which arose in the 11th century. Third, and linked to this, is a body of popular beliefs that involves the worship of local deities and spirit protectors.

Bön has its deepest roots in the earliest religious beliefs of the Tibetan people. Centred on an animist faith shared by all central Asian peoples, religious expression took the form of spells, talismans, oaths, incantations, ritual drumming and sacrifices. Rituals often revolved around an individual who mediated between humans and the spirit world.

The earliest form of Bön, sometimes referred to as Black Bön, also Dud Bön (the Bön of Devils) or Tsan Bön (the Bön of Spirits), was concerned with counteracting the effects of evil spirits through magical practices. Bönpo priests were entrusted with the wellbeing and fertility of the living, with curing sicknesses and affecting the weather. A core component was control of the spirits, to ensure the safe passage of the soul into the next world. For centuries Bönpo priests controlled the complex burial rites of the Yarlung kings. Bön was the state religion of Tibet until the reign of Songtsen Gampo (630–649).

Bön is thought to have its geographical roots in the kingdom of Shang-Shung, which is located in western Tibet, and its capital at Kyunglung (Valley of the Garuda). Bön's founding father was Shenrab Miwoche, also known as Tonpa Shenrab, the Teacher of Knowledge, who was born in the second millennium BC in the mystical land of Olma Lungring in Tajik (thought to be possibly the Mt Kailash area or even Persia). Buddhists often claim that Shenrab is merely a carbon copy of Sakyamuni (Sakya Thukpa), and certainly there are similarities to be found. Biographies state that he was born a royal prince and ruled for 30 years before becoming an ascetic. His 10 wives bore him 10 children who formed the core of his religious disciples.

announced that he would be reincarnated as his own successor. The 16th Karmapa died in 1981, and his disputed successor fled to India in 1999 (see The Karmapa Connection, p144). Other Kagyupa schools, the Drigungpa and Taglungpa, are based at Drigung Til and Talung Monasteries in Ü.

For a modern overview of Tibetan Buddhism, try *Introduction to Tibetan Buddhism* by John Powers or *Essential Tibetan Buddhism* by Robert Thurman.

Sakyapa Order

With the second diffusion of Buddhism in the 11th and 12th centuries, many Tibetan monasteries became centres for the textual study and translation of Indian Buddhist texts. One of the earliest major figures in this movement was Kunga Gyaltsen (1182–1251), known as Sakya Pandita (literally 'scholar from Sakya').

Sakya Pandita's renown as a scholar led to him, and subsequent abbots of Sakya, being recognised as a manifestation of Jampelyang (Manjushri), the Bodhisattva of Insight. Sakya Pandita travelled to the Mongolian court in China, with the result that his heir became the spiritual tutor of Kublai Khan. In the 13th and 14th centuries, the Sakyapa order became embroiled in politics and implicated in the Mongol overlordship of Tibet (see the Priests & Patrons: the Reign of the Sakyapas box, p203). Nevertheless, at the same time, Sakya emerged as a major centre for the scholastic study of Buddhism, and attracted students such as Tsongkhapa, who initiated the Gelugpa order.

The *sengye*, or snow lion, is one of Tibet's four animals and acts as a mount for many Tibetan protector deities. The other three animals are the garuda *(khyung)*, dragon *(druk)* and tiger *(dak)*.

Many of the tales of Shenrab Miwoche deal with his protracted struggles with the demon king Khyabpa Lagring.

Bön was first suppressed by the eighth Yarlung king, Drigum Tsenpo, and subsequently by King Trisong Detsen. The Bön master Gyerpung Drenpa Namkha (a *gyerpung* is the Bön equivalent of a lama or guru) struggled with Trisong Detsen to protect the Bön faith until the king finally broke Shang-Shung's political power. Following the founding of the Samye Monastery, many Bön priests went into exile or converted to Buddhism, and many of the Bön texts were hidden.

The modern Bön religion is known as Yungdrung (Eternal Bön). A *yungdrung* is a swastika, Bön's most important symbol. (Yungdrungling means 'swastika park' and is a common name for Bön monasteries.) *The Nine Ways of Bön* is the religion's major text. Bönpos still refer to Mt Kailash as Yungdrung Gutseg (Nine-Stacked-Swastika Mountain).

To the casual observer it's often hard to differentiate between Bönpo and Buddhist practice. It can be said that in many ways Bön shares the same goals as Buddhism but takes a different path. The word 'Bön' has come to carry the same connotation as the Buddhist term 'dharma' *(chö)*. Shared concepts include those of samsara, karma and rebirth in the six states of existence. Even Bön monasteries, rituals and meditation practice are almost identical to Buddhist versions. Still, there are obvious differences. Bön has its own Kangyur, a canon made up of texts translated from the Shang-Shung language, and Bönpos turn prayer wheels and circumambulate monasteries anticlockwise. The main difference comes down to the source of religious authority: Bönpos see the arrival of Buddhism as a catastrophe, the supplanting of the truth by a false religion.

Bönpo iconography is unique. Tonpa Shenrab is the most common central image, and is depicted as either a monk or a deity. He shares Sakyamuni's *mudra* (hand gesture) of 'enlightenment' but holds the Bön sceptre, which consists of two swastikas joined together by a column. Other gods of Bönpo include Satrid Ergang, who holds a swastika and mirror; Shenrab Wokar and his main emanation, Kuntu Zangpo, with a hooklike wand; and Sangpo Bumptri.

Complementing these gods is a large number of local deities – these are potentially harmful male spirits known as *gekho* (the protectors of Bön) and their female counterparts, *drapla*. Welchen Gekho is the king of the harmful *gekho*, and his consort Logbar Tsame is the queen of the *dralpa*.

A spirit trap is a series of interlocking threads around a wooden frame, often placed on a tree, which is supposed to ensnare evil spirits and which is burnt after its job is done.

Many Sakyapa monasteries contain images of the Sakyapa protector deity Gompo Gur and photographs of the school's four head lamas: the Sakya Trizin (in exile in the US), Ngawang Kunga (head of the Sakyapa order), Chogye Trichen Rinpoche (head of the Tsarpa subschool) and Ludhing Khenpo Rinpoche (head of the Ngorpa subschool).

Gelugpa Order

It may not have been his intention, but Tsongkhapa (1357–1419), a monk who left his home in Kokonor at the age of 17 to study in central Tibet, is regarded as the founder of the Gelugpa (Virtuous School) order, which came to dominate political and religious affairs in Tibet.

Tsongkhapa studied with all the major schools of his day, but was particularly influenced by the Sakyapa and the Kadampa orders. The Kadampa order had its head monastery at Netang, near Lhasa, and it was here that the 11th-century Bengali sage Atisha (Jowo-je) spent his last days. The Kadampa had sustained the teachings of Atisha, which are a sophisticated synthesis of conventional Mahayana doctrine with the more arcane practices of Tantric Buddhism, and emerged as a major school, emphasising scholastic study. It may never have matched the eminence of the Kagyupa and Sakyapa orders, but in the hands of Tsongkhapa the teachings of the Kadampa order established a renewal in Tibetan Buddhism.

The Tibetan Book of Living and Dying by Sogyal Rinpoche is an excellent background to *The Tibetan Book of the Dead* and the Dzogchen tradition. Sogyal has had contact with Western students, and several travellers recommend the book for beginners and advanced practitioners.

After experiencing a vision of Atisha (Jowo-je), Tsongkhapa elaborated on the Bengali sage's clerical-Tantric synthesis in a doctrine that is known as *lamrim* (the graduated path). Tsongkhapa basically advocated a return to doctrinal purity and monastic discipline as prerequisites to advanced Tantric studies. He did not, as is sometimes maintained, advocate a purely clerical approach to Buddhism, but he did reassert the monastic body as the basis of the Buddhist community, and he maintained that Tantric practices should be reserved only for advanced students.

Tsongkhapa established a monastery at Ganden, which was to become the head of the Gelugpa order. Other monasteries were also established at Drepung, Sera and Shigatse. Although the abbot of Drepung was the titular head of the order (and is to this day), it was the Dalai Lamas who came to be increasingly identified with the order's growing political and spiritual prestige.

Bön

In Tibet the establishment of Buddhism was marked by its interaction with the native religion Bön. This shamanistic faith, which encompassed gods and spirits, exorcism, talismans and the cult of dead kings among other things, had a major influence on the direction Buddhism took in Tibet.

The swastika is an ancient symbol of Buddhism and is often found painted on houses to bring good luck. Swastikas that point clockwise are Buddhist; those that point anticlockwise are Bön.

Many popular Buddhist symbols and practices, such as prayer flags, sky burial, the rubbing of holy rocks, the tying of bits of cloth to trees and the construction of spirit traps, all have their roots deep in Bön tradition. The traditional blessing of dipping a finger in water or milk and flicking it to the sky derives from Bön and can still be seen today in the shamanistic folk practices of Mongolia.

But it was Bön that was transformed and tamed to the ends of Buddhism and not vice versa. The Bön order, as it survives today, is to all intents and purposes the fifth school of Tibetan Buddhism. Major Bön monasteries include Menri and Yungdrungling (see p190) in central Tibet, and Tsedru (p262) and Tengchen (p263) in eastern Tibet. Other pockets of Bön exist in the Changtang region of northern Tibet and the Aba region of northern Sichuan (Kham). The main centre of Bön in exile is at Dolanji, near Solan, in India's Himachal Pradesh.

IMPORTANT FIGURES OF TIBETAN BUDDHISM

This is a brief iconographical guide to some of the gods and goddesses of the vast Tibetan Buddhist pantheon, as well as to important historical figures. It is neither exhaustive nor scholarly, but it may help you to recognise a few of the statues you encounter during your trip. Tibetan names are given first, with Sanskrit names provided in parentheses. (The exception is Sakya Thukpa, who is generally known by his Sanskrit name, Sakyamuni.)

Buddhas

SAKYAMUNI (SAKYA THUKPA)

Sakyamuni is the Historical Buddha (the Buddha of the Present Age), whose teachings set in motion the Buddhist faith. In Tibetan-style representations he is always pictured sitting cross-legged on a lotus-flower throne. His tight curled hair is dark blue and there is a halo of enlightenment around his head. The Buddha is recognised by 32 marks on his body, including a dot between his eyes, a bump on the top of his head, three folds of skin on his neck and the Wheel of Law on the soles of his feet. In his left hand he holds a begging bowl; and his right hand touches the earth in the 'witness' *mudra* (hand gesture). He is often flanked by his two principal disciples Sariputra and Maudgalyana.

Sakyamuni (Sakya Thukpa)

MARMEDZE (DIPAMKARA)

The Past Buddha, Marmedze, came immediately before Sakyamuni and spent 100,000 years on earth. His hands are shown in the 'protection' *mudra* and he is often depicted in a trinity with the Present and Future Buddhas.

ÖPAGME (AMITABHA)

The Buddha of Infinite Light resides in the 'pure land of the west'. The Panchen Lama is considered a reincarnation of this buddha. He is red, his hands are held together in his lap in a 'meditation' *mudra* and he holds a begging bowl.

TSEPAME (AMITAYUS)

The Buddha of Longevity, like Öpagme, is red and holds his hands in a meditation gesture, but he holds a vase containing the nectar of immortality. He is often seen in groups of nine.

Tsepame (Amitayus)

MEDICINE BUDDHAS (MENLHA)

A medicine buddha holds a medicine bowl in his left hand and herbs in his right and rays of healing light emanate from his body. He is often depicted in a group of eight.

DHYANI BUDDHAS (GYALWA RI NGA)

Each of the five Dhyani buddhas is a different colour, and each of them has different *mudras*, symbols and attributes. They are Öpagme, Nampar Namse (Vairocana), Mikyöba (or Mitrukpa; Akhshobya), Rinchen Jungne (Ratnasambhava) and Donyo Drupa (Amoghasiddhi).

JAMPA (MAITREYA)

Jampa, the Future Buddha (Milo Fo in Chinese), is passing the life of a bodhisattva until it is time to return to earth in human form 4000 years after the disappearance of Sakyamuni. He is normally seated in European fashion, with a scarf around his waist, often with a white stupa in his hair and his hands by his chest in the *mudra* of turning the Wheel of Law. Jampa is much larger than the average human and so statues of Jampa are often several storeys high.

Jampa (Maitreya)

Bodhisattvas

These are beings who have reached the state of enlightenment but vow to save everyone else in the world before they themselves enter nirvana. Unlike buddhas, they are often shown decorated with crowns and princely jewels.

CHENRESIG (AVALOKITESHVARA)

Chenresig (Avalokiteshvara)

The glorious gentle one, Chenresig (Guanyin to the Chinese) is the Bodhisattva of Compassion. His name means 'he who gazes upon the world with suffering in his eyes'. The Dalai Lamas are considered to be reincarnations of Chenresig (as is King Songtsen Gampo), and pictures of the Dalai Lama and Chenresig are interchangeable, depending on the political climate. The current Dalai Lama is the 14th manifestation of Chenresig.

In the four-armed version (known more specifically in Tibetan as Tonje Chenpo), his body is white and he sits on a lotus blossom. He holds crystal rosary beads and a lotus and clutches to his heart a jewel that fulfils all wishes. A deer skin is draped over his left shoulder.

There is also a powerful 11-headed, 1000-armed version, known as Chaktong Chentong. The head of this version is said to have exploded when confronted with myriad problems to solve. One of his heads is that of wrathful Chana Dorje (Vajrapani), and another (the top one) is that of Öpagme (Amitabha), who is said to have reassembled Chenresig's body after it exploded. Each of the 1000 arms has an eye in the palm. His eight main arms hold a bow and arrow, lotus, rosary, vase, wheel, staff and a wish-fulfilling jewel.

JAMPELYANG (MANJUSHRI)

Jampelyang (Manjushri)

The Bodhisattva of Wisdom, Jampelyang is regarded as the first divine teacher of Buddhist doctrine. He is connected to science and agriculture and school children; architects and astrologers often offer prayers to him. His right hand holds the flaming sword of awareness, which cuts through delusion. His left arm cradles a scripture on a half-opened lotus blossom and his left hand is in the 'teaching' *mudra*. He is often yellow and may have blue hair or an elaborate crown. He is sometimes called Manjughosa.

DRÖLMA (TARA)

A female bodhisattva with 21 different manifestations or aspects, Drölma is also known as the saviouress. She was born from a tear of compassion that fell from the eyes of Chenresig and is thus considered the female version of Chenresig and a protector of the Tibetan people. She also symbolises purity and fertility and is believed to be able to fulfil wishes. Images usually represent Green Tara, who is associated with night, or Drölkar (White Tara), who is associated with day (and also Songtsen Gampo's Chinese wife). The green version sits in a half-lotus position with her right leg down, resting on a lotus flower. The white version sits in the full lotus position and has seven eyes, including ones in her forehead, both palms and both soles of her feet. She is often seen as part of a longevity triad, along with red Tsepame (Amitayus) and three-faced, eight-armed female Namgyelma (Vijaya).

Drölma (Tara)

Protector Deities

Protectors are easily recognised by their fierce expressions, bulging eyes, warrior stance (with one leg outstretched in a fencer's pose), halo of flames and Tantric implements. They either stand trampling on the human ego or sit astride an animal mount, dressed in flayed animal or human skins. They represent on various levels the transformed original demons of Tibet, the wrathful aspects of other deities and, on one level at least, humankind's inner psychological demons.

CHÖKYONG (LOKAPALAS)

The Chökyong (or the Four Guardian Kings) are normally seen at the entrance hallway of monasteries and are possibly of Mongol origin. They are the protectors of the four cardinal directions: the eastern chief is white with a lute; the southern is green with a red beard and holds a sword; and the western is red and holds a green *naga*. The Chinese connect them to the four seasons.

Namtöse (Vaishravana), the protector of the north, doubles as the god of wealth (Jambhala) and can be seen with an orange body (the colour of 100,000 suns) and clumpy beard, riding a snow lion, and holding a banner of victory, a jewel-spitting mongoose and a lemon.

Nagpo Chenpo (Mahakala)

DORJE JIGJE (YAMANTAKA)

Dorje Jigje is a favourite protector of the Gelugpa order. A wrathful form of Jampelyang, he is also known as the destroyer of Yama (the Lord of Death). He is blue with eight heads, the main one of which is the head of a bull. He wears a garland of skulls around his neck and a belt of skulls around his waist, and holds a skull cup, butchers' chopper and a flaying knife in his 34 arms. He tramples on eight Hindu gods, eight mammals and eight birds with his 16 feet.

Tamdrin (Hayagriva)

NAGPO CHENPO (MAHAKALA)

A wrathful Tantric deity and manifestation of Chenresig, Nagpo Chenpo (Great Black One) has connections to the Hindu god Shiva. He can be seen in many varieties with anything from two to six arms. He is black ('as a water-laden cloud') with fanged teeth, wears a cloak of elephant skin and a tiara of skulls, carries a trident and skull cup and has flaming hair. In a form known as Gompo (or Yeshe Gompo), he is believed by nomads to be the guardian of the tent.

TAMDRIN (HAYAGRIVA)

Another wrathful manifestation of Chenresig, Tamdrin (the 'horse necked') has a red body. His right face is white, his left face is green and he has a horse's head in his hair. He wears a tiara of skulls, a garland of 52 severed heads and a tiger skin around his waist. His six hands hold a skull cup, a lotus, a sword, a snare, an axe and a club, and his four legs stand on a sun disc, trampling corpses. On his back are the outspread wings of Garuda and the skins of a human and an elephant. He is sometimes shown embracing a blue consort. He has close connections to the Hindu god Vishnu and is popular among herders and nomads.

Chana Dorje (Vajrapani)

CHANA DORJE (VAJRAPANI)

The name of the wrathful Bodhisattva of Energy means 'thunderbolt in hand'. In his right hand Chana Dorje holds a thunderbolt *(dorje* or *vajra),* which represents power and is a fundamental symbol of Tantric faith. He is blue with a tiger skin around his waist and a snake around his neck. He also has a peaceful, standing aspect. Together with Chenresig and Jampelyang, he forms part of the trinity known as the Rigsum Gonpo.

Palden Lhamo (Shri Devi)

PALDEN LHAMO (SHRI DEVI)

The special protector of Lhasa, the Dalai Lama and the Gelugpa order, Palden Lhamo is a female counterpart of Nagpo Chenpo. Her origins probably lie in the Hindu goddess Kali. She is blue, wears clothes of tiger skin, rides on a saddle of human skin, and has earrings made of a snake and a lion. She carries a club in her right hand and a skull cup full of blood in

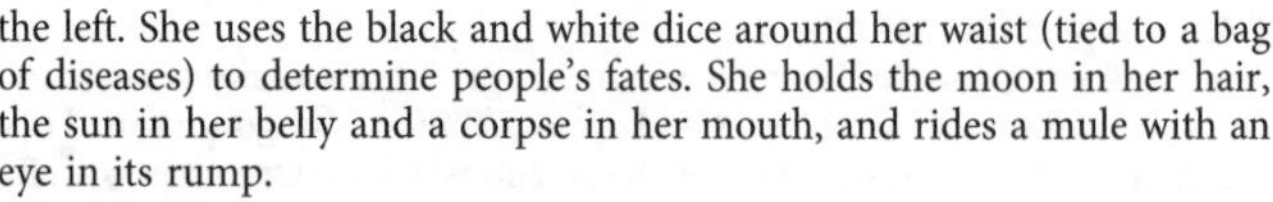
the left. She uses the black and white dice around her waist (tied to a bag of diseases) to determine people's fates. She holds the moon in her hair, the sun in her belly and a corpse in her mouth, and rides a mule with an eye in its rump.

Guru Rinpoche

DEMCHOK (CHAKRASAMVARA)

This meditational deity has a blue body with 12 arms, four faces and a crescent moon in his top knot. His main hands hold a thunderbolt and bell, and others hold an elephant skin, an axe, a hooked knife, a trident, a skull, a hand drum, a skull cup, a lasso and the head of Brahma. He also wears a garland of 52 heads, an apron of bone and clothes made from tiger skin.

Historical Figures

GURU RINPOCHE

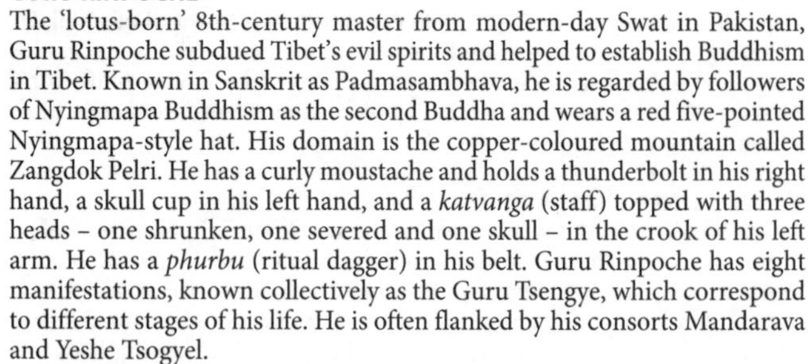
The 'lotus-born' 8th-century master from modern-day Swat in Pakistan, Guru Rinpoche subdued Tibet's evil spirits and helped to establish Buddhism in Tibet. Known in Sanskrit as Padmasambhava, he is regarded by followers of Nyingmapa Buddhism as the second Buddha and wears a red five-pointed Nyingmapa-style hat. His domain is the copper-coloured mountain called Zangdok Pelri. He has a curly moustache and holds a thunderbolt in his right hand, a skull cup in his left hand, and a *katvanga* (staff) topped with three heads – one shrunken, one severed and one skull – in the crook of his left arm. He has a *phurbu* (ritual dagger) in his belt. Guru Rinpoche has eight manifestations, known collectively as the Guru Tsengye, which correspond to different stages of his life. He is often flanked by his consorts Mandarava and Yeshe Tsogyel.

Tsongkhapa

TSONGKHAPA

Founder of the Gelugpa order and a manifestation of Jampelyang, Tsongkhapa (1357–1419) wears the yellow hat of the Gelugpas. Also known as Je Rinpoche, he is normally portrayed in the *yab-se sum* trinity with his two main disciples, Kedrub Je and Gyatsab Je. His hands are in the 'teaching' *mudra* and he holds two lotuses. He was the founder and first abbot of Ganden Monastery and many images of him are found there.

Fifth Dalai Lama

FIFTH DALAI LAMA

The greatest of all the Dalai Lamas, the fifth (Ngawang Lobsang Gyatso; 1617–82) unified Tibet and built the bulk of the Potala. He was born at Chongye (in the Yarlung Valley) and was the first Dalai Lama to exercise temporal power. He wears the Gelugpa yellow hat and holds a thunderbolt in his right hand and a bell *(drilbu)* in his left. He may also be depicted holding the Wheel of Law (symbolising the beginning of political control of the Dalai Lamas) and a lotus flower or other sacred objects.

KING SONGTSEN GAMPO

Tibet was unified under Songtsen Gampo, who introduced Buddhism to the country early in the 7th century. He has a moustache and wears a white turban with a tiny red Öpagme poking out of the top. He is flanked by Princess Wencheng Konjo, his Chinese wife, on the left, and Princess Bhrikuti, his Nepali wife, on his right.

King Songtsen Gampo

KING TRISONG DETSEN

The founder of Samye Monastery reigned from 755 to 797. He is normally seen in a trio of kings with Songtsen Gampo and King Ralpachen (r 817–36).

He is regarded as a manifestation of Jampelyang and so holds a scripture on a lotus in the crook of his left arm and a sword of wisdom in his right. Images show him with features similar to Songtsen Gampo's but without the buddha in his turban.

Milarepa

MILAREPA

A great 11th-century Tibetan magician and poet, Milarepa (c 1040–1123) is believed to have attained enlightenment in the course of one lifetime. He became an alchemist in order to poison an uncle who had stolen his family's lands and then spent six years meditating in a cave in repentance. During this time he wore nothing but a cotton robe and so became known as Milarepa (Cotton-Clad Mila). Most images of Milarepa depict him smiling, sitting on an antelope skin, wearing a red meditation belt and holding his hand to his ear as he sings. He may also be depicted as green because he lived for many years on a diet of nettles. Milarepa's guru was the translator Marpa.

Food & Drink

Tibet is unlikely to become a hot destination for foodies. Though you won't starve, Tibetan food will probably not be a highlight of your trip. In Lhasa there are a few restaurants that have elevated a subsistence diet into the beginnings of a cuisine but outside the urban centres, Tibetan food is more about survival than pleasure. On the plus side, fresh vegetables and packaged goods are now widely available and you are never far away from a good Chinese *fanguan* (饭馆) or *canting* (餐厅) (restaurant, or ཟ་ཁང་; *sakhâng* in Tibetan).

Want to cook some dharma food for a visiting *rinpoche*? Try *Tibetan Cooking: Recipes for Daily Living, Celebration, and Ceremony* by Elizabeth Kelly or *The Lhasa Moon Tibetan Cookbook* by Tsering Wangmo. Both books offer recipes for everything from *momos* to Milarepa-style nettle soup.

STAPLES & SPECIALITIES

Tibetan

Tellingly, the basic Tibetan meal is tsampa, a kind of dough made with roasted-barley flour and yak butter (if available) mixed with water, tea or beer – something wet. Tibetans skilfully knead and mix the paste by hand into dough-like balls – not as easy as it looks! Tsampa with milk powder and sugar makes a pretty good porridge and is a fine trekking staple, but only a Tibetan can eat it every day and still look forward to the next meal.

Outside of Lhasa, Tibetan food is limited to greasy *momos* and *thugpa*. *Momos* are small dumplings filled with meat or vegetables or both. They are normally steamed but can be fried and are pretty good.

More common is *thugpa*, a noodle soup with meat or vegetables or both. Variations on the theme include *hipthuk* (squares of noodles and yak meat in a soup) and *thenthuk* (more noodles). Glass noodles known as *phing* are also sometimes used. The other main option is *shemdre* (sometimes called curried beef), a stew of potatoes and yak meat on a bed of rice. In smarter restaurants in Lhasa or Shigatse you can try dishes like *damje* or *shomday* (varieties of fried rice with yak meat, raisins and yoghurt), *droma drase* (rice with sweet potato, sugar and butter) and *shya vale* (fried pancake-style pasties with a yak-meat filling).

In most restaurants you can simply wander out into the kitchen and point to the vegetables and meats you want fried up. The main snag with this method is that you'll miss out on many of the most interesting sauces and styles and be stuck with the same dishes over and over.

In rural areas and markets you might see strings of little white lumps drying in the sun that even the flies leave alone – this is dried yak cheese and it's eaten like a boiled sweet. For the first half-hour it is like having a small rock in your mouth, but eventually it starts to soften up and taste like old, dried yak cheese.

Also popular among nomads is *yak sha* (dried yak jerky). It is normally cut into strips and left to dry on tent lines and is pretty chewy stuff.

Chinese

Han immigration into Tibet may be a threat to the very essence of Tibetan culture but it's done wonders for the restaurant scene. Even most Tibetans admit that Chinese food is better than tsampa, *momos* and *thugpa*. Chinese restaurants can be found in almost every settlement in Tibet these days, but dishes are around 50% more expensive than Chinese restaurants elsewhere in China.

Tasty Travel

Tibetan food isn't all that popular among travellers. Top-end Tibetan restaurants in particular are very big on yak offal, with large sections of menus sumptuously detailing the various ways of serving up yak tongues, stomachs and lungs. The situation isn't helped by dishes such as *luokwa*, a 'combination of sheep's lungs, wheat flour, garlic, pepper and salt'. Probably lots of salt...

Chinese food in Tibet is almost exclusively Sichuanese, the hottest of China's regional cuisines. Sichuanese dishes are usually stir-fried quickly over a high flame and so tend to be very hygienic.

Chinese snacks are excellent and make for a fine light meal. The most common are *shuijiao* (ravioli-style dumplings) ordered by the bowl or weight (half a *jin,* or 250g, is enough for one person), and *baozi* (thicker steamed dumplings), which are similar to *momos* and are normally ordered by the steamer. Both are dipped in soy sauce, vinegar or chilli (or a mix of all). You can normally get a bowl of noodles anywhere for around Y5; *shaguo mixian* is a particularly tasty form of rice noodles cooked in a clay pot. *Chaomian* (fried noodles) and *dan chao fan* (egg fried rice) are not as popular as in the West but you can get them in many Chinese and backpacker restaurants.

If you find yourself kicking your heels up in Chengdu, several local hostels will teach you to stir-fry a multicourse Sichuan feast for around Y75 to Y100 (which includes the food). Places include Holly's Hostel (see p93) and Sim's Cozy Guesthouse (p91).

Muslim

The Muslim restaurants found in almost all urban centres in Tibet are an interesting alternative to Chinese or Tibetan food. These are normally recognisable by a green flag hanging outside or Arabic script on the restaurant sign. Most chefs come from the Linxia area of Gansu. The food is based on noodles, and, of course, there's no pork.

Dishes worth trying include *ganbanmian,* a kind of stir-fried spaghetti bolognaise made with beef (or yak) and sometimes green peppers, and *chaomianpian,* fried noodle squares with meat and vegetables. *Xinjiang banmian* (xinjiang noodles) are similar but the sauce comes in a separate bowl, to be poured over the noodles. You can often go into the kitchen and see your noodles being handmade on the spot.

Muslim restaurants also offer good breads and excellent *babao cha* or *babao wanzi* (eight treasure tea), which is made with dried raisins, plums and rock sugar, and only releases its true flavour after several cups.

One popular Sichuanese sauce is *yuxiang,* a spicy, piquant sauce of garlic, vinegar and chilli that is supposed to resemble the taste of fish (probably the closest thing you'll get to fish in Tibet).

Breakfasts

You can get decent breakfasts of yoghurt, muesli and toast at backpacker hotels in Lhasa, Gyantse and Shigatse, but elsewhere you are more likely to be confronted by Chinese-style dumplings, fried bread sticks (油条; *youtiao*) and tasteless rice porridge (稀饭; *xifan*). One good breakfast-type food that is widely available is scrambled eggs and tomato *(fanqie chaojidan).*

Self-Catering

There will be a time when you'll need to be self-sufficient, whether you're staying overnight at a monastery or are caught between towns on an overland trip. Unless you have a stove, your main saviour will be instant noodles. After a long trip to Mt Kailash and back you will know the relative tastes of every kind of packet of instant noodles sold in Tibet. Your body will also likely be deeply addicted to MSG. Even the faintest smell of noodles will leave you gagging. It's a good idea to stock up on instant coffee, hot chocolate and soups, as flasks of boiling water are offered in every hotel and restaurant.

Vegetables such as onions, carrots and bok choy (even seaweed and pickled vegetables) can save even the cheapest pack of noodles from culinary oblivion, as can a packet of mixed spices brought from home.

To re-create a little taste of Tibet when you get home, Lhasa's Oh Dan Guest House (see p121) offers *momo*-making courses for Y20.

DRINKS

Nonalcoholic Drinks

The local beverage that every traveller ends up trying at least once is yak-butter tea (see p78). Modern Tibetans use an electric blender to mix their yak butter tea.

YAK-BUTTER TEA

Bö cha, literally 'Tibetan tea', is unlikely to be a highlight of your trip to Tibet. Made from yak butter mixed with salt, milk, soda, tea leaves and hot water all churned up in a wooden tube, the soupy mixture has more the consistency of bouillon than of tea (one traveller described it as 'a cross between brewed old socks and sump oil'). When mixed with tsampa (roasted-barley flour) and yak butter it becomes the staple meal of most Tibetans and you may well be offered it at monasteries, people's houses and even while waiting for a bus by the side of the road.

At most restaurants you mercifully have the option of drinking *cha ngamo* (sweet, milky tea) but there will be times when you just have to be polite and down a cupful of *bö cha* (without gagging). Most nomads think nothing of drinking up to 40 cups of the stuff a day. On the plus side it does replenish your body's lost salts and prevents your lips from cracking. As one reader told us, 'Personally we like yak-butter tea not so much for the taste as the view'.

Most distressing for those not sold on the delights of yak-butter tea is the fact that your cup will be refilled every time you take even the smallest sip, as a mark of the host's respect. There's a pragmatic reason for this as well; there's only one thing worse than hot yak-butter tea – cold yak-butter tea.

The more palatable alternative to yak-butter tea is sweet, milky tea, or *cha ngamo*. It is similar to the tea drunk in neighbouring Pakistan. Chinese green tea, soft drinks and mineral water are available everywhere. The most popular Chinese soft drink is Jianlibao, a honey-and-orange drink (sometimes translated on restaurant menus as 'Jellybowl'). On our research trips we have never suffered any adverse effects from drinking copious amounts of *chang*. However, you should be aware that it is often made with contaminated water, and there is always some risk in drinking it.

Many Sichuanese dishes include *huajiao* (wild Asian flower pepper), a curious mouth-numbing spice.

Alcoholic Drinks

The Tibetan brew is known as *chang,* a fermented barley beer. It has a rich, fruity taste and ranges from disgusting to pretty good. Connoisseurs serve it out of a jerry can. Those trekking in the Everest region should try the local variety, which is served in a big pot. Hot water is poured into the fermenting barley and the liquid is drunk through a wooden straw – it is very good. Sharing *chang* is a good way to get to know local people, if drunk in small quantities.

The main brands of beer available in Tibet are Snow and Lhasa Beer, as well as the usual suspects like Budweiser. Lhasa Beer is brewed in Lhasa, originally under German supervision and now in a joint venture with Carlsberg. Look out also for Lhasa Ice Beer and Tibet Spring Green Barley Beer. Domestic beer costs around Y4 in a shop, Y8 in most restaurants and Y12 in swanky bars.

Outside of Lhasa, few Chinese restaurants have menus in English and when they do the prices are often marked up by as much as 50%.

Supermarkets in Lhasa stock several types of Chinese red wine, including Shangri-La, produced in the Tibetan areas of northeast Yunnan using methods handed down by French missionaries at the beginning of the 19th century. A bottle costs around Y50.

EAT YOUR WORDS – TIBETAN

Useful Phrases

I'm vegetarian.

ང་དཀར་ཟས་ཡིན། *nga karsay yin*

I don't eat meat.

ང་ཤ་ཟ་གྱི་མེད། *nga sha sagi may*

I'll have what they're having.

ཁོང་ཚོས་མཆོད་ཡག་དེ་ན་བཞིན་ང་ལ་དགོས། *khongtsö chöyate nashin ngala gö*

Not too spicy, please. སྨན་སྣ་ཞེ་དྲགས་མ་རྒྱག་རོགས་གནང་།	*menna shayta magyâronâng*
The meal was delicious! ཁ་ལག་ཞིམ་པོ་ཞེ་དྲགས་བྱུང་།	*khala shimbu shayta choong!*

Food Glossary

dumplings	མོག་མོག	*momo*
fried noodles	རྒྱ་ཐུག	*gyâthuk*
noodles	ཐུག་པ	*thukpa*
omelette	སྒོང་འབྲས་བརྔོས་པ་/ཨོམ་ལེཊ་	*gongdre ngöpâ; omlet*
roasted-barley flour	རྩམ་པ་	*tsâmpa*
salt	ཚྭ་	*tsha*
sugar	བྱེ་མ་ཀ་ར་/ཅི་ནི་	*chayma kara/ chini*
stir-fried vegetable dishes	ཚལ་བརྔོས་པ་	*tsay ngöpâ*
yak meat	གཡག་ཤ་	*yâksha*

Drinks

beer (bottled)	བྷི་ཡར་/ཕི་ཆུ་	*beeyar*
beer (home-brew)	ཆང་	*châng*
boiled water	ཆུ་འཁོལ་མ་	*chu khöma*
butter tea	བོད་ཇ་/ཇ་སྲུས་མ་	*böja; cha süma*
mineral water	བུལ་ཏོག་ཆུ་	*butogchu*

EAT YOUR WORDS – CHINESE

Useful Phrases

I don't want MSG.	我不要味精.	*Wǒ bùyào wèijīng.*
I'm vegetarian.	我吃素.	*Wǒ chī sù.*
Not too spicy.	不要太辣	*Bùyào tàilà.*
(cooked) together	一块儿	*yīkuàir*

Food Glossary

SNACKS

beef noodles in a soup	牛肉面	*niúròu miàn*
boiled dumplings	水饺	*shuǐjiǎo*
egg soup	蛋花汤	*dànhuā tāng*
fried Muslim noodles and beef	干拌面	*gānbàn miàn*
fried noodle squares	炒面片	*chǎomiànpiàn*
fried noodles with vegetables	蔬菜炒面	*shūcài chǎomiàn*
fried rice with beef	牛肉丝炒饭	*niúròusī chǎofàn*
fried rice with egg	鸡蛋炒饭	*jīdàn chǎofàn*
fried rice with vegetables	蔬菜炒饭	*shūcài chǎofàn*
Muslim noodles	拉面	*lāmiàn*
steamed meat buns	包子	*bāozi*
steamed white rice	米饭	*mǐfàn*
vermicelli noodles in casserole pot	砂锅米线	*shāguō mǐxiàn*
wonton (soup)	馄饨(汤)	*húntun (tāng)*
xinjiang noodles	新疆拌面	*xīnjiāng bànmiàn*

MAIN DISHES

baby bok choy	小白菜	*xiǎo báicài*
broccoli	西兰花	*xīlánhuā*
crispy chicken	香炸鸡块	*xiāngzhá jīkuài*

double-cooked fatty pork	回锅肉	*huíguō ròu*
dry-fried runner beans	干煸四季豆	*gānbiān sìjìdòu*
egg and tomato	番茄炒蛋	*fānqié chǎodàn*
'fish-resembling' eggplant	鱼香茄子	*yúxiāng qiézi*
'fish-resembling' pork	鱼香肉丝	*yúxiāng ròusī*
fried green beans	素炒扁豆	*sùchǎo biǎndòu*
fried vegetables	素炒蔬菜	*sùchǎo sùcài*
greens	油菜/空心菜	*yóucài/kōngxīncài*
home-style tofu	家常豆腐	*jiācháng dòufu*
pork and green peppers	青椒肉片	*qīngjiāo ròupiàn*
pork and sizzling rice crust	锅巴肉片	*guōbā ròupiàn*
pork in soy sauce	京酱肉丝	*jīngjiàng ròusī*
red-cooked eggplant	红烧茄子	*hóngshāo qiézi*
spicy chicken with peanuts	宫爆鸡丁	*gōngbào jīdīng*
spicy tofu	麻辣豆腐	*málà dòufu*
spinach	菠菜	*bōcài*
sweet and sour pork fillets	糖醋里脊	*tángcù lǐjī*
'wooden ear' mushrooms and pork	木耳肉	*mùěr ròu*

Drinks

beer	啤酒	*píjiǔ*
boiled water	开水	*kāi shuǐ*
mineral water	矿泉水	*kuàng quán shuǐ*
Muslim tea	八宝琬子	*bābǎo wǎnzi*
tea	茶	*chá*
hot	热的	*rède*
ice cold	冰的	*bīngde*

Environment

The Tibetan plateau has global ecological significance, not only as the earth's highest ecosystem and one of its last remaining great wildernesses but also as the source of Asia's greatest rivers. Furthermore, it is thought that the high plateau affects global jet streams and even influences the Indian monsoon. The Dalai Lama would like to see Tibet turned into a 'zone of peace' and perhaps even the world's largest national park.

The Tibetan Buddhist view of the environment has long stressed the intricate and interconnected relationship between the natural world and human beings, a viewpoint closely linked to the concept of death and rebirth. Buddhist practice in general stands for moderation and against overconsumption, and forbids hunting, fishing and the taking of animal life. Tibet's nomads, in particular, live in a fine balance with their harsh environment.

Geographically speaking, the Qinghai-Tibet plateau makes up almost 25% of China's total landmass, spread over five provinces.

THE LAND

The Tibetan plateau is one of the most isolated regions in the world, bound to the south by the 2500km-long Himalaya, to the west by the Karakoram and to the north by the Kunlun and Altyn Tagh ranges, some of the least explored ranges on earth. Four of the world's 10 highest mountains straddle Tibet's southern border with Nepal. The northwest in particular is bound by the most remote and least explored wilderness left on earth, outside the polar regions. With an average altitude of 4000m and large swathes of the country well above 5000m, the Tibetan plateau (nearly the size of Western Europe) deserves the title 'the roof of the world'.

The high plateau of Tibet is the result of prodigious geological upheaval. The time scale is subject to much debate, but at some point in the last 100 million years the entire region lay beneath the Tethys Sea. And that is where it would have stayed had the mass of land now known as India not broken free from the protocontinent Gondwana and drifted off in a collision course with another protocontinent known as Laurasia. The impact of the two land masses sent the Indian plate burrowing under the Laurasian landmass, and two vast parallel ridges, over 3000km in length and in places almost 9km high, piled up. These ridges, the Himalaya and associated ranges, are still rising at around 10cm a year. You may well find locals near Shegar selling fossils of marine animals – at an altitude of more than 4000m above sea level!

The TAR is made up of the municipality of Lhasa and six prefectures (Ali, Shigatse, Nagchu, Shannan, Nyingtri and Chamdo) and is divided into 70 counties.

The Tibetan Autonomous Region (TAR), with an area of 1.23 million sq km, covers only part of this geographical plateau (the rest is mostly parcelled off into the Qinghai and Sichuan provinces). It encompasses the traditional Tibetan provinces of Ü (capital, Lhasa), Tsang (capital, Shigatse) and Ngari, or western Tibet, as well as parts of Kham (eastern Tibet). The TAR shares a 3482km international border with India, Bhutan, Nepal and Myanmar (Burma), and is bordered to the north and east by the Chinese provinces of Xinjiang, Qinghai, Sichuan and Yunnan.

The dry, high altitudes of the Tibetan plateau make for climatic extremes – temperatures on the Changtang have been known to drop 27°C in a single day!

Much of Tibet is a harsh and uncompromising landscape, best described as a high-altitude desert. Little of the Indian monsoon makes it over the Himalayan watershed. Shifting sand dunes are a common sight along the Samye Valley and the road to Mt Kailash.

Ütsang (the combined provinces of Ü and Tsang, which constitute central Tibet) is the political, historical and agricultural heartland of Tibet. Its relatively fertile valleys enjoy a mild climate and are irrigated by wide rivers such as the Yarlung Tsangpo and the Kyi-chu.

Towards the north of Ütsang are the harsh, high-altitude plains of the Changtang (northern plateau), the highest and largest plateau in the world, occupying an area of more than one million sq km. This area has no river systems and supports very little in the way of life. The dead lakes of the Changtang are the brackish remnants of the Tethys Sea that found no runoff when the plateau started its skyward ascent.

For an account of George Schaller's trips to the Changtang and some wonderful photographs, check out his coffee-table book, *Tibet's Hidden Wilderness: Wildlife and Nomads of the Chang Tang Reserve*. For a more academic background to the region's natural history try his *Wildlife of the Tibetan Steppe*.

Tibet has several thousand lakes (*tso* in Tibetan), of which the largest are Nam-tso, Yamdrok-tso, Manasarovar (Mapham yum-tso), Siling-tso and Pangong-tso, the last crossing the Indian border into Ladakh. Nam-tso is the second-largest saltwater lake in China and one of the most beautiful natural sights in Tibet; the largest is Koko Nor (Qinghai Lake in Chinese; Tso-Ngon) in Qinghai province.

Ngari, or western Tibet, is similarly barren, although here river valleys provide grassy tracts that support nomads and their grazing animals. Indeed, the Kailash range in the far west of Tibet is the source of the subcontinent's four greatest rivers: the Ganges, Indus, Sutlej and Brahmaputra. The Ganges, Indus and Sutlej Rivers all cascade out of Tibet in its far west, not far from Mt Kailash itself. The Brahmaputra (known in Tibet as Yarlung Tsangpo) meanders along the northern spine of the Himalaya for 2000km, searching for a way south, before coiling back on itself in a dramatic U-turn and draining into India not far from the Myanmar border.

In the arid climate of much of Tibet, water takes on a special significance. The *lu* (water spirits) guard the wellbeing of the community and are thought to be very dangerous if angered.

Kham, which encompasses the eastern TAR, western Sichuan and northwest Yunnan, marks a tempestuous drop in elevation down to the Sichuan plain. The concertina landscape produces some of the most spectacular roller-coaster roads in Asia, as Himalayan extensions such as the Hengduan Mountains are sliced by the deep gorges of the Yangzi (Dri-chu in Tibetan; Jinsha Jiang in Chinese), Salween (Gyalmo Ngul-chu in Tibetan; Nu Jiang in Chinese) and Mekong (Dza-chu in Tibetan; Lancang Jiang in Chinese) headwaters.

The Yarlung Tsangpo crashes through a 5km-deep gorge here (the world's deepest) as it swings around 7756m Namche Barwa. Many parts of this alpine region are lushly forested and support abundant wildlife, largely thanks to the lower altitudes and effects of the Indian monsoon.

WILDLIFE

The vast differences in altitude in Tibet give rise to a spread of ecosystems from alpine to subtropical.

Animals

The Tibetan antelope was adopted as the mascot of the 2008 Beijing Olympic Games.

If you are not trekking in Tibet and your travels are restricted to sights off the Friendship Hwy, you are unlikely to see much in the way of wildlife. On the road out to Mt Kailash, however, it is not unusual to see herds of fleet-footed Tibetan gazelles *(gowa)*, antelope *(tso)* and wild asses *(kyang)*, particularly along the northern route. During the breeding season antelope converge in groups numbering several hundred.

Trekkers might conceivably see the Himalayan black bear or perhaps the giant Tibetan brown bear searching for food in the alpine meadows. Herds of blue sheep *(nawa na)* are frequently spied on rocky slopes and outcrops, but the argali, the largest species of wild sheep in the world, now only survives in the most remote mountain fastnesses of western Tibet.

Wolves in a variety of colours can be seen all over the Tibetan plateau. Much rarer than the all-black wolf is the white wolf, one of the great sacred animals of Tibet. Smaller carnivores include the lynx, marten and fox.

Marmots *(chiwa* or *piya)* are very common and can often be seen perched up on their hind legs sniffing the air curiously outside their burrows – they make a strange birdlike sound when distressed. The pika *(chipi)*, or Himalayan mouse-hare, a relative of the rabbit, is also common. Pikas have been observed at 5250m on Mt Everest, thus earning the distinction of having the highest habitat of any mammal.

A surprising number of migratory birds make their way up to the lakes of the Tibetan plateau through spring and summer. Tibet has over 30 endemic birds; 480 species have been recorded on the plateau. Birds include the black-necked crane (whose numbers in Tibet have doubled over the last decade), bar-headed goose and lammergeier, as well as grebes, pheasants, snow cocks and partridges. Watching a pair of black-necked cranes, loyal mates for life, is one of the joys of traipsing near the wetlands of northern and western Tibet. Flocks of huge vultures can often be seen circling monasteries looking for a sky burial.

Two of the best places to go bird-watching are the lakes Yamdrok-tso and Nam-tso; a section of the latter has been designated a bird preserve, at least on paper. April and November are the best times.

ENDANGERED SPECIES

About 80 species of animal that are threatened with extinction have been listed as protected by the Chinese government. These include the almost-mythical snow leopard *(gang-zig)*, ibex *(king)*, white-lipped deer *(shawa chukar)*, musk deer *(lawa)*, Tibetan antelope *(chiru)*, Tibetan wild ass *(kyang)*, bharal, or blue sheep *(nawa na)*, black-necked crane, argali and wild yak *(drong)*. Omitted from the list is the very rare Tibetan brown bear *(dom gyamuk)*, which stands up to 2m tall and can only be found in the forests of southern Tibet and the remote Changtang plateau.

The Tibetan red deer was recently 'discovered' only 75km from Lhasa after a 50-year hiatus, as was a hitherto unknown breed of ancient wild horse in the Riwoche region of eastern Tibet. The horses bear a striking resemblance to those shown in Stone Age paintings.

Wild yaks are mostly encountered in the Changtang, north of the 34th parallel. The biggest bull yaks are reputed to be as large as a Land Cruiser. Even rarer is the divine giant white yak, thought by Tibetans to inhabit the higher reaches of sacred mountains.

The *chiru*, a rare breed of antelope, was recently placed on the Red List (www.redlist.org), a list of threatened species maintained by the World Conservation Union. Numbers in Tibet have dropped from over a million *chiru* 50 years ago to as few as 70,000 today. Poachers kill the animal for its *shatoosh* wool (wool from the animal's undercoat).

The illegal trade in antelope cashmere, musk, bear paws and gall bladders, deer antlers, and other body parts and bones remains a problem. You can often see Tibetan traders huddled on street corners in major Chinese cities selling these and other medicinal cures. When the Dalai Lama expressed disapproval of Tibetans wearing animal pelts on their *chubas* (Tibetan cloaks) a few years ago, a movement inside Tibet resulted in the mass burnings of thousands of tiger, leopard and other hides as a sign of devotion.

Plants

Juniper trees and willows are common in the valleys of central Tibet and it is possible to come across wildflowers such as the pansy and the oleander, as well as unique indigenous flowers such as the *tsi-tog* (a light-pink, high-altitude bloom).

The east of Tibet, which sees higher rainfall than the rest of the region, has an amazing range of flora, from oak, elm and birch forests to bamboo, subtropical plants and flowers, including rhododendrons, azaleas and magnolias. It was from here that intrepid 19th-century plant hunters FM Bailey, Frank Kingdon Ward and Frank Ludlow took the seeds and cuttings of species that would eventually become staples in English gardening.

NATURE PRESERVES

Nature preserves officially protect over 20% of the TAR, although many exist on paper only. The preserve with the highest profile is the Qomolangma Nature Preserve (opposite), a 34,000-sq-km protected area straddling the 'third pole' of the Everest region. The park promotes the involvement of the local population, which is essential as around 67,000 people live within the park.

Yak-tail hair was the main material used to produce Father Christmas (Santa Claus) beards in 1950s America!

Tibet's newest preserve is the Changtang Nature Preserve, set up in 1993 with the assistance of famous animal behaviourist George Schaller. At 247,120 sq km (larger than Arizona), this is the largest nature reserve in the world after Greenland National Park. Endangered species in the park include bharal, argali sheep, wolves, lynxes, gazelles, snow leopards, wild yaks, antelopes, brown bears and wild asses.

Other reserves include the Great Canyon of the Yarlung Tsangpo Nature Reserve (formerly the Medog reserve) to the south of Namche Barwa, the Dzayul (Zayu) Reserve along the far southeast border with Assam, and

YAKETY-YAK

Fifty years ago an estimated one million wild yaks roamed the Tibetan plateau. Now it is a rare treat to catch a glimpse of these impressive black bovines, which weigh up to a tonne, whose shoulder heights reach over 1.8m and whose sharp, slender horns span 1m. Wild yaks have diminished in number to 15,000 as a result of the increased demand for yak meat and a rise in hunting. Although eating yak meat is not sacrilegious in Tibetan culture, hunting wild yaks is illegal.

Few, if any, of the yaks that travellers see are *drong* (wild yaks). In fact, most are not even yaks at all but rather dzo, a cross between a yak and a cow. A domestic yak rarely exceeds 1.5m in height. Unlike its wild relative, it varies in shade from black to grey and, primarily around Kokonor in Qinghai, white. Seeing only one yak of a certain colour in a herd is considered a bad omen, while seeing two or more yaks of the same colour is considered a sign of luck.

Despite their massive size, yaks are surprisingly sure-footed and graceful on steep, narrow trails, even while burdened by loads of up to 70kg. Yaks panic easily, though, and will struggle to stay close together. This gregarious instinct allows herders to drive packs of animals through snow-blocked passes, and thus to create a natural snowplough.

With three times more red blood cells than the average cow, the yak thrives in the oxygen-depleted high altitudes. Its curious lung formation, surrounded by 14 or 15 pairs of ribs rather than the 13 typical of cattle, allows a large capacity for inhaling and expelling air; thus the Latin name *Bos grunniens,* which translates literally as 'grunting ox'. In fact, a descent below 3000m may impair the reproductive cycle and expose the yak to parasites and disease. Cloaked in layers of shaggy, coarse hair and blanketed by a soft undercoat, the yak uses its square tongue and broad muzzle to forage close to the soil in temperatures that frequently drop to minus 40°C.

Tibetans rely on yak milk for cheese, as well as for butter for the ubiquitous butter tea and offerings to butter lamps in monasteries. The outer hair of the yak is woven into tent fabric and rope, and the soft inner wool is spun into *chara* (a type of felt) and used to make bags, blankets and tents. Tails are used in both Buddhist and Hindu religious practices. Yak hide is used for the soles of boots and the yak's heart is used in Tibetan medicine. In the nomadic tradition, no part of the animal is wasted and even yak dung is required as a fundamental fuel, left to dry in little cakes on the walls of most Tibetan houses. So important are yaks to the Tibetans that the animals are individually named, like children.

Herders take great care to ensure the health and safety of their animals. Relocation three to eight times a year provides adequate grazing. Every spring the yaks' thick coats are carefully trimmed. Nomads rely on unique veterinarian skills, which they use to lance abscesses, set broken bones and sear cuts.

The yak, with its extraordinary composition and might, has been perhaps the sole enabler of the harsh life of Tibet's *drokpas,* or nomads, and the two coexist in admirable harmony.

the Kyirong and Nyalam Reserves near the Nepali border. Unfortunately, these reserves enjoy little protection or policing.

The film *Mountain Patrol: Kekexili* tells the story of four Tibetans from Yushu who band together to protect the local Tibetan antelopes. The film was shot on location at Kekexili (Hoh Xil in Mongolian) nature reserve in the Tibetan grasslands of southern Qinghai (Amdo). For more info see www.nationalgeographic.com/mountainpatrol.

ENVIRONMENTAL ISSUES

Modern communist experiments, such as collectivisation and the changing of century-old farming patterns (for example, from barley to wheat and rice), upset the fragile balance in Tibet and resulted in a series of great disasters and famines in the 1960s (as, indeed, they did in the rest of China). By the mid-1970s, the failure of collectivisation was widely recognised and Tibetans have since been allowed to return to traditional methods of working the land.

Other natural resources are less easily renewed. When the Tibetan government-in-exile sent three investigative delegations to Tibet in the early 1980s, among the shocking news they returned with was that Tibet had been denuded of its wildlife. Stories of People's Liberation Army (PLA) troops machine-gunning herds of wild gazelles circulated with convincing frequency. Commercial trophy-hunting, often by foreigners paying tens of thousands of US dollars, has had an effect on the numbers of antelope and argali sheep in particular.

If you are interested in identifying Tibetan medicinal plants, check out *Tibetan Medical Thangkas of the Four Medical Tantras,* a lavish coffee-table book available in most Lhasa bookshops. Also see *Flowers of the Himalaya* by Oleg Polunin and Adam Stainton for some examples of Tibetan flora.

Rapid modernisation threatens to bring industrial pollution, a hitherto almost unknown problem, onto the high plateau. Several cement factories at Lhasa's edge created clouds of noxious smoke, which blanketed parts of western Lhasa until the factories were shut down in the 1990s. Mass domestic tourism (92% of tourists to Tibet are Chinese) is also beginning to take its toll, with litter and unsustainable waste management a major problem in areas like Nam-tso and the Everest region.

Tibet has enormous potential for hydroelectricity, although current projects at Yamdrok-tso and elsewhere have been criticised by both Tibetans and foreign environmental groups. For more information, see p181. Reports of a planned 'super-dam' (which could generate twice as much electricity as the Three Gorges Dam) on the Yarlung Tsangpo (Brahmaputra) in the remote southeast of Tibet has the Indian government downstream deeply concerned. China's latest mega-engineering project is a plan

QOMOLANGMA NATURE PRESERVE

The Qomolangma Nature Preserve (QNP) was established in 1989 by the government of the Tibetan Autonomous Region (TAR) to conserve the natural and cultural heritage of the Mt Everest region.

Bordering Nepal's Sagarmatha, Langtang and Makalu-Barun National Parks and their buffer zones, the 34,000-sq-km preserve is part of the only protected area to straddle both sides of the Himalaya. QNP's park managers hold regular exchanges with their counterparts in Nepal to share experiences and promote conservation cooperation across political boundaries.

More than 7000 foreign tourists visit the QNP each year, and their numbers are growing. The goal of the QNP is to encourage tourism and generate local benefits and employment while protecting the environment. Entry fees to core preserve areas are invested in maintaining access roads and controlling litter at major mountaineering and trekking camps.

Funding for various environmental and economic-development activities comes from national and regional governments. QNP also collaborates with a number of international organisations. The **Mountain Institute** (www.mountain.org; 1828 L St NW, Ste 725, Washington, DC 20036) is one such organisation; it supports QNP in conserving local environment and culture and improving village livelihoods through its multiyear Qomolangma Conservation Project (QCP). In Tibet, you can get information on the project from **Christopher La Due** (☎ 891-636 4037; qcp@mountain.org; Ste 1306, Lhasa Tashi Norbu Hotel, 24 South Tuanjie Xingcun Lane, Lhasa, TAR 850000), director of the institute's Peak Enterprise Program.

As early as 1642, the fifth Dalai Lama issued an edict protecting animals and the environment.

For more on environmental issues in Tibet, visit Tibet Environmental Watch at www.tew.org.

to construct a 300km pipeline to divert water from the Yalong, Dada and Jinsha Rivers in western Sichuan (Kham) to the Yellow River. The US$37 billion project is set to begin in 2010.

The region also has abundant supplies of geothermal energy thanks to its turbulent geological history. The Yangpachen Geothermal Plant already supplies Lhasa with much of its electricity. Portable solar panelling has also enjoyed some success; the plateau enjoys some of the longest and strongest sunlight outside the Saharan region. Experimental wind-power stations have been set up in northern Tibet.

Deforestation has long been a pressing problem in eastern Tibet: around US$54 billion worth of timber has been felled in the Tibetan region since 1959. The effect on sediment and runoff levels for rivers downstream, especially in flood-prone China, has finally sunk in and logging activity has eased considerably in recent years.

Environmentalists remain concerned about the new train line to Tibet. The line touches six protected areas and effectively blocks the seasonal migration routes of the endangered Tibetan antelope. Engineers claim that the 33 passageways built under the raised track allow wildlife to cross the line safely, though whether the antelope will learn to use the underpasses is another question. There are also fears that the possibility of seismic disruption (a magnitude 8.1 earthquake struck in 2001 near the Kunlun Shan pass) and the effects of global warming will affect the track in the coming years. Maintenance of the track may prove to be an even bigger job than construction.

Environmentalists also fear that the line will speed up mining exploitation in the region. Mining has traditionally been inimical to Tibetans, who believe it disturbs the earth spirits. In May 2007 several Tibetans were arrested in Bamei (Garthar) in Kham (Western Sichuan) after violent demonstrations against Chinese mining operations on the sacred peak of Yala Shan.

In the long term, climate change is expected to affect Tibet as much as it will the earth's low-lying regions. Chinese scientists recently announced that Tibet's glaciers are retreating at a rate of 9% in the Everest region and up to 17% at Mt Amnye Machen near the source of the Yellow River in Qinghai. China recently lowered the official height of Everest by 1.3m, citing a shrinkage in the ice cap around the peak. The UN has warned that Tibet's glaciers could disappear within a century, with 80% predicted to disappear by 2035.

The results of the glacial melting will be initial flooding and erosion, followed by a long-term drought. With almost half the world's population (85% of Asia) getting its water from the rivers flowing off the Tibetan plateau (the Ganges, Yarlung Tsangpo/Brahmaputra, Indus, Karnali, Sutlej, Yangzi, Huanghe/Yellow River, Mekong, Salween and Irrawady Rivers), changes to Tibet's environment will have global resonance.

Gateway Cities

Many visitors to Tibet will transit through either Chengdu or Kathmandu, or both, en route so this chapter offers basic information on these two cities. For more detail see Lonely Planet's *China, China's Southwest* and *Nepal* guides.

KATHMANDU

☎ 01 / pop 822,000 / elev 1300m

Crowded, hectic Kathmandu has long been a popular destination for travellers, but there are a couple of drawbacks to entering Tibet from here, namely the uncertainty of getting a Chinese visa (especially with extra days on it so you can travel after your organised tour) and the potential hassles involved in arranging a group tour. For detailed information on the topics, see p328 and p334.

The Thamel district of Kathmandu is a travellers' mecca and the place to get a good meal (in any number of Asian cuisines), repair a sleeping bag, buy a backpack, shop for souvenirs or purchase hard-to-find books on Tibet (including Indian reprints of some very rare editions). But it's also a bit of a zoo, with too many vehicles, beggars, Tiger-balm pedlars and trekking touts all sharing the same narrow, footpath-less roads. A few days here is plenty.

During the June to August monsoon season (when most visitors travel to or from Tibet) it is usually humid and rainy in Kathmandu.

INFORMATION

Bookshops

Pilgrims Book House (☎ 4424992; www.pilgrimsbooks.com), north of the Kathmandu Guest House in Thamel, and **New Tibet Book Store** (☎ 4415788; Tridevi Marg), east of Thamel, have the best selections.

Money

Check exchange and commission rates at both banks and licensed moneychangers as they do vary. The US dollar is worth around Rs 63 (63 rupees).

Himalaya Bank (Tridevi Marg; 🕑 10am-7.30pm Sun-Fri) Changes travellers cheques and gives cash advances on Visa cards.

Standard Chartered Bank Has two ATMs in Thamel, one inside the grounds of the Kathmandu Guest House.

Tours to Tibet

Many agencies in Thamel offer budget tours to Tibet (most leave Tuesday and Saturday) and these are currently the only way to get into Tibet. See p335 for more details about tour operators. The following agencies are the most reliable, although none is especially recommended.

Eco Trek (☎ 4423207; www.holyhimalaya.com; Thamel) Tours often run in conjunction with Indian pilgrim groups. A potentially interesting way to visit Mt Kailash.

Green Hill Tours (☎ 4700803; www.greenhilltours.com; Thamel)

Royal Mount Trekking (☎ 4241452; Durbar Marg)

Tashi Delek Nepal Treks & Expeditions (☎ 4410746; www.tashidelektreks.com; Thamel) Often the cheapest.

Other travel companies in Thamel offering tours to Tibet include **Earthbound Expeditions** (www.trektibet.com) and **Adventure Silk Road** (www.silkroadgroup.com), although there are many more.

Travel Agencies

Wayfarers (☎ 4266010; www.wayfarers.com.np; Thamel) Excellent and reliable agency for air tickets and local tours.

DANGERS & ANNOYANCES

Nepal has been affected by political and social unrest for many years now. Though not as frequent as before, strikes *(bandh)* can still happen, shutting down businesses and making getting to the airport difficult at these times. Don't believe your taxi driver when he says he can drop you off a few minutes' walk from the terminal – it will be more likely take you 30 minutes or more.

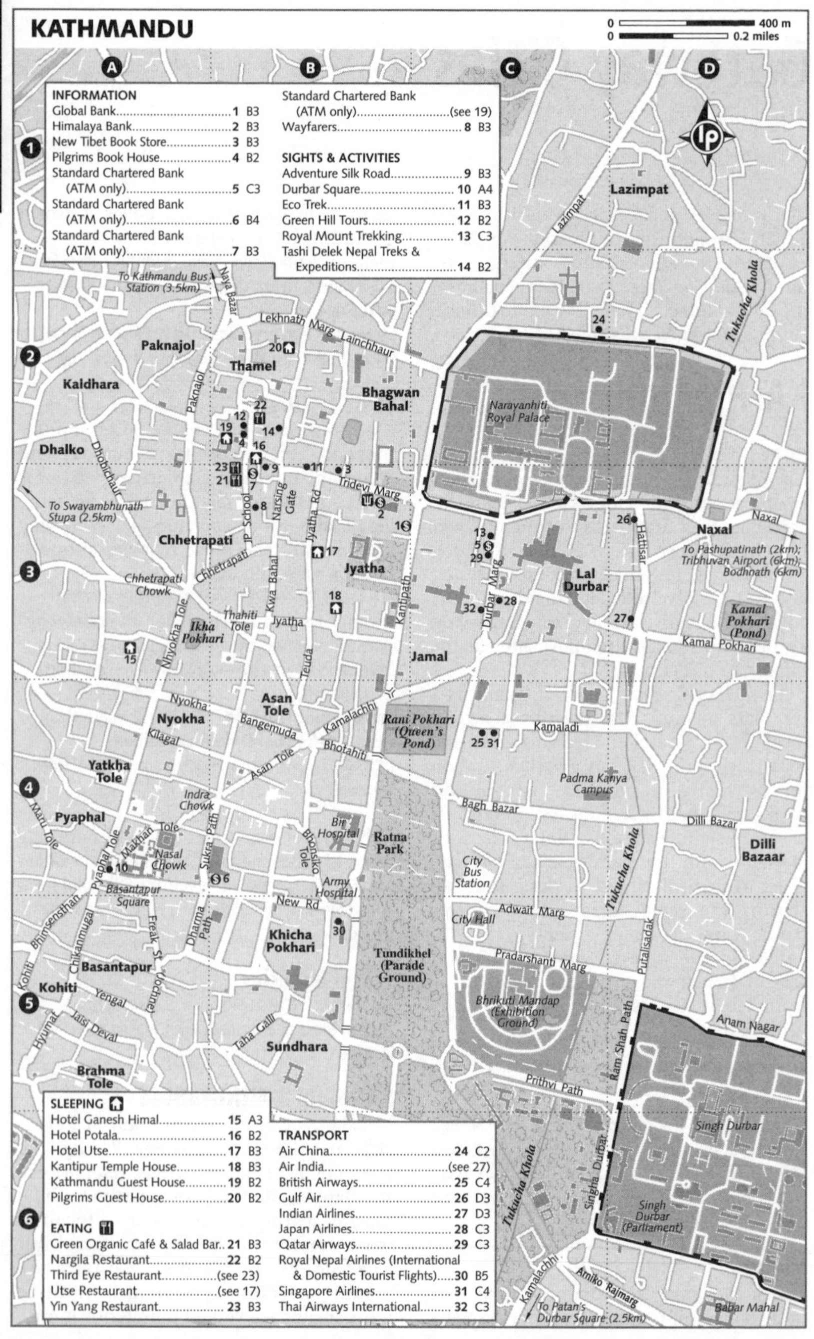
KATHMANDU
0 400 m
0 0.2 miles
A
B
C
D
1
2
3
4
5
6
INFORMATION
Global Bank....1 B3
Himalaya Bank....2 B3
New Tibet Book Store....3 B3
Pilgrims Book House....4 B2
Standard Chartered Bank (ATM only)....5 C3
Standard Chartered Bank (ATM only)....6 B4
Standard Chartered Bank (ATM only)....7 B3
Standard Chartered Bank (ATM only)....(see 19)
Wayfarers....8 B3
SIGHTS & ACTIVITIES
Adventure Silk Road....9 B3
Durbar Square....10 A4
Eco Trek....11 B3
Green Hill Tours....12 B2
Royal Mount Trekking....13 C3
Tashi Delek Nepal Treks & Expeditions....14 B2
SLEEPING
Hotel Ganesh Himal....15 A3
Hotel Potala....16 B2
Hotel Utse....17 B3
Kantipur Temple House....18 B3
Kathmandu Guest House....19 B2
Pilgrims Guest House....20 B2
EATING
Green Organic Café & Salad Bar....21 B3
Nargila Restaurant....22 B2
Third Eye Restaurant....(see 23)
Utse Restaurant....(see 17)
Yin Yang Restaurant....23 B3
TRANSPORT
Air China....24 C2
Air India....(see 27)
British Airways....25 C4
Gulf Air....26 D3
Indian Airlines....27 D3
Japan Airlines....28 C3
Qatar Airways....29 C3
Royal Nepal Airlines (International & Domestic Tourist Flights)....30 B5
Singapore Airlines....31 C4
Thai Airways International....32 C3
Lazimpat
To Kathmandu Bus Station (3.5km)
Naya Bazar
Lekhnath Marg
Lainchhaur
Paknajol
Thamel
Kaldhara
Bhagwan Bahal
Narayanhiti Royal Palace
Tukucha Khola
Dhalko
Dhobichaur
Tridevi Marg
To Swayambhunath Stupa (2.5km)
Narsing Gate
Jyatha Rd
JP School
Chhetrapati
Jyatha
Kantipath
Durbar Marg
Hattisar
Naxal
To Pashupatinath (2km); Tribhuvan Airport (6km); Bodhnath (6km)
Lal Durbar
Chhetrapati Chowk
Kwa Bahal
Thahiti Tole
Ikha Pokhari
Nhyokha Tole
Teuda
Jamal
Kamal Pokhari (Pond)
Kamal Pokhari
Nyokha
Asan Tole
Bangemuda
Kamalachhi
Rani Pokhari (Queen's Pond)
Kamaladi
Kilagal
Bhotahiti
Asan Tole
Yatkha Tole
Padma Kanya Campus
Indra Chowk
Bagh Bazar
Dilli Bazar
Pyaphal
Maru Tole
Makhan Tole
Nasal Chowk
Bir Hospital
Bhonsiko Tole
Ratna Park
Dilli Bazaar
Pyaphal Tole
Sukra Path
Basantapur Square
City Bus Station
Army Hospital
New Rd
Adwait Marg
City Hall
Bhimsensthan
Chikanmugal
Freak St (Jochne)
Dharma Path
Khicha Pokhari
Tundikhel (Parade Ground)
Pradarshanti Marg
Basantapur
Kohiti
Yengal
Jaisi Deval
Hyumat
Bhrikuti Mandap (Exhibition Ground)
Putalisadak
Ram Shah Path
Anam Nagar
Taha Galli
Sundhara
Brahma Tole
Prithvi Path
Singh Durbar
Tukucha Khola
Singha Durbar
Singh Durbar (Parliament)
Kamalachhi
Amiko Rajmarg
To Patan's Durbar Square (2.5km)
Babar Mahal

Public disorder and violent crime are both growing problems and locals warn not to be complacent as you wander the streets, especially at night. Check news reports and your own country's travel warnings for the current situation.

SIGHTS

Kathmandu's **Durbar Square** (admission Rs 200) is a collection of Newari-styled buildings that have been designated a World Heritage Site. Unfortunately the chaos that has plagued Nepal in recent years has settled on the area with a vengeance and it is really not very pleasant sightseeing as you dodge cars and motorcycles. Attempts are being made to make the area pedestrian-only but until they succeed, head out to Patan's **Durbar Square** (admission Rs 200), which has equally impressive architecture, but is still blocked to vehicular traffic.

The **Patan Museum** (admission Rs 250; 10.30am-4.30pm), within the square, has a knockout collection of Hindu and Buddhist religious artefacts (mostly statues of various deities). With detailed English text accompanying every display, it's a fantastic primer on the iconography of the two religions and especially useful for those planning to visit a lot of temples in Tibet. Just having explanations and examples of Buddhist *mudras* (hand gestures) is worth the price of admission. Patan is south of Thamel, about a 20-minute taxi ride (Rs 170).

To the west of central Kathmandu, a short taxi ride or 30-minute walk, is the great Buddhist stupa of **Swayambhunath** (admission Rs 75), also known as the Monkey Temple.

East of Kathmandu is the huge Tibetan chörten at **Bodhnath** (Boudha), which serves as a focus for the exiled Tibetan community. Here you'll find Tibetan hotels, restaurants, souvenir shops and half a dozen monasteries. There are good views of the Kathmandu Valley from the upper levels. It's a 6km taxi ride (Rs 160) from Thamel.

Pashupatinath (admission Rs 250), set along the ghats (steps) of the Bagmati River, is a major cremation site, and the most sacred Hindu site in Kathmandu. A taxi will cost around Rs 100.

Every evening around dusk, thousands of **birds** return to the forested grounds of the Narayanhiti Royal Palace. The sight and sound is like something out of Hitchcock's *The Birds*.

SLEEPING

There are dozens of places to stay in the tourist ghetto of Thamel. Listed here are just a few to get you started. Discounts are available everywhere these days, especially during the low season (May to September) – just ask.

Kathmandu Guest House (☎ 4413632; www.ktmgh.com; s US$2-55, d US$4-65;) The cheapest rooms in the old wing come without bathroom, while US$20 to US$30 will get you a bathroom and basic midrange comfort. Rooms over US$50 have air-con but even in summer it's not really necessary. Pretty much everything is overpriced here (and check your bill carefully every time), but the large quiet grounds, which include a well-tended garden and a courtyard restaurant (wi-fi enabled), provide an oasis that many travellers feel they need in this hectic city. There's also massage service, morning yoga classes and a mini-cinema. Just don't use the internet here, the international phone service, or ask for a taxi unless you want to pay double what you would just down the street. Reservations are strongly recommended.

Hotel Potala (☎ 4419159; s/d without bathroom Rs 125/250) Close to the heart of Thamel is this small and friendly Tibetan-run place. The hotel was closed at the time of writing for renovations, so expect prices to rise when it reopens.

Pilgrims Guest House (☎ 4440565; pilgrimsghouse@yahoo.com; s/d without bathroom US$4-6, s & d with bathroom US$6-10;) There's a good range of options here, from the top-floor rooms with a sofa, balcony and lots of light, to the cheapest singles, which are little more than a box. The place has a nice outdoor garden restaurant.

Hotel Ganesh Himal (☎ 4263598; htlganesh@wlink.com.np; Chhetrapati; s US$9-14, d US$12-17) Rooms here can be humid in summer, but otherwise it's a great little budget option, with cosy accommodation, garden seating, and an interior that includes colourful marble floors. The hotel is a five- to 10-minute walk southwest of Thamel.

our pick **Hotel Utse** (☎ 4226946; utse@wlink.com.np; s US$15-24, d US$21-30; discounts of 20%) The Utse is a well-run Tibetan hotel in Jyatha, with spotlessly clean and comfortable rooms. Romantically minded couples looking for some quaint and cosy styling on the cheap would be happy here. The restaurant (below) serves delicious Tibetan food.

Kantipur Temple House (☎ 4250131; www.kantipurtemplehouse.com; s US$50-70, d US$60-90; discounts of 25-40%) Along a short alley at the southern end of Jyatha is this gorgeous, well-run hotel built in the style of an old Newari temple. It's a tasteful, quiet retreat, and ecofriendly to boot.

EATING

Thamel is rich in backpacker-friendly cafés, bakeries and restaurants, so it's possible to get something to eat any time of day. All restaurants are open for at least lunch and dinner.

Utse Restaurant (☎ 4257614; Tibetan dishes Rs 60-80; 🕑 breakfast, lunch & dinner) In the hotel of the same name in Jyatha, this is one of the longest-running restaurants in the Greater Thamel area. The design is a lovely Tibetan teahouse style, which is appropriate as the restaurant turns out excellent Tibetan dishes. Menu in English.

Nargila Restaurant (☎ 4700712; mains Rs 60-110; 🕑 breakfast, lunch & dinner) North of the central *chowk* (intersection) on the 1st floor, this is one of the very few places to offer good Middle Eastern food. It's a fine place for taking a break from the bustle outside. Menu in English.

Green Organic Café & Salad Bar (☎ 4215726; dishes Rs 149-249) Just down from the Third Eye Restaurant is this funky 2nd-floor restaurant serving wholesome and delicious dishes like buckwheat noodle salads and veggie burgers, and obscure beverages like red rhododendron juice. It's not strictly vegetarian, so if you need soy and your companion wants chicken you can still enjoy a good meal together. Menu in English.

our pick **Third Eye Restaurant** (☎ 4260160; mains Rs 200-230; 🕑 breakfast, lunch & dinner) The Indian cuisine is excellent and the breakfasts (Rs 160 to 180) rank as some of the most delicious and filling in Thamel. Menu in English.

Yin Yang Restaurant (☎ 4425510; mains Rs 250) Just south of the intersection, this Thai restaurant is one of Thamel's most highly regarded. Menu in English.

SHOPPING

The Thamel area is rich in shops selling camping gear and clothing. What you purchase won't be genuine, but it should last at least one trip through Tibet.

GETTING THERE & AWAY

For details on flying to Kathmandu, see p330.

Air China (☎ 4440650; ktmddca@wlink.com.np; Dhobidhara) is a 10-minute walk east of Thamel, but it won't sell you a ticket to Lhasa without a Tibet Tourism Bureau (TTB) permit (see p323).

Other international airlines that operate out of Kathmandu:

Air India (☎ 4415637; Hattisar)
Gulf Air (☎ 4435322; Hattisar)
Indian Airlines (☎ 4410906; Hattisar)
Royal Nepal Airlines (☎ 4220757; Kantipath)
Thai Airways International (☎ 4223565; Durbar Marg)

The following have sales offices in Kathmandu:

British Airways (☎ 4222266; Kamaladi)
Japan Airlines (☎ 4224854; Durbar Marg)
Singapore Airlines (☎ 4220759; Kamaladi)

GETTING AROUND

Taxis are reasonably priced and most of the drivers will use the meter for short trips around town, which rarely come to more than Rs 50. In the evening you may have to negotiate a fare.

Three-wheeled autorickshaws are common and cost as little as half the taxi fare. Cycle rickshaws cost Rs 30 to 50 for most rides around town. Always agree on a price before you get in.

To/From the Airport

Kathmandu's **Tribhuvan International Airport** (☎ 4472265) is about 2km east of town. The international airport departure tax is Rs 1695, or Rs 1356 to neighbouring countries India, Pakistan, Bhutan and Bangladesh.

You'll find an organised taxi service in the ground-floor foyer area immediately after you leave the baggage collection and customs section. The taxis from the airport have a fixed fare of Rs 350 to Thamel or Rs 200 to the Durbar Marg.

Hotel touts outside the international terminal will offer you a free lift to their hotel, but you are less likely to get a discounted room rate this way as touts receive a hefty commission.

You should be able to get a taxi from Thamel to the airport for Rs 200.

CHENGDU 成都

☎ 028 / pop 4.1 million / elev 500m

Chengdu is the main gateway to Tibet and the largest and most important city in southwest China. Most travellers end up spending at least a day or two here while arranging a flight and permit necessary for Lhasa. Temperatures can hit an uncomfortable 35°C during muggy July and August. A new subway is under construction, so expect some traffic disruption until it opens in 2010.

INFORMATION

The best source for up-to-the-minute restaurant, bar and entertainment listings in Chengdu is the free magazine *Go West*. The website www.randomstuff.biz is also useful.

Bank of China (Zhongguo Yinhang; Renmin Nanlu; 8.30am-5.30pm Mon-Fri, 8.30am-5pm Sat & Sun) Changes money and travellers cheques and offers cash advances on credit cards on weekdays. There is another branch on Renmin Donglu and just north of Xinnanmen bus station. All have ATMs.

Chengdu Bookworm (☎ 8552 0117; www.chengdubookworm.com; 2-7 Yujie Donglu; 9am-1am;) Even if you don't have time to make use of this excellent lending library, it's worth coming to Chengdu's expat cultural hub for the café, restaurant and live weekend music.

Global Doctor Chengdu Clinic (Huanqiu Yisheng Chengdu Zhensuo; ☎ 8522 6058, 24hr emergency 139-8225 6966; Ground fl, Kelan Bldg, Bangkok Garden Apts, Section 4, 21 Renmin Nanlu)

Public Security Bureau (Gong'anjü; PSB; ☎ 8640 7067; 136 Wenwu Lu; 9am-noon & 1-5pm Mon-Fri) The foreign affairs entrance is on Tianzuo Jie; visa extensions are possible but take five days.

Tourist Booths (Lüyou Zixun Fuwu Zhongxin; 9am-9.30pm) Several but the best ones are on Chunxi Lu and next to the Xinnanmen bus station.

US Consulate (Meiguo Lingshiguan; ☎ 8558 3992; http://chengdu.usconsulate.gov; 4 Lingshiguan Lu) In the south of town.

Tours to Tibet

You can only buy an air or train ticket from Chengdu to Tibet with a TTB permit and so most travellers go through the travel agencies based at the main backpacker hotels. The following agencies can provide tickets and permits:

Dreams Travel (Mengzhilü; ☎ 8557 0315; www.dreams-travel.com; 242 Chengdu Wuhouci Dajie) Opposite Wuhou Temple.

Mix Hostel (Chengdu Lüyouji Qingnian lüshe; ☎ 8322 2271; www.mixhostel.com; 23 Renjiawan, Xinghui Xilu) For air ticket and TTB packages.

Sim's Cozy Guesthouse (Chengdu Guanhua Qingnian Lüshe; ☎ 8196 7573; www.gogosc.com; 42 Xizhu Shijie)

Windhorse Tour (Yema Lüxingshe; ☎ 8559 3923; www.windhorsetour.com; Room 508 Linsan Hotel, Sanduan Renmin Nanlu) Contact Helen. Not connected to Tibet Wind Horse Adventure in Lhasa.

SIGHTS

To fill in the time while you wait for your ticket and permit to Lhasa take a taxi or bus out to the **Giant Panda Breeding Research Base** (大熊猫繁殖研究中心; Daxiongmao Fanzhi Yanjiu Zhongxin; admission Y30; 8am-6pm), 12km northeast of the city. Feeding is around 9.30am, which is when the bears are most active. It's easiest to take one of the tours run by the budget guesthouses; they cost around Y50, which includes the entrance fee.

For a distinctly Sichuanese experience visit the teahouses in **People's Park** (人民公园; Renmin Gongyuan; admission free, tea Y5-20; 6am-8pm) or the **Wenshu Temple** (文殊院; Wenshu Yuan; Renmin Zhonglu; admission Y5; 8am-6pm). The monastery itself (Chengdu's largest) and the surrounding alleys are also worth a visit.

South of the river, on a street across from the entrance of the **Wuhou Temple** (武侯祠; Wuhou Ci; admission Y30; 6.30am-8pm), is a small Tibetan neighbourhood.

One of the most interesting places to wander is the large **Qingshiqiao Market** (青石桥市场; Qingshiqiao Shichang; Xinkai Jie). Shops and stalls sell brightly coloured seafood, flowers, cacti, birds, pets and a thousand dried foods.

SLEEPING

Budget

Many of the following guesthouses will pick you up from the train station for free or from the airport for around Y70. For more options see www.chengdusleeps.com.

our pick **Sim's Cozy Guesthouse** (Guanhua Qingnian Lüshe; ☎ 8691 4422; www.gogosc.com; 42 Xizhu Shijie; 12-bed dm Y15-20, 4- & 6-bed dm Y25-35, s from Y50, d Y70-

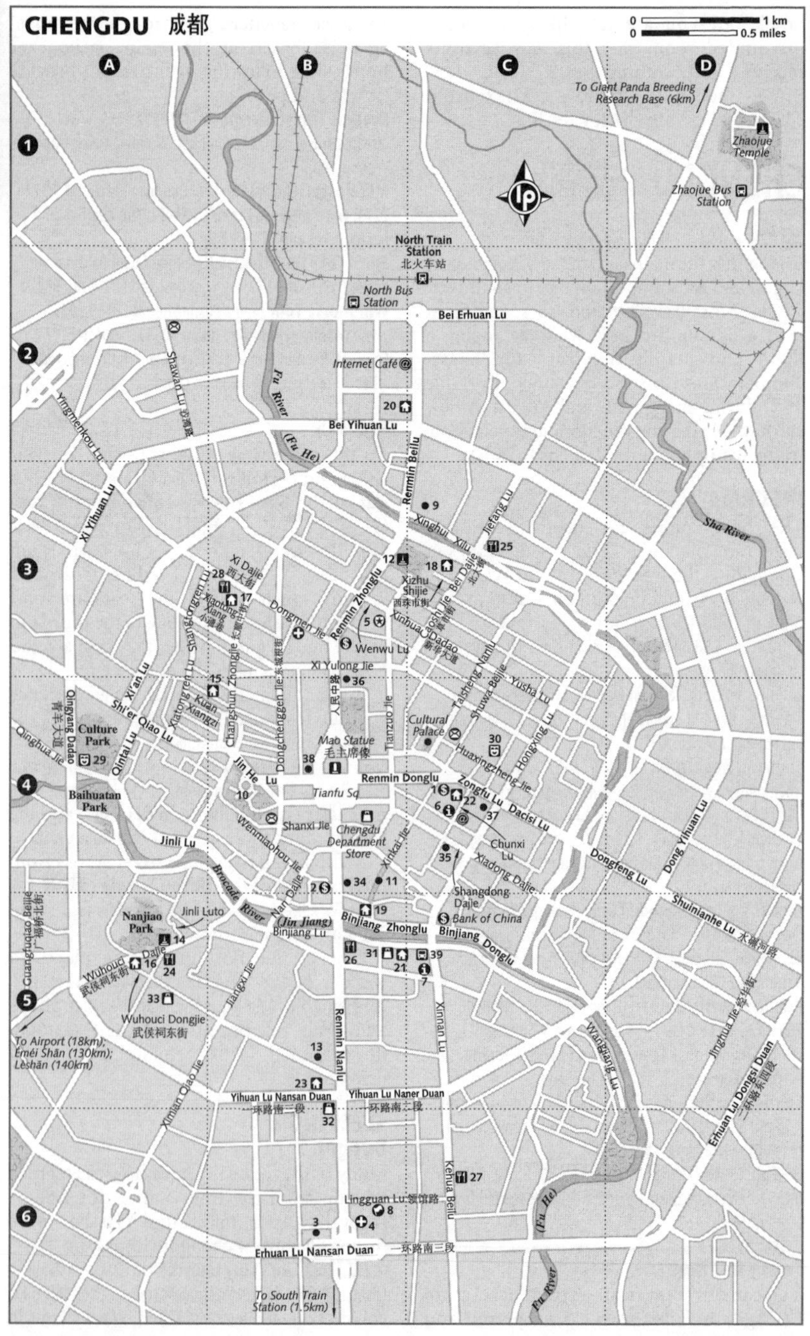

CHENGDU 成都
0 1 km
0 0.5 miles
To Giant Panda Breeding Research Base (6km)
Zhaojue Temple
Zhaojue Bus Station
North Train Station
北火车站
North Bus Station
Bei Erhuan Lu
Internet Café
Shawan Lu 沙湾路
Fu River
(Fu He)
Bei Yihuan Lu
Yingmenkou Lu
Xi Yihuan Lu
Renmin Beilu
Xinghui Xilu
Jiefang Lu
Sha River
Xi Dajie
西大街
Shangtongren Lu
Xiaotong Xiang
小通巷
Dongmen Jie
Renmin Zhonglu
Xizhu Shijie
西珠市街
Xinhua Dadao
新华大道
Bei Dajie
北大街
Wenwu Lu
Xi Yulong Jie
人民中路
Xi'an Lu
Shi'er Qiao Lu
Xiatongren Lu
Kuan Xiangzi
Changshun Zhongjie
Dongchenggen Jie 东城根街
Tianzuo Jie
Taisheng Nanlu
Shuwa Beijie
Yusha Lu
Hongxing Lu
Qingyang Dadao
青羊大道
Culture Park
Qinghua Jie
Qintai Lu
Cultural Palace
Mao Statue
毛主席像
Huaxingzheng Jie
Jin He Lu
Renmin Donglu
Baihuatan Park
Tianfu Sq
Zongfu Lu
Dacisi Lu
Dong Yihuan Lu
Shanxi Jie
Chengdu Department Store
Chunxi Lu
Jinli Lu
Wenmiaohou Jie
Xinkai Jie
Xiadong Dajie
Dongfeng Lu
Brocade River
(Jin Jiang)
Nan Dajie
Shangdong Dajie
Shuinianhe Lu 水碾河路
Guangfuqiao Beijie
广福桥北街
Nanjiao Park
Jinli Luto
Binjiang Zhonglu
Binjiang Lu
Bank of China
Binjiang Donglu
Wuhouci Dajie
武侯祠东街
Jiangxi Jie
Wuhouci Dongjie
武侯祠东街
Xinnan Lu
Wangjiang Lu
Jinghua Jie 经华街
To Airport (18km); Éméi Shān (130km); Lèshān (140km)
Renmin Nanlu
Erhuan Lu Dongsi Duan
二环路东四段
Ximian Qiao Jie
Yihuan Lu Nansan Duan
一环路南三段
Yihuan Lu Naner Duan
一环路南二段
Kehua Beilu
Lingguan Lu 领馆路
Erhuan Lu Nansan Duan
二环路南三段
(Fu He)
Fu River
To South Train Station (1.5km)

INFORMATION
Bank of China ATM
中国银行 (see 39)
Bank of China 中国银行 1 C4
Bank of China 中国银行 2 B4
Chengdu Bookworm 3 B6
Global Doctor Chengdu Clinic
环球医生成都诊所 4 B6
PSB (Foreign Affairs Section)
省公安厅外事科 5 B3
Tourist Booth
旅游咨询服务中心 6 C4
Tourist Booth
旅游咨询服务中心 7 C5
US Consulate 8 B6

SIGHTS & ACTIVITIES
Dreams Travel 梦之旅 (see 16)
Mix Hostel 驴友记青年旅舍 9 C3
People's Park 10 B4
Qingshiqiao Market
青石桥市场 11 B4
Sim's Cozy Guesthouse
观华青年旅舍 (see 18)
Wenshu Temple 文殊院 12 B3
Windhorse Tour 13 B5
Wuhou Temple 武侯祠 14 A5

SLEEPING
Dragon Town Youth Hostel
龙堂客栈 15 B4
Holly's Hostel
九龙鼎青年客栈 16 A5
Loft 四号工厂青年旅馆 17 B3
Sim's Cozy Guesthouse
观华青年旅舍 18 C3
Sofitel Wanda Chengdu
索菲特万达大饭店 19 B5
Tibet Hotel 西藏大酒店 20 B2
Traffic Hotel 交通饭店 21 B5
Xinchun Binguan 鑫春宾馆 22 C4
Yulin Binguan 玉林宾馆 23 B5

EATING
Are Zangcan 阿热藏餐 24 A5
Chen Mapo Doufu
陈麻婆豆腐 25 C3
Highfly Café 高飞咖啡 26 B5
Peter's Tex-Mex
皮得德州扒房 27 C6
Wenshu Temple 文殊院 (see 12)
Xiaohui Douhua 小讳豆花 28 B3

ENTERTAINMENT
Green Ram Temple 青羊宫 29 A4
Jinjiang Theatre 锦江剧场 30 C4

SHOPPING
Airwolf 非狼户外 (see 31)
Mountain Dak Outdoor Sports Club
高山户外旅游探险用品 31 B5
Outdoor Shops
户外用品商店 32 B5
Tibetan Shops 西藏专卖店 33 A5

TRANSPORT
Air China 中国民航 34 B4
China Southern Airlines
中国南方航空 35 C4
Dragonair 港龙航空公司 36 B4
KLM Office 37 C4
Sichuan Airlines
四川航空公司 38 B4
Xinnanmen Bus Station
新南门汽车站 39 C5

200;) Run by a Singaporean-Japanese backpacker couple, this exceptional hostel is in a traditional-style building a stone's throw from the Wenshu Temple. There's a wide range of rooms (with or without air-con, bathrooms, wi-fi etc), the staff are phenomenal and there's a lovely pond-side bar.

Loft (Sihao Gongchang Lüguan; 8626 5770; www.lofthostel.com; 4 Tongren Lu, Xiaotong Xiang; 4-/6-bed dm Y20/15, s & d without/with bathroom Y60/120;) Exposed brick walls, minimalist furnishings and sexy black-tiled bathrooms make this the coolest place in town. The common room has free internet, movies and a pool table. The staff here are so relaxed and friendly it's hard to tell at first glance who's an employee and who's a traveller.

Holly's Hostel (Jiulongding Qingnian Kezhan; 8554 8131; hollyhostelcn@yahoo.com; 246 Wuhouci Dajie; 4-bed dm without bathroom Y20, 6-bed dm with bathroom & air-con Y30, d Y120;) This charming guesthouse can be found in the heart of the bustling Tibetan quarter. The rooms look a bit old but they're large and clean, and the staff are friendly. The top-floor café has a lovely, leafy terrace.

Traffic Hotel (Jiaotong Fandian; 8545 1017; www.traffichotel.com; 6 Binjiang Lu; dm Y30, d/tr with bathroom Y240/290;) Conveniently placed next to the Xinnanmen bus station, this used to be the first choice for accommodation in Chengdu but it's facing some stiff competition these days. The three- or four-bed rooms are comfortable and air-conditioned and the shared bathrooms are super clean. The location is perfect if you are taking the bus to Kangding and beyond.

Dragon Town Youth Hostel (Longtang Kezhan; 8664 8408; www.dragontown.com.cn; 27 Kuan Xiangzi; dm Y30-40, s Y100-150, d 100-160;) Down a narrow alley in a beautiful four-storey building that dates back to the Qing dynasty, this has to be one of Chengdu's best budget options. The higher-end doubles feature antique Chinese furniture.

Midrange & Top End

Yulin Binguan (8557 8839; 9 Yihuan Lu, Nansan Duan; d Y148-280;) Something for all price ranges here, including one wing with the niftiest midrange digs in town. Rooms are small but bathrooms are modern. A cheaper wing with stinky halls has clean but snoringly bland rooms.

Xinchun Binguan (8672 6622; fax 8667 2382; 23 Chunxi Lu, Bei Duan; s Y280-340, d 340; discounts of up to 50%;) Tucked down one the city's bustling pedestrian shopping streets, this option is very central and rooms are sleekly modern and gleaming clean.

Tibet Hotel (Xizang Dajiudian; 8318 3388; fax 8319 3838; 10 Renmin Beilu; s/d Y648/1330;) The location is not the most convenient but the rooms are well decorated in Tibetan style. This hotel continually garners positive reviews from travellers.

Sofitel Wanda Chengdu (Suofeite Wanda Dajiudian; 6666 9999; www.sofitel.com; 15 Binjiang Zhonglu;

r from Y1500, discounted Y900; ☒ ☒ ☒) From service to facilities, this is the best hotel in town (for the moment at least).

EATING

Xiaohui Douhua (☎ 8625 2753; Section 12, 86 Xi Dajie; dishes Y2-10) Endless combinations of tofu and noodles here. Try the crispy beef tofu (牛肉豆花; *niurou douhua*) and the thick, succulent and spicy sweet noodles (甜水面; *tianshui mian*).

Chen Mapo Doufu (Pockmarked Grandma Chen's Bean Curd; Jiefang Lu; dishes from Y5) A Chengdu institution that specialises in its signature *mapo doufu* – soft, fresh bean curd with a fiery sauce of garlic, minced beef, salted soybean, chilli oil and fiery Sichuan pepper.

Wenshu Temple (Renmin Zhonglu; dishes Y6-10) The excellent vegetarian restaurant at this Buddhist temple is a special treat for nonmeat-eaters. Menu in English.

Are Zangcan (☎ 8557 0877; 234 Wuhouci Dajie; dishes Y10-70) Right across the street from Wuhou Temple, this Tibetan restaurant serves up everything from veggie *momos* (dumplings) to yak stew, with a nice outdoor terrace.

Highfly Cafe (Gaofei Kafei; ☎ 8544 2820; 18 Linjiang Zhonglu; dishes from Y12; 🕑 9am-late) An old-timer, it still serves great breakfast, pizzas and delicious calorie-laden fudge brownies, and offers free internet access. Menu in English.

Peter's Tex-Mex (Pide Dezhou Pafang; ☎ 8522 7965; 117 Kehua Beilu; dishes from Y15; 🕑 7.30am-11pm) More than just the best Tex-Mex food in the city, it's among the best you'll have anywhere. Menu in English.

ENTERTAINMENT

A night out at the Sichuanese opera is a must-do in Chengdu. Most of the budget guesthouses run tours for around Y80 to Y90 and some can even get you backstage.

Jinjiang Theatre (Jinjiang Juyuan; Huaxingzheng Jie) This combination teahouse, opera theatre and cinema has opera performances on weekend afternoons (Y120 per person), and the attached teahouse often has performances for Y15.

Green Ram Temple (Qingyang Gong; Wenhua Park) This Taoist temple also offers excellent nightly performances.

SHOPPING

For a last-minute Chinese-made tent or Gore-Tex jacket, try **Mountain Dak Outdoor Sports Club** (Gaoshan Huwai Lüyou Tanxian Yongpin; Bianjiang Lu) and **Airwolf** (Feilang Huwai; Bianjiang Lu), both near the Traffic Hotel.

A TOUCH OF SILK

A silk lining for your sleeping bag will keep it clean and add extra warmth that you'll appreciate on the plateau. If you're passing through Chengdu, you can buy silk in the Chengdu Department Store, on central Tianfu Sq, for about Y20 per metre (get 4m) and arrange for a tailor to make you a liner for less than US$1.

GETTING THERE & AWAY

Airline offices will not sell you a ticket to Lhasa without a TTB permit, so most people book their ticket through one of the backpacker agencies – see p91.

For details on flying to Chengdu, see p330.

Air China (Zhongguo Hangkong; ☎ 8666 1100; 41, Section 2, Renmin Nanlu)
China Southern Airlines (Zhongguo Nanfang Hangkong; ☎ 8666 3618; 19 Shangdong Dajie)
Dragonair (Ganglong Hangkong; ☎ 8676 8828; Sheraton Chengdu Lido Hotel, Section 1, 15 Renmin Zhonglu)
KLM (☎ 4008 808 222; 1603B, Bldg A, Times Plaza, 2 Zongfu Lu)
Sichuan Airlines (Sichuan Hangkong; ☎ 8666 6768; 6 Renmin Xilu)

Buses to destinations in western Sichuan, such as Kangding, depart from the Xinnanmen bus station.

GETTING AROUND

The most useful bus is route 16, which runs from Chengdu's north train station to the south train station along Renmin Nanlu. Regular buses cost Y1, while the double-deckers cost Y2. Taxis have a flag fall of Y5 (Y6 at night), plus Y1.4 per kilometre. Most budget accommodation rent bikes for about Y10 per day.

To/From the Airport

Shuangliu Airport is 18km west of the city. Airport bus 303 (Y10) runs every half-hour from the Air China office on Renmin Nanlu. A taxi costs around Y70, depending on the traffic.

Lhasa ལྷ་ས 拉萨

Lhasa, the remote abode of the Dalai Lamas, object of devout pilgrimage and heart and soul of Tibet, is still a city of wonders, despite the large-scale encroachments of modern Chinese influence. Your first hint that Lhasa is close is the Potala, a vast white-and-ochre fortress soaring over one of the world's highest cities. It's a sight that has heralded the marvels of the Holy City to travellers for close to four centuries and it still raises goose bumps.

While the Potala dominates the skyline, the Jokhang, some 2km to the east, is the real spiritual heart of the city. An otherworldly mix of flickering butter lamps, wafting incense and prostrating pilgrims, the Jokhang is the most sacred and alive of Tibet's temples. It is here and the encircling Barkhor pilgrim circuit that most visitors first fall in love with Tibet.

The old Tibetan quarter makes up a small area of Lhasa these days. The modern city is a Chinese boom town, where a new train line has fuelled massive growth in tourism, alongside new hotels, shops and supermarkets. The face of Lhasa is changing daily, with buildings rising and falling like the Shanghai stock market.

For all its modernisation Lhasa remains a fantastic cultural hybrid, its streets bustling with a diverse mix of people. As the gateway to the 'real' Tibet, out in the countryside, Lhasa deserves at least a week to see all the sights, soak up the backstreets and organise the adventures that beckon at the city limits.

HIGHLIGHTS

- Follow monks, mendicants and fellow pilgrims around the **Barkhor** (p102), Lhasa's fascinating medieval pilgrim circuit
- Join the shuffling lines of awed pilgrims around the glowing shrines of the **Jokhang** (p103), Tibet's holiest temple
- Go down into the bowels of the **Potala** (p108), the impressive but spiritless citadel of the Dalai Lamas, from the fifth to the 14th
- Take in a prayer meeting or some monk-debating at **Sera** (p133) and **Drepung** (p129), two of the largest and most intact of Tibet's great monasteries
- Catch the pilgrim bus for a day out to **Ganden Monastery** (p137) and test your sin on its fascinating kora (pilgrim path)
- Explore the traditional whitewashed architecture, teashops and craft workshops of Lhasa's backstreets on our **Old Town Walking Tour** (p117)
- Track down one of Lhasa's off-the-beaten-track temples, such as the **Meru Nyingba Monastery** (p103) or **Tengye Ling** (p114)

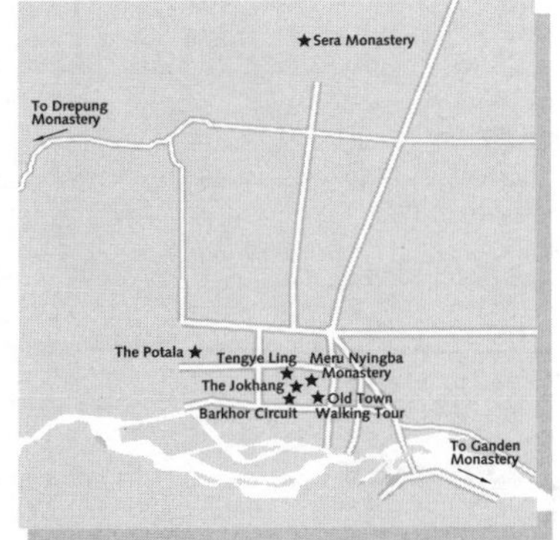

TELEPHONE CODE: 0891	POPULATION: 400,000	ELEVATION: 3595M

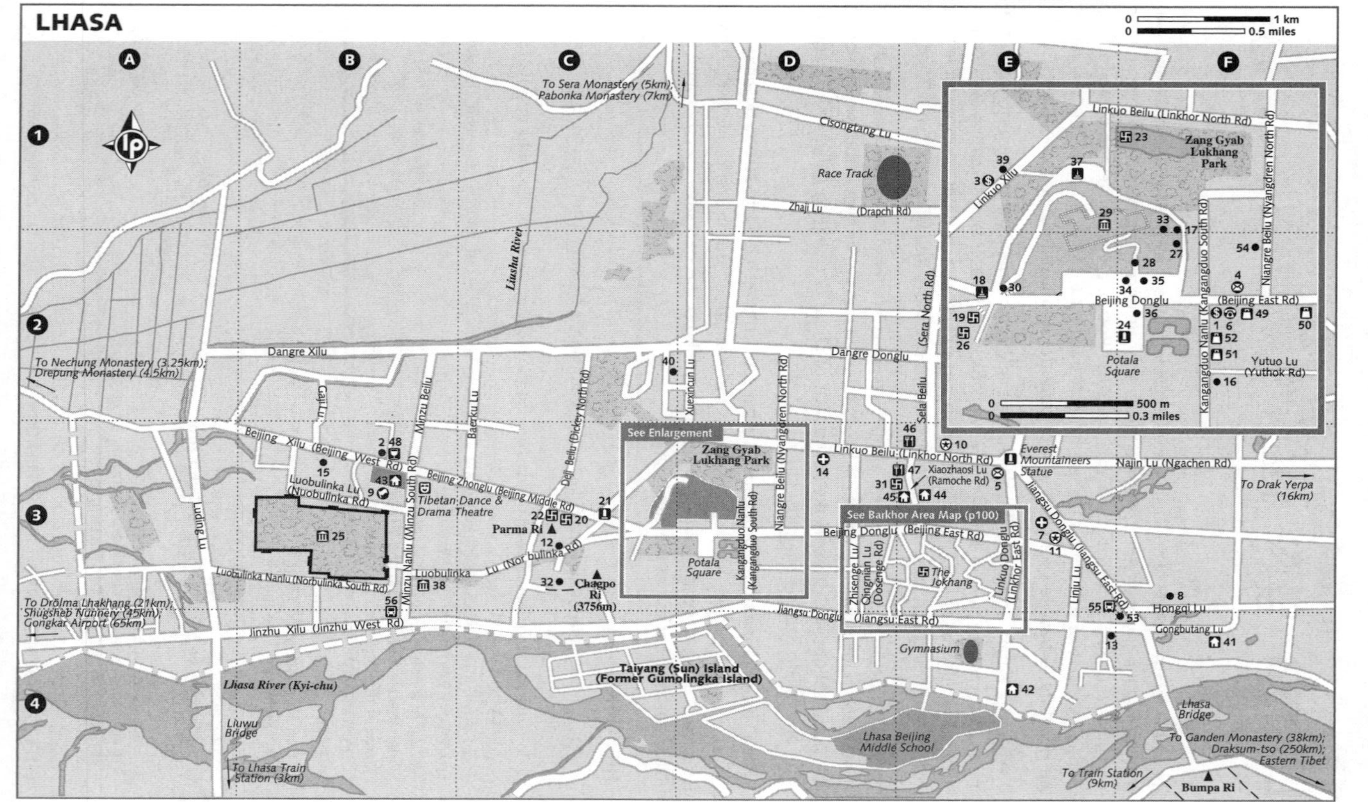
LHASA
0 1 km
0 0.5 miles
To Sera Monastery (5km); Pabonka Monastery (7km)
To Nechung Monastery (3.25km); Drepung Monastery (4.5km)
To Drölma Lhakhang (21km); Shugsheb Nunnery (45km); Gongkar Airport (65km)
To Lhasa Train Station (3km)
To Train Station (9km)
To Ganden Monastery (38km); Draksum-tso (250km); Eastern Tibet
To Drak Yerpa (16km)
Liusha River
Race Track
Cisongtang Lu
Zhaji Lu (Drapchi Rd)
Dangre Xilu
Dangre Donglu
Xuexincun Lu
Gaji Lu
Luding Lu
Beijing Xilu (Beijing West Rd)
Beijing Zhonglu (Beijing Middle Rd)
Tibetan Dance & Drama Theatre
Luobulinka Lu (Nuobulinka Rd)
Luobulinka Nanlu (Norbulinka South Rd)
Luobulinka Lu (Norbulinka Rd)
Minzu Beilu
Minzu Nanlu (Minzu South Rd)
Baerku Lu
Deji Beilu (Dickey North Rd)
Jinzhu Xilu (Jinzhu West Rd)
Parma Ri
Chagpo Ri (3756m)
See Enlargement
Zang Gyab Lukhang Park
Niangre Beilu (Nyangdren North Rd)
Kangangduo Nanlu (Kangangduo South Rd)
Potala Square
Linkuo Beilu (Linkhor North Rd)
Sela Beilu
(Sera North Rd)
Xiaozhaosi Lu (Ramoche Rd)
Everest Mountaineers Statue
Najin Lu (Ngachen Rd)
See Barkhor Area Map (p100)
Beijing Donglu (Beijing East Rd)
Zhisenge Lu/ Qingnian Lu (Dosenge Rd)
The Jokhang
Linkuo Donglu (Linkhor East Rd)
Jiangsu Donglu (Jiangsu East Rd)
Linju Lu
Hongqi Lu
Gongbutang Lu
Gymnasium
Lhasa Beijing Middle School
Taiyang (Sun) Island (Former Gumolingka Island)
Lhasa River (Kyi-chu)
Liuwu Bridge
Lhasa Bridge
Bumpa Ri
Linkuo Xilu
Beijing Donglu
Yutuo Lu (Yuthok Rd)
0 500 m
0 0.3 miles

INFORMATION
Agricultural Bank ATM 中国农业银行 ... 1 F2
Bank of China & ATM 中国银行 ... 2 B3
Bank of China (Main Office) 中国银行 ... 3 E1
China Post Main Office 中国邮政 ... 4 F2
China Post 中国邮政 ... 5 E3
China Unicom 中国联通 ... 6 F2
City People's Hospital 市人民医院 ... 7 E3
DHL 中外运敦豪 ... 8 F3
Nepali Consulate-General 尼泊尔领事馆 ... 9 B3
Public Security Bureau (Lhasa) 拉萨市公安局 ... 10 E3
Public Security Bureau (Tibet) 公安厅 ... 11 E3
Tibet Tourism Bureau (TTB) 西藏旅游局 ... 12 C3
Tibet University 西藏大学 ... 13 E4
Tibetan Autonomous Region People's Hospital 区人民医院 ... 14 D3
Xinhua Bookstore 新华书店 ... 15 B3
Xinhua Bookstore 新华书店 ... 16 F2
Yuzhou Wangba 宇宙网吧 ... (see 16)

SIGHTS & ACTIVITIES
Chapel ... 17 F1
Chörten (Former West Gate) ... 18 E2
Drubthub Nunnery ... 19 E2
Gesar Ling ... 20 C3
Golden Yak Statues ... 21 C3
Kunde Ling 功德林寺 ... 22 C3
Lukhang ... 23 F1
Monument to People's Liberation of Tibet ... 24 F2
Norbulingka 罗布林卡 ... 25 B3
Palha Lu-puk ... 26 E2
Phurbu Chok Hermitage Mani Lhakhang ... 27 F2
Potala Entry Gate ... 28 F2
Potala Palace 布达拉宫 ... 29 E1
Potala Ticket Booking Office ... 30 E2
Ramoche Temple 小昭寺 ... 31 D3
Rock Carvings ... 32 C3
Rock Carvings ... 33 F1
Stele ... 34 F2
Stele ... 35 F2
Stele ... 36 F2
Three Chörtens ... 37 E1
Tibet International Sports Travel 西藏圣地国际旅行社 ... (see 42)
Tibet Museum 西藏博物馆 ... 38 B3
Tibet Wind Horse Adventure 龙达国际旅行社 ... 39 E1
Tibet Yungdru Adventure 西藏云珠探险 ... 40 C2
Tsepak Lhakhang ... (see 31)

SLEEPING
Bhramaputra Grand Hotel 雅鲁藏布大酒店 ... 41 F4
Himalaya Hotel 喜玛拉雅饭店 ... 42 E4
Lhasa Hotel 拉萨饭店 ... 43 B3
Oh Dan Guest House Annex 欧丹旅馆 ... 44 E3
Pilgrimages Inn ... 45 E3

EATING
Holy Land Vegetarian Restaurant 神地素餐厅 ... 46 E3
Norzing Selchung Tashi Yamphel Restaurant ... 47 E3

DRINKING
Music Kitchen 音乐厨房 ... 48 B3

ENTERTAINMENT
Shöl Opera Troupe 雪巴拉姆 ... (see 42)

SHOPPING
Baiyi Supermarket 百益超市 ... 49 F2
Hongyan Supermarket 红艳超市 ... 50 F2
Lhasa Department Store 拉萨百货大楼 ... 51 F2
Photographic Shops ... 52 F2

TRANSPORT
Airport Buses ... (see 54)
Bus 97 & 91 Terminus ... 53 F4
CAAC 中国民航 ... 54 F2
City Train Ticket Office 火车票售票处 ... (see 12)
Eastern Bus Station 东郊客运站 ... 55 E3
Western (Main) Bus Station 西郊客运站 ... 56 B4

HISTORY

Lhasa rose to prominence as an important administrative centre in the 7th century AD, when Songtsen Gampo (c 618–49), a local ruler in the Yarlung Valley, continued the task initiated by his father of unifying Tibet. Songtsen Gampo moved his capital to Lhasa and built a palace on the site now occupied by the Potala. At this time the temples of Ramoche and the Jokhang were established to house Buddha images brought to Tibet as the dowries of Songtsen Gampo's Chinese and Nepali wives.

With the break-up of the Yarlung empire 250 years later, Buddhism enjoyed a gradual resurgence at monastic centres outside Lhasa and the centre of power shifted to Sakya, Nedong (Ü) and then Shigatse (Tsang). No longer the capital, Lhasa now languished in the backwaters of Tibetan history until the fifth Dalai Lama (1617–82) defeated the Shigatse kings with Mongol support.

The fifth Dalai Lama moved his capital to Lhasa. He built his palace, the Potala, on the site of the ruins of Songtsen Gampo's 7th-century palace. Lhasa has remained Tibet's capital since 1642, and most of the city's historical sights date from this second stage of the city's development.

Modern Lhasa in many ways provides the visitor with both the best and the worst of contemporary Tibet. Photographs of the city taken before October 1950 reveal a small town nestled at the foot of the Potala and linked by an avenue to another cluster of residences in the area of the Jokhang. The population of the city before the Chinese takeover is thought to have been between 20,000 and 30,000. Today the city has a population of around 500,000, and Chinese residents easily outnumber Tibetans, perhaps 2:1.

Shöl, the village at the foot of the Potala, has all but disappeared, and the old West Gate, through which most people entered the Holy City, was torn down during the Cultural Revolution to be replaced by a smaller, modern version in 1995. The area in front of the Potala has been made into a Tiananmen-style public square, complete with a 35m-tall monument to the 'liberation' of Tibet (under constant guard to prevent vandalism). What used to be the Tibetan picnic spot of Gumolingka Island is now a Chinese-style shopping and karaoke complex.

The Tibetan quarter is now an isolated enclave in the eastern end of town, comprising only around 4% of the total area of contemporary Lhasa. Even these lingering enclaves of tradition are under threat despite official protection. Lhasa has probably changed more in the last 20 years than in the thousand years before.

ORIENTATION

Lhasa is a surprisingly sprawling city and it now takes at least 20 minutes to drive through the western suburbs. The city divides clearly into a western (Chinese) section and an eastern (Tibetan) section, with the Potala Palace marking no-man's-land in the middle. The Tibetan eastern end of town is easily the most interesting place to be based and has all the budget and midrange accommodation popular with independent travellers.

The principal thoroughfare is the east– west Beijing Zhonglu (Dekyi Nub Lam), which becomes Beijing Donglu (Dekyi Shar Lam) in the east of town.

The Jokhang and Barkhor Square are between Beijing Donglu and Jiangsu Lu (Chingdröl Shar Lam) and are connected to these two main roads by the Tibetan quarter, a web of winding alleyways lined with the whitewashed façades of traditional Tibetan homes. This Tibetan area is not particularly extensive. Rather than worry about orientation it is more fun to simply slip away from the Barkhor circuit at some point and aimlessly wander the alleys. You won't stay lost for long.

STREET NAMES

In this edition we use Chinese street names, as that is what most locals (including many Tibetans) and almost all taxi drivers use. The traditional Tibetan names are included in brackets.

- Beijing Donglu (Dekyi Shar Lam)
- Beijing Zhonglu (Dekyi Nub Lam)
- Deji Lu (Dickey Lam)
- Jiangsu Lu (Chingdröl Shar Lam)
- Linkuo Lu (Linkhor Lam)
- Minzu Lu (Mirig Lam)
- Niangre Lu (Nyangdren Lam)
- Qingnian Lu (Dosenge Lam)
- Xiaozhaosi Lu (Ramoche Lam)
- Yutuo Lu (Yuthok Lam)
- Zangyiyuan Lu (Mentsikhang Lam)

Maps

The *Lhasa Tour Map* is a relatively useful 2006 English-language map of the city, available at the Xinhua bookshops (below), branches of China Post and the gift shops of most hotels. Other maps of Lhasa are available outside Tibet (p321).

INFORMATION

Useful information is scarce in Lhasa. The information boards at the Banak Shol, Snowlands and Kirey hotels (p120) can be useful if you're looking for trekking partners, a ride in a Land Cruiser, or even a second-hand Lonely Planet guidebook, though these days most of the notices are in Chinese.

Bookshops

The Nam-tso Restaurant (p123) at the Banak Shol hotel and the Summit Café (p125) both have some English-language books for exchange/rent and hotel gift shops stock a few glossy coffee-table souvenir books.

Xinhua Bookstore Yutuo Lu (Map p96); Beijing Xilu (Map p96) The most central branch, located about 10 minutes' walk west of Barkhor Square, has some maps, postcards and photo books. A new larger store is being built on Beijing Xilu.

Internet Access

The most popular internet cafés are those at the Snowlands, Kirey and Yak hotels (see Sleeping, p119), where you can surf the internet (Y5) and burn CDs (Y15 to 20), from 9am to midnight. If you have a laptop, the Summit Café (see p125) offers free wi-fi.

The following local places are cheaper, smokier and noisier:

Red Forest Net Café (Map p100; Beijing Donglu; per hr Y3; 24hr) Opposite the Banak Shol hotel.

Yuzhou Wangba (Map p96; 3rd fl, Xinhua Bookstore, Yutuo Lu; per hr Y3; 24hr)

Laundry

The Banak Shol and Kirey hotels offer a free laundry service to guests, but don't get the clothes all that clean. Most others will do laundry for a modest fee.

DANGERS & ANNOYANCES

If you fly straight into Lhasa, remember to take things easy for your first day or two: it's not uncommon to feel breathless, suffer from headaches and sleep poorly because of the altitude. Don't attempt the steps up to the Potala for the first few days, drink lots of fluids and read p351 for details on acute mountain sickness (AMS).

On a more mundane note, take care when re-opening things such as tubes of sunscreen after a flight in to Lhasa or even jars of Coffee-mate from a local shop, as the change in pressure can cause messy explosions of volcanic proportions.

Medical Services

Several hotels and pharmacies around town sell Tibetan herbal medicine recommended by locals for easing symptoms of altitude sickness. The most common medicine is known as *solomano* in Tibetan and *hongjingtian* (红景天) in Chinese, though locals also recommend *gaoyuanning* (高原宁) and *gaoyuankang* (高原康). A box of vials will cost you Y20 to 35; take three vials a day.

Military Hospital (Xizang Junqu Zongyiyuan; 西藏军区总医院; Map p129; ☎ 628 0557; Niangre Beilu) Travellers who have received medical attention confirm that this place is the best option (if you have an option).

Money

Bank of China branch (Zhongguo Yinhang; Map p100; Beijing Donglu; 🕑 9am-5pm Mon-Fri, 10.30am-3.30pm Sat & Sun) The most conveniently located bank changes cash and travellers cheques without fuss. It can't give a cash advance on a credit card but the ATMs normally work. It's between the Banak Shol and Kirey hotels.

Bank of China branch (Zhongguo Yinhang; Map p96; Beijing Xilu; 🕑 9am-5pm Mon-Fri, 10.30am-3.30pm Sat & Sun) Opposite the Lhasa Hotel.

Bank of China main office (Zhongguo Yinhang; Map p96; Linkuo Xilu; 🕑 9am-6.30pm Mon-Fri, 10am-4pm Sat & Sun) West of the Potala. This is the place for credit-card advances; there's a 3% commission and the maximum withdrawal is Y2000 per transaction. This is also the place to arrange a bank transfer (p322). There are ATMs inside and outside the building (the latter open 24 hours). Take a number as you walk in the door and expect to wait for ages.

Post

China Post main office (Zhongguo Zheng; Map p96; ☎ 624 1404; Beijing Donglu; 🕑 9am-8pm Mon-Sat, 9.30am-6.30pm Sun) The counter in the far left corner sells stamps and packaging for parcels. Leave parcels unsealed until you get to the post office as the staff will want to check the contents for customs clearance. Express Mail Service (EMS) is here. Postcards are sold in the shop to the east.

LHASA

LHASA'S PILGRIM CIRCUITS

For Tibetan pilgrims, who approach the Holy City with priorities somewhat different from those of the average Western visitor, the principal points of orientation are Lhasa's three koras (pilgrimage circuits): the Nangkhor, Barkhor and Lingkhor. For the visitor, all the koras are well worth following, especially during festivals, such as Saga Dawa (p319), when the distinction between tourist and pilgrim can become very fine. Remember always to proceed clockwise.

- Nangkhor – This kora encircles the inner precincts of the Jokhang.
- Barkhor – This traces the outskirts of the Jokhang in a circuit (p102) of approximately 800m. It is the most famous of Lhasa's pilgrimage circuits and probably the best introduction to the old town for newcomers.
- Lingkhor – This devotional route traditionally encompassed the entirety of the old city. Nowadays the Lingkhor includes a great deal of scenery that is of a decidedly secular and modern nature but it is still used by pilgrims. You can join the 8km-long circuit anywhere, but the most interesting section is covered in our Lingkhor Walking Tour (p118).
- Potala Kora (Tsekhor) – Another popular kora encircles the holy Potala, passing by an almost continuous circuit of prayer wheels, chörtens (stupas), rock paintings and the Lukhang Temple (p113).
- Other koras – There are excellent koras at Drepung (p132), Ganden (p139) and Sera (p135) Monasteries.

DHL (Zhongwaiyun Dunhao; Map p96; ☎ 635 6995; www.cn.dhl.com; Room 4, 2nd fl, Back Block, Norpel Ling Hotel/Baofa Jiudian, 6 Hongqi Lu) Free pick-up and delivery service.

Public Security Bureau (PSB)

Lhasa City PSB (Lasa Shi Gong'anju; Map p96; ☎ 624 8154; 17 Linkuo Beilu; 🕑 9am-12.30pm & 3.30-6pm Mon-Fri) Visa extensions of up to a week are given, but only a day or two before your visa expires.

Tibet PSB (Gong'anting; Map p96; ☎ 631 1442; cnr Beijing Donglu & Jiangsu Donglu; 🕑 9am-12.30pm & 3.30-6pm Mon-Fri) Travel permits are issued at this office but only to organised tour groups.

Telephone

The cheapest way to make an international call is through the various **private telephone booths** (🕑 8.30am-11pm), often advertised as 'Telecom Supermarkets'. Useful examples are in front of the Kirey Hotel or east of the Kyichu Hotel. Rates are Y2.4 per minute to the US, Y3.6 to Europe and Australia, or Y4.8 to other countries.

China Unicom (Zhongguo Liantong; Map p96; Beijing Donglu; 🕑 9am-6.30pm) Across from China Post, offers similarly cheap rates.

Travel Agencies

Most independent travellers in Tibet arrange their travel with one of several Foreign Independent Traveller (FIT) offices run by the Tibet Tourism Bureau (TTB). Despite being the same company, these offices operate independently and will quote you different rates.

FIT Banak Shol hotel (Map p100; ☎ 655 9938, 655 1841; fax 634 4397; fit0891@hotmail.com; 8 Beijing Donglu) Contact Xiaojin. Good prices, reliable and fairly transparent.

FIT Snowlands Hotel (Map p100; ☎ 634 9239; lhakpa88@yahoo.com; www.tibetfit.com; 2nd fl, Snowlands Hotel, 4 Zangyiyuan Lu) The main FIT office; contact Lhakpa or Samdup. Also goes under the name Tibet Changtang Yak Adventure, with an office next door.

Shigatse CITS (Map p100; ☎ 691 2080; Zangyiyuan Lu) Connected with FIT Banak Shol.

There are plenty of other travel agencies, though most cater to Chinese tourists who don't require travel permits (see p323). They are perhaps best used only for trips around Lhasa.

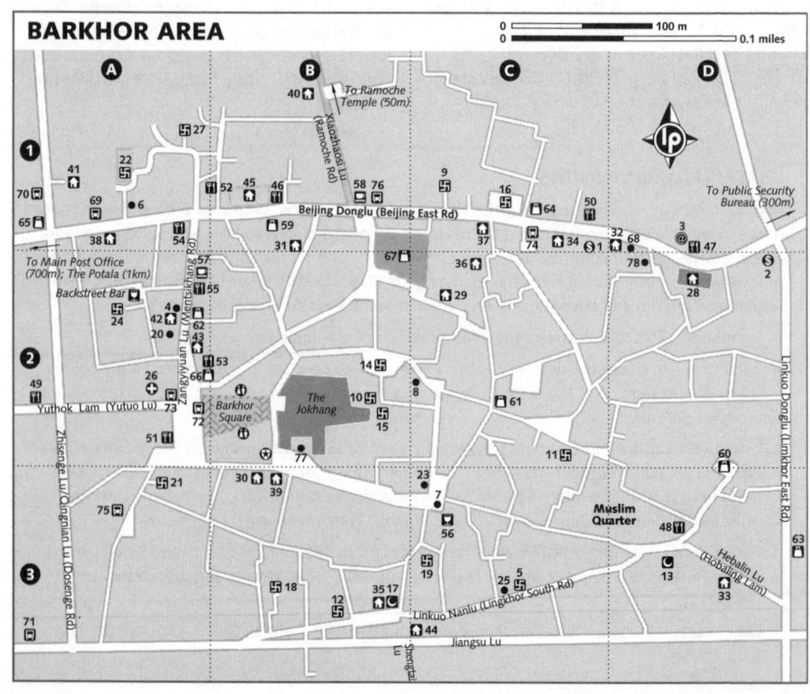

SIGHTS

The Barkhor བར་འཁོར་ 八廓

The first stop for most newcomers to Lhasa is the Jokhang in the heart of the Tibetan old town. But before you even venture into the Jokhang it's worth taking a stroll around the **Barkhor** (Map p100), Lhasa's most interesting kora (pilgrimage circuit), a quadrangle of streets that surrounds the Jokhang and some of the old buildings adjoining it. It is an area unrivalled in Tibet for its fascinating combination of sacred significance and push-and-shove market economics. This is both the spiritual heart of the Holy City and the main commercial district for Tibetans.

The Barkhor is the one part of Lhasa that has most resisted the invasions of the modern world. Pilgrims from Kham, Amdo and further afield step blithely around a prostrating monk and stop briefly to finger a jewel-encrusted dagger at a street stall; monks sit cross-legged on the paving stones before their alms bowls muttering mantras. It's a place you'll want to come back to time after time.

INFORMATION

- Bank of China 中国银行 1 C1
- Bank of Construction ATM 中国建设银行 2 D2
- Family & Independent Traveller Office (FIT) 散客旅游管理接待中心 (see 28)
- Family & Independent Traveller Office (FIT) 高原散客旅游管理接待中心 (see 43)
- Red Forest Net Café 红树林网城 3 D1
- Shigatse CITS 4 A2
- Telecom Booths 电话超市 (see 37)

SIGHTS & ACTIVITIES

- Ani Sangkhung Nunnery 5 C3
- Blind Massage Centre 6 A1
- Darchen Pole 7 C3
- Gedun Cheophel Artists' Guild 8 C2
- Gongkar Chöde Chapel (see 10)
- Gyüme (Lower Tantric College) 9 C1
- Jampa Lhakhang 10 B2
- Karmashar Temple 11 C2
- Lho Rigsum Lhakhang 12 B3
- Main City Mosque 拉萨清真寺 13 D3
- Mandala Museum (see 30)
- Mani Lhakhang 14 B2
- Meru Nyingba Monastery 15 B2
- Meru Sarpa Monastery 16 C1
- Mosque 清真寺 17 B3
- On the Tourist's Way 西藏日喀则中国国际旅行社 (see 33)
- Pode Kangtsang 18 B3
- Rabtse Temple 19 C3
- Raft Tibet (Tibet Wind Horse Adventure) 龙达国际旅行社 20 A2
- Rigsum Lhakhang 21 A3
- Shide Tratsang 22 A1
- Shrine 23 C3
- Tengye Ling 24 A2
- Thaizand Bicycle Tours 泰山单车 (see 37)
- Thangka Workshop 25 C3
- Tibet Chamdo International Travel 西藏昌都国际旅行社 (see 39)
- Tibetan Traditional Hospital (Mentsikhang) 藏医院 26 A2
- Tsome Ling 27 A1

SLEEPING

- Banak Shol 八郎学旅馆 28 D2
- Barkhor Namchen House 八廓龙乾家庭旅馆 29 C2
- Barkhor Norzeng Hotel 八角街诺增宾馆 30 B3
- Dhood Gu Hotel 敦固宾馆 31 B1
- Dongcuo International Youth Hostel 东措国际青年旅馆 32 D1
- Flora Hotel 哈达花神旅馆 33 D3
- Gang Gyan Hotel 刚坚拉萨饭店 34 C1
- Gorkha Hotel 郭尔喀饭店 35 B3
- House of Shambhala 香巴拉宫 36 C2
- Kirey Hotel 吉日旅馆 37 C1
- Kyichu Hotel 吉曲饭店 38 A1
- Mandala Hotel 满斋酒店 39 B3
- Oh Dan Guest House 欧丹宾馆 40 B1
- Phuntsok Khasang International Youth Hostel 平措康桑青年旅舍 41 A1
- Shangbala Hotel 香巴拉酒店 42 A2
- Snowlands Hotel 雪域宾馆 43 A2
- Xiongbala Hotel 雄巴拉大酒店 44 C3
- Yak Hotel 亚客宾馆 45 B1

EATING

- Dunya Restaurant 46 B1
- Feijie Restaurant 肥姐便餐 47 D1
- Islam Restaurant 伊斯兰饭庄 48 D3
- Kagui Nongmo Sakhang 白日自助餐馆 49 A2
- Lanqing Qingzhen Fanguan 兰青清真饭馆 50 C1
- Mandala Restaurant (see 39)
- Nam-tso Restaurant 纳木措餐馆 (see 28)
- New Mandala Restaurant 新满斋餐厅 51 A2
- Pentoc Tibetan Restaurant 52 B1
- Snowland Restaurant 雪域餐厅 53 A2
- Tashi I 54 A1
- Tashi II (see 37)
- Tengyelink Café 55 A2

DRINKING

- Dunya (see 46)
- Makye Amye 玛吉阿米餐吧 56 C3
- Summit Café 顶峰咖啡店 (see 42)
- Teahouse 57 A2
- Teahouse (see 5)
- Turquoise Dragon Teahouse 58 B1

ENTERTAINMENT

- Shangrila Restaurant (see 37)

SHOPPING

- Dorje Antique Shop 59 B1
- Dropenling 卓番林 60 D2
- Eizhi Exquisite Thangka Shop 61 C2
- Kyichu Art Gallery (see 38)
- Mani Thangka Arts 嘛呢唐卡艺术 62 A2
- Norling Supermarket 诺林超市 63 D3
- Outlook Outdoor Equipment 64 C1
- Sifang Supermarket 四方超市 65 A1
- Snow Leopard Carpet Industries 雪豹毯业有限公司 66 A2
- Tromsikhang Market 冲赛康市场 67 B2

TRANSPORT

- Bodi Chehang Bike Hire 博迪车行 68 D1
- Bus 301 & 302 to Lhasa Hotel & Drepung Monastery 69 A1
- Bus 503 to Sera Monastery 70 A1
- Bus 89 to Train Station 71 A3
- Buses to Ganden Monastery, Drak Yerpa & Samye 72 A2
- Buses to Tsurphu Monastery, Dranang, Tsetang & Shugsheb Nunnery 73 A2
- Government Bus to Shigatse 74 C1
- Lugu Bus Stand 75 A3
- Minibuses to Shigatse & Nagchu 76 B1
- Ticket Office for Bus to Ganden Monastery 77 B2
- Yueye Bike Rental 越野自行车出租 78 D2

BARKHOR SQUARE

For your first visit to the Barkhor, enter from Barkhor Square (八角广场; Bajiao Guangchang), a large plaza that was cleared in 1985. The square has become a focus for political protest and has been the scene of pitched battles between Chinese and Tibetans on several occasions, most noticeably in 1998 when several Tibetans were killed and a Dutch tourist was shot in the shoulder. Look for the video cameras recording everything from the rooftops above the square. The recent addition of several tacky fast-food joints at the west end of the square is a shame. At least the Chinese resisted the temptation to plunk a Mao statue in the middle of it all.

Close to the entrance to the Jokhang a constant stream of Tibetans follows the Barkhor circumambulation route in a clockwise direction. Look for the two pot-bellied, stone *sangkang* (incense burners) in front of the Jokhang. There are four altogether, marking the four extremities of the Barkhor circuit; the other two are at the rear of the Jokhang. Behind the first two *sangkang* are two joined enclosures. The northern **stele** is inscribed with the terms of the Sino-Tibetan treaty of 822. The inscription guarantees mutual respect of the borders of the two nations – an irony seemingly lost on the Chinese authorities. The southern one harbours the stump of an ancient willow tree, known as the hair of the Jowo, allegedly planted by Songtsen Gampo's Chinese wife, Princess Wencheng (Wencheng Konjo), and a stele erected in 1793 commemorating smallpox victims.

For your first few visits to the Barkhor circuit, it's best to let yourself be dragged along by the tide of pilgrims, but there are also several small, fascinating temples to pop into en route.

BARKHOR CIRCUIT

As you follow the flow of pilgrims past sellers of religious photos, felt cowboy hats and electric blenders (for yak-butter tea!), you'll soon see a small building on the right, set off from the main path. This is the **Mani Lhakhang**, a small chapel that houses a huge prayer wheel set almost continuously in motion. To the right of the building is the grandiose entrance of the former city jail and dungeons, known as the Nangtse Shar.

If you head south from here, after about 10m you will see the entrance to the **Jampa Lhakhang** (also Jamkhang or Water Blessing Temple) on the right. The ground floor of this small temple has a two-storey statue of Miwang Jampa, the Future Buddha, flanked by rows of various protector gods and the meditation cave of the chapel's founder. Pilgrims ascend to the upper floor to be blessed with a sprinkling of holy water and the touch of a holy *dorje* (thunderbolt).

VISITING MONASTERIES & TEMPLES

Most monasteries and temples extend a warm welcome to foreign guests and in remote areas will often offer a place to stay for the night. Please maintain this good faith by observing the following courtesies:

- Always circumambulate Buddhist monasteries and other religious objects clockwise, thus keeping shrines and chörtens (stupas) to your right.
- Don't take prayer flags or mani (prayer) stones.
- Refrain from taking photos during a prayer meeting. At other times always ask permission to take photos, especially when using a flash. The larger monasteries charge photography fees, though some monks will allow you to take a quick picture for free. If they won't, there's no point getting angry; you don't know what pressures they may be under.
- Don't wear shorts or short skirts in a monastery.
- Take your hat off when you go into a chapel (though there's generally no need to remove your shoes).
- Don't smoke in a monastery.
- Be aware that women are generally not allowed in protector chapels *(gönkhang)*; always ask before entering.

Continue down the alley following the prayer wheels, then pass through a doorway into the old **Meru Nyingba Monastery**. This small but active monastery is a real delight and is invariably crowded with Tibetans thumbing prayer beads or lazily swinging prayer wheels and chanting under their breath. The chapel itself is administered by Nechung Monastery, which accounts for the images of the Nechung oracle inside. The building, like the adjoining Jokhang, dates back to the 7th century, though most of what you see today is recently constructed.

On the west side of the courtyard up some narrow stairs is the small Sakyapa-school **Gongkar Chöde** chapel. Below is the **Jambhala Lhakhang**, with a central image of Marmedze (Dipamkara), the Past Buddha, and a small inner kora path. From here you can return north or head east to join up with the Barkhor circuit.

On the northeast corner of the Barkhor is the **Gedun Choephel Artists' Guild** (☎ 632 3825; 🕑 10am-7pm), an exhibition hall for a dozen modern Tibetan artists. It's a rare opportunity to view Tibetan modern art free from religious convention (and there are good views from the roof!).

The eastern side of the circuit has more shops and even a couple of small department stores that specialise in turquoise. In the southeast corner is a wall shrine and a *darchen* (prayer pole), which mark the spot where Tsongkhapa planted his walking stick in 1409. The empty southern square of the Jokhang used to host annual teachings by the Dalai Lama during the Mönlam festival. The circuit finally swings north by a PSB station back to Barkhor Square.

The Jokhang ཇོ་ཁང་། 大昭寺

The **Jokhang** (Dazhao Si; Map p100; admission Y70; 🕑 inner chapels 8am-12.30pm, sometimes 5.30-8pm, Mon-Sat), also known in Tibetan as the Tsuglhakhang, is the most revered religious structure in Tibet. Thick with the smell of yak butter, echoing with the murmur of mantras and bustling with awed pilgrims, the Jokhang is an unrivalled Tibetan experience. Don't miss it.

The chapels can be very busy, with long lines of pilgrims, so try to view the most popular ones just after the temple opens or just before it closes around noon. The complex is open in the afternoon but many chapels are closed then. Once you've left the complex you can't re-enter without buying another ticket. Photos are not allowed inside the chapels.

HISTORY

Estimated dates for the Jokhang's founding range from 639 to 647 AD. Construction was initiated by King Songtsen Gampo to house an image of Mikyöba (Akshobhya) brought to Tibet as part of the dowry of his Nepali wife Princess Bhrikuti. The Ramoche Temple was constructed at the same time to house another Buddha image, Jowo Sakyamuni (Sakya Thukpa), brought to Tibet by his Chinese wife Princess Wencheng. It is thought that after the death of Songtsen Gampo, Jowo Sakyamuni was moved from Ramoche for its protection and hidden in the Jokhang by Princess Wencheng. The image has remained in the Jokhang ever since (Jokhang, or Jowokhang, means 'chapel of the Jowo'), and it is the most revered Buddha image in all of Tibet.

Over the centuries, the Jokhang has undergone many renovations, but the basic layout is ancient and differs from that of many other Tibetan religious structures. One crucial difference is the building's east–west orientation, said to face towards Nepal to honour Princess Bhrikuti. A few interior carved pillars and entrance arches remain from the original 7th-century work of Newari artisans brought from the Kathmandu Valley in Nepal to work on the construction.

In the early days of the Cultural Revolution, much of the interior of the Jokhang was desecrated by Red Guards and it is claimed that a section was utilised as a pigsty. Since 1980 the Jokhang has been restored, and without the aid of an expert eye, you will see few signs of the misfortunes that have befallen the temple in recent years.

GROUND FLOOR

In front of the entrance to the Jokhang is a forecourt that is perpetually crowded with pilgrims polishing the flagstones with their prostrations. Several monuments stand in front of the Jokhang (opposite).

Just inside the entrance to the Jokhang are statues of the **Four Guardian Kings** (Chökyong), two on either side. Beyond this is the **main assembly hall** or *dukhang*, a paved courtyard that is open to the elements. During festivals the hall is often the focus of ceremonies. The throne on the left wall was formerly used by the Dalai Lamas. You'll see a line of pilgrims

THE JOKHANG

Approximate Scale 0 — 50 m

1 Sino-Tibetan Treaty Stele
2 Smallpox Stele and Ancient Willow Tree

GROUND FLOOR

3 Guardian Kings
4 Ticket Office
5 Throne of the Dalai Lamas
6 Naga Chapel
7 Nojin Chapel
8 Jampa Statue
9 Jampa Statue
10 Jampa Statue
11 Guru Rinpoche Statue
12 Chenresig Statue
13 Guru Rinpoche Statue
14 Chapel of Tsongkhapa & His Disciples
15 Chapel of the Buddha of Infinite Light (Öpagme)
16 Chörten
17 Chapel of the Eight Medicine Buddhas
18 Chapel of Chenresig (Avalokiteshvara)
19 Chapel of Jampa
20 Chapel of Tsongkhapa
21 Chapel of the Buddha of Infinite Light
22 Chapel of Jowo Sakyamuni
23 Chapel of Jampa
24 Chapel of Chenresig (Riding a Lion)
25 Guru Rinpoche Shrine and Rock Painting
26 Chapel of Tsepame
27 Chapel of Jampa
28 Chapel of the Hidden Jowo
29 Chapel of the Seven Buddhas
30 Chapel of the Nine Buddhas of Longevity (Tsepame)
31 Chapel of the Kings

FIRST FLOOR

32 Chapel of Lhobdak Namka Gyaltsen
33 Chapel of Sakyamuni
34 Chapel of Eight Medicine Buddhas
35 Chapel of Sakyamuni
36 Chapel of Five Protectors
37 Anteroom
38 Chapel of the Three Kings
39 Chapel of Songtsen Gampo
40 Chapel of Chenresig
41 Chapel of Sakyamuni
42 Prayer Wheel
43 Chapel of Guru Rinpoche & Sakyamuni
44 Chapel of Songtsen Gampo
45 Zhelre Lakhang (Inaccessible)
46 Chapel of Guru Rinpoche
47 Chapel of Samvara
48 Palden Lhamo Statues

OTHER CHAPELS

49 Drölma Chapel
50 Guru Rinpoche Chapel

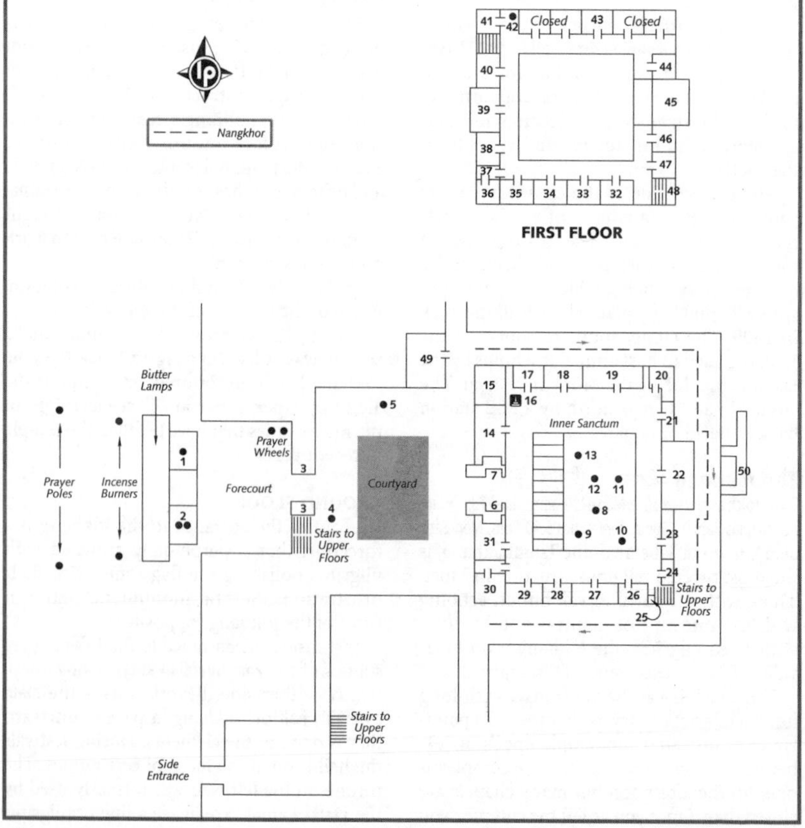

filing past the main Jokhang entrance as they walk the pilgrim circuit around the temple.

The inner prayer hall of the Jokhang houses the most important images and chapels. Most prominent are six larger-than-life statues that dominate the central prayer hall. In the foreground and to the left is a 6m statue of Guru Rinpoche. The statue opposite it, to the right, is of Jampa (Maitreya), the Future Buddha. At the centre of the hall, between and to the rear of these two statues, is a thousand-armed Chenresig (Avalokiteshvara). At the far right are two more Jampa statues, one behind the other, and to the far rear, behind Chenresig and facing the main Jowo statue, is another statue of Guru Rinpoche, encased in a cabinet.

Encircling this enclosed area of statues is a collection of chapels. Tibetan pilgrims circle the central area of statuary in a clockwise direction, visiting the chapels en route. There are generally long queues for the holiest chapels, particularly the Chapel of Jowo Sakyamuni. Pilgrims rub the doorways and chain-mail curtains, touch their heads to revered statues, throw seeds as offerings and pour molten yak butter into the heat of a thousand prayer lamps. The hushed atmosphere of respect is broken only by groups of Chinese tourists chattering into their mobile phones.

The chapels, following a clockwise route, are as follows. The numbers marked here refer to those marked on the Jokhang map.

Chapel of Tsongkhapa & His Disciples (14)

Tsongkhapa was the founder of the Gelugpa order, and you can see him seated centre, flanked by his eight disciples.

Chapel of the Buddha of Infinite Light (15)

This chapel is usually closed. Just outside is the large Tagba chörten (stupa).

Chapel of the Eight Medicine Buddhas (17)

The eight medicine buddhas are recent and not of special interest.

DEMONESS-SUBDUING TEMPLES

Buddhism's interaction with the pre-existing Bön – a shamanistic folk religion of spirits, ghosts and demons – combined with the wild and inhospitable nature of the Tibetan terrain has led to many metaphoric fables about Buddhism's taming of Tibet. The story of the early introduction of Buddhism to Tibet is attended by the story of a vast, supine demoness whose body straddled all of the high plateau.

It was Princess Wencheng, the Chinese wife of King Songtsen Gampo, who divined the presence of this demoness. Through Chinese geomantic calculations she established that the heart of the demoness lay beneath a lake in the centre of Lhasa, while her torso and limbs lay far away in the outer dominions of the high plateau. As in all such fables, the demoness can be seen as a symbol, of both the physical hardships of Tibet and the existing Bön clergy's hostility towards Buddhism; both had to be tamed before Buddhism could take root there. It was decided that the demoness would have to be pinned down.

The first task was to drain the lake in Lhasa of its water (read life-blood of the demoness) and build a central temple that would replace the heart of the demoness with a Buddhist heart. The temple built there was the Jokhang. A stake through the heart was not enough to put a demoness of this size out of action, however, and a series of lesser temples, in three concentric rings, were conceived to pin the extremities of the demoness.

There were four temples in each of these rings. The first are known as the *runo* temples and form a protective circle around Lhasa, pinning down the demoness' hips and shoulders. Two of these are Trandruk Monastery in the Yarlung Valley (p175) and Katsel Monastery (p161) on the way to Drigung. The second group, known as the *tandrul* temples, pin the knees and elbows of the demoness. Buchu Monastery (p250) near Bayi in eastern Tibet is one of these. And the final group, known as *yandrul* temples, pin the hands and feet. These last temples are found as far away as Bhutan (Paro and Bumthang) and Sichuan, though the location of two of them is unknown. You can see a representative image of the demoness and the temples that pin her down in the Tibet Museum (p116).

LHASA

Chapel of Chenresig (18)

This chapel contains the Jokhang's most important image after the Jowo Sakyamuni. Legend has it that the statue of Chenresig here sprang spontaneously into being and combines aspects of King Songtsen Gampo, his wives and two wrathful protective deities. The doors of the chapel are among the few remnants still visible of the Jokhang's 7th-century origins and were fashioned by Nepali artisans.

Chapel of Jampa (19)

In this chapel are statues of Jampa as well as four smaller bodhisattvas: Jampelyang (Manjushri), Chenresig (to the left), Chana Dorje (Vajrapani) and Drölma (Tara). Öpagme (Amitabha) and Tsongkhapa are also present here, as are two chörtens, one of which holds the remains of the original sculptor.

Chapel of Tsongkhapa (20)

This chapel's image of Tsongkhapa, founder of the Gelugpa order, was commissioned by the subject himself and is said to be a precise resemblance. It is the central image on top of the steps.

Chapel of the Buddha of Infinite Light (21)

This is the second of the chapels consecrated to Öpagme (Amitabha), the Buddha of Infinite Light. The outer entrance, with its wonderful carved doors, is protected by two fierce deities, red Tamdrin (Hayagriva; right) and blue Chana Dorje (Vajrapani; left). There are also statues of the eight bodhisattvas. Pilgrims generally pray here for the elimination of impediments to viewing the most sacred image of the Jokhang, that of Jowo Sakyamuni, which awaits in the next chapel.

Outside the chapel are statues of King Songtsen Gampo with his two queens and also Guru Rinpoche (with a big nose).

Chapel of Jowo Sakyamuni (22)

The most important shrine in Tibet, this chapel houses the image of Sakyamuni Buddha at the age of 12 years, brought to Tibet by Princess Wencheng. You enter via an anteroom containing the Four Guardian Kings, smiling on the left and frowning to the right. Inside are statues of the protectors Miyowa (Achala) and Chana Dorje (Vajrapani, blue). Several large bells hang from the anteroom's Newari-style roof. The carved doorway has been rubbed smooth by generations of pilgrims.

The 1.5m statue of Sakyamuni is embedded with precious stones, covered in silks and jewellery, and surrounded by silver pillars with dragon motifs. The silver canopy above was financed by a Mongolian khan. Pilgrims touch their forehead to the statue's left leg before being tapped on the back by a monk 'bouncer' when it's time to move on.

To the rear of Sakyamuni are statues of the seventh and 13th Dalai Lamas (with a moustache), Tsongkhapa and 12 standing bodhisattvas. Look for the 7th-century pillars on the way out.

THE SACRED GOAT

It is said that Princess Wencheng chose the site of the Jokhang, and that just to be difficult she chose Lake Wothang. The lake had to be filled in, but it is said that a well in the precincts of the Jokhang still draws its waters from those of the old lake. Over the years, many legends have emerged around the task of filling in Lake Wothang. The most prominent of these is the story of how the lake was filled by a sacred goat (the Tibetan word for goat, *ra*, is etymologically connected with the original name for Lhasa – Rasa). Look for a small image of the goat peeking out from the Chapel of Jampa (27) on the south wall of the Jokhang's ground-floor inner sanctum.

Chapel of Jampa (23)

The Jampa (Maitreya, or Future Buddha) enshrined here is a replica of a statue that came to Tibet as a part of the dowry of Princess Bhrikuti, King Songtsen Gampo's Nepali wife. Around the statue are eight images of Drölma, a goddess seen as an embodiment of the enlightened mind of Buddha-hood and who protects against the eight fears – hence the eight statues. There are some fine doorcarvings here.

Chapel of Chenresig Riding a Lion (24)

The statue of Chenresig on the back of a *sengye* (snow lion) is first on the left (it's not the largest of the icons within). The other eight statues of the chapel are all aspects of Chenresig.

Some pilgrims exit this chapel and then follow a flight of stairs up to the next floor, while others complete the circuit on the ground floor. If you're chapelled out (you've seen the important ones already), continue on upstairs, but look out first for a small hole in the wall on the left as you exit the chapel, against which pilgrims place their ear to hear the beating wings of a mythical bird that lives under the Jokhang.

Guru Rinpoche Shrine (25)

Two statues of Guru Rinpoche and one of King Trisong Detsen are next to the stairs. Beside the shrine is a rock painting of the medicine buddha protected by a glass plate.

Chapel of Tsepame (26)

Inside are nine statues of Tsepame (Amitayus), the red Buddha of Longevity, in *yabyum* (sexual and spiritual union) pose.

Chapel of Jampa (27)

This, another Jampa chapel, holds the Jampa statue that was traditionally borne around the Barkhor on the 25th day of the first lunar month for the Mönlam festival. Jampa's yearly excursion was designed to hasten the arrival of the Future Buddha. Jampelyang and Chenresig flank the Buddha.

The chapel is also named the 'Chapel of the Sacred Goat', after the rough 'self-arisen' (ie not man-made) image of the goat lurking in the first corner, beside the first protector deity (see the boxed text, opposite).

Chapel of the Hidden Jowo (28)

This is the chapel where Princess Wencheng is said to have hidden Jowo Sakyamuni for safekeeping after the death of her husband. You can see the cavity on the eastern wall, currently blocked by a bag of tsampa (roasted-barley flour). Inside is a statue of Öpagme (Amitabha) and the eight medicine buddhas with characteristic blue hair.

Other Chapels

From here there are several chapels of limited interest to non-Tibetologists. The **Chapel of the Seven Buddhas (29)** is followed by the **Chapel of the Nine Buddhas of Longevity (30)**, whose deities hold vases of immortality. The last of the ground-floor chapels is the **Chapel of the Kings (31)**, with some original statues of Tibet's earliest kings. The central figure is Songtsen Gampo, flanked by images of King Trisong Detsen (left) and King Ralpachen (right). Pilgrims touch their head to the central pillar. On the wall outside the chapel is a fine mural depicting the original construction of the Jokhang and the Potala, alongside performances of Tibetan opera, yak dances, wrestling, weightlifting and horse-racing.

FIRST FLOOR

At this point you should return clockwise to the rear of the ground floor (if you did not do so earlier) and climb the stairs to the upper floor of the Jokhang. The upper floor of the Jokhang's inner sanctum is also ringed with chapels, though some of them are closed.

As you begin the circuit, you will pass by several newly restored rooms that feature **Sakyamuni (33, 35)** accompanied by his two main disciples, and one featuring the **eight medicine buddhas (34)**. The **Chapel of Lhobdrak Namka Gyaltsen (32)** near the southeast corner features Pabonka Rinpoche, Sakyamuni, Tsongkhapa and Atisha (Jowo-je). The chapel in the southwest corner is the **Chapel of Five Protectors (36)** and has some fearsome statues of Tamdrin (Hayagriva), Palden Lhamo (Shri Devi) and other protector deities, attended by Tantric drumming in the anteroom. Next is the **Chapel of the Three Kings (38)**, dedicated to Songtsen Gampo, Trisong Detsen and Ralpachen. Also featured in the room are Songtsen Gampo's two wives, various ministers, and such symbols of royalty as the elephant and horse in the left corner.

Also worth a look is the **Chapel of Songtsen Gampo (39)**, the principal Songtsen Gampo chapel in the Jokhang. It is positioned in the centre of the west wall (directly above the entry to the ground-floor inner sanctum). The bejewelled king, with a tiny buddha protruding from his turban, is accompanied by his two consorts, his Nepali wife to the left and his Chinese wife to the right. His silver-embossed animal-headed *chang* (barley beer) container is placed opposite him behind a grill.

Most of the other rooms are hidden behind grills, the main exception being the meditation cell of **Chapel of Songtsen Gampo (44)** near the floor's northeastern corner, which has an incredible carved doorway smeared with decades' worth of yak butter. Murals to the right of the doorway depict the Jokhang. As you walk back to the stairs look at the unusual row of carved beams that look like half-lion, half-monkey creatures.

Back by the stairs, notice the round doorframes of the **Chapel of Guru Rinpoche (46)** and the

Chapel of Samvara (47), showing Samvara with consort, which date back to the 7th century.

Before you leave the 1st floor by the stairs in the southeast corner, ascend half a floor up to two statues of the protectress **Palden Lhamo (48)**, one wrathful, the other benign. There's also a photo of the Nechung oracle here. You can sometimes gain access to a Tantric chapel up on the 2nd floor.

OTHER CHAPELS

After you've explored the interior of the Jokhang, it's definitely worth spending some time on the **roof**, with its stunning views and small teahouse. The orange building on the north side holds the private quarters of the Dalai Lama. The outer halls and the roof are effectively open daily from sunrise to sundown.

It's worth finishing off a visit with a walk around the **Nangkhor** pilgrim path, which encircles the Jokhang's inner sanctum. If you're not utterly exhausted you could have a brief look at the **Drölma Chapel (49)**, featuring Drölma flanked by her green and white manifestations and others of her 21 manifestations. Pilgrims sometimes pop into the **Guru Rinpoche Chapel (50)**, a series of three interconnected shrines stuffed with images of Guru Rinpoche, at the back of the kora.

The Potala པོ་ཏ་ལ། 布达拉宫

Lhasa's cardinal landmark, the **Potala** (Budala Gong; Map p96; admission Y100; 9.30am-3pm before 1 May, 9am-3.30pm after 1 May, interior chapels close 4.30pm) is one of the great wonders of world architecture. As has been the case with centuries of pilgrims before you, the first sight of the fortress-like structure will be a magical moment that you will remember for a long time. It's hard to peel your eyes away from the place.

The Potala is a structure of massive proportions, an awe-inspiring place to visit, but still many visitors come away slightly disappointed. Unlike the Jokhang, which hums with vibrant activity, the Potala lies dormant like a huge museum, and the lifelessness of the highly symbolic building constantly reminds visitors that the Dalai Lama has been forced to take his government into exile. It's a modern irony that the Potala now hums with large numbers of chattering Chinese tourists staring with wonder at the building the generation before them tried in vain to destroy.

HISTORY

Marpo Ri, the 130m-high 'Red Hill', which commands a view of all Lhasa, was the site of King Songtsen Gampo's palace during the mid-7th century, long before the construction of the present-day Potala. There is little to indicate what this palace looked like, but it is clear that royal precedent was a major factor in the fifth Dalai Lama's choice of this site when he decided to move the seat of his Gelugpa government here from Drepung Monastery.

Work began first on the White Palace, or Karpo Potrang, in 1645. The nine-storey structure was completed three years later, and in 1649 the fifth Dalai Lama moved from Drepung Monastery to his new residence. However, the circumstances surrounding the construction of the larger Red Palace, or Marpo Potrang, are subject to some dispute. It is agreed that the fifth Dalai Lama died in 1682 and that his death was concealed until the completion of the Red Palace 12 years later. In some accounts, the work was initiated by the regent who governed Tibet from 1679 to 1703 and foundations were laid in 1690 (after the fifth Dalai Lama's death). In other accounts, the Red Palace was conceived by the fifth Dalai Lama as a funerary chörten and work was well under way at the time of his death. In any event, the death of the fifth Dalai Lama was not announced until he was put to rest in the newly completed Red Palace.

There is also some scholarly debate concerning the Potala's name. The most probable explanation is that it derives from the Tibetan name for Chenresig's 'pure land', or paradise, also known as Potala. Given that Songtsen Gampo and the Dalai Lamas are believed to be reincarnations of Chenresig, this connection is compelling.

Since its construction, the Potala has been the home of each of the successive Dalai Lamas, although since construction of the Norbulingka summer palace in the late 18th century, it has served as a winter residence only. It was also the seat of the Tibetan government, and with chapels, schools, jails and even tombs for the Dalai Lamas, it was virtually a self-contained world.

The Potala was shelled briefly during the 1959 popular uprising against the Chinese but the damage was not extensive. The Potala was spared again during the Cultural Revolution, reportedly at the insistence of Zhou Enlai, the Chinese premier, who is said to have deployed his own troops to protect it. The Potala was reopened to the public in 1980 and final touches to the US$4 million renovations were completed in 1995.

ENTRY PROCEDURES

A quota system is now in place to cope with the huge numbers of domestic tourists trying to visit the Potala during the summer months. From mid-April to November you need to go to an office at the southwestern gate by noon the day before your intended visit. Present your passport and get a reservation slip detailing a time for your visit the next day. One person can get slips for four people, so earn some good karma and take your friends' passports. After 2300 slips have been allotted (only 700 of which go to independent tourists) you'll be turned away, so start queuing early in peak seasons. There is talk of introducing an online booking system, which would make things a lot easier. It is expected that the entry fee will soon hit a cool Y300. During the winter months (December to mid-April) you can just buy a ticket on the spot.

The next day head to the main southern entrance and then proceed through the rebuilt village of Shöl up into the palace. Halfway up is the ticket office. From the roof you wind down into the labyrinthine bowels of the Potala, before exiting at the rear of the palace and descending to either the Lukhang or the western entrance. Much of your visit will be in one huge shuffling queue.

Photography of the interior of the Potala is forbidden and all rooms are wired with motion sensors and video cameras.

SHÖL

Nestled at the southern foot of Marpo Ri, the former village of Shöl (which means 'at the base of') was once Lhasa's red-light district, as well as the location of a prison, a printing press and some ancillary government buildings. Some of these buildings have been rebuilt, including an inn supposedly favoured by the sixth Dalai Lama and the residence of the monk police chief. Expect some kind of admission fee before long. There are plans for an exhibition hall, perhaps to include the famous three-dimensional mandala made of over 200,000 pearls that was formerly displayed inside the Potala.

Entry to the Potala is up two steep access ramps that will soon leave you wheezing in the oxygen-depleted air. The stairs lead past the ticket office to the large **Deyang Shar**, the external courtyard of the White Palace. At the top of the triple stairs leading up to the White Palace look out for the golden handprints of the fifth Dalai Lama on the wall to the left, and murals to the north depicting Songtsen Gampo's original Potala and the construction of the Jokhang.

ROOF OF THE WHITE PALACE

As you arrive on the roof, head right for the private quarters of the 13th and 14th Dalai Lamas. The first room you come to is the **throne room** (Simchung Nyiwoi Shar), where the Dalai Lamas would receive official guests. The large picture on the left of the throne is of the 13th Dalai Lama; the matching photo of the present Dalai Lama has been removed. There are some fine murals here, including a depiction of Bodhgaya (where the Buddha achieved enlightenment) and the mythical paradise of Shambhala (by the entry).

The trail continues clockwise into the **reception hall** (Dhaklen Paldseg), with a fine collection of bronze statues and fine hidden views from the balcony. Next comes the **meditation room**, which still displays the ritual implements of the present Dalai Lama on a small table to the side of the room. Protector gods here include Nagpo Chenpo (Mahakala), the Nechung oracle and Palden Lhamo. The final room, the **bedroom of the Dalai Lama** (Chimey Namgyal), has some personal effects of the Dalai Lama on show, such as his bedside clock. The mural above the bed is of Tsongkhapa, the founder of the Gelugpa order of which the Dalai Lama is the head. The locked door leads into the Dalai Lama's private bathroom.

RED PALACE

Third Floor

The first room in the main palace building is the **Chapel of Jampa** (Jamkhang), which contains an exquisite image of Jampa commissioned by the eighth Dalai Lama; it stands opposite the Dalai Lama's throne. To the right of the throne is a wooden Kalachakra mandala. The walls are stacked with the collected works of the fifth Dalai Lama. The chapel was unfortunately damaged in a fire in 1984 (caused by an electrical fault) and many valuable thangkas (religious paintings) were lost.

The **Chapel of Three-Dimensional Mandalas** (Loilang Khang) houses spectacular jewel-encrusted mandalas of the three principal

RED PALACE OF THE POTALA

Approximate Scale 0 50 m

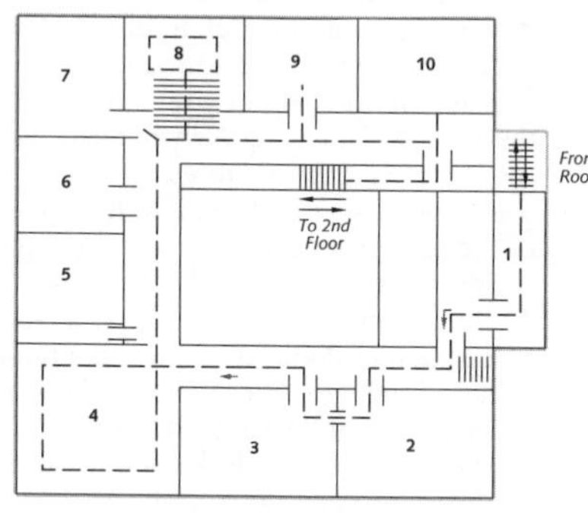

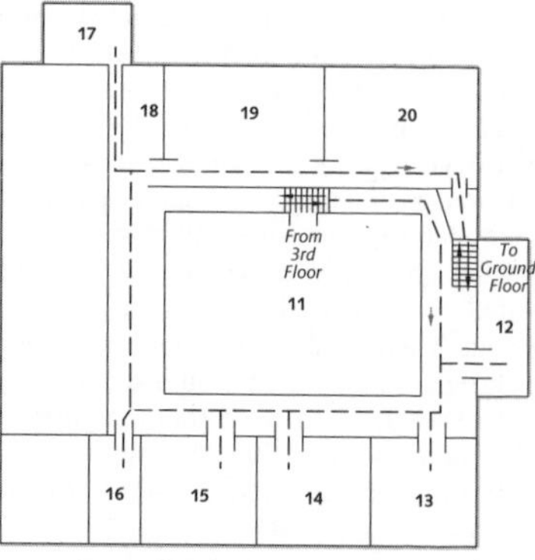

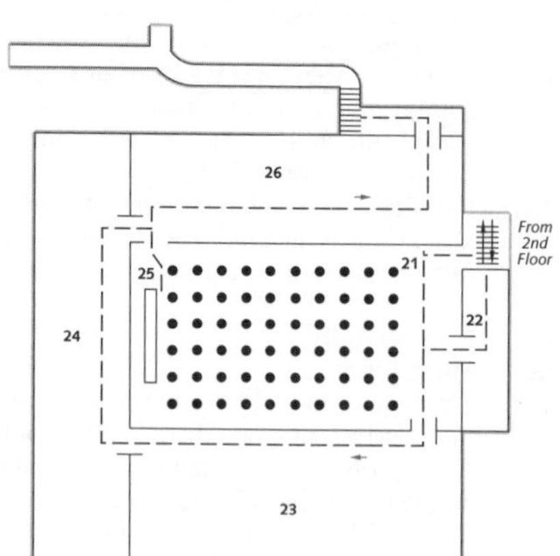

THIRD FLOOR

1 Chapel of Jampa (Jamkhang)
2 Chapel of the Three-Dimensional Mandalas (Loilang Khang)
3 Chapel of the Victory over the Three Worlds (Sasum Namgyal)
4 Chapel of Immortal Happiness (Chimey Dedan Kyil)
5 Tomb of the 13th Dalai Lama
6 Lhama Lhakhang
7 Tomb of the 7th Dalai Lama (Serdung Tashi Obar Khang)
8 Chapel of Arya Lokeshvara (Pakpa Lhakhang)
9 Tomb of the 8th Dalai Lama
10 Tomb of the 9th Dalai Lama

SECOND FLOOR

11 Rest Area
12 Chapel of Kalachakra (Dukhor Lhakhang)
13 Chapel of Sakyamuni (Thuburang Lhakhang)
14 Chapel of the Nine Buddhas of Longevity (Tsephak Lhakhang)
15 Treasures of the Potala Exhibition
16 Chapel of Sakyamuni (Zegya Lhakhang)
17 King Songsten Gampo's Meditation Chamber (Chogyal Drupuk)
18 Lima Lhakhang
19 Lima Lhakhang
20 Lima Lhakhang

GROUND FLOOR

21 Assembly Hall
22 Chapel of Lamrim
23 Rigsum Lhakhang
24 Chapel of the Dalai Lamas' Tombs (Serdung Zamling Gyenjikhang)
25 Throne
26 Chapel of the Holy Born (Trungrab Lhakhang)

— — — *Suggested Route*

Tantric deities of the Gelugpa order (Chana Dorje, Demchok and Yamantaka). Unfortunately you can no longer walk around to see the fine blackened murals near the throne of the seventh Dalai Lama.

The **Chapel of the Victory over the Three Worlds** (Sasum Namgyal) houses a library and displays examples of Manchu texts. The main statue is a golden thousand-armed Chenresig, while the main thangka is of the Manchu Chinese emperor Qianlong dressed in monk's robes, with accompanying inscriptions in four languages.

Next, the **Chapel of Immortal Happiness** (Chimey Dedan Kyil) was once the residence of the sixth Dalai Lama, whose throne remains; it is now dedicated to Tsepame, the Buddha of Longevity, who sits by the window. Next to him in the corner is the Dzogchen deity Ekajati (Tsechigma), with an ostrich-feather hat and a single fang.

From here a locked corridor leads off the main circuit to a gallery that overlooks the **tomb of the 13th Dalai Lama**. You could at one time look down on the chörten from above and then descend to look at it at ground level, but the room has been closed for years.

Also in the northwest corner is the **Lhama Lhakhang** and the golden **tomb of the Seventh Dalai Lama** (Serdung Tashi Obar Khang), constructed in 1757 and encased in half a tonne of gold. To the right stands a statue of the seventh Dalai Lama, Kalsang Gyatso.

In the northwest corner, steps lead up into the small but important **Chapel of Arya Lokeshvara** (Pakpa Lhakhang). Allegedly this is one of the few corners of the Potala that dates from the time of Songtsen Gampo's 7th-century palace. It is the most sacred of the Potala's chapels, and the image of Arya Lokeshvara inside is the most revered image housed in the Potala. The statue is accompanied on the left by the seventh Dalai Lama and Tsongkhapa, and on the right by the fifth, eighth and ninth Dalai Lamas and the protector Chana Dorje (Vajrapani). Relics include stone footprints of Guru Rinpoche and Tsongkhapa.

The last two rooms on this floor are the jewel-encrusted **tombs of the Eighth and Ninth Dalai Lama**, the former over 9m tall.

Second Floor

If you're exhausted already (not even halfway!), you can rest your legs at a reception area/teahouse in the middle of the floor.

The first of the chapels you come to on the 2nd floor is the **Chapel of Kalachakra** (Dukhor Lhakhang). It is noted for its stunning three-dimensional mandala, which is over 6m in diameter and finely detailed with over 170 statues. A statue of the Tantric deity Dukhor (Kalachakra) stands in the far right corner, though access to the room is limited.

The **Chapel of Sakyamuni** (Thuburang Lhakhang) houses a library, the throne of the seventh Dalai Lama and some fine examples of calligraphy.

In the **Chapel of the Nine Buddhas of Longevity** (Tsepak Lhakhang), look for the murals by the left window – the left side depicts Tangtong Gyelpo (see p30) and his celebrated bridge (now destroyed) over the Yarlung Tsangpo near Chushul. The images of coracle rafts halfway up the wall add an intimate touch. There are also nine statues of Tsepame here.

Passing the **Chapel of Sakyamuni** (Zegya Lhakhang), continue to the northwestern corner where you'll find a small corridor that leads to **King Songtsen Gampo's meditation chamber** (Chogyal Drupuk), which, along with the Chapel of Arya Lokeshvara on the 3rd floor, is one of the oldest rooms in the Potala. The most important statue is of Songtsen Gampo himself, to the left of the pillar. To his left is his minister Tonmi Sambhota (said to have invented the Tibetan script) and to the right are his Chinese and Nepali wives. The king's Tibetan wife (the only one to bear a son) is in a cabinet by the door. The fifth Dalai Lama lurks behind (and also on) the central pillar. Queues for this chapel can be long.

The last three rooms are all linked and are chock-a-block full of 3000 pieces of Chinese statuary, many donated by a Khampa businessman in 1995.

First Floor

This floor has been closed to visitors for years and is unlikely to reopen soon.

Ground Floor

As you round the steps, enter the beautiful **assembly hall**, which is the largest hall in the Potala and is its physical centre. Note the fine carved pillar heads. The large throne that dominates one end of the hall was the throne of the sixth Dalai Lama. Four important chapels frame the hall.

The first chapel on this floor is the **Chapel of Lamrim**. *Lamrim* means literally 'the graduated path', and refers to the graduated stages that mark the path to enlightenment. The central figure in the chapel is Tsongkhapa, the founder of the Gelugpa order, with whom *lamrim* texts are usually associated. Outside the chapel a fine mural depicts the Forbidden City, commemorating the fifth Dalai Lama's visit to the court of Emperor Shunzhi in Beijing.

The next chapel, the long **Rigsum Lhakhang**, is dedicated to eight Indian teachers who brought various Tantric practices and rituals to Tibet. The central figure is a silver statue of Guru Rinpoche (one of the eight), who is flanked by his consorts Mandarava and Yeshe Tsogyel (with a turquoise headdress), as well as statues of the eight teachers on his left and a further eight statues of him in different manifestations on the right. As you exit the chapel, take an up-close look at the fine wall murals.

In the west wing of the assembly hall is one of the highlights of the Potala, the awe-inspiring **Chapel of the Dalai Lamas' Tombs** (Serdung Zamling Gyenjikhang). The hall is dominated by the huge 12.6m-high chörten of the great fifth Dalai Lama, gilded with some 3700kg of gold. Flanking it are two smaller chörtens containing the 10th (right) and 12th (left) Dalai Lamas, who both died as children. Richly embossed, the chörtens represent the concentrated wealth of an entire nation. One of the precious stones is a pearl said to have been discovered in an elephant's brains and thus, in a wonderful piece of understatement, 'considered a rarity'. Eight other chörtens represent the eight major events in the life of the Buddha.

The last chapel is the **Chapel of the Holy Born** (Trungrab Lhakhang). Firstly, in the corner, is the statue and chörten of the 11th Dalai Lama, who died at the age of 17. There are also statues of the eight medicine buddhas, a central Sakyamuni and fifth Dalai Lama, and then Chenresig, Songtsen Gampo and the first four Dalai Lamas.

Around the Potala

A morning visit to the Potala can easily be combined with a circuit of the Potala kora and an afternoon excursion to some of the temples nearby. One of the best ways to visit the following sights is on our Lingkhor Walking Tour – see p118.

POTALA KORA

The pilgrim path that encircles the foot of the Potala makes for a nice walk before or after a visit to the main event. Recent renovations by the city authorities have largely secularised the walk, doing away with many of the stalls frequented by pilgrims, but there are still plenty of people here, especially in the mornings. From the western chörten (formerly the western gate to the city), follow the prayer wheels to the northwest corner, marked by three large chörtens.

The northeast corner is home to several rock paintings and a delightful prayer hall occupied by nuns. Just past here, spin the large prayer wheel of the Phurbu Chok Hermitage Mani Lhakhang and then swing past the Chinese-style square, where pilgrims often prostrate in front of the Potala. Look out for the three 18th-century *doring* (stele); the two to the north side of the road commemorate victories over the Central Asian Dzungars (left) and Nepali Gorkhas (right). The single southern obelisk is said to have been erected by King Trisong Detsen in the eighth century.

DRUBTHUB NUNNERY & PALHA LU-PUK

Southwest of the Potala an unmarked road leads around the eastern side of Chagpo Ri, the hill that faces Marpo Ri, site of the Potala. Take this road past stone carvers and rock paintings to **Drubthub Nunnery** (Map p96). The nunnery is dedicated to Tangtong Gyelpo, the 15th-century bridge-maker, medic and inventor of Tibetan opera, who established the original nunnery on the top of Chagpo Ri. Gyelpo's white-haired statue graces the nunnery's main hall.

After the nunnery, head next door to the **Palha Lu-puk** (Map p96; admission Y20; 8am-8pm), where stairs lead up to an atmospheric cave temple said to have been the 7th-century meditational retreat of King Songtsen Gampo.

The main attraction of the cave is its relief rock carvings, some of which are over a thousand years old, making them the oldest religious images in Lhasa. Altogether there are over 70 carvings of bodhisattvas in the cave and on the cave's central column; the oldest are generally the ones lowest on the cave walls. Songtsen Gampo is depicted on the west side.

The yellow building above the Palha Lu-puk is a chapel that gives access to the less interesting meditation cave *(drubpuk)* of King Songtsen Gampo's Chinese wife, Princess Wencheng.

LUKHANG

The **Lukhang** (Map p96; admission Y10; 9am-5pm) is a little-visited temple on a small island in a lake, behind the Potala. The lake is in the recently remodelled and very pleasant **Zang Gyab Lukhang Park** (Map p96).

The lake was created during the construction of the Potala. Earth used for mortar was excavated from here, leaving a depression that was later filled with water. *Lu* (also known as *naga*) are subterranean dragon-like spirits that were thought to inhabit the area, and the Lukhang, or Chapel of the Dragon King, was built by the sixth Dalai Lama to appease them (and also to use as a retreat). You can see Luyi Gyalpo, the *naga* king, at the rear of the ground floor of the Lukhang. He is riding an elephant, and protective snakes rise from behind his head. The *naga* spirits were finally interred in the nearby Palha Lu-puk (opposite).

The Lukhang is celebrated for its 2nd- and 3rd-floor murals, which date from the 18th century. Bring a torch (flashlight). The 2nd-floor murals tell a story made famous by a Tibetan opera, while the murals on the 3rd floor depict different themes on each of the walls – Indian yogis demonstrating yogic positions (west), 84 *mahisaddhas* or masters of Buddhism (east), and the life cycle as perceived by Tibetan Buddhists (north), with the gods of Bardo, the Tibetan underworld, occupying its centre. Look for the wonderful attention to detail, down to the hairy legs of the sadhus and the patterns on the clothes.

The 3rd floor also contains a statue of an 11-headed Chenresig and a meditation room used by the Dalai Lamas. To reach the 3rd floor, walk clockwise around the outside of the building and enter from the back via a flight of stairs. Finish off a visit with a kora of the island.

For a detailed commentary on the murals check out Ian Baker and Thomas Laird's coffee-table book *The Dalai Lama's Secret Temple: Tantric Wall Paintings from Tibet.*

PARMA RI

Several hundred metres west of Chagpo Ri, **Parma Ri** (Map p96) is a much smaller hill with a couple of interesting sights. At the foot of the hill, close to Beijing Zhonglu, is one of Lhasa's four former royal temples, **Kunde Ling** (Map p96; admission Y10; 9am-7pm). The *ling* (royal) temples were appointed by the fifth Dalai Lama, and it was from one of them that regents of Tibet were generally appointed. There are only a couple of restored chapels open, but it's a friendly place and worth a visit. Look for the upstairs mural of the original Kunde Ling, 80% of which has been destroyed.

On the north side of Parma Ri is the **Gesar Ling** (Map p96; admission Y5; 9.30am-7pm), a Chinese construction that dates back to 1793 and was recently renovated. It is the only Chinese-style temple in Lhasa. The main yellow-walled temple has a statue of the mythical Tibetan warrior Gesar (associated with Guandi, the Chinese God of War) along with Guru Rinpoche on the left and Ekajati, the Dzogchen deity, on the right. A separate yellow chapel has a statue of an orange Jampelyang with Sakyamuni, Chana Dorje (Vajrapani) and Chenresig.

Ramoche Temple ར་མོ་ཆེ 小昭寺

The **Ramoche** (Xiaozhaosi; Map p96; admission Y20; 8am-4.30pm) is the sister temple to the Jokhang, constructed around the same time but in Chinese style. It was built to house the Jowo Sakyamuni image that is now in the Jokhang. The principal image in Ramoche is Mikyöba (Akshobhya), brought to Tibet in the 7th century as part of the dowry of King Songtsen Gampo's Nepali wife, Princess Bhrikuti. The image represents Sakyamuni at the age of eight years. By the mid-15th century the temple had become Lhasa's Upper Tantric College. It is said to have been badly damaged by Red Guards during the Cultural Revolution, but the complex has since been restored with Swiss assistance.

As you enter the temple, past pilgrims doing full-body prostrations and the first of two inner koras, you'll see a **protector chapel** to the left, featuring masks and puppets on the ancient pillars and an image of Dorje Yundroma covered in beads on a horse. The main chapel is full of fiercesome protector deities in *yabyum* pose, as befitting a Tantric temple.

The fabulously ornate Mikyöba (Akshobhya) image can be seen in the inner **Tsangkhang**, protected by the four guardian kings and a curtain of chain mail, which pilgrims rub for good luck.

As you exit the Ramoche, look for a doorway just to the right by a collection of yak-butter and incense stalls, leading to a delightful chapel, the **Tsepak Lhakhang**. The central image is Tsepame, the buddha associated with longevity, flanked by Jampa and Sakyamuni. There are smaller statues of Dorje Chang

(Vajradhara) and Marmedze (Dipamkara), and a protector chapel next door. This hidden corner is very popular with pilgrims.

Another highlight is the pedestrian-only **Ramoche Lam** (aka Xiaozhaosi Lu), probably the most interesting street in Lhasa, jam-packed with teahouses, restaurants and stalls selling everything from saddles, cloaks and Tibetan tents to handmade potato chips and Tibetan scriptures. It's well worth a stroll.

Gyüme རྒྱུད་སྨད་གྲྭ་ཚང་

The **Gyüme** (Map p100; 15 Beijing Donglu), or Lower Tantric College, is across from the Kirey Hotel. It is easy to miss this working temple; look for an imposing entrance set back from the road. It's a surprisingly impressive place and little visited by foreigners.

Gyüme was founded in the mid-15th century as one of Tibet's foremost Tantric training colleges. In Lhasa, its importance was second only to the monasteries of Sera and Drepung. More than 500 monks were once in residence, and students of the college underwent a physically and intellectually gruelling course of study. The college was thoroughly desecrated during the Cultural Revolution, but a growing number of monks are now in residence.

The main *dukhang* (assembly hall) has statues of Tsongkhapa, the 13th Dalai Lama and Sakyamuni. Look for the monks' alms bowls encased in crafted leather, hanging from the pillars. Behind are huge statues of Tsongkhapa and his two main disciples, and next door is a fearsome statue of Dorje Jigje (Yamantaka). The 2nd- and 3rd-floor chapels are sometimes open.

Other Temples

Down the alleys off Beijing Donglu are three obscure temples, which can be visited if you've seen everything else.

Tsome Ling (Map p100) is the most interesting of the three. One of the four *ling* (royal) temples of Lhasa (along with Kunde Ling and Tengye Ling), this small site consists of two temples. To the east of the residential courtyard is the Karpo Potrang (White Palace), built in 1777, and to the west is the Marpo Potrang (Red Palace), built at the beginning of the 19th century. Both buildings have fine murals and are well frequented by pilgrims. Of equal interest is the small embroidery and Tibetan mattress workshop on site.

The obscure and rarely visited **Tengye Ling** (Map p100) chapel is a Nyingmapa-sect temple dedicated to the red-faced deity Tseumar, as well as Pehar (a protector linked to Samye) and Tamdrin (Hayagriva). The crates of *baijiu* (rice wine) stacked in the corner are there to refill the cup in Tseumar's hand; the chapel smells like a distillery. Look for the wonderful old photo of the Dalai Lama's pet elephant, stabled in the Lukhang behind the Potala. The chapel is hidden in the backstreets west of the Snowlands Hotel and is hard to find; enter through the gateway marked by juniper and *baijiu*-sellers, just south of the Backstreet Bar.

The badly ruined temple of **Shide Tratsang** (Map p100) is connected to Reting Monastery and was once one of the six principal temples encircling the Jokhang. It's in a housing courtyard, down a back alley near Tashi I restaurant, and remains a rare example of what Lhasa looked like before the renovation teams moved in.

The **Rigsum Lhakhang** (Map p100) is a small chapel hidden in a housing courtyard southwest of Barkhor Square. It's dedicated to the Rigsum Gonpo trinity of Jampelyang, Chenresig and Chana Dorje (Vajrapani). Look for the line of prayer wheels disappearing down the alley.

Die-hards can track down the hard-to-find **Pode Kangtsang** (Map p100), in the south of the old town, with its old upper-floor murals and large thangkas. It's accessed from the south.

The Norbulingka ནོར་བུ་གླིང་ཁ 罗布林卡

The **Norbulingka** (Luobulinka; Map p96; Minzu Lu; admission Y60, Tibetans Y3; 9am-6.30pm), the summer palace of the Dalai Lamas, is about 10 minutes' walk south of the Lhasa Hotel in the western part of town. It ranks well behind the other points of interest in and around Lhasa. The gardens are poorly tended and the palaces themselves are something of an anticlimax, since most rooms are closed to the public. Avoid the thoroughly depressing **zoo** (admission Y10).

This said, the Norbulingka is worth a visit if you don't mind the high entry fee, and the park is a great place to be during festival times and public holidays. In the seventh lunar month of every year, the Norbulingka is crowded with picnickers for the Shötun festival, when traditional Tibetan opera performances are held.

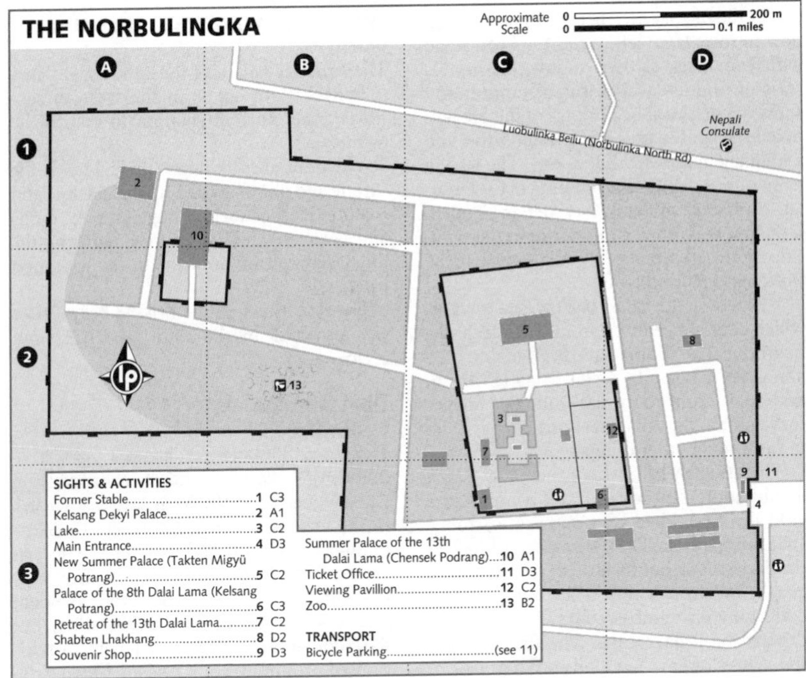

HISTORY

The seventh Dalai Lama founded the first summer palace in the Norbulingka (whose name literally means 'jewel park') in 1755. Rather than use the palace simply as a retreat, he decided to use the wooded environs as a summer base from which to administer the country, a practice that was repeated by each of the succeeding Dalai Lamas. The grand procession of the Dalai Lama's entourage relocating from the Potala to the Norbulingka became one of the highlights of the Lhasa year.

The eighth Dalai Lama (1758–1804) initiated more work on the Norbulingka, expanding the gardens and digging the lake, which can be found south of the New Summer Palace. The 13th Dalai Lama (1876–1933) was responsible for the three palaces in the northwest corner of the park, and the 14th (present) Dalai Lama built the New Summer Palace in 1956.

In 1959, the 14th Dalai Lama made his escape from the Norbulingka disguised as a Tibetan soldier (see p40). Unfortunately, all the palaces of the Norbulingka were damaged by Chinese artillery fire in the popular uprising that followed the Dalai Lama's flight. At the time, the compound was surrounded by some 30,000 Tibetans determined to defend the life of their spiritual leader. Repairs have been undertaken but have failed to restore the palaces to their full former glory.

PALACE OF THE EIGHTH DALAI LAMA

This palace (also known as Kelsang Potrang) is the first you come to. It was used as a summer palace by the eighth Dalai Lama and by every succeeding Dalai Lama up to the 13th. Only the main audience hall is open; it features 65 hanging thangkas and some lovely painted furniture.

NEW SUMMER PALACE

The New Summer Palace (Takten Migyü Potrang) in the centre of the park was built by the present (14th) Dalai Lama between 1954 and 1956 and is the most interesting of the Norbulingka palaces. You can only enter the walled complex from its east side.

The first of the rooms is the **Dalai Lama's audience chamber**. Note the wall murals, which depict the history of Tibet in 301 scenes that flow in rows from left to right. As you stand with your back to the window, the murals start on the left wall with Sakyamuni and show the mythical beginnings of the Tibetan people (from the union of a bodhisattva and a monkey in the Sheldrak Cave). The wall in front of you depicts the building of the circular monastery of Samye, as well as Ganden, Drepung and other monasteries to the right. The right wall depicts the construction of the Potala and Norbulingka.

Next come the **Dalai Lama's private quarters**, which consist of a meditation chamber and a bedroom. The rooms have been maintained almost exactly as the Dalai Lama left them, and apart from the usual Buddhist images they contain the occasional surprise (a Soviet radio, among other things).

The **assembly hall**, where the Dalai Lama would address heads of state, is home to a gold throne backed by wonderful cartoon-style murals of the Dalai Lama's court (left, at the back). Look out for British representative Hugh Richardson in a trilby hat, and several Mongolian ambassadors. The right wall depicts the Dalai Lamas. The first five lack the Wheel of Law, symbolising their lack of governmental authority. Last are the meeting rooms of the Dalai Lama's mother.

South of the New Summer Palace is the artificial lake commissioned by the eighth Dalai Lama. The only pavilion open here at the time of research was the personal **retreat of the 13th Dalai Lama** in the southwestern corner, featuring a library, a thousand-armed Chenresig statue, and a stuffed tiger in the corner! The seats overlooking the duck pond are a fine spot for a picnic.

SUMMER PALACE OF THE 13TH DALAI LAMA

The summer palace of the 13th Dalai Lama (Chensek Potrang) is in the western section of the Norbulingka, northwest of the awful zoo.

The ground-floor assembly hall holds the throne and photo of the 13th Dalai Lama and is stuffed full of various buggies, palanquins and bicycles. The fine murals depicting the life of Sakyamuni are hard to see without a torch.

Nearby, the smaller **Kelsang Dekyi Palace** was also built by the 13th Dalai Lama but is closed.

Tibet Museum བརྒྱལ་སྟོན་ཁང་ 西藏博物馆

This grand-looking new **museum** (Xizang Bowuguan; Map p96; Minzu Nanlu; ☎ 681 2210; adult/student Y30/5; 🕒 9am-6.30pm May-Oct, 10.30am-5pm Nov-Apr), in the west of town just opposite the Norbulingka, isn't too bad as long as you can filter out the blatant propaganda. The adult ticket includes a useful audio tour (student ticketholders pay an extra Y10 for this), but the commentary suffers from terrible Americanised pronunciation (Da-*lai* La-*maaarr!*).

The halls start logically with prehistory, which highlights the Neolithic sites around Chamdo and rock paintings at Rutok and Nam-tso. The 'Tibet is Inalienable in History' hall is full of boring seals and misleading Chinese political spin, but it's worth seeking out the Guge kingdom shields and the 18th-century gold urn and ivory slips that were used by the Chinese to recognise their version of the Panchen Lama (see p196). The more interesting third hall covers Tibetan script

THE BUMPA RI TREK

The demanding but excellent five-hour return trek up imposing Bumpa Ri, the holy peak to the southeast of Lhasa, is worth attempting if you're fit and acclimatised. It's straight up and then straight down, but offers unparalleled views over the Holy City, either from the top or just part of the way.

From the Eastern Bus Station it's a 10-minute walk south over the Lhasa Bridge to the base of the hill, where a path ascends to a chörten and incense-burning site. From here faint trails head straight up the hillside to the third small ridge, where a faint trail branches to the right. In general, aim for the pylon, to meet up with the main trail. After an hour you reach a ridge with views of the summit spires ahead. It's another hour's climb from here to the summit, following the trail to the right of the spires, over a spur and then up a gully to the two main summits, festooned in prayer flags. From the top it's a two-hour descent back down the way you came.

(with some fine 8th-century birch-paper scriptures), opera masks, musical instruments, divination guides, medical thangkas and statuary. The next hall concentrates on thangkas. The final hall has a good display of folk handicrafts, ranging from coracle boats to nomad tents, with some fine traditional Tibetan locks and leather bags used for carrying salt or tsampa.

The top floor has an inappropriate collection of Chinese jade and a hall of stuffed Tibetan wildlife, with a collection of python and leopard skins that were confiscated from local poachers. There are toilets and an overpriced shop. Photos are not allowed but everyone takes them anyway.

ACTIVITIES

Braille Without Borders Blind Massage Centre (Map p100; ☎ 632 0870; 4th fl, Room 59, Beijing Donglu; 9am-9pm) This worthy enterprise, set up by the Braille Without Borders organisation (p327), offers hour-long traditional massages (Y80) by blind therapists. The centre is in a courtyard, down an alley across from the Tashi I Restaurant. Call in advance. Ask at the Kyichu Hotel if you can't find it.

Thaizand Bicycle Tours (Map p100; ☎ 691 0898; thaizand@hotmail.com; Kirey Hotel, 105 Beijing Donglu) This small operation operates good bicycle tours ranging from day trips around Lhasa to fully supported overland rides to Kathmandu.

Tibet Wind Horse Adventure (Map p96; ☎ 136-3890 0332; www.windhorsetibet.com; Zangyiyuan Lu) Offers full-service rafting trips between June and October, either a half-day on the Tolung-chu (Y600), one/two days on the Drigung-chu (Y760/1520) or an ambitious five-day trip on the Reting Tsangpo. It also offers day trips on horseback in the Drigung and Tolung Valley regions (Y760). Trips are managed by Aussie adventurer Chris Jones. Pop into the Raft Tibet office (Map p100) near the Snowlands Hotel between June and September for details. See also p284.

WALKING TOURS

Old Town Walking Tour

The fragile Tibetan **old town** shelters the soul of Lhasa, far from Chinese influence. This walk takes in craft workshops, backstreet chapels and pilgrim paths, passing en route some of Lhasa's last remaining traditional architecture.

At the first turn of the **Barkhor circuit** (**1**; p102) take a left and then quick right, past strips of dried yak meat and yellow bags of yak butter to the bustling **Tromsikhang Market** (**2**). After a quick look around the modern market (the original Tibetan-style building was demolished in 1997), head north to the main road, Beijing Donglu, and then right to visit the **Gyüme Lower Tantric College** (**3**; p114).

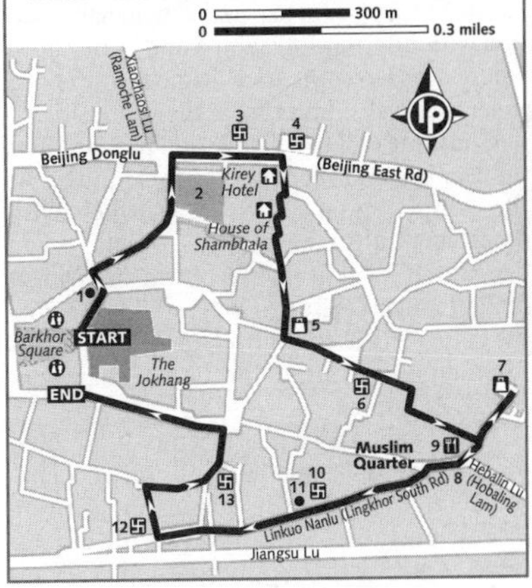

About 50m further down the road, opposite the Kirey Hotel, are the deceptively long white walls of the small but active **Meru Sarpa Monastery** (**4**; admission free). The building in the middle of the central housing compound houses a traditional wood-block printing press. In the northwest corner is an atmospheric chapel with a statue of thousand-armed Chenresig.

Take the alley down the east side of the Kirey Hotel into the old town and follow the winding branch to the right, past the yellow walls of the House of Shambhala (p123), which has a nice rooftop restaurant. As you continue south you'll pass Tibetan craftspeople making statues, cabinets, masks and Tibetan banners. At the junction there's the **Eizhi Exquisite Thangka Shop** (**5**) to the left; you want to take a left here but first look down the alleyway to

WALK FACTS

Start Barkhor Square
Finish Barkhor Square
Distance 3km
Duration Two to three hours

OLD TOWN WALKING TOUR

the right to see the brassware shop, a Tibetan tailor and a noodle-making workshop.

As you head southeast past a small market, curve right to the quiet but interesting **Karmashar Temple (6)**, once the home of the Karmashar, Lhasa's main oracle. Look for the Karmashar statue in the far right corner of the back chapel, decorated with bangles, beads and hair clips, and for the spooky faded icon painted on a pigskin bag in the main hall, pacified with offerings of tsampa and barley beer. There are also some nice original murals on the upper walls. Enter from the south side.

Continue east to a T-junction past outdoor pool tables and blaring video teahouses. At the T-junction take a left to visit the stylish **Dropenling crafts centre** (7; p125), where you can watch local craftsmen from the **Ancient Art Restoration Centre** (🕑 9am-1pm & 2-6pm) across the courtyard, as they grind up mineral paints for thangka-painting and hammer away at metal sculptures.

After loading up with souvenirs, head south towards the **Muslim quarter (8)**, the focus of Lhasa's 2000-strong Muslim population. During Friday lunchtime weekly prayers the quarter is full of men with wispy beards and skullcaps (non-Muslims are denied entry to the mosque itself). Many women here wear black-velvet headscarfs, characteristic of the Linxia region of China's Gansu province. Try a bowl of Muslim noodles at the **Islam Restaurant** (9; p124) if you're feeling peckish.

As you face the mosque, turn right and head southwest past Muslim tea stalls and butcher shops, along part of the Lingkhor pilgrim circuit to the yellow walls of the **Ani Sangkhung Nunnery** (10; 29 Linkuo Nanlu; admission Y30; 🕑 8am-5pm).

This small, friendly and active nunnery is the only one within the precincts of the old Tibetan quarter. The site of the nunnery probably dates back to the 7th century, but it housed a monastery until at least the 15th century. The principal image, upstairs on the 2nd floor, is a thousand-armed Chenresig. A small alley to the side of the main chapel leads down to the former meditation chamber of Songtsen Gampo, the 7th-century king of Tibet. The busy nuns run a great teahouse in the courtyard. Just next to the entrance is an excellent and very friendly **thangka workshop (11)**.

Continue past a second mosque to the **Lho Rigsum Lhakhang (12)**, one of four chapels surrounding the Jokhang at cardinal points. The lovely chapel, almost completely ignored by tourists, has a central statue of Tsepame (Amitayus) flanked by the four main bodhisattvas and its own inner kora. The site is looked after by monks from Ganden Monastery.

Take a right here headed north and then a right, then a left. At the junction you can see the **Rabtse Temple (13)**, affiliated to Sera Monastery.

The alley north takes you to the southeast corner of the Barkhor circuit, where you can continue clockwise to Barkhor Square.

Lingkhor Walking Tour

This walk follows the most interesting section of the city's main pilgrimage circuit, the Lingkhor (see p99). It's best walked in the morning, when you'll be joined by hundreds of Tibetan pilgrims.

The hardest part of this walk is finding the starting point. Take a taxi to Ladefense Restaurant (拉芳舍; Lafang She) or the next-door Xuefeng Binguan hotel (雪峰宾馆) on Jiangsu Lu, opposite the bridge to Sun Island, and look for a scruffy looking alleyway head-

WALK FACTS

Start Jiangsu Lu (Chingdröl Shar Lam)
Finish Potala Palace
Distance 3-4km
Duration Two to three hours

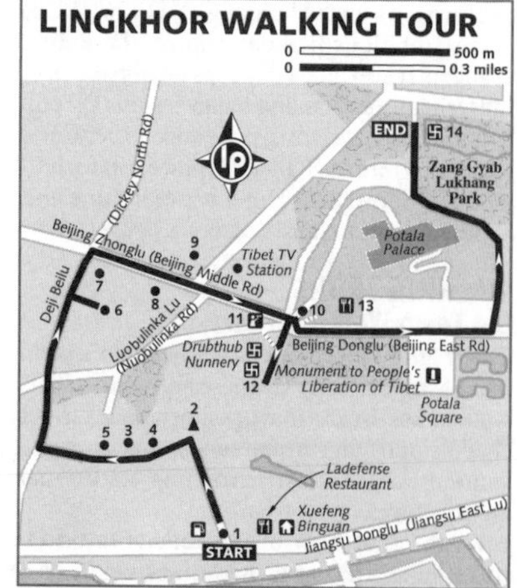

ing north. The alleyway is next to a petrol station and marked by an **incense burner (1)**.

After a couple of hundred metres the alleyway hits the base of **Chagpo Ri** (**2**; 3746m), the Iron Mountain, and continues west past a motley collection of rock paintings, shrines, stone mantras, carved yak skulls, *tsa-tsa* (clay icons) and even flower pots, discarded for good luck. A forest of prayer flags marks a crest in the path and you descend to a collection of **stone carvers (3)**, who tap away in front of sheets of slate. Detour to the right to walk clockwise around a large **chörten (4)**, built entirely of the carvers' mani stones.

Just west of here, at the southwest end of the hill, is a lovely collection of painted **rock carvings** (**5**; admission Y10) centred around a huge image of Tsepame. Altogether there are over 5000 carvings on Chagpo Ri, a tradition that started back in the 7th century and continued for the next thousand years. Pilgrims perform full body prostrations in front of the images, besides several rooms full of glowing butter lamps.

From here head west to Deji Lu (Dickey Lam in Tibetan) and head north through modern Lhasa. Just before you hit Beijing Zhonglu (the second crossroads) follow the alleyway to the right to visit the friendly **Kunde Ling** (**6**; p113). Back at the intersection with Beijing Zhonglu, pilgrims rub their backs, shoulders and hips against a series of polished **holy stones (7)**, in hopes of their healing properties. A couple of minutes' walk east along Beijing Zhonglu is the Chinese-style **Gesar Ling** (**8**; p113), which is also worth a quick visit.

Continue east to the **Golden Yaks statue (9)**, erected for the 40th anniversary of the 'liberation' of Tibet, and pass the Tibet TV station before reaching the former western **city gate** (**10**; Daggo Kani), at the corner of the Potala Palace. Black-and-white photos displayed in the Brahmaputra Grand Hotel (p122) show British Army troops entering the city through the original gate during the invasion of 1903–04.

Climb up to the **viewpoint (11)** just above the white chörten for one of Lhasa's classic photo opportunities. The hilltop behind you was once the site of Lhasa's principal Tibetan medical college, known as the Mentsikhang. Founded in 1413, the college was destroyed in the 1959 popular uprising. An army post means you can no longer climb to the mountain-top for the fine views.

From here, head down the nearby alley, past the Drubthub Nunnery, to visit **Palha Lu-puk** (**12**; p112), the site of Lhasa's earliest religious icons.

Either end the walk here with a well-deserved cup of sweet tea in the hot and humid **cave teahouse (13)** just east of the city gate or, if you have the energy, finish with a quick circuit of the Potala kora (see p112), stopping in at the fabulous murals of the **Lukhang** (**14**; p113) en route.

FESTIVALS & EVENTS

If at all possible, try to time your visit to Lhasa with one of the city's main festivals (p318). The **New Year** and **Saga Dawa** festivals in particular see thousands of pilgrims flood into town, and the city's pilgrim circuits take on a colourful, party atmosphere.

The Saga Dawa festival sees huge numbers of pilgrims making circuits around Lhasa late into the night. The entire 2km length of Deji Lu overflows with thousands of beggars, as rich Tibetans hand out alms from gigantic wads of one-mao notes.

A couple of months later, during the **Chökor Düchen** festival, Lhasa residents trek up to the summit of Gambo Ütse Ri, the high peak behind Drepung Monastery. In olden days even the Dalai Lama would ascend the peak, riding atop a white yak.

SLEEPING

The Tibetan-style accommodation around the old town is easily the most interesting place in which to be based. Several new midrange and upmarket options here means there's now something for everyone. Apart from the hotels listed here there are dozens of shiny, characterless Chinese-style hotels scattered around town. You might find yourself in one of these if you arrive on a tour or book a hotel online.

Prices given here (and throughout this book) apply to the high season from May to early October (see p314). If things are quiet (and certainly from mid-October to April), expect a discount of 25% to 50% on the room rates listed here.

Several new hostels, popular with the ever-increasing number of Chinese backpackers, are giving the long-established Tibetan places a run for their money. Note that most of the budget places don't accept reservations. You may have to hunt around for a room in the peak months of July and August and during Chinese holidays.

Budget

Apart from the places mentioned below, there is an increasing number of small and simple family-run guesthouses hidden in the backstreets of the Tibetan quarter, mostly frequented by Chinese backpackers. See also the Yak Hotel (opposite) for cheap dorm beds.

Dongcuo International Youth Hostel (Dongcuo Guoji Qingnian Lüguan; Map p100; ☎ 627 3388; www.yhalasa.com; 10 Beijing Donglu; dm Y15-20, s/d/tr/q without bathroom Y80/90/105/120, s/d/t with bathroom Y100/140/180; 💻) This Chinese-run hostel attracts both foreign backpackers and Chinese adventurers and has a quite different feel from the Tibetan-run places. Rooms are smallish but well maintained, with wooden floors and crisp white sheets, though a few don't have any exterior windows. The bunk-bed style dorms vary in size – the best deal is a bed in a triple for Y35. Hot water is available from 8pm to 7am in the rooms with bathrooms, or 24 hours in the common showers.

Banak Shol (Balangxue Lüguan; Map p100; ☎ 632 3829; 8 Beijing Donglu; dm/s/d Y20/30/60, d with bathroom Y100-160) Once *the* place to stay back in the early days of independent travel, the Banak Shol is looking pretty tired these days. It's still got several things going for it, including the good Nam-tso Restaurant (p123), reliable luggage storage and pleasant wooden verandas, but the staff seem jaded, the walls of the cheaper rooms are paperthin, and most rooms look onto either the noisy main road or a courtyard that seems perpetually full of reversing Land Cruisers. The doubles with a hot-water bathroom are among the cheapest such rooms in Lhasa, but they aren't terribly well maintained. Other plus points include an efficient branch of FIT and free laundry (though the staff won't touch your crusty socks after a week's trekking!). The majority of the guests these days are Chinese backpackers. The hotel doesn't accept reservations.

Snowlands Hotel (雪域宾馆 Xueyu Binguan; Map p100; ☎ 632 3687; fax 632 7145; 4 Zangyiyuan Lu; dm/d/tr Y25/60-80/105, d/deluxe d with bathroom Y250/350; 💻) Snowlands is another of Lhasa's old-timers. It was a favourite with backpackers and carpet-traders back in the 1980s, but the mood has changed a bit since then. Despite the almost perfect location beside Barkhor Square, Snowlands is quieter than both the Yak and the Banak Shol, largely because the standards are lower. The cheaper rooms suffer from paper-thin walls, the shower block is hit-and-miss and there's a frustrating lack of washbasins. Quiet but dark doubles with bathroom are discounted to Y100 in the low season and come with a heater. The deluxe rooms offer new beds and Tibetan décor. Laundry costs Y2 per piece.

Kirey Hotel (Jiri Lüguan; Map p100; ☎ 632 3462; 105 Beijing Donglu; dm/d/t Y25/60/90, d with bathroom Y80-100; 💻) The third of Lhasa's old-timers, the Kirey deserves more custom than it gets. It is friendly and clean, and has reliable hot water (9am to 9pm) in the shower block around the back. The Tashi II restaurant is on the premises and there's lots of balcony sitting space and a good internet café. Laundry service is free – put your washing in the bags provided and hand it in to reception before 9am. The main grumbles we have are the scarcity of sinks and the crummy shared toilets. The dim doubles with private bathroom at the back of the courtyard aren't really up to much either, though the upstairs rooms are better. The Y60 doubles offer perhaps the best value.

Barkhor Namchen House (Bakuo Longqian Jiating Lüguan; Map p100; ☎ 656 3009; info@shangrilatours.com; dm Y25, s Y60-70, d Y70; 💻) This promising new Tibetan-style guesthouse is a better budget choice. The old-town location just off the Barkhor is near perfect, the staff are friendly, and the common bathrooms and hot showers are superclean. The lounge area catches the winter sun and offers internet access, or head to the good rooftop restaurant for fine views. Some rooms have limited natural light; the upper-floor rooms are brighter. All rooms share the bathroom block.

Phuntsok Khasang International Youth Hostel (平措康桑青年旅舍; Pingcuo Kangsang Qingnian Lüshe; Map p100; ☎ 691 5222; www.tibetinn.cn; 48 Qingnian Lu; dm Y30-60, s/d/tr Y180/210/240) Lhasa's second Chinese-run youth hostel feels a bit too much like *Cell Block H* for us, with grafittied hallways and rooms set around an echoey courtyard. Useful perks include free breakfast, sitting areas, a laundry service and baggage storage. Prices swing wildly with the season, tripling from May to August, but are decent value in the low season (high-season rates are listed here). All of the 70 rooms, even dorms, have their own bathrooms and there are some Japanese-style rooms.

Barkhor Norzeng Hotel (Bajiaojie Nuoseng Binguan; Map p100; ☎ 633 5199; fax 691 6038; dm Y30-50, d/tr Y150/220) The top floor of the Namsel Department Store is not where you'd expect to find this decent modern option. The interior views of the department store aren't quite what you came to Lhasa for, but the spacious rooms are comfortable and bathrooms are clean. The five-bed room with bathroom is a bargain at Y50 per bed. The cheapest rooftop rooms look like they'd be hot in summer, but are cheap at Y30 per bed and you can use the hot shower in another room for Y5. The hotel is accessed down an alley beside the department store. The rooftop Tibetan restaurant has awesome views over the Jokhang without another tourist in sight.

Flora Hotel (Hadahuashen Lüguan; Map p100; ☎ 632 4491; www.florahtl.piczo.com; Hebalin Lu; dm Y35, s/d/tr with bathroom Y150/200) The Flora is a well-run and reliable hotel in the interesting Muslim quarter (it's run by a Nepali Muslim). Nice touches include a minibar at local-shop prices, a stock of foreign magazines and a laundry service. The decent but slightly cramped four-bed dorms out the back (with attached toilet and shared hot shower) offer a quiet alternative to the backpacker hotels of Lhasa. There's also a good but rather glum Nepali restaurant here. Prices generally include breakfast. Credit cards and bookings are accepted.

Oh Dan Guest House Annex (Oudan Lüguan; Map p96; ☎ 633 8104; 38 Xiaozhaosi Lu; s/d/tr without bathroom Y40/60/90) Ah, this new place could be so good. The Tibetan-style courtyard architecture lends a cosy vibe, the three-bed rooms are spacious, and the clean common hot showers come with heat lamps. Unfortunately the Tibetan-style mattresses were infested with bedbugs during our last visit, the lights were dim and it can be noisy. These may just be teething troubles (it opened at the time of writing) so give it a chance, but check the mattresses first.

Pilgrimages Inn (Miaojixiang Lüguan; Map p96; ☎ 634 1999; www.mjixiang.com; 15 Xiaozhaosi Lu; s/d/tr Y60/80/110, d with bathroom Y220) Like so many of Lhasa guesthouses, this Taiwanese-run place is built around an echoey internal courtyard, which makes it noisy. The sterile red carpets and white walls scream out for some homey touches but the rooms are clean, comfortable and good value, with a clean shared Western-style bathroom. The rooms with bathroom have better quality beds and some even have views of the nearby Ramoche Temple.

Mandala Hotel (Manzhai Jiudian; Map p100; ☎ 633 8940; fax 632 4787; 31 South Barkhor; s/d/tr with bathroom Y168/268/368) If you're more interested in what's going on outside your window than inside the room, then try the Mandala, with its superb location just off the Barkhor. The rooms are certainly nothing special, with tired carpets and dim lighting, but the views of the Barkhor circuit (from rooms 305 to 311 and 205 to 211) are priceless. If you do get a bum room just head to the Nepali-style rooftop restaurant to savour the Jokhang views over a cup of masala tea. The Mandala is one of the few budget places to accept reservations.

Midrange

See also the Banak Shol and Snowlands hotels in the Budget listings (opposite) for good-value midrange rooms.

Yak Hotel (Yake Binguan; Map p100; ☎ 632 3496; 100 Beijing Donglu; dm Y30, d without bathroom Y200, d with bathroom Y450-550; 💻 ❄) The wildly popular and well-run Yak has gone seriously upscale in recent years, though the popular (but cramped) dorm rooms are still hanging on, just. For a double with bathroom choose between the colourful Tibetan-style décor of the back block or the larger but noisier deluxe rooms overlooking the main street. Useful perks include good internet access, an open-air rooftop Nepali restaurant and bicycle hire (Y30 per day). Rooms are often occupied by tour groups, so book ahead.

Gorkha Hotel (Guo'erka Fandian; Map p100; ☎ 627 2222; tibetgorkha7l@hotmail.com; 45 Linkuo Nanlu; dm Y80, tr without bathroom Y240, r Y388, ste Y867-889; 💻) This atmospheric Nepali–Tibetan venture is a nice blend of cultures, from the Tibetan-style entry murals and traditional architecture to the photographs of Nepali royalty and fine Nepali-style restaurant on the roof. The back block housed the Nepali consulate in the 1950s. The rooms are set around a pleasant courtyard but are dark and some are better than others, so take a look at a few. All in all, it's a good choice. The hotel is in the south of the old town, near several lovely old temples. A small chapel on the roof is dedicated to the deity Ekajati.

Oh Dan Guest House (Oudan Binguan; Map p100; ☎ 634 4999; ohdan_guesthouse@yahoo.com; 15 Xiaozhaosi Lu; d with/without bathroom Y368/258, discounts of 30-60%; 💻 ❄) One of several hotels owned by the Oh Dan group, this is a good lower midrange Tibetan-run choice with an interesting location on the pedestrian street leading to the Ramoche Temple (taxis can't go up this street during the day). The rooms are spacious and clean, though only the top-floor rooms get much natural light. The English-speaking staff are helpful; for Y20 they'll even teach you how to make *momos* (dumplings)! The cosy restaurant is a nice refuge and serves good breakfasts (try the breakfast burrito) and Nepali dishes.

our pick **Kyichu Hotel** (Jiqu Fandian; Map p100; ☎ 633 1541; www.kyichuhotel.com; 149 Beijing Donglu; s/d/tr Y380/480/560, ste Y680;) The two-star Kyichu is a friendly and well-run choice that's very popular with repeat travellers to Tibet. The 52 rooms are simple but pleasant, with Tibetan carpets and private bathrooms, but the real selling points are the location and excellent service. There's also a good restaurant, a small library of books and, that rarest of Lhasa commodities – a lovely garden retreat (with wi-fi). Ask for a garden-view room at the back, as these are the quietest. A 20% winter discount is given from November to April. Reservations are essential in summer. Credit cards are accepted.

Dhood Gu Hotel (Dungu Binguan; Map p100; ☎ 632 2555; www.dhodguhotel.com; near the Tromsikhang market; s/d/tr Y420/520/640, Potala-view d Y600, ste Y940;) If you're looking for a dash of style, this comfortable Nepali-run three-star place is another good choice, with ornate Tibetan-style décor, a decent restaurant (Y40 buffet) and a superb location in the old town. Breakfast is included and rooms come with modern bathrooms, though the singles are cramped and some rooms lack views. The rooftop bar has fine Potala views. Credit cards are accepted.

Xiongbala Hotel (Xiongbala Dajiudian; Map p100; ☎ 633 8888; xingbl@public.ls.xz.cn; 28 Jiangsu Lu; s/d Y468/518, discounts of 20%;) This is a relatively new and well-run three-star Chinese hotel with a good location on the southern edge of the old town. Facilities include a coffee bar, sauna, business centre and several restaurants. West-facing rooms offer views of the Potala from the 5th floor.

Himalaya Hotel (Ximalaya Fandian; Map p96; ☎ 632 1111; fax 623 2675; 6 Linkuo Donglu; s/d Y536/728, deluxe r Y827, discounts of up to 40%) The overhauled rooms in this modern Chinese hotel make this a decent choice, particularly when discounted to Y400. Heat lamps in the bathrooms and photos of Tibet on the walls add a vague sense of style, though the single rooms are small. Most rooms have oxygen machines. The location isn't very convenient. Credit cards are accepted.

Shangbala Hotel (Xiangbala Jiudian; Map p100; ☎ 632 3888; www.tibetshangbalahotel.com; 1 Danjielin Lu; s/d Y580/680, discounts of up to 40%) Not to be confused with the Xiongbala Hotel, this modern blockhouse is totally out of place in its Tibetan surroundings, but it's popular with groups who want to be close to the Barkhor. Rooms are bland but reassuring, with clean bathrooms and good views from the 4th floor. You can't beat the location, just off Zangyiyuan Lu.

Loads of new hotels are being built around town. The new three-star block of the **Gang Gyan Hotel** (Gangjian Lasa Fandian; Map p100; 83 Beijing Donglu) is bound to be popular when it opens in 2008.

A new 16-room Tibetan-style hotel is being built next to Dropenling (see p125) and should be well done. Standard rooms, suites and rooms without bathroom are planned.

Top End

Brahmaputra Grand Hotel (Yaluzangbu Dajiudian; (Map p96; ☎ 630 9999; www.tibethotel.cn; Section B, Yangcheng Plaza, Gongbutang Lu; s/d Y980/1800;) The brainchild of China's Hongyan supermarket baron, Tibet's first five-star hotel occupies a space somewhere between hotel and ethnographic museum. The excellent lighting accentuates hundred of exhibits, from antique opera masks to armour, to create a mood that is at once grand and intimate, and that's just the corridors! You could easily spend an hour wandering the exhibits, even if you're not staying here. The rooms are comfortable and well designed but less remarkable than the public areas; ask for an upper-floor room with a view over the city. The cheapest singles are worth avoiding.

Lhasa Hotel (Lasa Fandian; Map p96; ☎ 683 2221; www.lhasahotel.com.cn; 1 Minzu Nanlu; standard/deluxe d Y1051/1368, Tibetan-style d Y1602, Tibetan ste Y2410;) In 1997 Holiday Inn pulled out of Tibet under increasing pressure from pro-Tibetan groups, and handed this hotel back to the government, who presumably didn't spend a lot of time agonising over its new name. Standards have certainly slid since then and only tour groups and the relatively clueless stay here these days. There is still a selection of restaurants, a clinic with both Western and Tibetan doctors, satellite TV and a dirty pool (summer only), but the putting-green carpets don't exactly scream cool and the staff appear to be a little glum. Still, it's a city landmark. Credit cards are accepted.

House of Shambhala (Map p100; ☎ 632 6533; www.houseofshambhala.com; 7 Jiri Erxiang; d incl breakfast US$60-90) Hidden in the old town in a historic Tibetan building, the Shambhala is Tibet's first real boutique hotel. The 10 rooms, decorated in wood and stone with antique Tibetan furniture, are perfect for those who prefer atmosphere over modern amenities. You'll have to fend off a lot of New Age nonsense, especially at the small spa. As with much of the hotel, the witty restaurant menu serves up its fare with a generous slice of bullsh** – try the 'Guru Rinpoche chicken tikka' or the 'Heinrich Harrer schnitzel'! The fabulous rooftop terrace is a great place to relax over a 'flaming dakini' (lassi yoghurt, Cointreau and rum set ablaze; Y88). Just don't take it as seriously as the owners seem to.

Several top-end hotels are planned in Lhasa over the coming years. The St Regis and Banyan hotels are due to open in 2010, with perhaps the Best Western and Crowne Plaza to follow.

EATING

The best places for breakfast are probably the Dunya and Nam-tso restaurants. All the eateries listed serve lunch and dinner, but you will struggle to find a meal after about 9.30pm.

Most individual travellers eat in the Tibetan quarter around the Barkhor Square area and there are plenty of great restaurants to try.

WESTERN

our pick **Tashi I** (Map p100; cnr Zangyiyuan Lu & Beijing Donglu; mains Y10-25; 8am-10pm) We've been coming to this Lhasa institution for over 20 years now and, despite increased competition, it's still a favourite. The service is friendly, the prices are cheap and everything on the revitalised menu is decent. Special praise is reserved for the *bobis* (chapati-like unleavened bread), which come with seasoned cream cheese and fried vegetables or meat. Tashi's cheesecakes (Y6) have been eclipsed by other restaurants' desserts in recent years but they are still a treat. Menu in English.

Tashi II (Map p100; ☎ 632 3462; Beijing Donglu; mains Y10-25) Located in the Kirey Hotel, Tashi II offers the same menu as Tashi I but is quieter and has a spruced-up interior. Menu in English.

Dunya Restaurant (Map p100; ☎ 633 3374; www.dunyarestaurant.com; 100 Beijing Donglu; dishes Y18-40) With sophisticated décor, excellent and wide-ranging food (from yak enchiladas to Indonesian noodles), this cosy foreign-run place feels like a 'real' restaurant. It's pricier than most other places in town but the food is authentic, from the oregano-flavoured pizza crust to the Italian imported pasta. The homemade sandwiches and soups are good for lunch, and this is one place where you can tuck into a salad without worrying about getting sick. Menu in English.

our pick **Nam-tso Restaurant** (Map p100; Banak Shol hotel; mains Y20, set breakfast Y20-25) This old-timer is still one of the top hotel-restaurants. Prices are a little higher than at the Tashi restaurants, but dishes stretch to vegetarian lasagne, burritos and yak burgers, and the sunny roof seating is one of the few places in town to sit outdoors. The chicken sizzler (Y25) is the classic Lhasa meal. The restaurant's breakfasts (muesli brought in from Kathmandu, among other things) have also achieved a devoted following. Menu in English.

Snowland Restaurant (Xueyu Canting; Map p100; ☎ 632 0821; Zangyiyuan Lu; dishes Y25-35) Attached to the Snowlands Hotel, this is a more upmarket and very popular place that serves a mix of excellent Continental and Nepali food in very civilised surroundings. The Indian dishes are particularly good, especially the small but tasty chicken tikka masala (Y20). The cakes are easily the best in town. Menu in English.

TIBETAN, CHINESE & MUSLIM

Kagui Nongmo Sakhang (Map p100; ☎ 632 7902; Yutuo Lu; mains Y6-20) This traditional Tibetan-style restaurant is a great place to take a Tibetan friend and try out local dishes without feeling overwhelmed (there's a picture menu for easy ordering). It has a good range of Tibetan and Chinese dishes, from curried potatoes to sweet-and-sour ribs, and the friendly Tibetan staff are very helpful.

Lanqing Qingzhen Fanguan (Map p100; Beijing Donglu; dishes Y6-45) There are several Muslim restaurants in the old town but this one is unique in having cosy Tibetan-style seating in the side room. The Xinjiang specialty *xiaopanji* (小盘鸡; Y25) – chicken in a sauce with potatoes and carrots on a bed of noodles – is bony but very tasty. The photo menu on the wall is a help, though the images bear only a passing resemblance to the real thing.

For lunch try one of the noodle dishes, such as *chaomianpian* (fried noodle squares) or *ganbanmian* (a kind of stir-fried spaghetti bolognaise) – see p77 for details.

Pentoc Tibetan Restaurant (Map p100; dishes Y7-12) For something more authentically Tibetan, charming English-speaking Pentoc runs this local teahouse restaurant after working in Tashi I for many years. The menu includes breakfast (eggs, Tibetan bread, pancake, curd) and it's a good place to try homemade Tibetan standards, such as *momos*, *thugpa* (noodles), *shemdre* (rice, potato and yak meat), plus butter tea and *chang* (barley beer). It's 20m down an alleyway off Beijing Donglu, on the left. Menu in English.

Feijie Restaurant (Map p100; Beijing Donglu; dishes Y7-20) Across from the Banak Shol hotel, this simple Sichuanese restaurant offers good, cheap Chinese dishes and is one of the few to have an English menu.

Norzing Selchung Tashi Yamphel Restaurant (Map p96; Xiaozhaosi Lu; dishes Y10-25) Superconvenient if you're visiting the next-door Ramoche Temple, this pleasant upstairs Tibetan restaurant offers great views over the street below from the low Tibetan-style tables. Try the set meal of *shemdre* (rice, potato and yak meat) for Y10 or choose something more adventurous from the photo menu, such as the tiger-skin chillies.

Islam Restaurant (Yisilan Fanzhuang; Map p100; ☎ 633 9258; noodles Y6-10, meat dishes Y15-35) For the most authentic Muslim food head to the Muslim district and particularly the Islam Restaurant. Invest in a cup of Muslim tea (*babao wanzi;* Y3) and a bowl of Xinjiang noodles (Y10) and watch the chefs at work in the open kitchen – but note that the English menu is more expensive than the Chinese.

Holy Land Vegetarian Restaurant (Shendi Su Canting; Map p96; ☎ 636 3851; 10 Linkuo Beilu; dishes Y10-25) Vegetarians don't need to worry about the 'soy fish' or 'soy chicken feet', this is 100% vegetarian food, dressed up to resemble meat dishes. The wooden tables and Buddhist images on the wall give the place a simple Zen-like atmosphere. The English and picture menus help things along.

NEPALI

With the arrival of half-a-dozen Nepali restaurants, Lhasa now rivals Kathmandu in its range of foreign foods (though prices are a bit higher). All offer a mix of Indian, pseudo-Chinese and Western dishes for about Y25, with Indian veggie dishes cheaper at Y10 to 12. If you're hankering for enchiladas, chocolate pudding, peach lassis and other Nepali backpacker favourites, make a beeline for these places.

New Mandala Restaurant (Map p100; ☎ 634 2235; west of Barkhor Sq; dishes Y15-25) This Nepali-run restaurant is definitely a winner for its fine views over the Barkhor, either from the 2nd floor or the sunny rooftop. The inside features some lovely and ornate Tibetan murals. It also sells packaged Nepali foods such as muesli and soup mixes. The owner runs the Tashi restaurants in Shigatse and Tsetang. Menu in English.

Mandala Restaurant (Map p100; ☎ 632 9645; Mandala Hotel, 31 South Barkhor; dishes Y15-30) Perfect for a post-kora meal, this cosy place on the Barkhor circuit offers a wide range of dishes from Indian curries to pizza, plus a few special-occasion Tibetan dishes and decent breakfasts. The Indian dishes can be a bit bland, so ask for the 'real' spices if that's how you like it. In summer grab a seat on the rooftop for awesome views of the Jokhang. Menu in English.

Tengyelink Café (Map p100; ☎ 632 3866; Zangyiyuan Lu; dishes Y25) This warm and cosy restaurant is popular with both foreigners and Tibetans, so get here early for a good table. The Chinese and Western dishes are joined by a good range of Tibetan, Thai and even Korean options. Service is good and it's a well-run place. The cakes are discounted after 9pm. Menu in English.

DRINKING

Bars

There's not a great deal in the way of entertainment options in Lhasa. In the evening most travellers head to one of the restaurants in the Tibetan quarter and then retire to the roof of the Yak or Banak Shol hotels (see Sleeping, p119) for a cold Lhasa Beer.

Makye Amye (Map p100; ☎ 632 8608; Barkhor; drinks Y8-23, mains Y20-38) The past is tastier than the present at this watering hole overlooking the Barkhor. If the stories are to be believed, this was once a drinking haunt of the licentious sixth Dalai Lama, who met the famed Tibetan beauty Makye Amye here and composed a famous poem about her. Tour groups and Chinese tourists are drawn to the views of the Barkhor from the window tables and fine rooftop terrace, but the food is just so-so.

Dunya (Map p100; 100 Beijing Donglu; beer Y12) The upstairs bar at this popular restaurant (see p123) is a favourite of both local expats and tour groups. Friday's happy hour means a Y2 discount between 7pm and 9.30pm.

Music Kitchen (Yinyue Chufang; Map p96; ☎ 681 2980; 77 Beijing Xilu; beer Y12-15) Part of a string of bars and restaurants across from the Lhasa Hotel, this Tibetan-owned place was one of the city's first and still boasts some of the best music in town, with live bands at the weekend, a full dinner menu, and just the right aroma of late-night booze and depravity.

Teahouses & Cafés

Summit Café (Dingfeng Meiyishu Kafeidian; Map p100; ☎ 691 3884; www.thetibetsummitcafe.com; 1 Danjielin Lu; coffee Y15-25; 7.30am-10pm;) With authentic espresso coffee and smoothies, sofas that you could lose yourself in, free wi-fi and melt-in-your-mouth desserts, this American-style coffeehouse is caffeine nirvana for Starbucks-addicts and latte lovers. It's in the courtyard of the Shangbala Hotel, off Zangyiyuan Lu.

There are several Tibetan teahouses around town where you can grab a cheap cup of *cha ngamo* (sweet tea). Most of them are grungy Tibetan-only places, blasted by high-decibel kung fu videos, but there are a few exceptions. **Turquoise Dragon Teahouse** (Map p100; cnr Beijing Donglu & Xiaozhaosi Lu) is a Tibetan-style place with a fine balcony overlooking Beijing Donglu. The bustling local **teahouse** (Map p100; Zangyiyuan Lu) underneath the Tashi Takgay Hotel is very central and full of colour, though the **Ani Sangkhung Nunnery teahouse** (Map p100; 29 Linkuo Nanlu) is probably the nicest for a quiet cup of tea.

ENTERTAINMENT

Unfortunately there is little in the way of cultural entertainment in Lhasa. Restaurants like the Shangrila in the courtyard of the Kirey Hotel have free song-and-dance performances for diners (buffet Y50). For authentic performances of Tibetan opera and dancing you'll probably have to wait for one of Lhasa's festivals (p318).

Shöl Opera Troupe (Map p96; ☎ 632 1111; 6 Linkuo Donglu) Performs a selection of Tibetan operas nightly at 7.30pm at the Himalaya Hotel. Tickets for the 90-minute show cost Y100, and there's a small museum on site.

For something a bit earthier there are several Tibetan *nangma* dance halls around town, which offer a mildly nationalistic mix of disco, traditional Tibetan line dancing, lots of beer and a bit of Chinese karaoke thrown in for good measure. Locations change regularly, so ask a Tibetan friend for the best places.

SHOPPING

You can get most things in Lhasa these days, though items such as medical supplies, books, water-purifying tablets and deodorant are still not easy to find.

Lhasa Department Store (Lasa Baihuo Dalou; Map p96; cnr Kangangduo Nanlu & Yutuo Lu) A good one-stop shop for most supplies, especially clothes, though it's a little pricier than elsewhere.

Photography

It is still a good idea to bring your own film supplies, but these days most flavours of memory card, camera batteries and print film are relatively easy to find in Lhasa (although bring your own slide film). A profusion of **photographic shops** (Map p96; Kangangduo Lu) to the east of the Potala Square offer digital prints from around Y1 per print.

Souvenirs

The Barkhor circuit (p102) is lined with stalls selling everything a visiting Tibetan or tourist might possibly need. Expect to be asked an outrageous initial price and then settle down for some serious and persistent haggling. Popular purchases include prayer wheels, rings, daggers, prayer scarves and prayer flags, all of which are fairly portable. Most of the stuff on offer is actually made in Nepal and sold by Chinese or Hui Muslim traders. Items of Tibetan clothing, such as *chubas* (long-sleeved sheepskin cloaks), Tibetan dresses, cowboy hats, Chinese silk jackets, Tibetan brocade and fur hats, are good buys.

The majority of shops in the Barkhor sell jewellery, most of it turquoise and coral and almost all of it fake (p325).

There are a couple of thangka workshops (Map p100) just south of the Barkhor circuit and several others in the surrounding backstreets.

Dropenling (Map p100; ☎ 636 0558; www.tibetcraft.com; 11 Chaktsalgang Lam; 10am-8pm) Run by the Tibetan Artisans Initiative, this nonprofit enterprise aims to bolster traditional Tibetan handicrafts in the face of rising Chinese and Nepali imports. Products are of high quality and employ traditional techniques (natural dyes, wool not acrylic cloth etc) updated with contemporary designs. Prices are fixed, with proceeds going back to artisans in the form of wages and social funds. Artefacts for sale include woolly carpets from the Wangden region of southern Tsang, UNDP-supported weavings and silverware, Tibetan aprons, leather appliqué bags, table runners and horse blankets. Credit cards are accepted (with a 4.2% fee), as are US dollars, and it can arrange international shipping. See also p117.

Snow Leopard Carpet Industries (Map p100; ☎ 632 1481; snowleopardcarpet@yahoo.com; 2 Zangyiyuan Lu) Next to the Snowland Restaurant, this place sells a collection of high-quality carpets and can arrange delivery abroad.

Mani Thangka Arts (Map p100; ☎ 657 7307; Zangyiyuan Lu) Opposite the Shangbala Hotel, Mani Thangka Arts features thangkas made with mineral paints by local artist Phurbu Tsering. Most of the other thangka shops are owned by Chinese traders who sell Nepali imports.

For higher-quality items at higher prices, try shops like the **Dorje Antique Shop** (Map p100; Beijing Donglu), opposite the Yak Hotel, and the **Kyichu Art Gallery** (Map p100; 149 Beijing Donglu) in the Kyichu Hotel.

There are several Tibetan dress shops on Beijing Donglu where you can get a formal Tibetan dress made or buy off the rack. One good place is opposite the Kyichu Hotel.

Supermarkets

Lhasa's glittering new supermarkets now offer a staggering range of imported goods, from frozen squid to ripe pineapples, alongside a bewildering array of dried yak meat. **Baiyi Supermarket** (Baiyi Chaoshi; Map p96; Beijing Donglu; 🕑 10am-9pm), next to Lhasa Department Store, boasts Lhasa's best range of foodstuffs, though the nearby **Hongyan Supermarket** (Map p96; Beijing Donglu; 🕑 9am-10.30pm) and **Sifang Supermarket** (Map p100; Beijing Donglu; 🕑 9am-10pm), the latter closest to the old town, are also good.

Tromsikhang Market (Map p100) This bazaar-style area in the old town has the widest selection of dried fruits and nuts and is the place to buy such Tibetan specialties as tsampa and yak butter.

The old town has a couple of Tibetan-run Nepali supermarkets selling everything from imported muesli and chocolate spread to Indian spices and peanut butter, though at prices higher than in Nepal.

Norling Supermarket (Nuolin Chaoshi; Map p100; 20 Linkuo Donglu) Located near the Muslim quarter, this has one of the widest selections.

Cheese-heads desperate for a lactose fix can try the Dunya (p123) and Nam-tso (p123) restaurants for locally made yak cheese by the pound.

Travel & Trekking Equipment

To find basic items, such as thermoses and water canisters, the best places are the lanes that run from the Tromsikhang Market down to the Barkhor circuit. Cheap pots and pans (ideal for instant noodles) are available at the stalls on the east side of the Potala, north of the Airway Hotel. For hard-to-find items such as, sunscreen and deodorant, dig around in the Nepali-stocked shops dotted around the Barkhor circuit.

Outlook Outdoor Equipment (Map p100; ☎/fax 633 8890; 11 Beijing Donglu; 🕑 9.30am-9pm) This fine trekking shop across from the Kirey Hotel has Western-quality sleeping bags, Gore-Tex jackets and tents, plus hard-to-find imported knick-knacks like altimeters, trekking socks and Primus cook sets. Gear is also available for rent (Y10 for a stove, Y25 for a tent).

There are now dozens of other trekking shops on Beijing Donglu and Zangyiyuan Lu, though most offer low-quality Nepali- or Chinese-made knock-offs.

GETTING THERE & AWAY

While there are a number of ways to get to Lhasa, the most popular routes are by air from Chengdu (in Sichuan), by train from Xining, and overland or by air from Kathmandu. For details of getting *into* Tibet, see p333.

Air

Flying *out* of Lhasa is considerably easier and cheaper than flying in. No permits are necessary – just turn up to the **Civil Aviation Authority of China office** (CAAC; Zhongguo Minhang; Map p96; ☎ 683 3446; 1 Niangre Lu; 🕑 9.30am-8pm) and buy a ticket. In August and around national holidays (p318), you'd be wise to book your ticket at least a week in advance.

To book a ticket you need to complete a form, get a reservation and then pay the cashier (cash only). You can buy onward tickets from Chengdu here, but not at discounted prices.

Bus & Minibus

TO/FROM CHINA

The arrival of the train has pushed the sleeper buses into irrelevancy. There are still daily sleeper services to Golmud (Y150 to 200, 20 hours), Xining (Y340, 2½ days) and even Chengdu (Y500, three days and four nights, via Golmud) but these must surely be an endangered species.

TO/FROM NEPAL

With the twice-weekly Lhasa–Kathmandu bus off limits to foreigners (see p335), you're left with hiring a Land Cruiser or looking out for the occasional advertisements posted around the Tibetan quarter for seats in nonstop minibuses or Land Cruisers to Zhangmu. Seats cost around Y350 to 450 for the overnight trip.

AROUND TIBET

Buses to popular pilgrim destinations leave early in the morning from the west side of Barkhor Square. Buses leave around 6.30am and 7.30am for Ganden Monastery (Y20 return, 1½ hours), 7am for Tsurphu Monastery (Y25 return, 2½ hours), 7.30am for Drak Yerpa (Y20 return), and 7.30am for Tsetang (Shannan; Y30) and Dranang (Y25). For Samye one direct bus runs via the bridge east of Tsetang (Y40, 3½ hours, 6am), while a second runs to the ferry only (Y25, 7.30am); see p172. For the direct bus buy your ticket the day before from the tin shack just north of the square on Zangyiyuan Lu. Buses depart when full, so expect lots of hanging around.

At the time of research the main **Western Bus Station** (Xijiao Keyunzhan; Map p96) wasn't selling bus tickets to foreigners. In case this changes there are services to Shigatse (Y50 to 60, 3½ hours, every 30 minutes), Tsetang (Y30 to 40, every 30 minutes), Nagchu (Y53, six hours, hourly) and Chamdo (nonsleeper Y280, three days). You might have more luck getting on one of the private minibuses or cars that wait to the side of the buses. A seat in a car costs about double the bus fare.

Your best bet to Shigatse are the private buses that leave from between the Yak and Kirey hotels on Beijing Donglu between 8am and 9am. Some are reluctant to take foreigners but most are more than happy to take your money. Private buses also depart from here around 7.30am for Nagchu (Naqu; Y53) and Damxung (Dangxiong; Y44).

A government bus to Shigatse (Y55) waits east of the Kirey Hotel to pick up passengers at around 8.30am, though staff are reluctant to sell foreigners a ticket. For Gyantse you'll probably have to take a bus to Shigatse and change there.

The **Eastern Bus Station** (Dongjiao Keyunzhan; Map p96) has frequent minibuses to Lhundrub (Linzhou; Y15) and Medro Gongkar (Mozhu Gongka; Y15), from outside the main station. Inside there are daily buses to Drigung Til (Y30, 7am) and Reting Monastery (Y40, 8am), among others. The frequent buses to Bayi (Y80 to Y100) are normally off limits to foreigners.

Lhasa's chaotic **Lugu Bus Stand** (Map p100) is southwest of the Barkhor Square and has several departures daily to Chushul, Yangpachen and Nyemo, but timings are awkward and information hard to find.

Lhasa's **Northern Bus Station** (Beijiao Qiche Keyunzhan; Map p129) has sleeper buses to Ali in western Tibet, operated by Tibetan Antelope Travel and Transportation Co (see p226). Officials wouldn't sell tickets to foreigners at the time of research but in case things change buses run every other day at around 5pm and take around 60 hours nonstop. Berths cost Y651, Y701 or Y751, depending on the location in the bus (the cheaper berths are at the back). Buses also run from this station to Zhangmu, Yadong, Markham, Zhongdian and Shigatse, but foreigners can't take them.

Rental Vehicles

Rental vehicles have emerged as the most popular way to get away from Lhasa in recent years, even though you can still travel along many of the main routes by public transport.

At the time of research, all Land Cruiser trips were supposed to be organised through the government-owned FIT (p100), though for trips around the Lhasa region (which require no permits) there is nothing to stop you negotiating with a private driver or other travel agency.

The popular seven-day trip to the Nepali border via Yamdrok-tso, Gyantse, Shigatse, Sakya and Everest Base Camp (see p20) costs between Y5500 and Y6500. The price includes permits and a guide but not entry fees nor the Y405 vehicle fee to enter the Qomolangma Nature Preserve. A return six-day trip to Everest Base Camp costs around Y5000.

If you are heading to the Yarlung Valley, a three- or four-day trip to Samye, Mindroling Monastery, Tsetang and back again costs Y2500 to Y2800 (including a guide and permits), or add on Gyantse and Shigatse for a total of Y4000.

For the rates of other popular Land Cruiser trips, see p163 and p152. For general advice on vehicle rental see p343.

Train

After years of waiting, it's now possible to do the hitherto impossible; take a train up onto the Tibetan plateau all the way to Lhasa. There are daily trains to/from Beijing, Xining/Lanzhou and Chengdu/Chongqing, and services either daily or every other day to Xi'an, Shanghai and Guangzhou. See p339 for fares and other details. All trains from Lhasa depart in the morning and all trains to Lhasa arrive in the evening. The train station is 4km southwest of town. A service to Shigatse is due to begin in 2009.

You can buy train tickets up to 10 days in advance at the Lhasa **train station ticket office** (7am-10pm) or the more centrally located **city ticket office** (Map p96; Luobulinka Lu; 8am-6pm) next to the TTB office.

To get from the train station into town take bus 89 (see right) to the centre or take bus 91 over the Lhasa Bridge to the terminus near the Eastern Bus Station and then hop on bus 97 to Beijing Donglu. To get *to* the station catch bus 89 just south of the Barkhor on Jiangsu Lu or take bus 91/97 in the opposite direction. Buses run every 20 minutes from 6.30am to 10.30pm. A taxi costs around Y30.

GETTING AROUND

For those travellers based in the Tibetan quarter of Lhasa, most of the major inner-Lhasa sights are within fairly easy walking distance. For sights such as the Norbulingka over in the west of town, it's better to take a taxi or rent a bicycle.

To/From Gongkar Airport

Recently renovated Gongkar airport is 65km from Lhasa, via the US$78 million tunnel and bridge that opened in 2005.

Airport buses (☎ 682 6282) leave seven times a day (Y25, 1¼ hours) between 7.30am and 1pm from beside the CAAC building. From the airport, buses wait for flights outside the terminal building. Buy tickets on the bus.

A taxi to the airport costs around Y150.

Bicycle

Bicycles are a great way to get around Lhasa once you have acclimatised to the altitude.

Thaizand Bicycle Tours (Map p100; ☎ 691 0898; thaizand@hotmail.com; Kirey Hotel, 105 Beijing Donglu) rents quality mountain bikes for Y60 per day, with a helmet and pads.

Yueye Bike Rental (Map p100; Beijing Donglu; 8am-9pm) down the alley beside the Banak Shol hotel rents decent Giant-brand mountain bikes for Y30 per day. The nearby **Bodi Chehang Bike Hire** (Map p100; Beijing Donglu; 9.30am-9.30pm) also rents bikes for Y20 per day. Other rental places on Zangyiyuan Lu charge around Y30 per day. The Yak Hotel (p121) is another possibility.

Bicycle theft is a problem in Lhasa, so be sure to park your bike in designated areas (Y1). A lock and chain is a good idea.

Minibus & City Buses

Buses (Y1) and private minibuses (Y2) are frequent on Beijing Donglu, and if you need to get up to the area around the Lhasa Hotel or the bus station this is the cheapest way to do it.

Useful bus routes:

Bus 89 From the train station to the Eastern Bus Station, via the Western Bus Station, TTB office, Potala Palace, Lhasa Department Store and Jiangsu Lu

Bus 106 From Beijing Donglu to the Potala, TTB office and Norbulinka

Bus 109 From Beijing Donglu to the Western Bus Station, via the CAAC office, Linkuo Xilu, Bank of China, Beijing Zhonglu and Norbulinka; returning to Beijing Donglu via Luobulinka Lu

Minibus 205 From Beijing Donglu to the Eastern Bus Station

Minibus 301 From the Eastern Bus Station to Beijing Donglu, CAAC, Zang Gyab Lukhang Park, Bank of China, Lhasa Hotel and the turn-off to Drepung Monastery

Pedicab

There is no shortage of pedicabs plying the streets of Lhasa, but they require endless haggling and are only really useful for short trips (around Y5). At least most are Tibetan owned. *Always* fix the price before getting in.

Taxi

Taxis charge a standard fare of Y10 to anywhere within the city.

AROUND LHASA

Within easy cycling distance of central Lhasa are the impressive Gelugpa monasteries of Sera and Drepung. Both are must-sees, even if you have only a brief stay in Lhasa.

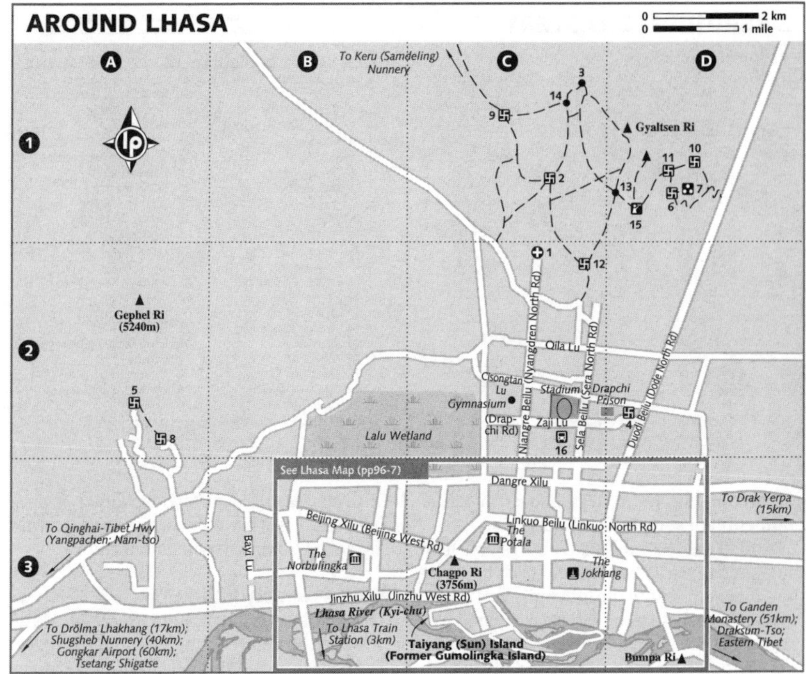

INFORMATION

Lhasa Military Hospital 1 C2

SIGHTS & ACTIVITIES

Chapsung Nunnery 2 C1
Dadren Ritrö Hermitage 3 C1
Drapchi Monastery 扎基寺 4 D2
Drepung Monastery 5 A2
Keutsang Ritrö 6 D1
Keutsang Ruins 7 D1
Nechung Monastery 8 A2
Pabonka Monastery 9 C1
Phurbu Chok Monastery 10 D1
Rakadrak Hermitage 11 D1
Sera Monastery 12 C2
Sera Ütse 13 D1
Tashi Chöling Hermitage 14 C1
Viewpoint 15 D1

TRANSPORT

Northern Bus Station 北郊客运站 16 C2

See the Ü map (p145) for the location of Drak Yerpa, Drölma Lhakhang and Shugsheb Nunnery.

DREPUNG MONASTERY འབྲས་སྤུངས 哲蚌寺

About 8km west of central Lhasa, **Drepung** (Zhebang Si; admission Y50, 8.30am-6.30pm) was once one of the world's largest monasteries. The word Drepung literally translates as 'rice heap', a reference to the huge numbers of white monastic buildings that once piled up on the hillside. It suffered through the ages with assaults by the kings of Tsang and the Mongols, but was left relatively unscathed during the Cultural Revolution and there is still much of interest intact. Rebuilding and resettlement continue at a pace unmatched elsewhere in Tibet and the site once again resembles a small village, with around 600 monks resident.

The best way to visit the chapels is to follow the pilgrims or, failing that, the yellow signs. Interior photography costs Y10 to 20 per chapel. A restaurant near the bus stop serves reviving tea by the glass, as well as bowls of *shemdre* (rice, potato and yak meat; Y6) and *momos*. The upstairs seating is very pleasant.

History

Drepung was founded in 1416 by a charismatic monk and disciple of Tsongkhapa called Jamyang Chöje. Within just a year of

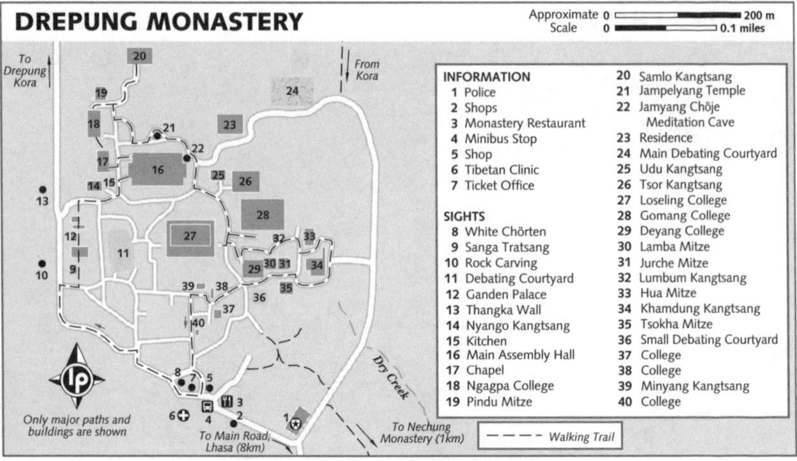

completion the monastery had attracted a population of some 2000 monks.

In 1530 the second Dalai Lama established the Ganden Palace, the palace that was home to the Dalai Lamas until the fifth built the Potala. It was from here that the early Dalai Lamas exercised their political as well as religious control over central Tibet, and the second, third and fourth Dalai Lamas are all entombed here.

Ganden Palace

From the car park, follow the kora clockwise around the outside of the monastery until you reach the steps up to the Ganden Palace.

The first hall on the left is the **Sanga Tratsang**, a recently renovated chapel housing statues of the protectors Namse (Vairocana), Nagpo Chenpo (Mahakala), Dorje Jigje (Yamantaka), Chögyel (Dharmaraja), Palden Lhamo (Shri Devi; on a horse) and the Nechung oracle, all arranged around a central statue of the fifth Dalai Lama.

Head up across the main courtyard, where performances of *cham* (a ritual dance) are still performed during the Shötun festival. The upper floor of the main building has three chapels that make up the apartments of the early Dalai Lamas. The second of the three chapels, to the right, has wonderfully detailed **murals** and the throne of the fifth Dalai Lama, next to a thousand-armed statue of Chenresig. The third is a simple living room.

From here descend and cross over to a final chapel whose entrance is defaced by a partially removed Cultural Revolution–era painting of Chairman Mao, complete with political slogans. Signs lead past a refreshment stand and a corner shrine to Drölma to the exit to the north.

Main Assembly Hall

The main assembly hall, or *tsogchen,* is the principal structure in the Drepung complex. The hall is reached through an entrance on the west side, just past a **kitchen**, whose medieval-looking giant cauldrons and ladles look like a set from the film *The Name of the Rose.*

The huge interior is very atmospheric, draped with thangkas and supported by over 180 columns, some of which are adorned with ancient armour.

The back-room chapel features the protector deities Chana Dorje (Vajrapani, blue) and Tamdrin (Hayagriva, red), and contains statues of Sakyamuni with his two disciples, the Buddhas of the Three Ages, and nine chörtens above. The walls and pillars are lined with statues of the eight bodhisattvas. To the front centre there is also a youthful-looking statue of Lamdrin Rinpoche (a former abbot of Drepung recognisable by his black-rimmed glasses); next to it is his chörten. To the east is Tsongkhapa, the founder of the Gelugpa sect.

Sculptures of interest in the main hall include a two-storey Jampelyang (Manjushri), accompanied by the 13th Dalai Lama; Sakyamuni; Tsongkhapa; Jamyang Chöje, Drepung's founder, in a cabinet to the right; and to the right Sakyamuni, flanked by five of the Dalai Lamas. At either end of the altar is a group of eight *arhats* (literally 'worthy ones').

Back by the main entrance, steps lead up to the 1st and 2nd floors. At the top of the stairs is the **Hall of the Kings of Tibet**, featuring the fifth Dalai Lama, and then a chapel containing the head of a two-storey **Jampa** statue. Pilgrims prostrate themselves here and drink from a sacred conch shell.

Continue moving clockwise through the **Sakyamuni Chapel**, stuffed with chörtens, and then descend to the **Miwang Lhakhang**. This chapel contains the assembly hall's most revered image, a massive **statue of Jampa**, the Future Buddha, at the age of 12. The statue rises through three floors of the building from a ground-floor chapel that is usually closed, and is flanked by Tsongkhapa to the left and Jamyang Chöje to the right. The chörtens behind contain the remains of the second Dalai Lama and Jamyang Chöje. At the front right are statues of seven of the Dalai Lamas.

To the right of the Sakyamuni Chapel is a **Drölma chapel**. Drölma is a protective deity, and in this case the three Drölma images in the chapel (to the immediate right) are responsible for protecting Drepung's drinking water, wealth and authority respectively. There are also some fine examples of Tibetan Kangyur **scriptures** here. The central statue is a form of Sakyamuni, whose amulet contains one of Tsongkhapa's teeth.

Exit the building from the western side of the 2nd floor.

Ngagpa College

Ngagpa is one of Drepung's four colleges, and was devoted to Tantric study. The chapel is dedicated to Dorje Jigje (Yamantaka), a Tantric meditational deity who serves as an opponent to the forces of impermanence. The cartoon-style Dorje Jigje image is said to have been fashioned by Tsongkhapa himself. Working clockwise, other statues include Palden Lhamo (first clockwise), Nagpo Chenpo (third), Drölma (fourth), Tsongkhapa (fifth), the fifth Dalai Lama (seventh), the Nechung oracle and, by the door, Dorje Drakden (p132). Look for Chögyel to the right, his hand thrusting out of the glass cabinet.

To get a feel for what Drepung was like before the renovation teams arrived, detour briefly up to the **Samlo Kangtsang**, unrestored and surrounded by melancholic ruins.

As you follow the pilgrim path (clockwise) around the back of the assembly hall you will pass the small **Jampelyang Temple**, where pilgrims pour yak butter on the wall and then

MONASTERIES IN TIBET

The great Gelugpa monasteries of Drepung, Sera and Ganden, collectively known as the *densa chenmo sum,* once operated like self-contained worlds. Drepung alone, the largest of these monasteries, was home to around 10,000 monks at the time of the Chinese takeover in 1951. Like the other major Gelugpa institutions, Drepung operated less as a single unit than as an assembly of colleges, each with its own interests, resources and administration.

The colleges, known as *dratsang,* were (and still are) in turn made up of residences, or *kangtsang*. A monk joining a monastic college was assigned to a *kangtsang* according to the region in which he was born. For example, it is thought that 60% of monks at Drepung's Loseling College were from Kham, while Gomang college was dominated by monks from Amdo and Mongolia. This gave the monastic colleges a distinctive regional flavour and meant that loyalties were generally grounded much deeper in the colleges than in the monastery itself.

At the head of a college was the abbot or *khenpo,* a position that was filled by contenders who had completed the highest degrees of monastic studies. The successful applicant was chosen by the Dalai Lama. Beneath the abbot was a group of religious leaders who supervised prayer meetings and festivals, and a group of economic managers who controlled the various *kangtsang* estates and funds. There was also a squad of huge monks known as *dob-dobs,* who were in charge of discipline and administering punishments.

In the case of the larger colleges, estates and funds were often extensive. Loseling College had over 180 estates and 20,000 serfs who worked the land and paid taxes to the monastery. Monasteries were involved in many forms of trade. For the most part, these holdings were not used to support monks – who were often forced to do private business to sustain themselves – but to maintain an endless cycle of prayer meetings and festivals that were deemed necessary for the spiritual good of the nation.

peer in to see a holy rock painting and get hit on the back with a holy iron rod. Just a little further, tucked in on the right, is the tiny **meditation cave** of Jamyang Chöje, with some fine rock paintings.

Loseling College

Loseling is the largest of Drepung's colleges, and studies here were devoted to logic. The **main hall** houses a throne used by the Dalai Lamas, an extensive library, and a long altar decorated with statues of the fifth, seventh and eighth Dalai Lamas, Tsongkhapa and former Drepung abbots. The chörten of Loseling's first abbot is covered with offerings. There are three chapels to the rear of the hall. The one to the left houses 16 *arhats,* which pilgrims walk under in a circuit. The central chapel has a large image of Jampa and interesting photos and a self-arisen image of the Nechung oracle; the chapel to the right has a small but beautiful statue of Sakyamuni.

On the 2nd floor you'll come to a small chapel full of angry deities and then you pass under the body of a stuffed goat draped with one-mao notes before entering the spooky *gönkhang* (protector chapel). There are more protective deities here, including Nagpo Chenpo, Dorje Drakden and Dorje Lekpa.

If you have time, pop into the small debating courtyard west of Loseling College. Monks sometimes do their music practise in the garden here, blowing huge horns and crashing cymbals.

Gomang College

Gomang is the second largest of Drepung's colleges and follows the same layout as Loseling. The **main hall** has a whole row of images, including Jampa, Tsepame and the seventh Dalai Lama. Again, there are three chapels to the rear: the one to the left houses three deities of longevity, but more important is the **central chapel**, chock-a-block with images. As at Loseling, there is a single protector chapel on the upper floor. Women are not allowed into this chapel.

Deyang College & Other Colleges

The smallest of Drepung's colleges, this one can safely be missed if you've had enough. The principal image in the main hall is Jampa, flanked by Jampelyang, Drölma, the fifth Dalai Lama and others.

East of here is a cluster of friendly colleges that the tour groups never reach, including the Lamba Mitze, Lumbum Kangtsang, **Jurche Mitze**, once home to students from Inner Mongolia, and then round to the **Khamdung Kangtsang**, the upstairs of which is defaced with faded Mao slogans and images. More buildings sport English signs saying that visitors are welcome.

If you're here in the afternoon, save some time to watch the monk-debating (lots of handslapping and gesticulation) between 2.30pm and 4.30pm in the main **debating courtyard** at the northeast corner of the monastery (photos Y15).

Drepung Kora

This lovely kora climbs up to around 3900m and probably should not be attempted until you've had four or five days to acclimatise in Lhasa. The walk takes about an hour at a leisurely pace (it is possible to do it more quickly at hiking speed). Look for the path that continues uphill from the turn-off to the Ganden Palace. The path passes several rock paintings, climbs up past a high wall used to hang a giant thangka during the Shötun festival (p319), peaks at a valley of prayer flags, and then descends to the east via an encased Drölma statue and several more rock carvings. There are excellent views along the way.

Getting There & Away

The easy way to get out to Drepung is by minibus 301, 302 and 303, which run from Beijing Donglu to the foot of the Drepung hill. From here a coach runs up to the monastery (Y1). Direct minibuses (Y3) run early in the morning from in front of Barkhor Square.

A taxi from the Barkhor is Y20 to Y30.

NECHUNG MONASTERY གནས་ཆུང་གྲྭ་ཚང་ 乃琼寺

Only 10 minutes' walk downhill from Drepung Monastery, **Nechung** (Naiqiong Si; admission sometimes Y25; 9am-4pm) is worth a visit for its historical role as the seat of the Tibetan State Oracle until 1959. The oracle was the medium of Dorje Drakden, an aspect of Pehar, the Gelugpa protector of the Buddhist state, and the Dalai Lamas would make no important decision without first consulting him. The oracle was not infallible, however; in 1904 the oracle resigned in disgrace after failing to predict the invasion of the British under Younghusband. In 1959 the State Oracle fled to India with the Dalai Lama.

THE NECHUNG ORACLE

Every New Year in Lhasa until 1959, the Dalai Lama consulted the Nechung oracle on important matters of state. In preparation for the ordeal, the oracle strapped on eye-shaped bracelets and an elaborate headdress of feathers, so heavy that it had to be lifted onto his head by two men.

The oracle would then whip himself into a trance in an attempt to dislodge the spirit from his body. Eyewitness accounts describe how his eyeballs swelled and rolled up into his sockets, and how his mouth opened wide, his tongue curling upward as his face reddened. As he began to discern the future in a steel mirror, the oracle would answer questions in an anguished, tortured, hissing voice, and the answers would be interpreted and written on a small blackboard. After the trance the oracle would faint from the ordeal and have to be carried away.

Nechung is an eerie place associated with possession, exorcism and other pre-Buddhist rites. The blood-red **doors** at the entrance are painted with flayed human skins and scenes of torture line the top of the outer courtyard. Tantric drumming booms from the depths of the building like a demonic heartbeat. For images of Dorje Drakden, the protective spirit manifested in the State Oracle, see the back-room chapel to the left of the main hall. The statue on the left shows Dorje Drakden in his wrathful aspect, so terrible that his face must be covered; the version on the right has him in a slightly more conciliatory frame of mind. The sacred tree in between the two is the home of Pehar.

The far right chapel has an amazing **spirit trap** and an image of the Dzogchen deity Ekajati, recognisable by her single fang. On the 1st floor is an audience chamber, whose throne was used by the Dalai Lamas when they consulted with the State Oracle. The 2nd floor features a huge new statue of a wrathful Guru Rinpoche. There are some fine murals in the exterior courtyard.

Nechung is easily reached on foot after visiting Drepung, en route to the main road. A path leads past stonecarvers to the monastery.

SERA MONASTERY སེ་ར་དགོན་པ་ 色拉寺

Sera Monastery (Sela Si; admission Y55; ⌚ 9am-5pm), approximately 5km north of central Lhasa, was one of Lhasa's two great Gelugpa monasteries, second only to Drepung. Its once-huge monastic population of around 5000 monks has now been reduced to several hundred and building repairs are still continuing. Nevertheless the monastery is worth a visit, particularly in the morning when the monastery is at its most active, but also between 3pm and 5pm (not Sundays), when debating is usually held in the monastery's debating courtyard. Chapels start to close at 3pm, so it makes sense to see the monastery chapels before heading to the debating.

Interior photography costs Y15 to Y30 per chapel; video fees are an outrageous Y850. Near the monastery entrance there is a simple but pleasant restaurant-teahouse.

History

Sera was founded in 1419 by Sakya Yeshe, a disciple of Tsongkhapa also known by the honorific title Jamchen Chöje. In its heyday, Sera hosted five colleges of instruction, but at the time of the Chinese invasion in 1959 there were just three: Sera Me specialised in the fundamental precepts of Buddhism; Sera Je in the instruction of itinerant monks from outside central Tibet; and Sera Ngagpa in Tantric studies.

Sera survived the ravages of the Cultural Revolution with light damage, although many of the lesser colleges were destroyed.

Sera Me College

Follow the pilgrims clockwise, past the Shampa Kangtsang and Tsa Kangtsang residential halls and several minor buildings, to the Sera Me College. This college dates back to the original founding of the monastery.

The central image of the impressive **main hall** is a copper Sakyamuni, flanked by Jampa (left) and Jampelyang. To the rear of the hall are four chapels. To the left is a dark chapel dedicated to the dharma protector of the east, Ta-og (in an ornate brass case and wearing a hat), alongside Dorje Jigje. Don't miss the **masks**, iron thunderbolts and antique bows hanging from the ceiling. Women cannot enter this chapel. To the left of the entrance is a three-dimensional wooden mandala.

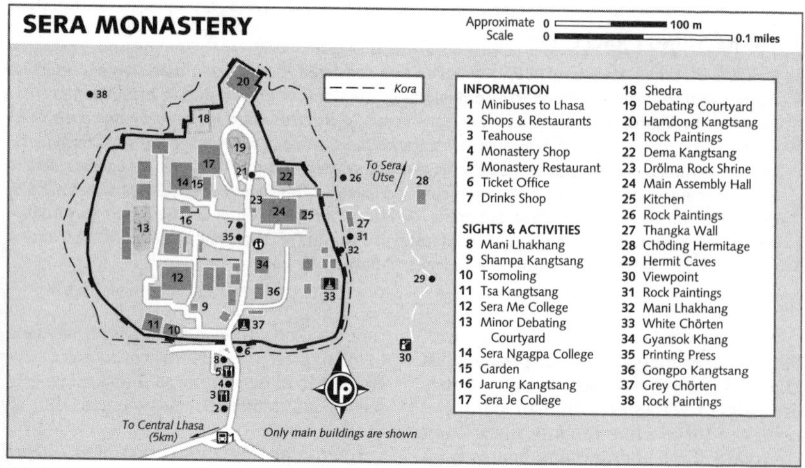

Continue to the central chapel, which contains statues of the Past, Present and Future Buddhas, as well as 16 *arhats* depicted in their mountain grottos.

The next chapel is home to Miwang Jowo, a central Sakyamuni statue that dates from the 15th century and is the most sacred of the college's statues. At the back are Tsepame and eight bodhisattvas. The entrance to the chapel is guarded by the protectors Tamdrin (Hayagriva; red) and Miyowa (Achala; blue). The last chapel is dedicated to Tsongkhapa and there are also images of several Dalai Lamas, as well as of Sakya Yeshe, Sera's founder and first abbot.

There are two chapels on the upper floor. The first, after you mount the stairs, is dedicated to Sakyamuni, depicted in an unusual standing form. The second is a Drölma chapel with 1000 statues of this protective deity. The third has 1000 statues of Chenresig, as well as a huge brass pot in the corner.

Sera Ngagpa College

A Tantric college, Ngagpa is also the oldest structure at Sera. The **main hall** is dominated by a statue of Sakya Yeshe (wearing a black hat), behind the throne, surrounded by other famous Sera lamas. There are three chapels to the rear of the hall, the first featuring Jampa and thousand-armed Chenresig, the second with 16 *arhats* and a large Sakyamuni statue, and the third with a statue of the protective deity Dorje Jigje, as well as Namtöse (Vaishravana), the guardian of the north, to the right, who rides a snow lion and holds a mongoose that vomits jewels. There are also a couple of rooms upstairs featuring Tsepame and the eight medicine buddhas (Menlha).

After exiting, most pilgrims pay a visit to the **Jarung Kangtsang** residential college.

Sera Je College

This is the largest of Sera's colleges, generally accessed from the side. It has a breathtaking **main hall**, hung with thangkas and lit by shafts of light from high windows. Several chörtens hold the remains of Sera's most famous lamas.

To the left of the hall is a passage leading, via a chapel dedicated to the Past, Present and Future Buddhas, to the most sacred of Sera Monastery's chapels, the **Chapel of Tamdrin**. Tamdrin (Hayagriva) is a wrathful meditational deity whose name means 'horse headed'. He is the chief protective deity of Sera, and there is often a long line of shuffling pilgrims waiting to touch their forehead to his feet in respect. The ornate brass shrine recalls the temples of the Kathmandu Valley. Take a look at the weapons, hats and masks hanging from the ceiling. There is a second chapel for him on the upper floor, but there he is in another aspect with nine heads.

The first chapel to the rear of the hall is devoted to a lovely statue of Sakyamuni, seated below a fine canopy and ceiling mandala. Pilgrims climb steps to the right to touch his left leg. The next two chapels are dedicated to Tsongkhapa, with Sakyamuni and Öpagme

(Amitabha); and to Jampelyang, flanked by Jampa and another Jampelyang. From here head to the upstairs chapels.

To the northeast of Sera Je is Sera's **debating courtyard**. There is usually debating practise here in the afternoons from around 3pm to 5pm, which provides a welcome relief from peering at Buddhist iconography. You will hear it (with much clapping of hands to emphasise points) as you approach Sera Je. Foreign photographers circle the site like vultures at a sky burial.

Hamdong Kangtsang

Hamdong served as a residence for monks studying at Sera Je College. The back left chapel contains a bearded image of a Sera lama who died in 1962; in a case to the right is an image of Drölma, who is said to protect Sera's water supply. Look for three **photos of Ekai Kawaguchi**, the Japanese monk who studied here in disguise (p17) in 1901.

As you walk downhill, note the wonderful **rock paintings** depicting Jampelyang, Chenresig, Chana Dorje (Vajrapani) and Green Tara.

Main Assembly Hall (Tsogchen)

The main assembly hall is the largest of Sera's buildings and dates back to 1710. The central hall is particularly impressive and is noted for its wall-length thangkas and two-storey statue of Jampa. He is surrounded by other figures, including Dalai Lamas on the right, while to the left is the large throne of the 13th Dalai Lama. Behind the throne is a figure of Sakyamuni accompanied by the 13th Dalai Lama and Sakya Yeshe, the founder of Sera.

Of the three chapels to the rear of the hall, the central is the most important, with its 6m-high Jampa statue. The statue rises up to the upper floor, where it can also be viewed from a central chapel. Also on the upper floor (to the far left of the central chapel) is a highly revered statue of a thousand-armed Chenresig. Pilgrims put their forehead to a pole that connects them directly and literally to the heart of compassion. The pilgrim path enters the building from the back so this may be the first chapel you come across, before descending to the prayer hall.

Printing Press

Before leaving the monastery it's worth having a look at the printing blocks in this new hall. Photos are Y5. Prints made on site are for sale. A small building to the side holds a sand mandala.

Sera Kora

The Sera kora takes less than an hour and is well worth the time. It starts outside the entrance and heads west, following an arc around the monastery walls. On the eastern descent, look out for several brightly coloured **rock paintings**. The largest ones on the eastern side of the monastery are of Dorje Jigje, Tsongkhapa and others. Next to the rock paintings is a support wall used to hang a giant thangka during festivals.

A path leads up the side steps of this wall to the **Chöding hermitage**. The hermitage was a retreat of Tsongkhapa, and predates Sera. There is not a great deal to see, but it is a short walk and the views from the hermitage are worthwhile. A path continues south around the hillside past a holy spring to a point that has fine views of Sera and Lhasa beyond.

Getting There & Away

Sera is only a half-hour bicycle ride from the Barkhor area of Lhasa. Leave your bicycle next to the monastery restaurant.

Alternatively, head down to the intersection of Beijing Donglu and Zhisenge/Qingnian Lu and catch minibus 503 (Y2, every 10 minutes) from just north of the intersection. Minibuses 501 and 502 also run to Sera.

PABONKA MONASTERY ཕ་བོང་ཁ་དགོན་པ་

Pabonka Monastery (admission free; dawn-dusk) is one of the most ancient Buddhist sites in the Lhasa region. It is infrequently visited, but is only a one-hour walk (or short taxi ride) from the Sera Monastery turn-off and is worth the effort.

Built on a flat-topped granite boulder, Pabonka may even predate the Jokhang and Ramoche. It was built in the 7th century by King Songtsen Gampo. The Tibetan king Trisong Detsen, Guru Rinpoche and Tibet's first seven monks all meditated here at various times, and it was also here that the monk Thonmi Sambhota reputedly invented the Tibetan alphabet. It was destroyed in 841 by the anti-Buddhist King Langdharma and rebuilt in the 11th century. The fifth Dalai Lama added an extra floor to the two-storey building. It suffered damage in the Cultural Revolution and has undergone repairs in recent years.

The first building you come across is the **Rigsum Gonpo Temple**, jam-packed with shrines,

DIY: TREKKING THE DODE VALLEY

From Sera Monastery you can make a great half-day trek up to the Sera Ütse retreat above the monastery and then around the ridge to the little-visited retreats of the Dode Valley. You shouldn't attempt the trek until you are well acclimatised to the altitude.

From Sera the steep relentless climb up to the yellow-walled **Sera Ütse** retreat takes at least an hour (look up and see how far it is before you set off). Take the path towards the Chöding hermitage (see p135) and branch off to the left before you get there, climbing the ridge via a switchback path until you reach the yellow building perched high above the valley. Sera Ütse was a retreat used by Tsongkhapa (his *drubpuk,* or meditation cave, can be visited) and is currently home to two monks. You can also reach the retreat directly from Pabonka's Tashi Chöling hermitage (opposite).

From the Ütse continue east along a level trail for 10 minutes to a superb **viewpoint**, probably Lhasa's most scenic picnic spot. From here the main trail continues east down into the Dode Valley, though it's possible for fit climbers to detour straight up the hillside to the summit, a knob of rock covered in prayer flags.

The main trail descends past a balancing rock to the small **Rakadrak** retreat, where you can visit three simple caves associated with Tsongkhapa. Five minutes' walk below Rakadrak is the larger **Keutsang Ritrö**, a retreat complex home to 23 monks. The original hermitage lies in ruins in an incredible location on the side of the sheer cliff-face to the east. A painting inside the main chapel (to the right) depicts the original. As you leave the complex a path to the left leads to the dramatic ruins but the trail is dangerous and ends in a sheer drop. The far section of the ruins can only be reached from the other side of the cliff.

From the Keutshang Ritrö follow the dirt road downhill and after 10 minutes branch left for the short uphill hike to the **Phurbu Chok Monastery** and its hilltop Rigsum Gonpo Lhakhang (an hour detour in total from the road). You can spot two nunneries from here; Negodong to the east and Mechungri to the southeast. Back at the junction, descend to the main road to flag down bus 601, which terminates at Linkuo Beilu, just north of the Ramoche Temple.

On the ride back it's worth getting off at Zaji (Drapchi) Lu to visit **Drapchi Monastery**, an active and unusual monastery that is located near Lhasa's most notorious political prison. Huge amounts of rice wine and *chang* (barley beer) are offered continuously to the local protectress Drapchi Lhamo and the site has an almost animist feel to it.

whose most famous relic is the blue and gold carved mantra *'om mani padme hum'* ('hail to the jewel in the lotus') that faces the entrance on the far side of the hall. The central shrine contains a 1300-year-old 'self-arising' (not man-made) carving depicting Chenresig, Jampelyang and Chana Dorje (Vajrapani) – the Rigsum Gonpo trinity after which the chapel is named. The stone carvings were buried during the Cultural Revolution and only dug up in 1985.

Continue uphill, turn left at the row of chörtens, and continue clockwise around the Pabonka rock (said to represent a female tortoise) to the **Palden Lhamo Cave** on the west side, where King Songtsen Gampo once meditated. Images inside are of Songtsen Gampo (with a turban), his two wives, Guru Rinpoche, Trisong Detsen (to the side) and a rock carving of the protectress Palden Lhamo.

Pabonka Potrang sits atop the ancient rock. There is nothing to see on the ground floor, but the upper floor has an intimate assembly hall with a picture of the current Pabonka Lama and a 'self-arising' Chenresig statue hidden behind a pillar to the right. The inner protector chapel holds an ancient conch shell *(dungkhar)* wrapped in a *kathak* (prayer scarf) and in a glass case. The four-pillared Kashima Lhakhang next door is lined with various lamas, three kings and their wives. The cosy rooftop quarters of the Dalai Lama have a statue of the meditational deity Demchok (Chakrasamvara) and offer fine views.

Further above the Pabonka Potrang are the remains of 108 chörtens and the yellow **Jasa Potrang**, or temple of Princess Wencheng (the Chinese wife of King Songtsen Gampo). The two ground-floor rooms are dedicated to five manifestations of Tsongkhapa and the medicine buddhas, and an upper-floor chapel has a small statue of Wencheng herself in the far right, near an image of Thonmi Sambhota (who reputedly invented the Tibetan alphabet here). Songsten Gampo's Nepali wife Bhrikuti is also present, as are images on the other side of the room of Green and White Drölma, of whom the two wives are thought to be emanations.

Walks Around the Monastery

A few intrepid (and fit) travellers use Pabonka as a base for walks further afield. The half-day kora around Pabonka, Tashi Chöling hermitage and Chupsang Nunnery makes a nice addition to a visit to Sera Monastery. Midday can be hot here, so bring enough water.

For those who aren't so fit, an easier 20-minute walk from Pabonka leads up to **Tashi Chöling hermitage**. There's not a lot left to see at the hermitage, but it offers good views. Pilgrims drink holy spring water from the upper chapel before making a kora of the hermitage. To get here from the back of the Pabonka kora, follow the path diagonally up the hillside, following the electricity poles.

From Tashi Chöling, the trail drops into a ravine and follows this down for 30 minutes to **Chupsang Nunnery**. There are some 80 nuns resident at Chupsang and it's a very friendly place. It's about 40 minutes' walk from the nunnery to the main road into Lhasa.

An alternative route from Tashi Chöling is to hike for 40 minutes northeast up the ravine to the cliffside hermitage of **Dadren Ritrö**. You can see the hermitage from the trail. From here, trekkers can follow trails across the ridge for an hour or two to Sera Monastery or Sera Ütse (see the boxed text, opposite).

Keru (or Samdeling) Nunnery is a tough four-hour trek from Tashi Chöling or Pabonka (allow around two hours for the descent). This is a serious day trek and should not be attempted until you are well adjusted to the altitude. The faint trail heads northwest from Tashi Chöling and follows a steep ridge. The nunnery, home to more than 80 nuns, is at an altitude of over 4200m.

Getting There & Away

To get to Pabonka, take minibus 502 or 503 to the Sera Monastery turn-off on Nangre Beilu. Rather than take the turn right to Sera, look for a left turn a little up the road before the military hospital. After five minutes take a right at the canal; after 15 minutes take the branch to the left and you'll see Pabonka up ahead to the left, perched on its granite boulder. The 'monastery' to the right is actually Chupsang Nunnery.

GANDEN MONASTERY དགའ་ལྡན་ 甘丹寺

Ganden (Gandan Si; adult/student Y45/35; dawn-dusk), just 50km northeast of Lhasa, was the first Gelugpa monastery and has been the main seat of this major Buddhist order ever since. If you only have time for one monastery excursion outside Lhasa, Ganden would probably be the best choice. With its stupendous views of the surrounding Kyi-chu Valley and fascinating kora, Ganden is an experience unlike the other major Gelugpa monasteries in the Lhasa area.

The monastery was founded in 1409 by Tsongkhapa, the revered reformer of the Gelugpa order, after the first Mönlam festival was performed here. Images of Tsongkhapa flanked by his first two disciples, Kedrub Je and Gyatsab Je, are found throughout the monastery. When Tsongkhapa died in 1411, the abbotship of the monastery passed to these disciples. The post came to be known as the Ganden Tripa and was earned through scholarly merit, not reincarnation. It is the Ganden Tripa, not, as one might expect, the Dalai Lama, who is the head of the Gelugpa order.

Ganden means 'joyous' in Tibetan and is the name of the Western Paradise (also known as Tushita) that is home to Jampa, the Future Buddha. There is a certain irony in this because, of all the great monasteries of Tibet, Ganden suffered most at the hands of the Red Guards, possibly because of its political influence.

Today it is the scene of extensive rebuilding, but this does not disguise the ruin that surrounds the new structures. In 1959 there were 2000 monks at Ganden; today there are just a couple of hundred. The destruction was caused by artillery fire and bombing in 1959 and 1966. New chapels and residences are being opened all the time, so even pilgrims are sometimes unsure in which order to visit the chapels.

Ganden was temporarily closed to tourists in 1996 after violent demonstrations against the government's banning of Dalai Lama photos. There were further scuffles in 2006 when monks smashed a statue of the controversial deity Dorje Shugden (see p139).

Interior photography fees are Y20 per chapel; video fees are an amazing Y1500. For

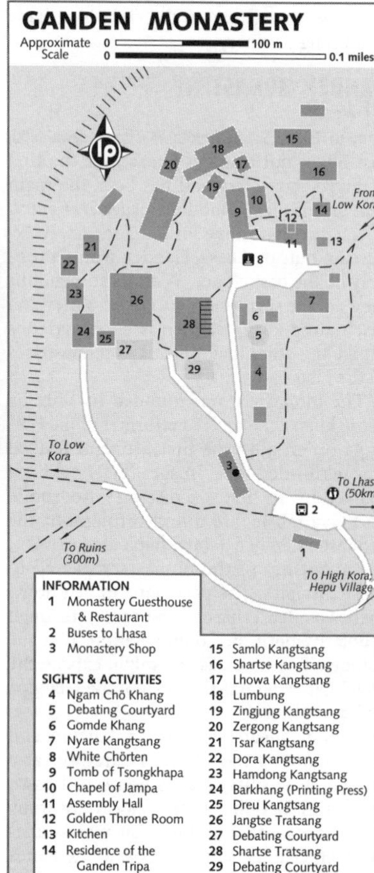

details of the trek from Ganden to Samye, see p288.

Ngam Chö Khang

The first chapel you reach from the parking area is Ngam Chö Khang. It is built on the site of Tsongkhapa's original assembly hall *(dukhang)*, and has a small shrine with images of Tsongkhapa. On the left is a protector chapel *(gönkhang)*, that houses four protective deities. The largest image is of Dorje Jigje.

Debating Courtyard

Southeast of the Gomde Khang residence is the debating courtyard. You should be able to hear the clapping of hands as you pass if there is a debate in progress.

Tomb of Tsongkhapa

The red fortress-like structure of Tsongkhapa's mausoleum, also known as the Serkhang, is probably the most impressive of the reconstructed buildings at Ganden. It's above the prominent white chörten.

The main entrance leads to a new prayer hall with a small sand mandala and an inner Sakyamuni chapel. The protector chapel to the right is the domain of the protective deity Chögyel (to the far right). Women are not allowed into this chapel.

Exit this building, turn to the left and take the stairs leading to the upper floors. The holiest shrine here is the Yangpachen Khang (or Serkhang) chapel, which houses Tsongkhapa's funeral chörten. The chapel is named after the stone in the back left, covered in offerings of yak butter, which is said to have flown from India. Both the original tomb and the preserved body of Tsongkhapa inside it were destroyed by Red Guards. The new silver-and-gold chörten was built to house salvaged fragments of Tsongkhapa's skull. The images seated in front of the chörten are of Tsongkhapa flanked by his two principal disciples. The room also holds several holy relics attributed to Tsongkhapa. Pilgrims line up to buy votive inscriptions written in gold ink by the monks. Protective amulets and incense are sold outside the chapel and one-mao notes are stuffed in the grill outside as offerings.

You can climb up to the roof for good views.

Chapel of Jampa

This small chapel (Jampa Lhakhang), just across from the exit of the Tomb of Tsongkhapa, holds two large images of the Future Buddha, plus the eight bodhisattvas.

Assembly Hall

The recently renovated assembly hall has statues of the 16 *arhats* and two huge statues of Tsongkhapa. Stairs lead up to the inner sanctum, the **Golden Throne Room (Ser Trikhang)**, which houses the throne of Tsongkhapa, where pilgrims get thumped on the head with the yellow hats of Tsongkhapa and the Dalai Lama.

There are two entrances on the north side of the building. The west one gives access to a 2nd-floor view of the Tsongkhapa statue, and the east one (sometimes closed) houses a library (Tengyur Lhakhang).

Residence of the Ganden Tripa

To the east of the Golden Throne Room and slightly uphill, this residence (also known as Zimchung Tridok Khang) contains the living quarters and throne of the Ganden Tripa. Other rooms include a protector chapel, with statues of Demchok, Gonpo Gur (Mahakala) and Nangjoma (Vajrayogini); a Tsongkhapa chapel; and a room with the living quarters of the Dalai Lama (note the photo of the 13th Dalai Lama). To the right is the 'Nirvana Room', which has a large shrine to Kurt Cobain (only kidding, it's Tsongkhapa again, who is said to have died in this room). The upper-floor library has a round platform used for creating sand mandalas.

Other Buildings

From here, the pilgrim trail winds through various renovated *kangtsangs* (residences), which offer some good opportunities to meet the local monks away from the tourist trail.

Lumbung Kangtsang is also known as the Amdo Kangtsang. Tsongkhapa himself was from Amdo (modern-day Qinghai), and many monks came from the province to study here.

The other main buildings are the **Jangtse Tratsang**, an active college with an impressive main prayer hall, and the **Shartse Tratsang**, both large, recently reconstructed colleges. In the morning (between 7.30am and 11am) and early afternoon (1.30pm to 3pm) listen out for debating in the enclosed courtyard south of the Shartse Tratsang.

Below the main assembly hall, the innocuous-looking **Nyare Kangtsang** houses a controversial statue of the deity Dorje Shugden. Worship of the deity has been outlawed by the Dalai Lama and in 2006 monks stormed the building and smashed the statue, leading to the arrest of two monks. The statue was replaced in 2007 with the support of a Chinese government more than happy to fan the flames of a sectarian split between local monks and the Dalai Lama. The standoff remains tense and the chapel is under the guard of a bored-looking PSB officer. The statue is in the third chapel, in the far right corner, with a red face and third eye, wearing a bronze hat and riding a snow lion.

Ganden Kora

The Ganden kora is a simply stunning walk and should not be missed. There are superb views over the braided Kyi-chu Valley along the way and there are usually large numbers of pilgrims and monks offering prayers, rubbing holy rocks and prostrating themselves along the path.

There are actually two parts to the walk: the high kora and the low kora. The high kora climbs Angkor Ri south of Ganden and then drops down the ridge to join up with the lower kora.

To walk the **high kora**, follow the path southeast of the car park, away from the monastery. After a while the track splits – the left path leads to Hepu village on the Ganden–Samye trek; the right path zigzags up the ridge to a collection of prayer flags. Try to follow other pilgrims up. It's a tough 40-minute climb to the top of the ridge, so don't try this one unless you're well acclimatised. Here, at two peaks, pilgrims burn juniper incense and give offerings of tsampa before heading west down the ridge in the direction of the monastery, stopping at several other shrines en route.

The **low kora** is an easier walk of around 45 minutes. From the car park the trail heads west up and then around the back of the ridge behind the monastery. The trail winds past several isolated shrines and rocks that are rubbed for their healing properties or squeezed through as a karmic test. At one point, pilgrims all peer at a rock through a clenched fist in order to see visions.

A **sky-burial site** is reached shortly before the high point of the trail. Some pilgrims undertake a ritual simulated death and rebirth at this point, rolling around on the ground.

Towards the end of the kora, on the eastern side of the ridge, is **Tsongkhapa's hermitage**, a small building with relief images of Atisha, Sakyamuni, Tsepame and Palden Lhamo. These images are believed to have the power of speech. Above the hermitage is a coloured rock painting that is reached by a narrow, precipitous path. From the hermitage, the kora drops down to rejoin the monastery.

Sleeping & Eating

The simple **Monastery Guesthouse** (dm Y15-40) is used mostly by trekkers headed to Samye. Better quality rooms have recently been built above the well-stocked monastery shop just down from the car park. The **monastery restaurant** has low-grade *thugpa* (Tibetan noodles; Y3) and some fried dishes.

Getting There & Away

Ganden (Y20 return, 1¼ hours) is one of the few sights in Ü that is connected to Lhasa by public transport. At least one bus leaves from in front of the Barkhor Square some time between 6am and 7am (a second bus often leaves between 7am and 7.30am), returning between 12.30pm and 1.30pm. A new paved road switchbacks the steep final 9km to the monastery, making the last few kilometres of the cycling trip here a lot less painful.

On the way back to Lhasa, the pilgrim bus normally stops at Sanga Monastery, set at the foot of the ruined Dagtse Dzong (or Dechen Dzong; *dzong* means 'fort').

A Land Cruiser for a day trip to Ganden costs around Y400; a taxi will be cheaper. Guides and permits are not required.

DRAK YERPA བྲག་ཡེར་པ་ 叶巴寺

For those with an interest in Tibetan Buddhism, **Drak Yerpa hermitage** (Yeba Si; admission sometimes Y20), about 16km northeast of Lhasa, is one of the holiest cave retreats in Ü. Among the many ascetics who have sojourned here are Guru Rinpoche and Atisha (Jowo-je), the Bengali Buddhist who spent 12 years proselytising in Tibet. King Songtsen Gampo also meditated in a cave, after his Tibetan wife established the first of Yerpa's chapels. The peaceful site offers lovely views and is a great day trip from Lhasa.

At one time the hill at the base of the cave-dotted cliffs was home to Yerpa Drubde Monastery, the summer residence of Lhasa's Gyutö College at the Ramoche Temple. The monastery was destroyed in 1959.

Monks have begun to return to Yerpa but numbers are strictly controlled by the government, which tore down several 'unauthorised' chapels as recently as 1998.

The Caves

As you ascend from the parking lot, take the left branch of the stairway to visit the caves in clockwise fashion. The first caves are the **Rigsum Gompo Cave** and the **Tendrel Drubpuk**, the cave where Atisha (portrayed in a red hat) meditated. At one nearby cave pilgrims squeeze through a hole in the rock wall; at another they take a sip of holy water.

The yellow **Jamkhang** has a two-storey statue of Jampa flanked by Chana Dorje (Vajrapani) to the left and Namse (Vairocana) and Tamdrin (Hayagriva) to the right. Other statues are of Atisha (Jowo-je) flanked by the fifth Dalai Lama and Tsongkhapa. The upper cave is the **Drubthub-puk**, recognisable by its black yak-hair curtain. Continuing east along the ridge a detour leads up to a chörten that offers fine views of the valley.

The next chapel surrounds the **Lhalung-puk**, the cave where the monk Lhalung Pelde meditated after assassinating the anti-Buddhist king Langdharma in 842.

The largest chapel is the **Dawa-puk** (Moon Cave), where Guru Rinpoche (which is the main statue) is said to have spent seven years meditating. Look for the painting of Ekajati (Tsechigma) in the left corner of the anteroom and the stone footprints of Guru Rinpoche and Lhalung in the inner room, to the right.

Heading west, climb to the **Chögyal-puk**, the Cave of Songtsen Gampo. The interior chapel has a central thousand-armed Chenresig (Avalokiteshvara) statue known as Chaktong Chentong. Pilgrims circle the central rock pillar continually. A small cave and statue of Songtsen Gampo are in the right-hand corner.

Below the main caves and to the east is the **Neten Lhakhang**, where the practice of worshipping the 16 *arhats* was first introduced. Below here is where Atisha is said to have taught. Further east is the holy mountain of Yerpa Lhari, topped by prayer flags and encircled by a kora.

There are several caves and retreats higher up the cliff-face and some fine hiking possibilities in the hills if you have time. With a sleeping bag and some food it's generally possible to spend the night in one of the chapels (normally the Dawa-puk).

Getting There & Away

A daily pilgrim bus leaves from the Barkhor Square at around 7.30am for the caves (Y20 return), returning around 1pm. Bus drivers often call the site 'Drayab'. The newly paved road crosses the low 3980m Ngachen-la before turning into the side valley at Yerpa village and passing two ruined *dzongs* (forts) and a large disused dam en route to the caves. The bus does a final circuit of a large ruined chörten before screeching to a halt in a great cloud of dust.

DRÖLMA LHAKHANG སྒྲོལ་མ་ལྷ་ཁང་ 卓玛拉康

This small but significant **monastery** (Zhuomalakang; admission free; dawn-dusk) is full of ancient relics and hidden treasures. It's only

30 minutes by bus southwest of Lhasa and is worth a stop for those interested in Tibetan Buddhism.

As you take the Lhasa–Tsetang road out of Lhasa, you'll pass a blue **rock carving** of Sakyamuni Buddha at the base of a cliff about 11km southwest of town (it's easily missed coming from the south). Nyetang village and the monastery are about 6km further on.

Drölma Lhakhang is associated with the Bengali scholar Atisha (982–1054). Atisha came to Tibet at the age of 53 at the invitation of the king of the Guge kingdom in western Tibet and his teachings were instrumental in the so-called second diffusion of Buddhism in the 11th century. Drölma Lhakhang was established at this time by one of Atisha's foremost disciples, Drömtonpa, who also founded the Kadampa order, to which the monastery belongs. Atisha died at Netang aged 72.

The monastery was spared desecration by the Red Guards during the Cultural Revolution after a direct request from Bangladesh (which now encompasses Atisha's homeland). Apparently, Chinese premier Zhou Enlai intervened on its behalf.

The first chapel to the left is a *gönkhang* (protector chapel), decorated with severed stags' heads. As you enter and exit the main monastery building look for the two ancient guardian deities ,which may even date back to the 11th-century founding of the monastery.

From the entry, pass into the first chapel, the **Namgyel Lhakhang**, which contains a number of chörtens. The black-metal Kadampa-style chörten to the right reputedly holds the staff of Atisha and the skull of Naropa, Atisha's teacher. Statuary includes Atisha and the eight medicine buddhas.

The eponymous middle **Drölma Lhakhang** houses a number of relics associated with Atisha. The statues at the top include an 11th-century statue of Sakyamuni and statues of the 13th Dalai Lama (left), Green Tara, and Serlingpa (right), another teacher of Atisha. A 13th-century statue of Chenresig was allegedly stolen from here recently by art thieves. The lower central statue behind the grill is an image of Jampa that was reputedly saved from Mongol destruction when it shouted 'Ouch!'. There are also 21 statues of Drölma, after whom the monastery and the chapel are named.

The final **Tsepame Lhakhang** has original statues of Tsepame, cast with the ashes of Atisha, flanked by Marmedze (Dipamkara), the Past Buddha, Jampa (the Future Buddha) and the eight bodhisattvas. The small central statue of Atisha in a glass case is backed by his original clay throne. As you leave the chapel, look out for two sunken white chörtens, which hold Atisha's robes.

Upstairs is the throne room of the Dalai Lama, as well as a living room in the far left featuring a fine tree-of-life thangka depicting the Gelugpa lineages. To the right is a library.

Really keen *gompa* stompers can plod out a further hour west from Drölma Lhakhang to **Ratö Monastery**. This Gelugpa institution is renowned for its fine wall murals. It is reached via a track that heads west from the main road, south of Drölma Lhakhang.

Getting There & Away

Any bus heading to/from destinations south of Lhasa (eg to Shigatse, Samye Monastery, Tsetang) will take you past the entrance to Drölma Lhakhang. Alternatively, visit on the way back from Shigatse or the Yarlung Valley, since you can get back to Lhasa by flagging down anything that comes by.

SHUGSHEB NUNNERY ཤུག་གསེབ་ཨ་ནི་དགོན་པ་ 雄色尼姑寺

elev 4410m

Trekkers and anyone who likes to get off the beaten track will love this excursion to Tibet's largest nunnery, set in a large natural bowl about 65km south of Lhasa and home to over 280 nuns. The region is a favourite of bird-watchers.

From the end of the motorable road it's a steep 45-minute hike up to the village-like **nunnery** (Xiongse Nig Si; no admission fee). The central hall contains a three-dimensional mandala of Drölma and statues of Guru Rinpoche, Dorje Semba (Vajrasattva), White Tara and several old lamas. Both Nyingma and Dzogchen schools are represented here. Stairs to the right lead upstairs to a chapel with a statue of Machik Labdronma (holding a double drum), the famous 11th-century adept who opened up the valley. There is also a black-and-white photo of one of her reincarnations.

You can hike up the hill, following the electric poles, for 45 minutes to the **Gangri Tokar shrine** (Drubkhang), where Longchenpa, an important 14th-century Dzogchen lama, once meditated. The chapel has a cave shrine and a sacred tree stump in front of a rock image of the Dzogchen deity Rahulla.

From here fit and acclimatised hikers can climb for a couple of hours up past meditation caves (marked by prayer flags) to the ridgeline behind. The views of the Kyi-chu Valley are fantastic from here and if the weather is clear you'll get views of snowcapped 7191m Nojin Kangtsang and other Himalayan peaks to the south. From the ridgeline you can continue northwest across a boulder field for 15 minutes to a small hill (5160m) topped by a chörten that offers epic views northwards as far as Lhasa. Alternatively you could continue east along the ridge to summit the bowl's main peak.

It's possible to stay the night at the nunnery **guesthouse** (dm Y10-20). The small teahouse below the main complex offers simple meals.

Getting There & Away

A nunnery bus (Y15) leaves at 7am from Lhasa's Barkhor Square on Monday, Wednesday and Saturday, returning to Lhasa around 5pm. At the time of research it crossed the Kyi-chu just before the tunnel to Gongkar airport, since the more direct bridge, 10km south of Drölma Lhakhang, was closed to traffic.

The bus passes the picturesque cliffside Samanga Monastery en route to the nunnery and stops briefly at the small Öshang Lhakhang on the way back, though this may change when the more direct bridge is repaired. On the way back to Lhasa the nunnery bus pauses at the Drölma Lhakhang (p140) for a quick tour of the chapels, before terminating in Lhasa at the Palha Lu-puk (p112).

Ü

The traditional province of Ü is very much the historical, cultural and modern heartland of Tibet and, along with Tsang to the west, forms the power centre of central Tibet. The Tibetans trace the very birth of their nation to the valleys of the Yarlung and Yarlung Tsangpo (Brahmaputra), in particular the Monkey Cave above Tsetang. The nearby Yumbulagang Palace is claimed as Tibet's oldest building. Centuries later Guru Rinpoche meditated at caves in Sheldak and Chimphu and battled demons on the bank of the nearby Yarlung Tsangpo, before founding Tibet's first monastery at nearby Samye. It was from the Yarlung Valley that the earliest Tibetan kings launched their 6th-century unification of the plateau and it is in the nearby Chongye Valley that they lie buried.

It's not all ancient history. With a gorgeous turquoise hue, Nam-tso, an immense salt-water lake, is far and away the region's most popular natural attraction. The dramatic desert landscapes of the Yarlung Tsangpo, Tibet's most important river, are a surreal highlight. Mysterious Lhamo La-tso, a hard-to-reach lake southeast of the capital, is the only place where access remains a real challenge.

For those wanting to explore Tibet by themselves, there's fantastic scope for independent exploration. The valleys of the Yarlung Tsangpo shelter a wealth of monasteries that rarely see a foreigner. Reting Monastery remains one of the most serene in Tibet. Travellers with limited time have discovered a gem of a destination in Drigung Til Monastery and the hot springs at nearby Tidrum. Ü is best experienced on foot, whether on day hikes to side monasteries or on the classic multiday treks from Ganden to Samye (p288), or Tsurphu to Yangpachen (p292). With most of the sights in this chapter not requiring those pesky travel permits, this is the place to get out of the Land Cruiser, stick your thumb out and go exploring.

HIGHLIGHTS

- Get a taste of the northern Changtang at the turquoise waters, snowy peaks and nomads' tents of stunning high-altitude lake **Nam-tso** (p147)
- Soak up the fabulous location and spectacular circular complex of **Samye** (p168), Tibet's first monastery
- Hike the Yarlung Valley, including the iconic **Yumbulagang** (p175) – the first building in Tibet – and the ruins of **Rechung-puk** (p176)
- Overnight at one of central Tibet's peaceful monasteries – either beside the sand dunes of **Dorje Drak** (p165), beneath the juniper-clad hills of **Reting** (p151) or at the vibrant monastic centre of **Mindroling** (p167)
- Squeeze, drag and giggle yourself silly through the sacred cave complexes of **Drak Yangdzong** (p166), an adventurous overnight pilgrim destination

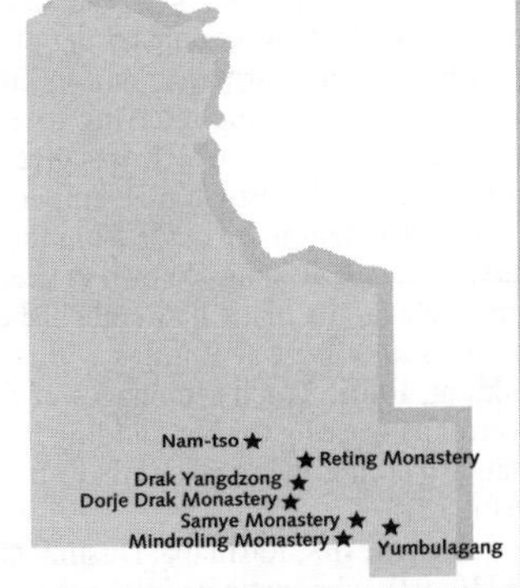

Permits

The good news is that travel in Lhasa prefecture (central and northern Ü) does not require a travel permit. This includes such places as Tsurphu, Nam-tso, Reting, Drigung Til, Lhundrub and Nyemo. In theory most of the Yarlung Tsangpo Valley (formally Shannan prefecture) does require permits (see p323), but the only place where you might actually be asked for one is at Samye and the Yarlung Valley around Tsetang. The area around the airport at Gongkar does not require permits, so you could use it as a base from which to explore the surroundings.

NORTHERN Ü དབུས་བྱང་

The featured sights in this section are often visited on separate trips: to the northwest (Tsurphu and Nam-tso), north (Lhundrub, Talung and Reting) and east (Tidrum and Drigung Til). You can also combine destinations for a five-day Land Cruiser trip to Nam-tso, Reting Monastery and the Lhundrub Valley, or a six-day trip to Nam-tso, Reting and Drigung Til/Tidrum.

Although you'll need to be self-sufficient with food and have some time, it's possible to get to all the sights in this section through a persistent combination of hitching and hiking. (For information on the risks associated with hitchhiking, see p344.) Permits are not required for the sights in this section.

TSURPHU MONASTERY མཚུར་ཕུ་དགོན་པ་ 楚布寺

elev 4480m

Around 65km west of Lhasa, **Tsurphu Monastery** (Chubu Si; admission Y45) is the seat of the Karmapa branch of the Kagyupa order of Tibetan Buddhism. The Karmapa are also known as the Black Hats, a title referring to a mythical crown, a copy of which was given to the fifth Karmapa by the Chinese emperor Yong Lo in 1407. Said to be made from the hair of *dakinis* (celestial beings, known as *khandroma* in Tibetan), the black hat, embellished with gold, is now kept at Rumtek Monastery in Sikkim, India. You'll see images of the 16th Karmapa wearing the hat, holding it with his hand to stop it flying away (that's how powerful it is).

It was the first Karmapa, Dusum Khyenpa (1110–93), who instigated the concept of reincarnation and the Karmapa lineage has been maintained this way ever since.

The respected 16th Karmapa fled to Sikkim in 1959 after the popular uprising in Lhasa and founded a new centre at Rumtek. He died in 1981 and his reincarnation, Ogyen Trinley Dorje, an eight-year-old Tibetan boy from Kham, was announced amid great controversy by the Dalai Lama and other religious leaders in 1992 (see p146). Over 20,000 Tibetans came to Tsurphu to watch the Karmapa's coronation that year. In December 1999, the 17th Karmapa undertook a dramatic escape from Tibet into India via Mustang and the Annapurna region.

Tsurphu has an annual festival around the time of the Saga Dawa festival, on the ninth, 10th and 11th days of the fourth Tibetan month (around May). There is plenty of free-flowing *chang* (Tibetan barley beer), as well as ritual *cham* dancing and the unfurling of a great thangka on the platform across the river from the monastery.

History

Tsurphu was founded in 1187 by Dusum Khyenpa, some 40 years after he established the Karmapa order in Kham, his birthplace. It was the third Karmapa monastery to be built and, after the death of the first Karmapa, it became the head monastery for the order.

The Karmapa order traditionally enjoyed strong ties with the kings and monasteries of Tsang, a legacy that proved a liability when conflict broke out between the kings of Tsang and the Gelugpa order. When the fifth Dalai Lama invited the Mongolian army of Gushri Khan to do away with his opponents in Tsang, Tsurphu was sacked (in 1642) and the Karmapa's political clout effectively came to an end. Shorn of its political influence, Tsurphu nevertheless bounced back as an important spiritual centre and is one of the few Kagyud institutions still functioning in the Ü region. When Chinese forces invaded in 1950, around 1000 monks were in residence. Now there are about 300 monks.

Viewing the Monastery

The large **assembly hall** in the main courtyard houses a chörten (stupa) containing relics of the 16th Karmapa, as well as statues of Öpagme (Amitabha), Sakyamuni (Sakya Thukpa), and the eighth and 16th Karmapas. Upstairs are the private quarters of the

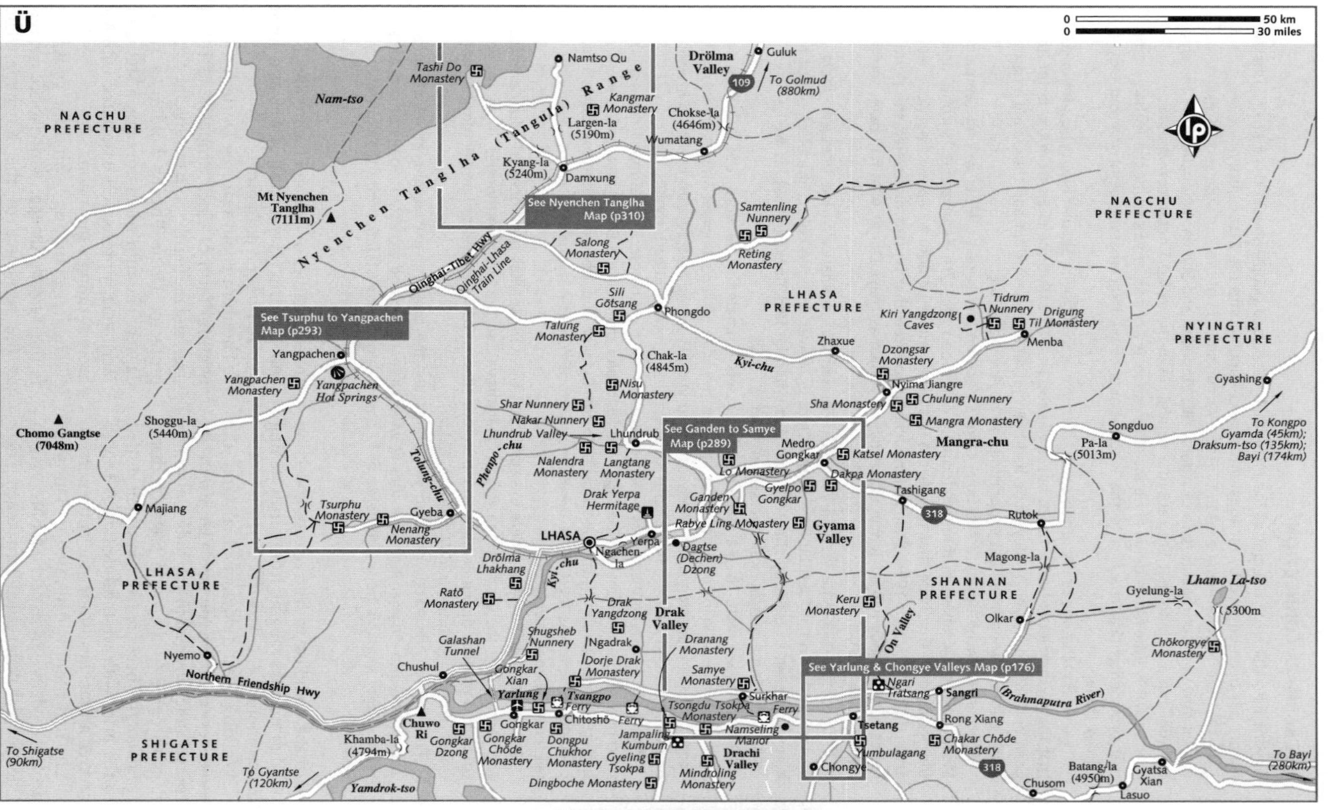
Ü
0 50 km
0 30 miles
NAGCHU PREFECTURE
Nam-tso
Tashi Do Monastery
Namtso Qu
Nyenchen Tanglha (Tangula) Range
Kangmar Monastery
Largen-la (5190m)
Kyang-la (5240m)
Damxung
Wumatang
Chokse-la (4646m)
Drölma Valley
Guluk
109
To Golmud (880km)
Mt Nyenchen Tanglha (7111m)
See Nyenchen Tanglha Map (p310)
NAGCHU PREFECTURE
Qinghai-Tibet Hwy
Qinghai-Lhasa Train Line
Salong Monastery
Samtenling Nunnery
Reting Monastery
Sili Gōtsang
Phongdo
LHASA PREFECTURE
Talung Monastery
Chak-la (4845m)
Kyi-chu
Zhaxue
Kiri Yangdzong Caves
Tidrum Nunnery
Drigung Til Monastery
Menba
NYINGTRI PREFECTURE
Dzongsar Monastery
Nyima Jiangre
Chulung Nunnery
Sha Monastery
Mangra Monastery
Mangra-chu
Gyashing
To Kongpo Gyamda (45km); Draksum-tso (135km); Bayi (174km)
Songduo
Pa-la (5013m)
See Tsurphu to Yangpachen Map (p293)
Yangpachen
Yangpachen Monastery
Yangpachen Hot Springs
Chomo Gangtse (7048m)
Shoggu-la (5440m)
Tolung-chu
Tsurphu Monastery
Gyeba
Nenang Monastery
Majiang
Nisu Monastery
Shar Nunnery
Nakar Nunnery
Lhundrub Valley
Lhundrub
Phenpo-chu
Nalendra Monastery
Langtang Monastery
Drak Yerpa Hermitage
See Ganden to Samye Map (p289)
Medro Gongkar
Katsel Monastery
Lo Monastery
Dakpa Monastery
Gyelpo Gongkar
Ganden Monastery
Rabye Ling Monastery
Gyama Valley
Tashigang
318
Rutok
LHASA
Yerpa
Ngachen-la
Dagtse (Dechen) Dzong
Magong-la
Drölma Lhakhang
Kyi-chu
Ratō Monastery
LHASA PREFECTURE
Drak Yangdzong
Drak Valley
Keru Monastery
SHANNAN PREFECTURE
Gyelung-la
Lhamo La-tso
5300m
Olkar
On Valley
Shugsheb Nunnery
Ngadrak
Dranang Monastery
Galashan Tunnel
Dorje Drak Monastery
Samye Monastery
Chōkorgye Monastery
Nyemo
Chushul
Gongkar Xian
See Yarlung & Chongye Valleys Map (p176)
Ngari Tratsang
Sangri
Northern Friendship Hwy
Yarlung Tsangpo
Ferry
Surkhar
Brahmaputra River
Chitoshō
Tsongdu Tsokpa Monastery
Ferry
Chuwo Ri
Gongkar
Namseling Manor
Tsetang
Rong Xiang
Jampaling Kumbum
To Shigatse (90km)
SHIGATSE PREFECTURE
Khamba-la (4794m)
Gongkar Dzong
Gongkar Chōde Monastery
Dongpu Chukhor Monastery
Gyeling Tsokpa
Drachi Valley
Yumbulagang
Chakar Chōde Monastery
To Bayi (280km)
To Gyantse (120km)
Yamdrok-tso
Dingboche Monastery
Mindroling Monastery
Chongye
318
Chusom
Batang-la (4950m)
Gyatsa Xian
Lasuo

Ü

THE KARMAPA CONNECTION

Anyone who thinks of Tibetans as lofty, spiritually absorbed people should think again. Tibetan history has been dogged by factional intrigue, continuing into the 21st century.

In 1981 the 16th Karmapa died in Chicago. Administration of the Karmapa sect in Sikkim was passed down to four regents, two of whom, Situ Rinpoche and Shamar Rinpoche, have become embroiled in a dispute that has caused a painful rift in the exiled Tibetan community.

In early 1992 the four regents announced the discovery of a letter written by the 16th Karmapa that provided critical clues as to the whereabouts of his reincarnation, eight-year-old Ogyen Trinley Dorje.

Two weeks after one of the regents was killed in a road accident, Shamar Rinpoche announced that the mystery letter was a fraud, but it was too late. By early June clues from the letter had been deciphered, Ogyen Trinley Dorje had been found in eastern Tibet and the Dalai Lama had made a formal announcement supporting the boy's candidature.

Shamar Rinpoche opposed the Dalai Lama's decision and began a letter-writing campaign. Meanwhile, the Chinese authorities formally enthroned the 17th Karmapa at Tsurphu, using the occasion to announce that they had a 'historical and legal right to appoint religious leaders in Tibet'. In March 1994, Shamar Rinpoche announced that he had discovered the rightful reincarnation, a boy named Tenzin Chentse (also known as Thaye Dorje), who had been spirited out of China to Delhi.

In December 1999, the then 14-year-old 17th Karmapa dramatically fled Tibet into India. In a letter left behind at Tsurphu he told the Chinese he was going to collect the black hat of the Karmapa (taken to India by the 16th Karmapa when he fled Tibet in 1959), as well as several relics, including a human skull encased in silver.

The stakes are high. The Karmapa sect has assets estimated to be worth US$1.2 billion and up to one million followers, including many in the USA. Sikkim's Rumtek Monastery (now the head Karmapa monastery) was briefly occupied in 1993 by Indian troops to break up brawling by monks divided over the issue. Both Karmapas have received death threats.

The flight of the Karmapa was a particular blow for the Chinese. The Karmapa ranks as the third-most important lama in Tibet after the Panchen Lama and the Dalai Lama and is the only high-level reincarnation recognised by both the Chinese and Tibetan authorities. China's fury over the escape was levelled at the Karmapa's tutor Yongzin Nyima who spent 15 months in jail for his alleged involvement.

For the moment, at least, there is a stalemate. The Karmapa has been granted refugee status and residence at the Gyuto Monastery in Dharamsala, but the Indian authorities, in an attempt to avoid a political dispute with China, have not allowed him to travel to Rumtek (until recently China did not recognise India's claim to Sikkim).

For more on the starkly differing viewpoints, see the pro-Karmapa website at www.rumtek.org and the pro–Shamar Rinpoche sites at www.karmapa.org and www.karmapa-issue.org. Mick Brown's very readable book *The Dance of 17 Lives* is a good investigation into the controversy.

Karmapa, complete with an eclectic collection of English books ranging from birdwatching to astronomy.

Walking west (clockwise) around the monastery complex you pass a large *darchen* (prayer pole) covered in yak hide and prayer flags to come to the main **protector chapel** *(gönkhang)*. There are five rooms, all stuffed to the brim with wrathful deities. A row of severed animal heads lines the entry portico.

The first room is dedicated to Tsurphu's protector deity, an aspect of blue Nagpo Chenpo (Mahakala) called Bernakchen. There are also statues of Palden Lhamo (Shri Devi) and Tamdrin (Hayagriva), as well as a spirit trap and several dead birds.

The third room features Dorje Drolo, a wrathful form of Guru Rinpoche astride a tiger, and the fourth room features the Kagyud protector Dorje Phurba holding a ritual dagger. The fifth room contains a statue of Tseringma, a protectress associated with Mt Everest, riding a snow lion.

The large building behind the *gönkhang* is the **Serdung Chanpo**, which once served as the residence of the Karmapa. The side chapel features new statues of all 16 previous Karmapas.

The **Lhakhang Chenmo**, which is to the right of the Serdung Chanpo, houses a new 20m-high statue of Sakyamuni that rises through three storeys; this replaced a celebrated 13th-century image destroyed during the Cultural Revolution.

Behind the Serdung Chanpo and Lhakhang Chenmo is the sprawling **Chökang Gang Monastery**, the residence of the exiled regent of Tsurphu.

The outer walls of the monastery are marked at four corners by four coloured chörtens.

Tsurphu Kora

The Tsurphu kora, a walk of around two hours, is quite taxing if you are not acclimatised to the altitude. It ascends 150m, past springs, shrines and meditation retreats, providing splendid views of Tsurphu below.

To follow the kora take the track west of Tsurphu that leads up past walls of mani stones to a walled garden (see p292). Bear right here up to a sky burial site *(dürtro)* and follow the cairns that snake up the hill to a small pass marked by prayer flags. The kora then winds in and out of the ridges above the monastery and detours up to the Samtenling retreat, before descending eastward into a gully to the chörten at the northeastern corner of the monastery.

Sleeping

The small **Monastery Guesthouse** (dm Y25), opposite the main assembly hall, has damp and dark dorm rooms with four or six beds on concrete floors.

Getting There & Away

About 40km west of Lhasa, the road to Tsurphu crosses the Tolung-chu near the railroad bridge. From here it's another 25km up a rough dirt track to the monastery.

A minibus goes to Tsurphu (one way/return, Y15/25, two hours) from Lhasa's Barkhor Sq around 7am, leaving when full. It heads back to Lhasa at around 2pm, but confirm this with the driver. If you miss the monastery bus then take Lhasa city bus 108 to its terminus at Gyeba village at the mouth of the valley and hitch from there. (We got a lift with an electricity company car that stopped every 400m to read the meter and hand out electricity bills – it took hours!).

You could hire a Land Cruiser for Y500 return or, better, tag a visit here onto a trip to Nam-tso. You should organise this in advance with your travel agency. Some will let you detour to Tsurphu for free, others will add up to Y150 to the price of the tour. The road to Tsurphu passes **Nenang Monastery**, home to the young 11th Powa Rinpoche, which is worth a quick stop if you have your own transport.

NAM-TSO གནམ་མཚོ་ 纳木错

elev 4730m

Approximately 240km northwest of Lhasa, **Nam-tso** (Namucuo; admission Y80) is the second-largest saltwater lake in China and one of the most beautiful natural sights in Tibet. It is over 70km long, reaches a width of 30km and is 35m at its deepest point. When the ice melts in late April, the lake is a miraculous shade of turquoise and there are magnificent views of the nearby mountains. The wide open spaces, dotted with the tents of local *drokpas* (nomads), are intoxicating.

The Nyenchen Tanglha (Tangula) range, with peaks of more than 7000m, towers over the lake to the south – it was these mountains that Heinrich Harrer and Peter Aufschnaiter crossed on their incredible journey to Lhasa (their expedition is documented in the book *Seven Years in Tibet*).

Whatever you do, do not sign up for a lift out here until you have been in Lhasa for at least a week. It is not unusual for visitors to get altitude sickness on an overnight stay out at the lake. The sudden altitude gain of 1100m is not to be treated lightly.

For more on the trek to Nam-tso over the Kyang-la, see p308. Those seeking detailed information on Nam-tso should refer to *Divine Dyads: Ancient Civilization in Tibet* by John Vincent Bellezza (though this book may be hard to find).

Tashi Do Monastery བཀྲ་ཤིས་མདོ་དགོན་པ་

Most travellers head for Tashi Do, situated on a hammerhead of land that juts into the southeastern corner of the lake. Here at the foot of two wedge-shaped hills are a couple of small chapels with views back across the clear turquoise waters to the huge snowy Nyenchen Tanglha massif (7111m).

The first **chapel** is the smaller but more atmospheric of the two. The main statue is of Luwang Gyelpo, the king of the *nagas* (snake spirits). Pilgrims test their sin by lifting the heavy stone of Nyenchen Tanglha, the god who resides in the nearby mountain of the same name (and who is also the protector of Marpo Ri, on which the Potala is built).

The second, main **chapel** features a central Guru Rinpoche statue and the trinity of Öpagme, Chenresig and Pema Jigme, known collectively as the Cholong Dusom. Protectors include Nyenchen Tanglha on a horse and the blue-faced Nam-tso, the goddess of the lake, who rides a water serpent. Both gods are rooted deep in Bön belief. Several other chapels and retreats are honeycombed into the surrounding cliffs.

There are some fine walks in this area. The short **kora** takes less than an hour. It leads off west from the accommodation area to a

NOMADS

One attraction of a trip to Nam-tso is the opportunity to get a peek at the otherwise inaccessible life of Tibet's *drokpas,* seminomadic herders who make their home in the Changtang, Tibet's vast and remote northern plateau. (You may also get the chance to visit a *drokpa* camp along the road from Sok to Nagchu or on the trek from Ganden to Samye.)

Nomad camps are centred on their spider-like brown or black yak-hair tents. These are usually shared by one family, though a smaller subsidiary tent may be used when a son marries and has children of his own. The interior of a nomad tent holds all the family's possessions. There will be a stove for cooking and boiling water and also a family altar dedicated to Buddhist deities and various local protectors, including those of the livestock, tent pole and hearth. The principal diet of nomads is tsampa (roasted-barley flour) and yak butter (mixed together with tea), dried yak cheese and sometimes yak meat.

Tending the herds of yaks and sheep is carried out by the men during the day. Women and children stay together in the camp, where they are guarded by one of the men and the ferocious Tibetan mastiffs that are the constant companions of Tibet's nomads. The women and children usually spend the day weaving blankets and tanning sheepskins.

With the onset of winter it is time to go to the markets of an urban centre. The farmers of Tibet do the same, and trade between nomads and farmers provides the former with tsampa and the latter with meat and butter. Most nomads these days have a winter home base and only make established moves to distant pastures during the rest of the year.

Nomads' marriage customs differ from those of farming communities. When a child reaches a marriageable age, inquiries are made, and when a suitable match is found the two people meet and exchange gifts. If they like each other, these informal meetings may go on for some time. The date for a marriage is decided by an astrologer, and when the date arrives the family of the son rides to the camp of the prospective daughter-in-law to collect her. On arrival there is a custom of feigned mutual abuse that appears to verge on giving way to violence at any moment. This may continue for several days before the son's family finally carry off the daughter to their camp and she enters a new life.

The nomads of Tibet have also traditionally traded in salt, which is collected from the Changtang (northern plateau) and transported south in bricks, often to the border with Nepal, where it is traded for grain (see the documentary *The Saltmen of Tibet*, p17). These annual caravans are fast dying out. Traditional life suffered its greatest setback during the Cultural Revolution when nomads were collectivised and forcibly settled by the government. In 1981 the communes were dissolved and the collectivised livestock divided equally, with everyone getting five yaks, 25 sheep and seven goats.

Drokpas now number around two million across the plateau, half of their pre-1950 population. Government incentives are forcing the settlement of nomads, further reducing their numbers and grazing grounds. The introduction of the motorbike has further transformed nomad life. Pressure also comes in the form of enforced migration dates and winter housing, as well as attitude changes within the *drokpas* themselves as young people are fleeing the grasslands in search of a 'better life' in urban centres. How far into the 21st century their way of life will persist is a matter for debate among Tibetologists.

hermit's cave hidden behind a large splinter of rock. The trail continues round to a rocky promontory of cairns and prayer flags, where pilgrims undertake a ritual washing, and then continues past several caves and a *chaktsal gang* (prostration point). The twin rock towers here look like two hands in the *namaste* greeting and are connected to the male and female attributes of the meditational deity Demchok (Chakrasamvara). Pilgrims squeeze into the deep slices of the nearby cliff face as a means of sin detection. They also drink water dripping from cave roofs and some ingest 'holy dirt'.

From here the path curves around the shoreline and passes a group of ancient rock paintings, where pilgrims test their merit by attempting to place a finger in a small hole with their eyes closed. At the northeastern corner of the hill is the **Mani Ringmo**, a large mani (prayer) wall at whose end is a chörten with a *chakje* (handprint) of the third Karmapa. From here you can hike up to the top of the hill for good views.

If you have enough time, it's well worth walking to the top of the larger of the two hills. There are superb views to the northeast of the Tanglha (Tangula) range, which marks the modern border between Tibet and Qinghai (Amdo).

Sleeping & Eating

The good news is that there are now half a dozen places to stay at Tashi Do, which these days resembles a tented village. The bad news is that development has also brought generators, motorbikes and rising levels of rubbish – all of which are beginning to take their toll.

Bedding is provided at all places but nights can get very cold, so it's a good idea to bring a sleeping bag and warm clothes. Between the altitude, cold and the barking dogs, most people sleep fitfully at best. Accommodation is only available between April and October. There are plenty of decent camping spots far away from the hubbub if you are prepared for the cold.

Tent restaurants offer Sichuanese dishes at slightly inflated prices. Several places sell delicious locally made yoghurt.

There's not much between the following places to stay. Things to check for include the thickness of the mattress, cleanliness of the duvet and proximity of rabid dogs.

Gesang's (dm Y25) The latest arrival, with proper beds in spacious five-person tents, but it's close to psychotically barking dogs, so bring your ear plugs.

Tashi Island Hotel (扎西岛宾馆; Zhaxidao Binguan; dm Y25-35) Perhaps the best place at present, with pleasant partitioned four-bed tents or larger octagonal tents, the latter close to a noisy generator.

Fangniu Binguan (☎ 0891-650 1854; dm Y35-70) Has proper beds in a clean, sterile cabin (Y60 to Y70) or a four-person tent (Y45 to Y50), or thinner mattresses in black yak-hair tents, embroidered with crane motifs (Y35).

Yang's Binguan Sheep Guesthouse (羊宾馆; Yang Binguan; dm Y25-50, r Y100) Closest to the chapels. Choose here between good beds in an ugly portacabin or foam beds in a three- or five-person tent. There's a decent restaurant.

Damshung Pema Hotel (当雄县白马宾馆; Dangxiong Xian Baima Binguan; ☎ 0891-611 2098; dm Y30-48, s/d/tr with bathroom Y268/318/318;) Located in the southern half of the gateway town of Damxung (4220m). This is the best place to stay in town if it's late. The Tibetan atmosphere makes a pleasant change, with rooms with bathroom decorated with Tibetan carpets and traditional furniture. The dorm rooms share squat toilets but no showers.

Damxung is a popular lunch spot en route to Nam-tso. There are several good Muslim noodle joints as you enter the town from the south, including the **Linxia Shuangcheng Qingzhen Fanguan** (临夏双城清真饭馆; dishes Y6-10).

Getting There & Away

There is no public transport to Nam-tso. Most Lhasa travel agencies offer minibus tours for around Y150 to Y200 per person, which often includes the Y80 entry ticket. Most are day trips, which gives you just enough time to rush around the kora, get a gigantic altitude headache and then pile back in the minibus; opt for an overnight trip if you can. It's a four-hour drive to Nam-tso from Lhasa.

Land Cruiser hire for a two-day return trip costs Y1200 to Y1500 and can fit four passengers, (guides not required). Many groups stop off at the hot-spring pool at Yangpachen (see p295) or Tsurphu Monastery en route, often for no extra charge. It's possible to return to Lhasa via Reting Monastery and either Drigung Til or the Lhundrub Valley, making for an interesting and adventurous loop for around Y2800.

The nearest place served by public transport is Damxung (Dangxiong). Public buses depart from Lhasa (Y44) at around 7.30am from west of the Yak Hotel. Nagchu-bound buses also pass through Damxung. From Damxung, private minibuses (Y30) depart for Lhasa from the turn-off to Nam-tso half-hourly until noon. You might also find a seat in a taxi (Y40). From Damxung, you'll have to hitch the 62km to Tashi Do.

Some intrepid travellers have made it all the way out to Nam-tso on a mountain bike, though the shiny wheels seem to drive most nomads' dogs even more berserk than normal. The road is now paved all the way to Tashi Do.

By road it's 9km to the checkpost where you pay the entry fee, a further 16km steep uphill journey to the 5190m Largen-la, 7km to a junction and then a circuitous 30km to Tashi Do. Around 4km before the checkpost, a motorable dirt road offers a possible detour to Kyang-rag Monastery (see p309). Another road leads north from the ticket gate to Kangmar Monastery.

LHUNDRUB VALLEY ལྷུན་གྲུབ་གཞུང་

☎ 0894 / elev 3800m

Few travellers get to this lovely valley, around 70km from Lhasa, though it offers plenty of scope for adventurous DIY exploration. Also known as Phenpo, the valley is easy to get to (though less easy to get around) and is dotted with interesting monasteries. The light traffic and dirt roads make it a particularly good destination for mountain bikers.

Lhundrub ལྷུན་གྲུབ་ 林周

The main town in the valley is Lhundrub (Linzhou), which serves as a useful base. The northwestern section of town has the main shops and restaurants, the centre has the interesting **Ganden Chökhorling Monastery**, and the southeast has the minibus stand.

If you need to stay the night, the **Xinxin Zhaodaisuo** (鑫鑫招待所; ☎ 612 2666; d/tr without bathroom Y60/90) offers the best budget accommodation, whereas the **Government Guesthouse** (政府招待所; Zhengfu Zhaodaisuo; ☎ 612 2326; d with bathroom Y160) has the best rooms in town.

Minibuses to Lhundrub (Y15, one hour) run every 20 minutes from Lhasa's Eastern Bus Station, departing when full. The last bus back to Lhasa returns around 7pm.

Nalendra Monastery ན་ལེན་ཊ་དགོན་པ་

Ruins still dwarf the rebuilding work at Nalendra Monastery, founded in 1435 by the lama Rongtonpa (1367–1449), a contemporary of Tsongkhapa. It was largely destroyed in 1959.

To get an idea of the original layout, look closely at the mural on the immediate left as you enter the **main assembly hall**. The impressive *gönkhang* (women cannot enter) has a central Gompo Gur, a form of Nagpo Chenpo (Mahakala) and protector of the Sakyapa school, as well as statues of Pehar (on an elephant) and Namse (Vairocana, on a snow lion), both in the left corner. Look for the three huge wild yak heads in varying states of decay.

The main hall has a statue of Rongtonpa in a glass case. The inner sanctum features Rongtonpa in the front centre, flanked by two Sakyapa lamas, and an inner kora. It's worth catching one of the atmospheric prayer meetings, which are followed by a mass slurping of butter tea.

Other chapels worth popping into include the Tsar Kangtsang, still under renovation, the *shedra* (monastic college), the Jampa Kangtsang (with its interesting statue of skeletons in a *yabyum* pose), and the ruins of the *dzong* (fort) outside the monastery gate to the west.

Nalendra and Langtang monasteries are an excellent half-day trip by tractor (Y50 to Y100) or by motorbike (Y60 per bike); both are available for hire if you ask around in Lhundrub.

Alternatively, you can walk from Lhundrub to Nalendra in half a day, stopping at Langtang en route. From Lhundrub minibus stand, head south over the bridge and follow the dirt tracks as they swing west by the irrigation canal, paralleling the mountain ridge. You can see the former road to Lhasa snaking up the mountainside to the south.

Langtang Monastery གླངས་ཐར་དགོན་

On the way back from Nalendra it's worth stopping off at Langtang Monastery, visible from afar due to its huge Kadampa-style chörtens. The monastery was founded in 1093 and once had 200 monks. Today only two chapels and the ruins of the main assembly hall remain, served by 33 monks. Like Nalendra, Langtang was built as a Kadampa monastery but was subsumed into the Sakyapa school. The main hall has a central statue of Jampa (Maitreya), the Future Buddha, with Sakya Pandita (Kunga Gyaltsen, 1182–1251) to the left. Sadly, the famous *sungjolma* (speaking) statue of Drölma (Tara) was stolen a decade ago. The protector chapel to the left has a central image of Langtangpa, the 11th-century founder of the monastery, but it's often locked these days.

Langtang is a 1½ hour walk from Lhundrub. Nalendra is a further 90-minute hike away.

Other Monasteries

From Nalendra it's also possible to hike north across the valley for half a day to **Shar Nunnery** (famed for its impressive Kadampa-style chörtens), sleep the night there and return the next day to Lhundrub via **Nakar Nunnery**. You will need a sleeping bag and food. You could also do this in a half-day motorbike tour or add it on to a visit to Nalendra for a long day excursion (Y100 to 150).

Other monasteries worth exploring at the northern end of the valley include ruined **Lhundrub Dzong** and, 7km further, **Nisu Monastery**, both visible from the main road. The latter is recognisable by its row of eight yellow-topped chörtens. At the head of the valley the road switches back up to the Chak-la (4845m) and then winds down past nomads' tents for 13km towards Talung Monastery.

TALUNG MONASTERY སྟག་ལུང་དགོན་པ་ 达龙寺

elev 4150m

Dynamited by Red Guards and now in ruins in the green fields of the Pak-chu Valley, the sprawling monastic complex of Talung (or Taglung; Dalong Si in Chinese) is around 120km north of Lhasa by road. Rebuilding is currently underway, but not on the scale of other, more important, monasteries in the area.

Talung was founded in 1180 by Tangpa Tashipel as the seat of the Talung school of the Kagyupa order. At one time it may have housed some 7000 monks (it currently has 160), but was eventually eclipsed in importance and grandeur by its former branch, the Riwoche Tsuglhakhang in eastern Tibet (p261).

The site's most important structure was its **Tsuglhakhang** (grand temple), also known as the Red Palace. The building was reduced to rubble but its impressively thick stone walls remain.

To the south is the main assembly hall, the Targyeling Lhakhang. Look out for the destroyed set of three chörtens, one of which contained the remains of the monastery's founder.

To the west in the main monastery building, the Choning (Tsenyi) Lhakhang is used as a debating hall and has a statue of the bearded Tashipel to the right. The fine *cham* masks are worn during a festival on the eighth day of the eighth month (the festival clothes are in a metal box in the corner). Snarling stuffed wolves hang from the ceiling of the protector chapel next door. The Jagji Lhakhang behind the Choning Lhakhang has fine new murals around a central mandala.

Down in the centre of the village is the renovated Tashikang Tsar, the residence of the local reincarnation Tsedru Rinpoche, who died in 2007.

An hour's walk north of the turn-off to Talung brings you to **Sili Götsang**, an amazing eagle's-nest hermitage perched high above the main road.

If you need to spend the night, there is a very basic **monastery guesthouse** (dm Y15) and a small shop that sells instant noodles, beer and candles (there's no electricity).

The monastery is 2.5km west of the main road to Phongdo. For information on reaching the monastery, see p152.

RETING MONASTERY ར་སྒྲེང་དགོན་པ་ 热振寺

elev 4100m

Pre-1950 photographs show **Reting Monastery** (Rezhen Si; admission Y30) sprawled gracefully across the flank of a juniper-clad hill in the Rong-chu Valley. Like Ganden Monastery, it was devastated by Red Guards and its remains hammer home the tragic waste caused by the ideological zeal of the Cultural Revolution. Still, the site is one of the most beautiful in the region. The Dalai Lama has stated that should he ever return to Tibet it is at Reting, not Lhasa, that he would like to reside.

The monastery dates back to 1056. It was initially associated with Atisha (Jowo-je) but in its later years it had an important connection with the Gelugpa order and the Dalai Lamas. Two regents – the de facto rulers of Tibet for the interregnum between the death of a Dalai Lama and the majority of his next reincarnation – were chosen from the Reting abbots. The fifth Reting Rinpoche was regent from 1933 to 1947. He played a key role in the search for the current Dalai Lama and served as his senior tutor. He was later accused of collusion with the Chinese and died in a Tibetan prison.

The sixth Reting Rinpoche died in 1997. In January 2001 the Chinese announced that a boy named Sonam Phuntsog had been identified out of 700 candidates as the seventh Reting Rinpoche. Significantly, the announcement came just two days after the Karmapa set off on his flight from Tibet to India (p146). The Dalai Lama refuses to recognise the choice, and denounces it as part of a long-term strategy by the Chinese government to control religious leadership in Tibet.

The young *rinpoche* currently resides under Public Security Bureau (PSB; Gong'anju) surveillance at his official residence, 2km below the monastery by the riverside. Foreign groups staying the night at Reting must register with the PSB.

Viewing the Monastery

The current main assembly hall, or **Tsogchen**, is half its original size. Enter the hall to the right to get to the main inner shrine, the Ütse (women not allowed). The central statue of Jampai Dorje is an unusual amalgam of the gods Jampelyang (Manjushri), Chana Dorje (Vajrapani) and Chenresig (Avalokiteshvara). To the left is an ancient thangka of Drölma that, according to our monk guide, was brought here by Atisha himself. A wooden box beside the altar holds the giant molar of Sangye Wösong, the Buddha before Sakyamuni.

To the left of the Ütse entrance is a rare mural of the 14th (current) Dalai Lama (though it doesn't really resemble him); to the right of the entrance is a picture of the current Reting Rinpoche and a footprint and photo of the fifth Reting Rinpoche. In front of the entrance is a platform used for creating sand mandalas. Behind the Ütse is a storeroom stuffed with Tantric drums.

As you leave the chapel look for a second hall to your right. The hall contains a gold chörten with the remains of the sixth Reting Rinpoche, Tenzin Jigne. Lining the back wall are statues of all six previous Reting Rinpoches. The metal box in the right corner holds a giant thangka, unveiled once a year. The main courtyard is often full of yak hides, drying in the sun.

The monastery is still graced by surrounding juniper forest, said to have sprouted from the hairs of its founder Dromtompa. A 40-minute **kora** leads from the guesthouse around the monastery ruins, passing several stone carvings, a series of eight chörtens and an active sky burial site. Further up the hillside is the *drubkhang* (meditation retreat) where Tsongkhapa composed the Lamrim Chenmo (Graduated Path), a key Gelugpa text. The large escarpment draped with prayer flags to the right is the Sengye Drak (Lion's Rock), where there are several more retreats.

A pleasant hour-long walk northeast of Reting leads to the village-like **Samtenling Nunnery**, home to over 240 nuns. The main chapel houses the meditation cave of Tsongkhapa; to the right is a stone footprint of Tsongkhapa and hoofprint belonging to the horse of the protectress Pelden Lhamo. The trail branches off to the nunnery from the sky burial site to the northeast of the monastery.

The **monastery guesthouse** (dm Y35) offers basic dormitory rooms and simple meals.

Getting There & Away

Talung and Reting monasteries are most easily visited together in a rented vehicle. The cost of a two-day Land Cruiser trip should be Y1000 to Y1300. A guide and permits are not necessary. You could add a detour to Drigung Til Monastery and make a nice four-day loop for a few hundred yuan more.

A public bus departs for Reting (Y40, four hours) daily at 8am from the Lhasa Eastern Bus Station, passing near Talung and returning the following day. More frequent transport goes to Lhundrub, from where you'd have to rely on hitching (for information on the risks of hitching, see p344), though with enough time you shouldn't have any major problems.

Reting is 25km from the crossroads settlement of Phongdo (Pangduo Xian), which has a ruined *dzong* and is overlooked by a mountain of near perfect conical proportions.

ROAD TO DRIGUNG TIL MONASTERY

Increasingly popular destinations for independent travellers are the Drigung Til Monastery and Tidrum Nunnery, around 120km northeast of Lhasa. Though they can be reached by bus, rented transport or hitching, the valleys retain an untouched and timeless

(Continued on page 161)

GARRY WEARE

Chörten (p208) at Rongphu Monastery, with the north face of Mt Everest towering in the background

The glittering roof of Tashilhunpo Monastery (p191), the traditional seat of the Panchen Lama

CHRIS BEALL

Chanting begins early in life at Nechung Monastery (p132)

BRADLEY MAYHEW

BRADLEY MAYHEW

Devout woman spinning a prayer wheel at Rongphu Monastery (p207)

Walking the kora (p194) at Tashilhunpo Monastery

CHRIS BEA

GAVIN QUIRKE

A still moment in the perpetual motion of the Barkhor circuit (p102)

JULIET COOMBE

Tibetan woman adorned with turquoise and coral jewellery (p48)

Khampa men with their traditional red hair braids (p49)

BRADLEY MAYHEW

KEREN SU

The last rays of sunshine at Shigatse (p190), with Tashilhunpo Monastery towering above the town

The turquoise-blue waters of Yamdrok-tso (p181) stand in contrast to the colours of the sky

ANTHONY PLUMME

ANTHONY PLUMMER

A colourful collection of prayer flags on the shore of Nam-tso (p147)

Traditional Tibetan farms (p46), sheltered in a tranquil green valley

KEREN SU

RICHARD I'ANSON

Wrathful and peaceful deities depicted in the entrance to the main assembly hall at Sakya Monastery (p201)

A monk worshipping at the huge Buddha portrait carved into the rock at Drepung Monastery (p129)

KEREN SU

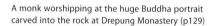

HILARY SMITH

Spinning a prayer wheel (p65), one of the integral parts of a Tibetan monastery

BRADLEY MAYHEW

A traditional sand mandala (p60) before it is swept away a week or so later as a symbol of impermanence and nonattachment

JULIET COOMBE

Traditional Tibetan instrument (p55)

Yak butter (p78) for sale in the market, Lhasa

JULIET COOMBE

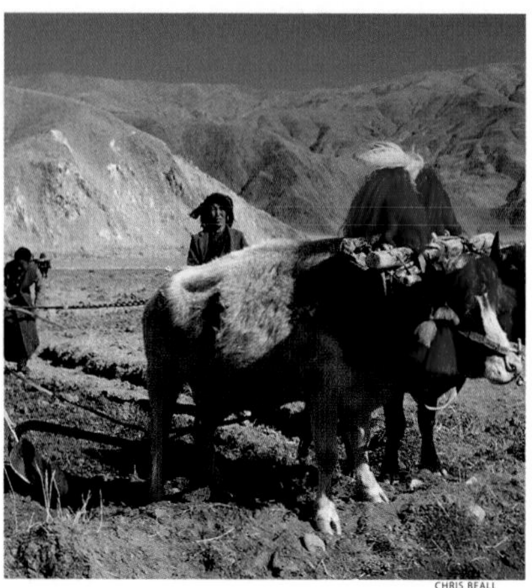

CHRIS BEALL

Farmers and their colourfully decorated yaks (p84)

Unusual grey, red and white stone houses display a form of Tibetan secular architecture (p59)

CRAIG PERSHOUSE

Traditional white rural housing in the small town of Nyalam (p211)

ANDREW PEACOC

(Continued from page 152)

quality that makes them seem much further from Lhasa than they actually are.

Gyama Valley རྒྱ་མ་སྣང་ 甲玛

This valley, 60km east of Lhasa, is famed as the birthplace of Tibet's greatest king, Songtsen Gampo, who lived here until he became king at the age of 15. It's an easy half-day excursion by bus from Lhasa and it's also a perfect place to explore on bike.

From the main highway it's 2km south to the **Gyelpo Gongkar**, a chapel just east of the tarmac road and dedicated to Songtsen Gampo and his two wives. The original building dates from the 7th century and resembles a small Yumbulagang. A black and white photo inside shows the original building, which was destroyed in the Cultural Revolution.

From here it's an hour-long walk south to the **Rabye Ling Monastery** and, in the village behind, the huge Kadam-style funeral **chörten** of Sangye On (1251–96), a master of the Talung School and founder of the Riwoche Tsuglhakhang (see p261). The small monastery boasts some fine murals and a stone mantra that is said to have appeared naturally at the moment of Songtsen Gampo's birth.

From here, continue 10 minutes north along the paved road to the three **Dumburi chörtens** and the nearby shrine and natural springs that mark the birthplace of King Songtsen Gampo. Archaeologists have linked the nearby ruins of Jampa Mingyur Ling to the palace that Songtsen Gampo's father built after leaving the Chongye Valley. From here it's a 5km (1¼ hour) walk back to the main road.

To get to the valley, take a frequent Medro Gongkar–bound minibus from Lhasa's Eastern Bus Station (Y15, 40 minutes) and get off at kilometre marker 4572, 8km before Medro Gongkar.

KILOMETRE MARKERS ALONG THE KYI-CHU

Lhasa to Medro Gongkar marker	Feature
4632	Lhasa Bridge
4611	Dagtse/Dechen Dzong & Sanga Monastery
4610/09	Dagtse bridge, turn-off to Lhundrub
4592/1	Turn-off to Ganden Monastery
4587	Large chörten surrounded by three others
4584/3	Lhamo Monastery
4572	Gyama village & valley
4569	Roadside chörten
4564	Medro Gongkar

Medro Gongkar མལ་གྲོ་གུང་དཀར་ 墨竹工卡

☎ 0891 / pop 2000 / elev 3600m

On the wide banks of the Kyi-chu, 75km northeast of Lhasa, Medro Gongkar (Mozhu Gongka) is just a pit stop en route to Drigung. If you have time it's worth stopping at **Katsel Monastery**, 3km from town on the road to Drigung. Legend has it that this Kagyupa order monastery was founded by the 7th-century King Songtsen Gampo who was led here by the Buddha disguised as a doe with antlers. The temple is also significant as one of the original demoness-subduing temples (p105) – it pinned the monster's right shoulder.

There are several places to stay in Medro Gongkar, as well as lots of Chinese restaurants.

Jama Trigang Tashi Guesthouse (Jiama Zhikang Zhaxi Lüguan; 甲玛志康扎西旅馆; ☎ 613 2666; dm Y10-15, tr per bed Y30-35) There are plenty of room types here but the best bet are the triples. It's near the east end of town, where the minibuses depart for Nyima Jiangre.

Wenxin Zhaodaisuo (温馨招待所; ☎ 135-1899 1821; dm/s/d Y20/40/60) Another decent place, with clean rooms, good beds, washbasins in each room and squat toilets down the hall. It's opposite the Agricultural Bank – enter via the road transport compound.

Minibuses go between Lhasa's Eastern Bus Station and Medro Gongkar (Y15, one hour) every 20 minutes or so until around 8pm. Smaller minibuses continue, when full, up to Nyima Jiangre (Y10) from the east end of town.

Nyima Jiangre (Drigung Qu) འབྲི་གུང་ཆུས་

☎ 0891 / pop 1500

As you continue along the upper Kyi-chu Valley from Katsel Monastery you pass two enormous ruined chörtens on the right. Halfway up the valley you come to Nyima Jiangre village, set at the auspicious confluence of three rivers. Shortly before the town is a large new dam and reservoir.

A 20-minute walk northwest of town is the Drigungpa-school **Dzongsar Monastery**. Apart from the usual statues of Guru Rinpoche and Sakyamuni inside the main assembly hall, there is a two-armed standing Chenresig, as well as the founder of the Drigung school, Jikten Gonpo (and his golden footprints). Below the hall in a protector chapel is an icon of Abchi, the white female protector of the region. Behind the monastery two chörtens stand sentinel over the beautiful upper Kyichu Valley, now partially flooded by the new dam below.

Also nearby is **Sha Monastery**, 2km southeast of Drigung Qu, dedicated to the Dzogchen suborder. As you go in past two *dorings* (inscribed pillars), one of which dates from the 9th century, look up at the remains of a stuffed snow leopard. To the right is a side protector chapel with the Dzogchen trinity of Dorje Lekpa, Rahulla and Ekajati, and a mask depicting the mountain deity Tseringma. This chapel contains the hoofprints of the goat that allegedly carried both Dorje Lekpa and the inscribed pillars to the monastery. Continue through an unusual courtyard encircling a huge chörten, to an upstairs chapel above the entrance.

For a good day hike, walk an hour northeast up a side valley from Sha Monastery to the Nyingmapa-sect **Chulung Nunnery**. From here return to the main valley and then head up the main Mangra-chu valley for another hour to the Gelugpa school **Mangra Monastery**. Figure on around four hours' walking in total.

Gongkar Tashi Dromkhang (工卡扎西旅馆; Gongka Zhaxi Lüguan; dm Y10) is a pleasant upper-floor teahouse, whose traditional seats become beds when the last customer leaves. It's a nice bet but only if it's not busy, as there's not a great deal of privacy.

The **Amdo Naibeykhang** (安多招待所; Anduo Zhaodaisuo; dm Y20, d per bed Y50) at the east edge of town has one pleasant Tibetan-style living room with Tibetan-style beds, plus simpler dorm rooms. It also has the town's only real toilet.

For food, the **Tashi New House Restaurant** (扎西康萨饭馆; Zhaxi Kangsa Fanguan) is a cosy teahouse that offers sweet tea and *shemdre* (yak, potatoes and rice). For Chinese dishes try the Amdo Canguan at the main junction.

It's approximately 35km to Drigung Til from Nyima Jiangre.

DRIGUNG TIL MONASTERY འབྲི་གུང་མཐིལ་ 直贡梯寺

elev 4150m

Although it suffered some damage in the Cultural Revolution, **Drigung Til Monastery** (Zhigongti Si; admission Y30) is in better shape than most of the other monastic centres in this part of Ü. First established in 1167, it is the head monastery of the Drigungpa school of the Kagyupa order and the most famous sky burial site in central Tibet. By 1250 it was already vying with Sakya for political power – as it happened, not a particularly good move as the Sakya forces joined with the Mongol army to sack Drigung Til in 1290. Thus chastened, the monastery subsequently devoted itself to the instruction of contemplative meditation. There are around 200 monks at Drigung Til these days.

Drigung Til sprouts from a high, steep ridge overlooking the Zhorong-chu Valley. A steep thread of a path makes its way up into the monastic complex, although there is also vehicle access from the eastern end of the valley. The 180-degree views from the main courtyard are impressive and a serene stillness pervades the site.

The **main assembly hall** is probably the most impressive of the buildings. The central figure inside is Jigten Sumgon, the founder of the monastery. Guru Rinpoche (in the corner) and Sakyamuni are to the left. Upstairs on the 1st-floor Serkhang (golden room or chapel) you can see statues of Jigten Sumgon and his two successors, all wearing red hats. Jigten's footprint is set in a slab of rock at the foot of the statue. From the 1st floor you can go upstairs to a balcony and a circuit of prayer wheels. Steps lead up from here to the chörtens of two previous abbots.

The monastery **kora** heads up the hill to the main *dürtro*. This is the holiest sky burial site in the Lhasa region – people travel hundreds of kilometres to bring their deceased relatives here. Tourists are no longer welcome to view the sky burials, though monks say that it's fine to hike up to the site when no sky burials are taking place. It's possible to see the circular platform of stones where the bodies are cut up and the adjacent buildings where the shaved hair of the dead is stored (the site is purified once a year in the sixth lunar month and the hair is removed). If the birds are circling, don't go up to the site.

As you follow the kora along the ridge and back down to the monastery, ask the monks for the path to the *gönkhang*. This **protector chapel** is dedicated to Abchi, the protectress of Drigung, who can be seen to the left of the main statue of Jigten Sumgon. To the right of the chapel there is another statue of Abchi riding a horse, which is next to Tseringma, the goddess of Mt Everest, riding a snow lion. Also look out for the pair of yak horns on the left wall of the chapel, after which Drigung is said to be named (a *dri* is a female yak and *gung* means 'camp'). The name may also derive from the hillside, which is said to be in the shape of a yak.

It's possible to stay at the comfortable **Monastery Guesthouse** (dm/d Y15/30) in the main courtyard. You can get simple meals at the monastery kitchen and there's a small shop.

Getting There & Away

Most travellers get to Drigung Til and Tidrum by rented vehicle. The trip takes around three hours from Lhasa. It's worth spending at least one night in Tidrum or Drigung, more if you want to do any hiking. A two- or three-day trip will cost around Y1500. It is also possible to visit Drigung as part of a loop taking in Reting (around Y1500 to Y1900), or as a longer four- to five-day trip taking in Nam-tso and Reting (around Y2500).

Alternatively, a public bus (Y30) runs daily from the Lhasa Eastern Bus Station to Drigung Til, departing at 7am. The bus normally continues to Tidrum (Y35). It leaves Tidrum the next day at 9am, picks up passengers at Menpa (the village below Drigung) and continues to Lhasa via Nyima Jiangre (Y15).

If you are hitching, first catch one of the frequent minibuses between Medro Gongkar and Nyima Jiangre (Y10, one hour) and hitch from there. (For information on the risks associated with hitchhiking, see p344.)

TIDRUM NUNNERY གཏེར་སྒྲོམ་བཙུན་དགོན་ 德仲寺

elev 4325m

Around three hours' walk (or a half-hour drive) from the main valley, northwest of Drigung Til and 13km up a side valley, is Tidrum Nunnery (Dezhong Si). Tidrum, with its **medicinal hot springs** (tourist/local Y5/2), has a great location in a narrow gorge at the confluence of two streams. The entire valley is festooned with prayer flags. The small nunnery has strong connections to Yeshe Tsogyal, the wife of King Trisong Detsen and consort of Guru Rinpoche. The Kandro-la, the resident spiritual leader of the nunnery, is considered a reincarnation of Yeshe Tsogyel.

The delightful hot springs are surrounded by wooden canopies and there are separate men's and women's pools. Bring a towel, swimming costume and flip-flops.

If you have a day to spare, you could do a tough day hike up to the Kiri Yangdzong caves, associated with Yeshe Tsogyel. The trail ascends to 5180m to visit the caves and then descends steeply down a scree slope to Dranang Monastery. Take a guide from the nunnery as the trail can be hard to find.

For a short walk, head north up the gorge behind the nunnery for about 1½ hours until you get to Dranang Monastery, where the valley divides.

Sleeping & Eating

There are two simple guesthouses beside the springs – both share a squalid outdoor toilet. Choose between the overpriced **Government Guesthouse** (dm Y20-40, d Y60-120) or the shabby **Nunnery Guesthouse** (dm Y15-20) next door. In general Drigung is a better place to stay.

A shop sells biscuits and beer, and the restaurant above the government guesthouse serves hearty bowls of *thugpa* (noodle soup; Y6).

Getting There & Away

For information on reaching Tidrum Nunnery, see the directions for Drigung Til (left).

YARLUNG TSANGPO VALLEY ཡར་ཀླུང་གཙང་པོའི་གཞུང་ 雅鲁流域

The serene waters of the braided Yarlung Tsangpo meander through a swathe of land flanked by dramatic sand dunes and rich in Tibetan history. It's only a couple of hours by bus or taxi from Lhasa and the ease of travel means you can jump on and off public transport to visit any combination of sights near the roadside. With more time you could spend days exploring the various side valleys on foot or by mountain bike.

The road through the valley is sealed all the way to Tsetang and beyond and there are sights at every turn; check the kilometre markers to keep track of what is coming up.

GONGKAR གོང་དཀར་ 贡嘎

☎ 0891 / elev 3600m

Gongkar (Gongga) county's main claim to fame is its airport but there are also a couple of interesting monasteries west of the airport, along the 'old' road to Lhasa. Note that there are three places called Gongkar: the airport, the monastery 10km to the west and the county town, about 10km to the east.

Information

Bank of China (Zhongguo Yinhang; 🕑 9.30am-5.30pm Mon-Fri, 11am-4pm Sat & Sun) Five minutes' walk south of the airport; changes cash and travellers cheques and has a 24-hour ATM. It cannot change RMB back into foreign currency (see p322).

Gongkar Chöde Monastery གོང་དཀར་ཆོས་སྡེ་དགོན་ 曲德寺

Surprisingly large, the Sakyapa-school **Gongkar Chöde Monastery** (Qude Si; admission Y20), founded in 1464, is famous for its 16th-century Kyenri-style murals. It lies 400m south of the highway, around 10km from the airport, back along the old road to Lhasa.

The **assembly hall** has statues of Sakya Pandita, Drölma, Guru Rinpoche and the monastery founder Dorje Denpa (1432–96). To the left of the hall is the *gönkhang*, whose outer rooms have black murals depicting a sky burial. The inner hall has a statue of the Sakyapa protector Gonpo Gur and some amazing spirit traps (in a case to the right). The inner sanctum has fine Kyenri-style murals of the Sakyapa founders by the entrance, and an inner kora *(nangkhor)*. Art specialists say the murals show a marked Chinese influence. The chapel to the right of the assembly hall has particularly fine images of the Past, Present and Future Buddhas.

The upper floor has more lovely old murals, including some showing the original monastery layout. On either side of the roof is the Kyedhor Lhakhang, which has fine protector murals in *yabyum* (Tantric sexual union) pose, and the Kangyur Lhakhang.

As you walk clockwise around the main monastery building, look for the *shedra* (monastic college) on the northern side. The monks attend thangka-painting classes in the morning here and practice debating in the afternoon.

Die-hards can hike a further 5km up the side valley to visit the 13th-century **Dechen Chokhor Monastery** on the hillside.

A further 13km along the road to Chushul are the impressive ruins of the Potala-like **Gongkar Dzong** and neighbouring Sundruling Monastery.

KILOMETRE MARKERS ALONG THE YARLUNG TSANGPO

Chushul to Tsetang marker	Feature
72	Chuwo Ri, one of Ü's four holy mountains
73	Monastery on side of Chuwo Ri
80-81	Ruins of Gongkar Dzong & Shedruling Monastery
84	Gongkar Chöde Monastery
90	Bridge and tunnel to/from Lhasa
93-94	Gongkar airport
100	Dakpo Tratsang Monastery
102-103	Gongkar Xian town, Mao statue & Rame monastery
112	Ferry to Dorje Drak Monastery
117-18	Chitoshö village, ruined *dzong* & Dongphu Chukhor Monastery
138	Ferry to Drak Valley, for Drak Yangdzong Caves
142	Dranang Xian & turn-off to Dranang Monastery (2km)
147	Road to Mindroling Monastery (8km)
148-149	Tsongdu Tsokpa Monastery
155	Samye ferry
161	Namseling Manor turn-off
170	Sand dunes
190	Tsetang town

Gongkar Xian 贡嘎县

This country town (Gongga Xian; *xian*), 9km east of the airport, is of note for hosting Tibet's only public **Chairman Mao statue**, located next to a school west of the centre. The 12m tall icon, erected in 2006, has more to do with the town's economic connections to Mao's home province of Hunan than with a major ideological statement.

Rame Monastery (Remai Si), at the north end of town, is one of the earliest Sakyapa monasteries in Tibet, dating from the late 12th century, though its glory days are long gone. There are now 44 monks here.

Sleeping & Eating

There are a couple of decent places to stay near the airport if you want to use Gongkar as a base from which to explore the valley.

Hangkong Binguan (航空宾馆; ☎ 618 2109; 2nd fl, cnr main & airport rds; d Y30-50) Budget travellers can choose between two simple guesthouses opposite each other above the main road junction. Each of the neglected rooms here has a basic bathroom with cold water. There's an internet café on the ground floor. The Lantian Binguan across the road is much the same, but without the attached bathrooms.

Hunan Binguan (湖南宾馆; ☎ 739 3282; Zangxing Lu, Gongkar Xian; ordinary/standard d Y80/128, discounts of 30%) Rooms at this clean modern hotel at Gongkar Xian, 9km east of the airport, come with Western bathroom, though only the pricier standard rooms have a shower.

Airport Hotel (机场宾馆; Jichang Binguan; ☎ 624 6608; Gongkar airport; standard/deluxe d incl breakfast Y200/280;) All rooms come with cleanish carpet, dim bathroom and hot-water boiler. The cheaper standard rooms in the south block are a little darker but better value. The hotel is right by the terminal building.

Gongkar has dozens of cheap Chinese restaurants, all overpriced but with decent food.

Getting There & Away

Airport buses run from the office of the Civil Aviation Authority of China (CAAC) in Lhasa to Gongkar seven times a day (Y25, 75 minutes). Return buses to Lhasa are timed to coincide with the arrival of flights, with the last departing around 4pm. One bus a day also runs to Shigatse (Y60, 9am). Taxis to Lhasa cost around Y120.

Plenty of buses stop at Gongkar en route to Tsetang (Y20) or Lhasa (Y20). Minibuses run when full from Gongkar Xian to Chitoshö village (Y5).

A chartered minibus from the airport to Gongkar Chöde Monastery costs around Y40 return, or Y10 one way to Gongkar Xian.

DORJE DRAK MONASTERY རྡོ་རྗེ་བྲག་དགོན་པ་ 多吉扎寺

elev 3550m

Along with Mindroling Monastery, Dorje Drak (Duojizha Si) is one of the two most important Nyingmapa monasteries in Ü. With a remote and romantic location, it is less accessible than Mindroling and consequently gets few Western visitors.

Dorje Drak was forcibly relocated to its present site in 1632 by the kings in Tsang and then sacked by the Dzungar Mongols in 1717. The monastery is headed by a line of hereditary lamas known as the Rigdzin, named after the first Rigdzin Godemachen, who are thought to be reincarnations of Guru Rinpoche. The 10th Rigdzin Lama currently resides in Lhasa.

The main assembly hall has statues of Guru Rinpoche and Pema Trinley, the fourth Rigdzin. The Samsum Namgyel Gönkhang to the right has five butter sculptures representing the chapel's five protectors. A cabinet holds the monastery's treasures, including a fragment of a staff belonging to Milarepa that was smashed in the Cultural Revolution. The upstairs chapel sells lovely ground juniper incense.

A demanding 1½ hour **kora** leads around the back of the *dorje* (thunderbolt symbol) shaped rock behind the monastery, up to a ruined retreat atop the rock. The path overlooks some dramatic sand dunes and the views from the retreat are simply stunning.

Tibetan-style beds are available at the **Monastery Guesthouse** (dm Y15). There are lots of duvets but it's a good idea to bring a sleeping bag and some food. A small shop sells soft drinks and instant noodles.

The monastery, on the northern bank of the Yarlung Tsangpo, can be reached via a ferry from kilometre marker 112 on the Lhasa–Tsetang road. Boats run in the morning and late afternoon (Y3, 30 minutes) or you can charter a boat for Y60. Hard-core trekkers can approach Dorje Drak from Lhasa, a trek of around four days.

A new road being built along the northern shore of the Yarlung Tsangpo, from the Gongkar tunnel to Samye via Dorje Drak, looks set to change transport patterns, as well as the site's remoteness.

DRAK YANGDZONG 扎央宗

For an adventurous off-the-beaten track trip, pack your sleeping bag and a torch (flashlight) and take the ferry across the Yarlung Tsangpo to explore the cave complexes of the Drak valley. The best advice we can give you is to try and visit the sites with a band of Tibetan pilgrims. Note that the Drak Valley is not the same as the valley behind Dorje Drak Monastery.

There are several sacred spots in the valley and all are visited by pilgrims en route to the caves. The first stop is at the **Dromochen Lhakhang**, which commemorates the birthplace of Nubchen Sangye Yeshe, a 9th-century Tantric master who was one of the 25 disciples of Guru Rinpoche.

Next comes **Tsogyel La-tso**, the spirit lake of Guru Rinpoche's consort Yeshe Tsogyel. The golden-roofed chapel has a statue of Tsogyel, as well as a photo of her current reincarnation who lives in Amdo.

Passenger trucks continue to Ngadrak village, where some terminate. There are several shops here and a large Karma Kagyupa monastery. Look for the stone footprint of Yeshe Tsogyel by one of the assembly hall pillars.

The dirt road continues up the valley, past Gyarong village at the base of the ruined fortress Pema Dzong, and turns west up the valley at Ngalu village for the final climb to **Chusi Nunnery**.

From the nunnery it's a tough 1½ hour climb up to the **Drak Yangdzong caves** (Zhayangzong). The large first cave has a chapel, an interesting side mural of Mindroling Monastery and a couple of resident nuns, who will act as your guide through the caves (Y5). Access to the upper caves is via a 10m ladder secured with strips of yak hide. Note that the caves are very narrow at times and are absolutely no place for those with claustrophobia, vertigo or a tendency to eat too many doughnuts. The spiritual and physical heart of the complex is a tiny Guru Rinpoche cave.

Back into the daylight (and after a quick round of butter tea) pilgrims continue to a side cave, smaller but with more rock formations.

To visit the separate **Dzong Kumbum** cave complex you need to make your way back to Ngadrak village, 1½ hours' walk down the main valley. Pilgrims generally start the trek the following morning early at around 3am and return in the afternoon after visiting the four main caves. You can shave off some of the trek by hiring a tractor for the first section. The next day pilgrims take the bus down to the ferry.

Sleeping

Chusi Nunnery Guesthouse (dm Y10) Cosy clean rooms and a small teahouse-restaurant make this a wonderful place to stay for a night or two.

Comfortable Hotel (舒心招待所; Shuxin Zhaodaisuo; ☎ 790 6815; dm Y15) This simple guesthouse in Ngadrak village is a decent place to overnight before visiting the second cave complex or catching the passenger truck back to the ferry.

Getting There & Away

Take the 7am bus from Lhasa's Barkhor Sq to Dranang (Y25) and get off at the ferry, a couple of kilometres before Dranang (note: this is not the same dock as the ferry to Dorje Drak). Boats make the hour-long crossing (Y5) when there are 25 passengers. At the far side, everyone piles into a converted truck for the ride up the Drak Valley to Ngadrak village. If you're lucky, you can share transport with pilgrims going all the way to the caves (Y15). Otherwise you may have to hike the final couple of hours.

When heading back, it's best to spend the night at Ngadrak and take the morning bus down to the ferry, otherwise you'll likely have to wait hours for a ferry or be forced to charter one (Y120).

Trekkers can access the Drak Yangdzong cave complex on foot from the Dorje Drak Valley over the Gur-la.

DONGPHU CHUKHOR MONASTERY

རྡོ་ཕུད་ཆོས་འཁོར་གླིང་ 顿配曲果寺

This forgotten 11th-century Sakyapa monastery (Dunpei Quguo Si) lies just five minutes' walk south of the main highway. The surrounding Tibetan village of **Chitoshö** is one of the most traditional in the region and well worth a stroll, though almost nothing remains of its hilltop *dzong*.

The main assembly hall has a fine mural of the fifth Dalai Lama outside the vestibule and an unusual side chapel dedicated to the five Dhyani Buddhas, arranged around a central statue of Nampa Namse. On the upper floor a throne and image of Chenresig marks the spot where the 23-year-old current Dalai Lama spent the night en route to exile in India in 1959.

Chitoshö village is 23km east of Gongkar airport. Buses shuttling between Tsetang and Lhasa drop off and pick up passengers here.

DRANANG MONASTERY & VALLEY

གྲྭ་ནང་གཞུང་ 扎塘寺

About 48km east of Gongkar airport is the turn-off to the 11th-century **Dranang Monastery** (Zhatang Si; admission Y25). This small Sakyapa monastery of only 18 monks is of interest mainly to art specialists for its rare murals, which combine Indian (Pala) and inner Asian (Western Xia) styles. Bring a torch to see the murals.

The assembly hall has central statues of Dorje Chang (Vajradhara; with crossed arms) and the monastery's founder, Drapa Ngonshe. Look for the interesting oracle costume and mirror (to the left of Dorje Chang) in which the oracle would discern his visions. The inner sanctum holds all that remains of the murals, the best of which are on the back (western) wall.

A side protector chapel is accessed by steps outside and to the left of the main entrance. The chapel (whose central image is that of a yak's head) has a passage at the back that leads to a rooftop chapel and kora.

To get to the monastery, walk 2km south from the highway, through the modern town of Dranang into the old town, until the road curves to the right. If you need to spend the night, try the **Zhuzhou Binguan** (株洲宾馆; dm Y50, d Y120-266), a clean modern place at the junction with the main highway. The dorms are in spacious triples.

Also worth visiting if you have a particular interest are the ruins of the **Jampaling Kumbum**, on the hillside a half-hour walk southeast of Dranang. The 13-storey chörten, built in 1472, was one of the largest in Tibet with an attendant monastery of 200 monks before it was dynamited by the Chinese in 1963. A climb up the hillside above the ruins gives an overview of the scale of the site, which is one of the most eloquent testaments to the tragic loss of Tibetan culture over the last half-century. Rebuilding efforts are limited to a two-storey Jampa chapel. Check out the little brass toe on the throne – all that remains of the original Jampa statue after which the complex was named.

To get to Jampaling, walk south out of Dranang Monastery and after a couple of minutes turn left, following a path to the base of the ruins visible on the hillside above.

Explorers with a tent and supplies could easily spend a couple of days in the Dranang Valley, hiking up the valley past the village and monastery of **Gyeling Tsokpa**, 8km from Dranang, to **Dingboche Monastery**, 14km from Dranang.

A direct minibus (Y25) runs to Dranang from Barkhor Sq in Lhasa every day at 7am. Otherwise, take any Tsetang-bound bus to the Dranang junction, from where it's a short three-wheel motor rickshaw ride or 20-minute walk to the monastery. The pilgrim bus from Samye to Lhasa also stops here briefly (see p172).

MINDROLING MONASTERY

སྨིན་གྲོལ་གླིང་དགོན་པ་ 敏珠林寺

A worthwhile detour from the Lhasa–Tsetang road, between the Dranang turn-off and the Samye ferry crossing, is **Mindroling Monastery** (Minzhulin Si; admission Y25). It is the largest and most important Nyingmapa monastery in Ü.

Although a small monastery was founded at the present site of Mindroling as early as the 10th century, the date usually given for the founding of Mindroling is the mid-1670s. The founding lama, Terdak Lingpa (1646–1714), was highly esteemed as a *terton* (treasure finder) and scholar, and counted among his students the fifth Dalai Lama. Subsequent heads of the monastery were given the title Minling Trichen; the current titleholder lives in exile in Dehra Dun, India. The monastery was razed in the Mongol invasion of 1718 and later restored.

Mindroling has *cham* dancing on the 10th day of the fifth Tibetan lunar month and the fourth day of the fourth lunar month. The latter festival features the creation of a sand mandala nine days later.

The central **Tsuglhakhang** is an elegant brown stone structure on the west side of the courtyard. As you walk clockwise, the first chapel is the **Zhelre Lhakhang**, with statues of

Guru Rinpoche and Terdak Lingpa (with a white beard and excellent hat). The bare main hall itself has another statue of Terdak Lingpa, along with Dorje Chang and a row of Kadam-style chörtens – the monastery originally belonged to the Kadampa school. The inner chapel has a large Sakyamuni statue. Only the statue's head is original; the body was ripped apart by Chinese troops for its relics.

Upstairs, the **Tresor Lhakhang** houses several treasures, including a stone hoofprint and a famed old thangka with the gold footprints and handprints of Terdak Lingpa, which was given to the fifth Dalai Lama.

The top floor holds the Lama Lhakhang, with some fine ancient murals of the Nyingma lineages, plus a central statue of Kuntu Zangpo (Samantabhadri). The Dalai Lama's quarters remain empty.

The other main building, to the right, is the **Sangok Potrang**, used for Tantric practices. To the left of the main entrance is a famous 'speaking' mural of Guru Rinpoche. Flanking the left wall is a huge thangka that is unfurled once a year on the 18th day of the fourth lunar month.

A new white **chörten** has recently been built with Taiwanese funds just outside the monastery, to replace an original 13-storey chörten destroyed in the Cultural Revolution. It's possible to climb past the ground-floor statue of Jampa to its upper floors.

Nice walks lead off from the kora around the Tsuglhakhang, west up the valley through the village to the ruins of what used to be a nunnery.

On the main road, 1.5km towards Tsetang, is the small **Tsongdu Tsokpa Monastery**. The original monastery across the road has been converted into a housing block.

Sleeping & Eating

It's possible to stay the night at the **Monastery Guesthouse** (dm Y15), though you'd do well to bring a sleeping bag. Beware of dogs if you leave your room at night. A new guesthouse is being built outside the southern gate. A small shop sells noodles, Pepsi and the like.

Getting There & Away

There is little direct transport to Mindroling. One possibility is to take the Lhasa–Tsetang bus and get off at kilometre marker 147 by the English sign to the monastery. The monastery is around 8km south of the road, up the Drachi Valley, and the last section involves a climb (it's not too punishing). You won't see the monastery until you round a ridge and are below it. You should be able to hitch a lift from the highway turn-off.

One daily bus leaves the monastery around 8am for Tsetang (Y10), returning in the afternoon.

Mindroling is easily slotted into a Yarlung Valley excursion if you have a rented vehicle.

SAMYE MONASTERY བསམ་ཡས་དགོན་པ་ 桑耶寺

☎ 0893 / elevation 3630m

Samye Monastery (Sangye Si) is deservedly the most popular destination for travellers in the Ü region. Surrounded by barren mountains and dramatic sand dunes and approached via a beautiful river crossing, the monastery has a magic about it that causes many travellers to stay longer than they had intended.

As Tibet's first monastery and the place where Buddhism was established, the monastery is also of major historical and religious importance. No journey in Ü is complete without a visit to Samye.

For details of the popular trek between here and Ganden, see p288.

Permits

A travel permit is theoretically needed to visit Samye and you can only get one by organising a tour and guide (see p323). At the time of research there were only occasional permit checks at the ferry point on the Tsetang side and at the Monastery Guesthouse. No-one is checked for weeks and then suddenly a bunch of travellers are fined. You'll have to ask other travellers or just give it a try.

If you are stopped without a permit, you may be subject to a fine of up to Y500, but if you play the 'dumb foreigner' card well enough you should be able to negotiate this down to Y100 or less.

History

Samye was Tibet's very first monastery and has a history that spans more than 1200 years. It was founded in the reign of King Trisong Detsen, who was born close by (see p292), though the exact date is subject to some debate – probably between 765 and 780. Whatever the case, Samye represents the Tibetan state's first efforts to allow the Buddhist faith

SAMYE MONASTERY

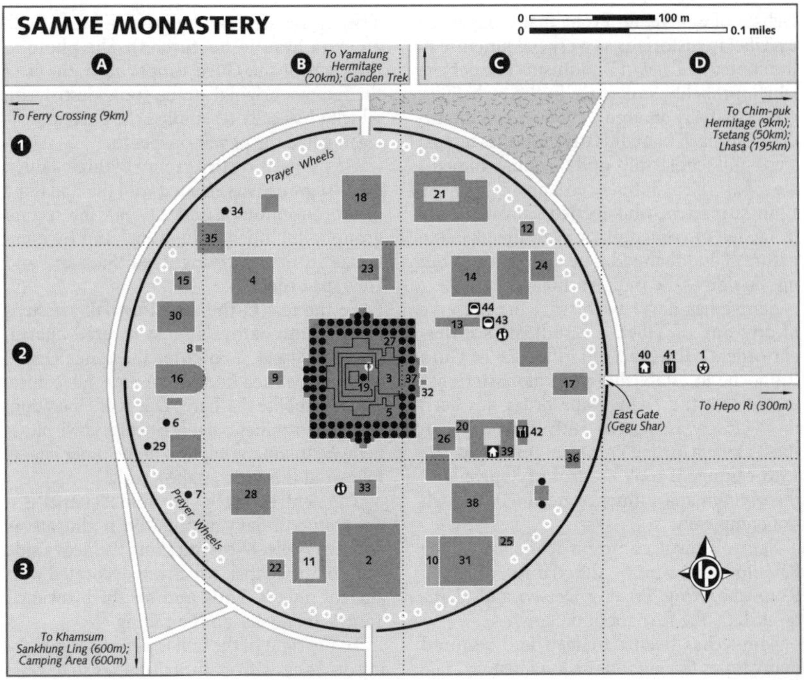

INFORMATION

Public Security Bureau.....1 D2

SIGHTS & ACTIVITIES

Aryapalo Ling.....2 B3
Assembly Hall.....3 B2
Black Chörten.....4 B2
Chenresig Chapel.....5 B2
Chörten.....6 A2
Chörten.....7 A3
Chörten.....8 A2
Chörten.....9 B2
Debating Courtyard.....10 C3
Drayur Gyagar Ling.....11 B3
Dzogchen Lhakhang.....12 C1
Gheku.....13 C2
Green Chörten.....14 C2
Jampa Lhakhang.....15 A2
Jampa Ling.....16 A2
Jampel Ling.....17 C2
Jangchub Semkye Ling.....18 B1
Jowo Khang.....19 B2
Kitchen.....20 C2
Kordzo Pehar Ling.....21 C1
Mani Lhakhang.....22 B3
Moon Temple.....23 B2
Namdok Trinang Ling.....24 C2
Ngamba Ling.....25 C3
Old Guesthouse.....26 C2
Protector Chapel.....27 B2
Red Chörten.....28 B3
Sacred Tree.....29 A2
Samtenling (Closed).....30 A2
Shetekhang.....31 C3
Stele.....32 C2
Sun Temple (Destroyed).....33 B3
Tree Shrine.....34 B1
Triple Mani Lhakhang.....35 A1
Tsangmang Ling.....36 C2
Ütse.....37 B2
White Chörten.....38 C3

SLEEPING

Friendship Snowland Hotel.....(see 41)
Monastery Guesthouse.....39 C2
Tashi Guesthouse.....40 D2

EATING

Friendship Snowland Restaurant.....41 D2
Monastery Restaurant.....42 C2

TRANSPORT

Bus Ticket Office.....43 C2
Bus to Lhasa, Trucks to Ferry.....44 C2

to set down roots in the country. The Bön majority at court, whose religion prevailed in Tibet prior to Buddhism, were not at all pleased with this development.

The victory of Buddhism over the Bön-dominated establishment was symbolised by Guru Rinpoche's triumph over the massed demons of Tibet at Hepo Ri, just to the east of Samye. It was this act that paved the way for the introduction of Buddhism to Tibet.

Shortly after the founding of the monastery, Tibet's first seven monks (the 'seven examined men') were ordained here by the monastery's Indian abbot, Shantarakshita (Kende Shewa), and Indian and Chinese scholars were invited to assist in the translation of Buddhist texts into Tibetan.

Before long, disputes broke out between followers of Indian and Chinese scholarship. The disputes culminated in the Great

Debate of Samye, an event that is regarded by Tibetan historians as a crucial juncture in the course of Tibetan Buddhism. The debate, which probably took place in the early 790s, was essentially an argument between the Indian approach to bodhisattvahood via textual study and scholarship, and the more immediate Chan (Zen) influenced approach of the Chinese masters, who decried scholarly study in favour of contemplation on the absolute nature of buddhahood. The debates came out on the side of the Indian scholars.

Samye has never been truly the preserve of any one of Tibetan Buddhism's different orders. However, the influence of Guru Rinpoche in establishing the monastery has meant that the Nyingmapa order has been most closely associated with Samye. When the Sakyapa order came to power in the 15th century it took control of Samye, and the Nyingmapa influence declined, though not completely.

Samye's most common icons are of the Khenlop Chösum – the trinity of Guru Rinpoche, King Trisong Detsen and Shantarakshita, the first abbot of Samye.

Samye has been damaged and restored many times throughout its long history. The most recent assault on its antiquity was by the Chinese during the Cultural Revolution. Extensive renovation work has been going on since the mid-1980s and there are now 190 monks at Samye.

The Ütse

The central building of Samye, the **Ütse** (admission Y40; 8am-5.30pm), comprises a unique synthesis of architectural styles. The ground and 1st floors were originally Tibetan in style, the 2nd floor was Chinese and the 3rd floor Indian. The corner parapets with green and gold *dorje* designs are also unique.

Just to the left of the main entrance is a **stele** dating from 779. The elegant Tibetan script carved on its surface proclaims Buddhism as the state religion of Tibet by order of King Trisong Detsen. The doorway is flanked by two ancient stone lions and two stone elephants.

From here the entrance leads into the first of the ground-floor chambers: the **assembly hall**. As you enter the hall you pass a statue of Tangtong Gyelpo to the left and a row of figures greet you straight ahead: the translator Vairocana, Shantarakshita, Guru Rinpoche, Trisong Detsen and Songtsen Gampo (with an extra head in his turban). The photo to the right of the Guru Rinpoche statue is of the famous original statue (now destroyed), which physically resembled the guru and allegedly had the power of speech.

On the right are two groups of three statues: the first group is associated with the Kadampa order (Dromtompa and Atisha); the second group is multidenominational and includes lamas from the Nyingmapa, Sakyapa and Gelugpa orders.

To the rear of the assembly hall are steps leading into Samye's most revered chapel, the **Jowo Khang**. You enter the inner chapel via three painted doors – an unusual feature. They symbolise the Three Doors of Liberation: those of emptiness, signlessness and wishlessness. A circumambulation of the inner chapel follows at this point (take a torch).

The centrepiece of the inner chapel is a 4m statue of Sakyamuni. Ten bodhisattvas and two protective deities line the heavy side walls of the chapel, which are decorated with ancient murals. Look also for the blackened Tantric mandalas on the ceiling.

To the right of the hall is a *gönkhang*, reeking of *chang*, with statues of deities so terrible that they must be masked. Watch out for the stuffed snake over the blocked exit.

Before ascending to the 1st floor, take a look at the **Chenresig Chapel**, outside and to the left of the main assembly hall, which features a dramatic 1000-armed statue of Chenresig.

The structure of the 2nd floor echoes the inner chapel and houses an image of Guru Rinpoche in a semiwrathful aspect, flanked by Tsepame and Sakyamuni, with Shantarakshita and Trisong Detsen flanking them. Look up to see the Chinese-influenced bracketing on the beams. There is an inner kora around the hall.

Some of the murals outside this hall are very impressive (photos Y10); those on the southern wall depict Guru Rinpoche, while those to the left of the main door show the fifth Dalai Lama with the Mongol Gushri Khan and various ambassadors offering their respects. Also on this floor are the Dalai Lama's quarters (left) and another protector chapel and Tsepame (Amitayus) chapel (right).

The 3rd floor is a recent addition to the Ütse. It holds statues of four of the five Dhyani Buddhas, with a mandala of the fifth (Namse) on the ceiling.

Walk around the back to a ladder leading up to the 4th floor. This chapel holds the sacred core of the temple, as well as an image of Dukhor (Kalachakra), a Tantric deity, but it is generally locked. As you descend from the 3rd floor look for a rare mural of the 14th (current) Dalai Lama beside the stairwell.

Back on the ground floor you can follow the prayer-wheel circuit of the Ütse, and look at the interesting murals showing the founding of the monastery. You can also ascend to the outer roof for views over the complex.

Ling Chapels & Chörtens
དགོན་ཁང་དང་མཆོད་རྟེན་

As renovation work continues at Samye, the original *ling* (royal) chapels (the lesser, outlying chapels) are slowly being restored. Wander around and see which are open. Following is a clockwise tour of those open at the time of research.

The square in front of the Monastery Guesthouse has some interesting bits and pieces. The stubby isolated building to the north constitutes the remains of a nine-storey tower used to display festival thangkas.

From the eastern gate *(gegyu shar)* follow the prayer wheels south to the **Tsemang Ling**, once the monastery printing press, and look for the sacred stone in the centre of the chapel. If you pass the residential college of the **Shetekhang** around 9.30am or 6pm, listen out for the sounds of debating in the attached courtyard. The restored **Aryapalo Ling** was Samye's first building and has a lovely ancient feel. The statue of Arya Lokeshvara is similar to one seen in the Potala Palace (see p109). The **Drayur Gyagar Ling** was originally the centre for the translation of texts, as depicted on the wall murals. The main statue on the upper floor is of Sakyamuni, flanked by his Indian and Chinese translators.

The **Jampa Ling** on the west side is where Samye's Great Debate was held. On the right as you go in, look out for the mural depicting the original design of Samye with zigzagging walls. There is an unusual semicircular inner kora here that is decorated with images of Jampa. Just north of here is a chörten that pilgrims circumambulate; south is a **sacred tree** to which pilgrims tie stones. The **triple Mani Lhakhang** to the north has lovely murals.

The green-roofed Chinese-style **Jangchub Semkye Ling** to the north houses a host of bodhisattvas around a statue of Marmedze, with a 3-D wooden mandala to the side. Take a torch to see the central Asian style murals.

East of here is the **Kordzo Pehar Ling**, the home of the oracle Pehar until he moved to Nechung Monastery outside Lhasa. Pilgrims stick passport photos of themselves onto the locked entrance of the ground-floor chapel, which is flanked by two ancient-looking leather bags. The upstairs portico has some old cane helmets. The inner chapel reeks of alcohol, hooks hang from the ceiling and demons' hands reach out from their cases, as if trying to grab you.

It is also possible to enter the four reconstructed concrete chörtens (white, red, green and black), though there is little of interest inside.

THE SAMYE MANDALA

Samye's overall design was based on that of the Odantapuri Temple of Bihar in India, and is a highly symbolic mandalic representation of the universe. The central temple represents Mt Meru (Sumeru), and the temples around it in two concentric circles represent the oceans, the continents and the subcontinents that ring the mountain in Buddhist cosmology. The complex originally had 108 buildings (an auspicious number to Tibetans). The 1008 chörtens on the circular wall that rings the monastery represent Chakravala, the ring of mountains that surrounds the universe.

Hepo Ri ཧད་པོ་རི་ 哈不日神山

Hepo Ri is the hill some 400m east of Samye, where Guru Rinpoche vanquished the demons of Tibet. King Trisong Detsen later established a palace here. Paths wind up the side of the hill from the road leading from Samye's east gate. A 30-minute climb up the side ridge takes you to an incense burner, festooned with prayer flags and with great views of Samye below. Head south along the ridge and descend from here. Early morning is the best time for photography.

AROUND SAMYE

Chim-puk Hermitage མཆིམས་ཕུ་སྒྲུབ་ཁང་ 青朴寺

Chim-puk hermitage is a warren of caves northeast of Samye that was once a meditation retreat for Guru Rinpoche. It is a popular day hike for travellers spending a few days at Samye. If you are lucky, you might find a pilgrim truck heading up there in the early morning, or you could hire a tractor in Samye (Y50). Ask at the reception of the Monastery Guesthouse. Otherwise the walk takes around four or five hours up and three hours down. Take plenty of water.

There is a small monastery built around Guru Rinpoche's original **meditation cave** halfway up the hill. Follow the pilgrims around the various other shrines. It's possible to stay the night here if you have a sleeping bag and food.

If you are feeling fit and acclimatised, it is possible to climb to the top of the peak above Chim-puk. You'll probably only have enough time to do this if you get a lift to Chim-puk or stay the night there. To make this climb from the Guru Rinpoche cave follow the left-hand valley behind the caves and slog it uphill for 1½ hours to the top of the ridge, where there are several clumps of prayer flags. From here you can drag yourself up along a path for another 1½ hours to the top of the conical peak, where there are a couple of meditation retreats and fine views of the Yarlung Tsangpo Valley. On clear days you can see several massive Himalayan peaks to the southeast.

Yamalung Hermitage གཡའ་མ་ལུང་ 聂玛隆圣洞

It is possible to head up the valley directly behind Samye to the Yamalung hermitage, around 20km from Samye. See p291 for details. It's really too far to hike there and back in a day but you could probably hire a tractor to take you there for around Y50 return. The recent upgrading of the road to Yamalung might bring regular transportation along this road.

Sleeping

Monastery Guesthouse (☎ 736 2761; dm Y20-40, d/tr Y100/150) Most travellers end up at this pleasant guesthouse, just in front of the Ütse compound. Rooms are simple but spacious and there's a common hot shower (Y5) at the back. The higher the floor, the better quality the room, with pilgrims at the bottom and tour groups top of the heap.

Friendship Snowland Hotel (Xueyu Tongbao Canguan, Gangjong Pönda Sarkhang; ☎ 799 3449; dm Y25) Proper mattresses (not just foam) are on offer here, in concrete rooms above the cosy restaurant of the same name, though it's worryingly close to the PSB office. Note that the eastern gate is closed at dusk, after which you can get to the hotel from the south or north gates.

Tashi Guesthouse (Zhaxi Zhaodaisuo; ☎ 790 6048; dm Y30) Pleasant five-bed dorms with clean foam beds, above a shop by the east gate.

There is fine camping in an orchard 10 minutes' walk south of the Ütse, near the Tibetan-style Khamsum Sankhung Ling. Take your own water.

Eating

Monastery Restaurant (dishes Y7-15) Loads of atmosphere, monks galore and decidedly average food at this place attached to the guesthouse. Menu in English.

Friendship Snowland Restaurant (☎ 799 3449; meals Y8-18) The backpacker-inspired menu at this pleasant Tibetan-style restaurant includes banana pancakes ('bread' on the menu), as well as the normal menu gibberish ('Tibet in the Pig'?). Decent Chinese and Tibetan dishes are available (spinach in ginger, ginseng chicken), as well as breakfasts, and it's actually cheaper than the Monastery Restaurant. It's outside the eastern gate of the monastery complex. Menu in English.

The shops on either side of the guesthouse are well stocked. Grab a cold beer and retire to the roof of the Monastery Guesthouse for wonderful moonlight views of the Ütse.

Getting There & Away

While it appears that Samye is easily reached by road from Lhasa, keep in mind that the main highway is south of the river, so if you come from Lhasa you need to cross over to the north bank, either by ferry (to the west) or bridge (to the east).

The only regular direct bus service from Lhasa to Samye, via the bridge at Tsetang, is a daily pilgrim bus (Y40, 3½ hours), which departs from Barkhor Sq at around 6am. Buy your ticket the day before from the tin shack just north of the square opposite Snowlands Restaurant. The return bus leaves around 2pm and stops at Tsetang (Y15), Dranang Monastery (p167) and Rame Monastery (p165) en route, making a total trip of around five hours. Buy your ticket well in advance from the shack in the monastery compound.

Many travellers still opt for the ferry across the Yarlung Tsangpo, at least one way. A bus service runs from just west of Barkhor Sq to the Samye ferry, departing around 8am (Y25,

2½ hours), or take any Tsetang-bound bus. River crossings (per person Y10, one hour) operate whenever there are enough people or a bunch of foreigners charter the boat for Y90. It is 9km from the ferry drop-off point to Samye and everyone – Tibetans included – jumps on a truck or tractor for the ride (Y5, 20 minutes).

Trucks leave Samye for the ferry terminal whenever there are enough passengers, often around 8am and 2pm. Buses to Tsetang and Lhasa wait for their passengers on the other side of the river, as does the PSB. This generally works out quicker than taking the pilgrim bus back to Lhasa.

NAMSELING MANOR རྣམ་སྲས་གླིང་ 朗色林庄园

Perhaps the only building of its type still standing in Tibet, this ruined multistorey family mansion is a minor site. You might find it worth a visit if you have your own transport.

There are a few murals left, but the ruins are unstable in places so you should take care when exploring. The building is 3km south of the main highway near kilometre marker 161. Renovations are planned, along with an admission fee (Y20).

TSETANG རྩེད་ཐང་ 泽当

☎ 0893 / pop 52,000 / elev 3515m

An important Chinese administrative centre and army base, Tsetang (Zedang) is the fourth-largest city in Tibet and the capital of huge Shannan (Lhoka) prefecture. For travellers, Tsetang is of interest mainly as a jumping board for exploration of the Yarlung Valley. Unfortunately the local PSB has put up so many obstacles to travel in the area that for the time being we're tempted to advise permitless budget travellers to give the place a wide berth. Expect hassles buying a bus ticket, finding a budget hotel and even visiting the local sights.

Tsetang is divided into a characterless modern Chinese town and a small traditional Tibetan town, clustered to the east around Gangpo Ri, one of Ü's four sacred mountains. The former *dzong* and village of Nedong has been subsumed into Tsetang's southern suburbs.

Information

Bank of China (Zhongguo Yinhang; Naidong Lu; 9.30am-6pm Mon-Fri, 10.30am-4.30pm Sat & Sun) Changes cash and travellers cheques and has an ATM.

Changxiang Wangba (Naidong Lu; per hr Y3; 24hr) Internet café.

China Post (Zhongguo Youzheng; 12 Naidong Lu; 9.30am-7pm)

Public Security Bureau (Gong'anju; PSB; Naidong Lu; 9am-12.30pm & 3-6pm) Best avoided.

Zhijianyuan Wangcheng (cnr Naidong Lu & Gaisang Lu; per hr Y4; 24hr) Internet café on 2nd floor above a restaurant.

Sights & Activities

MONASTERY KORA

There are a couple of small monasteries in the Tibetan quarter that are worth a brief visit. Pilgrims visit them in a clockwise circuit.

From the market on Bairi Jie head east to a small square and continue down the street to the right of the bank. After 200m you'll come to **Ganden Chökhorling Monastery**. This 14th-century monastery was originally a Kagyupa institution, but by the 18th century the Gelugpas had taken it over, which is why the central statue is of Tsongkhapa.

From here head north and then east to **Ngamchö Monastery**, a somewhat livelier place. On the top floor are the bed and throne of the Dalai Lama. A side chapel is devoted to medicine, with images of the eight medicine buddhas. The protector chapel displays fine festival masks, representing snow lions, stags and demons.

A kora leads from the monastery around the base of Gangpo Ri up to a bundle of prayer flags and round to a throne-shaped incense burner. From here a side trail ascends the hill to the Monkey Cave, while the main kora descends to **Sang-ngag Zimche Nunnery** (admission Y10). The principal image here is of a 1000-armed Chenresig, dating back to the time of King Songtsen Gampo. According to some accounts, the statue was fashioned by the king himself.

GANGPO RI གོང་པོ་རི 贡不日神山

Gangpo Ri (4130m) is of special significance for Tibetans as the legendary birthplace of the Tibetan people, where Chenresig in the form of a monkey mated with the white demoness Sinmo to produce the beginnings of the Tibetan race. The **Monkey Cave**, where all this took place, can be visited near the summit of the mountain. Do it in the spirit of a demanding half-day walk in the hills, rather than as a trip specifically to see the Monkey Cave, as the cave itself is rather disappointing.

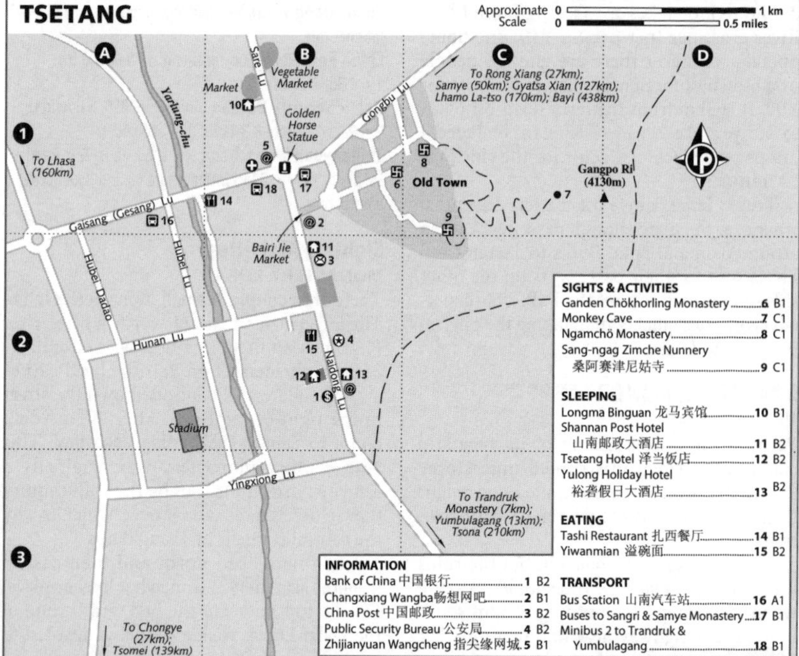

The most direct trail leads up from the Sang-ngag Zimche Nunnery, climbing about 550m to the cave. If in doubt, follow the prayer flags.

Sleeping & Eating

Finding good budget accommodation is a real problem in Tsetang. The town's cheaper hotels are prevented from accepting foreigners by a strong PSB presence, and those that will accept you will notify the PSB of your presence within minutes of you checking in.

Shannan Post Hotel (Youzheng Dajiudian; ☎ 782 1888; 10 Naidong Lu; d incl breakfast Y238-328, discounts of 50%) The rooms may be a bit knackered but this is still probably your best budget bet. The cheaper rooms come with a squat toilet but the promised hot water is unreliable.

Longma Binguan (☎ 783 5388; 28 Sare Lu; d with bathroom Y268-488, tr Y388, discounts of 40-60%) The cheaper ordinary rooms *(putong biaozhun)* here are much the same as the pricier versions and are often discounted to Y150, making them a good deal. Get a room overlooking the inner courtyard, not the noisy market.

Yulong Holiday Hotel (Yulong Jiri Dajiudian; ☎ 783 2888; 16 Naidong Lu; r Y580, discounts of 50-60%;) This new three-star place was offering great discounts at the time of research for its clean modern rooms. You can even listen to your favourite Chinese pop tunes in the power shower. Or not.

Tsetang Hotel (Zedang Fandian; ☎ 782 5555; fax 782 1855; 21 Naidong Lu; d Y480-680;) This is Tsetang's premier tour-group lodging, with money exchange (guests only), piped-in oxygen and comfortable four-star rooms. The souvenir shop sells slide film. Credit cards are accepted.

Yiwanmian (Naidong Lu; snacks Y5-10; 24hr) This clean and bright place across from the PSB office offers a wide range of excellent snacks. Try the *shaguo jiaozi* (砂锅饺子), ravioli in a boiling broth.

Tashi Restaurant (☎ 783 1958; Gaisang Lu; mains Y20-30) Branch of the Tashi Restaurant in Shigatse (not Tashi's in Lhasa) that offers up Nepali-style Western goodies, such as pizza, curries and good breakfasts, in a nice Tibetan-style hall. Menu in English.

Getting There & Away

Buses run hourly between Tsetang and Lhasa's main Western Bus Station (Y30, 2½ hours) until around 6pm, passing Dranang (Y10) and Gongkar airport (Y20) en route. Private cars also do the run at dangerous speeds for Y50 per seat.

During research for this guide, the bus station at Tsetang stopped selling tickets to foreigners. In case this changes, there are daily buses to Tsomei (Y50), Gyatsa (Y60), Tsona (Y50) and Shigatse (Y80), and services to Nangartse (Y50, Monday, Wednesday and Friday). Two buses a day run to Chushul (Y25, two hours), via Gongkar Chöde Monastery (Y20, 1½ hours).

Private buses to Samye (Y15, 45 minutes) and Sangri (Y5, one hour) depart at 8am from near the main roundabout and foreigners are allowed on these.

YARLUNG VALLEY ཡར་ཀླུང་གཞུང་ 雅砻河谷

Yarlung is considered the cradle of Tibetan civilisation. It was from Yarlung that the early Tibetan kings unified Tibet in the 7th century and their massive burial mounds still dominate the area around Chongye. Yumbulagang, perched on a crag like a medieval European castle, is another major attraction of the area and the site of Tibet's oldest building.

The major attractions of the Yarlung Valley can just about be seen in a day, but this is a beautiful part of Tibet for extended hiking and day walks. The main problem is the Tsetang PSB, who seem intent on limiting tourism to guided groups.

Some travellers band together in Lhasa for a three- or four-day trip out to the Yarlung Valley by way of Tsetang, taking in Samye and Mindroling en route. The total cost (including permits and guide) for a Land Cruiser for such a trip is around Y2800. It's more cost-effective to add a Yarlung extension onto a trip to the Nepali border if you are heading that way.

Permits

Travel permits (see p323) are theoretically needed to visit anywhere outside Tsetang town, though there weren't any formal permit checks in the valley during our last few research visits. The only place you are likely to be checked is in Chongye, and then only if you stay the night.

Trandruk Monastery ཁྲ་འབྲུག་དགོན་པ་ 昌珠寺

Around 7km south of the Tsetang Hotel, **Trandruk** (Changzhu Si; admission Y70, photos Y75; dawn-dusk) is one of the earliest Buddhist monasteries in Tibet, having been founded at the same time as the Jokhang and Ramoche in Lhasa. Dating back to the 7th-century reign of Songtsen Gampo, it is also one of Tibet's demoness-subduing temples (see p105; Trandruk pins down the demoness' left shoulder). In order to build the monastery here, Songtsen Gampo had first to take the form of a hawk *(tra)* in order to overcome a local dragon *(druk)*, a miracle which is commemorated in the monastery's name.

Trandruk was significantly enlarged in the 14th century and again under the auspices of the fifth and seventh Dalai Lamas. The monastery was badly desecrated by Red Guards during the Cultural Revolution.

The entrance of the monastery opens into a courtyard area ringed by cloisters. The building to the rear of the courtyard has a ground plan similar to that of the Jokhang, and shares the same Tibetan name, Tsuglhakhang.

The principal chapel, to the rear centre, holds a statue of Tara known as Drölma Sheshema (under a parasol), next to the five Dhyani buddhas. The Tuje Lhakhang to the right has statues of Chenresig, Jampelyang and Chana Dorje, who form the Tibetan trinity known as the Rigsum Gonpo. The stove to the right is said to have belonged to Princess Wencheng (Wencheng Konjo), the Chinese consort of Songtsen Gampo.

Upstairs and to the rear is a central chapel containing a famous thangka of Chenresig made up of 29,000 pearls, as well as an ancient appliqué thangka showing Sakyamuni.

Minibus 2 (Y1) runs here every 20 minutes from the main roundabout, picking up passengers along Naidong Lu.

Yumbulagang ཡུམ་བུ་བླ་སྒང་ 雍布拉康

A fine, tapering finger of a structure that sprouts from a craggy ridge overlooking the patchwork fields of the Yarlung Valley, **Yumbulagang** (Yongbulakang; admission Y60; 7am-7pm) is considered the oldest building in Tibet. At least that is the claim for the original structure – most of what can be seen today dates from 1982. It is still a remarkably impressive sight, with a lovely setting.

The founding of Yumbulagang stretches back into legend and myth. The standard line is that it was built for King Nyentri Tsenpo, a historic figure who has long since blurred into

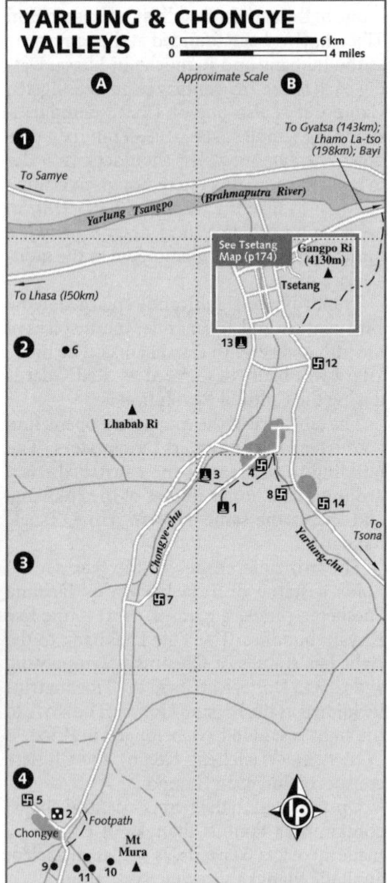

SIGHTS & ACTIVITIES

Bhairo-puk	1	B3
Chingwa Tagtse Dzong	2	A4
Gongtang Bumpa Chörten	3	B3
Rechung-puk Monastery 日琼布寺	4	B3
Riwo Dechen Monastery	5	A4
Sheldrak Cave	6	A2
Tangboche Monastery 唐布齐寺	7	A3
Tashi Chöeden Monastery 扎西曲登寺	8	B3
Tomb of Songtsen Gampo	9	A4
Tomb of Trisong Detsen	10	A4
Tombs of the Tibetan Kings 藏王墓群	11	A4
Trandruk Monastery 昌珠寺	12	B2
Tsechu Bumpa Chörten	13	B2
Yumbulagang 雍布拉康	14	B3

mythology. Legend has him descending from the heavens and being received as a king by the people of the Yarlung Valley. More than 400 Buddhist holy texts (known collectively as the 'Awesome Secret') are said to have fallen from the heavens at Yumbulagang in the 5th century. Murals at Yumbulagang depict the magical arrival of the texts.

There has been no conclusive dating of the original Yumbulagang, although some accounts indicate that the foundations may have been laid more than 2000 years ago. It is more likely that it dates from the 7th century, when Tibet first came under the rule of Songtsen Gampo.

The plan of Yumbulagang indicates that it was originally a fortress and much larger than the present structure. Today it serves as a chapel and is inhabited by around eight monks who double as guards – in 1999 some 30 statues were stolen from the main chapel. Its most impressive feature is its **tower**, and the prominence of Yumbulagang on the Yarlung skyline belies the fact that this tower is only 11m tall.

The ground-floor **chapel** is consecrated to the ancient kings of Tibet. A central buddha image is flanked by Nyentri Tsenpo on the left and Songtsen Gampo on the right. Other kings and ministers line the side walls. There is another chapel on the upper floor with an image of Chenresig, similar to the one found in the Potala. There are some excellent murals by the door that depict, among other things, Nyentri Tsenpo descending from heaven, Trandruk Monastery, and Guru Rinpoche arriving at the Sheldrak meditation cave (in the mountains west of Tsetang).

Perhaps the best part is a walk up along the ridge above the building, if only to get some peace from the syrupy Chinese pop music that blasts up from the car park below. There are fabulous views from a promontory topped with prayer flags. It is an easy five-minute climb and no entry fee is required.

Yumbulagang is 6km from Trandruk Monastery. Minibus 2 (Y2), originating from the Tsetang roundabout and passing Trandruk Monastery, terminates here.

Rechung-puk Monastery རལ་ཆུང་ཕུ་ 日琼布寺

A popular pilgrimage site associated with the illustrious Milarepa (1040–1123), the remains of Rechung-puk Monastery are set high on a dramatic escarpment that divides the two branches of the Yarlung Valley.

Milarepa, founder of the Kagyupa order, is revered by many as Tibet's greatest songwriter and poet. It was his foremost disciple, Rechungpa (1083–1161), who founded Rechung-puk as a cave *(puk)* retreat. Later a monastery was established at the site, eventually housing up to 1000 monks. This now lies in ruins. For pilgrims, the draw of the monastery is the atmospheric **cave of Black Heruka**, where they are thumped on the back with the stone footprint of Rechungpa.

See below for how to visit the ruins as part of a day-long hike around the valley.

Tangboche Monastery ཐང་པོ་ཆེ 唐布齐寺

A minor site thought to date back to 1017, Tangboche Monastery is about 15km south-west of Tsetang on the way to Chongye. Atisha, the renowned Bengali scholar, stayed here in a meditation retreat. The monastery's **murals**, which for most visitors with an interest in things Tibetan are the main attraction, were commissioned by the 13th Dalai Lama in 1913. They can be seen in the monastery's main hall – one of the few monastic structures in this region that was not destroyed by Red Guards.

Tangboche is easily visited if you are travelling by rented transport between Tsetang and Chongye. You should be able to see the building on the left once you're about 15km out of Tsetang.

CHONGYE VALLEY འཕྱོང་རྒྱས་གཞུང་

Most visitors to the Chongye Valley go as a day trip from Tsetang and combine it with attractions in the Yarlung Valley. It is possible to stay in the town of Chongye but you leave yourself open to potential permit hassles.

Chongye is a beautiful valley enclosed by rugged peaks. The views from some of the burial mounds are superb. It is also well worth climbing up to Riwo Dechen Monastery and the ruins of the old *dzong* behind it for more views of the mounds.

Chongye Town འཕྱོང་རྒྱས་གྲོང་རྡལ་ 琼结镇

☎ 0893 / pop 3000

Chongye is not a town in which you'll want to linger, but it makes a decent base for treks in the area.

There are buses almost hourly between Tsetang and Chongye town (Y5), from where most of the important sights are easily accessible on foot. Hitching here is not that easy, though by no means impossible.

Chongye Burial Mounds འཕྱོང་རྒྱས་སྲོང་བཙན་བང་བས་ 藏王墓群

The Tombs of the Kings at Chongye represent one of the few historical sites in the country that gives any evidence of a pre-Buddhist culture in Tibet. Most of the kings interred here are now firmly associated with the rise of Buddhism on the high plateau, but the methods of their interment point to the Bön faith. It is thought that the burials were probably officiated at by Bön priests and were accompanied

DIY: TREKKING THE YARLUNG VALLEY

Perhaps the best way to see the lesser sights of the Yarlung Valley is on foot, visiting a handful of pilgrimage sites, none of which are more than 40 minutes' walk apart. Bring water and a packed lunch for a fine day trip.

After visiting **Trandruk Monastery** and **Yumbulagang**, take Minibus 2 for 2km north from Yumbulagang and get off at kilometre marker 373. Follow the side road westwards for 15 minutes, then curve to the left to visit the small **Tashi Chöden Monastery**, home to 20 monks.

From here, head north along the base of the hillside for 25 minutes and take a left where the canal branches left. A faint path climbs the ridge for 15 minutes up to **Rechung-puk** (see opposite). Alternatively, carry on north to Khurmey village, from where it is an equally steep 20-minute walk up to the monastery, passing a white chörten.

After visiting the main **Heruka cave**, head over the back (west) side of the ridge, pick your way down through the ruins, past a looted chörten, to the minor road at the base of the ridge. Follow this southwest for 10 minutes to a small village. A path leads from here up to a cleft in the rock, decorated with prayer flags – this is the **Bhairo-puk**. The tiny cave is home to a couple of hermits and houses a stone handprint and statue of the translator Vairocana.

From here descend back to the village and head west along a dirt track towards the large **Gongtang Bumpa chörten** and then join the main road from Tsetang to Chongye and hitch (p344) back to Tsetang.

by sacrificial offerings. Archaeological evidence suggests that earth burial, not sky burial, might have been widespread in the time of the Yarlung kings, and may not have been limited to royalty.

Accounts of the location and number of the mounds differ. Erosion of the mounds has also made some of them difficult to accurately identify. It is agreed, however, that there is a group of 10 burial mounds just south of the Chongye-chu.

The most revered of the mounds, and the closest to the main road, is the **Tomb of Songtsen Gampo**. It is the largest of the burial mounds and has a small **Nyingmapa temple** (admission Y30) atop its 13m-high summit. The furthest of the group of mounds, high on the slopes of Mt Mura, is the **Tomb of Trisong Detsen**. It is about a one-hour climb, but there are superb views of the Chongye Valley.

Chingwa Tagtse Dzong འཕྱིང་བ་སྟག་རྩེ་རྫོང་

The *dzong* can be seen clearly from Chongye town and from the burial mounds, its crumbling ramparts straddling a ridge of Mt Chingwa. Once one of the most powerful forts in central Tibet, it dates back to the time of the early Yarlung kings. The *dzong* is also celebrated as the birthplace of the great fifth Dalai Lama. There is nothing to see in the fort itself, but again you are rewarded with some great views if you take the 40-minute or so walk up from Chongye. Paths lead up from the centre of town, from the nearby ruins of the red chapel and from the gully behind Riwo Dechen Monastery.

Riwo Dechen Monastery
འཕྱོང་རྒྱས་རི་བོ་བདེ་ཆེན་ 日乌德庆寺

The large, active, Gelugpa-sect Riwo Dechen Monastery sprawls across the lower slopes of Mt Chingwa below the fort. There are some nice walks up to the ridge north of the monastery and then down to the fort.

Riwo Dechen Monastery can be reached by a half-hour walk from Chongye's atmospheric old Tibetan quarter. Turn west at the town's T-junction and ask for the 'gompa'. Halfway up is a grand, new chörten. It is sometimes possible to stay the night at the monastery – a magical experience.

LHAMO LA-TSO བླ་མའི་བླ་མཚོ་ 拉姆拉措

One of Ü's most important pilgrimage destinations, Lhamo La-tso (Lamu Lacuo) is around 115km northeast of Tsetang. *La* is a Tibetan word that means 'soul' or 'life spirit'. *La* resides in both animate and inanimate forms, including lakes, mountains and trees. In the case of Lhamo La-tso, *la* is identified with the spirit of Tibet itself.

The Dalai Lamas have traditionally made pilgrimages to Lhamo La-tso to seek visions that appear on the surface of the oracle lake. The Tibetan regent journeyed to the lake in 1933 after the death of the 13th Dalai Lama and had a vision of a monastery in Amdo that led to the discovery of the present Dalai Lama. The lake is considered the home of the protectress Palden Lhamo.

The gateway to Lhamo La-tso is the dramatic, but mostly ruined, **Chökorgye Monastery** (却柯杰寺; Quekejie Si; 4500m), wedged between three mountains, Zhidag (north), Palden Lhamo (south) and Begtse (east) in the Tsi-chu Valley. Founded in 1509 by the second Dalai Lama, Gendun Gyatso (1476–1542), the monastery served later Dalai Lamas and regents as a staging post for visits to the lake. Some 500 monks were in residence until the place was flattened by the Chinese during the Cultural Revolution; a handful have returned and the main hall has been rebuilt.

On the nearby slope is a mani wall that consecrates a footprint stone of the second Dalai Lama.

Just short of the mountain pass that overlooks Lhamo La-tso is a ritual *shökde* (throne) built for the Dalai Lamas. It is now buried under a mound of *kathak* (silk scarves). It's a 15-minute walk from the *shökde* to the pass and another 1½ hours to get down to the lake, which is encircled by a kora.

Permits

A visit to Lhamo La-tso requires four permits (three days to process), which are only available with the help of a tourist company in Lhasa. Even then, obtaining permissions can be tricky. The only place you are likely to be checked is at Chökorgye Monastery or a hotel in Gyatsa Xian. We weren't checked during our visit, but because we were without a permit we didn't hang around too long.

Sleeping & Eating

Chökorgye Monastery (dm Y50) The nearest accommodation to Lhamo La-tso. It has basic dorm rooms at outrageous prices. There are good camping spots behind the temple walls if you have a tent.

Gyatsa Holy Lake Hotel (d Y160) Of the several hotels in Gyatsa Xian (for those who have a permit), this one, on the eastern edge of town, is the best.

Getting There & Away

The approach to Lhamo La-tso begins from Tsetang, usually by hired vehicle. From Tsetang it is 27km to the village of Rong Xiang, where a bridge crosses the Yarlung Tsangpo to Sangri. Continuing east from Rong Xiang, the road passes **Chakar Chöde Monastery** (恰嘎曲德寺; Qiaga Qude Si), situated above the road next to a large purple water tank. Most of the monastery stands in ruins, but the main hall has been rebuilt and features a statue of Sakyamuni. Check out Songtsen Gampo's sword on the pillar to the left. If the main hall is locked, you can get a key from the caretaker who lives next door.

It's slow going for 32km to Chusom (Qusong; 3880m), where the **Mansion of Lhagyari** (拉加里王府; Lajiali Wangfu) – a three-storey, mud-brick pile – looms above the road. You can scamper up to the 13th-century ruins in about five minutes. The interior bears some painted crossbeams, but is pretty unstable.

From Chusom the road climbs 36km to Batang-la (4950m) and then descends 26km to Lasuo village, where you can stay in a basic **guesthouse** (dm Y20) if it is late. Another 26km brings you to Gyatsa (加查; Jiazha) Xian, where a bypass leads 3km to a bridge that spans the Yarlung Tsangpo. Traffic is sparse but you might be able to hitch a ride from here up to Chökorgye Monastery; otherwise it's a 55km walk of two days, via Tseju village. Keep a low profile in Gyatsa Xian if you have no permit.

Altogether, it takes about six hours to drive from Tsetang to Chökorgye Monastery.

From the monastery, 4WD vehicles can drive (one hour) up a twisting mountain road to the *shökde*. Without transport, you can walk to the pass from the monastery in four hours – you have to be fit, acclimatised and well equipped to attempt it.

The most interesting way to reach the lake is to trek from Rutok (six days, via Dzingchi and Magong-la) or from Sangri, both routes via Gyelung-la. Coming from Sangri it's 42km along a driveable road to Olkhar, where you can break the journey at a hot-spring pool. For detailed information on this trek see Gary McCue's *Trekking in Tibet – A Traveler's Guide*. A four- or five-day trip from Lhasa to Lhamo La-tso in a hired vehicle, including permits and guide, will cost around Y4000.

Tsang གཙང་

With most of its major sights relatively close to Lhasa, and on or near the paved Friendship Hwy, the traditional province of Tsang draws the crowds. This is no reason to avoid it. After all, this is the region that has Everest, the highest mountain in the world, the Gyantse Kumbum, Tibet's most stunning architectural wonder, and many of the country's most important monasteries. The latter include the fortress-like Sakya Monastery, seat of the first Tibetan government with a lama ruler, and Tashilhunpo, seat and burial site of the Panchen Lamas.

Getting off the tourist path is relatively easy, though if you're travelling by Land Cruiser tour you should arrange this from the start. Phuntsoling and Shalu monasteries are two very worthwhile diversions. Both are intensely atmospheric, highly photogenic and have important places in Tibetan history.

Tsang doesn't hurt for outstanding scenery, either. There's Everest, of course, but also the turquoise waters of Yamdrok-tso, the snaking valleys of the Yarlung Tsangpo, wide meadowlands dotted with whitewashed villages, and stunning views from passes that get up to 5100m. The adventurous take this all in slowly by cycling down the Friendship Hwy, or trekking: Everest Base Camp to Tingri (p299) is the most popular trekking route in Tsang, though there are others.

After Shegar and the turn-off for Mt Everest, the attractions dry up. Though most travellers are headed for Kathmandu, a round trip from Lhasa should allow you to see more in a short time. How short? A week is bare minimum, while three weeks gives time for day hikes out to little-visited monasteries, one longer trek and (well-deserving) repeat visits to the larger monastic compounds.

HIGHLIGHTS

- Marvel at the turquoise waters of **Yamdrok-tso** (opposite), one of Tibet's most sacred lakes
- Worship before a 26m gold Buddha at **Tashilhunpo Monastery** (p191), a walled complex the size of a village
- Climb the dazzling **Gyantse Kumbum** (p187), a monumental chörten with mural-filled chapels
- Absorb the holy atmosphere inside ancient **Sakya Monastery** (p201)
- Get off the beaten track at photogenic **Phuntsoling Monastery** (p200), set at the base of a monstrous sand dune
- Sleep in nomad tents and gaze upon the north face of **Mt Everest** (p209)

History

Tsang lies to the west of Ü and has shared political dominance and cultural influence over the Tibetan plateau with its neighbour. With the decline of the Lhasa kings in the 10th century, the epicentre of Tibetan power moved to Sakya, under Mongol patronage from the mid-13th to the mid-14th centuries.

After the fall of the Sakya government, the power shifted back to Ü and then again back to Tsang. But, until the rise of the Gelugpa order and the Dalai Lamas in the 17th century, neither Tsang nor Ü effectively governed all of central Tibet, and the two provinces were rivals for power. Some commentators see the rivalry between the Panchen Lama and Dalai Lama as a latter-day extension of this provincial wrestling for political dominance.

Permits

Most of Tsang's sights involve detours from the Friendship Hwy and you need permits to visit these areas. At the time of writing the only way to get permits was by travelling with an organised Land Cruiser tour. Check the situation before you leave as many expect a relaxation of the rules after the 2008 Olympics.

Getting Around

The main road through Tsang, the Friendship Hwy, is paved all the way to Tingri. The dirt road from Tingri to Nyalam is in good shape, but after Nyalam it's a mess to the Nepali border. The southern route via Yamdrok-tso was being upgraded at the time of writing and should be paved all the way from Chushul to Shigatse by the end of 2007. Land Cruiser trips (the usual way to travel through the region) take this more scenic route, but there is less public transport here for the independent traveller.

Public transport runs along the Northern Friendship Hwy as far as Shegar. By 2009 the Qinghai–Tibet train could be open from Lhasa to Shigatse.

Note that at the time of writing, foreigners were not permitted to take any form of public transport from Lhasa's main bus station. This may change, so we have included information where it exists.

The entries in this chapter follow a southwesterly route through Tsang from Lhasa to the border with Nepal, taking in the main attractions of the area on the way.

YAMDROK-TSO ཡར་འབྲོག་མཚོ་ 羊卓雍措

elev 4441m

Dazzling Yamdrok-tso (Yang Zhuoyong Cuo) is normally first seen from the summit of the Kamba-la (4700m). The lake lies several hundred metres below the road, and in clear weather is a fabulous shade of deep turquoise. Far in the distance is the huge massif of Mt Nojin Kangtsang (7191m).

DOWN THE DRAIN

Yamdrok-tso is one of Tibet's holiest lakes and an important centre for pilgrimage. It's also, incongruously, the site of Tibet's largest hydroelectric plant.

Yamdrok-tso has an unusual location, locked 4441m above sea level in a high bowl above the Yarlung Tsangpo (Brahmaputra River). In the mid-1980s the Chinese leadership sanctioned a plan to build a 6km tunnel below the surface of the lake that would send the waters dropping some 846m. The hydroelectric project, capable of generating 90 megawatts of power, would be a gift to the Tibetan people, according to then premier Li Peng.

But the gift was not greeted with the enthusiasm that may have been expected. Not only was it a painful effrontery to Tibetan religious sensibilities but, as many complained bitterly, the energy produced would mostly be directed to military bases and Chinese communities around Lhasa. Work was temporarily halted after opposition by the Panchen Lama, but with the lama's death in 1989 the project was back on track. By 1997 the turbines had started to produce electricity for the Lhasa region. You can see the pumps from the Lhasa–Shigatse road, 15km southwest of Chushul.

A decade later, the plant is still generating controversy with every watt of power. Much of the ongoing concern is over the environment. Yamdrok-tso is a dead lake with no outlet and no perennial source of water. While it is unlikely the Chinese will allow Yamdrok-tso to completely drain, diverting river water (as has been promised, though never done) to replenish what is lost would change the consistency of the lake's waters. Like the vast herds of gazelle in Ngari, the famed turquoise-blue waters of Yamdrok-tso, and the ecosystem it now supports, may one day be things of the past.

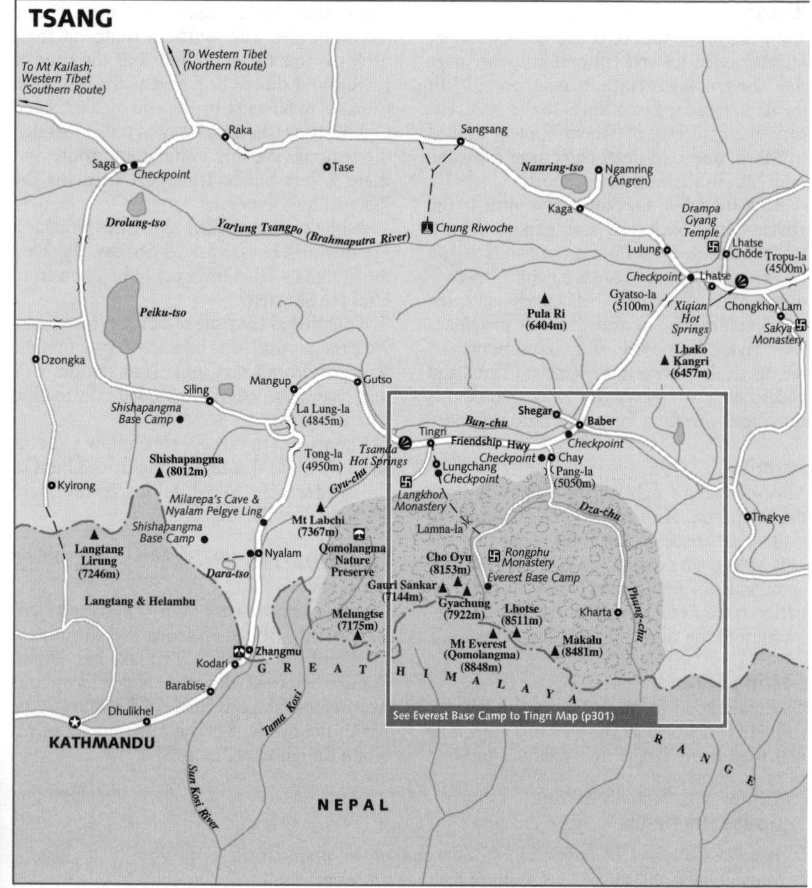

Yamdrok-tso is shaped like a coiling scorpion. It doubles back on itself on the western side, effectively creating a large island within its reaches. For Tibetans, it is one of the four holy lakes (the others are Lhamo La-tso, Namtso and Manasarovar) and home to wrathful deities. Devout Tibetan pilgrims circumambulate the lake in around seven days.

Most Western travellers are content with a glimpse of the lake from the Kamba-la and views from the town of Nangartse, where you can stay the night.

Permits

At the time of writing you could only travel as far as the Kamba-la due to road construction (access via Gyantse was also restricted), but the new road was expected to be open by the time you read this. Permits are currently required. If you travel with a Land Cruiser tour staff will arrange the permits for you.

Nangartse སྣ་དཀར་རྩེ་

☎ 0893 / elev 4400m

Nangartse is the largest town on the lakeside and a popular stop for the night. It's not a particularly attractive place but there is a small monastery in the south of town, an old Tibetan quarter and a small *dzong* (fort) to the north (famed as the birthplace of the mother of the fifth Dalai Lama). There are also opportunities for walks, such as to Samding Monastery. You can't actually walk to the lakeshore as you will soon find yourself up to

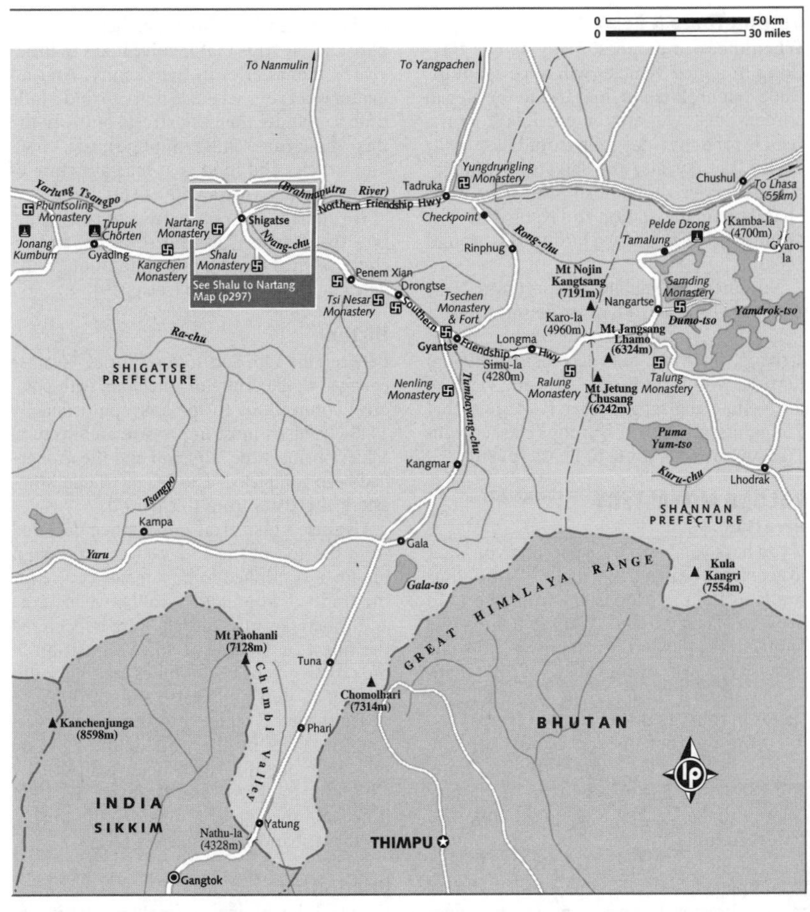

your knees in bog, but the views are still good and bird-watchers in particular will have a field day during the summer months.

There are a number of cheap guesthouses and restaurants in town as this is a popular stopping point for Land Cruiser tours. All are within 200m of each other on the main road.

Samding Monastery བསམ་སྡིང་དགོན་པ་

On the shores of Yamdrok-tso, about 10km east of Nangartse, Samding is situated on a ridge that separates the northern arm of the lake from Dumo-tso (a smaller lake between the northern and southern arms of Yamdrok-tso). It provides excellent views of the Dumo plain and the mountains to the south. You can walk here from Nangartse in about two hours.

Samding is noted for the unusual fact that it is traditionally headed by a female incarnate lama named Dorje Phagmo (Diamond Sow). When the Mongolian armies invaded Samding in 1716, Dorje Phagmo changed her nuns into pigs to help them escape. Her current incarnation works for the government in Lhasa.

It's possible to visit the main *dukhang* (assembly hall), to the right of the courtyard, which is dominated by a statue of Sakyamuni (Sakya Thukpa). There's also a footprint of the ninth Dorje Phagmo here, plus an eerie protector chapel and several chapels upstairs. There are 31 monks in residence.

Getting There & Away

When the road reopens, many people travelling in rented vehicles will once again include Yamdrok-tso in their trip to the Nepali border. But it will also be possible to rent a vehicle for a four-day loop from Lhasa visiting the lake, Gyantse and Shigatse. Semiregular bus service should also resume between Lhasa's main bus station and Nangartse. The distance between the two locations is around 140km.

Note there is no public transport from Nangartse to Gyantse, 100km to the southwest.

Leaving Yamdrok-tso is as spectacular as arriving, since you have to cross the 4960m Karo-la, with its awesome roadside views of the Nojin-Kangtsang Glacier. It was here that Younghusband's British troops clashed with Tibetan forces en route to Lhasa (p186).

RALUNG MONASTERY ར་ལུང་དགོན་པ་

elev 4350m

If you have your own transport and you want to get off the beaten track, make a 5km detour south to Ralung Monastery from the road between Nangartse and Gyantse. Ralung was founded in 1180 and gets its name from the monastery's 'self-arising' image of a *ra* (goat).

The original *tsuglhakhang* (great temple) stands in ruins, as does a chörten (stupa) visible from the roof. As you wander around, look for images of the founder, Tsanpa Gyare, and the Drukpa Rinpoche (the monastery belongs to the Drukpa Kagyud school), who resides in India.

When the road between Gyantse and Ralung is completed, irregular bus service should resume. Previously, buses ran every four days between Gyantse and Ralung village.

GYANTSE རྒྱལ་རྩེ་ 江孜

☎ 0892 / pop 15,000 / elev 3980m

One of the more pleasant towns around Tibet, Gyantse (Jiangzi), located in the Nyang-chu Valley, is famed for the Gyantse Kumbum, the largest chörten in Tibet. The white chörten, a magnificent tiered structure, contains a seemingly endless series of mural-filled chapels and offers outstanding views from its upper levels.

Most people rush through Gyantse, stopping only to see the *kumbum* (100,000 Buddha images), but the Gyantse Dzong, which dominates the town's skyline, should not be missed, especially if you are feeling a little Buddha-burnout from endless monastery visits. For those with more time, there are some pleasant day trips that involve hikes to little-visited monasteries in the vicinity. And no matter what your schedule is, try to find a little time to wander the back streets of town: the mix of pilgrims, children, pop music, cows, motorcycles and mud is as true a picture of contemporary Tibetan life as you'll find.

If you happen to be in Tibet in early June, note that Gyantse has a horse-racing and archery festival during this time, though the date could change again (see p319).

History

Between the 14th and 15th centuries, Gyantse emerged as the centre of a fiefdom, with powerful connections to the Sakyapa order. By 1440 Gyantse's most impressive architectural achievements – the *kumbum* and the *dzong* – had been completed. The Pelkor Chöde Monastery also dates from this period.

Gyantse's historical importance declined from the end of the 15th century, although the town continued to be a major centre for the trade of wood and wool between India and Tibet. Gyantse carpets were considered the finest in Tibet. The town's position at the crossroads of trade routes leading south to Bhutan, west to Shigatse and northeast to Lhasa turned Gyantse into the third-largest town in Tibet by the time of the Chinese takeove,r but it's since been eclipsed by Chamdo, Bayi, Ali and Tsetang. In 1904 it became the site of a major battle during Younghusband's advance on Lhasa.

Orientation

Gyantse 'downtown' is small, consisting of a few wide streets. Yingxiong Nanlu (Hero South Rd) is 'main street' and has a decent selection of shops, restaurants and hotels.

To the north and west is the old Tibetan part of town, concentrated around the main road leading to Pelkor Chöde Monastery past the *dzong*, which looms over the town on a high ridge. To the south and east is an incipient Chinese quarter with government buildings and more shops, restaurants and a couple of hotels.

Information

There's an **internet bar** (wangba; Yingxiong Nanlu; per hr Y8) in the south of town with decent connection speeds. For cash withdrawals the **Agricultural Bank of China** (Weiguo Lu) has an

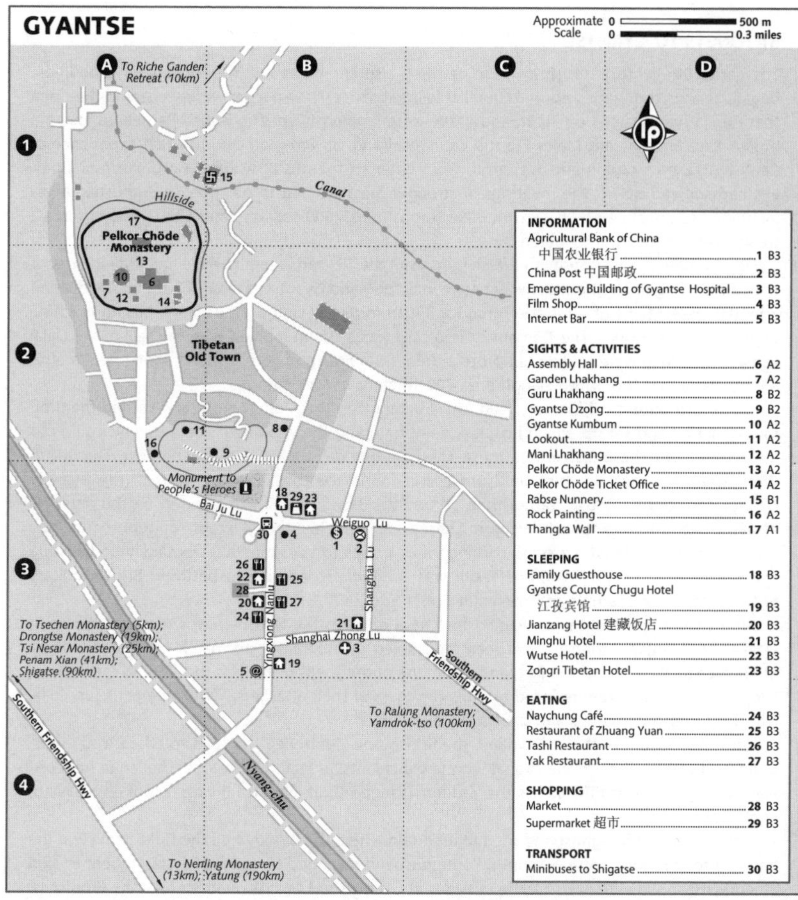

ATM that accepts foreign cards on the Plus, Visa or MasterCard network. There are private telecom booths around town for cheap phone calls.

Sights

PELKOR CHÖDE MONASTERY

དཔལ་འཁོར་མཆོད་རྟེན་དགོན

The sprawling compound in the far north of town houses **Pelkor Chöde Monastery** (Pelkor Chötengön; ☎ 817 2680; admission Y40; 🕑 9am-6pm, some chapels closed 1-3pm) and the monumental Gyantse Kumbum, a chörten filled with fine paintings and statues. Both are deservedly top of the list on most travellers' must-sees.

Founded in 1418, the red-walled Pelkor Chöde was once a compound of 15 monasteries that brought together three different orders of Tibetan Buddhism – a rare instance of multidenominational tolerance. Nine of the monasteries were Gelugpa, three were Sakyapa and three belonged to the obscure Büton suborder whose head monastery was Shalu (p199) near Shigatse.

A climb up the nearby Gyantse Dzong will give you a clear birds-eye view of the original extent of the monastery and a sense of what a bustling place it must have been. Today, however, much of the courtyard, enclosed by high walls that cling to the hills backing onto the monastery, is bare and many buildings are empty. But the monastery has not yet become a mere museum. There's a small but visible population of monks and a steady

BAYONETS TO GYANTSE

The early-20th-century British invasion of Tibet, also known as the Younghusband expedition, began, as wars sometimes do, with unreliable intelligence. Newspapers were spreading the claim that Russia had designs on Tibet, and many were lapping it up. The British Raj feared losing a buffer state and so sent Major Francis Younghusband, an army officer with rich experience of Central Asia, on a diplomatic mission to Tibet. After six months of waiting, no Chinese or Tibetans had showed up for the meetings. A stronger message had to be sent. Younghusband was instructed to advance on Lhasa with 3000 troops (plus 7000 servants and 4000 yaks) to force a treaty on the recalcitrant Tibetans.

Despite previous brushes with British firepower, the Tibetans seem to have had little idea what they were up against. About halfway between Yatung and Gyantse, a small Tibetan army bearing a motley assortment of arms confronted a British force carrying light artillery, Maxim machine guns and modern rifles. The Tibetans' trump card was a charm marked with the seal of the Dalai Lama, which they were told would protect them from British bullets. It didn't. Firing began after a false alarm and the British slaughtered 700 Tibetans in four minutes.

The British buried the Tibetan dead (the Tibetans dug them up at night and carried them off for sky burial) and set up a field hospital, dumbfounding the wounded Tibetans, who could not understand why the British would try to kill them one day and save them the next. The British then continued their advance to Gyantse, but found the town's defensive fort (the Gyantse Dzong) deserted. Curiously, rather than occupy the *dzong,* the British camped on the outskirts of Gyantse and waited for officials from Lhasa to arrive. While they waited, Younghusband sped off up to the Karo-la with a small contingent of troops to take on 3000 Tibetans who had dug themselves in at over 5000m. The result was the highest land-based battle in British military history and a fine example of frozen stiff upper lip.

After nearly two months of waiting for Lhasa officials, the British troops received orders to retake the Gyantse Dzong (it had been reoccupied by Tibetans) and march on Lhasa. Artillery fire breached the walls of the fort, and when one of the shells destroyed the Tibetan gunpowder supply the Tibetans were reduced to throwing rocks at their attackers. The *dzong* fell in one day, with four British casualties and over 300 Tibetan dead.

With the fort under their command, the British now controlled the road to Lhasa. Younghusband lead 2000 troops to the capital with few incidents. In fact, the greatest challenge he faced was getting all the troops across the Yarlung Tsangpo (Brahmaputra River): it took five days of continual ferrying.

Once in Lhasa Younghusband tried to ascertain where the bloody hell the Dalai Lama was (he had fled to Mongolia). After a month, Younghusband managed to get the Tibetan regent to sign an agreement allowing British trade missions at Gyantse and Gartok (near Mt Kailash). (Ironically, the troops discovered that British goods were already trickling into the bazaars – one British soldier wrote that he found a sausage machine made in Birmingham and two bottles of Bulldog stout in the Barkhor.) But the treaty and others that followed in 1906 were largely meaningless as Tibet simply had to no capacity to fulfil them.

As for Younghusband himself, the most significant event of the campaign was yet to come. On the evening before his departure, as he looked out over Lhasa, he felt a great wave of emotion, insight and spiritual peace. Younghusband had always been a religious man, but this moment changed him forever. 'That single hour on leaving Lhasa was worth all the rest of a lifetime,' he later quipped.

For more information on this chapter in Tibet's history, try Charles Allen's book *Duel in the Snows: The True Story of the Younghusband Mission to Lhasa.*

stream of prostrating, praying, donation-offering pilgrims doing the rounds almost any time of the day.

The **assembly hall** is straight ahead as you walk into the compound, and most people begin their explorations here. The entrance is decorated with statues of the Four Guardian Kings, instead of the usual paintings, and a large Wheel of Life mural. Just by the entrance on the left is a particularly spooky protector chapel, with murals depicting sky burial in fairly graphic details. Look for the huge *tor-*

mas (sculptures made out of tsampa) in a case outside the entrance.

The hall is quite dark inside and if you want a good look at the various murals and thangkas, it is a good idea to bring a torch. The main chapel is located to the rear. There is an inner route around the chapel, which is lined with fine murals. The central image is of Sakyamuni, who is flanked by the Past and Future Buddhas.

To the left of the main chapel is the **Dorjeling Lhakhang**, with a four-headed Nampa Namse (Vairocana) and the other four Dhyani (or Wisdom) Buddhas.

Moving to the upper floor, the first chapel to the left is noted for a three-dimensional mandala, wall paintings of the Indian-looking *mahasiddhas* (highly accomplished Tantric practitioners) and lacquered images of key figures in the Sakyapa lineage. Each of the 84 *mahasiddhas* is unique and shown contorted in a yogic posture. Unfortunately, the room is seldom opened. Other chapels, which are open in the mornings, are dedicated to Jampa (Maitreya), Tsongkhapa and the 16 *arhats* (literally 'worthy ones'). Some chapels have fairly kitschy modern displays. Photos cost Y10 per chapel.

A new and easily overlooked **Ganden Lhakhang** chapel to the left of the *kumbum* is worth a quick peek for the largest Tsongkhapa statue in Tibet.

GYANTSE KUMBUM རྒྱན་སྐུ་འབུམ

Commissioned by a Gyantse prince in 1427, the **Gyantse Kumbum** (Gyen Kumbum; admission incl with entry to Pelkor Chöde) is the town's foremost attraction. The 35m-high chörten, with its white layers trimmed with decorative stripes and its crown-like golden dome, is awe-inspiring. But the inside is no less impressive, and in what seems an endless series of tiny chapels you'll find painting after exquisite painting (*kumbum* means '100,000 images').

The Gyantse Kumbum has been described as the most important of its kind in Tibet. There are only two contemporaries, ruined and remote, in the Buddhist world: Jonang Kumbum (p200), 60km northeast of Lhatse, and the even more remote Chung Riwoche in the west of Tsang. However, it is commonly held that neither could ever compare with the style and grandeur of the Gyantse Kumbum.

You can enter the *kumbum* and follow a clockwise route that leads murmuring pilgrims up through the six floors, taking in the dozens of rather tiny chapels that recede into the walls along the way. Much of the statuary in the chapels was damaged during the Cultural Revolution but the murals have weathered well. They date back to the 14th century, and if they were not created by Newari (Nepali) artisans then they were obviously influenced by Newari forms. Experts also see evidence of Chinese influence and, in the fusion of these Newari and Chinese forms with Tibetan sensibilities, the emergence of a syncretic but distinctly Tibetan style of painting.

Whatever the case, there are an awful lot of murals to see and it is difficult not to hurry through floors. You really won't be missing out if you stop and linger in just a few of the chapels to have a close look at the wall frescoes. In fact, you will probably enjoy the experience more and gain a greater appreciation for Tibetan art if you examine some of the wall figures in detail.

Depending on the position of the sun, certain chapels are sometimes illuminated with a warm, soft light that allows flashless photographs. There is a photography charge of Y10 for interior shots.

First Floor

This floor has four main chapels, two storeys high, and oriented according to the cardinal points. The four chapels are dedicated to: Sakyamuni (along with two disciples, medicine buddhas and Guru Rinpoche) in the south; Sukhavati, the 'pure land of the west' and home of red Öpagme (Amitabha) in the west; Marmedze (Dipamkara, the Past Buddha) in the north; and Tushita, another 'pure land' and home of Jampa (Maitreya), in the east. In between are some excellent murals depicting minor Tantric and protector deities. Statues of the Four Guardian Kings in the east mark the way to the upper floors.

Second Floor

The first four chapels in clockwise order from the stairs are dedicated to Jampelyang (known in Sanskrit as Manjushri), Chenresig (Avalokiteshvara), Tsepame (Amitayus) and Drölma (Tara). Most of the other chapels are devoted to wrathful protector deities, including Drölkar (White Tara; 12th chapel from the stairs), Chana Dorje (Vajrapani; 14th chapel) and Mikyöba (Akshobhya; 15th chapel), a blue buddha who holds a *dorje* (thunderbolt).

Third Floor

This floor is also dominated by a series of two-storey chapels at the cardinal points portraying the four Dhyani Buddhas: red Öpagme (Amitabha) in the south; yellow Rinchen Jungne (Ratnasambhava) in the west; green Donyo Drupa (Amoghasiddhi) in the north ;and blue Mikyöba (Akshobhya) in the east. There are several other chapels devoted to the fifth Dhyani Buddha, white Namse (Vairocana). Again, most of the other chapels are filled with wrathful deities.

Fourth Floor

The 11 chapels on this floor are dedicated to teachers, interpreters and translators of obscure orders of Tibetan Buddhism. Exceptions are the Three Kings of Tibet on the north side (eighth chapel clockwise from the steps) and Guru Rinpoche (10th chapel).

Upper Floors

The 5th floor, which is also known as the Bumpa, has four chapels and gives access to the roof of the *kumbum*. Hidden steps behind a statue on the western side lead up to the 6th floor and take you onto the veranda at the level of the eyes painted on the wall. There is also a series of murals painted around a central cube, but most people are taken in by the outstanding views, especially looking south over the old town where, in the background, the white-walled Gyantse Dzong is perched atop a colossal outcrop.

The top floor of the *kumbum* portrays a Tantric manifestation of Sakyamuni, but you will likely find the way up locked.

TSANG

GYANTSE DZONG

Like most Tibetan towns, Gyantse radiates old-world charm when its whitewashed buildings are viewed from on high. So the stiff 20-minute climb to the top of the **Gyantse Dzong** (☎ 817 2116; admission Y40) is worth the effort for the great lookouts. In addition to Gyantse, clear views are afforded of the entire fertile Nyang-chu Valley and down into the compound of the Pelkor Chöde Monastery.

Many of the 14th-century fort's buildings and rooms are open for exploration, and a few have interesting murals and friezes, though most are bare. There's a kitschy attempt to re-create the old **tax office** behind the ticket booth, and a little further on to the left you'll find a dungeon, chapel and torture room with dioramas that leave nothing to the imagination. Bring a torch to explore the spooky lower chambers beneath the chapel.

Entry to the *dzong* is via a gate, just north of the main roundabout. Land Cruisers can drive up about halfway to the top.

OTHER SIGHTS

Hidden behind the hill that runs between the monastery and the *dzong* is **Rabse Nunnery**, a delightful place decorated with prayer flags, chörtens and *mani lhakhangs*. The 'correct' way to visit is along the clockwise pilgrim trail that goes around the back of the Pelkor Chöde Monastery. To start, follow the road up beside the monastery and then swing right onto the dirt kora path. Bring a compass as the way back takes you through a maze of streets in the old town (but what views of the fort in the distance!). Bring water and lunch, too, as once you get out to this splendid open area you're going to want to continue to Riche Ganden Retreat (p190). A round trip from central Gyantse to Rabse and back takes about two hours.

Sleeping

All the following have English signage out the front.

BUDGET

our pick **Jianzang Hotel** (Jianzang Fandian; ☎ 817 3720; Yingxiong Nanlu; tr per bed with/without bathroom Y50/40, d Y180-200, discounts of 20%) The Jianzang once again gets our vote as the best place in town. Rooms are clean, spacious and good value. Some rooms have squat toilets; others are Western-style and there are shared hot showers for the cheaper rooms. The best rooms, with wood floors and little touches of Tibetan décor, are in the new block overlooking the main road (it's quiet at night).

Wutse Hotel (Wuzi Fandian; ☎ 817 2909; fax 817 2880; Yingxiong Nanlu; dm Y50, s/d/tr with bathroom Y280/200/288, discounts of 30%) A popular place set around a courtyard. The quads are old but serviceable and there are reasonably clean toilets and showers. The private rooms have wood floors, 24-hour hot water and cosy beds with white cotton quilts.

Family Guesthouse (Jiangzi Liangshiju Zhaodaisuo; ☎ 817 4666; Weiguo Lu; s/d/tr per bed Y60/40/25) The carpets are old and stained but otherwise the rooms and shared bathrooms (no showers) are clean and fine for a night's stay. The guesthouse is on the corner of Yingxiong Nanlu and Weiguo Lu, on the 2nd floor. The owner (who also owns the next door Zongri Tibetan Hotel) speaks some English.

MIDRANGE

Gyantse County Chugu Hotel (Jiangzi Chugu Binguan; ☎ 817 3165; Yingxiong Nanlu; s & d Y150) The newest courtyard hotel in Gyantse, with 24-hour hot water, wood-floor rooms and friendly staff.

Zongri Tibetan Hotel (Jiangzi Zongshan Fandian; ☎ 817 5555; ngawangrangchuan_n@hotmail.com; 1 Weiguo Lu; d incl breakfast Y320, discounts of 30-50%) With 24-hour hot water, clean Western-style rooms and usual discounted rates of Y140 to Y160 a room, this is a solid-value midrange option. A top-floor restaurant (dishes Y10 to Y30) offers almost 360 degree views of Gyantse. Step outside onto the rooftop (access via the back of the restaurant) for the perfect shot of the Gyantse Dzong.

Minghu Hotel (Minghu Fandian; ☎ 817 2468; 1 Shanghai Lu; d/tr Y369/380, discounts of 20-30%) A clean and quiet two-star Chinese-style hotel with comfy beds and 24-hour hot water. Most travellers probably won't find the jump in quality over cheaper courtyard places so great to justify the extra expense, however.

Eating

For a small town, Gyantse has a good range of decent restaurants. Most will cook at any time.

Naychung Café (☎ 892 2223; Yingxiong Nanlu; mains Y10-30; 🕑 breakfast, lunch & dinner) Newly opened at the time of writing, the Naychung serves the usual traveller-friendly Nepalese, Tibetan, Chinese and Western fare. The food is a little better than average and the friendly, competent staff and the bistro atmosphere make this a good choice for a relaxing meal at the beginning or end of the day. Menu in English.

Yak Restaurant (☎ 817 4971; Yingxiong Nanlu; mains Y15-30; 🕑 breakfast, lunch & dinner) The Yak offers backpacker treats like French toast (Y12), pizza, yak burgers, sizzlers (dishes served on a hot, sizzling plate) and Western breakfasts. Menu in English.

Tashi Restaurant (☎ 817 2793; Yingxiong Nanlu; mains Y15-40) The Nepalese curries and the Tibetan dishes are not as good as you get in Lhasa but are tasty enough when you're this far from home. Menu in English.

Restaurant of Zhuang Yuan (☎ 139-8059 6328; Yingxiong Nanlu; dishes Y15-50) The owners of the Zhuang Yuan know how to promote themselves, and you'd likely find yourself stepping in for a look even without our recommendation. The Chinese dishes are tasty and while the prices are not cheap, portions are large, although single travellers will spend much more here than elsewhere for a complete meal. Menu in English.

SELF-CATERING

Yingxiong Nanlu is filled with small shops selling drinks, fresh fruit and basic snack foods. There are a couple of **supermarkets** (cnr Weiguo Lu & Yingxiong Nanlu), and a **market** (Yingxiong Nanlu) directly opposite the Restaurant of Zhuang Yuan selling veggies and meat, including roasted chicken (great to take for lunch on a long hike).

Getting There & Away

Minibuses to Gyantse depart from in front of Shigatse's main bus station between 10am and 8pm (Y20, 1½ hours). Alternatively you can get a seat in a taxi for around Y25 (one hour).

Minibuses from Gyantse back to Shigatse leave from the main intersection in Gyantse. Gyantse is 90km from Shigatse.

Getting Around

All of Gyantse's sights can be reached comfortably on foot, but there are rickshaws and even taxis if you need them. Negotiate all prices before you head out.

AROUND GYANTSE

There are several excellent adventurous half-day trips to sights around Gyantse that could warrant an extra day or two in town.

Tsechen Monastery & Fort རྩེ་ཆེན་དགོན་པ་

The traditional village of Tsechen is located about 5km northwest of Gyantse and is a nice half-day trip from town. There is a small monastery above the village, but the main reason to hike out here is to climb the ruined fortress, wander along the defensive walls and enjoy great views of the (often flooded) river valley below. It's a good idea to bring a picnic.

The fortress is believed to have been built as early as the 14th century and was used by the British during their 1904 invasion, although it was already partly ruined by then. Hike up to the right side of the fortress and then cross over to the highest ramparts on the left. Across the highway and behind a hill are more monastic ruins.

To get to Tsechen you can either walk, hitch (see p344) or take a taxi along the Southern Friendship Hwy toward Shigatse. The village is just past the turn-off south to Yatung. On the way back it's possible to cut through fields to the river and follow the dirt roads back to the Gyantse bridge. You might get a lift back on a tractor for a couple of yuan; otherwise it's an hour-long walk.

Riche Ganden Retreat རི་ཆེ་དགའ་ལྡན

Hidden in a fold of a valley north of town, this ruined and little-visited monastery is a fine 10km (two-hour) hike from Gyantse. The last section is the only steep part, as you drop into a ravine and then climb from a ruined manor house and herders' camp. Watch out for the dogs here.

There are ruins all around the site, including what was once the main Drölma Lhakhang; compare it with the black-and-white photos taken of the monastery before it was destroyed. Today there are eight Gelugpa monks here. The central Tsongkhapa statue has a glass plate in his chest, which holds an older image of Tsongkhapa.

To get to Riche walk up the road beside the Pelkor Chöde Monastery and turn right onto the dirt track (a kora route) heading towards the Rabse Nunnery. Shortly you'll see a misspelled sign for Riche Ganden directing you north. The way is obvious and clear across an open valley.

Other Monasteries

If you have your own transport, there are several minor monasteries you can visit on the road connecting Gyantse and Shigatse.

Places to explore include **Drongtse Monastery** and chörten, 19km from Gyantse, **Tsi Nesar Monastery**, 25km from Gyantse, a **monastery** at the county capital Penam Xian, 41km from Gyantse, and another **monastery** 62km from Gyantse, 8km before the turn-off to Shalu Monastery.

YUNGDRUNGLING MONASTERY
གཡུང་དྲུང་གླིང་

Just visible across the river from the road between Lhasa and Shigatse is the Bönpo **Yungdrungling Monastery**. It was once the second most influential Bön (p70) monastic institution in Tibet and home to 700 monks. The number is now limited to 35 by the Chinese government and consists largely of different factions of Bönpos from the Aba region of northern Sichuan.

To many, Yungdrungling looks much like a Buddhist monastery, but note the swastikas swirling anticlockwise and the reluctance of your guide and driver to enter the grounds (many Tibetan Buddhists have an aversion to Bön). The monks welcome visitors and one or two can even speak English. If someone is around who has a key, you can visit the large *dukhang*, with its impressive thrones of the monastery's two resident lamas. There are 1300 small iron statues of Shiromo (the equivalent of Sakyamuni) along the walls – look for the deity's characteristic swastika mace. You may also be able to visit a couple of chapels behind the main hall, including the Namjya Lhakhang. Just remember to make the rounds in an anticlockwise direction.

The monastery is 170km west of Lhasa on the north bank of the Yarlung Tsangpo (Brahmaputra River), just east of where the Nangung-chu meets it. Cross the bridge and follow the road 2km north along the Nangung-chu to a footbridge. From here it's about 1.5km up to the monastery (take the path diagonally up the hillside after crossing the stream). If the water level of the Nangung-chu is not too high, you can also take the dirt road 100m to the right after crossing the Yarlung Tsangpo.

SHIGATSE གཞིས་ཀ་རྩེ་ 日喀则

☎ 0892 / pop 80,000 / elev 3840m

About 250km southwest of Lhasa, or 90km northwest of Gyantse, lies Shigatse (Rikaze), Tibet's second-largest town and the traditional capital of Tsang province. Shigatse is a sprawling place, with dusty, uneven streets humming with traffic (even the pedestrian-only lane). As you drive in across the plains, the site of the Potala-lookalike Shigatse Dzong, high on a hilltop overlooking the town, will probably fire up your imagination, but the fort is empty and most of what you see dates from a 2007 reconstruction. It is the Tashilhunpo Monastery, to the west of town, that is the real draw. Since the Mongol sponsorship of the Gelugpa order, Shigatse has been the seat of the Panchen

Lama, and this seat was traditionally based in the monastery.

The town, formerly known as Samdruptse, has long been an important trading and administrative centre. The Tsang kings exercised their power from the *dzong* and the fort later became the residence of the governor of Tsang. The modern city is divided into a tiny old Tibetan town huddled at the foot of the fort, and a rapidly expanding modern Chinese town that has all the charm of, well, every other expanding modern Chinese town.

During the second week of the fifth lunar month (around June/July), Tashilhunpo Monastery becomes the scene of a three-day festival and a huge thangka is unveiled (p319).

Information

INTERNET ACCESS

Internet bars (网吧; wangba) go in and out of business quickly in Shigatse.

China Telecom Internet Bar (Shandong Lu; per hr Y4; 24hr) Has been around for a while and, though it's somewhat dark and smoky inside, the connection speeds are decent.

Tien Le Internet Bar (Shandong Lu; per hr Y5 24hr) Has good connection speeds and window seats for those who need a little fresh air.

MONEY

Bank of China (Zhongguo Yinhang; Shanghai Zhonglu; 9am-6.30pm Mon-Fri in summer, 9.30am-6pm in winter, 10am-5pm Sat & Sun) Next door to the Shigatse Hotel across the intersection, changes travellers cheques and cash and gives credit-card advances. There's a 24-hour ATM outside.

PERMITS

At the time of writing, the **Public Service Bureau** (PSB, Gong'anju; Qingdao Xilu) was not issuing permits for individual travel. Check with other travellers and on Lonely Planet's Thorn Tree forum for the latest information.

POST

China Post (Zhongguo Youzheng; cnr Shandong Lu & Zhufeng Lu) It's possible to send international letters and postcards from here, but not international parcels.

TELEPHONE

The cheapest places to make calls are the many private telecom booths around town.

China Telecom (Zhongguo Dianxin; Zhufeng Lu; 9am-6.30pm Mon-Fri, 9.30am-6.30pm Sat & Sun) You can send faxes and make international phone calls here, around the corner from the post office.

TRAVEL AGENCIES

FIT (☎ 883 8068, 899 0505; Zhufeng Lu) Branch office of the Lhasa government agency, situated next to the carpet factory. At the time of writing FIT could not arrange any travel for foreigners (due to restrictions on permits), except direct trips to the Tibet–Nepal border.

Sights

TASHILHUNPO MONASTERY

བཀྲ་ཤིས་ལྷུན་དགོན 扎什伦布寺

One of the few monasteries in Tibet that weathered the stormy seas of the Cultural Revolution, **Tashilhunpo** (Tashi Lhüngön; Zhashilunbu Si; ☎ 882 2114; Qingdao Xilu; admission Y55; 9am-7pm in summer, 10am-noon & 3-6pm in winter) remains relatively unscathed. It is a real pleasure to explore the busy cobbled lanes twisting around the aged buildings. Covering 70,000 sq metres, the monastery is essentially a walled town in its own right.

From the entrance to the monastery, visitors get a grand view. Above the white monastic quarters is a crowd of ochre buildings topped with gold – the tombs of the past Panchen Lamas. To the right, and higher still, is the **great white wall** that is hung with massive, colourful thangkas during festivals. Circumnavigating the compound is a one-hour kora that takes you into the hills behind the monastery.

As you explore the various buildings, you'll see a lot of photos of the ninth, 10th and 11th Panchen Lamas. The ninth is recognisable by his little moustache. The 11th is the disputed Chinese-sponsored lama, a young boy.

History

The monastery is one of the six great Gelugpa institutions, along with Drepung, Sera and Ganden in Lhasa, and Kumbum (Ta'er Si) and Labrang in Amdo (modern Gansu and Qinghai provinces). It was founded in 1447 by a disciple of Tsongkhapa, Genden Drup. Genden Drup was retroactively named the first Dalai Lama and he is enshrined within Tashilhunpo. Despite its association with the first Dalai Lama, Tashilhunpo was initially isolated from mainstream Gelugpa affairs, which were centred in the Lhasa region.

The monastery's standing rocketed, however, when the fifth Dalai Lama declared his teacher – then the abbot of Tashilhunpo – to be a manifestation of Öpagme (Amitabha). Thus Tashilhunpo became the seat of an important

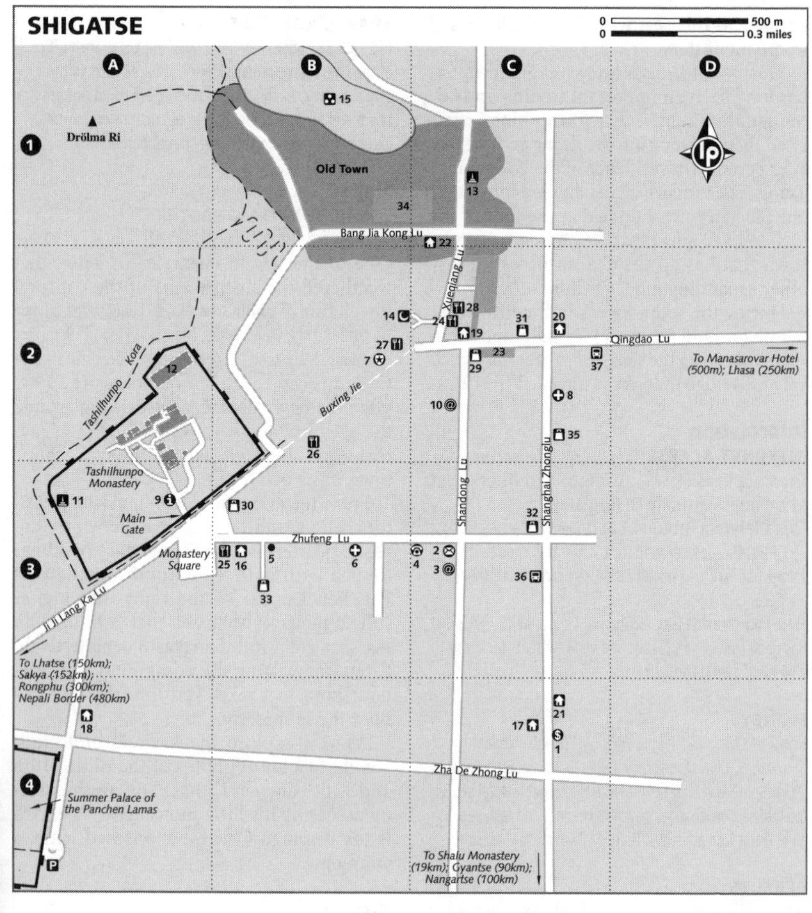

lineage: the Panchen ('great scholar') Lamas (see p196). Unfortunately, with the establishment of this lineage of spiritual and temporal leaders – second only to the Dalai Lamas themselves – rivalry was introduced to the Gelugpa order.

The monastery has a very high profile as the largest functioning monastic institution in Tibet. The monks here can be somewhat cool and there is conjecture that many of the English-speaking monks are in cahoots with the Chinese authorities.

Information

Morning is the best time to visit as more of the chapels are open. After 11am most tourists start to head out for lunch leaving many buildings practically empty.

Severe restrictions are in place on photography inside the monastic buildings. The going cost for a photograph varies, but be prepared for a pricey Y75 fee per chapel, and as high as Y150 in the assembly hall. Video camera fees are an absurd Y1000 to Y1500 in some chapels.

The monastery lends itself to wandering but, with rooms on rooms, tombs beside tombs, winding staircases, ladders and secret passages, after a while you probably won't know where you are, even with our map. At these moments you can always wait for a tour group to come in and eavesdrop on the guide to help orientate yourself again.

INFORMATION
Bank of China 中国银行 1 C4
China Post 中国邮政 2 C3
China Telecom Internet Bar
中国电信网吧 3 C3
China Telecom
中国电信 4 C3
FIT 5 B3
Hospital 医院 6 B3
PSB 公安局 7 B2
Tibet-Shigatse Regional People's Hospital 8 C2
Ticket Booth 9 A3
Tien Le Internet Bar 10 C2

SIGHTS & ACTIVITIES
Chörten 11 A3
Festival Thangka Wall 12 A2
Mani Lhakhang 13 C1
Mosque 14 B2
Shigatse Dzong 15 B1

SLEEPING
Gang Gyan Shigatse Orchard Hotel
日喀则刚坚宾馆 16 B3
Post Hotel 17 C4
Qomolongma Friendship Hotel 18 A4
Samdruptse Hotel 19 C2
Shambhala Hotel
西藏刚坚日喀则香巴拉宾馆 20 C2
Shigatse Hotel 西藏日喀则饭店 21 C4
Tenzin Hotel 22 C1

EATING
Fruit & Vegetable Market 23 C2
Gongkar Tibetan Restaurant 24 C2
Kailash Traditional Restaurant 25 B3
Songtsen Tibetan Restaurant 26 B2
Tashi Restaurant 27 B2
Tenzin Restaurant .... (see 22)
Zhengxin Restaurant 28 C2

SHOPPING
Department Store 29 C2
Photo Shop 30 B3
Photography Shops 31 C2
Sifang Supermarket 32 C3
Tibet Gang Gyen Carpet Factory 33 B3
Tibetan Market 34 B1
Toread Outdoor 35 C2

TRANSPORT
Main Bus Station 36 C3
Minibuses & Taxis to Lhasa 37 C2

Chapel of Jampa (Jamkhang Chenmo)

Walk through the monastery and bear left for the first and probably most impressive of Tashilhunpo's sights: the Chapel of Jampa. An entire building houses the world's largest **gilded statue**, a 26m figure of Jampa (Maitreya), the Future Buddha. The statue was made in 1914 under the auspices of the ninth Panchen Lama and took some 900 artisans and labourers four years to complete.

The impressive, finely crafted and serene-looking statue looms high over the viewer. Each of Jampa's fingers is more than 1m long, and in excess of 300kg of gold went into his coating, much of which is also studded with precious stones. On the walls surrounding the image there are a thousand more gold paintings of Jampa set against a red background.

Victory Chapel (Namgyel Lhakhang)

This chapel is a centre for philosophy and houses a large statue of Tsongkhapa flanked by Jampa and Jampelyang (Manjushri). If it's not open, try to convince one of the monks to let you in.

Tomb of the 10th Panchen Lama (Sisum Namgyel)

This dazzling gold-plated funeral chörten holds the remains of the 10th Panchen Lama, who died in 1989. His image is displayed in front of the tomb. The ceiling of the chapel is painted with a Kalachakra (Dukhor in Tibetan) mandala and the walls are painted with gold buddhas.

Tomb of the Fourth Panchen Lama (Kundun Lhakhang)

The 11m silver-and-gold funerary chörten of the fourth Panchen Lama (1570–1662) was the only tomb chörten to escape destruction during the Cultural Revolution.

From here you pass through a dark walkway that leads out to the Kelsang Temple complex.

Kelsang Temple

The centrepiece of this remarkable collection of buildings is a large **courtyard**, which is the focus of festival and monastic activities. This is a fascinating place to sit and watch the pilgrims and monks go about their business. Monks congregate here before their lunchtime service in the main assembly hall. A huge prayer pole rears up from the centre of the flagged courtyard and the surrounding walls are painted with buddhas. There are splendid photo opportunities here.

The **assembly hall** is one of the oldest buildings in Tashilhunpo, dating from the 15th-century founding of the monastery. The massive throne that dominates the centre of the hall is the throne of the Panchen Lamas. The hall is a dark, moody place, with rows of mounted cushions for monks, and long thangkas, depicting the various incarnations of the Panchen Lama, suspended from the ceiling. The central inner chapel holds a wonderful statue of Sakyamuni, while the chapel to the right holds several images of Drölma (Tara).

You can also visit the huge new **Tomb of the Fifth to the Ninth Panchen Lamas (Tashi Langyar)**, built by the 10th Panchen Lama to replace tombs destroyed in the Cultural Revolution. The central statue is of the ninth Panchen Lama. The 10th Panchen Lama returned to Shigatse from Beijing to dedicate the tomb in 1989. He fulfilled his prediction that he

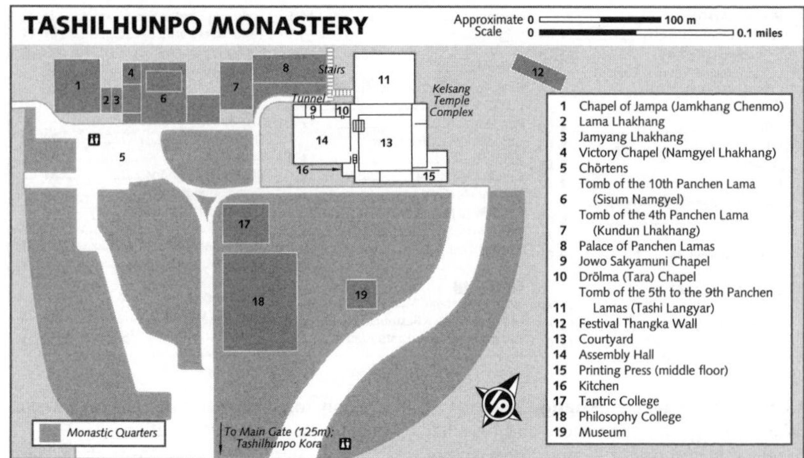

would die on Tibetan soil just three days after the ceremony.

There are a dozen other chapels in the complex. Follow the pilgrims on a clockwise circuit, ending up in a tangle of chapels above the assembly hall. Here in the far left (upper) corner chapel you'll find views of the two-storey Jampa statue below and, to the right, the tombs of the first and third Panchen Lamas and first Dalai Lama. Then descend to the middle floor and do another clockwise circuit taking in the interesting **printing press** and monastic **kitchen**.

Other Buildings

As you leave Tashilhunpo, it is also possible to visit the monastery's two remaining colleges. They are on the left-hand side as you walk down towards the main gate. The first is the **Tantric College** and the second is the brown **Philosophy College**. Neither is particularly interesting, but you might be lucky and find yourself in time for debating, which is held in the courtyard of the Philosophy College.

Tashilhunpo Kora

The kora around Tashilhunpo takes just an hour to walk and provides a chance to mingle with pilgrims, turn a few hundred prayer wheels, donate cash to beggars (the other pilgrims will insist you do so) and take some great photos of the monastery from above. About the only negative is that the route is garbage ridden in many spots.

From the main gate, follow the monastery walls in a clockwise direction and look out for an alley on the right. The alley curves around the western wall and climbs into the hills above the monastery where streams of prayers flags spread over the dry slopes like giant colourful spider limbs. The views of the compound below are wonderful from here. In about 20 minutes you pass the 13-storey white tower used to hang a giant thangka at festival time. The path then splits in two: down the hill to complete the circuit of the monastery, and along a ridge to the Shigatse Dzong, a walk of around 20 minutes. There is a small flat rock outcrop at this point for relaxing on and taking in the views.

SHIGATSE DZONG གཞིས་ཀ་རྩེ་རྫོང

Once the residence of the kings of Tsang and later the governor of Tsang, very little remained of the *dzong* after it was destroyed in the popular uprising of 1959. Construction on a new building began several years ago and Shigatse is now once again graced with an impressive hilltop fort that bears a close resemblance to the Potala, albeit on a smaller scale.

The *dzong* was empty and closed at the time of writing and there was no word on when it would open.

SUMMER PALACE OF THE PANCHEN LAMAS བདེ་ཆེན་སྐལ་བཟང་ཕོ་བྲང་ 德庆格桑颇彰

Though it ranks far below Tashilhunpo, if you have extra time in Shigatse, pay a visit to this walled **palace complex** (admission Y15; 9.30am-12pm

& 4-6pm) on the south end of town. Recent efforts at rehabilitating the straggly gardens are taking fruit, as is the restoration or reworking of wall murals. While the new paintings cannot compare to the masterly works of the past, they are still quite lovely and, covering every surface of the rooms as they do with vibrant colours and fantastic images, form a rather awesome whole.

The palace was built in 1844 by the seventh Panchen Lama, Tenpei Nyima. At the time of writing you could walk around the gardens and enter the palace itself. Only the first hall and the staircase seemed open to visitors but you could still enter many rooms and watch the artists at work. If the entire building is open when you arrive, look for the 10th Panchen Lama's **sitting rooms** on the 1st floor and his **audience chamber** on the 2nd floor.

The palace is about 1km south of Tashilhunpo. Follow the road to the end and turn right into the gated compound.

Sleeping

Shigatse has a good range of decent hotels, most with flush toilets and 24-hour hot water. All the following have English signage out the front.

BUDGET

Tenzin Hotel (Tianxin Luguan; ☎ 882 2018; fax 883 1565; 8 Bangjiakonglu; q per bed Y40, d/tr without bathroom Y180/120, standard/deluxe d with bathroom Y280/320, discounts of 20-30%) Popular with both backpackers and Land Cruiser groups, though a little noisy for our tastes, especially on the lower floors. The shared bathrooms are excellent and have 24-hour hot water. The restaurant has a good range of Indian, Western and Nepalese dishes (Y15 to Y35).

Shambhala Hotel (Xiangbala Fandian; ☎ 882 7668; fax 883 3681; Qingdao Lu; s without bathroom Y60, d/tr with bathroom per bed Y60/40) With its clean rooms, 24-hour hot water and courteous staff, this is one of the best budget choices in town. Showers are available for Y5 for rooms without bathrooms. The facilities are clean, though the ancient metal showerheads will probably remind you of *M*A*S*H*.

Qomolongma Friendship Hotel (Zhufeng Youyi Binguan; ☎ 882 1929; fax 882 2984; Puzhang Lu; d Y100) Cheap doubles run by apathetic staff who seem eager to return to the front desk to watch TV. It's fine if you are on a budget but really need your own bathroom.

Samdruptse Hotel (Sangzhuzi Fandian; ☎ 882 2280; 2 Qundao Lu; d/tr without bathroom Y180/150, d with bathroom Y280, discounts of 30%) This bright, quiet, modern hotel features courteous staff and rooms with wood floors and decent cotton bedding. The cheaper doubles and triples can sometimes be paid per bed.

MIDRANGE & TOP END

Gang Gyan Shigatse Orchard Hotel (Rikezi Gangjian Binguan; ☎ 882 0777; fax 883 0171; 77 Zhufeng Lu; d/tr without bathroom Y168/188, s/d with bathroom Y288/388, discounts of 30%; ⌘) Right next to the carpet factory is this well-managed hotel offering large Western-style rooms with comfortable beds and furnishings. The shared bathrooms are clean but the showers' water supply is iffy; rooms with private bathrooms have a good supply of water. Breakfast is included, but best of all is the location of the hotel, less than 100m from the entrance of the Tashilhunpo Monastery.

Post Hotel (Youzheng Binguan; ☎ 882 2938; 12 Shanghai Zhonglu; tw Y260, discounts of 30%) All rooms are twins in this modern, well-managed place across from the Shigatse Hotel. You wouldn't expect it looking at the glossy surfaced lobby, but a few rooms are a bit tattered, so check carefully before you pay.

Shigatse Hotel (Rikaze Fandian; ☎ 882 2525; fax 882 1900; 12 Shanghai Zhonglu; s/d/tr Y560/560/660, discounts of 20%) Recently remodelled and sporting a very fancy looking Tibetan-style lobby and atrium, the Shigatse is often booked solid by affluent tour groups. Rooms are furnished Tibetan- and Western-style, and there's in-house dry cleaning and laundry, and a games room.

Eating

Shigatse is swarming with good restaurants generally open for lunch and dinner.

our pick **Gongkar Tibetan Restaurant** (☎ 882 1139; Xueqiang Lu; dishes Y10-20) Hang out with the people and enjoy good food. In addition to the standard *momos* (dumplings) and noodle dishes, you'll find easy-to-resist dishes such as yak-tongue soup. Menu in English.

Zhengxin Restaurant (Xueqiang Lu; dishes Y10-20; breakfast, lunch & dinner) On a street with a few other Chinese restaurants, the Zhengxin stands out mostly for its English menu and friendly owners. The food is tasty enough but not outstanding. Menu in English.

Kailash Traditional Restaurant (☎ 899 5923; Zhufeng Lu; dishes Y10-30; breakfast, lunch & dinner) At

THE PANCHEN LAMAS

As the second-highest ranking lamas in the land, the Panchen Lamas' authority often rivalled that of the Dalai Lamas. So great is their prestige, in fact, that the Panchen Lamas assist in the process of choosing new Dalai Lamas (and vice versa). And as with the latter, the Panchen lineage results from the rebirth of previous lamas, which in the 20th century has lead to a long series of unfortunate events.

The ninth Panchen Lama (1883–1937) spent his last days in the clutches of a Chinese nationalist warlord after attempting to use the Chinese as leverage in gaining greater influence in Tibet. His reincarnated self never knew anything but Chinese interference and control.

After the ninth's death, the usual search went on for his replacement. In 1951, the Chinese forced Tibetan delegates in Beijing to endorse their choice. (They even claimed that in 1949, the 11-year-old future Panchen Lama had written to Mao Zedong asking him to 'liberate' Tibet.) Though little more than a tool of Beijing when he arrived at Tashilhunpo Monastery in 1951, by 1965 the Panchen Lama had become a 'big rock on the road to socialism'. By the year of his death, 1989, he had become a hero to his people. What happened?

It seems that the Panchen Lama had a change of heart about his Chinese benefactors after the 1959 Lhasa uprising. In September 1961, the Panchen Lama presented Mao with a 70,000-character catalogue of the atrocities committed against Tibet, and a plea for increased freedoms. The answer was a demand that he denounce the Dalai Lama as a reactionary and take the latter's place as spiritual head of Tibet. Not only did the Panchen Lama refuse but, in 1964, with tens of thousands of Tibetans gathered in Lhasa for the Mönlam festival, he said to the crowds that he believed Tibet would one day regain its independence and the Dalai Lama would return as its leader.

It must have come as quite a shock to the Chinese to see their protégé turn on them. They responded in time-honoured fashion by throwing the Panchen Lama into jail, where he remained for 14 years, suffering abuse and torture. His crimes, according to the Chinese authorities, included participating in orgies, 'criticising China' and raising a private insurrectionary army. A 'smash the Panchen reactionary clique' campaign was mounted, and those close to the Panchen Lama were subject to 'struggle sessions' and in some cases were imprisoned.

After emerging from prison in early 1978, the Panchen Lama rarely spoke in outright defiance of the Chinese authorities, but continued to use what influence he had to press for the

the end of Zhufeng Lu next to the park is this new travellers' hang-out with cosy Tibetan-style seating and decent Nepalese curries, Western breakfasts and sandwiches. Menu in English.

Tashi Restaurant (☎ 883 5969; Buxing Jie; dishes Y10-30; breakfast, lunch & dinner) Another popular travellers' hang-out with a wide range of comfort foods. This Nepali-run restaurant has everything from yoghurt muesli to pizza and Nepali curries. Staff sometimes give you the impression they've been doing this kind of work for a few too many years. Menu in English.

Songtsen Tibetan Restaurant (☎ 883 2469; Buxing Jie; dishes Y20-35; breakfast, lunch & dinner) A similar but brighter, friendlier Tibetan-style place on the pedestrian-only street. Sit by the window and people watch as you dine on Indian, Nepalese, Tibetan or Western fare, or just enjoy a hearty Western breakfast at the start of the day. Menu in English.

SELF-CATERING

Shigatse has a number of shops selling drinks and snacks along Zhufeng Lu and Shandong Lu. There's a traditional market behind the defunct department store selling fruit, vegetables, meats and breads.

Jin Long Supermarket, on the ground floor of the defunct department store, has a small selection of goods. **Sifang Supermarket** (cnr Zhufeng Lu) has a wider selection.

Shopping

The **market** (Bangjiakonglu) in front of the Tenzin Hotel is a good place to pick up souvenirs, such as prayer wheels, rosaries and thangkas. There are also dozens of souvenir and craft shops along the pedestrian-only street. Bargain hard.

Tibet Gang Gyen Carpet Factory (☎ 882 2733; 9 Zhufeng Lu; 9am-1pm & 3-7pm) Beside the Gang Gyan Hotel, 100m down a dirt track (follow the enormous signs), this French joint venture exports 100% Tibetan wool preservation of Tibetan cultural traditions. (He argued, for example, against the building of a hydroelectric power plant at Yamdrok-tso, one of Tibet's most sacred lakes.) It is believed that shortly before his death he again fell out with the Chinese, arguing at a high-level meeting in Beijing that the Chinese occupation had brought nothing but misery and hardship to his people. Accordingly, many Tibetans believe that he died not of a heart attack, as was reported, but by poisoning. However, others maintain that, exhausted and perhaps despairing, the Panchen Lama came home in 1989 to die – as he always said he would – on Tibetan soil.

Of course, the story doesn't end here. In May 1995 the Dalai Lama identified Gedhun Choekyi Nyima, a six-year-old boy from Amdo, as the latest reincarnation of the Panchen Lama. Within a month the boy had been forcibly relocated to a government compound in Beijing, causing him to be dubbed the 'world's youngest political prisoner', and an irate Chinese government had ordered the senior lamas of Tashilhunpo to come up with a second, Chinese-approved choice. Chadrel Rinpoche, the abbot who led the search that identified Gedhun, was later imprisoned for six years for 'splitting the country' and 'colluding with separatist forces abroad' (ie consulting the Dalai Lama), and Tashilhunpo was closed to tourists for a few months.

Tashilhunpo's lamas eventually settled on Gyancain Norbu, the son of Communist Party members, who was formally approved in a carefully orchestrated ceremony.

Beijing's interest is not only in controlling the education of Tibet's number-two spiritual leader, but also influencing the boy who could later be influential in identifying the reincarnation of the Dalai Lama. Meanwhile, Dalai Lama–appointed Panchen Lama, now 18, remains under house arrest at an undisclosed location in China.

There are a number of groups campaigning to free the Panchen Lama. Check out the websites of the **Tashilhunpo Monastery in exile** (www.tashilhunpo.org), which offers a reward for information on the whereabouts of the boy, the **Australia Tibet Council** (www.atc.org.au) and the **Canada Tibet Committee** (www.tibet.ca).

The Search for the Panchen Lama by Isabel Hilton is a look at the political intricacies of Tibet, with an emphasis on the controversial Panchen Lama and China's abduction of his current reincarnation.

carpets to the USA and Europe. It's fun to visit just to look around as women work on the carpets, singing as they weave, dye, trim and spin; you are free to take photographs. Expect to pay a few hundred US$, plus shipping, for a carpet measuring 185cm by 90cm. Note that almost half the profits go to Tashilhunpo Monastery.

Toread Outdoor Sports (☎ 882 3195; Shanghai Zhonglu) If you are headed off on a trek but totally unprepared, you can pick up basic equipment such as tents, stoves and jackets here.

There are a couple of photo shops next to each other across from Monastery Square and also on Qingdao Lu where you can burn CDs.

Getting There & Away

Minibuses to Lhasa (Y50) leave from a stand on Qingdao Lu on the eastern side of Shigatse. You can also catch the similar public bus service, which runs from the main bus station. Foreigners will be able to buy bus tickets to Lhasa on the minibuses, but not tickets on buses to Lhasa from the main bus station.

Going between Lhasa and Shigatse, taxis do the trip for Y50 to Y70 per person (four hours) and wait for fares near the spot where the minibuses depart.

At the main bus station there are daily morning minibuses to Sakya (Y40, four hours) and Lhatse (Y40, five hours).

Minibuses to Gyantse (Y20, 1½ hours) run when full from outside the main bus station from morning till late evening. Taxis run when full for Y25 per seat.

There are daily (sometimes twice daily) buses running to Saga (Y150, 16 hours), and two or three buses daily to Shegar (Y75, seven hours).

Getting Around

Shigatse is not that large and can be comfortably explored on foot. For trips out to the

KILOMETRE MARKERS ALONG THE FRIENDSHIP HIGHWAY

The following towns, geographical features and points of interest along with their appropriate kilometre markers (signifying distance from Shanghai) may be of help to travellers, hitchhikers and mountain bikers.

Lhasa to Shigatse

Marker	Feature
4646	Lhasa's eastern crossroads to Golmud or Shigatse
4656	Blue Buddha rock painting
4661	sign to Nyetang Tashigang Monastery
4662/3	Netang village and Drölma Lhakhang
4673	bridge (closed at time of writing) on left to Shugsheb Nunnery
4683	new bridge and tunnel to Gongkar airport
4695-7	Chushul (Tibetan 'End of River')
4703	bridge over the Yarlung Tsangpo to Nangartse and Tsetang; shops and restaurants
4712	hydroelectric project on the far side of the river; the structure shaped like a golf ball atop the hill is a radar and meteorological centre
4717/8	ruined fortress on left and village
4724	village, ruined *dzong* and monastery
4732	valley begins to narrow into rocky gorge
4757	road to Nyemo to north; restaurants; bridge
4768	suspension footbridge to left
4779	bridge over to south side of river
4800	checkpoint; turn-off to Rinbu (Rembu); old road to Shigatse; shops
4820	Traduka; bridge to Yungdrungling Monastery and Yangpachen; restaurants
4835	Drakchik Ferry
4840	Huda village
4869	Ansa Monastery on hillside to south
4875	bridge north to Nanmulin (potato-growing region)
4900-5	Shigatse

Shigatse to Tingri

Marker	Feature
4900-5	Shigatse
4913	turn-off to Ngor Monastery
4917	Nartang Monastery
4928	Gyeli village
4932/3	very gentle mountain pass of Tra-la (3970m)
4936	Kangchen Monastery to right
4956/7	interesting ruined Trupuk Chörten 1km to the north
4960/1	Gyading; ruined fort; restaurants and shops
4972	Dilong village
4977/8	turn-off to Phuntsoling Monastery
4994	Daoban
5000	marker showing 5000km from Shanghai; small monastery and ruined *dzong*

Shigatse Hotel or bank, you might want to use a pedicab (Y5). A ride anywhere in town in one of the many taxis will cost Y10.

AROUND SHIGATSE

There are many sights around Shigatse, but few are visited by Western travellers. En route to Lhatse stop at **Nartang Monastery**, a 12th-century Kadampa monastery famed for wood-block printing the Nartang canon in the 18th century, and **Kangchen Monastery**. Both are signposted in English just off the Friendship Hwy. There's a trek from Shalu to Nartang (p296). It is possible to visit Gyantse as a day trip from Shigatse. It's a very pleasant ride through a lightly wooded valley dotted with small villages.

5009	village and start of climb to pass
5014	Tropu-la (Tsuo-la; 4500m)
5028	Sakya bridge; turn-off to Sakya; rebuilt hilltop monastery
5036	ruined *dzong*
5041	village and turn-off to Xiqian Hot Springs
5052	Lhatse
5058	checkpoint and turn-off to western Tibet
5063	start of climb to pass, with a height gain of around 1000m
5083	Gyatso-la (5100m)
5114	views of Everest and the Himalaya
5121	hermitage across river
5124	bridge; to nunnery and fortress
5128/29	Qiabu village, fort and caves
5133	Baber (Baipa) and turn-off to Shegar
5139	Shegar checkpoint
5145	turn-off to Everest Base Camp
5155	ruined *dzong* to left
5162	village
5170	village
5193-4	Tingri

Tingri to Nyalam

Marker	Feature
5193-4	Tingri
5199	paved road ends
5206	turn-off for Tsamda Hot Springs
5216	two small Tibetan guesthouses in village
5221-9	various ruins by side of road
5232-3	Gutso village; guesthouse and restaurant
5237	village on west side of the river
5254	village and small guesthouse and restaurant
5258	ruins by road
5263	start climb to La Lung-la
5265	turn-off to Saga and Mt Kailash via Peiku-tso
5276	La Lung-la (4845m)
5282	bridge, road workers' hostel
5289	Tong-la (Yarle Shung; 4950m) and view of Cho Oyu and Mt Everest
5292	short cut down the hillside, used by Land Cruiser drivers
5303	roadworkers' hostel and village
5311	village, with ruins behind
5334	Gangka village and track to Milarepa's Cave
5345	Nyalam
5376	approximate checkpoint
5378	Zhangmu
5386	Nepali border

Shalu Monastery ཞྭ་ལུ་དགོན་པ་ 夏鲁寺

It's a treat for the traveller when a sight is both a pleasure to explore and of great importance in local history and culture. Such is the **Shalu Monastery** (Xialu Si; admission Y40), which dates back to the 11th century. The monastery rose to prominence in the 14th century when its abbot, Büton Rinchen Drup, emerged as the foremost interpreter and compiler of Sanskrit Buddhist texts of the day. (A suborder, the Büton, formed around him.) It also became a centre for training in skills such as trance walking and *thumo* (generating internal heat to survive in cold weather), feats made famous by the flying monks of Alexandra David-Neel's book *Magic and Mystery in Tibet*.

In the abstract, the design of the monastery represents the paradise of Chenresig (Avalokiteshvara), a haven from all worldly suffering. In the concrete, Shalu is the only monastery in Tibet that combines Tibetan and Chinese styles in its design. Much of the original structure was destroyed by an earthquake in the 14th century and, as this was a time of Mongol patronage (see p203), many Han artisans were employed in the reconstruction. The green-tiled Chinese style, clearly visible as you approach, is one of the monastery's most easily recognisable features.

What remained of the original 11th century Tibetan-style monastery was largely destroyed in the Cultural Revolution, but the Chinese-influenced inner Serkhang has survived reasonably well. If you enjoy looking at murals, Shalu has some fine ones from the 14th century that fuse Chinese, Mongol and Newari styles. The best murals line the walls of a corridor that rings the central assembly hall; bring a powerful torch (flashlight) to really appreciate these.

The inner Serkhang contains a **kanjyur lhakhang** (scripture chapel), with lovely 14th-century mandala murals. The west chapel has a black stone statue of Chenresig Kasrapani, the monastery's holiest relic. The northern chapel has more fine murals, including one in the left corner depicting the monastery's founder. There are a couple of upper chapels, including the Mudu Lhakhang, which holds the **funeral chörten** of Büton.

From Shalu you can make the trek to Nartang (p296) or take an hour's walk up to **Ri-puk Hermitage**, a former meditation centre built around a spring. There are pleasant views of the Shalu Valley from here.

GETTING THERE & AWAY

Shalu Monastery is just a few kilometres off the Shigatse–Gyantse road and a side-trip here should not add to the cost of a Land Cruiser trip. If taking a Gyantse-bound minibus from Shigatse, get off at kilometre marker 19 or 21 and take a dirt road heading south. Both approaches will lead you to Shalu village in an hour. As you walk through the small village look for the monastery (its green-tiled roof is a dead giveaway) on the right down an alley.

There are a number of shops outside Shalu Monastery gates selling soft drinks, water and noodles.

PHUNTSOLING MONASTERY & JONANG KUMBUM ཕུན་ཚོགས་གླིང་ ཇོ་ནང་སྐུ་འབུམ་

If you're travelling down the paved Friendship Hwy and want to get a taste of what off-the-beaten track looks like, consider a few hours' diversion to **Phuntsoling Monastery** (admission Y30). Not only is the drive here along the winding Yarlung Tsangpo highly scenic, but so is the monastery itself, situated at the bottom of a gargantuan sand dune. A ruined red fort, seated high above the monastery on a rocky crag, just adds to the fantastic photogenic atmosphere.

Phuntsoling Monastery was once the central monastery of the Jonangpa. This Kagyu sect is especially known for the examination of the nature of emptiness undertaken at the monastery by its greatest scholar, Dolpopa Sherab Gyaltsen (1292–1361). He was one of the first proponents of the hard-to-grasp notion of *shentong*. Roughly, this is based on the idea that the Buddha-mind (which transcends all forms) is not ultimately empty, even though all forms are empty illusions.

Shentong has been debated among Buddhist philosophers for seven centuries. The Gelugpa school did not share Dolpopa's view, to the point where in the 17th century the fifth Dalai Lama suppressed the Jonangpa school and forcibly converted Phuntsoling into a Gelugpa institution.

You can visit the monastery's large **assembly hall**, which is dominated by a statue of Chenresig (Avalokiteshvara). Other statues include those of the 10th Panchen Lama, Tsongkhapa and the fifth Dalai Lama. The inner sanctum of the hall contains a statue of Mikyöba (Akshobhya), while the murals on the roof tell the story of the life of Sakyamuni.

The highlight of the monastery is a walk up to the ruined **fortifications** behind the monastery, which offer stunning views of the valley. Look for the ruined *dzong* on a cliff across the Yarlung Tsangpo.

A festival is held at Phuntsoling around the middle of the fourth lunar month (or June/July) every year, and sees lamas and pilgrims from all over the county gathering in the courtyard for prayers and celebrations. Unfortunately the event is closed to foreigners and if you show up on this day, the PSB will quickly escort you off the premises.

From Phuntsoling you can head south up the valley for a two-hour walk to the ruins of the **Jonang Kumbum**. The former 20m-high chörten was built by Dolpopa in the 14th century and was the spiritual centre of the Jonangpas. It was said to be one of the best-preserved monuments in Tibet, resembling the Gyantse Kumbum, before it was wrecked during the Cultural Revolution.

Lhatse Chöde ལྷ་རྩེ་མཆོད་སྡེ་

If you continue on the road past Phuntsoling Monastery, in a couple hours you'll reach Lhatse Chöde, with its small monastery and ruined *dzong*. (You can also reach the village by going 1km east of Lhatse on the Friendship Hwy to the 5052km mark and then heading north.) To the east of the village is **Drampa Gyang Temple**, one of Songtsen Gampo's demoness-subduing temples (p105). In this case it pins the troublesome demoness' left hip.

Getting There & Away

Phuntsoling Monastery can be visited on the way from Shigatse to Lhatse. Take the dirt-road detour north of the Friendship Hwy at kilometre marker 4977/8. The monastery is 34km northwest from here (less than an hour's drive). It's a 61km journey from Phuntsoling to Lhatse but it's probably faster and more comfortable just to return to the Friendship Hwy, unless you plan to also visit Lhatse Chöde.

SAKYA ས་སྐྱ་ 萨迦

☎ 0892 / elev 4280m

A detour to visit the small town of Sakya (Sajia) is pretty much *de rigueur* for any trip down the Friendship Hwy. The town is southeast of Shigatse, about 25km off the Southern Friendship Hwy, accessed via a good dirt road through a pretty farming valley. The draw here is the **Sakya Monastery**, which, like Shalu, has great appeal to the eye (the high-walled monastery compound is dubbed the 'Great Wall of Tibet' by some) and the spirit (the dim, smoky assembly hall exudes sanctity like few others). Also like Shalu, Sakya occupies an important place in Tibetan history (see p203)

Sakya actually has two monasteries, on either side of the Trum-chu. The heavy, brooding, fortress-like monastery south of the river is the more famous and if you only have time to visit one, make it this. The hillside northern monastery, mostly reduced to picturesque ruins, is undergoing restoration work.

One characteristic feature of the Sakya region is the colouring of its buildings. Unlike the standard whitewashing that you see elsewhere in Tibet, Sakya's buildings are ash grey with white and red vertical stripes. The colouring symbolises the Rigsum Gonpo (the trinity of bodhisattvas) and stands as a mark of Sakya authority. Sakya literally means 'pale earth'.

Unfortunately, a great deal of ugly development has occurred in the southern half of Sakya in recent years, robbing the town of much of its charm. At the same time, however, a new Tibetan village (with a lovely debating hall and monks' quarters) is being constructed down by the river. Pretty much any photograph you take pointed towards the hills to the north is going to look good.

Permits

You need a travel permit from the PSB to visit Sakya, and at the time of writing there were officers inside the monastery checking to make sure you had one as soon as you paid and entered.

Sights

SAKYA MONASTERY

The immense, grey, thick-walled **southern monastery** (☎ 824 2352; admission Y45; 9am-6pm) is one of Tibet's most impressive man-made sights, and one of the largest monasteries. The monastery was established in 1268 and is designed defensively, with watchtowers on each of the corners of its high walls. Before the Cultural Revolution, Sakya Monastery had one of the largest monastic communities in Tibet. At the time of writing there was much reconstruction work underway, and many areas were closed to visitors. As usual, morning is the best time to visit as more chapels are open.

Directly ahead from the east-wall main entrance is the entry to the inner courtyard. The dusty, somewhat pedestrian looking courtyard is a bit of a disappointment after the grandeur of the outside walls, but things pick up again as you enter the main **assembly hall (Lhakhang Chenmo)**, a huge structure with walls 16m high and 3.5m thick.

At first glance the assembly hall may strike you as being like most others in Tibet: a dark interior illuminated with shafts of sunlight and the warm glow of butter lamps; an omnipresent smell of burning butter from the lamps; slick stone floors (again from the butter); rows of red mounted cushions covered with old patterned rugs; tall columns decorated with colourful thangkas and photographs; and an array of gilded statues representing buddhas, bodhisattvas, Tibetan kings and holy men. But even weary tour groups seem to quickly recognise the age, beauty and sanctity of Sakya. Plan to spend time here just soaking up the atmosphere. You'll find few that are its equal.

A few things to look specifically for in the hall are the huge drum in the far left corner and the massive sacred pillars that hold up the ceiling. Some are made of entire tree trunks and are famous throughout Tibet. One reputedly was a gift from Kublai Khan!

The walls of the assembly hall are lined with towering **gilded buddhas**, which are unusual in that many also serve as reliquaries for former Sakya abbots. The buddha in the far left corner contains relics of Sakya Pandita; the one next to it houses those of the previous abbot of Sakya. The largest central buddha contains remains of the founder of the monastery. To the right of the central buddha are statues of Jampelyang (Manjushri), a seated Jampa (Maitreya) and a Dorje Chang (Vajradhara) that seemed to us to radiate holiness. Sakya's famous library is accessible from this hall but hidden from sight and it is rarely opened up to tourists.

As you exit the assembly hall the chapel to the right (south) is the Purkhang Chapel. Central images are of Sakyamuni and of Jampelyang (Manjushri), while wall paintings behind depict Tsepame (Amitayus) to the left, Drölma (Tara) and white Namgyelma (Vijaya) to the far left, as well as a medicine buddha, two Sakyamunis and Jampa (Maitreya). Murals on the left wall depict Tantric deities central to the Sakya school.

To the north of the inner courtyard is a chapel containing 11 gorgeous **silver chörtens**, which are also reliquaries for former Sakya abbots. Look to the left corner for the **sand mandala** inside a dirty glass case. A sometimes-locked door leads into another chapel with additional amazing chörtens and murals. Bring a torch as the room is even dimmer than others.

There are several chapels upstairs but these may be closed for construction when you ar-

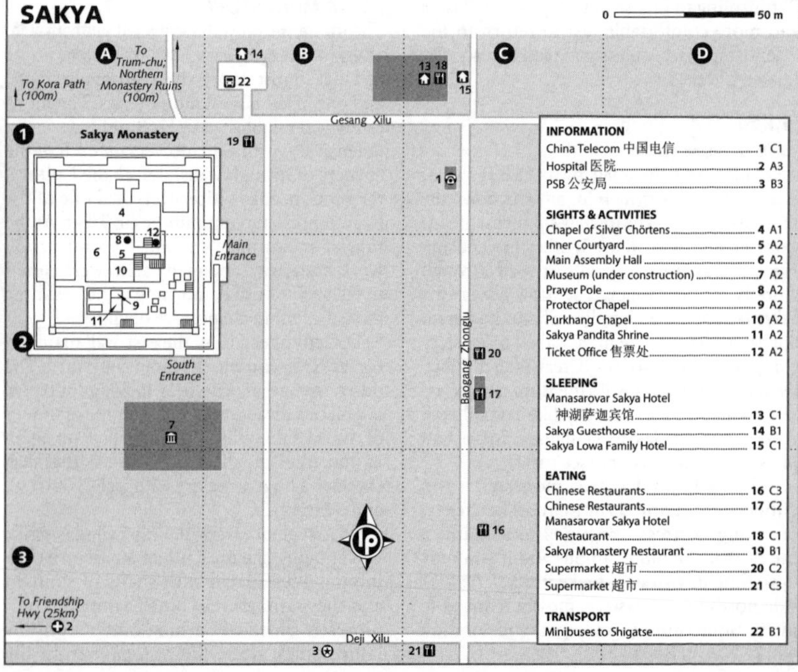

PRIESTS & PATRONS: THE REIGN OF THE SAKYAPAS

The 11th century was a dynamic period in the history of Tibetan Buddhism. Renewed contact with Indian Buddhists brought about a flowering of new orders and schools. During this time, the Kagyupa order was founded by Marpa and his disciple Milarepa, and in Sakya, the Kön family established a school that came to be called the Sakyapa. One interesting distinction between the latter school and others is that the abbotship was hereditary, restricted to the sons of the Kön family.

By the early 13th century, the Tsang town of Sakya had emerged as an important centre of scholastic study. The most famous local scholar was a Sakya abbot, Kunga Gyaltsen (1182-1251), who came to be known as Sakya Pandita, literally 'scholar from Sakya'.

Such was Sakya Pandita's scholastic and spiritual eminence that when the Mongols threatened to invade Tibet in the mid-13th century he represented the Tibetan people to the Mongol prince Godan (the son of Genghis Khan). Sakya Pandita made a three-year journey to Mongolia, arriving in 1247, and after meeting with Godan offered him overlordship of Tibet. Resistance was pointless, Sakya Pandita noted. The Mongols were set on conquest, and their easy victories over the Western Xia and other kingdoms left no doubt what Tibet's fate would be if it put up a fight.

After Sakya Pandita's death in 1251, one of his nephews became the abbot of Sakya and therefore (with Mongol support) the ruler of all Tibet. This was the first religious government with a lama as head of state, and set an important precedent for Tibetan government. However, the association between Tibetan lamas and Mongol masters also set a precedent of outside rule over Tibet that the Chinese have used to justify current claims over the high plateau.

As it was, Mongol overlordship and Sakya supremacy were relatively short-lived. Mongol corruption and rivalry between the Sakyapa and Kagyupa orders led to the fall of Sakya in 1354, when power fell into the hands of the Kagyupa and the seat of government moved to Nedong in Ü.

Sakya was to remain a powerful municipality, however, and, like Shigatse, enjoyed a high degree of autonomy from successive central governments. Even today, you can see homes across the plateau painted with the red, white and blue-black stripes associated with Sakya Monastery.

rive. On the right-hand side of the east-wall entrance are stairs leading up to a 2nd-floor chapel of five chörtens. Another flight of stairs in the left corner of the courtyard leads up to another couple of chapels. A long flight of stairs outside the central complex leads up to a single rooftop protector chapel.

There are a couple of chapels open outside of this central complex (but still within the compound), the most interesting of which is the very spooky **protector chapel** of the Pakspa Lhakhang. If the thick incense doesn't get you, the terrifying monsters, the huge *cham* masks and the stuffed wolves that wait in the dark recesses just may. To the left is a **shrine** dedicated to Sakya Pandita.

It may be possible to climb up onto the wall-walk of the monastery for superb views of the surrounding valley, but ask first.

NORTHERN MONASTERY RUINS

Very little is left of the original monastery complex that once sprawled across the hills north of the Trum-chu, but it is still worth climbing up through the Tibetan village and wandering around what does remain. The northern monastery predates the southern monastery (the oldest temple situated at the northern monastery was built in 1073), and it is alleged to have contained 108 buildings, like Ganden. It may once have housed some 3000 monks who concentrated on Tantric studies.

A new Tibetan village is hastily being constructed across the river at the base of the mountains and is adding to the charm of the area. Centred in the village is a large new **debating hall** with monks' quarters. Work was in progress at the time of writing but the wood and brick structure was looking like it was going to fit into its environment very nicely.

After passing through the new village, head for the white chörtens, or the ruins even further to the left. Near the chörtens are the three main complexes that are still open: the main **Labrang Shar**, the **Namja Choede** to the left and the **Rinche Gang** nunnery to the far right. Remember to walk in a clockwise fashion as this is a kora route.

Sleeping

Accommodation is limited but you have the option of showers and a toilet if you want them. Several inexpensive family-run guesthouses were being built around the Lowa Family Hotel at the time of writing. With the exception of the Sakya Guesthouse, you'll find English signs outside all these places.

Sakya Guesthouse (☎ 824 2233; dm Y15-20) The rooms are basic but bearable if you have a sleeping bag (the guesthouse mostly serves the great unwashed masses of pilgrims), but you probably won't be able to stay here without PSB permission.

Manasarovar Sakya Hotel (Shenhu Sajia Binguan; ☎ 824 2222; dm/tr Y50/380, d Y220-280, discounts of 20-30%) En suite plumbing has finally come to Sakya, for better or worse, with this large modern hotel. Rooms are carpeted (though a bit tatty in places), clean and comfortable, with hot showers, Western-style bathrooms and comfy beds. The eight-bed dorm rooms are decent enough; one even comes with en suite toilet and shower. There are superb views from the hotel's rooftop.

Sakya Lowa Family Hotel (☎ 824 2156; s/d per bed Y120/60) Recently opened, the Lowa seems to be part of a ripple (goodness knows it's not yet a wave) of better quality guesthouses hitting Tibet. Rooms are clean, fresh and furnished with decent beds, new TVs and a few with yak-dung stoves. Walls are brightly painted and accented with traditional motifs. There are no showers but you can use the courtyard's pump, which is actually a pretty fun way to wash yourself when the weather is warm.

Eating

Sakya has a number of Chinese restaurants, all set up by Sichuanese immigrants. All restaurants serve lunch and dinner, and have no fixed opening hours.

Sakya Monastery Restaurant (☎ 824 2988; dishes Y7-15) This Tibetan eating place is owned by the monastery and serves up fried rice, *thugpa* (noodles) and milk tea.

Manasarovar Sakya Hotel Restaurant (☎ 824 2222; dishes Y15-35; ⏰ breakfast, lunch & dinner) For Western food, such as omelettes, burgers, sizzlers and pizza. There are also Tibetan, Nepalese and Indian dishes. Menu in English.

SELF-CATERING

For drinks and basic supplies there are several small supermarkets scattered about town.

Getting There & Away

There's one daily minibus between Shigatse bus station and Sakya (Y40, four hours). The return bus departs from Sakya around 11.30am. Another option is to take a Lhatse-bound bus from Shigatse to the Sakya turn-off and then walk or hitch the remaining 25km. See p344 for information regarding the risks associated with hitching.

LHATSE ལྷ་རྩེ་ 拉孜

☎ 0892 / pop 2000 / elev 3950m

Approximately 150km southwest of Shigatse and some 30km west of the Sakya turn-off, the bleak town of Lhatse (Lazi) is best considered a pit-stop for lunch or supplies, or a venue for acclimatising or for staying overnight on the way to better destinations. Lhatse is more or less a one-street town with a small square near the town centre. The 3km-long main street runs east–west and used to be part of the Friendship Hwy, but this has now been diverted to the north. Passing Land Cruiser traffic will mostly be heading to Everest Base Camp, the Tibet–Nepal border or the turn-off for Ali in western Tibet (p224), about 6km out of town.

There's little to see in Lhatse save the small **Changmoche Monastery** at the western end of town. Nearby is the Xiqian Hot Springs, Lhatse Chöde and Drampa Gyang Temple.

Sleeping

In addition to the following (which all have English signage), at the time of writing a couple of Tibetan-style guesthouses were under construction in the eastern end of town as you first drive in from Shigatse. They may be worth a look when ready. There are also a few grubby, characterless hotels around the middle of town to consider if everything else is full. If you are coming from Lhasa or Shigatse, your stay here may be your first introduction to Tibet's infamous pit toilets.

Lhatse Tibetan Farmers Hotel (☎ 832 2333; d/tr per bed Y60/50) Located on the east side of town, this courtyard guesthouse is popular with Land Cruiser drivers and guides. It looks quaint on the outside but the rooms are pretty basic, with hard mattresses, bare furnishings and a single dim bulb. The 2nd-floor rooms are somewhat better but often booked by tour groups. The guesthouse's Tibetan-style restaurant is a very cosy place, with decent Tibetan and Western food (Y10 to Y25).

Dewang Hotel (☎ 832 2888; d/tr Y120) The rooms at this family-run courtyard are superior (they even come with TV) to the Farmers Hotel and, other than the pit toilets, even fairly fussy travellers should be OK here. The hotel is diagonal across the road from the Farmers Hotel. The sign outside reads 'Plain Sailing'.

Shanghai Hotel of Lazi (☎ 832 3678; fax 832 3786; d Y360, discounts of 30%) This is the top hotel in Lhatse and, while overpriced, is the place to stay if you need Western comforts like good bed sheets, flush toilets and showers. The hotel is obvious on the south side of the town square. There is a very large sign in English as you drive through town announcing its presence and directing you to it.

Eating

Guesthouses all have their own inexpensive Tibetan-style restaurants (with English menus) and most travellers eat at these. You can also try the many Chinese and Muslim restaurants that line the south side of the main street.

Lhatse Kitchen (☎ 832 3678; dishes Y10-35; breakfast, lunch & dinner) Just left of the Shanghai Hotel of Lazi, the Kitchen serves a range of tasty Nepali, Indian and Western dishes in an upscale Tibetan-style setting. Menu in English.

Getting There & Away

Daily morning minibuses (Y40, five hours) run between Shigatse and Lhatse. Two or three buses a day from Shigatse pass through on the way to Shegar. There's no public transport all the way out to Mt Kailash, though daily (sometimes twice-daily) buses from Shigatse pass through on the way to Saga.

AROUND LHATSE

For the small traditional village of Lhatse Chöde, just north of Lhatse, see p201.

Xiqian Hot Springs ཚོངས་པ་ཆུ་ཚན

Tibetans come from far and wide to bathe in the healing waters of these **hot springs** (wenquan; baths per person Y60), which are said to cure a multitude of ills, especially skin irritations (so be careful who you share the pools with). The facilities have been upgraded in recent years and the odourless spring water is now piped into two large indoor pools, set under a canopy roof. It's a pleasant enough place for a dip, especially in the cooler months or in the evenings.

The hot springs are 10km east of Lhatse. Turn north off the Friendship Hwy at the town of Xiqian (or Xiqin; kilometre marker 5041) and continue 750m north. The sign reads 'Shi Chen Hot Spring Holiday Resort', which is a bit of a stretch, though at the time of writing a new guesthouse was being built beside the pool house. It may be worth checking out as the area is much more pleasant than Lhatse (there's a large grassy park with a stream running through it adjacent to the guesthouse). It's a good idea to agree beforehand about including the springs in your itinerary if you want to visit by hired Land Cruiser.

BABER & SHEGAR ཤེལ་དཀར

☎ 0892 / elev 4250/4150m

There's a bit of confusion about this area but Baber (also Baipa) is the name many give to the small settlement lining 1km of the Friendship Hwy at kilometre marker 5133. This is where most travellers spend the night before heading off to Everest Base Camp and also where you can buy your permit for the Qomolangma Nature Preserve, which includes Everest Base Camp, Rongphu Monastery and Cho Oyu Base Camp. The **Qomolangma Service Centre** (☎ 826 2835; 24hr) is in the Qomolangma Nature Preserve San Chen Guesthouse. To get here take the turn-off to Shegar and, after crossing the river, turn right at the first road. The hotel is plainly seen across a field.

Shegar (also known as New Tingri, but not to be confused with Tingri) is reached by turning off the Friendship Hwy at Baber and heading 7km northwest. It's worth a visit for the ruins of **Shegar Dzong** (Crystal Fort), once the capital of the Tingri region. The remains of the *dzong's* defensive walls snake incredibly over the pinnacle that looms over town. A 2km kora trail leads up from the western side of town to the top of the impossibly steep crag (think Mt Crumpit in *The Grinch Who Stole Christmas*). Along the way you can see Mt Everest in the distance. Morning light is best for taking photographs.

On the way up you'll pass the **Shegar Chöde Monastery**, a small Gelugpa institution built in 1269. A painting inside depicts the monastery at its height, when it had around 800 monks. These days only a few remain, but they are happy to have visitors sit and chat with them in the courtyard. Keep an eye out for the 'longevity sheep' (sheep that were saved from slaughter) that hang out in the courtyard.

Sleeping & Eating

Shegar has a few guesthouses, but the town is pretty grubby, with piles of rubbish everywhere and stray dogs roaming the streets. Baber is better and most groups spend the night here before heading out early the next morning to catch dawn over the Himalayas at Pang-la.

Most guesthouses and hotels in town have attached restaurants. Most of these have English menus and signs outside announcing the type of food they serve (one even has its menu scrawled on the outside wall). You can pick up water and noodles and biscuits in the shops near the Kangjong Hotel.

If the Kangjong is full, try the place signed **Tibetan Guesthouse Cheap And Best Service** (☎ 826 2880; dm per bed Y25) at the beginning of town (coming from Lhatse) on the right, or the **Chengdu Manor Hotel** (dm per bed Y30) a little further down the road and also on the right. Both places have basic rooms with shared pit toilets and simple restaurants (dishes Y10 to Y35) serving Chinese and Tibetan food.

Tibetan Tingri Snowlands Kangjong Hotel (d Y60-100) The best place in town, with basic but clean rooms set around a courtyard. There's a free shower block and fairly clean pit toilets. The cheaper doubles can be rented per bed (Y30). The more expensive doubles are a step up in comfort and quality, though they, too, have shared bathrooms (but in a separate room at the end of the hall). The hotel is in the middle of town at the crossroads to Shegar. The hotel's restaurant and sitting area has wall-to-wall comfy sofas arranged around a warm stove. Simple but good food is available (Y10 to Y15 per dish) and you can kick back with a thermos of sweet tea. It's a great place to meet other travellers.

Baber has two Western-style hotels but they are substandard.

Consider the **Qomolangma Hotel Tingri** (☎ 826 2775; fax 826 2818; d/tr Y240/468, discounts of 10%) on the other side of the river on the way to Shegar only if you have to have private bathrooms.

Getting There & Away

Baber is around 81km from Lhatse. There are two or three buses (Y75, seven hours) a day between Shegar and Shigatse with a stop in Baber. If you are hitching or cycling, you may have a hard time getting past the checkpoint 6km to the south as you will be asked to show both a passport and PSB permit.

EVEREST REGION

Everest's Tibetan name is generally rendered as Qomolangma, and some 27,000 sq km of territory around Everest's Tibetan face have been designated as the Qomolangma Nature Preserve (p85). For foreign travellers, Everest Base Camp has become one of the most popular trekking destinations in Tibet, offering the chance to gaze on the magnificent north face of the world's tallest peak, **Mt Everest** (珠穆朗玛峰, Zhumulangma Feng; 8850m). The Tibetan approach provides far better vistas than those on the Nepali side, and access is a lot easier as there is also a road all the way up.

The most satisfying way to get to Everest Base Camp is to make the popular three- or four-day trek from the Friendship Hwy at Tingri (p299). If you drive up by Land Cruiser, note that it's not possible to go all the way to Everest Base Camp anymore. All vehicles must stop at the tent camp a few kilometres past Rongphu Monastery. From here passengers must trek or take a horse and cart the last glorious 4km.

At the time of writing, the road to Everest Base Camp from Chay was closed for repairs and Land Cruiser traffic was redirected along a track near Tingri. The old route should be open by the time you read this and will sport a new paved surface, which will undoubtedly bring even more traffic to the mountain.

Permits

You need two permits to visit Everest Base Camp. The first is the usual PSB travel permit (only available if you were on a Land Cruiser tour at the time of writing). The second, a park-entry permit for Qomolangma Nature Preserve, can be bought at the Qomolangma Nature Preserve San Chen Guesthouse in Baber (p205) or in the Snow Leopard Guest House (p210) in old Tingri (if coming from Nepal). The permit costs Y400 per vehicle, plus Y180 per passenger. Make sure you are clear with your agency if this cost is included in your trip (it usually isn't).

Your passport and PSB permit will be scrutinised at the checkpoint 6km west of Shegar. The park permit is checked at the Chay checkpoint, 3km after the turn-off from the Friendship Hwy. If you are hiking or driving in from Tingri, there is a checkpoint at Lungchang.

WHAT'S IN A NAME?

In 1856, Andrew Waugh, surveyor general of India, released the most important finding of the mapping of the 'Great Arc' of mountains from the south of India to the Himalayas: Peak XV was the highest mountain in the world and would henceforth be known as 'Mount Everest', in honour of Waugh's predecessor, Sir George Everest (actually pronounced eve-rest).

Waugh's proposal met with much initial opposition, including from Everest himself who thought a local name should be used. In response Waugh claimed that there was no 'local name that we can discover'. But this was almost certainly untrue, even if Waugh himself didn't know it. Very likely there were many scholars who knew the Tibetan name for the mountain: Qomolangma, which can be interpreted as 'Goddess Mother of the Universe' or (more literally, if less poetically) 'Princess Cow'. As early as 1733, the French produced a map on which Everest is indicated as Tschoumou Lancma. In addition, on the very day Waugh's paper on Everest was presented to the Royal Geographic Society, another was read that revealed the local Nepali name to be Deodhunga.

Still, the Everest contingent gained the upper hand (even the writer of the Nepali paper wanted the great man's name used) and in 1865 the Royal Geographic Society declared 'Mt Everest' would henceforth designate the world's highest mountain. Of course, this has had little effect on what the Tibetans and Chinese call the mountain.

Dangers & Annoyances

Whatever you do, don't attempt to walk to Everest Base Camp directly after arriving in Tingri from the low altitudes of the Kathmandu Valley. The altitude gain of over 2600m leaves most people reeling from the effects of acute mountain sickness (AMS, also known as altitude sickness). Even those coming from Lhasa often have trouble.

It's also important to realise just how high and remote you are, and to carry warm clothing and some kind of rain gear no matter what time of year you visit and no matter how short your walk. Unlike on the Nepali side, there is no rescue service up here in the shadow of Everest. Get caught wearing shorts and a T-shirt when a sudden rain or snowfall hits and you could be in serious trouble.

The Chinese maintain a small military presence at Everest Base Camp to deal with any potential trouble, which include attempts to camp or trek past the base camp.

Baber to Rongphu & Tent Camp

The Everest access road begins around 6km west of the Shegar/Baber checkpoint, shortly after kilometre marker 5145. The 91km drive takes around two or three hours. The locations this drive takes you through can be seen on Map p301.

About 3km from the Friendship Hwy you get to the village of Chay, where your entry permit is checked. From Chay, it's a winding drive up to Pang-la (5050m). The views here are stupendous on a clear day, and feature a huge sweep of the Himalaya range, including Makalu, Lhotse, Everest, Gyachung and Cho Oyu.

The road then descends past a couple of photogenic villages and ruins down into the fertile Dzaka Valley and the village of Tashi Dzom (also known as Peruche), where you can get lunch or a bed for the night at several places.

The dirt road then runs up the wide valley, passing the small villages of Lha Shing, Rephel, Pelding and Puba before reaching Pasum, which also offers accommodation. The next main village is Chödzom (more accommodation) and from here the road turns south towards Rongphu (or Rong-puk or also Rongbuk). The first views of Everest appear half an hour before you arrive at Rongphu.

Rongphu Monastery རོང་ཕུ་ཆེ་དགོན་པ

elev 4900m

Though there were probably monastic settlements in the area for several hundred years previously, **Rongphu Monastery** (admission free) is the main Buddhist centre in the valley and once coordinated the activities of around a dozen smaller religious institutions, all of which are now ruined. It was established in 1902 by a Nyingmapa lama. While not of great antiquity, Rongphu can at least lay claim to being the highest monastery in Tibet and thus the world.

Renovation work has been ongoing at the monastery since 1983, and some of the interior **murals** are superb. The monastery and its large **chörten** make a great photograph with Everest thrusting its head skyward in the background.

The **Monastery Guesthouse** (dm per bed Y40, d Y80) offers basic quads but the doubles are a decent choice if the conditions at the tent camp bother you. There's a cosy restaurant serving up pancakes (bring your own jam or honey), egg, meat, noodle and rice dishes to order for around Y10 each.

Across from the Monastery Guesthouse, the rooms are aging poorly at the **Government Hotel** (☎ 0892-858 4535; d per bed Y300). Despite the price, you won't get a private bathroom or a shower.

Tent Camp

New to the Everest scene is this group of nomad tents lining both sides of the dirt road between Rongphu and Base Camp. It's the furthest point vehicles can drive to and is a fun place to stay.

All tents charge the same per-bed fee (Y40) and all offer very simple meals and drinks. A few have beer for sale if you are in the mood to celebrate.

Be careful with your belongings as the tents are open all the time and offer no security. It's

THE ASSAULT ON EVEREST

There had been 13 attempts to climb Everest before Edmund Hillary and Sherpa Tenzing Norgay finally reached the summit as part of John Hunt's major British expedition of 1953. Some of these attempts verged on insanity.

In 1934 Edmund Wilson, an eccentric ex-British army captain, hatched a plan to fly himself from Hendon direct to the Himalaya, crash land his Gypsy Moth halfway up Everest and then climb solo to the summit, despite having no previous mountaineering experience (and marginal flying expertise). Needless to say he failed spectacularly. When his plane was impounded by the British in India he trekked to Rongphu in disguise and made a solo bid for the summit. He disappeared somewhere above Camp III, and his body and diaries were later discovered by the mountaineer Eric Shipton at 6400m. A second solo effort was later attempted by a disguised Canadian from the Tibet side. It was abandoned at 7150m.

From 1921 to 1938, all expeditions to Everest were British and were attempted from the north (Tibetan) side, along a route reconnoitred by John Noel – disguised as a Tibetan – in 1913. In all, the mountain claimed 14 lives. Perhaps the most famous early summit bid was by George Mallory and Andrew Irvine (just 22), who were last seen going strong above 7800m before clouds obscured visibility. Their deaths remained a mystery until May 1999 when an American team found Mallory's body, reigniting theories that the pair may have reached the top two decades before Norgay and Hillary. In 2005 teams were sent up to gather evidence, and the results prompted the writers at www.everestnews.com to publish an intriguing theory in support of a Mallory summit. It was Mallory, who when asked why he wanted to climb Everest famously quipped 'because it is there'.

With the conclusion of WWII and the collapse of the British Raj, the Himalayas became inaccessible. Tibet closed its doors to outsiders and, in 1951, the Chinese invasion clamped the doors shut even more tightly. In mountaineering terms, however, the Chinese takeover had the positive effect of shocking the hermit kingdom of Nepal into looking for powerful friends. The great peaks of the Himalaya suddenly became accessible from Nepal.

In 1951, Eric Shipton led a British reconnaissance expedition that explored the Nepali approaches to Everest and came to the conclusion that an assault via Nepal might indeed be met with success. Much to their dismay, the British found that the mountain was no longer theirs alone. In 1952 Nepal issued only one permit to climb Everest – to the Swiss. The Swiss, who together with the British had virtually invented mountaineering as a sport, were extremely able climbers. British climbers secretly feared that the Swiss might mount a successful ascent on their first attempt, something that eight major British expeditions had failed to achieve. As it happened, the Swiss climbed to 8595m on the southeast ridge – higher than any previous expedition – but failed to reach the summit.

The next British attempt was assigned for 1953. Preparations were particularly tense. It was generally felt that if this attempt were unsuccessful, any British hopes to be the first to reach the best to leave everything in your Land Cruiser if possible.

This is the furthest point vehicles can drive to and is an incredibly scenic place to stay. You're hemmed in by high grey ridges to the east and west and as you look up the street, Everest's north face dominates the skyline. This is prime real estate and it's yours for a pittance.

Don't expect any privacy at the camp, though: tents sleep six people (your host and perhaps a relative or two will be sharing the space with you) in an open area around the central stove. Also, at night, when all the stoves are burning yak dung, the insides can get very smoky. People with allergies, lung problems, or sensitive noses should consider sleeping at Rongphu. The views are just as good there.

Everest Base Camp ཇོ་མོ་གླང་མའི་ག་ཞམ་རོག་

elev 5150m

Endowed with springs, Everest Base Camp was first used by the 1924 British Everest expedition. The site has a couple of permanent structures and a small army base. Clamber up the small hill festooned with prayer flags for great views of the star attraction, then have your photo taken at the base camp marker, which disappointingly

summit would be dashed. There was considerable backroom manoeuvring before the expedition set off. As a result, Eric Shipton, who had led three previous expeditions (including one in 1935), was dropped as team leader in favour of John Hunt, an army officer and keen Alpine mountaineer, though relatively unknown among British climbers.

Shipton's 1951 expedition had at the last minute accepted two New Zealand climbers. One of them was Edmund Hillary, a professional bee-keeper and a man of enormous determination. He was invited again to join Hunt's 1953 expedition. Also joining the expedition was Tenzing Norgay, a Sherpa who had set out on his first Everest expedition at the age of 19 in 1935 and who had subsequently become infected with the dream of conquering the world's highest peak.

On 28 May 1953, Hillary and Norgay made a precarious camp at 8370m on a tiny platform on the southeast approach to the summit, while the other anxious members of the expedition waited below at various camps. That night the two men feasted on chicken noodle soup and dates. At 6.30am the next morning they set out.

Almost immediately they were in trouble, confronted with a vast, steep sweep of snow. It was the kind of obstacle that had turned back previous expeditions, but Norgay agreed with Hillary that it had to be risked. It was a gamble that paid off. The next major obstacle was a chimney-like fissure, which the two men squirmed up painfully. Struggling onwards they suddenly found themselves just metres away from a snow-clad dome. At 11.30am, 29 May, they stepped up to the top of Mt Everest and stood at the closest point to the heavens it is possible to reach on foot.

By 2007, over 3000 people had reached the peak of Everest (including George Mallory II, Mallory's grandson), while more than 200 climbers had died in the attempt. The first woman to reach the summit was Junko Tabei from Japan on 16 May 1975. The youngest person was 15-year-old Sherpa Temba Tseri from Nepal, who reportedly reached the top in May 2001 after losing five fingers to frostbite in a previous attempt. The oldest person to make the climb was Toshio Yamamoto at 63 years and 311 days. The Nepali side is the easier and more frequently used.

In other firsts, 2005 saw a helicopter summit of the mountain by Frenchman Didier Delsalle. In 2006, Tormod Granheim and Tomas Olsson attempted to ski Everest's North Face. Olsson died in the attempt, falling over 1700m.

Of all the controversies that Everest generates in the world of mountaineering, its height is not one that should still be an issue. But in May 1999 an American expedition planted a global positioning system (GPS) at the top of Everest and pegged the height at a controversial 8850m – 2m higher than the 8848m accepted since 1954. The Chinese dispute this claim (and indeed recently lowered the height by 1.5m due to melting of the summit ice cap – see p85), and will have the opportunity to make their case to the world when they attempt to carry the Olympic torch to the summit in 2008.

For the latest news on Everest, check out www.everestnews.com.

does not even mention the word 'Everest'. It reads 'Mt Qomolangma Base Camp' and the Chinese below indicates that it is 5200m above sea level. (Other measurements have it at 5020m or 5150m.) The springs are just to the left of this marker.

Since the dirt road is closed to traffic for the last few kilometres, it's very enjoyable walking to Everest Base Camp. The way up is gentle and the altitude gain is less than 200m: most people can cover the distance in less than an hour. Along the way you pass scree slopes, jagged ridges, and broad glacial valleys flowing with muddy water. If the altitude is bothering you, hire a horse and cart (Y50) at the tent camp. The ride includes an hour stay at Base Camp.

Note that you can get mobile phone reception at Tent Camp and Base Camp. Call a friend. They'll be thrilled.

GETTING THERE & AWAY

There is no public transport to Everest Base Camp. It's either trek in or hire a Land Cruiser.

TINGRI དིང་རི་ 定日

pop 500 / elev 4250m

The village of Tingri (Dingri), 142km from Lhatse, comprises a half-kilometre of brick Tibetan homes, restaurants, guesthouses and shops lining the Friendship Hwy. Sometimes called Old Tingri, it overlooks a sweeping plain bordered by towering Himalayan peaks and is a usual overnight stop for Land Cruiser traffic heading to or from the Nepali border. For newcomers from Kathmandu, the discomforts of the sudden altitude gain are likely to make it an unpleasant stay.

Ruins on the hill overlooking Tingri are all that remain of the Tingri Dzong. This fort was destroyed in a Nepali invasion in the late 18th century. On the plains between Shegar and Tingri, dozens more ruins that shared the same fate can be seen from the Friendship Hwy.

It is possible to trek between Everest Base Camp and Tingri (p299).

Sleeping & Eating

Most places offer basic double rooms around a main courtyard with pit toilets, a hot shower block and a cosy Tibetan restaurant or teahouse. All have English signage out the front.

Amdo Hotel (☎ 826 2701; s/d Y35/25) In the middle of town, with an English sign reading 'On More Hotel'. There are hot showers (guests/nonguests Y10/15) and a restaurant (dishes Y10 to Y20) that serves decent Tibetan food though some travellers have complained that the kitchen is not very clean.

Lhasa Guesthouse (☎ 890 6396; s Y100, d per bed Y30-45) Prices rise with the quality of mattresses here. An extra Y10 (nonguests Y15) gets you a hot shower. The restaurant (dishes Y5 to Y25) gets better reviews for the cleanliness of its kitchen. The hotel is east of Amdo.

Himalaya Guest House (d per bed Y40) This is a new family-run place with cute cloth-covered walls that make the cheap doubles look rather cheery. It's on the east side of town on the right as you drive in from the Baber. Showers are included in the price.

Tingri Snowland Guesthouse (☎ 892 6017; d per bed Y40) About 800m west of the centre of town, Snowland has excellent views of the Himalayas when you step outside your room into the courtyard. Rooms have cloth-covered walls and are bright and clean. The restaurant has a large menu. Showers are included in the room price.

Snow Leopard Guest House (☎ 826 2711; d with/without bath Y318/180, tr/q Y168/200) Some Land Cruiser drivers and guides try to swing their customers here but look at a few other places in town first before deciding if this place is acceptable. It's a bit tatty and stained for the money.

Namtso Restaurant (☎ 826 2708; dishes Y14-30; ⏰ breakfast, lunch & dinner) In the far west side of town, this place serves burgers, pizza, curries and breakfasts. There are also several Chinese restaurants in town catering largely to the local army garrison.

AROUND TINGRI

Langkhor Monastery གླང་འཁོར་དགོན་པ་

If you've got time on your hands, you could head out to Langkhor Monastery, 20km southwest of Tingri. The monastery is associated with Padampa Sangye, an Indian ascetic who was an important figure in the second diffusion of Buddhism on the Tibetan plateau. There's not much to see here, but it's a good chance to hire a pony and cart for the bumpy ride out there. Most villagers have a cart, but not everyone will be interested in taking you. Try to negotiate under Y100. It's not a comfortable 4½-hour return ride (bring some padding!), but you'll get to see some fantastic scenery this way.

Tsamda Hot Springs མཚམས་མདའ་ཆུ་ཚན་

The odourless, iron-rich springs are about 12km west of Tingri, and are piped directly into the pools of the **Tsamda Snow Leopard Hot Spring Hotel** (☎ 892 6030; dm Y40, d Y200-280). Most travellers are not very impressed with the public pools, but you can rent a private room with bath for Y50 for a couple hours if the place is not busy. The private bath is a bit rough, too, and stained red in places from the iron in the water, but it's just the thing for cleaning yourself off after a day or two at Everest Base Camp.

The hotel makes for a better stop than Tingri. There's a common room on the 2nd floor with outstanding views, and some pleasant easy walks around the nearby hills. And the hot-spring water, despite the basic setup, is actually very good quality and the perfect temperature for soaking in.

The springs are 1km off the Friendship Hwy and are signposted in English near kilometre marker 5206.

NYALAM གཉའ་ལམ་ 聂拉木

☎ 0892 / elev 3750m

Nyalam (Nielamu) is a rainy, humid one-street town with a Chinese façade. It's about 30km from the Nepali border, 152km from Tingri, and is a usual overnight spot for Land Cruiser trips to or from Nepal. It's also a base for trekking in the southern Shishapangma region.

There are several **internet bars** (网吧; wangba; per hour Y5) around town, including one across from the Nyilam Nga Dhom Hotel. There are numerous private telecom booths around town for cheap calls.

For those who want to trek, Gary McCue has a section on the area in his book *Trekking in Tibet – A Traveler's Guide*. One possible day hike takes you up the valley behind Nyalam to Dara-tso, a holy lake from which glaciers of the Langtang and Jungal Himal, and maybe even Shishapangma (the only mountain over 8000m planted squarely in Tibet), are visible on a clear day.

Snowland Hotel can help organise porters and sells basic Chinese-made trekking gear from its shop across the road.

Sights

Wandering around town recording the crazy English signs (Deliciously Fresh Bathroom, The mature and steady is a Rongcheng of Restaurant, the Hotel of Coloured Beans) can pass an hour.

The only cultural sight close to Nyalam is **Milarepa's Cave**. Milarepa was a famous Buddhist mystic and composer of songs (Tibet's St Francis of Assisi) who lived in the late 11th and early 12th centuries. During his time spent in long meditation in this cave he renounced all luxuries and survived on a diet of local weeds (famously turning green as a result).

At the time of writing the cave was more or less closed due to construction. Expect a shiny new monastery when you arrive, with possible guesthouses. Most people can safely miss the cave without disappointment, though if the guesthouses are built they could make

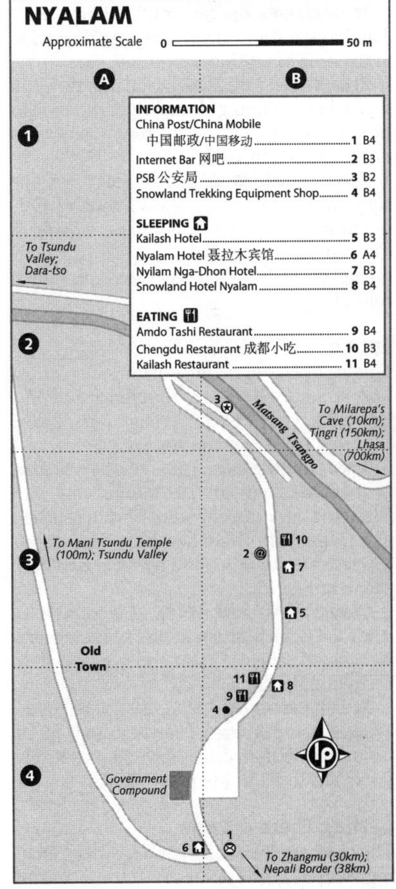

for a more interesting overnight location than bland Nyalam.

The cave is signposted 'Milaraba Buddist Practice Cave' and is 10km north of Nyalam, at Gangka village.

Sleeping

None of the guesthouses have showers (浴室; *yushi*), but you can have one at Chengdu Restaurant for Y20 between 8am and 11pm. All hotels have English signage out the front.

Nyilam Nga-Dhon Hotel (☎ 827 2113; new block d Y100, old block dm per bed Y30) The rooms in the new block are decent enough for a night's stay. The inferior old-block rooms are thinwalled and cramped. The owners are friendly, and there's a clean toilet and washing block.

Snowland Hotel Nyalam (☎ 827 2111; d per bed Y30) The Snowland was undergoing reconstruction at the time of writing. Prices may rise.

Kailash Hotel (☎ 827 2488; d/tr Y50/30) New kid on the block offering clean, bright rooms with new furnishings. East-facing rooms have wonderful mountain views.

Nyalam Hotel (☎ 827 2507; per bed Y30-50) The sign outside this place reads 'Hotel of Coloured Beans' and we hope it never changes. The rooms set around the courtyard are spartan but clean. It's often very busy with Indian tour groups.

Eating

Finding a place to eat in Nyalam is simple: just look around. All serve at least lunch and dinner and have no fixed opening hours. Below are just a few to get you started.

Amdo Tashi Restaurant (dishes Y15-20; ⏲ breakfast, lunch & dinner) There are two rooms, one with Western tables and one with Tibetan couches. The menu makes a similar split – you can get a muesli breakfast or good *tenthuk* (noodles). Menu in English.

Chengdu Restaurant (☎ 827 2350; dishes Y15-20) The food is fairly tasty and the Chinese menu has a good range of meat and veggie dishes. Menu in English.

Kailash Restaurant (☎ 827 2485; dishes Y20-25; ⏲ breakfast, lunch & dinner) There's a range of Tibetan and Western dishes including set breakfasts (Y20 to Y25). Menu in English.

Getting There & Away

The only way here is by Land Cruiser, hitching (see p344) or cycling.

NYALAM TO ZHANGMU

The landscape along the 30km route from Nyalam to Zhangmu should be touted as one of Tibet's great natural wonders. From Nyalam, the road drops like a stone off the Tibetan plateau into a deep gorge of evergreen forests, waterfalls and thundering rivers. Such noise and colour and drama after the dry, serene landscape of Tibet is a joy to the senses. Perhaps most amazing are the dozen or more falls, many well over 200m long, any one of which would be considered a great attraction anywhere else. During the summer monsoons, the road is submerged in a sea of cloud – no doubt one of the reasons why Nyalam means 'gateway to hell' in Tibetan.

At the time of writing the road was under heavy construction. Landslides and washouts and long waits were common. Expect work to last for years.

ZHANGMU (DRAM) འགྲམ་ 樟木

☎ **0892 / elev 2250m**

Zhangmu, also known as Dram in Tibetan and Khasa in Nepali, hugs the rim of what seems a never-ending succession of hairpin bends down to the customs area at the border of China and Nepal. After Tibet, it all seems incredibly green and wet.

Zhangmu is a typical border town, much larger than Nyalam, and has a restless, reckless feel to it. There is one far-too-narrow main road through town and it gets backed up frequently. During these times the squealing of Tata truck brakes as the vehicles inch their way down will drive you insane. The town is sadly a poor way to enter or leave Tibet.

Information

For showers head to **Bath House** (Y10; ⏲ 9am-11.30pm). For an internet bar (网吧; wangba) head to **Lian Tian Internet** (per hour Y5; ⏲ 12pm-3am). Note that staff may try to charge foreigners Y10.

Moneychangers deal openly in front of the Zhangmu Hotel and change any combination of Chinese yuan, US dollars or Nepali rupees at better rates than on the Nepali side. **Bank of China** (⏲ 9.30am-1.30pm & 3.30-6.30pm Mon-Fri, 11am-2pm Sat & Sun), way up the hill, will change cash and travellers cheques into yuan and also yuan into dollars, euros or pounds if you have an exchange receipt, but doesn't deal in Nepali rupees.

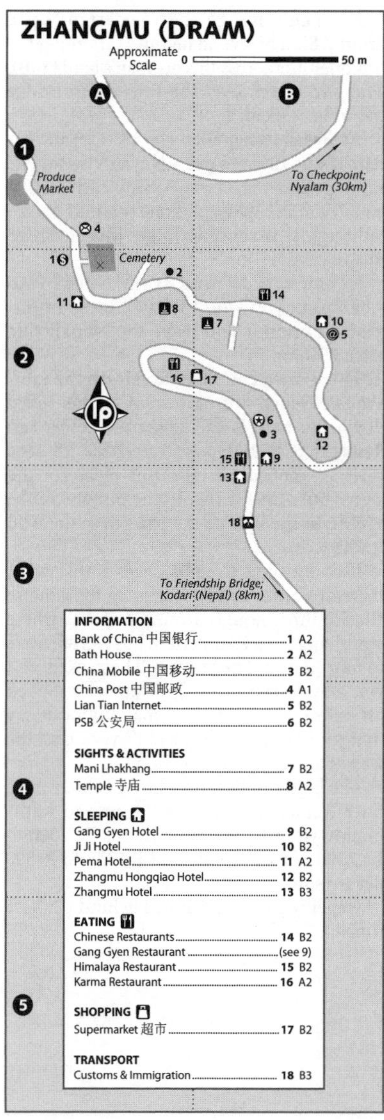

China Post near the bank has an ATM outside accepting foreign cards on the Visa and Plus networks. For telephone calls try the many private telecom booths around town.

PERMITS

Located above China Mobile, the **Zhangmu PSB** (Gong'anju; ☎ 874 2264) won't give you an Alien Travel Permit to head north into Tibet unless you have a guide, a driver and the mysterious Tibetan Tourism Bureau (TTB) permit – effectively making it impossible for independent travellers to come up from Nepal without having booked a tour in Kathmandu. The checkpoint just north of town makes sure of this. The PSB cannot extend your visa.

Sleeping

Try to get a room off the road, preferably facing the mountains, as the noise from traffic can be awful.

Zhangmu Hongqiao Hotel (☎ 874 2261; dm Y32, d with/without bathroom Y262/152) For the cheapest beds in town, this local hotel is good value. Dorm rooms are small but clean and the Western-style doubles will do for a night's stay. It's a five-minute walk uphill from customs.

Pema Hotel (☎ 874 2106; fax 874 2605; dm Y40, d with/without bathroom Y300/180) Rooms are small and boxy and the whole place looks like a school dormitory, but the mountain views make up for this. The musty dorms are in the basement and the doubles are up a tiny spiral staircase on the top floor. The hotel is in the north of town – look for its pedestrian overpass, but note you check-in on street level.

Gang Gyen Hotel (☎ 874 2188; dm without bathroom Y50, d with bathroom Y300) The dorms are spacious and reasonably clean, though the shared bathrooms can be a bit smelly. Hot showers are available and are free for guests (Y10 for nonguests). The doubles with bathroom are cosy if overpriced. The hotel is just a stone's throw from customs, however, which may be important if you have heavy bags.

Ji Ji Hotel (☎ 874 5688; tr per bed Y50, d with/without bathroom Y160/100) Rooms are clean and basic. There are no showers for the dorms but you can grab one just up the road at Bath House.

Zhangmu Hotel (☎ 874 2221; fax 874 2220; d/tr Y480/580, deluxe Y680, discounts of 15%) The modern rooms in this government-run hotel are luxurious by Tibetan standards, and back rooms have great mountain views, but it's overpriced. Like the Gang Gyen, though, it's as close to customs as you can get. The hotel runs a legitimate massage centre (foot massage US$6) two doors up the road.

Eating

There is no shortage of restaurants in Zhangmu. Wander up the hill for an excellent selection of Western, Chinese, Tibetan and Nepali cuisine. All restaurants serve lunch and dinner and have no fixed opening hours. Many restaurants fix lunch boxes, which come in handy on the long ride to Kathmandu.

Gang Gyen Restaurant (Ground floor, Gang Gyen Hotel; dishes Y15-35; breakfast, lunch & dinner) Looking a little like a Western sports bar, this popular establishment serves a full range of Nepali, Chinese, Tibetan and Western mains, including steaks and breakfast foods. The curries are thick and delicious. The sign above the restaurant reads 'Base Camp Western Food & Coffee Bar'. Menu in English.

Himalaya Restaurant (☎ 874 3068; opposite Gang Gyen Hotel; dishes Y15-25; breakfast, lunch & dinner) A cheery place for decent Tibetan, Nepali or Chinese food. Menu in English.

Karma Restaurant (☎ 893 5050; dishes Y15-30; breakfast, lunch & dinner) Another travellers' restaurant serving Western, Tibetan, Nepalese and Chinese dishes. Not as good as Gang Gyen but a little cheaper and friendlier. Menu in English.

Shopping

There are countless small shops on the main road selling drinks and snacks, and equally important in Zhangmu, umbrellas. There's a small basic supermarket five minutes' walk up the hill from customs.

Getting There & Away

TO KATHMANDU

At **Chinese immigration** (9.30am-6.30pm, sometimes closed 1.30-3.30pm) you will need to fill in an exit form and health declaration and you may be asked for your travel permit.

From customs, go on to Kodari in Nepal, around 8km below Zhangmu. Cars and pickups offer lifts across this no-man's land (Y10). The last stretch over the Friendship Bridge has to be walked.

At **Nepali immigration** (8.30-4pm) in Kodari it's possible to get a Nepali visa for the same price as in Lhasa (US$30 cash, or the equivalent in rupees, plus one passport photo) although it is sensible to get one in Lhasa just in case.

If you are coming from Nepal into Zhangmu, you won't find Chinese immigration open if you leave the Nepali side after 3.30pm.

There are a couple of hotels on the ramshackle Nepali side of town. A further 12km down the road is the adventure resort **Last Resort** (☎ 4439501; www.tlrnepal.com; full board US$25-35). You can't miss this place for the signs, but also for the insane bungee venue visible to the side of the road over the wild Bhote Kosi.

If continuing straight on to Kathmandu there are buses every hour or so to Barabise (Rs 55, three hours) around halfway, where you change to a Kathmandu bus (Rs 86, three to four hours). The buses will be packed, and you may mysteriously find yourself dropped off before you reach Kathmandu; locals say that sometimes the bus will drive you all the way in and sometimes it won't.

The better option is to hire a vehicle from near Nepali immigration. A ride to Kathmandu (four to five hours) costs Rs 1500 to Rs 2000 per car, or around Rs 375 to Rs500 per person.

Nepal is an odd 2¼ hours behind Chinese time.

Western Tibet (Ngari)

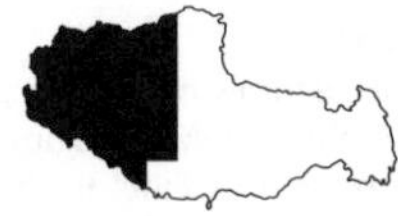

མངའ་རིས་

Vast, scarcely populated and with an average altitude of over 4500m, Ngari is a frontier in one of the remotest corners of Asia. The main attractions of what is likely to be a three-week trip are a mountain and a lake – but what a mountain and what a lake! Sacred Mt Kailash and Lake Manasarovar are two of the most far-flung and legendary travel destinations in the world. Many of the pilgrims on the road have been planning a visit all their lives.

The landscape of Ngari is dominated by the Himalaya range to the south and the huge salt lakes of the Changtang plateau to the north. In between are immense stretches of yellow steppe, dusty badlands, sandy deserts, and the mineral-rich trans-Himalayan ranges stained purple, rust and green. For those not overly fussed by the spiritual significance of Mt Kailash, going to one of the most isolated and beautiful corners of the globe is likely to be an attraction in itself.

Days are long in transit, and until recently, Western travellers were quite rare. Even now few travel the more out-of-the-way northern route or visit the otherworldly ruins of the ancient Guge kingdom at Tsaparang, a day's journey from Mt Kailash. The truly intrepid who visit secluded monasteries, hidden valleys and isolated archaeological sites can be counted on one hand.

Travel in Ngari is still not easy or comfortable, but improved roads and telephone lines (and mobile-phone reception) have made it more accessible. There's a bus service from Lhasa to Ali, a small but growing network of public transport, and an airport planned for 2010. Change is coming, which makes now the time to visit Ngari.

HIGHLIGHTS

- Join the pilgrims looking to erase the sins of a lifetime on the three-day trek around holy **Mt Kailash** (p226)
- Hike the sandy shores of sacred **Lake Manasarovar** (p229), or just marvel at the turquoise waters and snowcapped-mountain backdrop
- Camp anywhere in this otherworldly landscape, but especially by the lakes **Tagyel-tso** (p222), **Dawa-tso** (p223) and **Peiku-tso** (p220)
- Explore the ruins of an ancient kingdom at **Tsaparang** (p235), one of Asia's unknown wonders
- Spot wild asses, gazelle and blue sheep on the **northern route** (p221) to Ali

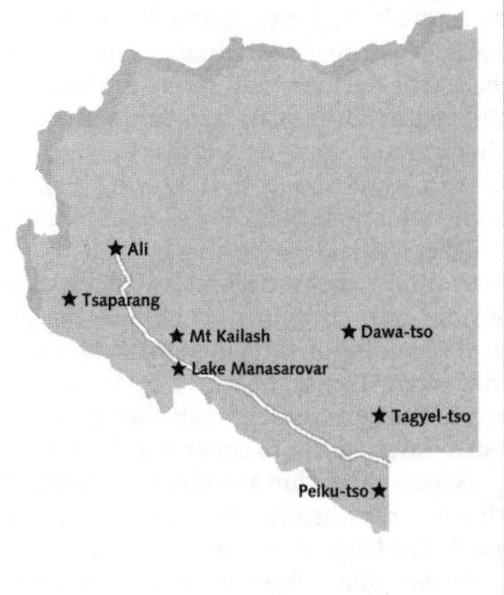

History

Most histories of Tibet begin with the kings of the Yarlung Valley region and their unification of central Tibet in the 7th century. But it is thought that the Shangshung (or Zhangzhung) kingdom of western Tibet probably ruled the Tibetan plateau for several centuries before this. According to some scholars, the Bön religion made its way into the rest of Tibet from here. The Shangshung kingdom may also have served as a conduit for Tibet's earliest contacts with Buddhism. There is little material evidence of the Shangshung kingdom in modern Tibet, though the Khyunglung Valley, on the Sutlej River near Tirthapuri hot springs, marks the site of the old kingdom.

The next regional power to emerge in Ngari was the Guge kingdom in the 9th century. After the assassination of the anti-Buddhist Lhasa king Langdharma, one of the king's sons, Namde Wosung, established this kingdom at Tsaparang, west of Lake Manasarovar and Mt Kailash. The Guge kingdom, through its contacts with nearby India, led a Buddhist revival on the Tibetan plateau and at its peak was home to over 100 monasteries, most of them now in ruins.

In the late 16th century, Jesuit missionaries based in the enclave of Goa took an interest in the remote kingdom of Guge, mistaking it for the long-lost Christian civilisation of Prester John (a legendary Christian priest and king who was believed to have ruled over a kingdom in the Far East). The Jesuits finally reached Tsaparang in 1624 after two failed attempts, but if their leader, Father Antonio de Andrede, had expected to find Christians waiting for him, he was disappointed. Nevertheless, he did meet with surprising tolerance and respect for the Christian faith. The Guge king agreed to allow de Andrede to return and set up a Jesuit mission the following year. The foundation stone of the first Christian church in Tibet was laid by the king himself.

Ironically, the evangelical zeal of the Jesuits led not only to their own demise but also to the demise of the kingdom they sought to convert. Lamas, outraged by their king's increasing enthusiasm for an alien creed, enlisted the support of Ladakhis in laying siege to Tsaparang. Within a month the city fell, the king was overthrown and the Jesuits imprisoned. The Guge kingdom collapsed.

At this point, Ngari became so marginalised as to almost disappear from the history books – with one notable exception. In the late Victorian era, a handful of Western explorers began to take an interest in the legend of a holy mountain and a lake from which four of Asia's mightiest rivers flowed. The legend, which had percolated as far afield as Japan and Indonesia, was largely ridiculed by Western cartographers. However, in 1908 the Swedish explorer Sven Hedin returned from a journey that proved there was indeed such a mountain and such a lake, and that the remote part of Tibet they occupied was in fact the source of the Karnali (a major tributary of the Ganges), Brahmaputra (Yarlung Tsangpo), Indus (Sengge Tsangpo) and Sutlej (Langchan Tsangpo) Rivers. The mountain was Kailash and the lake, Manasarovar.

Permits

Foreigners are supposed to have a fistful of permits: an Alien Travel Permit, military permit, Tibet Tourism Bureau (TTB) permit, foreign affairs permit… If you arrange a Land Cruiser trip in Lhasa, the travel agency will organise all these for you but it can take a week.

Technically you can get around most of the region with just an Alien Travel Permit (p324). In the past, you could obtain one by getting to Ali (by hitching or bus) and surrendering yourself immediately to the Public Security Bureau (PSB; Gong'anju) office. In return for a fine (Y300 to 350) you would receive a travel permit for most places in the prefecture (eg Mt Kailash, Manasarovar, Purang, the Guge kingdom, Rutok, Gertse and Tsochen). At the time of research some travellers were being turned back, so check for the latest word before you head off.

Western Tibet is a politically sensitive area and is periodically closed to foreigners, due either to political unrest on the Mt Kailash kora or military tension along the contested borders of China, India and Pakistan.

When to Go

May, June and from mid-September to early October are probably the best times to head out to Ngari. Rates for Land Cruiser hire are cheapest in November. Drölma-la on the Mt Kailash kora is normally blocked with snow from late October or early November until early April.

The festival of Saga Dawa (p229) during May or June is a particularly popular time

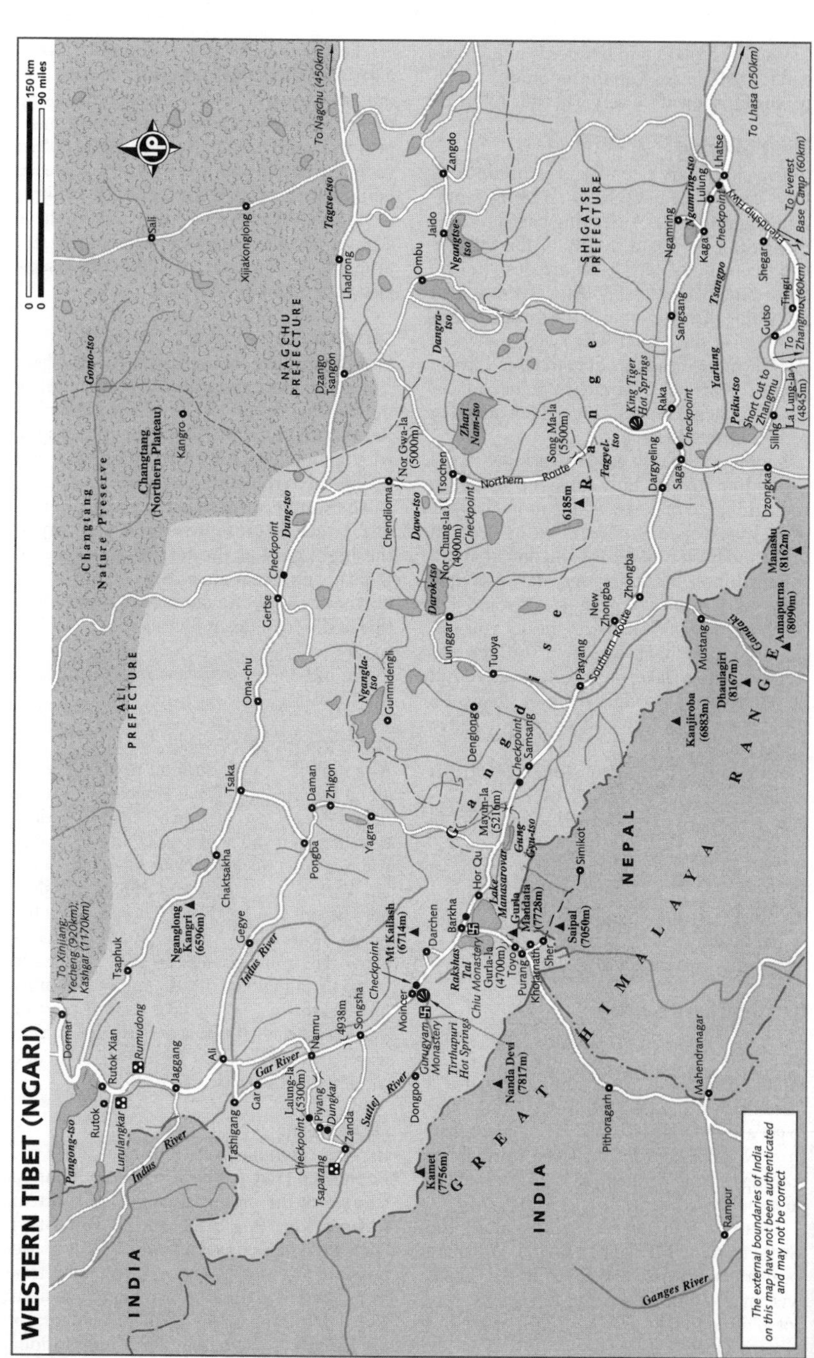
WESTERN TIBET (NGARI)
0 150 km
0 90 miles
INDIA
Pangong-tso
Rutok
Rutok Xian
Rumudong
Rulangkar
Dormar
To Xinjiang: Yecheng (920km); Kashgar (1170km)
Indus River
Jaggang
Tsaphuk
Ali
Tashigang
Gar
Gar River
Namru
Lalung-la (5300m)
Piyang
Dungkar
Checkpoint
Tsaparang
Zanda
4938m
Songsha
Sutlej River
Dongpo
Gurugyam Monastery
Tirthapuri Hot Springs
Moincer
Checkpoint
Mt Kailash (6714m)
Darchen
Barkha
Rakshas Tal
Chiu Monastery
Gurla-la (4700m)
Toyo
Purang
Khojarnath
Sher
Gurla Mandata (7728m)
Saipal (7050m)
Simikot
Lake Manasarovar
Hor Qu
Gung Gyu-tso
Mayum-la (5216m)
Nganglong Kangri (6596m)
Gegye
Chaktsakha
Tsaka
Pongba
Daman
Zhigon
Yagra
Checkpoint
Samsang
Denglong
Gunmidengl
Ngangla-tso
Oma-chu
Gertse
Checkpoint
Dung-tso
ALI PREFECTURE
Changtang Nature Preserve
Changtang (Northern Plateau)
Kangro
Gomo-tso
NAGCHU PREFECTURE
Dzango Tsangon
Lhadrong
Tagtse-tso
Xijiakonglong
Saji
To Nagchu (450km)
Zangdo
Ombu
Jaido
Ngangtse-tso
Dangra-tso
Zhari Nam-tso
Nor Gwa-la (5000m)
Chendiloma
Dawa-tso
Tsochen
Checkpoint
Northern Route
Nor Chung-la (4900m)
Darok-tso
Lunggar
Tuoya
Paryang
Southern Route
New Zhongba
Zhongba
6185m
Song Ma-la (5500m)
Tagyel-tso
King Tiger Hot Springs
Dargyeling
Saga
Checkpoint
Raka
Checkpoint
Sangsang
Ngamring
Ngamring-tso
Kaga
Lulung
Checkpoint
Lhatse
SHIGATSE PREFECTURE
Yarlung Tsangpo
Friendship Hwy
To Lhasa (250km)
To Everest Base Camp (60km)
Shegar
Tingri
Gutso
To Zhangmu (60km)
Peiku-tso
Short Cut to Zhangmu
La Lung-la (4845m)
Siling
Dzongka
Manaslu (8162m)
Annapurna (8090m)
Gandaki
Mustang
Dhaulagiri (8167m)
Kanjiroba (6883m)
G a n g d i s e R a n g e
NEPAL
GREAT HIMALAYA RANGE
Nanda Devi (7817m)
Kamet (7756m)
INDIA
Pithoragarh
Mahendranagar
Rampur
Ganges River
The external boundaries of India on this map have not been authenticated and may not be correct

to visit Mt Kailash and hundreds of pilgrims and tourists descend on the mountain, which means for some it's a very bad time to go.

What to Bring

Warm clothes are essential, even in summer. Days can be hot though, so do bring something light to wear. A sleeping bag is recommended, as is a tent. Many of the villages and towns in western Tibet are dusty, dirty, depressing places to stay. After spending all day riding through some of the most glorious scenery on the planet why sleep anywhere else? If you are heading out to trek Mt Kailash, a tent is essential. If you're hitching, a facemask will help keep out some of the dust. See p345 for other ideas.

Supplies are fairly easy to get now in the expanding towns but consider bringing some things to make travelling more flexible. A package or two of muesli (with powdered milk) and fresh fruit means you don't have to suffer Chinese breakfast every day. A couple of loaves of bread and peanut butter and jam (or canned luncheon meat) means you can stop and have lunch wherever you like: beside a turquoise lake, or flowing river, or out in yellow fields beside a flock of sheep. All the above supplies can easily be purchased in Lhasa (see p126).

It's also worth bringing along a few treats ,such as peanuts, sachets of hot chocolate, chocolate bars and dehydrated food, from home.

The only places to change money in Ngari are banks in Ali and, less reliably, Purang – it's much easier to change US dollars as cash rather than travellers cheques. It's best just to bring what you expect to spend.

Getting There & Away

Most travellers approach Ngari from Lhasa because it's the easiest place to organise permits and find travelling companions for a Land Cruiser tour (still the most common way to get around). Ngari can also be approached from Nepal. Check for the latest word about coming in from Xinjiang as it's a long way to go to be turned back.

There's a nonstop bus service along the northern route between Lhasa and Ali and a local-transport network based in Ali. However, at the time of writing foreigners were not allowed to take any buses into or around western Tibet.

The rare traveller still tries to hitch out to Ngari, but check the latest situation with permits as there are several checkpoints along the way where you need to show your passport and travel permit. Note drivers are often very reluctant to pick up foreigners as special permits are needed. If you do decide to hitch, be honest when asked by drivers if you have a travel permit so they can assess their risk properly. For information on the risks associated with hitching, see p344.

FROM LHASA

From Lhasa there are two approaches to Ngari: a southern route and a northern. Both follow the same road west to Lhatse and beyond to Raka. About 6km past Raka the routes split, with the southern route continuing west and the northern route heading north.

The southern route is the more popular one, largely because it is the fastest way to the highlights of the territory. Although there are no stellar attractions on the longer northern route, the scenery is superb and this is the road taken by the Lhasa–Ali bus (p226).

See p21 for an overview of the routes to Mt Kailash.

FROM XINJIANG

Although it's a very difficult road, the route along the Xinjiang–Tibet Hwy sees its share of hitchhikers, cyclists and other independent travellers. But you're always taking a risk that you might get turned back in Ali, so check the latest word on permits and PSB permissiveness before you head out. There's a bus between Yecheng and Ali when road conditions allow. The route passes through the remote Aksai Chin region; with the unpredictability of breakdowns, it can take several days or more (especially if you are trying to hitch) to travel the 1100km from Yecheng to Ali. For a rundown of the route, see p338.

FROM NEPAL

If you're coming from Kathmandu on the Friendship Hwy (or heading to Kathmandu because of the permit situation), a shortcut to/from Saga (via the beautiful Peiku-tso) takes a full day's travel off your trip. It is also possible to enter Ngari on a four-day trek from Simikot in the Humla region of western Nepal to Purang on the Chinese border near Mt Kailash. This route is open only to tour groups that trek in from Humla, which is a restricted region.

SOUTHERN ROUTE

There are now bridges over all the major rivers along the shorter southern route, which has boosted traffic (though sand can still be a problem in places). At the time of writing the road from Sangsang to Raka was being upgraded but should be ready by the time you read this.

Lhatse to Saga (306km)

This is a full day's journey of about eight hours driving. Just past the Lhatse checkpoint (6km after Lhatse itself), the road leaves the paved Friendship Hwy and bears northwest onto a dirt road. The kilometre marker at the start of this route is 2141.

Just a couple of kilometres after leaving the Friendship Hwy the road crosses the Yarlung Tsangpo and then runs for an hour or so through alternating scenery: barren canyons (that swell in the summer rains) and green meadowland with scattered Tibetan villages on the edges. The photogenic **Lang-tso** (Ox Lake), which you pass in the first hour, has been stocked by the Chinese for sport fishing, a sore point with local Tibetans. (Tibetans don't catch or eat fish because of the Buddhist prohibition on taking life.)

Past the lake the road climbs up to the Ngamring-la (4500m). At kilometre marker 2085, 60km from Lhatse, the road passes through the very small town of **Kaga** (Kajia), next to the **Ngamring-tso**, which often appears brown because of the nearby mountains reflecting off its surface. A turn-off runs round the east side of the lake to the larger settlement and army base of **Ngamring** (Angren), visible on the northeast side of the lake and about 6km off the main route. Ngamring has food and accommodation if you need it.

Within 10km of passing Kaga, 70km west of Lhatse, you'll leave behind the last trees for many days, and soon after you'll also leave behind the last agricultural fields. The scenery now begins to look like a dreamy Cézanne landscape, with broken hills of tan and rust and purple folding in on each other as if slashed onto a canvas with a heavy impasto.

About 500m beyond kilometre marker 2060, prayer flags mark the start of a path to the **Drapsang Monastery**, which overlooks the road from a steep fairy-tale-like crag. The road then makes a zigzag ascent past photogenic nomads' camps and their flocks to the Sang-la (4700m), then down to a valley time forgot, and up again to the 4800m Karla before dropping down over one hour to Sangsang.

Sangsang, 122km west of Lhatse, is a small grubby town of a few hundred souls. The **Hotel Sangsang** (d/q per bed Y35/25), at the T-junction, is bearable for an overnight stay and has a good Chinese restaurant. There are a couple of other very basic restaurants, truck-stop guesthouses and one grocery store on the left just north of the T-junction. If you have time, you could visit the small Nyingma-school **Wösaling nunnery**, which overlooks the town from the northern end.

By the time you read this, the road from Sangsang to Raka should be paved. The route passes through a succession of wide alleys: stop in one and take a couple of hours to hike to the top of a treeless foothill for outstanding views. Back on the road you follow a gorge into the spectacular wide ravine of the Raka Tsangpo with its dark, craggy peaks. Emerging from this ravine the road skirts a lake and then crosses a flood plain, which is prone to flood damage during the monsoon. The route then climbs a couple of passes, before dropping down again and passing through the tiny settlement of **Raka** (4900m, kilometre marker 1912), about 6km before the junction of the northern and southern routes, and 120km from Sangsang.

The rooms in the misspelt **Lhato Hotal Teahoese** (d Y30) are rustic but clean and have their own yak-dung stoves for heat. The hotel is on the right as you drive through the village (the whole community is about two blocks long), and has a pretty decent Chinese restaurant and Tibetan teahouse. There are a couple of other restaurants and guesthouses in town, most with English signage. If you're taking the northern route, this is pretty much the last hotel for 240km, though you are able to camp at Tagyel-tso. Confusingly, many maps show Raka (or Raga) right at the crossroads; in fact the turn-off is 6km away.

If you are heading to Saga, it's another 60km.

Zhangmu to Saga (280km)

The scenic short cut from Zhangmu on the Nepali border to Saga (Sajia) on the southern route to Ngari saves 250km (at least a day of travel) and is used by Land Cruiser groups visiting Ngari directly from Nepal.

See p211 and p212 for more details on the first part of this route. Past Nyalam the road climbs to the 4950m Tong-la and then the 4845m La Lung-la. Not long after, the short cut branches west off the Friendship Hwy (kilometre marker 5265-66; 113km from Zhangmu), rounding some hills at the entrance of a vast stony plain. From here to Saga is about 170km or four hours of driving.

Siling (Seylong) village is reached in the first hour and here travellers must pay Y65 per person and Y40 per car for entry to the western section of the Qomolongma Nature Reserve. The nearby village has a fine monastery and ruined *dzong* (fort).

To the south come views of **Shishapangma** (8012m), known to the Nepalese as Gosainthan, the only 8000m-plus mountain planted completely inside Tibet. The road provides access to the mountain's north base camp before skirting the beautiful turquoise lake **Peiku-tso** (4591m), about an hour's drive from Siling. This is one of Tibet's magical spots, and there's fine camping by the lakeshore, with stunning views of snowcapped Shishapangma and Nepal's Langtang range. If you do plan to camp, bring your own drinking water and be well acclimatised. Also try to find a sheltered camp site as winds whip up in the afternoon. To the west of the lake is an eroded canyon to explore.

The bumpy route then follows a narrow gorge before passing the turn-off to the scenic but off-limits Kyirong Valley. After passing the small Drolung-tso you climb to a pass and then drop steeply down to the bridge across the Yarlung Tsangpo. From here it's 3km to Saga, where you join the southern route.

Saga ས་དགའ་ 萨嘎

☎ 0892 / elev 4600m

The dirty, sprawling town of Saga is the last of any size on the southern route and your last chance to eat a lavish meal. The town is expanding in all directions, but for this book's purposes we concentrate on the northeast part at the T-junction where the Saga Hotel is sited. The road going north at the junction heads toward Zhongba and Mt Kailash, while the road south leads to Lhatse. The road west heads into the new centre of town, where you connect with the road to Zhangmu (see p219).

There's an **internet bar** (网吧; wangba; per hr Y5; ⌚ 11am-11pm) in the lobby of the Saga Hotel, and hot showers at the **bathhouse** (linyu; Y10; ⌚ 10am-11pm) just west of the Saga Hotel about 50m down the road.

Saga Hotel (萨嘎宾馆; Saga Binguan; ☎ /fax 820 2888; d with bathroom Y320, d/t without bathroom Y280/180, discounts of 20-30%) is a decent place with clean, Western-style rooms sporting comfortable beds and modern bathrooms. The detractions are shouting staff and scruffy hallways. Next door is the **Moon Star Restaurant** (☎ 820 3008; dishes Y10-40) serving good Chinese food, though dishes are mostly sized to suit groups.

Xingyue Guesthouse (Xingyue Jiudian; ☎ 820 3008; dm Y40) is a basic guesthouse at the eastern tip of the T-junction, just up from the Saga Hotel. It's popular with Land Cruiser drivers and guides.

There are a number of cheap Tibetan guesthouses on the road heading north from the T-junction. Try **Yajiang Yajie Hotel** (Yajiang Binguan; ☎ 890 0855; d/tr per bed Y30/25) about 500m north of the Saga Hotel, or the nearby Shancheng Comfortable Hotel.

Note that all hotels except Xingyue Guesthouse have English signage out the front.

Saga has numerous small Chinese restaurants along the northern road with dishes better sized to fit a single traveller's needs than Moon Star. Though there are no English menus, owners are friendly and usually willing to help out. 'Fried rice? Fried noodles?'

West of the Saga Hotel is a fruit shop and several small grocery stores for drinks and snacks.

There are daily (sometimes twice daily) buses running between Saga and Shigatse (Y150, 16 hours).

Saga to Zhongba (145km)

There are several ruined monasteries along this stretch, including one just 1km out of Saga. **Dargyeling Monastery**, 42km from Saga (kilometre marker 1820), is the best preserved and worth a stop.

From here, you cross a river and then pass the ruins of a large monastery, 12km from Dargyeling Monastery. The road then climbs to a pass marked by hundreds of miniature chörtens, before dropping 23km to Zhongba.

Zhongba འབྲོང་པ

'Old' Zhongba is a tiny, dusty town on the main road with a couple of basic guesthouses, restaurants and a small monastery. ('New'

Zhongba, 25km northwest, is a small Chinese town with a couple of shops, hotels and restaurants and has little to recommend it.) Given the choice between here and Paryang, take 'Old' Zhongba.

The rustic **Yak Hotel** (☎ 0892-858 1011; dm Y40), on the eastern side of the pass, is the best there is.

Zhongba to Paryang (110km)

From Zhongba, the road deteriorates and the kilometre markers disappear. This section is particularly prone to invasion from the sand dunes on either side of the road and many trucks get stuck briefly here. You shouldn't have any real problems in a Land Cruiser.

A photogenic section of dunes, lake and mountains kicks in 60km from Zhongba. About 23km before Paryang you crest a pass and drop past more dunes to Paryang. Photos taken along this route can often get steppe, streams, desert dunes and snowcapped mountains in the same shot.

Paryang པར་ཡངས་

elev 4750m

Guides have said that while many groups spend a night in Paryang on the way to Mt Kailash, none want to spend the night here on the return. The reason is obvious: it looks more like a refugee camp than a village, with stray dogs roaming everywhere, and garbage piles burning day and night.

If you must pass a night here, there are a few guesthouses. The **Shishabama Hotel** (dm/d Y40/100), run by a friendly Tibetan family, has freshly painted rooms, though bedsheets have a few stains. From the Chongqing Restaurant (below) head up the road, turn right at the T-junction and walk a few blocks until you see a large white compound on the left.

In the centre of the village, **Chongqing Restaurant** (重庆饭店; Chongqing Fandian; dishes Y10-30) serves pretty good food considering where you are. Menu in English.

Paryang to Hor Qu (223km)

The route is a pleasant four-hour drive, passing through yellow steppe, with craggy, snowcapped Himalayan peaks off to the south when the weather is clear. Pick any foothill that strikes your fancy and go for a stroll.

There is a tricky section of sandy road 12km west of Paryang but all the major river crossings now have bridges. There's a checkpoint along the way, where you must show your passport and permits.

After the Mayun-la (5216m), the road improves as you cross from Shigatse to Ngari prefectures and descends to the long Gung Gyu-tso, which nomads consider poisoned and will not let their herds drink from. Magical Mt Kailash comes into view approximately 90km after the Mayun-la, just before the town of Hor Qu.

Hor Qu ཧོར་ཆུས་

elev 4560m

Hor Qu is another expanding village with little to recommend it but the views. The 7728m Gurla Mandata is to the southwest, as is Lake Manasarovar, though the lake is a long hike away. Some trekkers walking the Lake Manasarovar kora (p311) spend the night here but most tour groups should give it a miss and continue to Darchen or, better, Chiu Monastery at Lake Manasarovar.

Yang-tso Guesthouse (白雪湖日光旅馆; Baixuehu Riguang Lüguan; ☎ 136-3897 5385; q per bed Y30) is a clean and decent family-run place at the east end of town. The cosy teahouse is a good place to relax and observe family life. The sign at the entrance to the compound reads 'White-Snow Lake ZL Sunlight Guesthouse'. The pit toilets have no roof but this grants you the most magnificent views of Gurla Mandata to the southwest.

Pu Lan Guesthouse (普兰旅馆; Pulan Lüguan; ☎ 136-3897 6303; q per bed Y40) offers slightly better rooms with cheap wood floors, but it's not as friendly a place as the Yang-tso.

To the right of Yang-tso Guesthouse, the rustic **Big Wineshop of Jin Mantang** (dishes Y10-30) serves decent rice and noodle dishes. Electricity is on from 9pm to midnight in Hor Qu, so hang around to watch a DVD. Menu in English.

From Hor Qu, it's 22km to the crossroads settlement of Barkha (Barga), where you turn south to Chiu Monastery (one hour driving from Hor Qu) on the shores of Lake Manasarovar, or continue west to Darchen.

NORTHERN ROUTE

The northern route is the longer of the two routes from Lhasa to Ngari but there's more traffic and public transport along it. Although it's no freeway, the dirt road is at least maintained by teams of road crews working hard for their Y900 a month. The first part, like the southern route, follows the road from Lhatse to the turn-off near Raka (see p219). From Raka, there is basically no accommodation before Tsochen, 240km away. If you're travelling by Land Cruiser, seriously consider camping most of the time as the towns are uniformly dismal. On the other hand there's no shortage of grassy riverside spots with beautiful mountain views. You'll see a lot of seminomadic herders along this route, as well as marmots, blue sheep, wild asses and antelope.

King Tiger Hot Springs & Tagyel-tso
སྟག་རྒྱལ་ཆུ་ཚན

Only 21km north of the Raka junction are the Tagyel Chutse, or **King Tiger Hot Springs**, a wild collection of gushing geysers, bubbling hot springs, puffing steam outlets and miscellaneous smoking holes in the ground. It's a fun place to explore and maybe even wash up at. If you head directly down to the riverbed from the top of the pass, you'll find a small bathing area built into the rocks.

From the hot springs, the road runs around the western side of a beautiful lake, then through a wide valley, one of the stretches of flat terrain in Ngari where you can see the road ahead of you for kilometres. From a low pass, the route descends to a much larger lake, the **Tagyel-tso**, the waters of which are a miraculous shade of the deepest blue imaginable and ringed with snowy peaks. This is a great place to camp if you're prepared for the cold and altitude (around 5170m). There are lots of flat spots by the lake, and you'll have plenty of marmots and grazing wild asses for company.

North to Tsochen

It's about 240km from Raka to Tsochen or five to six hours of driving. For 25km the road runs along the eastern side of Tagyel-tso before starting to climb to the 5500m Song Ma-la. At kilometre marker 322 look straight ahead at the copper-stained mountain range for the uncanny likeness of Jabba the Hut's face in the rocks.

A further 45km from the pass and the road crests a smaller pass and leads down to two joined lakes, past a small salt mine. Eventually you pop out into the wide sandy valley of the Yutra Tsangpo, where the road splits *Mad Max*–style into a dozen parallel tracks. At kilometre mark 179 there is a major checkpoint where your passport and permit will be checked. The town of Tsochen is just ahead across the plains.

Tsochen མཚོ་ཆེན་ 措勤

☎ 0897 / pop 1000

Tsochen (Cuoqin), 235km from the northern turn-off, 173km south of the northern road proper, is another bleak, dusty town lining the main road. At the east end (about 2km from the start) is a **Tibetan quarter**. Walk through this to reach a mass of mani stones, prayer poles and yak skulls that local pilgrims flock to daily at dusk.

From here, you are able to see the desert plateau to the north and a second mass of prayer flags about 1km away; just below here is the **Mentong Monastery**, a small but friendly place with 30 monks. Visitors can enter the main prayer hall and the Kuding Lhakhang, which has an inner chapel. The monastery belongs to the Kagyud school, so there are pictures of Milarepa, Marpa and the Karmapa.

One potential excursion from Tsochen is to **Zhari (Tsari) Nam-tso**, a huge salt lake 50km east of town towards the town of Tseri (Tsitri). You will need to have this visit pre-arranged with your driver before leaving Lhasa or arrange extra payment for the half-day trip.

The PSB (公安局; Gong'anju) maintains a strong presence in town and at the time of writing all foreign travellers had to go to the station to register. The station is about halfway up the road on the left from the start of town (coming from Lhasa). The process can be a long one.

There's an unmarked **guesthouse** (s/d per bed Y120/60) 150m past the petrol station on the right. Look for the white-tiled building and turn into its courtyard. Rooms, on the 2nd floor, are large and fairly well provided with TVs, washstands, sofas and clean bedding. The pit toilets across the compound are nasty.

Friendship Feria Hotel (☎ 290 1878; d Y180) is at the beginning of town on the left, before the petrol station. It looks fine on the outside but is, as WH Auden once wrote of motels, 'designed to disintegrate'.

The main street is lined with Chinese restaurants (dishes Y10 to 30), but don't expect to find an English menu. There are several grocery stores at the far end of town near the Tibetan quarter.

Tsochen to Gertse (257km)

From Tsochen to the junction of the northern road is a journey of about 180km; Gertse is another 77km, making a total drive of around seven hours. If you plan to stay in Gertse, take your time as the route is far more interesting and scenic than the town.

The ride out of Tsochen offers many opportunities for a quintessential Tibetan photo of flocks of sheep grazing on rolling yellow steppe backed by high rugged mountains. About 43km north of Tsochen, the road passes the 4900m **Nor Chung-la** (Small Wild Yak Pass) before descending to the dramatic turquoise waters of **Dawa-tso**, another superb camping spot. For the next 60km the route crosses from one attractive valley to another, sometimes connected by the river and gorge, at other times by minor passes.

The road crosses the scenic **Nor Gwa-la** (Wild Yak Head Pass), another pass of nearly 5000m, 94km (about 2½ hours of driving) north of Tsochen. From the pass the route descends to a bridge, 109km from Tsochen, at **Chendiloma**, where there is a small guesthouse and teahouse.

From about 10km before Chendiloma and for the next 50km, the road runs right beside a beautiful, snowcapped mountain range running north–south, crossing several of its glacial outwashes. The valley narrows towards its northern end before the road suddenly pops out onto a wide plain to meet the northern road proper (the one that links Amdo with Ali). It's a long 15km drive almost in a straight line towards the **Dung-tso,**with its purple mountain backdrop and salt marsh foreground that looks like whitecaps on the water from a distance.

From the junction it's two hours west to Gertse through a wide valley dotted with sheep, blue sheep and prayer flags. There's a minor checkpoint for drivers 24km before Gertse.

Gertse སྒེར་རྩེ་ 改则

☎ **0897**

Gertse (Gaize) is the biggest town along the northern route before Ali and looks like a strip of warehouses and junkyards when you first drive in. The main street of town begins from the roundabout and runs east–west about 1.5km. Even if you don't spend the night here, budget an hour to visit the long wall of chörtens, mani stones, prayer flags and yak horns that stretches off to the south of town.

There's mobile-phone reception in Gertse and numerous private telecom booths around town for cheap calls.

The **Government Guesthouse** (政府招待所; Zhengfu Zhaodaisuo; q/d per bed Y35/45, deluxe s/d Y180) is opposite the hospital west of the roundabout. There are three blocks here. The cheapest quads are a bit smelly and cramped and are favoured by truck drivers. The doubles have clean beds, TVs, and electricity till 2am. The deluxe doubles are a big step up, but the private bathrooms remain out of reach, locked up due to a lack of running water.

There are numerous Chinese and Tibetan restaurants (dishes Y10 to 35) along the main road. Most are open for lunch and dinner, and several for a breakfast of *baozi* (steamed meat-filled buns) and *xifan* (rice porridge).

A sleepy indoor market in the middle of town on the north side of the road offers such unexpected treats as bananas and pears.

Gertse to Gegye (368km)

It's a seven- to eight-hour drive from Gertse to Gegye, the next town of any size. Soon after leaving Gertse, you'll pass several small lakes set in a wide plain that switches between steppe and desert. Keep your eyes open for round, tomblike buildings that are actually tsampa (roasted barley) storage bins, and for the astonishingly varied colours of the mountains: rust, mustard, turmeric, green barley… Also look for the Chinese-built wells that look like the entranceways to pedestrian underpasses. **Oma-chu** (kilometre marker 982), a small village huddled beneath a rocky outcrop, is 50km west of Gertse.

After about 30km the road passes large Tarab-tso (or Dara-tso). It's another 75km to ramshackle **Tsaka** (about three hours from Gertse), a small salt-mining community. The centre of town has a guesthouse.

From Tsaka one route continues west to meet the Ali–Kashgar road just north of Pangong-tso. The road to Pongba heads south and climbs to the 4878m Gya-la, then passes nomads' tents and curves around salty Bar-tso, before crawling to another pass (4800m) that has a large cave on one side. The road then descends to **Pongba** (Shungba or Xiongba) via a wide plain marked with wavy lines made by vehicle tyres: it's like a giant Edvard Munch canvas. Pongba is a dismal wool-trading centre for the nomads of the region, 96km from the turn-off. Here you'll find a very basic truckers' guesthouse and a few restaurants.

In the last stretch, the road heads northwest from Pongba. Check out the fields of grasses of varying colours: honey, camel and mustard. The most amazing pictures are created by this natural palette, including one we saw that looked exactly like a cartoon desert island with a coconut tree growing in the centre. At kilometre marker 1202, the road enters a gorge and follows the Indus River to Gegye, 105km (two hours) from Pongba.

Gegye དགེ་རྒྱས་ 革吉

The formerly quiet little town of Gegye (Geji), nestled against a ridge, is expanding rapidly and an entirely new main street was almost completed at the time of writing. It was actually looking very nice as the buildings – though offices for companies such as China Telecom and the Agricultural Bank of China – were built in an attractive Tibetan style. The new and old main streets join at a T-junction just down from China Telecom. At the far end of the old main street, heading towards the hills, is the Tibetan quarter.

The government guesthouse **Gegye Binguan** (革吉宾馆; Geji Binguan; ☎ 0897-263 245; d Y90) is the best in town. Rooms have high ceilings, decent beds and TV. The bathrooms are locked though, so you must use the dirty squat ones outside. The hotel is on the old main street 150m up on the left. It's a large, official-looking building inside a compound with a white tiled arch.

Qile Guesthouse (奇乐招待所; Qile Zhaodaisuo; dm Y30) is a basic Tibetan-run guesthouse across the road from the Gegye Binguan, on the 2nd floor. There's a cosy teahouse at the end of the hallway.

The old main road contains a couple of small grocery stores, plenty of Chinese and Muslim restaurants (dishes Y10 to 30), and a couple of Tibetan teahouses. Don't expect an English menu anywhere.

Gegye to Ali

Ali is just 112km (three hours) from Gegye. At first the road follows the infant Indus River. Then at kilometre marker 1260 it crosses the river and soon enters a marshland with an abundance of birdlife, including golden ducks and large black-necked cranes.

The road then passes through a landscape of alternating dry canyons and marshland. At kilometre marker 1330 a misplaced factory suddenly appears out of nowhere. Ali soon emerges like a bizarre mirage. From afar it looks very large and modern and the shock is reinforced when you actually reach the town. There are clusters of modern-looking buildings, shops, neon signs, paved roads and hordes of taxis. Here you'll drive on your first bitumen road since Lhatse and it's an amazing experience to glide smoothly into town after five or six days bouncing around the northern plateau.

ALI ཨ་རི་ 阿里

☎ 0897 / elev 4280m

Ali, also known as Shiquanhe in Chinese and Senge Khabab (Town of the Lion) in Tibetan, is the capital of the Ali prefecture. There's nothing much to see, but it is a good place to clean up, have some decent food, top up supplies and check your email before heading off to the real attractions of Ngari.

Ali is thoroughly Chinese. There are plenty of Tibetans wandering the streets but, like you, they are probably visitors from further afield. The town is expanding rapidly, especially to the south of the river, and there's a big army presence. After the barren emptiness of the surrounding country, Ali, with its video-game parlours, department stores and karaoke bars, comes as a real shock to the system.

For views of the town, climb up to the prayer-flag-strewn hills to the north of town. Don't take pictures of the army compound to the west (recognisable by the huge army symbol painted on the hillside above it).

Information

For cheap international calls visit one of the many private telecom booths around town.

Agricultural Bank of China (Zhongguo Nongye Yinhang; ⏲ 10am-7pm Mon-Fri) Near the army post, west of the roundabout. Will change cash US dollars, euros and UK pounds only (no travellers cheques). There's an ATM outside on the Visa, MasterCard and Cirrus networks.

China Telecom Internet Bar (Zhongguo Dianxin Wangba; per hr Y4; ⏲ 24hr) Go through the gate and take the stairs to the left to the 2nd floor. Private booths are available with windows if you can't stand the smoke in the main room.

PSB (Gong'anju; ☎ 282 1542, 136-1897 7294; ⏲ 10am-1pm & 4.30-7pm Mon-Fri) Groups will need to register here. Individuals without permits may be fined Y350 and then

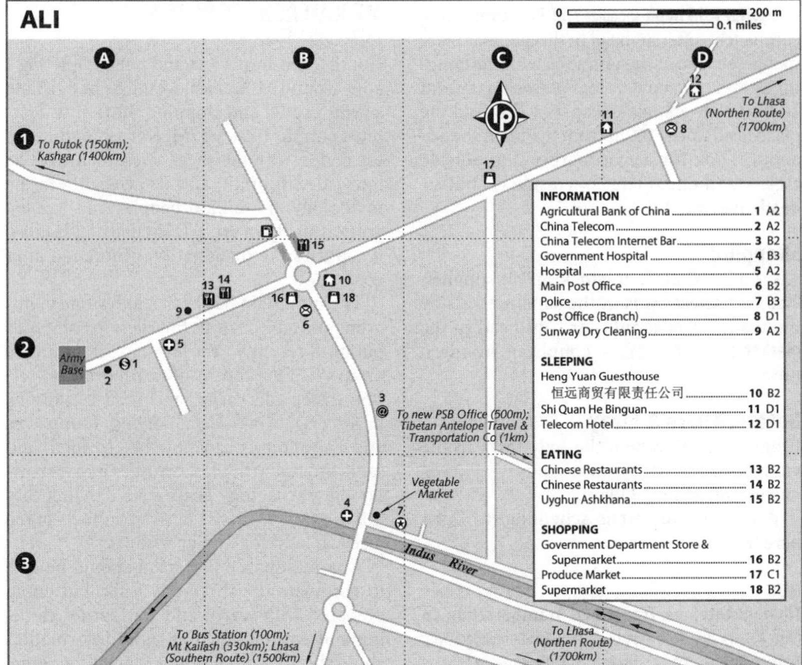

given a travel permit for the region for Y50, or they may be sent back to wherever they came from. Check with other travellers on the latest situation. The new office is way out in the southeastern suburbs; take a taxi and ask for the *xin gong'anju* – 新公安局. The office is on the ground floor, at the end of the corridor to the left. Note that at the time of writing the PSB were stopping travellers on the street asking to see passports and permits. There were also obvious undercover officers pretending to be fellow travellers.

Sunway Dry Cleaning (Saiwai Ganxidian; per piece Y4-5) Will do laundry; ask for normal wash (*shuixi;* 水洗) not dry-cleaning (*ganxi;* 干洗).

Sleeping & Eating

Your sleeping options are limited in Ali as many hotels are off-limits to foreigners.

Telecom Hotel (Ali Dianxin Binguan; ☎ 282 2998; d/tr Y150/130) This place has really dropped in quality (and fortunately in price) and while the rooms are still fine for a night's stay (they're clean but the furnishings are taking a beating), there's no running water, and you should expect discreet knocks on your door throughout the night from the local gals.

Heng Yuan Guesthouse (Heng Yuan Binguan; ☎ 282 8288; s/d/tr without bathroom Y180/185/188, d with bathroom Y300, discounts of 30%) A popular place with Land Cruiser tours, with large clean rooms lacking any style. The bathrooms in the more expensive doubles are very large but the water drips from the showerheads. The hotel has a decent inexpensive restaurant (dishes Y5 to 30) on the ground floor with an extensive Chinese menu. The *niurou mian* (beef noodles; Y5) is very cheap, as is the plate of *shuijiao* (dumplings; Y12). There's also a more expensive but quite pleasant (in a generic kind of way) teahouse-sports bar (drinks Y15 to Y30) on the 2nd floor with a widescreen TV.

Shi Quan He Guesthouse (Shiquanhe Binguan; ☎ 282 4977; d with bathroom Y300, s/d without bathroom Y80/160, tr per bed Y30; discounts of 15%) This charmless two-star hotel offers bright, Western-style rooms with small bathrooms (24-hour hot water), and very spartan rooms without. Rooms here are often booked out, especially the triples.

Ali has numerous Chinese restaurants south and west of the main junction and, given the town's remote location, they are surprisingly good value for money. There are also a few Tibetan places around. Don't expect English menus.

Uyghur Ashkhana (noodles Y10) For something completely different head to this popular place that greets you at the entrance with the hanging carcass of a cow. A loaf of thick naan and 10 beef skewers is a cheap Y11. To find the place head north 100m from the main roundabout. Look for a man barbecuing outside a glass building. (The cow inside is another dead giveaway.)

Shopping

Ali is a good place to stock up on supplies. The best selection is in the supermarkets by the main roundabout. For fruit head to the **market** (⌚ 7am-10pm), a couple of hundred metres east.

Getting There & Away

From Ali to Darchen, the only town in the vicinity of the Mt Kailash kora, it's a day's journey of around 330km.

A civilian airport is scheduled to open here in 2010.

BUS

Tibetan Antelope Travel and Transportation Co (藏羚羊旅运有限公司; Zanglingyang Lüyun Youxian Gongsi; ☎ 282 3828; ttt010406@sina.com) runs a bus service between Lhasa and Ali. The office is in the far southeast of town, not far from the new PSB building.

The sleeper bus runs every two or three days nonstop along the northern route and takes 60 hours. The tickets are priced from Y651 to Y751. Booking tickets two or three days in advance is essential. For details of the Lhasa services, see p127.

The company also runs buses to the following: Yecheng (Y500, 50 hours) every two days, road conditions permitting; Rutok Xian (Y50) once a day; Zanda (Y200) every two or three days; Darchen/Purang (Y230/280) every two days.

From the government bus station at the south end of town buses also run to Lhasa, Darchen, Purang, Zanda, Rutok and Yecheng.

Getting Around

Fleets of taxis are part of the mirage-in-the-desert shock of arriving in Ali. Within the city limits there's a standard taxi fare of Y5, but the centre of town is actually compact enough that you can walk anywhere.

MT KAILASH གངས་རིན་པོ་ཆེ་ 冈仁波齐峰

Going to western Tibet and not completing a kora around Mt Kailash would be like visiting a great capital and stopping short outside its most famous treasure. Mt Kailash dominates the region with the sheer awesomeness of its four-sided summit, and its centrality in the mythology of a billion people. And like the greatest works of art, a Taj Mahal or a *Hamlet*, it captures the imagination generation after generation.

The mountain has been a lodestone to pilgrims and adventurous travellers for centuries but until recently very few had set their eyes on it. With the means of transportation getting easier and easier, and road conditions improving, this is fast changing. Camp sites and guesthouses can now be crowded, and sadly littered with plastic bottles and instant-noodle packaging. There's no denying that this distracts from the sense of holiness of the place, at least for foreign visitors.

Any reasonably fit person should be able to complete the three-day walk, but come prepared with warm and waterproof clothing and equipment. For more information about the kora, including a map of the route, see p302.

History

Throughout Asia, stories exist of a great mountain, the navel of the world, from which flow four great rivers that give life to the areas they pass through. The myth originates in the Hindu epics, which speak of Mt Meru – home of the gods – as a vast column 84,000 leagues high, its summit kissing the heavens and its flanks composed of gold, crystal, ruby and lapis lazuli. These Hindu accounts placed Mt Meru somewhere in the towering Himalaya but, with time, Meru increasingly came to be associated specifically with Mt Kailash. The confluence of the myth and the mountain is no coincidence. No-one has been to the summit to confirm whether the gods reside there (although some have come close), but Mt Kailash does indeed lie at the centre of an area that is the key to the drainage system of the Tibetan plateau. Four of the great rivers of the Indian subcontinent originate here: the Karnali, which feeds into the Ganges (south); Indus (north); Sutlej (west); and Brahmaputra (Yarlung Tsangpo, east).

TO THE LAND OF SHIVERING SHIVA

'Are you cold?' I asked Mr Ranjan as we met in the hallway of the Saga Hotel. He was wearing a thick blue North Face jacket, ski gloves, ski pants, balaclava and a woven scarf wrapped up to his stubbly chin. I was wearing a short-sleeved shirt, sandals and jeans.

'I haven't been outside yet,' he answered. 'But the altitude is very high here I think. I can't take any chances falling ill. I am on my way to Kailash.'

He didn't need to tell me. On my walk around the holy mountain I'd seen hundreds of Indian pilgrims, and they had all been dressed literally exactly like him.

Hindus are a common sight around the Kailash area from June to September. For them, Mt Kailash is the abode of Shiva and Lake Manasarovar a mental creation of Brahma. An agreement between China and India allows a limited number of pilgrims to make the journey each year. The trip is so important that the quota is oversubscribed and places have to be determined by a lottery. I could see why Mr Ranjan was taking no chances with a stray breeze. If he missed this opportunity to do a *parikrama* (the Hindu equivalent of a kora) around Mt Kailash, there would not be another.

I had finished my own circuit around Mt Kailash not three days before and when he heard this Mr Ranjan suddenly became all flashing eyes and questions: Had I walked all the way around the sacred peak? What was it like? What did I *see*? I answered that yes I had circumambulated the peak, the route was an easy one to follow and I had seen the four sides of Mt Kailash: the northern peak, with its black granite face, was most beautiful.

These were not the answers he wanted, of course, but I didn't feel like admitting I had spent three days wanting to vomit from the effects of acute mountain sickness (AMS). *What was it like?* It was like being out of mind but not body. *What did I see?* I dreamt one night of Milarepa, riding a St Bernard, flying me down off the mountain on a beam of light.

'Are you going to take a horse around the mountain?' I asked to change the direction of the conversation. Most Indian pilgrims to Mt Kailash drive as far as they can up the Lha-chu Valley on the first day, and then switch to Tibetan horses, with herds of yaks and their handlers in tow with supplies.

But Mr Ranjan was clear that this was not the way to do things.

'I walk the holy ground with my own legs,' he said, not boasting, just matter-of-factly. 'Otherwise, why do I go?'

I agreed and at that our conversation ended. Mr Ranjan uttered a final 'God bless you', then walked to the end of the hallway, turned into the lobby, exited the front door and stepped into 25°C weather dressed like a snowman.

Mt Kailash, at 6714m, is not the mightiest of the mountains in the region, but with its hulking shape – like the handle of a millstone, according to Tibetans – and its year-round snowcapped peak, it stands apart from the pack. Its four sheer walls match the cardinal points of the compass, and its southern face is famously marked by a long vertical cleft punctuated halfway down by a horizontal line of rock strata. This scarring resembles a swastika – a Buddhist symbol of spiritual strength – and is a feature that has contributed to Mt Kailash's mythical status. The mountain is known in Tibetan as Kang Rinpoche, or 'Precious Jewel of Snow'.

Mt Kailash has long been an object of worship for four major religions. For Hindus, it is the domain of Shiva, the Destroyer and Transformer. To the Buddhist faithful, Mt Kailash is the abode of Demchok (Sanskrit: Samvara), a wrathful manifestation of Sakyamuni or Sakya Thukpa, thought to be the equivalent of Hinduism's Shiva. The Jains of India also revere the mountain as the site at which the first of their saints was emancipated. And in the ancient Bön religion of Tibet, Mt Kailash was the sacred Yungdrung Gutseg (Nine-Stacked-Swastika Mountain) upon which the Bönpo founder Shenrab alighted from heaven.

In May 2001 Spanish climbers gained permission to climb the peak, only to abandon their attempt in the face of international protests. Reinhold Messner also gained permission to scale the peak in the 1980s, but

PLANNING A LAND CRUISER TRIP TO MT KAILASH

Any pilgrimage worth its salt involves its fair share of trials and tribulations, but with careful planning it's possible to avoid many of the common pitfalls of arranging a trip to Mt Kailash.

Your first step should be to write up a detailed proposed itinerary for the trip, to give to both your agency and other prospective travellers. Mention all sights you wish to see so the agency will know which permits to apply for. Once you're on the road, it's usually too late.

If you've acclimatised in Lhasa, the slow rate of gain along the way shouldn't pose any serious problems. From Lhasa, most groups spend five to six days to get to Mt Kailash, often stopping en route at Shigatse and Sakya. After three or four days on the kora, a day is spent at Lake Manasarovar to rest up and enjoy the scenery. From the lake it's four days back to Lhasa, though you can do it in three.

If you plan to visit Thöling Monastery and Tsaparang, add at least three days to your proposal. An itinerary that takes in both the northern and southern routes will eat up around 21 days, though it will be hard to find other travellers to join you.

Costs usually come to about Y1000 per day but can be more, or less, depending on the month. This pays for your driver and guide, the Land Cruiser, most permits and fuel. It does not pay for your expenses, including meals, accommodation and entrance fees. Additional days cost Y500 to Y800, meaning it's often cheaper to book fewer days than you really plan to travel (there are of course limits to this).

abandoned his expedition in deference to the peak's sanctity when he got to the mountain.

Darchen 塔钦

Mt Kailash is accessed via the small town of Darchen (Taqin; elevation 4560m), the starting point of the kora. It is a dirty, forgettable little village, littered with various compounds. Most travellers linger long enough to organise their kora and then get out. The smart ones arrange to sleep at Lake Manasarovar just over an hour's drive away. If you need medical attention, however, there's a Swiss-funded Tibetan clinic in Darchen to the northwest.

The PSB (公安局; Gong'anju) is in the middle of town in an unmarked building 100m north of Tibet Manasarovar Travels Guesthouse. Groups will need to get their travel permit stamped here on arrival. 'Tickets' for the Mt Kailash kora (Y50) are available here. Travellers also need to register with the military, and the office for this is on the northeast side of town inside the police compound.

SUPPLIES

From June to September, nomad traders set up a row of tents in the south end of Darchen. Mostly they sell drinks, snacks and instant noodles at inflated prices.

For something better try to locate the *roudian* (butchery) in the centre of town and buy some fresh lamb. Then take it to a restaurant and ask the staff to boil it. In the cooler air of Mt Kailash it will last two days. There's also a woman who bakes traditional flat bread inside the compound of the Tibet Manasarovar Travels Guesthouse (opposite).

PORTERS & YAKS

Big groups often hire yaks to carry their supplies. These cost Y50 a day plus another Y80 for a guide. However, yaks will only travel except in pairs or herds, so you have to hire at least two. Most hikers get by with the services of local porters for Y80 a day.

DANGERS & ANNOYANCES

There are many stray dogs in Darchen and sometimes on the kora path. Most are friendly, but a Tibetan woman was killed by a pack a couple years ago and now many Tibetans won't hike alone.

SIGHTS & ACTIVITIES

If you've got extra time at Darchen, or you want to spend a day or two acclimatising before setting out on the Mt Kailash kora, you can find some interesting short walks in the area. The ridge to the north of the village obscures Mt Kailash, but an hour's walk to the top offers fine views of the mountain. To the south you will be able to see the twin lakes of Manasarovar and Rakshas Tal.

A dirt road just to the east of Darchen leads up to the **Gyangdrak Monastery**, largest of the Mt Kailash monasteries. Like other monasteries, it was rebuilt (in 1986) after the depredations of the Cultural Revolution. It is possible to drive here, but it's a fine 2½-hour walk. At the crossroads near a stream, head west if you want to visit **Selung Monastery**, a two-hour walk.

FESTIVALS & EVENTS

The festival of **Saga Dawa** marks the enlightenment of Sakyamuni, and occurs on the full-moon day of the fourth Tibetan month (in May or June). Saga Dawa is a particularly popular time to visit Mt Kailash, though you will have to share the Tarboche camping area with several hundred other foreigners, most of them on group tours. You can also expect that all the hotels in Darchen will be booked solid throughout this time. The rudeness of some tourists and their intrusive camera lenses can spoil the occasion. Other times offer a less colourful but more personally spiritual time to make your kora.

The highlight of the festival is the raising of the Tarboche prayer pole on the morning of Saga Dawa. Monks circumambulate the pole in elaborate costumes, with horns blowing. There are plenty of stalls, a fair-like atmosphere and a nonstop tidal flow of pilgrims around the pole. After the pole is raised at about 1pm everyone sets off on their kora.

How the flagpole stands when it is re-erected is of enormous importance. If the pole stands absolutely vertical all is well, but if it leans towards Mt Kailash things are not good; if it leans away towards Lhasa, things are even worse.

Particularly large numbers of pilgrims assemble at Mt Kailash every 12 years, in the Tibetan Year of the Horse. The next gathering is in 2014.

SLEEPING & EATING

Pectopath (☎ 139-8907 0383; dm Y30) The 10-bed dorm is clean and cosy, if slightly cramped. The attached teahouse is a great place to plan your kora and chat with other travellers. The owner, Diki, speaks some English. The guesthouse is west of the red compound of the Tibet Manasarovar Travels Guesthouse, or north of the nomads' tents across an empty lot.

The House of Support (☎ 139-8997 5186; dm Y40) Another friendly dorm with a cosy restaurant. It's beside Pectopath.

Tibet Manasarovar Travels Guesthouse (tr per bed Y60) Rooms are basic and clean and there's usually electricity after 9.30pm. The guesthouse is inside a large red compound in the southeast of town.

The **restaurant** (🕑 breakfast, lunch & dinner; dishes Y10-30) attached to the Tibet Manasarovar Travels Guesthouse serves decent Chinese food and you can get a cheap breakfast of *baozi* (meat-filled buns) and *xifan* (rice porridge) before heading off for the Mt Kailash trek.

Chinese restaurant (dishes Y15-25) This restaurant is just south of the Tibet Manasarovar Travels Guesthouse below the East-West Hotel.

GETTING THERE & AWAY

Darchen is 6km north of the main Ali–Paryang road, about 12km from Barkha, 107km north of Purang, 330km southeast of Ali and a lonely 1200km from Lhasa.

Land Cruiser trips are the most popular way to get to Darchen. During the peak season (July, August and September) you'll probably find three or four trips advertised on Lhasa's noticeboards at any one time. For tips on planning Land Cruiser trips, see opposite and p345.

There are buses every two days between Ali and Darchen (Y230), but none between Darchen and Saga. You may be able to get a ride back in a Land Cruiser. Ask around.

LAKE MANASAROVAR མཚོ་མ་ཕམ

elev 4560m

Lake Manasarovar, or Mapham Yum-tso (Victorious Lake) in Tibetan, is the most venerated of Tibet's many lakes and one of its most beautiful. With its sapphire-blue waters, sandy shoreline and snowcapped-mountain backdrop, Manasarovar is immediately appealing, and a welcome change of venue from the often-forbidding terrain of Mt Kailash.

According to ancient Hindu and Buddhist cosmology the four great rivers of the Indian subcontinent, the Indus, Ganges, Sutlej and Brahmaputra, arise from Manasarovar, though in reality only the Sutlej originates at the lake.

Manasarovar has been circumambulated by Indian pilgrims since at least 1700 years ago when it was extolled in the sacred Sanskrit literature the *Puranas*. A Hindu interpretation has it that *manas* refers to the mind of the supreme god Brahma, the lake being its outward manifestation. Accordingly, Indian pilgrims bathe in the waters of the lake and circumambulate its shoreline. Tibetans, who are not so keen on

KAILASH & MANASAROVAR BOOKS

There are numerous books about Mt Kailash, Lake Manasarovar and the surrounding area to whet your appetite for adventure. *The Sacred Mountain* by John Snelling reports on early Western explorers, including those who turned up in the early 1980s when the door to China and Tibet first creaked narrowly open. The Kailash chapters in German-born Lama Anagarika Govinda's *The Way of the White Clouds* (1966) includes a classic account of the pilgrimage during a trip to Tibet in 1948. There's also Sven Hedin's three-volume *Transhimalaya: Discoveries & Adventures in Tibet* (1909-13).

Books such as *Kailas: On Pilgrimage to the Sacred Mountain of Tibet* by Kerry Moran (with photos by Russell Johnson) and *Walking to the Mountain* by Wendy Teasdill may make you jealous that you didn't get to the mountain just a decade or two earlier. Both highlight the much greater difficulties (and, in their eyes, rewards) that one would experience on a pilgrimage as recently as the late 1980s.

The more scientifically inclined can turn to Swami Pranavananda's *Kailas Manasarovar,* an account of the author's findings over numerous stays in the region between 1928 and 1947. The book was reprinted in India in 1983 and you should be able to find a copy in a Kathmandu bookshop or online.

Charles Allen's *A Mountain in Tibet* investigates the hunt for the sources of the region's four great rivers and is perhaps the best introduction to the region.

the bathing bit, generally just walk around it. Legend has it that the mother of the Buddha, Queen Maya, was bathed at Manasarovar by the gods before giving birth to her son.

The Hindi poet Kalidasa once wrote that the waters of Lake Manasarovar are 'like pearls' and that to drink them erases the 'sins of a hundred lifetimes'. Be warned, however, that the sins of a hundred lifetimes tend to make their hasty exit by way of the nearest toilet. Make sure that you thoroughly purify Manasarovar's sacred waters before you drink them, however sacrilegious that may sound.

Manasarovar is linked to the smaller Rakshas Tal (known to Tibetans as Lhanag-tso) by the channel called Ganga-chu. The two bodies of water are associated with the conjoined sun and moon, a powerful symbol of Tantric Buddhism. On rare occasions, water flows through this channel from Lake Manasarovar to Rakshas Tal; this is said to augur well for the Tibetan people and most are pleased that water has indeed been flowing between the two lakes in recent years.

Most groups and individuals base themselves at the picturesque Chiu village, site of the Chiu Monastery, on the northwestern shore of the lake. For an overview of the Lake Manasarovar kora, see p311.

Sights & Activities

CHIU MONASTERY

Thirty-three kilometres south of Darchen, **Chiu Monastery** (admission free) enjoys a fabulous location atop a craggy hill overlooking Lake Manasarovar. The chapel here contains images of Sakyamuni and Guru Rinpoche, but most people love the lake views, the winding stone staircases and old wooden doorframes of this fairy-tale-like structure. On a clear day you can see Mt Kailash and 7728m Gurla Mandata, the huge peak on the southern horizon.

HOT SPRINGS

There are *wenquan (*hot springs) behind the monastery piped into a glass-roofed **bathhouse** (admission Y20) close to the village. The water is channelled from the hot springs into individual cubicles via open ducts. The odourless water is silky to the touch, much like the waters the Japanese describe as a 'beauty bath'.

Someday, a proper spa will be built here (and the view it will have of the lake!) but until then you must be satisfied with a good wash with great water in rather dodgy-looking tubs (bring a towel to sit on and wear sandals).

TREKKING

For a trek, walk along the ridge to the southeast of the monastery or make a half-day trek along part of the lake kora to the ruined chörten and prayer wall at Cherkip, returning via the shoreline cave retreats (see p311). There are fine views and lots of nesting birds along this route, but bring repellent against the annoying shoreline flies.

Sleeping & Eating

You need to register with the PSB in Darchen before spending the night. It's not necessary to go in person if you are on a Land Cruiser tour; the guide and driver can handle this.

There are a couple of simple, friendly guesthouses such as **White Horse Hostel** (d Y40) in Chiu village, on the bluff near the bathhouse. Our favourite, though, is an unmarked **guesthouse** (dm Y40) down on the sandy shore of the lake to the left of the Indian pilgrim Manasarovar Guesthouse compound. The guesthouse is run by a very sweet nomad family, and is striking for it's uncluttered space and rustic but cheery atmosphere. Sure it has pit toilets (pretty clean and with a fabulous view of the monastery) and mud-brick walls with old blue and white paint, but it's exactly the kind of unpretentious place we'd want for a simple lakeside retreat. There's a cosy teahouse inside where you can get simple noodle and rice dishes, and drinks.

Most other guesthouses can also provide simple meals.

Getting There & Around

You will have made it this far either by hitching or by hiring a Land Cruiser. There is no public transport and very little truck activity between Darchen and the monastery.

TIRTHAPURI HOT SPRINGS & KORA

ཏེ་ཏྲ་པུ་རི་ཆུ་ཚན་

On the banks of the Sutlej, only a few hours' drive northwest of Darchen, the Tirthapuri hot springs enjoy close associations with Guru Rinpoche. Pilgrims traditionally bathe here after completing their circuit of Mt Kailash, but the springs are growing weaker year by year and are now oddly diverted into a barren field. Tirthapuri has a one-hour kora route. It's somewhat interesting to follow, though most people can safely give this place a miss if time is tight.

Starting from the hot springs the trail climbs to a cremation point, an oval of rocks covered in old clothes and rags. From this point, an alternative longer kora climbs to the very top of the ridge, rejoining the trail near the long mani wall. The regular kora trail continues past a hole where pilgrims dig 'sour' earth for medicinal purposes. Further along, there's a 'sweet' earth hole. The trail reaches a miniature version of Mt Kailash's Drölma-la, marked with mani stones and a large collection of yak horns and skulls. Below, prayer flags hang right across the gorge and a series of rocky pinnacles are revered as *rangjung*, or self-manifesting or self-arising chörtens.

The trail passes the **Guru Rinpoche (Tirthapuri) Monastery**. Where the trail doubles back to enter the monastery there is a rock with a hole in it right below the solitary prayer wheel, which is a handy karma-testing station. Reach into the hole and pull out two stones. If both are white your karma is excellent; one white and one black means that it's OK; and if both are black you have serious karma problems. Perhaps another Mt Kailash kora would help?

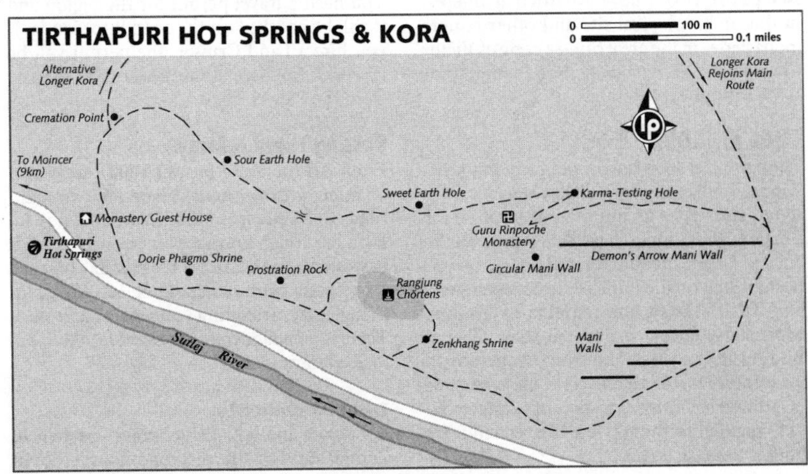

The monastery *dukhang* (assembly hall) has stone footprints of Guru Rinpoche and his consort Yeshe Tsogyel to the right of the altar. Outside the monastery a large circle of mani stones marks the spot where the gods danced in joy when Guru Rinpoche was enshrined at Tirthapuri. Beside it is a mani wall (a wall made of mani stones) over 200m long, the end result of a demon firing an arrow at the guru. (The guru stopped the arrow's flight and transformed it into this wall.) Finally, the kora drops back down to the river, passing a large collection of mani walls of various sizes on the way.

There are limited facilities at the hot springs, so you should be self-sufficient. The **monastery guesthouse** (d Y30) has a couple of rooms and you can camp further downstream (purify all river water here).

There is no public transport to Tirthapuri, which is 9km south of Moincer (Mensi), which in turn is 65km west of Darchen along the main road to Ali. There's a checkpoint at Moincer, which sometimes charges a fee to proceed to Tirthapuri. Moincer is the dormitory town for the coal mines 20km to the northeast and has a decent selection of shops, restaurants and the basic Meiman Zhaodaisuo guesthouse.

A further 14km west from Tirthapuri is the Bönpo-sect **Gurugyam Monastery**. The nearby upper Sutlej region, a further 10km away, is peppered with abandoned cave settlements and forms the **Kyunglung (Garuda) Valley**, the location of the early kingdom of Shangshung (see p216). If you have a particular interest in this archaeological site and other remote monasteries in the area, bring a copy of Victor Chan's *Tibet Handbook* and be prepared for some serious exploration.

GUGE KINGDOM གུ་གེ་རྒྱལ་རབ

The barren, eroded landscape around modern Zanda is unlike any you will have encountered so far, and seems an improbable location for a major civilisation to have developed. Yet the ancient Guge kingdom thrived here as an important stop on the trade route between India and Tibet. Today, the remains of Thöling Monastery, once a major centre of Tibetan Buddhism, and neighbouring Tsaparang, a 9th-century fortress etched into the very stone of a towering ridge, are two of western Tibet's highlights, though few Western tourists bother to make it this far.

Tsaparang is 20km west of Zanda, while Thöling Monastery is now merely an adjunct to the town. To visit both you need to budget at least three days (two merely for getting there and back from Darchen).

History

By the 10th century the Guge kingdom was a wealthy centre supporting several thousand people, and the great Guge king Yeshe Ö began to nurture an exchange of ideas between India and Tibet. The young monk Rinchen Zangpo (958-1055) was sent to study in India and returned 17 years later to become one of Tibet's greatest translators of Sanskrit texts and a key figure in the revival of Buddhism across the Tibetan plateau. Rinchen Zangpo built 108 monasteries throughout western Tibet, Ladakh and Spiti, including the great monasteries of Tabo (Spiti) and Alchi (Ladakh). Two of the most important were those at Tsaparang and Thöling. He also invited Kashmiri artists to paint the unique murals still visible today. It was partly at Rinchen Zangpo's behest that Atisha, a renowned Bengali scholar and another pivotal character in the revival of Tibetan Buddhism, was invited to Tibet. Atisha spent three years in Thöling before travelling on to central Tibet.

The kingdom fell into ruin just 50 years after the first Europeans arrived in Tibet in 1624, after a siege by the Ladakhi army (see p216).

Permits

You need a travel permit for the region and it will be checked on the road into Zanda. If you hire a Land Cruiser, the permit will be arranged in Lhasa. Otherwise, try to get one from the PSB in Ali.

Getting There & Away

From Ali there are buses (Y200) every two or three days to Zanda. There are two main roads to Zanda from the Darchen–Ali road. Both are rough and go over some very high passes. In a Land Cruiser it's possible to make it to Zanda from either Ali or Mt Kailash in a single day, providing you get an early start. There is no public transportation for the 21km to Tsaparang.

TO/FROM DARCHEN

It's about an eight-drive from Darchen to Zanda, though the distance is only about

243km. It's 65km from Darchen to Moincer, which is the turn-off to Tirthapuri, and then another 56km from there to the army base at Ba'er/Songsha, where there's a basic Tibetan restaurant. By the end of 2007 the road from Songsha to Moincer should be paved, though this won't cut off much time as the 122km from Songsha to Zanda is the hard part and takes six to seven hours of zigzagging down and up fantastically eroded gorges and gullies. The road then enters the wider Sutlej Valley and, after crossing a bridge, finally reaches Zanda.

TO/FROM ALI

Coming from Ali, the road is equally tough going, but highly scenic, and will also take around eight hours of driving though it's only around 200km. The first hour is on paved road that runs above and then through the super-flat Gar Valley. About 64km from Ali the route crosses a bridge to the western side of the valley. A further 10km and the road branches right off the main road. Now more like a trail, or wagon path, the road climbs huge switchbacks up to the 5300m Lalung-la (Laling Gutsa), then the Laochi-la before descending and climbing again to a third pass. About 65km from the turn-off there's a permit checkpoint (this used to be just outside Zanda).

From a plateau there are stunning 180-degree views of the Indian Himalaya, stretching from Nanda Devi in the south to the Ladakh range in the north. The route then drops down into deep, eroded wadi-like gullies before finally reaching the Sutlej Valley. Around 80km from the turn-off look for a village surrounded by eroded cliffs with hundreds of tombs carved into the soft rock.

The Sutlej Valley is a wonderland of eroded clifffaces that have taken on the most astonishing shapes. You'll swear over and over again that you're seeing the ancient ruins of a monastery, or a castle, or the high pillars that once held the roof of a mighty palace.

After crossing the valley and then a long bridge you wind up in the foothills to Zanda, 130km from the turn-off.

Zanda རྩ་མདའ་ 札达

☎ 08927 / elev 3650m

Zanda (Zhada), or Tsamda, is the bland, one-street town that has been built up the slopes from the Thöling Monastery. Be careful wandering around and taking pictures as the army maintains a strong and visible presence, with bases at both ends of town.

The **Cultural Affairs Bureau** (☎ 062 2110), just south of the entrance to the Hubei Hotel courtyard (Shuili Binguan), may issue permits for the caves at Dungkar (p237) – or get one at the PSB in Ali to be safe – and help you find a local who knows the way.

There are good hot showers *(yushi)* on the 2nd floor at **The Masses Bath** (Dazhong Yushi; Y20; 9am-1am) in the south end of town near the Chongqing Hotel. On the 1st floor you can get your **laundry** (per piece Y4-5) done. There's an **internet bar** (wangba; per hr Y8) in the shop just beside the laundry.

SLEEPING & EATING

Telecom Hotel (q with/without TV Y60/50) This place has big rooms with fairly comfy beds and a desk. The pit toilets at the back of the compound are reasonably clean.

The Letter Reaches the Guesthouse (☎ 139-8997 1972; s/d Y60/80) Friendly place with small rooms but decent beds. There's even a real sink and mirror in the common area for washing up. And yes, the crazy English name is what you will read on the sign over the door.

Chongqing Hotel (Chongqing Binguan; ☎ 136-2897 6950; d Y100) Rooms are in small cabins with TV and cheery flowery bedsheets. The cabins are set in a large quiet compound, which is right beside laundry, internet and hot showers.

The main street has at least half-a-dozen places to eat, mostly generic Chinese restaurants, though also a couple of Tibetan options, and one Muslim eatery. **Hong Man Tian Restaurant** (dishes 10-25) was newly painted and spruced up at the time of writing, though more importantly it was serving good Chinese food. There's an English sign out the front. Menu in English.

SHOPPING

There's a small grocery store up from China Telecom and an underground market just past that sells fresh fruit.

Thöling Monastery མཐོ་གླིང་

Founded by Rinchen Zangpo in the 10th century, **Thöling Monastery** (admission Y50) was once Ngari's most important monastic complex. It was still functioning in 1966 when the Red Guards shut down operations. Three main buildings survive within the monastery walls.

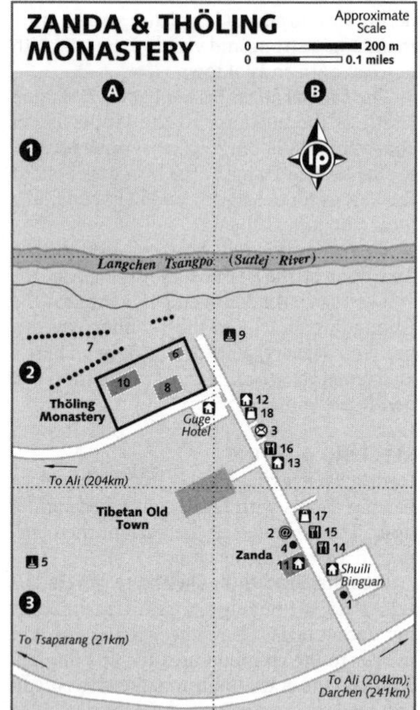

INFORMATION
China Post 1 B2
China Telecom .... (see 12)
Cultural Affairs Bureau 2 B3
Internet 网吧 3 B2
The Masses Bath 4 B2

SIGHTS & ACTIVITIES
Chörten 5 A2
Lhakhang Karpo 6 A1
Lines of Minature Chörtens 7 A1
Main Assembly Hall 8 A2
Serkhang Chörten 9 B1
Yeshe Ö's Mandala Chapel 10 A2

SLEEPING
Chong Qing Hotel 重庆宾馆 11 B2
Telecom Hotel 12 B2
The Letter Reaches the Guesthouse 13 B2

EATING
Bei Bei Quick Meal Shop 14 B2
Happy Restaurant for Travellers 15 B2
Hong Man Tian Restaurant 16 B2

SHOPPING
Supermarket 17 B2
Supermarket 18 B2

Even if you have little interest in Buddhist statues and murals, it is still fascinating to walk around the complex, with its cramped hallways and low doorframes, and open views across the Sutlej Valley from the courtyard.

MAIN ASSEMBLY HALL (DUKHANG)

The dimly lit chamber of the *dukhang* has especially fine wall murals, showing strong Kashmiri and Nepali influences; bring a powerful torch (flashlight) to enjoy the rich detail. The Kashmiri influences are noticeable in the shading on the hands and feet, the detail of the jewellery and dress, the tight stomach lines and non-Tibetan images of palm trees and *dhotis* (Indian-style loincloths). Scholarly opinion varies on whether the murals date from the 13th and 14th, or 15th and 16th centuries.

The main statues here are of the past, present and future buddhas (all of recent origin), and there's also a footprint of Rinchen Zangpo. The lower walls of the inner area have murals depicting the life of the Buddha and the founders of the monastery. Murals of the protectors Dorje Jigje (Yamantaka) and Namse (Vairocana) decorate the main entry.

WHITE CHAPEL (LHAKHANG KARPO)

The entry to this side chapel is marked by a finely carved deodar (cedar) doorframe that originated in India. Inside are detailed 15th- and 16th-century murals. The left wall in particular has been hit by water damage and a Swiss team is currently working on a restoration plan. The central statue is an old Sakyamuni Buddha; only his hands are of recent origin. Lining the sides are the eight medicine buddhas in various states of destruction. Male deities line the left wall; female bodhisattvas on the right. The far-right-corner murals depict sky burials.

YESHE Ö'S MANDALA CHAPEL (NAMNANG LHAKHANG)

Once the main building in the Thöling complex, Yeshe Ö's Mandala Chapel was also known as the Golden Chapel. Before its destruction in the Cultural Revolution, the square main hall had four secondary chapels at the centre of each wall. Figures of the deities were arrayed around the wall facing towards a central image atop a lotus pedestal, in the form of a huge three-dimensional Tibetan mandala (a circular representation of the three-dimensional world of a meditational deity). All the images have been destroyed but the four chörtens remain.

You enter the Mandala Chapel through the Gyatsa Lhakhang and finish off a visit by walking around an interior kora of empty chapels.

OUTSIDE THE MONASTERY WALLS

A few steps east of the monastery compound is the recently restored **Serkhang chörten**. A similar **chörten** stands in total isolation just to the west of the town. To the north, between the monastic compound and the cliff-face that falls away to the Sutlej River below are two long lines of miniature **chörtens**. The area is superbly photogenic at dusk.

Tsaparang ཙ་རེད་

The citadel of **Tsaparang** (admission Y106, plus Y10 for Chinese-speaking guide) has been gracefully falling into ruin ever since its slide from prominence in the 17th century. The ruins, which seem to grow organically out of the hills in successive levels, are crowned by a red Summer Palace atop a yellow cockscomb-like outcrop. It's a photogenically surreal landscape.

The site's early Tantric-inspired murals are of particular interest to experts on early Buddhist art. (See p232 for a history of the site.) For everyone else there are the views over the valley and the twisting paths and secret tunnels that worm their way through the fortress.

The ruins climb up the ridge through three distinct areas. At the bottom of the hill is the monastic area with the four best-preserved buildings and their murals. From there the trail to the top climbs through former residential quarters, where monks' cells were tunnelled into the clay hillside. Finally, the route burrows straight into the hillside through a tunnel before emerging in the ruins of the palace citadel at the very top of the hill. The vast, rough-hewn landscape of the Sutlej Valley that spreads out before you is both terrifying and sublime: you can't take your eyes off its beauty, but you know you wouldn't last a day alone in it.

Tsaparang is 21km west of Zanda, but unless you get lucky hitching a ride, the only way to get there is with a rented vehicle. Walking is risky as the dirt roads change every year because of the monsoons.

Early evening (particularly around 8pm) offers the best light. No photography is allowed inside the chapels. Bring a strong torch, lunch and water, and expect to spend at least half a day exploring the ruins; longer if possible.

SIGHTS

Chapel of the Prefect

Just inside the entrance to the complex is a small building that was a private **shrine** for Tsaparang's prefect or regent. The caretaker has named it the 'Drölma Lhakhang' after his own sculpture of Drölma (Tara) displayed here. The wall murals date from the 16th century, by which time the style evinced in other Tsaparang murals was in decline. The exuberant murals include fantastic multicoloured images of elephants, Garuda-like bird-people, hermits and snow lions, among others. The main mural on the back wall shows Sakyamuni flanked by Tsongkhapa and Atisha (Jowe-je). Small figures of the Buddha's disciples stand beside his throne.

Lhakhang Karpo

Slightly above the entrance, the large **Lhakhang Karpo**, or White Chapel, holds the oldest paintings at Tsaparang and is probably the most important chapel in Ngari. The murals of the chapel date back to the 15th or 16th century but their influences extend back to 10th-century Kashmiri Buddhist art, and for this reason are of particular interest to scholars of Buddhist art. Apart from Tsaparang, very little material evidence of early Kashmiri art remains (noticeably at Alchi Monastery in Ladakh). Lay people can spot the Kashmiri influence in the Hindu-inspired deities, with their slender torsos and thin waists, the detailed brocade of the figures' robes and the general richness of the colours.

The ceiling is beautifully painted, as are the many thin columns that support it. The carvings and paintings of Sakyamuni that top each column are particularly noteworthy. At one time, 22 life-size statues lined the walls; today only 10 remain and these are severely damaged. Even so, this chapel has fared better than most temples attacked during the Cultural Revolution. Originally each statue would have been framed by a *torana* (halo-like garland). Only partial sections of these remain (look in the far left corner and back recess), but you can still see the holes where these structures were once anchored to the walls.

The doors are flanked by two 5m-high guardian figures, red Tamdrin (Hayagriva) and blue Chana Dorje (Vajrapani). Again, both are damaged but even armless they hint at the lost marvels of the chapel.

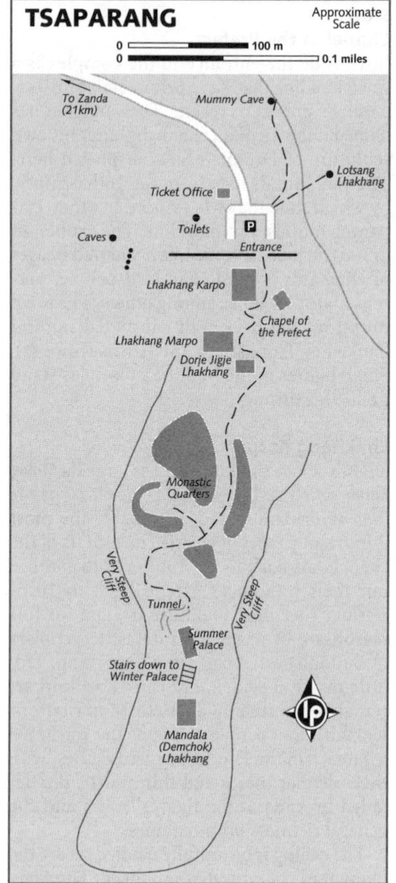

The huge figure of Sakyamuni that once stood in the recess, the Jowo Khang, at the back of the hall has been replaced by one of the caretaker's statues. On the side walls at the back were once row after row of smaller deities, each perched on its own small shelf.

Lhakhang Marpo

Above the Lhakhang Karpo is the equally large **Lhakhang Marpo**, or Red Chapel, which was built around 1470, perhaps 30 years earlier than the Lhakhang Karpo. The murals in this chapel were repainted around 1630, shortly before the fall of the Guge kingdom, so they are actually younger than those in the Lhakhang Karpo.

The beautiful original chapel door, with its concentric frames and carvings of bodhisattvas, mantras and elephants, has survived and is worth close inspection. Inside, many thin columns support the chapel roof, similar to those of the neighbouring Lhakhang Karpo. By the main door are images of Chenresig (Avalokiteshvara), Green Tara and an eight-armed White Tara, with Drölma and Jampelyang (Manjushri) to the right.

The statues that once stood in the chapel were placed towards the centre of the hall, not around the edges, and although only the bases and damaged fragments remain, the crowded feel to the space, the intense colours and the eerie silence combine to create a powerful atmosphere. You almost expect Indiana Jones to come striding out from behind the wreckage.

Although the wall murals have been damaged by vandalism and water leakage, they remain so remarkably brilliant it's easy to forget that they are actually over 350 years old. On the left wall are the famous murals chronicling the construction of the temple: animals haul the building's huge timber beams into place as musicians with long trumpets celebrate the completion of the temple. Officials stand in attendance (a Kashmir delegation wears turbans), followed by members of the royal family, the king and queen (under a parasol), Öpagme (Amitabha) and, finally, a line of chanting monks. The royal gifts frame the bottom of the scene.

Murals on the far right (northern) wall depict the life of the Buddha, showing him tempted by demons and protected by a naga serpent, among others. On the eastern wall are eight stylised chörtens, representing the eight events in Buddha's life.

The main deities in the chapel have very ornate *toranas,* decorated with birds and crocodiles, and topped with flying *apsaras* (angels). At the back of the hall, statues of the 35 confessional buddhas once sat on individual shelves; a handful of them still have bodies but all the heads have gone.

Dorje Jigje (Jikji) Lhakhang

The murals in the smaller **chapel** a few steps above the Lhakhang Marpo are also painted red and gold, and are almost solely devoted to wrathful deities such as Demchok (Chakrasamvara), Hevajra and the buffalo-headed

Dorje Jigje (Yamantaka), to whom the chapel is dedicated. On the left as you look back at the door is Namtöse (Vaishravana), the God of Wealth, who is depicted riding a snow lion and surrounded by square bands of Tibetan warriors.

Like the Chapel of the Prefect, the paintings here are of later origin, central Tibetan in style (rather than Kashmiri-influenced) and of lower quality; the golden years had passed by this point. All the statues that once stood here were destroyed.

Summer Palace

From the four chapels at the base of the hill, the path to the top climbs up through the monastic quarters and then ascends to the palace complex atop the hill via a tunnel. The **Summer Palace**, at the northern end of the hilltop, is empty, with a balcony offering wonderful views. The Sutlej Valley is just to the north. Across the smaller valley to the northeast is the ruined Lotsang Lhakhang.

The most interesting of the palace buildings is the small but well-preserved Mandala (Demchok) Lhakhang, the red-painted building in the centre of the hill-top ridge. The centrepiece of this small chapel was a wonderful three-dimensional mandala with Tantric murals, only the base of which survived the desecrations of the Cultural Revolution. It is currently being restored and is closed to visitors.

Winter Palace

Accessed by a steep and treacherous eroded staircase (now with a rough railing in place), the **Winter Palace** is an amazing ants' nest of rooms tunnelled into the clay below the Summer Palace. The rooms were built 12m underground in order to conserve warmth, and the eastern rooms have windows that open out onto the cliff-face. There are seven dusty chambers, all empty, linked by a cramped corridor. Branching off from the stairs you will see a dim passage that provided vital access to water during sieges and served as an emergency escape route for the royal family.

The easily missed stairs to the Winter Palace lead down from between the Summer Palace and the Mandala (Demchok) Lhakhang. Don't go down if you're prone to vertigo or claustrophobia.

Other Sights

North of the main entrance to Tsaparang a trail follows a green river valley down about 700m to a **cave** on the left that holds the mummified remains of several bodies. On the way back, visit the chörten and ruined chapel of the **Lotsang Lhakhang**. Only the feet of the main statue remain. Also worth a quick visit are the **caves** and **chörtens** to the west of the main site, near the public toilet behind the caretaker's compound.

DUNGKAR & PIYANG དུང་དཀར་

Caves with extensive wall paintings were discovered at remote Dungkar approximately 40km northeast of Zanda, during the early 1990s. At around 1100 years old, the cave paintings are possibly the oldest in Ngari and have much in common stylistically with the Silk Road cave murals of Dunhuang in China (particularly in their almost cartoon style, and the flying *apsaras,* painted on a blue background). There are three main caves, of which the best preserved is the mandala cave. You need to have an interest in early Tibetan and Silk Road art for the trip to be worthwhile. Lovely Dungkar village also has a ruined **monastery** above the town.

The PSB in Ali (p224) will usually give you a permit (Y50) to the caves, but if it doesn't, try the Cultural Affairs Bureau in Zanda (p233). It may give you a letter of introduction to the caretaker. Remember, though, that if he's not at home when you arrive, you won't get in as no-one else has the key.

Also note that you may not get there at all as most Land Cruiser drivers do not know the area and the dirt roads are unsigned and change every year after the monsoons. Your best bet is to bring a local with you, but this probably means bringing a local back with you to Zanda. Realistically plan on at least a full day to visit the caves.

A couple of kilometres north, further up the valley, the village of Piyang is worth the small detour. It lies at the foot of a large ridge honeycombed with thousands of caves and topped with ruined monastery buildings and walls.

RUTOK XIAN རུ་ཐོག 日土县

The new Chinese town of Rutok Xian (Ritu Xian), 132km from Ali, is a modern army post, but there are a couple of great sights nearby that warrant the trip. The road between Rutok and Ali was being upgraded at the time of writing, so the journey there in the future should be fairly quick.

About 8km north of Rutok Xian, the road hits the east end of lovely turquoise **Pangong-tso** (4241m). The long lake extends 110km into Ladakh in India.

The old Tibetan village of Rutok lies about 10km off the main road from a turn-off about 5km south of Rutok Xian. The drive passes the pretty **chörtens** of Bankor village en route. Lovely white-painted traditional Rutok huddles at the base of a splinter of rock, atop which is **Rutok Monastery**, flanked at both ends of the hill by the crumbling, but still impressive, ruins of **Rutok Dzong**. From here, you can see the reservoir below and Pangong-tso in the distance. The surrounding villages are largely deserted in summer, as herders have moved to higher pastures.

The intensely atmospheric main chapel of the monastery has a large statue of Jampa (Maitreya) and a bronze Garuda to the left. Clearly, at one time the whole eastern face of the hill was covered in monastic buildings. The monastery was destroyed during the Cultural Revolution and rebuilt in 1983-84; it now has just six monks.

Sights

ANCIENT PETROGLYPHS

In 1985 prehistoric rock carvings, or petroglyphs, were found at several sites in Rutok County. This was the first time such finds had been made in Tibet, although similar finds have since been made at numerous other sites.

The extensive collection of rock carvings at **Rumudong** is right beside the road, about 36km south of the old Rutok turn-off, or about 96km north of Ali. There are kilometre markers every 5km along this road. Travelling north from Ali, start looking on the east side of the road at kilometre marker 970 (though the kilometre markers may change with the upgraded road); the petroglyphs would be at around 967. There are two distinct groups on the rockface right beside the road, just before it crosses a bridge to travel along a causeway over the marshy valley floor of the Maga Zangbu-chu.

The first, and more extensive, group also features a number of more recent Buddhist carvings, some of them carved right over their ancient predecessors. The most impressive of the rock carvings features four extravagantly antlered deer racing across the rock and looking back at three leopards in hot pursuit. Also depicted are eagles, yaks, camels, goats, tigers, wild boars and human figures.

Less visited are the **Lurulangkar** paintings, about 12km southwest of Rutok. The relatively primitive carvings are right beside the road, up to a height of 4m above the ground, and show a variety of pre-Buddhist symbols and animals, including dogs, yaks, eagles, deer and goats. Human figures are shown standing in isolation or riding on horses. There are a number of hunting scenes showing dogs chasing deer and hunters shooting at them with bows and arrows.

Most people visit Rutok Xian as a day trip from Ali, though there are a couple hotels in town and many restaurants. There's no accommodation or any other facilities at old Rutok.

Getting There & Away

From Ali there are daily buses (Y50) to Rutok Xian, but there's no public transport to old Rutok and very little traffic on the road.

WESTERN NEPAL TO MT KAILASH

See Lonely Planet's *Trekking in the Nepal Himalaya* for details of the trek from Humla, a restricted region in the far west of Nepal, to Mt Kailash. This route is open only to tour groups that trek in from Humla and you will need a specially endorsed Chinese visa.

From the Nepali border at Sher, the road makes a long descent to a stream and then follows the Humla Karnali to the village of Khojarnath, 10km north.

Khojarnath འཁོར་ཆགས་

elev 3790m

For those travelling north from Nepal, Khojarnath, 21km south of Purang, is the first large village over the border in Tibet. It boasts the wonderful **Korjak Monastery** (admission Y30), an important monastery of the Sakya order. The blood-red compound, which dates back to 996, is sited in a narrow valley hemmed in by hulking dark-green mountains dotted with traditional villages. Korjak escaped the worst excesses of the Cultural Revolution and the damage sustained has been repaired with financial assistance from German and Italian sponsors.

The atmospheric main hall is entered via an ancient wooden door with particularly fine carvings. The hall itself is presided over by a figure of Jampa (Maitreya). To the far left is a small chamber with paintings from the earliest days of the monastery. Hanging from the ceiling to the right of the entrance are the stuffed carcasses of a yak, an Indian tiger, a snow leopard and a wolf.

The eight-pillared Rinchen Zangpo Lhakhang adjoining the main hall is dominated by the trinity of Chenresig (Avalokiteshvara), Jampelyang (Manjushri) and Chana Dorje (Vajrapani). To the right of these statues is a *rangjung* (self-manifesting or self-arising) speaking Tara. The revered 2ft-high statue once warned the monastery's abbot how to prevent flooding of the local area. During the Cultural Revolution the statue was buried for safekeeping.

When you finish inside do a final kora around the compound. Little appears to have changed here or in the surrounding valley for a millennium.

Khojarnath is 130km from Darchen or about 107km from Chiu Village on Lake Manasarovar. Travellers to these areas should try to pay a visit to Khojarnath. The drive south from Darchen or Lake Manasarovar is one of the most scenic in western Tibet. From the lake, the monastery is easy to work in as a day trip.

Purang སྤུ་ཧྲེང་

☎ 08060 / elev 3800m

Purang (Taklakot to the Nepalis) is a large trading centre comprising a number of distinct settlements separated by the Humla Karnali River, known in Tibetan as Mabja Tsangpo (Peacock River). Nepali traders come up from the Humla district and also the Darchula region in the extreme west of Nepal to trade a variety of goods, including rice, carried up from Nepal in huge trains of goods-carrying goats. Indian consumer goods and Nepali rice are traded for Tibetan salt and wool in the Darchula bazaar, a 15-minute walk south of Purang.

Purang is also the arrival point for the annual influx of Hindu pilgrims from India, intent on making a *parikrama* (the Hindu equivalent of a kora) of Mt Kailash, which devout Hindus consider the abode of Shiva.

The hill northwest of town is the site of a huge army base said to extend far into the mountain

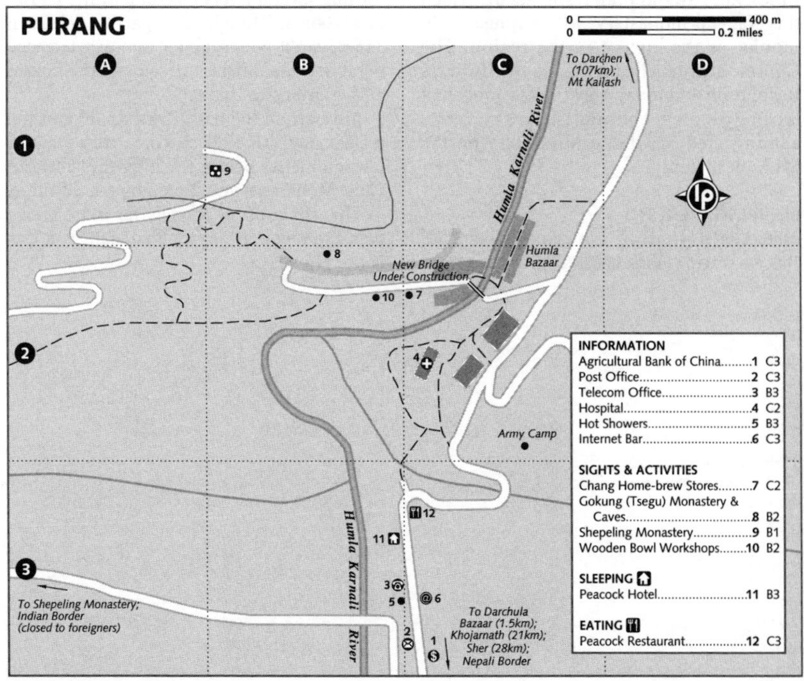

in a series of caves. It's even rumoured there are missiles here, aimed at New Delhi.

INFORMATION

There's an **internet bar** (wangba; per hr Y10; ⏰ 24hr) in a dark room on the 2nd floor in the middle of town, and **hot showers** (yushi; Y20; ⏰ 10am-11pm) directly across the hall.

DANGERS & ANNOYANCES

Be careful not to photograph the Chinese military base to the east or any of the small compounds in town. One guide we know was beaten by a group of soldiers after his tour group inadvertently photographed a restricted area.

SIGHTS

In the hills above the Humla Bazaar are many retreat **caves** formed around the cliffside **Gokung (Tsegu) Monastery**. Here, a ladder leads up to a couple of upper-floor cave chapels decorated with prayer flags. The dirt road from Humla Bazaar passes several **chang home-brew stores** and **bowl workshops**.

The ruined **Shepeling Monastery** towers over the town from its dramatic hilltop position. In 1949 the Swami Pranavananda described this Kagyud monastery, which housed 170 monks, as the biggest in the region. The Chinese army shelled it during the Cultural Revolution and today only the assembly hall is being restored. The monastery is currently administered by Chuku Monastery on the Mt Kailash kora.

SLEEPING & EATING

Peacock Hotel (孔雀宾馆; Kongque Binguan; ☎ 290 0139; d/tr per bed Y100/40, ste Y280) All rooms have decent beds and TV, but no bathrooms. If you want privacy, the best deal is to pay for all the beds in a triple.

There are a few other hotels and guesthouses in town, but the PSB may not let you stay at any of them.

Despite the proximity to Nepal, there's little flavour of the subcontinent in Purang's restaurants. **Peacock Restaurant** (☎ 290 0139; dishes Y10-25) This has a decent range of Chinese dishes and is a very neat and presentable establishment.

GETTING THERE & AWAY

Western trekkers arriving from Nepal usually arrange to be met at the border town of Sher for the 28km drive via Khojarnath to Purang.

Buses (Y230) run every two days from Ali to Purang via Darchen. From Purang it's 74km north to the Chiu Monastery on the shores of Lake Manasarovar and another 33km from there to Darchen, starting point for the Mt Kailash kora.

The road north from Purang passes the quaint village of Toyo before passing a number of small Tibetan settlements and fording several rivers en route to the Gurla-la (4700m). Though still part of Western Tibet, you'll be struck by the lush terraced fields and the different designs of the houses and chörtens in this area.

Just beyond the pass, Rakshas Tal and (on a clear day) Mt Kailash come into view. A few kilometres before reaching the village at Chiu Monastery you'll pass by a gold mine.

The way south is actually far more scenic than the way north as the first sight you face is the Himalaya.

Eastern Tibet (Kham)

ཁམས་

The eastern region of Tibet, known as Kham, is a land apart. Its climate, geography, flora and fauna all lend it a unique, almost magical atmosphere. The stone villages have more in common with neighbouring Bhutan, the chörtens (stupas) seem lifted from Mustang in Nepal and the forested scenery is more Swiss Alps than high Tibetan plateau. The traditional Tibetan province of Kham incorporates the eastern Tibetan Autonomous Region (TAR), western Sichuan and northwest Yunnan. This chapter covers only the eastern TAR, where travel permits are required. For information on overland travel through western Sichuan, see p267.

Geographically the region varies from the lush subtropical jungle and raging rivers of the southern borderlands to the arid plateau and purple gorges of the east, where the headwaters of some of Asia's greatest rivers – the Mekong, Salween and Yangzi – tumble off the Tibetan plateau. The glaciated peaks of Namche Barwa (7756m) and the remote gorges of the Yarlung Tsangpo, the world's deepest, form one of Asia's last secret corners.

Kham gains much of its charm from its people. Khampa cowboys, dressed in sheepskin cloaks and braided hair, cruise the region's highways on their motorbikes. Kham sometimes feels like the America's Wild West, with the cowboys and buffalos replaced by Khampas and yaks. There are two main routes through the region, offering a once-in-a-lifetime route in or out of Tibet. The busier and strategically important southern road takes in the best of the alpine scenery. The unpaved northern road is a higher roller-coaster ride past ancient temples, remote Bön monasteries and herding communities.

HIGHLIGHTS

- Take a perfect photo of **Draksum-tso** (p247), a sublime alpine lake with a fairy-tale island monastery
- View the magnificent scenery from **Nyingtri to Pomi** (p251), climbing from lush subtropical forest to alpine valleys and snowy passes
- Picnic by the stunning turquoise waters of **Rawok-tso** (p254), a mirror lake fringed with snow-capped peaks
- Peer up in awe at the towering statues of the remote **Riwoche Tsuglhakhang** (p261)
- Clamber up wooden ladders to cliff-top shrines at the amazing **Tsedru Monastery** (p262), Tibet's most spectacularly sited monastery
- Follow the pilgrims around the charming **Lamaling Temple** (p250), shaped like Guru Rinpoche's celestial paradise
- Join the monks in a debate at Chamdo's **Galden Jampaling Monastery** (p257), one of the largest monastic communities in Tibet

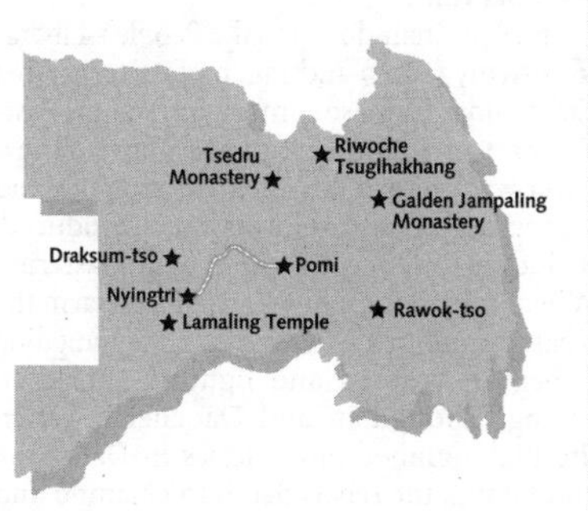

History

The area around Chamdo was one of the first settled in Tibet, as attested to by the 5000-year-old Neolithic remains at nearby Karo. Fossilised millet hints at a 5000-year tradition of agriculture in the region.

Kham was the home of many early lamas, including the founders of the Drigungpa and Karmapa schools. In 1070, many Buddhists fled persecution in central Tibet to Kham, where they set up influential monasteries, later returning to central Tibet to spearhead the so-called second diffusion of Buddhism in Tibet.

Lhasa's control over the region has waxed and waned over the centuries. Lhasa first gained control of Kham thanks to Mongol assistance, but the majority of the region has enjoyed de facto political independence. Until recently, much of Kham comprised many small fiefdoms ruled by kings (Derge), lamas (Litang) or hereditary chieftains (Batang). Relations with China were mostly restricted to the trade caravans, which carried bricks of Chinese tea in, and pastoral products out.

Chinese warlords such as Zhao Erfeng and Liu Wenhui swept through the eastern part of Kham (modern-day western Sichuan) in the late 19th and early 20th centuries, eventually to set up the Chinese province of Xikang (western Kham). Khampa rebellions occurred frequently, notably in 1918, 1928 and 1932, though not all were against the Chinese; in 1933 the Khampas tried to shake off Lhasa's nominal rule.

In 1950 Chamdo fell to the People's Liberation Army (PLA) and much of eastern Tibet came under Chinese control. In 1954 the eastern part of Kham east of the upper Yangzi River was merged into Sichuan province and a program of land reforms was introduced, including the collectivisation of monasteries. When in 1955 the Chinese tried to disarm the Khampas and settle the nomads, the Kangding Rebellion erupted and fighting spread to Litang, Zhongdian and Daocheng. When the PLA bombed monasteries in Daocheng and Litang, the rebels fled into Chamdo and later to India and Nepal, to organise armed resistance from Mustang (in Nepal) with CIA assistance.

Today eastern Tibet remains heavily Sinicised along the southern Sichuan–Tibet Hwy, where the controversial construction of new towns (with multicoloured roofs) is fast altering the face of the region. Off the main highways, Khampa life remains culturally strong.

Climate

Kham has a dramatically different climate from the rest of Tibet. The summer monsoon from Assam brings a lot of rain from early June to September, when much of the southern route is shrouded in mist and fog. Snowfall generally starts in October. Northern areas between Sok and Nagchu receive strong winds year-round and sudden blizzards even in summer. Nagchu is Tibet's coldest city; July temperatures range between 3°C and 15°C, with January temperatures bottoming out at minus 25°C. In March, while the northern road remains dry and bleak, southern farms around Pomi are already filled with verdant crops.

The best times to travel are from late March to early May, and from September to early November. At other months you can find the roads temporarily blocked for anything from a couple of hours to a few days.

Permits

The eastern part of the TAR is officially closed to foreigners unless you have a guide, private transport (normally a Land Cruiser) and a fistful of permits, including a military permit (p323). Once on the road nervous guides will often want to register your group with every county-level PSB office along your route, which can be a real pain.

One irritation is that the Public Security Bureau (PSB) in Lhasa generally doesn't write monastery names on their permits, only towns. The occasional obstructive local PSB office in eastern Tibet may then deny you access to a monastery because only the local town is listed on your permit…

Even with all the requisite permits you will still encounter problems visiting Sok Tsanden Monastery and, to a lesser extent, the Riwoche Tsuglhakhang. To stand the best chance of gaining access you'll need to insist that the specific monastery (not just the local town name) is listed on your permits.

Places close to the disputed Indian border such as Namche Barwa and the Tsangpo gorges are very difficult to get permits for; your agency will need military connections for these.

If you decide to hitch through eastern Tibet without a permit, you will have to keep a very low profile at all checkpoints and in larger towns and county capitals. If you're caught without a permit, you will most likely be fined between Y200 and Y500 and sent back in the direction from which you came. Hot spots that permitless travellers should avoid include Bayi, Markham and Chamdo. Generally speaking, it's easier to hitch *out* of the region than hitch in. See p337.

Getting There & Around

Lhasa is the logical place from which to launch an expedition to Kham. It's the closest gateway city and permits are relatively hassle-free to acquire, as long as you are on an organised tour. The most popular routes are the loop route along the southern road to Chamdo and back along the northern road to Lhasa, and the one-way shot along the southern road between Lhasa and Zhongdian (and vice versa).

For a two-week loop of Kham (taking in Draksum-tso, Bayi, Pasho, Riwoche and Sok), Foreign Independent Traveller (FIT) in Lhasa charges around Y16,000 for transport, guides and permits. A shorter six-day loop from

FOUR RIVERS, SIX RANGES: THE KHAMPA RESISTANCE

By the late 1950s thousands of Khampa warriors had begun to rebel against Chinese rule and reforms. News of the armed rebellion filtered through to central Tibet, but the Khampas' pleas for help fell on deaf ears. The Dalai Lama, keen to avoid conflict with the Chinese, asked the Khampas to disarm. Without organisation or cohesive leadership the rebellion was routed.

Yet a core of Khampa fighters managed to regroup in Lhoka, in southern Tibet, and in a rare moment of Khampa unity formed an organisation called Chizhi Gangdrung (Four Rivers, Six Ranges), the traditional local name for the Kham region. Soon 15,000 men were assembled, led by Gonbo Tashi, and a new flag was created.

The Khampas eventually attracted the attention of exiled Tibetan leaders in Kalimpong (India), as well as the Chinese Kuomintang (KMT or Nationalist Party; some Khampas were trained in Taiwan) and even the CIA, who liaised with the Tibetans through Thubten Norbu and later Gyalo Dhundup, both brothers of the Dalai Lama.

Before long, Tibetan leaders were liaising with CIA agents in Kolkata (Calcutta), arranging secret meetings through dead letter drops and secret messages. The first batch of six Khampa agents trekked over the border to Kalimpong, were driven to Bangladesh and then were flown to the Pacific island of Saipan, where they were trained to organise guerrilla groups. Agents were later parachuted behind enemy lines into Samye and Litang.

In 1957, guerrilla attacks were made on Chinese garrisons and road camps, and in 1958, 700 Chinese soldiers were killed by guerrillas near Nyemo. The movement met with the Dalai Lama in southern Tibet when he fled Lhasa in 1959 as the CIA readied three plane loads of arms – enough for 2000 people.

The flight of the Dalai Lama to India marked a setback for the resistance and the focus switched to a base in Mustang, an ethnically Tibetan area in Nepal, where initially at least the Nepalis turned a blind eye to the movement. Between 1960 and 1962 over 150 Tibetans were sent to Colorado for training.

Yet the resistance was living on borrowed time. The Americans never had much confidence in the Tibetans and by the mid-1960s CIA funding had dried up. By 1972 the international political climate had changed; US president Richard Nixon's visit to China and the coronation of Nepal's pro-Chinese king had left the Khampas out on a limb. Moreover, the resistance was riddled with feuds – most of the Khampa rebels had always been fighting more for their local valley and monastery than for any national ideal. In 1973 the Nepalis demanded the closure of the Mustang base and the Dalai Lama asked the rebels to surrender. It was the end of the Khampa rebellion and the end of Tibetan armed resistance to the Chinese.

For more on the CIA's funding of Tibetan resistance guerrillas and the diplomatic behind-the-scenes wrangling, read *Orphans of the Cold War: America and the Tibetan Struggle for Freedom* by John Kenneth Knaus. Knaus, a 44-year veteran of the CIA, was personally involved in training Tibetan agents in Colorado. For a Tibetan perspective, try *Warriors of Tibet* by Jamyang Norbu, a slim volume recalling the Khampa rebellion in Nyarong (western Sichuan).

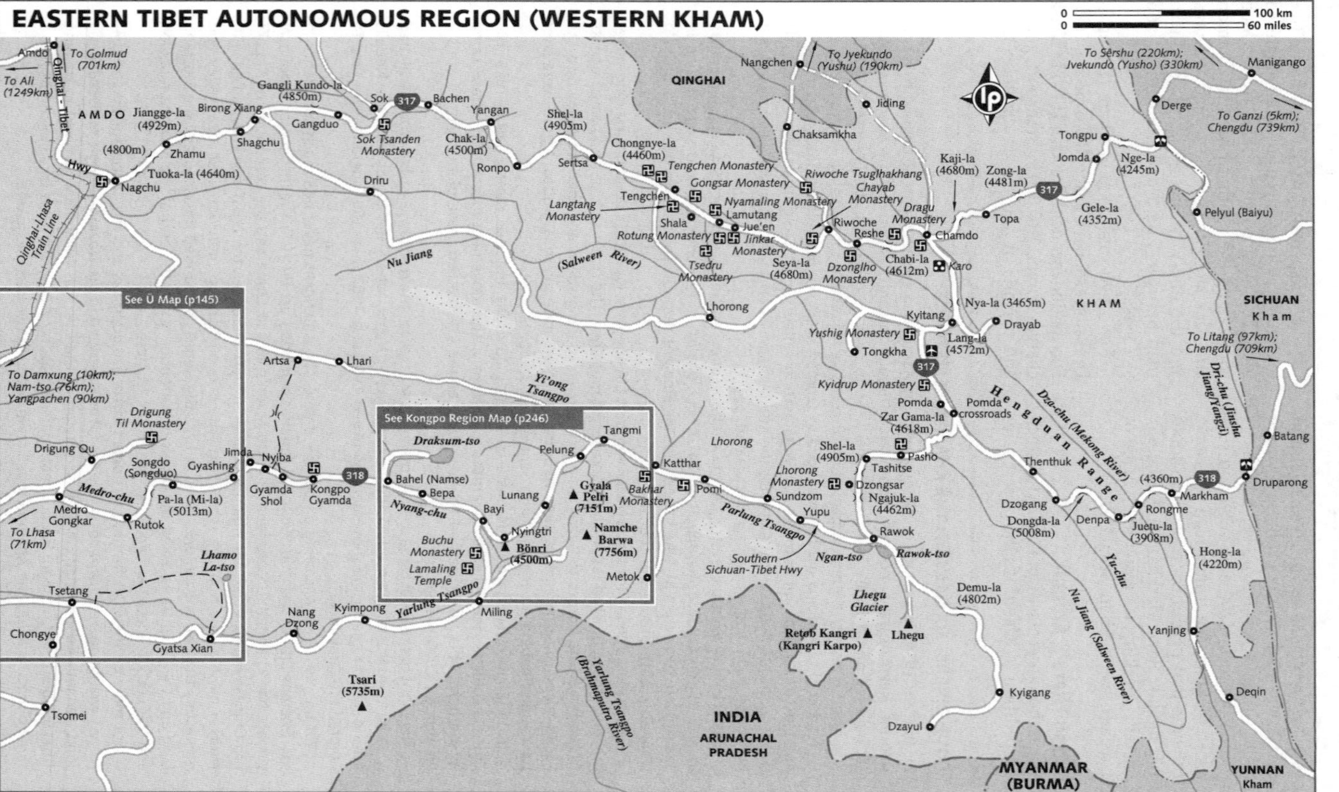
EASTERN TIBET AUTONOMOUS REGION (WESTERN KHAM)
0 100 km
0 60 miles
Amdo
To Golmud (701km)
To Ali (1249km)
Qinghai - Tibet Hwy
AMDO
Jiangge-la (4929m)
(4800m)
Zhamu
Tuoka-la (4640m)
Nagchu
Qinghai-Lhasa Train Line
Gangli Kundo-la (4850m)
Birong Xiang
Shagchu
Gangduo
Sok
317
Bachen
Sok Tsanden Monastery
Yangan
Chak-la (4500m)
Ronpo
Driru
Shel-la (4905m)
Sertsa
Chongnye-la (4460m)
Tengchen Monastery
Gongsar Monastery
Tengchen
Langtang Monastery
Shala
Nyamaling Monastery
Lamutang
Jue'en
Rotung Monastery
Jinkar Monastery
Tsedru Monastery
Nu Jiang
(Salween River)
Nangchen
To Jyekundo (Yushu) (190km)
QINGHAI
Jiding
Chaksamkha
Riwoche Tsuglhakhang
Chayab Monastery
Riwoche
Reshe
Seya-la (4680m)
Dzonglho Monastery
Dragu Monastery
Chamdo
Chabi-la (4612m)
Karo
Kaji-la (4680m)
Zong-la (4481m)
Topa
Tongpu
Jomda
Nge-la (4245m)
Gele-la (4352m)
Derge
To Sershu (220km); Jvekundo (Yusho) (330km)
Manigango
To Ganzi (5km); Chengdu (739km)
Pelyul (Baiyu)
Lhorong
Nya-la (3465m)
KHAM
Drayab
Kyitang
Yushig Monastery
Lang-la (4572m)
Tongkha
SICHUAN
Kham
To Litang (97km); Chengdu (709km)
Dri-chu (Jinsha Jiang/Yangzi)
Batang
Druparong
See Ü Map (p145)
To Damxung (10km); Nam-tso (76km); Yangpachen (90km)
Drigung Til Monastery
Drigung Qu
Songdo (Songduo)
Gyashing
Jimda
Medro-chu
Medro Gongkar
To Lhasa (71km)
Pa-la (Mi-la) (5013m)
Rutok
Lhamo La-tso
Tsetang
Chongye
Gyatsa Xian
Tsomei
Artsa
Lhari
Nyiba
Gyamda Shol
Kongpo Gyamda
318
Yi'ong Tsangpo
See Kongpo Region Map (p246)
Draksum-tso
Bahel (Namse)
Bepa
Nyang-chu
Bayi
Lunang
Pelung
Tangmi
Gyala Pelri (7151m)
Nyingtri
Bönri (4500m)
Namche Barwa (7756m)
Buchu Monastery
Lamaling Temple
Yarlung Tsangpo
Metok
Miling
Kyimpong
Nang Dzong
Tsari (5735m)
Katthar
Bakhar Monastery
Pomi
Lhorong
Kyidrup Monastery
317
Pomda
Pomda crossroads
Zar Gama-la (4618m)
Hengduan Range
Dza-chu (Mekong River)
Shel-la (4905m)
Pasho
Tashitse
Lhorong Monastery
Dzongsar
Ngajuk-la (4462m)
Sundzom
Yupu
Parlung Tsangpo
Southern Sichuan-Tibet Hwy
Ngan-tso
Rawok
Rawok-tso
Thenthuk
Dzogang
Dongda-la (5008m)
Denpa
(4360m)
Markham
Rongme
Juetu-la (3908m)
Hong-la (4220m)
Yu-chu
Nu Jiang (Salween River)
Demu-la (4802m)
Lhegu Glacier
Retob Kangri (Kangri Karpo)
Lhegu
Yanjing
Kyigang
Deqin
Dzayul
Yarlung Tsangpo (Brahmaputra River)
INDIA
ARUNACHAL PRADESH
MYANMAR (BURMA)
YUNNAN
Kham

WALK ON THE WILD SIDE

Warmer, wetter and more forested than anywhere else in Tibet, Kham's wide vertical range hides Tibet's largest concentration of rare animal and plant species. Takins, red pandas, musk deer, gorals, long-tailed leaf monkeys, Himalayan tahrs, tragopans, pheasants and Himalayan monals all live in the tropical and subtropical regions of Tibet's southeastern borderlands.

Eastern Tibet is also a botanical powerhouse and early on attracted the attention of intrepid 19th- and 20th-century British plant hunters. From May onwards the region is a riot of wildflowers, bursting with 190 species of rhododendrons, 110 types of gentians and 120 species of primula, not to mention such rare flowers as the blue poppy, discovered by the explorer/spy FM Bailey in the Rong-chu Valley in 1913. Many of the rhododendrons and azaleas found in the West descend from samples taken from eastern Tibet and neighbouring Yunnan, and many of the expeditions were actually funded by foreign seed companies.

Overlogging is a serious problem in the temperate forests of eastern Tibet, though logging was formally banned in the Tibetan areas of Sichuan and Yunnan in 1998 after a series of devastating floods downstream in lowland China. Pockets of ancient cypresses up to 2500 years old continue to hang on in the Nyingtri region.

Lhasa to Bayi and back, taking in Draksum-tso, Bayi, Miling, Gyatsa Xian, Tsetang and Samye, costs around Y6000. Finding others to share the cost of the car can be the hardest part of organising these fairly unusual trips. When arranging an itinerary with an agency it's important to specify in advance any detours off the main road, for example to Tsedru Monastery (p262) and Lhegu Glacier (p254).

For details of the trip from Lhasa to Zhongdian in Yunnan, see p337. For details of the routes into the region from Chengdu (Sichuan), via either Derge or Batang, see the Overland Routes From Sichuan chapter (p267).

The most remote and least travelled route into the region is the northeastern route from Qinghai to Riwoche, via the towns of Yushu (Jyekundo) and Nangchen. For details, see p337.

Long-distance buses travel the northern route and southern route, from Lhasa to Chamdo, Bayi (Y100), Markham (Y340) and Zhongdian (Y500), and local buses and private minibuses travel between many of the main towns, but unless the permit situation changes (see p242) you'll be lucky to be allowed on these buses.

A surprising number of cyclists without permits, but self-sufficient with tent and food, make it through the region.

MEDRO GONGKAR TO KONGPO GYAMDA (203KM)

The first major stop after the turn-off to Drigung Til (see p162) is **Rutok**, in the upper Medro-chu Valley, which has a monastery on the hillside north of town and several Tibetan teahouses. It is also the trailhead for the six-day trek to Lhamo La-tso (p179).

From Rutok the road climbs to impressive views from the high Pa-la (5013m; Mi-la), before winding down to Songdo (Songduo). About 65km after the pass, just before the village of Nyiba, a rickety bridge offers a worthwhile five-minute excursion up to a hillside **rock carving** of Sakyamuni (Sakya Thukpa).

A further 13km downstream brings you to a huge, photogenic boulder stuck in the middle of Nyang-chu, covered with prayer flags and topped with a rhododendron bush. Locals consider it the seat of the local protector deity Kongtsun Demo.

Five kilometres further, the village of Gyamda Shol was once an important stop on the old Lhasa–Chamdo caravan trail, which branches north from here over the mountains into the Yi'ong Tsangpo Valley. From here it's 13km to Kongpo Gyamda.

KONGPO GYAMDA ཀོང་པོ་རྒྱ་མདའ 工布江达

☎ **0894 / pop 4500 / elev 3400m**

There's little reason to stop in this modern town, unless you get a late start from Lhasa and need to spend the night. The town has a decent range of accommodation.

The **Kathok Nunnery**, located in the hills to the north of town, has eight nuns and a small chapel housing an image of Guru Rinpoche and King Trisong Detsen. Like most nunneries it's well tended. A path (a 30-minute

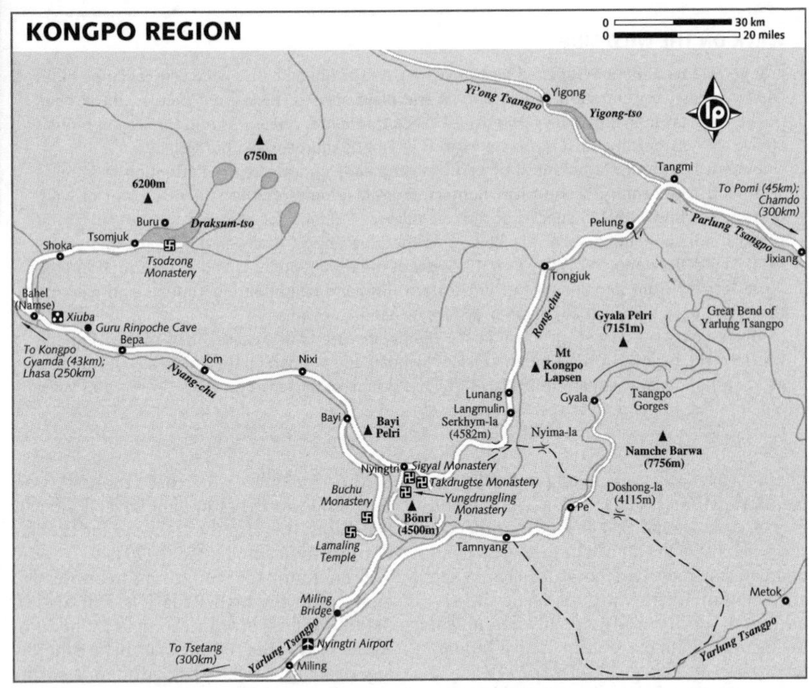

walk) leads up to the nunnery from the plaza just to the north of the Grain Department Guesthouse, climbing some steps and weaving through the old quarter to offer fine views.

The nunnery is backed by a cleft in the forested Baripo Mountain, which has a small **hermitage** marked by fluttering prayer flags; it takes 45 minutes to walk there from the nunnery.

You can get online at the **Xinhua Wangba** (心话网吧; per hr Y3; 24hr), a block north of the Grain Department Guesthouse.

The PSB office is at the eastern end of town.

Sleeping & Eating

Grain Department Guesthouse (粮食局新招待所; Liangshiju Xin Zhaodaisuo; ☎ 136-2894 9804; dm Y20) This is probably the best budget option, with decent dorm beds in rooms that come with an attached squat toilet. Rooms are cleaned infrequently, if at all, so expect piles of cigarette ash (and worse) in the corners of the rooms. This is the 'new' grain guesthouse, down a small side street; the old one on the main street isn't as good. The Qingquan Bathhouse (清泉淋浴; Qingquan Linyu) across the road offers hot showers for Y6.

Yinye Zhaodaisuo (银叶招待所; ☎ 541 2541; d Y30-60) Rooms on the 3rd floor are clean with good quality beds but there's no shower and the shared toilet at the end of the hall is seriously nasty. It's in a courtyard in front of a bank.

Huating Kangsha Dajiudian (华庭康厦大酒店; ☎ 541 3111; d Y380, discounted to Y130;) This plush place opened in 2006 as the best in town, with soft carpets, Western-style bathrooms and hot water in the evenings. It's down a side street towards the government offices.

The main street is lined with Sichuanese restaurants. There's a good Tibetan teahouse below the Grain Department Guesthouse.

Getting There & Away

Kongpo Gyamda is 277km from Lhasa. A bus (Y60, four hours, 8am) departs daily from Lhasa's Eastern Bus Station.

Buses to Lhasa (Y50 to Y80) leave at about 8am from Kongpo Gyamda's main street. Minibuses depart for Bayi (Y30) when full from the east of town.

KONGPO REGION

The Kongpo region is culturally, ecologically and linguistically quite distinct from the rest of Tibet. A former kingdom of the early Yarlung kings and rival to Lhasa, Kongpo has for centuries been vilified by central Tibetan rulers as a land of incest and poison, whose inhabitants would routinely drug unsuspecting strangers to steal their souls.

The distinctive traditional Kongpo dress features a round hat with an upturned rim of golden brocade for men (known as a *gyasha*) and a pretty pillbox hat with winged edges (known as a *dieu*) for women. Men and women wear brown woollen tunics, belted around the waist.

Kongpo is now the scene of a large-scale resettlement and rebuilding program. In 2006 alone over 290,000 people – 10% of Tibet's population – were moved into new homes across Tibet. Some of these new villages were built to settle newcomers from the eastern borderlands, moved here by the Chinese to protect ecosystems at the upper reaches of the Yangzi. The plan has some precedent. Forty years ago, during the Cultural Revolution, Kongpo was home to a vast network of prisons and gulags, some of which are still in use.

DRAKSUM-TSO བྲག་གསུམ་མཚོ་ 巴松措

elev 3470m

This beautiful alpine lake, known variously as Draksum-tso, Bagsum-tso and Pasum-tso, depending on the dialect (Basongcuo in Chinese), is a long day's drive from Lhasa and a 41km one-way detour off the Sichuan–Tibet Hwy. Apart from the sheer beauty of the lake and its surrounding 6000m peaks, the site has strong connections to Gesar of Ling, the semimythical ruler of eastern Tibet, and Guru Rinpoche, the Indian sage, both of whom are said to have resided at the lake.

A Y50 entrance fee to the area is payable at a toll gate 33km past the turn-off at Bahel, and 4km before of the lake. PSB officers here and at the hotel by the lake will want to see your travel permits.

The highlight of the lake is the charming **Tsodzong Monastery** (The Fortress in the Lake), a small Nyingmapa chapel sited on a photogenic island just off the southern shore. The island is an organic fusion of dozens of types of flora and a sprinkle of holy sights.

The monastery was founded by Sangye Lingpa in the 14th century. The main chapel has statues of a wrathful and peaceful Guru Rinpoche and smaller statues of Sakyamuni, Chenresig (Avalokiteshvara) and Kongtsun Demo, a local protector, on horseback. The statues were actually shot and then burned by Red Guards during the Cultural Revolution, before being restored by the famous local lama Dudjom Rinpoche and his son Chuni Rinpoche (now resident at Lamaling Monastery near Bayi – see p250). In the corner of the monastery is what is said to be a stone hoofprint of Gesar's horse. The steps to the monastery are flanked by ancient-looking male and female fertility symbols.

A small kora (ritual circumambulation circuit) around the monastery passes many hard-to-discern holy sites, including a tree said to resemble a conch horn, a sky-burial site, a 'body print' of Gesar, an underground treasury of the Karmapa, a tiger print and a tree whose leaves bear magical symbols.

Just to the west of the lake by a small pass, wooden boardwalks climb up to a fine viewpoint over the lake. There's plenty of scope for hikes around the lake and up side valleys, though permit hassles generally impede much independent exploration. You could walk a couple of hours east along the south shore or even further to Tsongo village for the best views of the mountains to the north. A two-day **kora** rings the lake. A motorboat trip around the island is Y25 per person or you can hire the boat for a one-hour lake tour (Y400).

Massive development is underway in the valley, spurred on by a new hydroelectric power station, that will doubtless take away some of the charm of the lower valley. Draksum-tso is very popular with busloads of mainland Chinese tourists and preparations are underway for more hotels and tourist facilities.

About 12km from the junction, the road up to the lake passes three tall 12-sided stone towers, which can be reached with a bit of scrambling. No-one quite knows for what purpose the enigmatic towers were built – they stand empty and entryless. Locals refer to them as *dudkhang* (demons' houses) and recite legends connecting them to Gesar of Ling.

A more accessible collection of **towers** (admission Y10) stands 7km east of Bahel, on the main Sichuan–Tibet highway at Xiuba. The five magnificent towers are said to date from the reign of Songtsen Gampo (r 630–49).

A further 7km towards Bayi, a series of wooden walkways lead up to a **Guru Rinpoche cave**, which pilgrims crawl through, returning to the surface through a small opening further up the hillside. Take a torch and much care, as there are a couple of hairy moments during the scramble. It's not an excursion for the claustrophobic or overweight.

Sleeping & Eating

Local officials try to force foreigners to pay a fee of Y100 for camping anywhere around the lake.

Draksum Lake Tourism Holiday Village (巴松措度假村; Basong Cuo Dujia Cun; ☎ 0894-541 3508; dm Y100-120, d Y240) This simple resort offers beds in comfortable but overpriced portacabin-style rooms with private bathrooms. Most rooms can't be locked. There's a Tibetan-style restaurant here.

It's possible to stay at Bahel (Namse) village, on the Sichuan–Tibet Hwy near the turn-off to Draksum-tso. **Draksum Dromkhang** (巴松湖旅馆; Basonghu Lüguan; ☎ 0894-541 3419; dm Y20) has beds in cosy but basic wooden rooms above a restaurant. There are several other equally basic places in town, as well as a public shower (淋浴; linyu, Y5) and an internet café. The junction is lined with Chinese-run fish restaurants, which Tibetans spurn for religious reasons.

Getting There & Away

The road to Draksum-tso branches off the main highway at Bahel Bridge (also known as Namse). On the right, high on the cliff, look for the Pangri Jokpa hermitage. After 4km the road passes the new dam site. A further 20km takes you past the first of the stone towers. The lake comes into view 35km from Bahel at Tsomjuk (Lake's Mouth). The road continues another 6km to Tsodzong island.

BAYI བརྒྱད་གཅིག 八一

☎ 0894 / pop 60,000 / elev 2990m

> To get to paradise you have to go through the inferno, and Bayi is the inferno.
>
> Hamid Sardar, quoted by Michael McCrae, *The Siege of Shangri-la*

Bayi, 80km east of Bahel, is a large Han Chinese military town of limited interest, except perhaps as a base from which to visit the surrounding sights. 'Bayi' in Chinese means '1 August', the founding date of the PLA, though some Tibetans joke that it really means 'Eight Chinese for every one Tibetan'. Bayi is expanding at a breathtaking pace and an entire new town is under construction in the eastern suburbs, alongside a huge pagoda-style temple.

Groups will need to register with the unwelcoming local PSB; travellers without a permit should steer well clear of the town.

Information

China Post (Zhongguo Youzheng; Zhuhai Lu; 🕑 9.30am-7pm)
China Telecom (Zhongguo Dianxin; ☎ 582 1048; Zhuhai Lu; 🕑 9.30am-7.30pm)
Eastern Express Internet Café (Dongfang Kuaiche Wangba; Aomen Lu; per hr Y3; 🕑 24hr)
Huaifeng Bathhouse (Huaifeng Linyu; Guangdong Lu; hot shower Y5; 🕑 10am-10pm)

Pelri Kora

At the eastern edge of the town rises Bayi Pelri, a holy mountain that is associated with Guru Rinpoche, who fought demons on the hill and then conjured up the surrounding farmland from a vast lake.

A pleasant kora rings the peak, though recent modernisation has robbed the walk of some of its charm. If you are on foot, follow the road that switchbacks up the hillside. If you have transport, continue to a saddle on the north side of the plateau, where a forest of prayer flags around a white chörten marks the point where the kora path leaves the tarmac road.

The boardwalk path leads around the back of Pelri, past several sacred sites where pilgrims hang hats, bowls and even miniature ladders, through forest back to the switchbacking road. There are superb views into the valley below.

Sleeping

Tibet Linzhi Holiday Hotel (Linzhi Jiari Jiudian; ☎ 582 0111; Guangdong Lu; dm Y60-80, d Y668, discounted to Y240; ❄ 💻) Budget travellers can buy a bed in the three economy rooms (with clean shared bathrooms) but only if they aren't occupied by drivers or guides. The doubles with bathroom are a comfortable midrange option.

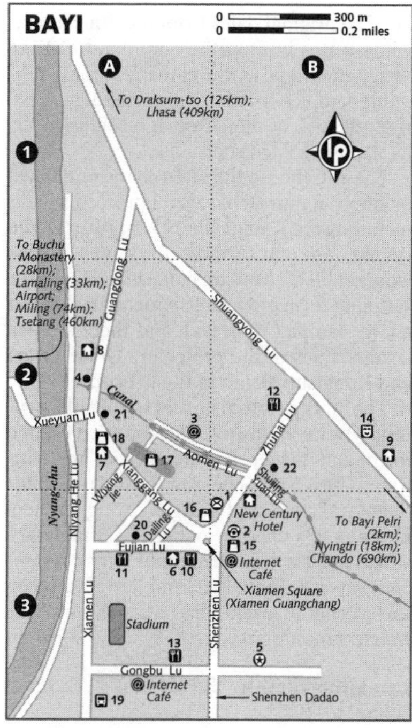

INFORMATION

China Post 中国邮政 ... 1 B3
China Telecom 中国电信 ... 2 B3
Eastern Express Internet Café 东方快车网吧 ... 3 A2
Huaifeng Bathhouse 淮风淋浴 ... 4 A2
PSB 公安局 ... 5 B3

SLEEPING

Kangfuyuan Hotel 康福源大酒店 ... 6 A3
Post Hotel 邮政大酒店 ... 7 A2
Tibet Linzhi Holiday Hotel 林芝假日酒店 ... 8 A2
Xiaofangcun Jiudian 小芳村酒店 ... 9 B2

EATING

Green Ser Aelpe Tibetan Kitchen 绿海明珠藏餐馆 ... 10 A3
Hengyuan Xiaochi Yeshicheng 恒源小吃夜食城 ... 11 A3
Lo Les Traditional Emotion Palace 拉列思民族风情宫 ... 12 B2
Xiangsihai Zidong Huoguo 香四海自动火锅 ... 13 A3

ENTERTAINMENT

Shangri-la Nongma 香格里拉民族歌舞城 ... 14 B2

SHOPPING

Kodak Express 柯达快速彩色 ... 15 A3
Lebailong Department Store 乐百隆 ... 16 A3
Market 市场 ... 17 A2
Toread 探路者 ... 18 A2

TRANSPORT

Bus Station 客运站 ... 19 A3
Buses to Kongpo Gyamda & Miling ... 20 A3
Buses to Lamaling & Miling ... 21 A2
Transport to Nyingtri, Lunang & Pomi ... 22 B2

Xiaofangcun Jiudian (☎ 582 5686; 18 Shuangyong Lu; d/ste Y200/380, discounted to Y120/200) A cool lobby bar, photos of Tibet on the wall and enthusiastic staff gives this place almost a boutique feel, which is quite something for Bayi! Rooms are bright and clean, with wooden floors and little sofas. You might have trouble persuading your guide to let you stay here as it isn't a tour-group hotel.

Kangfuyuan Dajiudian (☎ 582 1181; 3 Fujian Lu; d Y328, discounted to Y180;) When the rooms are discounted, this place offers the best value in town. The rooms are so large that you can pitch a tent in the corner and still have room for a game of Twister and the clean bathrooms offer the joys of reliable hot water and warming heat lamps. Prices include breakfast.

Post Hotel (Youzheng Dajiudian; ☎ 588 9666; cnr Xianggang Lu & Xiamen Lu; d with/without bathroom Y888/84, discounted to Y260/50) The six old block rooms in the annexe here (ask in Chinese for the *putongjian*) might be your only budget option. They come with decent shared bathrooms and a hot shower. The standard rooms have fairly grotty private bathrooms, but are sometimes discounted as low as Y100.

Eating

Green Ser Aelpe Tibetan Kitchen (☎ 582 8618; Xiamen Square; dishes Y8) Located on the southern side of the roundabout, this authentic Tibetan-style teahouse has a nonsensical name but passable *shemdre* (yak curry). It's best for a milk tea and a game of cards.

Lo Les Traditional Emotion Palace (Laliesi Minzu Fengqing Gong; ☎ 582 8588; Zhuhai Lu; dishes Y25-60, snacks Y10) although this is not the cheapest place in town, it is definitely the plushest, with regal Tibetan décor, fantastically dressed staff and live Tibetan music. The seats by the front window are more casual and have a cheaper snacks menu.

Xiangsihai Zidong Huoguo (☎ 583 1419; Gongbu Lu; buffet Y28) This is a great place for self-service, all-you-can-eat hotpot. Load up from the ingredients buffet and throw the lot in the spicy or mild broths (Y10 extra per table). It's idiot-proof.

For good Chinese food try the **Hengyuan Xiaochi Yeshicheng** (dishes Y10-20), a clean and tasty place on Fujian Lu, recommended by several Chinese travellers.

There are several other small **Tibetan teahouses** (Dailing Lu), across from the Kangfuyuan Dajiudian.

Entertainment

Shangri-la Nongma (☎ 582 8878; Shuangyong Lu; 🕑 9pm-4am) Enjoy some innocent *nangma* (entertainment club) fun with comedy acts, song-and-dance routines and stone-faced, waltzing locals.

Shopping

Xianggang Lu is the main shopping drag. The main produce market is south of the canal.

Toread (Tanluzhe; ☎ 582 4401; Xianggang Lu) Tents, sleeping bags and outdoor gear

Kodak Express (☎ 582 3276; Xiamen Square) For film and batteries

Lebailong Department Store (Xiamen Square; 🕑 9.30am-10pm) There's a good supermarket on the 2nd floor

Getting There & Away

Buses to Bayi (Y80 to Y100, seven hours) depart frequently from Lhasa's East Bus Station, though foreigners might have troubles buying a ticket.

Buses back to Lhasa (Y60 to Y80, hourly until 3pm) depart from **Bayi Bus Station** (Xiamen Lu), in the southwest of town. There are also buses every other day to Chamdo (Y240, two days), Chengdu (Y510) and Markham (Y340). One bus a day runs to Nang Dzong (Lang Xian; Y105, 7.30am), via Miling.

Private minibuses leave when full from in front of the Kangfuyuan Dajiudian for Kongpo Gyamda (Y30, 130km) and Miling (Y25). Private minibuses to Pe (Y50), Lamaling (Y10) and Miling (Y25) depart from beside the Post Hotel.

A car park near the New Century Hotel has frequent microbuses to Nyingtri (Y7) and Lunang (Y30), and daily Land Cruisers to Pomi (Y80 to Y100, five hours).

The new Nyingtri (Linzhi) airport, south of Bayi near Miling, has a weekly flight to Chengdu (Y1510), but it's rarely used by foreigners.

A taxi anywhere in town costs Y10.

AROUND BAYI

Buchu Monastery བོན་ཚོས་དགོན་པ་ 布久寺

Some 28km south of Bayi is the small but ancient Gelugpa monastery of Buchu (Bujiu Si). The original dates from the 7th century, when it was built at the command of King Songtsen Gampo as one of the demoness-subduing temples (p105); it pins the demoness' right elbow. The monastery is recognisable by its striking golden roof.

The entrance to the main chapel is flanked by unusual murals of several protector gods, including the Kongpo deity Kongtsun Demo (in the far right on horseback, next to the wheel of life). The main hall has statues of the standing form of Guru Rinpoche (right) and a large Jampa (Maitreya), and there are two small statues of the protectors Dorje Lekpa and Kongtsun Demo in the left corner.

The inner sanctum houses statues of Chenresig (Avalokiteshvara), with Songtsen Gampo in the left corner. Behind these is the trinity of Guru Rinpoche, the Indian translator Shantarakshita and King Trisong Detsen. Upstairs is a cheesy, modern 3-D mandala, which depicts the sacred mountains of Namche Barwa, Kailash, Tsari and Kawa Karpo on each corner. A lovely kora path surrounds the timeless monastery.

Lamaling Temple བླ་མ་གླིང་དགོན་པ་ 喇嘛宁寺

About 1.5km south of Buchu a paved road branches 4km west off the main road to the stunning Lamaling Temple (Lamaning Si). The monastery was the seat of the exiled Dudjom Rinpoche (1904-87), the former head of the Nyingma order. It is now looked after by his son-in-law Chuni Rinpoche and has over 100 monks and nuns.

The octagonal main Zangtok Pelri temple has been wonderfully restored (reconstruction began in 1989) and rises through four storeys, bringing to mind the Ütse of Samye Monastery. The building is draped in long strands of cannonball-sized wooden prayer beads. The grassy courtyard in front is home to a few doleful mountain goats brought here from Tsodzong Monastery at Draksum-tso. Don't get too close: they buck.

Take your shoes off before entering the temple. The ground floor has a statue of Guru Rinpoche, with two stone footprints of the guru on the altar (curiously, both the right foot!) and puppet-like images of the protector Tseumar to the left. A passageway behind the altar leads up to a mezzanine level with four protector chapels in each corner. The chapel above this houses statues of Chenresig (Avalokiteshvara), flanked by Jampelyang (Manjushri) and Chana Dorje (Vajrapani). The top-floor chapel contains a statue of Öpagme.

The other main building, to the right, is the assembly hall, where most religious services are held, on the 10th, 15th and 25th days of each lunar month. The hall is dominated by a huge statue of Sakyamuni and more images of Dudjom Rinpoche wearing his characteristic sunglasses. Pilgrims circumambulate both this building and the main temple.

If you want to stretch your legs, a trail leads off from the corner of the car park to an atmospheric prayer-flag-draped chörten and then winds up the hillside for about 40 minutes (follow the prayer flags) to Norbu Ri, where the original Lamaling Temple stood before it was destroyed in 1930 in an earthquake. Look out for the Sakyamuni footprint on a cloth above the door.

Nyingtri ཉིང་ཁྲི་ 林芝

☎ 0894 / pop 3100 / elev 2900m

This two-street town (Linzhi in Chinese) is much smaller than Bayi, 18km away, but is actually the county capital.

Neche Goshog Monastery (尼池寺; Nichi Si; admission Y5) is a small Bön monastery 1km southwest of Nyingtri. Turn right at the new wooden sign that says 'Classical Elegance of Nichi'. The small monastery, home to 50 monks, is famous for its 2000-year-old juniper tree that is sacred to Bönpos. The manicured courtyard includes a small side shrine dedicated to the Bön founder Tonpa Shenrab. Remember to visit the monastery in an anticlockwise direction.

En route between Bayi and Nyingtri look out for a group of 2500-year-old **cypress trees** (admission Y20) just north of the highway near Pagyi (Bajie) village.

The rooms at the **Telecom Guesthouse** (Dianxin Zhaodaisuo; ☎ 589 2340; dm Y20) are dark, damp and miserable; you are better off staying in Bayi. When we asked where the bathroom, was the caretaker swept her arm across the horizon. Permitless travellers should know that it's next to the PSB office.

Bönri བོན་རི་

Bönri is the Bön (p70) religion's most sacred mountain, a sprawling massif where Bön founder Tonpa Shenrab fought and defeated his arch-rival Khyabpa Lagring. Bönpo pilgrims come from all over Tibet to circumambulate the mountain in an anticlockwise direction.

The full 60km kora takes two or three days, climbing to the 4500m Bönri-la on the second day. The kora passes many sites connected to Tonpa Shenrab, as well as an ancient burial tumulus, a 9th-century stele and a cemetery for babies.

The most easily visited of the kora's Bön monasteries is **Taktse Yungdrungling Monastery**, 7km south of Nyingtri along a motorable road (take the left fork early on) and then another 1.5km up a side valley. The main monastery has a series of gods that will be unfamiliar even to visitors who are *au fait* with Buddhist iconography (was it us or is one deity holding a Rubik's cube?). The ruins behind the monastery hide some lovely ruined chörtens and water-driven prayer wheels.

The other accessible Bön site here is **Sigyal Monastery**, a two-hour hike from Nyingtri (alternatively, you can drive part of the way down the road to Yungdrungling Monastery and then hike an hour from there). Take a guide or ask villagers for directions. It's possible to hike from Nyingtri to Sigyal and then continue down to Yungdrungling, visiting both of the monasteries on a nice day trip.

NYINGTRI TO POMI (220KM)

From Nyingtri the road heads east and climbs through forest in the shadow of Bönri. A few kilometres out of town a side road turns right into a village from where it is a 3km uphill walk (along a motorable road) to **Takdrugtse Monastery**, another Bön pilgrimage site. The sanctuary contains a large central stone with 'tiger paw prints' on it. Long ago, legend says, monks decided to build a temple here after seeing an auspicious tiger *tak* (tiger) crouching on the rock.

The main road towards Pomi switchbacks up the forested hillside, past the final sections of the Bönri kora (prayer flags mark the end of the kora) and up to the 4582m **Serkhym-la** (Seji La). On a clear day there are dramatic views of shark-toothed Mt Namche Barwa (7756m) and Gyala Pelri (7151m).

About 7km past the pass, a short walkway (admission Y10) leads to fine views over the forested valley below. Get the same views 1km later, but without the tour groups or the admission fee.

Lunang ལུ་གླང་ 鲁郎

☎0894 / pop 3000 / elev 3400m

From the Serkhym-la the road descends past gorgeous alpine valleys lined with rhododendron bushes into the Rong-chu Valley and the logging town of **Lunang** (Lulang). The valley's lovely villages sport traditional wooden roofs held in place with stones, similar to those found in neighbouring Bhutan. There are fine views of Mt Kongpo Lapsen to the north. The surrounding valley is perfect for camping.

Lunang has a PSB office, a next-door bathhouse (open weekends only) and several Han Chinese restaurants, which serve up the pricey Sichuanese speciality *shiguoji* (石锅鸡; stone-pot chicken; Y80 to Y160). The local Tibetan community seems totally marginalised in Lunang.

Lulang Binguan (鲁郎宾馆; ☎589 9108; dm Y20-25, d Y140) The best place to stay is at the northern end of the main street, diagonally across from the PSB office. The plumbing is a bit iffy but rooms are comfortable and clean (avoid the ground-floor rooms).

Lulang Tese Shaguo (鲁郎特色砂锅; ☎589 3018; dm Y25) Beds in simple triple rooms are also available above this restaurant opposite the Lulang Binguan.

Lunang to Pomi

From Lunang the road descends to the riverside and after 40km passes a photogenic suspension bridge. When the tarmac ends the main landslide area begins. From here the air gets warmer, the insects get louder and you have to crane your head to see the sky between the towering cliffsides.

The next 17km to Tangmi, and the 10km after Tangmi, are loaded with treacherous bends and sheer drops. The hillsides are scarred by numerous landslides and are often hidden in subtropical fog. The plentiful hot springs around here are testament to the region's geological instability. Road washouts are common during the rainy season, so it's best to check conditions in Lunang before setting off.

Around 56km from Lunang, just past the Monpa community of **Pelung**, a prominent suspension bridge marks the start of the 40km (one-way) trek downriver to the **Great Bend of the Yarlung Tsangpo** (雅鲁藏布大拐弯; Yaluzangbu Daguaiwan). Trekkers need to pay up Y80 for an entry fee, Y400 as a refundable deposit and Y100 per day for a mandatory Monpa guide. Dormitory accommodation (Y20 to Y30) is available 30km down the track at Yumei Bridge and near the bend at Zhaqu (check with the ticket seller). Few foreigners have made this trek, though it's increasingly popular with adventurous Chinese backpackers.

If you don't have time for the three- or four-day trek, it's still worth following the trail for 40 minutes down to the foaming junction of the Rong-chu and Parlung Tsangpo Rivers. This marks the lowest part of the Sichuan–Tibet Hwy (at around 2000m) and is a fine place for a picnic.

The main highway swings north above the river junction and passes a drainpipe-straight waterfall before crossing a bridge at the spot

THE TSANGPO GORGES

Hidden deep behind the mountains south and east of the Sichuan–Tibet Hwy, the swollen Yarlung Tsangpo makes a dramatic U-turn and crashes over a series of spectacular falls, through what Chinese scientists claim is the world's deepest gorge. With 7756m Namche Barwa and 7151m Gyala Pelri towering over either side of the gorge, only 27km apart, the gorge records a depth of 5382m (almost three times the depth of the Grand Canyon), with a length of 496km. At one point the river narrows to a mere 20m, before bursting out into the Assamese plain as the vast Brahmaputra River.

The region remains one of the world's least explored areas, and is home to king cobras, leopards, red pandas, musk deer, monkeys, tigers and virgin forests.

A few Western explorers have trekked through the region (see p16), but the strategic border area is tightly monitored by the PLA and getting permits is very difficult. Chinese tour groups are allowed to trek between Pe and Gyala; the other main access point is the hike to the Big Bend from the bridge near Pelung (see above).

You may need to hurry. While the Chinese government publicly insists otherwise, Beijing reportedly has plans to build a huge hydroelectric station on the river, a move that would have significant environmental, social and political consequences for Tibet, China, India and Bangladesh.

where the Yi'ong Tsangpo joins the valley. A poor-quality side road heads 23km northwest up to the **Yigong-tso** (elevation 2150m), a stunning but hard-to-reach lake that was created by a landslide in 1900. Tea is produced in this area.

Just 3km past the junction, **Tangmi** (通麦; Tongmai) has a couple of simple but decent guesthouse-restaurants, including the **Guanghui Jiudian** (光辉酒店; ☎ 0894-542 3320; dm Y20-25). As you enter town from the west look for the **monument** dedicated to a group of road builders who were trapped in a mudslide in August 1969 – 10 died trying to drag their truck from the mire.

As the tarmac main road heads up the Parlung Tsangpo Valley, pine trees and settlements return and the scenery becomes increasingly spectacular. Princess Wencheng is said to have stayed in the district, known as Powo, during her journey to Lhasa in the 7th century to meet her new husband King Songtsen Gampo.

Some 64km from Tangmi is the 800-year-old **Bakhar Monastery** (also called Orgyen Sanga Chöling; 2680m), stunningly located on a grassy knoll above the river, overlooked by the spiky Kangmi mountain range. There is no guesthouse here, but if you have a tent the monks will point out a decent camping site. There's also excellent riverside camping 8km west of the monastery, at the foot of a forested knoll.

From the monastery it's just 35km along a good-condition road to Pomi, so there is no need to rush out of here. If you are on a hired Land Cruiser tour of Kham, this is one place to abandon the car for a while and explore the surrounds on foot.

From Lunang to Pomi is 160km.

POMI སྤོ་ཡུལ་

☎ 0894 / pop 11,000 / elev 2740m

Formerly called Tramo, this bustling county capital has well-stocked shops and several hotels and restaurants, making it the logical place to spend the night. The town itself is an eyesore but the surrounding scenery is stupendous and there is plenty of scope for exploring the nearby valleys, if you have enough time.

Information

Yuandatou Linyu (袁大头淋浴; shower Y5; 8am-midnight) Bathhouse next to the Jiaotong Lüguan.

Kuaile Wangba (快乐网吧; per hr Y5; 24hr) Internet café in a courtyard by the Xinhua Bookstore, near the central square.

Sights

Around 6km west of Pomi, on the opposite bank of the river, is the tranquil **Dodung Monastery**, set on a pine-clad hill overlooking the valley. The main prayer hall includes, to the right, a collection of *cham* (dance) masks and a flaccid snake (it's a fake). Upstairs are murals depicting the life story of two forms of Gesar, as well as Guru Rinpoche and Tsepame (Amitayus). The monastery is a branch of Chayab Monastery (see p262) and so there are some photos of the sixth Taksam Rinpoche. Several lovely mani *lhakhangs* (buildings holding prayer wheels) make up the rest of the lovely complex.

To reach the monastery from Pomi, cross the road bridge over the Parlung Tsangpo, opposite the Jiaotong Lüguan and take the right fork. A dirt road continues up the back of the hill into the monastery compound. A three-wheel rickshaw from Pomi costs around Y10.

Sleeping & Eating

Jiaotong Lüguan (交通旅馆; ☎ 542 2798; dm Y20, s/d without bathroom Y30/40, d with bathroom Y80-128) Not to be confused with the larger nearby hotel of the same name, this recently renovated place has a wide range of rooms and will often let you pay per bed in the rooms with bathroom, which is a good deal. It is above some shops opposite the bridge.

Jiaotong Dajiudian (交通大酒店; Traffic Hotel; ☎ 542 3040; d Y60-80, tr Y80, d with bathroom Y280, discounted to Y120) A decent option, the rooms with private bathrooms have hot water in the evenings. It is located at the west end of town, close to the bridge to Dodung Monastery.

Zhongxing Binguan (众兴宾馆; ☎ 542 3338; Zhamucun Lu; d/tr Y288/368, discounted to Y200/260;) Amazingly plush considering where you are, the spacious rooms are carpeted and have hot-water Western-style bathrooms. It's up the side street that branches north in the centre of town.

There are a couple of well-stocked supermarkets in the centre of town, as well as dozens of simple Sichuanese restaurants.

Getting There & Away

The bus station at the western end of town has buses every other day to Chamdo (Y160)

TIBET'S HIDDEN LANDS

The lotus-shaped Pemako region south of Pomi is a *beyul* (or *pelyul*), one of 16 'hidden lands' scattered throughout the Himalaya that were rendered invisible by Guru Rinpoche to provide hidden retreats in times of danger. Guidebooks on how to get to the hidden lands were written by Guru Rinpoche as *terma* (concealed teachings), to be rediscovered at a suitable time (in this case it was the 17th century) by *terton* (treasure seekers).

Spiritual realisation is said to be easily attained in such places, and, in some cases, the *beyul* also act as sanctuaries providing protection in times of war, religious persecution or famine. Many Khampas fled to Pemako when the Chinese invaded eastern Tibet in the 1950s.

or Chengdu (Y450). A ride to Pasho on the former costs Y80. Share jeeps parked by the main square run to Yigong (per seat Y100, 9am) and Bayi (per seat Y100), but can be chartered for other destinations.

POMI TO RAWOK (131KM)

From Pomi the road winds through pine forests in the shadow of craggy peaks until emerging at the spectacular Sundzom Valley, surrounded by snow-covered mountains. The valley's centrepiece is the small Sundzom Temple (43km east of Pomi), a 15th-century monastery that was home to 200 monks before the Cultural Revolution.

The condition of the road deteriorates as it climbs from Sundzom up the Parlung Tsangpo Valley. There are several stunning side valleys on this high alpine route, whose glaciers tumble down almost to the roadside. You soon get your first magical views of the blue waters and sandy beaches of Ngan-tso (both Rawok-tso and Ngan-tso are commonly referred to as Rawok-tso). There are wonderful camping and picnicking spots by the lake.

RAWOK ར་འོག 然乌

☎ 0895 / pop 2900 / elev 3880m

Rawok has the ramshackle and temporary feel of a frontier outpost, but without the charm. The short main drag is strewn with guesthouses and noodle joints, not to mention the occasional body part (we found a human skull lying ignored in the gutter a few years back). Still, the surrounding scenery is spectacular and there are opportunities for walking to the nearby lakes. Rawok is an increasingly popular stopover with Chinese overlanders, so get here early to score a hotel bed.

The old town is worth a wander. A road leads into the warren from the north end of the Rawok strip. From here you can work your way through to the large chörten, mani wall and small temple overlooking the lake in the southeast of town. The surrounding fields are full of wooden platforms for drying barley.

Even if you're not bound for Lhegu Glacier (see below), it's worth heading north of town and taking the side road southeast for around 6km to the second lake, Rawok-tso. The views here are excellent and it's a great place for a picnic. It's a popular location for Chinese tourists, who come to watch the sunrise.

Sleeping & Eating

Rawok is the logical place to stay en route between Pomi and Pasho. If the weather is clear, the best option is to camp around either of the two lakes. Apart from the places mentioned here, most of the restaurants offer basic plywood rooms upstairs.

Government Guesthouse (政府宾馆; Zhengfu Binguan; ☎ 456 2666; d Y80, tr without bathroom Y50; 💻) The pricier rooms here come with a bathroom but no shower. It's the only place in town with internet access.

Ranwu Binguan (然乌宾馆; r Y160; 🕑) Wooden floors, decent beds and electric blankets here, but it's still overpriced, especially as the shared squat toilets are filthy.

Rawok has lots of simple places to eat. A form of culinary apartheid exists, with the Chinese restaurants on the left-hand side of the road and the Tibetan restaurants on the right.

Getting There & Away

There's no public transport to Rawok, so if you haven't organised a tour you'll have to hitch. Traffic is meagre at best.

Rawok is 131km from Pomi and 92km from Pasho.

AROUND RAWOK

The most popular excursion from Rawok is to the **Lhegu Glacier** (来古冰川; Laigu Binchuan; admission Y20, parking Y10), 31km from Rawok. It's so popular, in fact, that you might find yourself racing a convoy of Beijing tourists. The main draw is the stunning scenery, some of the best along the entire southern road. The glacier itself is impressive, especially because it tumbles into a picturesque lake, but most of the ice flow is hidden by the mountain to the north, Retob Kangri (Kangri Karpo). To get full views you'll have to cross a stream and hike along the moraine for an hour or so.

To get to the glacier from Rawok, follow the road east to Rawok-tso, take the right fork 16km from Rawok and follow this rough dirt road for another 15km. From the car park it's a 20-minute walk up to views of the glacier, or ride a horse for Y20. With an early start it's possible to visit the glacier and then continue on to Pasho in the afternoon.

The left branch continues into the border region of Dzayul (Zayu), just 20km from Myanmar (Burma). Foreigners are not allowed on this road.

RAWOK TO PASHO (90KM)

From Rawok the road climbs north past nomads' camps and a small azure lake to the Ngajuk-la (Anju-la; 4462m), which marks a dramatic step up from the subtropical Parlung Tsangpo Valley onto the arid high plateau. The pass also marks the watershed between the waters of the Brahmaputra, flowing into India, and the Salween, flowing into Southeast Asia.

Around 13km from the pass it's worth detouring 2km west to the lovely village of Dzongsar, which has the small Sangha Lhakhang (recognisable by the stuffed sheep outside) and the fort-like ruins of Ramo Monastery. This is a very friendly village and you'll need to allocate extra time for yak-butter tea breaks with the locals. A 20-minute walk to the west leads to the active Lhorong Monastery. Be on the look out for dogs here. On the hillside further west is the ruined Yarlo Monastery.

Back on the main road, some 26km later look for the ruined *dzong* (fort) above the village of Tashitse. The traditional whitewashed villages along this section are particularly charming. As the road descends, the landscape changes colour from arid khakis to rocky purples and reds, reminiscent of Utah or Arizona.

PASHO དཔའ་ཤོད་ 八宿

☎ 0895 / pop 3700 / elev 3270m

Pasho (Basu), formerly known as Pema (Baima), is a pleasant modern town that makes for a good overnight stop.

Information

Wangyuan Wangba (网缘网吧; per hr Y3; ⌚ 24 hr) Internet café down a side street opposite the Government Hotel.

Sights & Activities

On the northwestern outskirts of the town is **Neru Monastery**, a Gelugpa monastery that's worth a visit if you have a couple of spare hours. The renovated central chapel holds the throne of the Pakhpala, a religious leader based in Chamdo, whose current incarnation is a government minister. It was the current Pakhpala who paid for the restoration of Neru Monastery. To the right of the main chapel is the funeral chörten of the monastery's last *trulku* (reincarnated lama) and the back room has a large seated Jampa (Maitreya) statue made by craftsmen from Chamdo. The top floor contains a *gönkhang* (protector chapel) loaded with old Khampa weaponry. The monastery is a 25-minute walk from the centre of town, across a pedestrian bridge, or you can drive here via the sturdier bridge west of town.

About 4km east of town, beside the main highway, is **Dola Monastery**. The older lower chapel is surrounded by chörtens and ancient yak-hide prayer wheels and is a great place to meet local pilgrims. A kora leads up the mountainside to a plateau and then descends west to Pasho town, with fine views of the arid valley. The leisurely half-day kora is chock-a-block with jovial pilgrims during the Saga Dawa festival (p319).

Sleeping & Eating

Fukang Lüguan (富康旅馆; ☎ 456 2581; dm Y15-20, d Y50) The choice here is between ground-floor quads or quieter upper-floor doubles that come with carpet and sofa. Either way this is the best budget bet. The Tibetan matriarch that runs the place is helpful and there's a public shower block in the front courtyard (Y5; open 8.30am to 11pm). The shared toilets are fukang awful.

Jiaotong Binguan (交通宾馆; Traffic Hotel; ☎ 465 2235; dm Y20-30, s Y40, d with bathroom Y160) There's a wide range of reasonably clean rooms on offer here at the bus station hotel in the western end of town. It's not the quietest option but it's fine if you arrive late or depart early on the bus. There's a public shower (Y5) out on the main street; turn right as you leave the hotel.

There are plenty of restaurants – try the decent **Piaoxiang Fandian** (飘香饭店), opposite the Jiaotong Binguan.

Huashun Supermarket (化顺连锁超市; 8.30am-midnight) In between the two main hotels, this supermarket has the best range of goods, from muffins to M&Ms.

Getting There & Away

The bus station has daily buses to Chamdo (Y80) at 8am. Buses headed to Markham (Y160 to Y180), Zhongdian (Y300) and Lhasa (Y240) from elsewhere in Tibet overnight in Pasho and may have empty seats. Private minibuses run to Pomi (Y100 per seat) when full from outside the bus station. A one-way charter to Rawok costs around Y150.

PASHO TO CHAMDO (270KM)

From Pasho the road east passes picturesque villages and chörtens reminiscent of those in Ladakh. The stretch of road 32km from Pasho is particularly susceptible to landslides, so check on road conditions before setting off. From here a bridge leads across the Ngul-chu (Nu Jiang, or Salween River) and disappears into a short tunnel (look for the ancient pilgrim track on the other side of the river as you exit). The road leaves the Salween Valley and starts an epic series of 72 switchbacks up to the 4618m **Zar Gama-la** (Yala Shankou), making this the highest single altitude gain of any motorable pass in Tibet.

From the pass the now paved road descends 13km to the Pomda crossroads (邦达; Bangda; elevation 4390m), where the southern Sichuan–Tibet Hwy branches off to Markham (p279). There are several good restaurants and good guesthouses here, including the **Bangda Xueyue Dajiudian** (邦达雪越大酒店; ☎ 0895-462 2416; dm Y30-35, s/d Y50/80) and **High Plateau Snowlion Hotel** (高原雪狮宾馆; Gaoyuan Xueshi Binguan; ☎ 0895-499 6166; d/tr Y50/60). Buses to Markham, Pasho, Bayi and Chamdo pass through here between 11am and noon. The distance between Pasho and Pomda is 97km.

Five kilometres from the crossroads lies the lovely village and monastery of Pomda, set at the edge of a wide valley. **Pomda Monastery** dates back 360 years but was destroyed in 1959 and rebuilt between 1984 and 1988. It is now home to 90 monks. The main entry hallway of the assembly hall has excellent murals depicting monastic dress codes and the *gelong* examination that all monks must pass. There is also a protector chapel and a debating courtyard, as well as a huge mani wall and mani *lhakhang* (prayer-wheel chapel).

Another 12km brings you to **Kyidrup Monastery**, home to seven monks and two nuns. A further 10km from here a bridge gives access to the yellow-painted and rather derelict Shongba Guen Tashi Chöling Monastery. It is visible from the highway, across a glorious grassy plain; a pleasant walk there takes about 25 minutes.

Chamdo airport is another 20km further north, from where it's still 130km to Chamdo town. There's a hotel at the airport (see p260). At over 4300m, this is reckoned to be world's highest civilian airport.

Around 6km north of the airport is a turn-off onto a dirt road that heads 7km to the remote and welcoming **Yushig Monastery**, home to 50 Kagyupa monks, and three *trulkus* (reincarnated lamas), one of whom is considered a manifestation of Rechungpa, a disciple of Milarepa (see p176). The main hall contains images of Sakyamuni, Marpa and Milarepa. The spirited debating that takes place here in the afternoons sounds more like a pub brawl than a theological discussion! The turn-off for the monastery is to the left (west) about 100m before the bridge. The wide plain here supports large herds of grazing yaks.

Some 16km north of the airport is the turn-off west for Lhorong (Luolong). This road follows the former caravan trail to Lhasa. Soon the main road rises to the 4572m Lang-la, the watershed between the Salween and Mekong drainages, and then descends dramatically 29km, past a hot-springs complex, to **Kyitang** (吉塘; Jitang) village. **Tra'e Monastery**, on the southeastern edge of the village, is worth a look. The kora around the ancient-feeling old chapel is lined with animal skulls. A new assembly hall is under construction next door. The turn-off for the 10-minute walk to the monastery is marked by a huge new white chörten. The barracks-style **Jixiang Binguan** (吉祥宾馆; dm Y15) at the north end of town offers basic rooms and pit toilets in an emergency. The Tibetan-style restaurant opposite is worth a look, if only for its interesting architecture. Kyitang is 65km from Chamdo.

Travelling north from Kyitang, you cross a ridge over the 3465m Nya-la to be met with views of the chocolate-coloured Dza-chu

(Lancang Jiang), or Mekong River. The road now parallels the Mekong, passing a Willy Wonka–esque landscape of spearmint green fields, raspberry purple hills and chocolate streams. Around 7km after the pass is a turn-off leading 42km southeast along a dirt track to **Drayab** (察雅; Chaya) and the **Endun Monastery**. The approach to Chamdo is marked by the mirage-like appearance of the Snow Beer brewery, 2km before town.

CHAMDO ཆབ་མདོ་ 昌都

☎ 0895 / pop 80,000 / elev 3300m

Chamdo (literally meaning 'river confluence'; Changdu in Chinese), at the strategic river junction of the Dza-chu and the Ngon-chu, is a surprisingly pleasant town. It is dominated by the hilltop Galden Jampaling Monastery, below which huddles the tiny Tibetan old town and a much larger, sprawling Chinese new town. Over 1000km from Lhasa and 1250km from Chengdu, the town is the major transport, administrative and trade centre of the Kham region. If you are on a long loop of eastern Tibet, this is the logical place to take a day off from the constant travel.

Chamdo has had a troubled relationship with nearby China. The Chinese warlord Zhao Erfeng (the 'Butcher of Kham') captured Chamdo in 1909 and ruled the region until the Tibetans recaptured it in 1917. Chamdo fell to communist troops in 1950 (see below).

Information

There is nowhere to change money in Chamdo.

Bentang Wangba (per hr Y3.5; 24hr) One of two internet bars across from each other in heart of the pedestrian market.

China Post (Zhongguo Youzheng; Zhong Lu; 9am-7.30pm)

China Telecom (Zhongguo Dianxin; Changdu Xilu; 10am-9pm) Sells phonecards.

Jihua Wangluo (per hr Y3.5; 24hr) Internet café near the Jinchuan Binguan.

Laundry (Jiejieshi Ganxidian; 9.30am-10.30pm) Dry cleaners in the pedestrian market that will wash clothes for Y3 Y4 per piece.

PSB (Gong'anju; ☎ 482 4794; Changdu Xilu; 9am-12.30pm & 3-6.30pm Mon-Fri) Thirty-day visa extensions are possible, provided you have travel permits to be in Chamdo.

Shengjie Bathhouse (Shengjie Linshi; Binjiang Lu; shower Y5, bath Y20; 9am-midnight)

Sights

GALDEN JAMPALING MONASTERY

དགའ་ལྡན་བྱམས་པ་གླིང་དགོན་ 强巴林寺

This active hilltop monastery (Qiangbalin Si) of around 1000 monks dominates Chamdo.

THE FALL OF CHAMDO

In spring 1950, Chamdo was in real trouble. Although there were still pockets of resistance at Derge and Markham, the communist Chinese had taken control of most of Kham without even a fight. Chinese armies were moving in on Tibet from Xinjiang and Xikang (now Sichuan) provinces in a strategy masterminded by, among others, Deng Xiaoping.

The first skirmish between Chinese and Tibetan troops took place in May 1950 when the People's Liberation Army (PLA) attacked Dengo on the Dri-chu (Yangzi River). Then on 7 October 1950 the PLA moved in earnest, as 40,000 troops crossed the Dri-chu and attacked Chamdo from three directions: Jyekundo to the north, Derge to the east and Markham to the south.

As panic swept through Chamdo, the city responded to the military threat in characteristic Tibetan fashion – a frenzy of prayer and religious ritual. When the local Tibetan leader radioed the Tibetan government in Lhasa to warn of the Chinese invasion, he was coolly told that the government members couldn't be disturbed because they were 'on a picnic'. To this the Chamdo radio operator is said to have replied *'skyag pa'i gling kha!'*, or 'shit the picnic!'. It was to be the last ever communication between the Chamdo and Lhasa branches of the Tibetan government.

The city was evacuated (with the Chamdo government commandeering most of the town's horses) but the PLA was one step ahead. Chinese leaders know that speed is of the essence (the Chinese described the military operation as 'like a tiger trying to catch a fly') and had already cut the Tibetans off by taking Riwoche. The Tibetans surrendered without a shot on 19 October. The Tibetan troops were disarmed, given lectures on the benefits of socialism, and then given money and sent home. It was the beginning of the end of an independent Tibet.

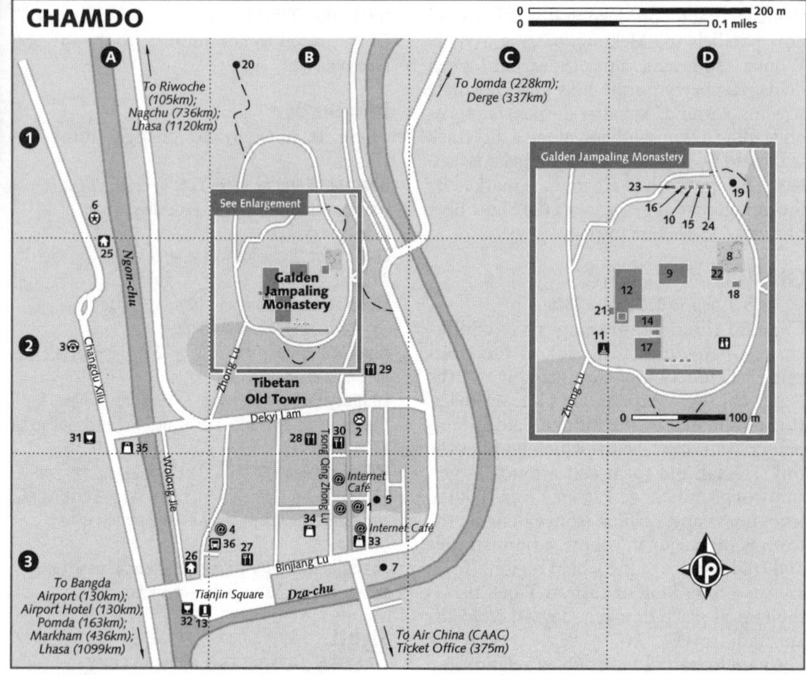

The monastery was founded in 1444 by Jangsem Sherab Zangpo, a disciple of Tsongkhapa. It was destroyed in 1912 and then rebuilt in 1917, after the Tibetan army retook Chamdo.

Pilgrims circumambulate the exterior of the walled compound in the mornings and it's worth following them on at least one circuit. Behind the monastery, to the north of town, trails lead up to a sky-burial site and views over the city. The steep paved road up to the east gate is one of the town's most interesting, lined with Tibetan teahouses, tailors and prayer-wheel repair workshops.

The first building on the right is the impressive **Tsenyi Lhakhang** (Dialectic College), behind which is a debating courtyard. Just to the left of the college is a side entrance; go in here, take an immediate left up the stairs and then turn right at the top. This leads to a *gönkhang* (protector chapel) packed with guns, knives and pistols – echoes of the region's warrior past.

Back outside, the monastery's enormous **kitchen** is well worth a look, but only men can enter.

The main **dukhang** (assembly hall) is particularly impressive, especially when it is packed with hundreds of murmuring monks. This is probably the largest assembly of monks you will see in Tibet these days, outside festival times. The glorious inner sanctum is dominated by Sakyamuni, Tsongkhapa and Atisha. The statue second to the left is the Pakhpala, the line of religious leaders that head the monastery. The bearded statue in the far right is of the monastery's founder.

In the main monastery courtyard is the *gönkhang,* lined with fantastic murals and statues of protector gods, along with lots of old armour. The Jamkhang to the south holds a large new statue of Jampa (Maitreya).

Behind the *gönkhang* is the **former residence of the Pakhpala**, whose 11th reincarnation currently works for the Tibetan government in Lhasa. The exit in the southwest corner leads to the **Tsenkhang** (earth spirit house), hidden around the back of the interior courtyard, with a fantastic collection of protectors strung up on a series of pillars like a crack squad of gravity-defying martial arts warriors. Look also for the skeleton and monkey outfits worn

INFORMATION
Bentang Wangba 奔腾网吧 ... 1 B3
China Post 中国邮政 ... 2 B2
China Telecom 中国电信 ... 3 A2
Jihua Wangluo 嘉华网络 ... 4 B3
Laundry 佳洁士干洗店 ... 5 B3
PSB 公安局 ... 6 A1
Shengjie Bathhouse 圣洁淋室 ... 7 B3

SIGHTS & ACTIVITIES
Debating Courtyard ... 8 D2
Dukhang (Assembly Hall) ... 9 D2
Dukhor (Kalachakra) Tratsang ... 10 D1
Eight Chörtens ... 11 C2
Former Residence of the Phakhpala ... 12 D2
Golden Eagle Statue ... 13 A3
Gönkhang (Protector Chapel) ... 14 D2
Guhyasamaja Tratsang ... 15 D1
Hevajra Tratsang ... 16 D1
Jamkhang ... 17 D2
Kitchen ... 18 D2
Prayer Flags ... 19 D1
Sky Burial Site ... 20 B1
Tsenkhang ... 21 C2
Tsenyi Lhakhang ... 22 D2
Vairocana (Namse) Tratsang ... 23 D1
Yamantaka Tratsang ... 24 D1

SLEEPING
Chamdo Hotel 昌都饭店 ... 25 A2
Jinchuan Binguan 金川宾馆 ... 26 A3
Post Hotel 邮政宾馆 ... (see 2)

EATING
Chinese Restaurants ... 27 B3
Fruit Stalls ... 28 B2
Shaguo Stalls 沙锅小吃店 ... 29 B2
Vegetable Market 中路菜市场 ... 30 B2

DRINKING
Come In Bar 来吧 ... 31 A2
Friendship Food Plaza 友谊美食广场 ... 32 A3

SHOPPING
Kodak Express 柯达快速彩色 ... 33 B3
One Polar Outdoor Shop 极地户外用品 ... 34 B3
Supermarket ... (see 26)
Toread 探路者 ... 35 A2

TRANSPORT
Bus Station 客运站 ... 36 B3

during cham dances, as well as a stuffed bear. Around the back is a small tsampa (roasted barley) mill.

Sleeping

Chamdo has lots of cheap hostels, but the PSB doesn't allow foreigners to stay in them.

Post Hotel (Youzheng Binguan; ☎ 484 4777; Changqing Jie; d Y50, d with bathroom Y80-120) This place, smack in the centre of town, offers cheap rooms with hot-water bathrooms but you'll pay for your cheap rates with broken fixtures and endlessly flushing toilets. The double rooms with toilet but no shower (Y50) are perhaps the best value.

Jinchuan Binguan (☎ 484 4998; Wolong Jie; d/q Y280/480, discounted to Y196/294) The four-bed interconnected rooms (联通房; *liantong fang*) here are a particularly good deal for Land Cruiser groups and come with two hot-water bathrooms. Rooms are arranged around a smoke-filled mahjong hall but it closes at 9pm. The carpets are a mosaic of cigarette burns.

Chamdo Hotel (Changdu Fandian; ☎ 482 5998; 22 Changdu Xilu; d Y380-480, discounted to Y300-380) Rooms at this three-star place are overpriced though comfortable. The cheaper rooms are small but have cave-like bathrooms. Hot water is available 24 hours.

Eating

There are several good cheap Chinese restaurants 70m east of the Jinchuan Binguan, and there's a collection of tasty shaguo stalls on the north side of the square in front of the Post Hotel (a *shaguo* is a boiling claypot soup or noodle dish).

There are good fruit stalls near the entrance to the large covered vegetable market, opposite the post office.

Drinking

Friendship Food Plaza (Youyi Meishi Guangchang; beer Y6-15, mains Y20-58) The open-air riverside seating here is very pleasant and it's a great place to people watch over a beer, though the Western food in particular is disappointing.

Come In Bar (Laiba; Changdu Xilu; 1pm-5am) A cosy place for a beer, either by the window or in the nooks upstairs. It's quiet in the afternoon and open late.

Shopping

The well-stocked **supermarket** (Wolong Jie) on the ground floor of the Jinchuan Binguan has items such as batteries, and normal foodstuffs.

Outdoor shops like **One Polar Outdoor Shop** (Jidi Huwai Yongpin; Pedestrian Market) and **Toread** (Tanluzhe; Changdu Xilu) offer down vests, camping gas canisters, sleeping bags and the like.

Kodak Express (Binjiang Lu; 10am-10pm) Burns digital photos onto a CD for Y10.

Getting There & Away

AIR

Air China operates a weekly flight (currently Monday) to Lhasa (Y930) and four flights a week to Chengdu (Y930). All are morning flights. The **ticket office** (中国民航售票处; Zhongguo Minhang Shoupiaochu; ☎ 482 1004; 9.30-11.30am) is 500m south of the Dza-chu River. Staff will sell you a ticket without checking for permits but you might still be asked for them at the airport when you check in.

Bangda (Pomda) airport is 130km south of Chamdo. Airport buses (Y40) depart from opposite the CAAC office at 3pm the day before flights, requiring an overnight stay at the extremely crummy **Airport Hotel** (邦达机场宾馆; Bangda Jichang Binguan; ☎ 0895-482 8228; dm/d/ste Y40/160/360). A taxi from Chamdo costs around Y200 and takes two hours.

BUS

Purchasing bus tickets at the **Chamdo Bus Station** (☎ 482 7351) is straightforward, though the staff may rat you up to the PSB if you don't have a permit. There are daily buses to Lhasa (Y310), overnighting in Pasho and Bayi en route. Buses to Bayi (Y220, two days) run every other day. There are also daily buses to Markham (Y130), Dzogang (Y65), Pasho (Y90), Jomda (Y70), Tengchen (Y100) and Riwoche (Y50). Buses to Nagchu (Y240, three days) run on Monday, Wednesday and Friday, overnighting in Tengchen and Sok en route.

Sleeper buses operate nonstop to Chengdu (Y450, 60 hours) every other day. Buses to Zhongdian (Y316, via Deqin) are more infrequent.

Getting Around

Taxis cost a flat Y5 to anywhere in town.

CHAMDO TO RIWOCHE (110KM)

The northern highway to Nagchu passes a weir 6km outside Chamdo and then crosses the river near a series of chörtens and a large mani *lhakhang*. Kiss the tarmac a fond farewell here. Soon the road leaves the Dza-chu (Mekong River) and swings south, eventually climbing past the stunningly located **Dragu (or Trugu) Monastery** (朱吉寺; Zhuji Si) perched on a grassy plateau at around 4200m and backed by granite bluffs and snow-capped peaks. The 50 or so monks are friendly and will point out the tiger and snow leopard pelts in the upper protector chapel. A huge thangka is unfurled on a platform outside the monastery gate during the Losar festival.

To drive to the monastery, take the steep 3km dirt road to the right just after some houses, before kilometre marker 1331, and about 38km past Chamdo. The best views of the monastery are actually from the main road.

The main road continues to climb for 17km through sections of 1500-year-old juniper forest to cross the 4612m Chabi-la (Zhutong-la), before making a long descent past herders' huts into a lovely alpine valley. About 88km past Chamdo, next to the road near Reshe village, is the restored **Dzonglho Monastery** (宗洛兴旺林寺; Zongluo Xingwanglin Si) If you fancy a walk, a suspension bridge leads across the river to the ruins of the original monastery, at the base of a bluff with the ruins of the old *dzong* atop it.

From Reshe, the road leads past several lovely chörtens and newly constructed villages for 22km to Riwoche town.

RIWOCHE རི་བོ་ཆེ 类乌齐县

☎ 0895 / pop 2800 / elev 3800m

It's important to realise early on that there are two places called Riwoche: Riwoche town (also known as Ratsaka and Leiwuqi), which is the *xian* (country capital) on the main highway, and the *zhen* (village) of Riwoche 26km northwest, which is home to the *tsuglhakhang* (literally 'grand temple'). Riwoche town is of little interest, but makes a decent base from which to visit the Riwoche Tsuglhakhang.

FLORA OR FAUNA?

In early summer (May and June) you will see nomads and entrepreneurs camped in the high passes of eastern Tibet, digging for a strange root known as *yartsa gunbu (Cordiceps sinensis)* that locals say is half-vegetable, half-caterpillar. It is actually a fusion of a caterpillar and the parasitic fungus that mummifies it. The Chinese name for the root is *dongchong xiacao* (冬虫夏草; 'winter-worm, summer-grass'), a direct translation of the Tibet name. The root is used in Tibetan and Chinese medicine as an aphrodisiac and tonic similar to ginseng and fetches anywhere from Y3000 to Y40,000 per kilo, making it one of the most expensive commodities in Tibet. The business is most lucrative in Tengchen county, where amazingly it accounts for more than 60% of the local GDP. Entire tent villages spring up on the grasslands during harvest time, equipped with restaurants and shops, and it's not unusual for fights to erupt between the local communities and outside speculators.

An interesting **nunnery workshop** in the southeastern suburbs manufactures prayer wheels and chörten spires. It's connected to the large Kaji Nunnery, 15km from Riwoche, some of whose 600 nuns you'll see wandering around town. The workshop is near the faux-Tibetan style 'cultural activities centre'.

Information

Feixiang Internet bar (飞翔网吧; Feixiang wangba; per hr Y4; 9am-midnight) In the square behind the Sunshine Hotel.

Meijie Yushi (美洁浴室; 9am-10pm, shower Y5) Public bathhouse in the same square

Sleeping

Zigong Binguan (自贡宾馆; s/d/tr Y40/40/54) This simple but clean place in the centre of town is the best of several cheapies. Rooms are small but clean, though the windowless single rooms are worth avoiding.

Dashan Binguan (大山宾馆; 450 4433; d/ste Y188/380, discounts of 30%) Spacious rooms, wooden floors, electric blankets and a hot shower here, but don't drop the soap in the squat toilet directly below it. It's clean and quiet, opposite the central government offices.

Sunshine Hotel (阳光酒店; Yangguan Jiudian; 450 9004;) This will be the best hotel in town when the current round of renovations finish.

Getting There & Away

One bus leaves Riwoche daily around 8am for Chamdo (Y50). There's no public transport between Riwoche town and the *tsuglhakhang* (great temple, 26km, 40 minutes).

Land Cruisers leave when full from Riwoche for the six-hour drive north to the former Tibetan kingdom of Nangchen (per seat Y100; 200km), across the border in Qinghai province, from where you can continue to Jyekundo (Yushu). The second half of the journey is unpaved and can be treacherous after heavy rain. It's an adventurous trip and well worth a try if you're properly prepared, but it would be wise to come with a back-up plan. See p337 for more on this route.

RIWOCHE TSUGLHAKHANG

རི་བོ་ཆེ་གཙུག་ལག་ཁང་ 类乌齐寺

From the western edge of Riwoche town a road branches northwest off the main highway, crosses the river and follows a wonderful new paved road north. A couple of kilometres before Riwoche village the road crests a ridge and you get your first views of the amazing golden-roofed *tsuglhakhang*.

Founded in 1276 by Sangye On, who relocated to Kham after the death of his master Sangye Yarjon (1203–72), the third leader of the Talung order, Riwoche started as an offshoot of Talung Monastery in Ü. Eventually it grew to eclipse its parent monastery and it now ranks as one of Tibet's most impressive monasteries. It is still the more vibrant of the two, retains the characteristic red, white and black vertical stripes of the Talung school, and is home to 305 monks.

Information

To be allowed into the main ground-floor hall you must first get permission from the village leader (乡政府领导; Xiang Zhengfu Lingdao) at the government compound, 300m south of the Tsuglhakhang. To see all three main floors you need to track down three different keys, from three different monks, which can take some time. It helps to have Riwoche Tsuglhakhang or at least Riwoche Zhen on your permit, rather than just 'Riwoche'.

The Temple

The huge *tsuglhakhang* towers over Riwoche village, dwarfing the medieval-looking pilgrims who circumambulate the massive structure. You enter through huge 20m doors into a breathtaking open inner courtyard. Photos are not allowed in the chapels.

The eye is immediately drawn to the huge statues that tower out of the half-light. The entry is flanked on the left by Jampa (Maitreya) and eight chörtens, and on the right by two dramatic protector masks that peer down at you from a high pillar. The left wall has statues of Tsepame (Amitayus), Guru Rinpoche (one peaceful and one smaller wrathful variety with a scorpion in his hand) and Sakyamuni. The west wall has the funerary chörten of a local rinpoche, three Sakyamunis, two abbots and the two early Talung lamas – Sangye Yarjon on the right and Sangye On to the left. The altars are fronted by elephant tusks and long banners made of petals. Along the right wall is a white statue of Namse (Vairocana) in front of a mandala, a gold chörten, a seated Jampa (Maitreya), Matrö Bodhisattva, Sakyamuni Buddha and finally two 1000-armed statues of Chenresig (Avalokiteshvara).

The middle floor is bare but has some fine murals and statues of Guru Rinpoche, a 1000-armed Chenresig (Avalokiteshvara) and Sakyamuni.

The top floor is where the real gems are kept. The most precious items are behind a locked grill, and include some beautiful antique statues and ancient saddles that the caretaker claims belonged to Gesar of Ling and his general. Look for the very old statue of Dorje Chang (Vajradhara), with the slender waist. The room is locked for security reasons, so you'll have to ask nicely to get in.

Monks' quarters lie to the north. It's worth walking up the hillside a little to get overviews of the site.

RIWOCHE TO TENGCHEN (148KM)

Back at Riwoche town the main highway west swings to the south and starts to climb, reaching **Chayab (Taksam or Dashang) Monastery** after 17km. This small but very charming Nyingma-school monastery is surrounded by over 100 chörtens, thousands of mani stones and a short kora. The design of the main chapel is similar to that of Lamaling Temple (p250) but on a much smaller scale. Look for a photo of the current Taksam Rinpoche, the reincarnation of Taksam Nuden Dorje, an 18th-century *terton* (treasure finder) who founded the monastery (and whose portrait is painted in the right-hand corner of the chapel). There are good camping sites nearby.

A further 8km along the highway, past the village of Pakhsa (Kamaduo), look for the ruins of Sibta Dzong to the left, above the village of Mardo. After another 4km, the road passes a striking white marble mountain before it crests the 4680m Seya-la (also known as the Chonyi-la or Dzekri-la). During the summer many nomads camp around here, employed in the lucrative search for medicinal roots (see p260).

The road descends through a series of red-rock gorges until, 95km from Riwoche, you reach **Jinkar Monastery** (金卡寺; Jinka Si), a small Gelugpa monastery of about 30 monks. To visit the monastery take the road to the left, just before the bridge. The kitchen and metal workshop to the side of the main assembly hall are particularly worth visiting.

From the western end of the monastery a path leads for about five minutes past a chörten and through barley fields, down to the remarkable **Rotung Monastery**, a tiny monastery of 40 monks surrounded by tens of thousands of votive-carved mani stones. Pilgrims circle the monastery from dawn to dusk.

About 13km past Rotung, easily visible above the road to the west, is **Nyamaling Monastery**. The short walk to this Gelugpa monastery affords excellent views of the valley.

If you've got time, one of the most amazing sites in the area is **Tsedru Monastery** (孜珠寺; Zizhu Si; 4474m), considered to be Tibet's largest and oldest Bön monastery. The monastery location, strung out along a ridgeline below a series of natural cliffs and caves is one of the most fantastical you can imagine. Once you've visited the main chapels (there's debating in the afternoon), walk up to the large natural arch to the left, where ancient wooden ladders lead up the cliff-face to a precarious ridgetop shrine that features a stone footprint of the monastery's founder inlaid in the floor. If you have time, it's also worth walking clockwise around the base of Ngon Ri, the mountain to the east. When you reach a small chapel on the south side climb the kora path to the peak for amazing views. The skies around the cliffs are full of soaring eagles and vultures, attracted by the sky-burial site in the valley below.

To get to Tsedru, take the turn-off by a village 6km past the village of Lamutang, cross the bridge, enter a gorge and take the dirt road that branches left. The incredible road switchbacks for 10km, gaining almost 1000m. You might not make it if it's been raining recently. All told, it's a half-day, 25km detour from the main road.

Back on the main road, keep your eyes open for more monasteries dotted along the next 30km stretch, including the hillside **Gongsar Monastery**, **Lharu Monastery**, and the impressive-looking Bön-sect **Langtang Gompa**, 7km before Tengchen.

The distance between Riwoche town and Tengchen is 148km.

TENGCHEN སྟེང་ཆེན་ 丁青

☎ 0895 / pop 8000 / elev 3820m

The largely Tibetan town of Tengchen (Dingqing) is a forlorn outpost of crumbling concrete blocks and half-broken facilities. The main source of income is the curious 'caterpillar fungus' (p260). Both Tengchen and the surrounding area of Khyungpo are strong centres of the Bön religion.

Information

Ewang Qingshen Wangba (E网情深网吧; per hr Y4; 10am-midnight) Internet café down an alley to the side of the Dinging Binguan.

Qiongbu Linshi (琼布淋室; shower Y10) Public bathhouse in the Qiongbu Hotel, across from the Dingqing Binguan.

Sights & Activities

The main reason to stop here is to visit the **Tengchen Monastery**, on a hillside 4km west of town. This interesting Bön monastery is actually made up of two separate institutions. The main building, founded in 1110, has an impressive assembly hall and upper-floor chapel. Bön deities here include Tonpa Shenrab and an amazing Palpa Phurbu, whose lower half consists of a ritual dagger.

To the east is the Ritro Lhakhang, built in 1180. The main chapel, the Serdung, contains three funerary chörtens, another many-armed Palpa Phurbu and a statue of Monlam Tai, the founder of the monastery. Another chapel displays a row of six Bön gods on a variety of mounts. There are fine views from the roof.

There are said to be **hot springs** in the valley that leads north of Tengchen, between the town and monastery.

Sleeping

Gonglu Binguan (公路宾馆; ☎ 459 3389; dm Y25-30) Simple but spacious rooms above the closest thing the town has to a bus station. There are no showers but you can wash with a basin and thermos of hot water. The beds aren't brilliant, but all in all this is the best value in town.

Dingqing Binguan (丁青宾馆; Y80-128) This place on the main junction has the edge over the competition because if you search long enough, you should find a room with both hot running water *and* electricity – score! Rooms off the main road are quieter. Check out the fantastic Chairman Mao statue in the lobby.

Government Guesthouse (迎宾宾馆; Yingbin Binguan; d Y160) The rooms at this remodelled place are comfortable, but way overpriced considering there's not even any running water. The overwhelming police presence makes a visit here feel like walking into the lion's den.

Getting There & Away

Buses to Chamdo (Y100) depart at 8am. Buses from Chamdo to Nagchu (Y180) overnight in Tengchen before continuing via Sok (Y130). Enquire and buy tickets at the Gonglu Binguan.

TENGCHEN TO SOK (270KM)

The 33km from Tengchen to the Chongnye-la (Chuni-la or Tsuni-la) launches you up into the highlands of northeastern Tibet, offering fabulous views across nomad camps and yak herds to the huge range of snowy peaks to the south. The 4460m pass itself gives views westward to the Nyenchen Tanglha (Tangula) range. The road then descends for 9km to the lovely village of Bajung, where you can explore the clifftop Bön-sect Yongdzong Monastery and the Gelugpa-sect Tashiling Monastery.

Just below Bajung, and 44km from Tengchen, is the modern town of **Sertsa** (色扎; Khardong), which offers restaurants, a couple of simple guesthouses and a large collection of mani stones in the southwest corner. About 14km from Sertsa keep an eye out for the Bön sect **Targye Monastery** perched dramatically across the valley on the face of a high ridge. Some 66km past Tengchen the unremarkable town of Choedo has some shops and another guesthouse.

Here the road swings north and starts to climb up to the stunning 4905m **Shel-la**, 102km past Tengchen and the highest and most dramatic pass along the northern route. Some 40km past the Shel-la brings you to **Ronpo** (荣布; Rongbu), a small crossroads that offers food and basic accommodation at the atmospheric **Changsheng Zangcan** (昌盛藏餐; ☎ 0896-391 0522; dm Y15-20). There is a large mani wall at the western end of town. The Gelugpa-school Rabde Monastery (热登寺; Redeng Si) is a 13km detour to the south.

The road climbs yet again to the 4500m Chak-la, where you turn a corner for a dramatic view of one of the Salween's many tributaries. The road then makes a long descent past scattered nomad camps and a chörten to **Yangan** (Ya'an) village, where there is a collection of basic teahouses.

From here it's another 48km to **Bachen** (巴青; Baqing), a dull country town bypassed by the main road. If it's late, you can stay at the **Da'ertang Xinyuan Binguan** (达尔塘信苑宾馆; ☎ 0896-361 2222; dm Y58), which has clean rooms but distant toilets. Bus passengers overnight at the aircraft hanger-like **Jiaotong Binguan** (交通宾馆; Traffic Hotel; ☎ 0896-398 6065; d Y100-160, tr Y120). There is a Bön monastery on

Bachen's western fringe. From Bachen it's 33km to Sok.

SOK སོག 索县

☎ 0896 / pop 4500 / elev 4000m

Sok's claim to fame is the impressive **Sok Tsanden Monastery**, perched on an outcrop in the southern suburbs. The monastery of 270 monks, founded by the Mongol leader Gushri Khan, looks like a miniature version of the Potala. The best views of the building are from the south, as you leave town.

The monastery was made off limits to foreigners in 2001 after tourists smuggled out a letter from the monks of Sok to the Dalai Lama. Local authorities remain very suspicious of foreign visitors and threaten a Y20,000 fine for anyone trying to sneak into the monastery! If you want to try to get permission to visit the monastery, make sure that Sok Monastery (not just the town) is specifically written on your travel permits. Even this is no guarantee of entry as police will contend that the matter is in local hands.

The Repung Nunnery to the northeast of town is also technically off limits.

Information

PSB (公安局; Gong'anju; ⌚ 10am-5pm) Inside a compound in the north of town, not far from the main crossroads.

Xinji Linyu Bathhouse (新纪淋浴; Xinji Linyu; shower Y8) Just south of the central crossroads.

Xinshiji Wangba (新世纪网吧; per hr Y5; ⌚ 24hr) Internet access below the Electricity Hotel.

Sleeping

None of Sok's hotels have running water.

Yala Xinyuan Jiudian/Telecom Hotel (亚拉信苑酒店/电信宾馆; ☎ 370 3000; dm Y30, d Y150-200; ❄) Easily the best choice, this place is located behind the China Telecom office on the west side of town and is also known as the Dianxin Binguan. The four-bed economy rooms are perfect for accommodating Land Cruiser groups. The doubles with TV and air-con are a bit overpriced considering all rooms use the same shared squat toilets. Guests can use the washing machine in the shared bathroom.

Electricity Hotel (电力宾馆; Dianli Binguan; ☎ 370 2694; dm Y35-50) The breathtakingly filthy corridors here hide surprisingly decent rooms. The rooms come with a private bathroom but you are not allowed to use it since there's no running water!

Dongpo Jiulou (东坡酒楼; mains Y18-38) The best restaurant in town is this relatively pricey option by the main junction.

Snowland Happy Tibet Restaurant (雪域幸福藏餐馆; Xueyu Xingfu Zangcanguan) The tea and *thugba* comes Tibetan-style at this place with a pleasant traditional interior.

Getting There & Away

Buses depart at 8am for Nagchu (Y75). Buses to Tengchen pass through at around 6pm, before overnighting in Bachen.

SOK TO NAGCHU (237KM)

South from Sok the road passes two monasteries and a picturesque roadside chörten before ascending gradually to the 4850m Gangli Kundo-la (Gangla Shankou). The road then descends 36km past a turn-off left to the county capital of Driru (Biru).

There's a restaurant at Birong Xiang, 2km further, but you get a better choice of restaurants 22km later at **Shagchu**, 135km from Sok. From here it's 100km of high plateau grassland, over a couple of gentle passes and past herds of yaks and black herders' tents, all the time staying above 4500m. You are now well and truly in the grasslands of northern Tibet.

At the final pass, just 4km before Nagchu, you crest the gateway of the 4640m Tuoka-la to see the city of Nagchu sprawling below you.

NAGCHU ནག་ཆུ 那曲

☎ 0896 / pop 70,000 / elev 4500m

Nagchu (Naqu) is one of the highest, coldest and most windswept towns in Tibet. Perched on the edge of the Changtang (northern plateau), it is an often dismal town of mud and concrete, but is still an important stop on both the road and railway line between Qinghai and Tibet. It's a literally breathtaking place: oxygen levels here are only 60% of those at sea level, so be prepared for headaches and watch for the symptoms of altitude sickness (AMS). Bring warm clothes, even in summer.

Nagchu has a **horse-racing festival** from 10 to 16 August, when the town swells with up to 10,000 nomads and their tents from all over the Changtang. Accommodation can be very tight at this time.

On the western outskirts of the town is the surprisingly large **Shabten Monastery** (founded 1814), a branch of Lhasa's Sera Monastery ,with 130 monks. The small Tsenkhang chapel is just across the canal. The **Samtenling Nunnery** is a 30-minute walk northwest of here above the Qinghai–Tibet Hwy. You might see the occasional northern nomad in the bazaars, trading fleeces for pots and pans and other goods.

Information

China Post (中国邮局; Zhongguo Youzheng; cnr Zhejiang Lu & Liaoning Lu; 9.30am-7pm)
China Telecom (中国电信; Zhongguo Dianxin; 14 Zhejiang Lu; 9.30am-12.30pm & 4-7pm) Situated 1½ blocks west of the Naqu Hotel.
Jishen Linyu (洁神淋浴; 10am-midnight; shower Y7) Bathhouse diagonally across from China Telecom.
Kangda Wangluo Shijie (康达网络世界; cnr Zhejiang & Chaodan Lu; per hr Y3-4, 24hr) Fast internet access.

Sleeping

Nagchu has several decent budget hotels on the main drag, though few accept foreigners.

Post Hotel (邮苑宾馆; Youyuan Fandian Binguan; 382 0999; cnr Zhejiang Lu & Liaoning Lu; d/tr Y120/150, d with bathroom Y288-388;) Next to the post office, the rooms with private bathroom are often discounted to Y200, or even Y120, which is a good deal. The manager had to fix the hot-water boiler, lights, shower head and entire electrical supply in our room; after that it was just fine! The cheaper rooms are darker and share a grim bathroom. Check everything works before you commit to a room.

Naqu Hotel (那曲饭店; Naqu Fandian; 382 2424; fax 382 1898; 262 Zhejiang Donglu; d Y238, d with Western-style toilets Y328-368, discounts of 25%;) This place is often booked out with groups, both local and foreign. The ordinary doubles are tired, with squat toilets, grubby carpets and a hot-water shower. The deluxe rooms (the higher end of the price range) are similar, but with nicer décor.

China Tibet Grassland Telecom Hotel (信苑酒店; Xinyuan Jiudian; 382 8888; cnr Zhejiang & Chaodan Lu) This is the town's best hotel, but is currently under renovation.

Erjie Baozidian (二姐包子店; Liaoning Lu) The *baozi* (dumplings) are the speciality in this clean and friendly restaurant place, but regular dishes are also available. It's 100m south of the Post Hotel.

Lhasa Nola Bozee (拉萨财神藏餐; Lasa Caishen Zangcan; Liaoning Lu; snacks Y7, mains Y15-25) Nearby is this cosy and clean Tibetan teahouse, with traditional-style seating and a menu that stretches to *shemdre* (yak curry) and *shomdre* (yoghurt and rice).

Changsheng Chaoshi (昌盛超市; Liaoning Lu) Located 50m south of the Post Hotel, this is the best supermarket in town.

Getting There & Away

The **main bus station** (382 2159) is in the south of town. A taxi from the town centre costs Y10. Buses run to Lhasa (Y55 to Y80, seven hours) until noon, and there are departures around 8am for Driru (Y75), Sok (Y70) and Lhari (Y75). Buses run to Chamdo (Y260) via Tengchen (Y180) every couple of days. Private cars run to Lhasa for about Y100 per seat.

The train station is 8km south of town. There are four trains to Lhasa (Y51 hard seat, 4½ hours) between noon and 5.30pm. There are also morning trains to Golmud (hard sleeper Y279) and beyond. The ticket office is open from 8am; get here early to buy tickets. A taxi here costs Y20.

NAGCHU TO LHASA (328KM)

The road south of Nagchu is the Qinghai–Tibet Hwy (Tso-Bö Lam), the busiest and most strategic highway in Tibet. The highland scenery along the road swings from completely dismal in bad weather to breathtakingly beautiful in good light.

One recommended place to break the trip and try some local yoghurt is the signposted Nakchu Dairy Cooperative in Guluk township, 100km from Nagchu (kilometre marker 3658). Further 5km south, on the west side of road is the **Drölma Valley** (admission Y50), a recently established ecotourism cooperative, whose profits are distributed among nomad families. The valley has a monastery and nunnery, and you can rent horses and trek to nearby Yam-tso, known as the 'mother of Nam-tso'. Accommodation is provided in Tibetan-style tents or the Pilgrim Lodge. The local English-speaker guide/fixer can even arrange a local elder to come to your tent at night and spin tales about King Gesar of Ling. See the website www.holylandnortherntibet.com for details.

From Goluk the road climbs to 4646m Chokse-la, where Tibetans throw into the air the paper prayers they bought at Nagchu bus station. One kilometre further is the Chörten Rango, a line of eight chörtens that commemorate the eight main events in the life of Sakyamuni.

From here on the plain is dotted with nomad tents and thousands of grazing yaks, offering quintessential north Tibetan scenery. You might spot endangered black-necked cranes along the roadside in May.

Damxung, 40km from the pass, is the turn-off for Nam-tso and a good place to get lunch (p149)

About 20km south of Damxung a side dirt road branches off to the east towards Reting Monastery (p151), past the cliffside monastery of Shalung, while the main highway follows the railway line south to Yangpachen, Tsurphu Monastery (p144) and Lhasa.

Overland Routes from Sichuan

Wild, mountainous and deliciously remote, the Tibetan areas of western Sichuan are a cultural and geographical extension of the Tibetan plateau in all but name. The area was once part of the eastern Tibetan region of Kham, before it became part of Sichuan province. It has long been the meeting point of the Chinese and Tibetan worlds and it was this region that first experienced the Chinese invasion and provided the stiffest resistance to it.

It is an irony that because it is part of Sichuan, Tibetan culture is in many ways better preserved here than in the Tibetan Autonomous Region (TAR) and subject to fewer religious restrictions. You'll see photos of the Dalai Lama freely displayed. Free of the regulations that dog travel in the TAR, travellers are here able to explore to their heart's content.

This chapter details overland routes through western Sichuan to the borders of Tibet. (For other land routes to Tibet, see p335.) The northern and southern roads offer the main sights, including the big monasteries of Ganzi, Derge and Litang. Off the main roads are several spectacularly situated and rarely visited monasteries. Hikers can find bliss in the sublime scenery of Yading Nature Reserve or on horseback in the lovely valleys around Derge.

Western Sichuan sees few visitors, partly because travel is still rough and time-consuming, but there are some real Tibetan cultural jewels here. And if you have the permits to continue over the high passes and deep gorges into remote eastern Tibet, you deserve to feel a little smug in the knowledge that you have completed one of the world's great road trips.

HIGHLIGHTS

- Watch traditional Tibetan block printing done by hand at **Bakong Scripture Printing Press** (p274) in Derge
- Jump off the bus and explore Tibetan monasteries at small towns such as **Rongbatsa** (p272) and Luhuo (p271)
- Explore the mountain valleys around remote **Dzogchen Monastery** (p273)
- Hire horses and ride with Khampa wranglers in the wild west town of **Tagong** (p270)
- Walk the kora of **Yading Nature Reserve** (p277) amid the region's stunning scenery
- Hike and then hitch out to **Tsopu Gou** (p279), a remote monastery by a holy alpine lake surrounded by prayer flags
- Play pool with wild-looking Khampas in the high-altitude town of **Litang** (p275), before exploring the large monastery

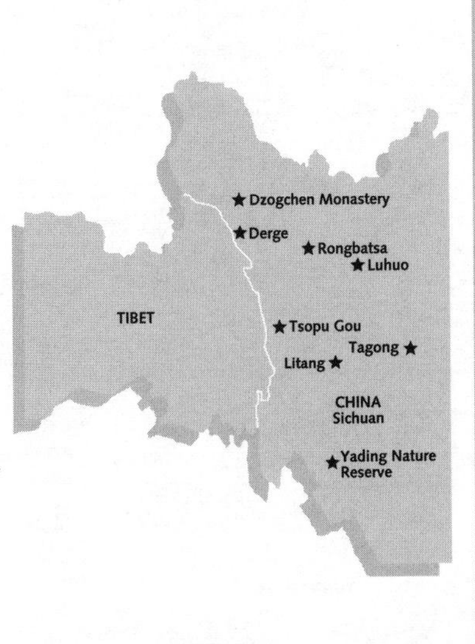

PERMITS

The good news is that no permits are required anywhere in western Sichuan. You will technically need permits to continue into the Tibetan Autonomous Region (TAR) and the only way to get these is to book a vehicle and guide, either in Lhasa or Chengdu. For more details, see p323 and p337.

KANGDING (DARTSEDO) 康定

☎ 0836 / pop 82,000 / elev 2616m

Kangding (Dartsedo or Dardo in Tibetan) is nestled in a deep river valley at the confluence of the Zheduo and Yala Rivers, known in Tibetan as the Dar-chu and the Tse-chu. (The 'do' of the town's Tibetan name means 'river confluence'.)

Arriving in Kangding, there is a tangible sense that you have reached the border of the Chinese and Tibetan worlds. The town has been a trade centre between the two cultures for centuries with the exchange of yak hides, wool, herbs and, especially, bricks of tea from Ya'an wrapped in yak hide. It also served as an important staging post on the road to Lhasa, as indeed it does today as western Sichuan's largest town.

Kangding was historically the capital of the local Tibetan kingdom of Chakla (or Chala) and later, between 1939 and 1951, the capital of the short-lived province of Xikang, when it was controlled by opium-dealing warlord Liu Wenhui. Today Kangding is largely a Han Chinese town.

Information

Agricultural Bank of China (Zhongguo Nongye Yinhang; Xi Dajie; 🕑 9am-5pm Mon-Fri) Can change US dollars and UK pounds and *sometimes* travellers cheques, but there's no ATM or cash advances on credit cards.

China Telecom (Zhongguo Dianxin; Yanhe Xilu) Next to the Black Tent Guesthouse; offers cheap international phone calls.

Internet cafés (Wangba; per hr Y2-3; 🕑 8am-midnight) There's one in an alley off Xi Dajie, or get online at Sally's Knapsack Inn (opposite).

Public Security Bureau (PSB; Gong'anju; ☎ 281 1415; Dongda Xiaojie; 🕑 8.30am-noon & 2.30-5.30pm Mon-Fri) Visa extensions in three to five days, maybe even the same day if you ask nicely.

Yala Snow Mountain Outdoor Shop (☎ 139 0516 2433; email 13905162433@e172.com) Mr Lin Yueluan

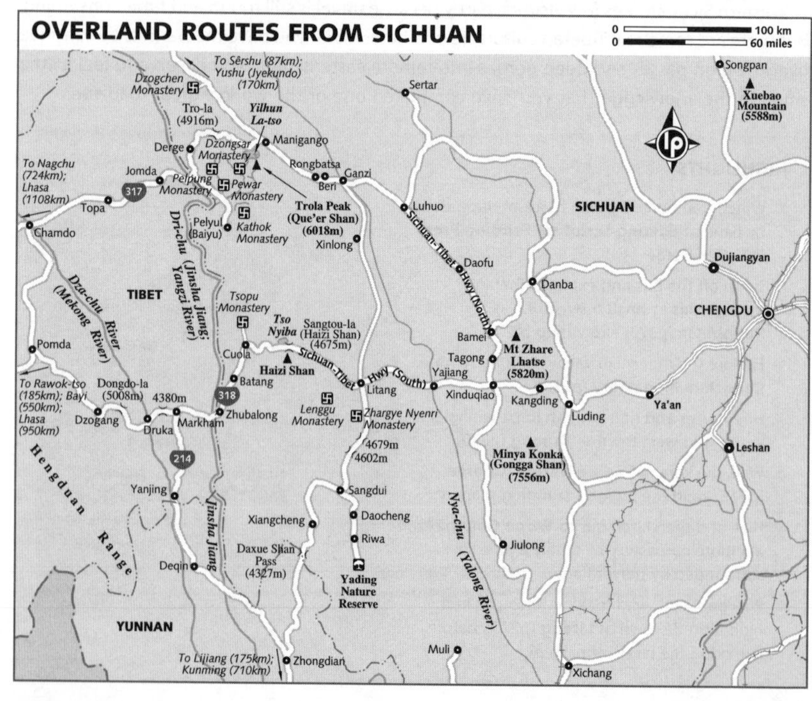

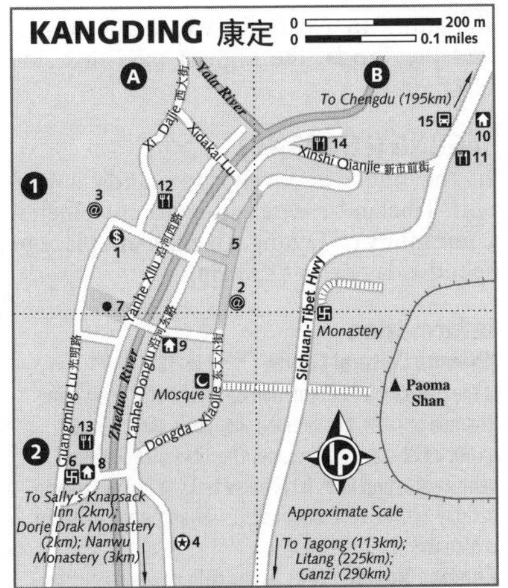

INFORMATION
Agricultural Bank of China 中国农业银行 1 A1
Internet Café 网吧 2 A1
Internet Café 网吧 3 A1
PSB 公安局 4 A2

SIGHTS & ACTIVITIES
Market 市场 5 A1
Ngachu Monastery 安觉寺 6 A2
People's Square 人民广场 7 A1

SLEEPING
Black Tent Guesthouse 西藏雨黑帐篷 8 A2
Love Song Hotel 情歌大酒店 9 A2
Qingyuan Dajiudian 请源大酒店 10 B1

EATING
Droma Yudia-Khampa Tibetan Eatery 11 B1
Hongkang Fandian 鸿康饭店 12 A1
Nine Bowls Vegetable of Country 九碗农家乡 13 A2
Sichuan Stalls 小吃店 14 B1

TRANSPORT
Bus Station 汽车站 15 B1

rents and sells trekking equipment, can advise on local trekking routes and can arrange guides and horses.

Sights

There are several minor monasteries in and around Kangding. Just behind the Black Tent Guesthouse, the **Ngachu Monastery** (Anjue Si) is a fairly quiet temple built in 1654. It is home to around 20 monks and a new Jampa Chapel.

The **Nanwu Monastery** in the west of town is the most active monastery in the area and has around 80 lamas in residence. To reach it, walk south along the main road and follow its bend to the left for 2km. South of town is the **Dorje Drak Monastery** (Jingang Si), which was under renovation at last look.

You can head up **Paoma Shan** for excellent views of Kangding and, if you're lucky, Mt Minya Konka (Gongga Shan; 7556m). Take particular care when wandering around Paoma Shan and try to avoid hiking on your own. A British tourist was murdered here in the spring of 2000.

In town, the **market** on Dongda Xiaojie is worth a look. Locals flock most evenings to **People's Square** for some Tibetan and Western-style dancing.

Festivals & Events

The **Zhuanshanjie**, or 'Walking around the Mountain' festival, takes place on Paoma Shan on the eighth day of the fourth lunar month to commemorate the birthday of Sakyamuni (Sakya Thukpa). White and blue Tibetan tents cover the hillside and there's plenty of wrestling and horse racing, with visitors from all over western Sichuan.

Sleeping

If you're only staying in Kangding a night, to catch an onward bus, it's convenient to be in the east of town near the bus station, although most guesthouses and attractions are over the river on the west side of town.

Black Tent Guesthouse (西藏雨黑帐篷; Xizang Yuhei Zhangpeng; ☎ 886 2107; 28 Yanhe Xilu; dm/d Y20/50) Next to Ngachu Monastery, this clean and sociable place is the spot to meet other travellers. Showers and toilets are clean, but there's only one of each.

Sally's Knapsack Inn (背包客栈; Beibao Kezhan; ☎ 283 8377; zanglingren666@163.com; dm Y20-30) Next to Dorje Drak Monastery, 2km south of town, this laidback hostel and café has colourful carved wooden beds and the most helpful staff in town. A taxi from the bus station costs Y5.

Qingyuan Dajiudian (☎ 669 9888; Yingbin Dadao; d Y380;) Some rooms here are missing lights, electric kettles and even room switches, but once you stumble on an intact room, they're terrific, with reliable hot water and heating. It's conveniently located right by the bus station, and a discounted room may run as low as Y120 to Y150.

Love Song Hotel (Qingge Dajiudian; ☎ 281 3333; fax 281 3111; 156 Dongda Xiaojie; d Y580) Service here can be pretty lethargic but the rooms and facilities are the best in town, despite being overpriced.

Eating

Nine Bowls Vegetable of Country (Jiuwan Nongjia Xiang; ☎ 287 5199; Yanhe Xilu; dishes from Y5; 11am-9pm) You can't miss this cubbyhole place – the sign next door says 'Chongqing Strange Taste Fish'! The hospitable manager speaks decent English. Menu in English.

Droma Yudia-Khampa Tibetan Eatery (☎ 282 3463; Xinshi Qianjie; dishes from Y10; 9am-9pm) A newer place with a large, warm dining room and comfy seating. It's got a huge menu of local, Nepali and Western food, and even breakfast.

Hongkang Fandian (☎ 283 5101; 14 Xi Dajie; dishes Y12-18; 9am-10pm) Outstanding Sichuan food is served in this modest but spotless restaurant – you really can order just about anything off the menu and not be disappointed.

In the evening, numerous covered stalls in the northern end of town offer arguably the widest selection of skewered meat, vegies and fish in Sichuan.

Getting There & Away

The completion of the Erlang Shan (Two-Wolf Mountain) tunnel has cut the ride to Chengdu down to a comfortable seven hours. Buses leave half-hourly for Chengdu from 6am to 5pm (Y105 to 125). In Chengdu, buses to Kangding leave from the Xinnanmen bus station.

Going west from Kangding, there are daily buses at 6.45am for Litang (Y80, seven hours), at 6.15am for Ganzi (Y107, 12 hours), at 6.30am for Batang (Y138, two days), at 7.30am for Derge (Y166, 24 hours) and at 6am for Xiangcheng (Y140, 14 hours). Local minibuses run to Yajiang, Daofu and Luhuo.

An airport is being built on the way to Tagong; it's slated for completion in 2009.

THE NORTHERN ROUTE

This is one of the two main routes of the Sichuan–Tibet Hwy, which links the Tibetan areas of western Sichuan with Tibet proper. Almost 300km longer than the southern route, the northern route extends from Kangding to Chamdo, via Derge, Ganzi and the Tro-la, the highest pass this side of Lhasa.

TAGONG (LHAGONG) 塔贡

In the midst of lovely grasslands dotted with Tibetan herders is the vibrant Tibetan community of Tagong, an excellent place to spend a day or so exploring.

Information

Khampa Cultural Centre (☎ 136-1813 0199) This is the place to get information on local treks, learn some Khampa phrases, get your laundry done and even get a *chuba* (Tibetan cloak) made. The Tibetan-Australian venture also organises local horse treks (Y150 per person per day with accommodation). A café and small museum is planned.

Khampa Nomad Treks (www.definitelynomadic.com) Established by a former Peace Corps worker, this company runs horse treks and artisan tours and sells crafts through the Khampa Nomad Arts Cooperative.

Sights

At the north end of town, the Sakyapa-school **Tagong Monastery** (admission Y10) blends Han Chinese and Tibetan styles and appears to have survived the ravages of time amazingly well, though two of the three main halls have been rebuilt recently. The holiest statue in the far right building is a replica of Lhasa's Jowo Sakyamuni Buddha, said to have been carved *in situ* when the original passed through en route to Lhasa in the 7th century. Note also the beautiful 1000-armed Chenresig (Avalokiteshvara) in the building to the left. Make sure you visit the stunning collection of over 100 chörtens behind the monastery; finish off your visit with a clockwise kora of the site.

The velvety hills around Tagong, topped with prayer flags and chörtens, offer views of the rolling grasslands and the stunning 5820m pyramid peak of Zhare Lhatse. Take a walk up to the hill above town, which is topped by a chörten surrounded by votive rags, amulets and beads left by pilgrims.

The grasslands are also the stage for an annual **horse-racing festival**, held at the beginning of the eighth lunar month (mid-July to August) and attended by thousands of local Tibetan herders.

A 20-minute walk west of town, over the river, leads to the *shedra* (Buddhist college), which has a large collection of Buddhist rock carvings in the plain below.

Sleeping & Eating

Snowland Guesthouse (雪城旅社; Xuecheng Lüshe; ☎ 286 6098; dm Y25) Top of the accommodation heap is this great guesthouse right next to the monastery. It's got wooden everything and rigid but comfy beds; best are the thick blankets. The shower and facilities are clean.

Travellers have recommended the Tibetan-style rooms at Gayla's Guesthouse, in the opposite corner of the monastery square from Sally's Kham Restaurant.

Sally's Kham Restaurant (☎ 139-9045 4752; tagongsally@yahoo.com) This travellers' gold mine serves Tibetan, Chinese and Western food and has internet access, CD burning, a bakery, and rental of bicycles and sleeping bags. English-speaking Sally is a good source for local travel information and can arrange one- or two-day horse treks for two people or more (Y100 to 120 per person per day).

Getting There & Away

One bus to Tagong (on its way to Daofu) runs daily from Kangding (Y33, three hours) at 6am. If you're heading to Ganzi (Y70), you can pick up the same bus the next day at about 10am as it passes through town.

Afternoon buses returning to Kangding can be flagged down in Tagong. You can also catch a minibus or shared taxi (Y20) to take you to the Xinduqiao crossroads, from where there are buses through to Kangding and Litang.

TAGONG TO GANZI

Several bustling but little-visited towns en route from Tagong to Ganzi offer impressive monasteries and some basic accommodation. The Khampa houses in this region, built from wood and stone, are particularly elegant.

Bamei (八美; Garthar in Tibetan) is a lunch stop about 20km north of Tagong; there's a pretty series of chörtens in the south of town. Bamei is famous as the birthplace of the 11th Dalai Lama. Just 8km northeast of town, along the road to Danba, is the **Garthar Chöde Monastery** (惠远寺; Huiyuan Si), built by the seventh Dalai Lama.

A further 72km north is **Daofu** (道孚; Tawu in Tibetan), home to the 450-year-old Gelugpa-school **Nyitso Monastery**, one of the largest monasteries in the region.

Luhuo (炉霍; Drango in Tibetan), 70km further, has **Drango Gompa**, which once had over 1000 monks. The monastery sits on the hillside in the Tibetan-style southern part of town and has a large, newly carved wooden statue of Jampa (Maitreya). The Tibetan name of Drango means 'head of the rock' and derives from Luhuo's strategic position at the confluence of two rivers.

About 20km before Ganzi the road rises to a high pass before dropping down past the lake and monastery of **Kasuo-tso**.

GANZI 甘孜

☎ 0836 / pop 61,400 / elev 3394m

The bustling market town of Ganzi (also spelled Kandze, Garze and Ganze) sits in a valley at 3400m, surrounded by the sleeping giants of the Trola (Chola) range, and is a natural place to break your trip. The gorgeous surrounding countryside is peppered with Tibetan villages and resurgent monasteries. A couple of isolated bombings took place in Ganzi and Chengdu between 1998 and 2002, a sign of the growing frustrations of local Tibetan communities.

Information

Dorjee Tsewang (☎ 135-6868 8297; bondorjee@yahoo.com) If you're looking for a local guide, English-speaking Dorjee Tsewang can arrange hiking and horse-riding treks, plus pretty much anything else. He lives in Rongbatsa, so email in advance.

Sights

Over 540 years old, **Garze Monastery** (甘孜寺; Ganzi Si; admission sometimes Y15) is just north of the town's Tibetan quarter and is the region's largest monastery, with over 500 monks. Encased in the walls of the main prayer hall are hundreds of small golden Sakyamuni statues. In a smaller hall just west of the main hall is an impressive statue of Jampa (Maitreya), dressed in silk.

To find the monastery, turn left out of the bus station and head north for about 10 minutes until you reach the Tibetan neighbourhood. A kora winds clockwise around and above the monastery. To follow it take one of the roads to the left when you reach the Tibetan quarter and look for a huge chörten and then a hall of prayer wheels, from where the path winds uphill.

Den Monastery in the southern part of town is smaller but older and much more atmospheric. The inner chapel is surrounded by three pilgrimage paths and houses fierce statues of the protector god Nagpo Chenpo (Mahakala). Upstairs are several Mao slogans left over from the Cultural Revolution and a small printing press.

For a nice half-day walk head south from the bus station over the Nya-chu (Yalong Jiang) river. The right fork leads through barley fields for 20 minutes to **Dongtong (Dontok) Monastery** and the new but impressive **Dingkhor chörten**. The left fork leads to **Pongo Monastery** after about an hour or so.

Ganzi has the region's best antique shops and many general stores selling Tibetan goods.

Sleeping & Eating

Accommodation options in Ganzi are limited as most of the hotels do not accept foreigners.

Pubu Living Buddha Family House (布绒朗寺旅店; Buronglang Si Lüdian; ☎ 899 5861; www.burongna.net; 233 Jiefang Lu; dm Y25) This small guesthouse was set up by the rinpoche (high lama) of nearby Burongna Monastery. Beds are in three-or four-bed rooms and food is available. Best of all, know your money is going to fund the construction of a home for elderly Tibetans.

Ruifeng Zhusudu (瑞丰住宿都; ☎ 752 5465; Binhe Donglu; s & d Y50) This place has plain, basic rooms with startlingly immense bathrooms but no hot water. Walk left out of the bus station, hang a right on Chuanzang Lu, continue until you cross the river and turn left onto Binhe Donglu (reads only 'He Donglu' on the street sign).

Chengxin Binguan (诚信宾馆; ☎ 752 5289; Dajin Jie; s/d without bathroom Y60/80, r with bathroom Y180) Opposite the bus station, this place has very clean rooms and great staff.

Himalaya Hotel (喜玛拉雅宾馆; Ximalaya Binguan; ☎ 752 1878; r with/without air-con Y170/150;) The small but spotless modern rooms at this friendly hotel are the nicest in Ganzi (discounted rooms cost from Y110 to 120).

Golden Yak Hotel (金牦牛酒店; Jinmaoniu Jiudian; ☎ 752 5188, 752 5288; 1 Dajin Tan; s/d Y150) This place, attached to Ganzi's bus station, has similar rates to the Himalaya Hotel but it's not as nice. Still, it's worth considering if you have an early bus the next morning.

Daba Zanghan Yijia Xin Fandian (大巴藏汉一家新饭店; 27 Dajin Tan; dishes Y8-10; 9am-10pm) The Sichuan dishes at this place are good.

The Muslim restaurants east of the bus station double as video bars and offer good noodles if you can stand the ear-shattering sounds of kung fu.

Getting There & Away

Buses to Ganzi (Y107, 12 hours) leave Kangding daily at 6.15am. From Ganzi, a bus leaves each morning at 6.30am for Kangding. There are also morning buses to Derge (Y50 to 70, seven hours, 8.30am) and an afternoon bus to Manigango (Y21, two hours, 2.30pm), or try for a seat on the bus from Kangding. Private minibuses to Derge are available for hire for Y450.

To reach Beri and Dargye Monasteries (see the next section), catch anything heading west or negotiate a taxi down to Y20.

You can also head north from Ganzi to Yushu (Tibetan: Jyekundo) in Qinghai, via the town of Sêrshu (Y92, nine hours, 6.30am).

GANZI TO DERGE

Beri

A 15km excursion from Ganzi, on the north side of the river, is the Gelugpa **Beri Monastery**. There are several other monasteries in the pretty village of Beri.

Rongbatsa

☎ 0836

Around 65km before Manigango, near the village of Rongbatsa, are the circular walls of **Dargye Monastery** (Dagei Si). The nearby hot springs, although more lukewarm than hot, may be the only bathroom you get for some time.

A local lama named Gyalten Rinpoche operates the excellent **Gyalten Rinpoche Guesthouse** (dm Y35), a couple of kilometres west of Dargye Monastery. Set against a backdrop of white-capped mountains, this wonderful guesthouse feels superbly isolated. The rooftop commands some breathtaking views of the valley and you can easily lose yourself here for a day or two. Simple meals are available. Beds are mattresses covered with Tibetan carpets; a sleeping bag is a good idea. To find the guesthouse, walk out of Dargye Monastery's west gate and look for a pond; beyond this a sign directs you up a dirt track to the guesthouse.

From the monastery it's a two-hour walk north along the Nya-chu (Yalong River) to **Hadhi Nunnery**, home to around 60 nuns who operate a basic shop and are reportedly happy to receive short-term guests.

Manigango 马尼干戈

☎ 0836

This scruffy crossroads town halfway between Ganzi and Derge can be a useful base for visiting Dzogchen Monastery (below) or Yilhun La-tso (right). A construction boom was underway at last check, so you might find upgraded places to stay

There is one guesthouse, **Manigange Shisudian** (马尼干戈食宿店; dm Y10-20), where all the buses stop. The rooms are comfortable if basic, but the toilets are half a mile up the road – make sure you bring a torch! The friendly staff can help with travel information, even horse hire (Y100 per day, plus Y100 for a guide). The restaurant here is good and cheap.

Next door, **Yulong Shenhai Binguan** (玉龙神海宾馆; dm Y15-30) is more modern and has its own public toilet – bonus! Look for the large red sign with white Chinese characters.

A daily bus passes through Manigango at 11am for Derge (Y35, three to four hours). Coming from Derge, a bus stops in Manigango at 11am and heads on to Ganzi (Y25, five to seven hours) and Luhuo (Y50, five hours), where it overnights before heading on to Kangding (Y130). A 9am bus leaves daily for Sêrshu.

Around Manigango

A 50km detour north from Manigango takes you to **Dzogchen Monastery** (竹庆佛学院; Zhuqing Foxueyuan), founded in 1684 and the home of the Dzogchen school (see p67), the most popular form of Tibetan Buddhism in the West. The monastery and *shedra* (monastic college) have a stunning location at the foot of a glacial valley. Several important high Nyingmapa lamas, now exiled abroad, originally came from nearby valleys.

The site includes the small town, 1.5km off the road, which has a few shops, chörten and a chapel with huge prayer wheels. Up the small gorge is the main monastery and 1km further is the *shedra*. It's possible to stay at the college for Y15, though you'll need a sleeping bag and your own food.

Getting here can be tricky. Buses to Yushu and Sêrshu pass the monastery but it's probably easier to hitch. If you do hitch, make sure you set out in the morning as there is not much traffic on the roads in the afternoon (for information on the risks associated with hitching, see p344).

The road crosses the Muri-la (4633m). A hired vehicle from Manigango (ask at the Manigange Shisudian; left) costs around Y250 return.

Manigango to Derge

Around 13km from Manigango the highway passes **Yilhun La-tso** (新路海; Xinlu Hai; admission Y20), a stunning, holy alpine lake bordered by chörtens and dozens of rock carvings. The lake is backed by the huge glaciers of 6018m Trola Peak (Que'er Shan) and it's possible to walk an hour or two up the left (east) side of the lakeshore for glacier views. The lake has many great places to camp (take mosquito repellent), though recent reports suggest the lakeshore has been fenced off by local tourist authorities. To get here you'll have to hitch to the turn-off where there's a bridge and trail 1km to the lake. A return taxi to the lake from Manigango costs Y70, including a couple of hours' wait time.

From the lake the road ascends to the wild and craggy scenery of the 4916m Trola before descending through deep gorges and some pretty Tibetan villages to arrive in Derge.

DERGE 德格

☎ 0836 / pop 58,000 / elev 4327m

Resting in a valley between the Tibetan border to the west and the Trola (Chola) range to the east, Derge forms the cultural heartland of Kham. While the Chinese influence is evident and growing rapidly here, the old town and surrounding villages are very much Tibetan.

There are many historically important monasteries in the valleys south of Derge, namely at Pelpung (Chinese: Babang), Dzongsar, Pewar (Baiya), Kathok and Pelyul

(Baiyu). For details on these monasteries and wonderful treks in the area see Gary McCue's book *Trekking in Tibet* and visit the travel section of the website www.khamaid.org.

Sights

At the heart of Derge is the 18th-century **Bakong Scripture Printing Press and Monastery** (德格印经院; Dege Yinjingyuan; admission Y25; 8.30am-noon & 2-6.30pm). The press houses more than 217,000 engraved blocks of Tibetan scriptures from all the Tibetan Buddhist orders, including Bön; the collection makes up an astonishing 70% of Tibet's literary heritage. These texts include ancient works about astronomy, geography, music, medicine and Buddhist classics, including two of the most important Tibetan sutras. A history of Indian Buddhism comprising 555 wood-block plates is the only surviving copy in the world (written in Hindi, Sanskrit and Tibetan).

Within the monastery, dozens of workers hand-produce over 2500 prints to order each day, as ink, paper and blocks fly through the workers' hands at lightning speed. Upstairs is an older crowd of printers who produce larger and more complex prints of Tibetan gods on paper or coloured cloth. If you catch them with a free moment, they'll print you one of your choice for Y10.

You can also examine storage chambers, paper-cutting rooms and the main hall of the monastery itself. Protecting the monastery from fire and earthquake is the guardian goddess Drölma (Tara). There are some nice murals in the two ground-floor chapels, so bring a torch. You can get a close-up look at the workers who carve the printing blocks (in relief) in the administrative building across from the monastery.

Admission to the monastery includes an obligatory guided tour. Photography is not allowed. To reach the printing house, turn left out of the bus station and right over the bridge. Continue up this road to the southeast of town and to the monastery's front door.

Just uphill behind the printing house, the large Sakyapa **Gonchen Monastery** is well worth a look. Restored during the 1980s, the three inner sanctums are dedicated to Guru Rinpoche, Sakyamuni and Jampa (Maitreya).

Also worth seeking out is the **Tangtong Gyelpo Chapel** (Tangyel Lhakhang) – as you head uphill to the printing press look out for the small alley leading to the right. For an introduction to the remarkable Tangtong Gyelpo, see p30

Sleeping

Dege Binguan (德格宾馆; ☎ 822 2157; dm Y20, d with bathroom Y180) The only place in town officially open to foreigners has clean, damp and overpriced doubles and fairly grim dorm rooms. Worse, you may be directed across the street to the expensive wing (Y280).

Wuzi Zhaodaisuo (物资招待所; dm Y20) Some travellers have managed to bag a bed at this place, directly opposite the bus station, which has nicer dorms, although they are still very basic. Look for the multicoloured bunting strung up outside.

Getting There & Away

From Derge a daily early-morning bus leaves for Kangding (Y166, two days) via Manigango (Y35, three hours), Ganzi (Y60, eight hours) and Luhuo (Y86, 10 to 12 hours), where it stops for the night before carrying on to Kangding the following day.

If you're travelling west, note that individuals are officially forbidden from travelling into the TAR without travel permits (see p323). The occasional sleeper bus trundles through Derge to and from Chamdo but rarely has empty berths. There is occasional transport west to the town of Jomda, just over the Tibetan border.

DERGE TO CHAMDO

From Derge it's 109km to Jomda (江达; Jiangda), crossing the Dri-chu (Jinsha Jiang or Yangzi River) at the Tibetan border. From here it's 228km to Chamdo via Topa and several high passes. If you are hitching along this route without a permit, you'll have to be careful at Jomda (where there is a guesthouse, a PSB office and an occasionally manned checkpost) and at the checkpost at the bridge over the Dri-chu. Your best bet is to travel through this checkpoint at night.

The occasional minibus travels between Derge, Jomda and Chamdo, but you will probably have to change rides when you get to Jomda.

THE SOUTHERN ROUTE

The southern route that goes from Kangding to Pomda is shorter than the northern route and passes equally stunning scenery. It offers fewer monasteries but includes the option of detouring south to Yading Nature Reserve and continuing on the rugged back-door route to Zhongdian (Gyeltang) in Yunnan.

LITANG 理塘

☎0836 / pop 51,300 / elev 4014m

Resting on open grassland framed by snowcapped peaks, Litang is a friendly and authentically Tibetan place in which to hang out for a couple of days. At over 4000m, it's not uncommon for travellers to feel the affects of altitude sickness (see p351).

The town is famed for its annual **horse-racing festival**, held from 1 to 7 August, when the town swells with tens of thousands of local Khampas and their colourful Tibetan tents. It's a great time to visit, though accommodation is impossible to come by at this time, so bring a tent. Every five years an even more spectacular event is staged. The festival was cut short in 2006 after a disputed race result ended in rioting. There were more political disturbances during the 2007 festival after one Khampa grabbed a microphone and called for the return of the Dalai Lama.

Litang is also famed as the birthplace of the seventh and 10th Dalai Lamas and also four of the Pabalas, Chamdo's religious leaders. After a visit to Litang the controversial sixth Dalai Lama wrote a famous poem about a crane, indicating through it that his reincarnation would be born in Litang. The area around Litang also has strong connections to the epic warrior Gesar of Ling and a statue of the man, complete with plastic palm trees, decorates a square in town.

There's some scope for hiking around Litang. Travellers are increasingly being approached by freelance guides at the bus station or outside the Crane Guest House, offering to organise walks or a visit to a nomad camp. Most have had good experiences; some have been disappointed. Ask around when you arrive to get the latest from other travellers.

Information

China Post (Zhongguo Youzheng; Tuanjie Lu Beiduan; 9-11.30am & 2-5.30pm) On the main north–south street.

Internet café (Wangba; Tuanjie Lu Beiduan; per hr Y3) Right next to China Post.

Sights

At the northern end of town is the large and recently restored **Litang Chöde Monastery** (理塘长青春科尔寺; Litang Changqing Chunke'er Si), built for the third Dalai Lama. Inside is a statue of Sakyamuni that is believed to have been carried from Lhasa by foot. A collection of chörtens and mani stone (prayer stone) carvings line the main entrance. The monastery was bombed by Chinese troops in 1956 during a Khampa rebellion.

On the eastern edge of Litang is a 33m-high **chörten**, supported by snow lions, which locals perpetually circumambulate. The entrance is on a side street off Xinfu Xilu.

A difficult-to-find 420-year-old building known as the Zenkhang marks the **birthplace of the seventh Dalai Lama**. The upper-floor sleeping room of the Dalai Lama has a statue and several relics of the man, and an interesting old Chinese army bag. It can be hard to find the lady with a key. Photos are not allowed.

There are **hot springs** (admission Y7) at the western edge of town, 4km from the centre. A taxi here costs Y7 one way.

Sleeping

Litang has decent food and lodging, making it a fine place to break a trip for a day or more. Many hotels have no showers or hot water and electricity everywhere can be unreliable.

Safe and Life International Hotel (平安涉外宾馆; Ping'an Shewai Binguan; ☎532 3861; Xingfu Xilu; 2-bed dm Y15, s Y30) Right across from the bus station, the location here is ideal if you have an early-morning bus, or arrive late at night. The owners speak no English but are eager to help. Rooms are cramped, beat-up, and can get cold and damp in winter. A communal shower in the courtyard has hot water from 8am to 11pm and the 1st-floor restaurant has an English-Chinese menu.

Crane Guest House (仙鹤宾馆; Xianhe Binguan; ☎532 3850; Xingfu Xilu; dm Y25, s/d with bathroom Y156/166) Handsdown the backpacker favourite. Here, the two- and three-bed dorms are cosy and the rooms with private bathroom have hot-water showers and heat lamps in the bathrooms. Some staff speak a little English and they often invite guests to sit around the fire and sip yak-butter tea. Take a left out of the bus station and head about 350m east into town; it's on the right-hand side of the road.

Nomad Homestay (☎ 532 2013, 135-0829 6651; Chengxihe Lu Bei'erduan; d/q Y60/100) Travellers have recommended this Tibetan-style family guesthouse, with 10 rooms annexed to a traditional stone home. The traditional Tibetan décor is joined by hot showers. Home-made Tibetan food is available. It's a 20-minute walk from the bus station.

High City Hotel (高城宾馆; Gaocheng Binguan; ☎ 532 2706; Genie Donglu; d/tr Y480/340;) This government-run hotel is the most upscale option in town, though the upkeep is a bit lax. The nice lobby has a killer karaoke setup loaded and ready at all times. Low-season rates start at Y120.

Travellers have recommended the new Potala Inn, in the east of town, with doubles around Y160, a large lounge and plenty of excursions on offer.

Eating & Entertainment

Litang has countless small restaurants, with the best selection on Xingfu Xilu around the Crane Guest House.

Wanglong Guan Tangbao (Genie Donglu; 8am-late evening) This is a good place for your morning *baozi* (dumplings).

If you want something to do at night, try the bar (*jiuba*) behind the High City Hotel. It's a big, saloon-style place that has Tibetan dancing performances on many nights. Drop by around 9pm to see what (if anything) is going on.

Just north of the bar is the Sichuan Fandian, one of the fanciest restaurants in town and getting good reviews from travellers.

Getting There & Away

Litang's bus station is a chaotic place, so double-check all times and prices. Getting tickets can take a lot of patience (and often a lot of time) so don't leave it until the last minute. The ticket window opens at 2pm. It's 284km to Kangding and 654km to Chengdu.

Buses leave Litang for Kangding (Y81, eight hours) and Batang (Y60, six hours) at 6.30am. At the time of writing, there was serious roadwork between Litang and Batang, so expect either heavy delays or a smooth new road along this route.

A back-door route to Yunnan runs south from Litang, through 400km of spectacular scenery to Zhongdian, from where another road leads into Tibet (see p337). Buses run to Xiangcheng (Chatreng; Y62, four hours, 6am) and Daocheng (Y47, three to four hours, 6am), the latter for Yading Nature Reserve.

AROUND LITANG

The **Zhargye Nyenri Monastery**, 18km from Litang along the road to Daocheng, is next to a holy outcrop of rock honeycombed with caves and covered in prayer flags, *kathaks* (prayer scarfs), sacred symbols, eagles' nests and a hard-to-make-out image of self-arising Jampa (Maitreya). Pilgrims come here to make an hour-long kora around the peak, past several caves and sin-testing spots, particularly on the second day of the eighth month. The monastery itself has images of Tsongkhapa, Drölma, Jampelyang and Marpa, plus fine murals by artists from Ganzi. To get to Zhargye Nyenri, take the morning bus to Daocheng or Xiangcheng, get off at the monastery and hitch back (for information on the risks associated with hitching, see p344). It's possible to stay the night here. Sadly two bears are kept chained up in the courtyard.

Lenggu Monastery is in a remote but stunning area 70km from Litang, between 6224m Mt Gambo Gonga (Genyen Peak, or Genie Feng) and 5807m Mt Xiaozha. The monastery was built by the first Karmapa in 1164. It's an adventure to get here as there's little public transport; from Litang branch left off the main road to Batang after 15km or so to the village of Lamaya in Reke district. From here walk or hire a horse to Legando village (a short day) or the monastery (a long day). It's a minimum three-day return trip but with more time you could make day trips to Xiaozha Lake and waterfall, and to Ruogen-tso. It's possible to stay with families in Lamaya and Zhamla villages and Legando. The region is part of Genie Natural Biological Tourism Protection Zone.

The road from Litang to Batang traverses the **Maoya Grasslands** and crosses the Sangtoula pass before dropping down to the twin lakes of **Tso Nyiba**, with a backdrop of the Haizi Shan, before continuing to Batang.

DAOCHENG (DABPA) 稻城

☎ 0836 / pop 7000 / elev 3800m

The county town of Daocheng (Dabpa in Tibetan) is mainly a jumping-off point for Yading Nature Reserve (right). Peak season for Chinese tourists is the first week of May, followed by the first week of October.

There are two **internet cafés** (per hr Y5; 24hr) on the renovated cobblestone street that leads off the main north–south drag.

The **Xiongdeng Monastery** is a large Gelugpa monastery about a two- to three-hour walk northeast of town. The monks are friendly and the views are good. Head east out of town to the bridge and then north up the hillside. You can hitch parts of the way on a passing tractor or you can hire a minibus from town for Y50.

After a trek in Yading, soak your weary limbs in the **Rapuchaka Hot Springs** (admission Y10), 4km southeast of town. A taxi here costs Y10 one way.

Sleeping

There are numerous excellent Tibetan-style B&Bs. Most offer beds from around Y20, basic pit toilets and no showers. Rates are flexible and are 30% higher in May.

Tongfu Hostel (同福客栈; Tongfu Kezhan; ☎ 572 8667; www.inoat.com; 1 Yazhuo Jie; dm Y20, d Y80-100) The backpacker-friendly Tongfu has a young, friendly owner who speaks a little English and is very helpful with tourist info.

Jinsui Binguan (金穗宾馆; ☎ 572 7179; d Y100-120;) Across the street, this option is open year-round, has simple rooms, and keeps the hot water and electricity running 365 days a year.

There are plenty of places to eat here but don't leave it too late; many restaurants shut by 8pm.

Khampa Restaurant (康巴藏餐; Kangba Zangcan; dishes Y6-25; 8.30am-8.30pm) This place has a good selection of Tibetan fare.

Getting There & Away

From Daocheng, buses run early in the morning to Kangding via Litang, and to Zhongdian. Daily buses to Xiangcheng and Litang (both Y47) leave at 6am and take three hours. A minibus or taxi to either of these places costs Y300.

If you take the bus between Litang and Xiangcheng, you may get dropped off at the junction of Sangdui, 28km from Daocheng. Microbuses shuttle people to Daocheng (45 minutes) for Y10 per person, or Y40 for the vehicle. About 5km north of Sangdui is the recently rebuilt Kagyud-school **Benpo Monastery**, which is well worth a visit.

An airport is being built 8km outside Daocheng, with direct flights to Chengdu planned.

YADING NATURE RESERVE 亚丁自然保护区

Six hours south of Daocheng, this stunningly beautiful **reserve** (Yading Ziran Baohuqu; admission Y150) is the real reason to detour all the way out here.

You'll need to time your trip well, as April and October see snowfalls, and early May and October see a flood of Chinese tourists during national holidays. September is a good time to visit.

The reserve is centred around the three peaks of Jampelyang (Yangmaiyong Shenshan; 5958m) to the south, Chana Dorje (Xiari Duoji Shenshan; 5958m) and Chenresig (Xiannairi Shenshan; 6032m). The mountains are named after the Rigsum Gonpo, the Tibetan Buddhist trinity of bodhisattvas. None have ever been climbed. The reserve is a strong contender as the inspiration for James Hilton's novel *Shangri-La*.

The region was once part of the old kingdom of Muli and was visited by the fifth Dalai Lama in the 17th century. Joseph Rock, *National Geographic*'s 'man in China', who counted the corpulent King of Muli as a close personal friend, visited in the 1930s and described the famed 'Bandit Monastery', whose 400 monks would regularly head out on plundering expeditions before returning to prayer and contemplation.

En route to the reserve you'll pass **Rewu Monastery** on the other side of the valley and then, after a high pass, **Konkaling Monastery** (Gongling Si), the largest in the region, before reaching the town of Riwa. Riwa is 60km from Daocheng and has accommodation.

Just south of Riwa, where the road branches, you have to pay the hefty park entry fee. Yading village and the entrance to the park is 35km further on.

Among Chinese tourists the most popular way to see the reserve is by horse. Horse treks generally cost Y180 for the first day, Y120 to 150 for each day after that, depending on your bargaining skills. Most foreigners just walk.

There are several inns here, including the friendly **Gedong Hotel** (☎ 0836-572 7119; dm Y30), offering basic beds and food in a Tibetan home. It's signposted on the main road before you reach the park entrance. The owners can advise on the two-hour hike up to Qingwa Lake.

Inside the park there's simple accommodation at **Tsongu Monastery** (r Y40-60). A basic wooden **guesthouse** (☎ 136-9814 2416; dm Y30) was being built near here at the time of research and may be worth checking out. The owner plans to offer horses for hire.

The Kora

From the entrance it's a 45-minute walk through dripping forests and past chörtens to **Tsongu Monastery** (Chonggu Si), currently under renovation, where there is simple accommodation.

Two hours' walk southeast is Luorong Pasture (Luorong Muchang; 4188m), where there is normally another **tent hotel** (beds Y30) and restaurant. From here it's three hours to alpine Milk Lake (Niunai Hai; 4720m). Five Colours Lake (Wuse Hai) lies just over the side ridge.

From this point most Chinese tourists return the way they came but it is possible to do a kora of the mountain. For this you'll need camping equipment for one night. From the lake the kora climbs for one hour to a wide 4400m triple pass; it then branches right and descends to meadows, a popular place to camp. There are shepherds' huts here, where guides or porters normally stay the night.

From the valley a trail leads west to the main road, but the kora continues two hours northeast to Drölma-la (4375m). The trail continues four hours downhill, beneath the north face of Chenresig and past spectacular **Drölma-tso** (Tara Lake, sometimes called Pearl Lake) en route back to Tsongu Monastery. It's also possible to do a day hike to Drölma-tso from Tsongu Monastery.

Getting There & Away

The reserve is about 110km from Daocheng and takes about 2½ hours to reach. There is no public transportation here, although someone occasionally gets a bus to the park up and running during the high-season summer months, but this service cannot be counted on. Most people just arrange a ride through their accommodation. Alternatively, minibuses ply Gongga Lu Yiduan, Daocheng's main street, all day; fellow travellers will be trolling for a ride here as well, so you could hook up with them and split the cost to the reserve. Out of season it's not a bad idea to organise for your driver to take you back at a pre-arranged time. Snows can block the road without warning in April and October.

BATANG 八塘

☎ 0836 / pop 10,000 / elev 2589m

Lying 32km from the Tibetan border and 197km from Litang, low-lying Batang is the closest town to Tibet that is open to foreigners. An easy-going and friendly place with lots of streetside barbecue grills and outdoor seating, the modern town is surrounded by suburbs of beautiful ochre Tibetan houses. When it's still the end of winter in Litang it's already spring in Batang. If you are here in November, ask about the colourful *cham* dances held outside town on the 26th of the ninth Tibetan month.

Many travellers try to sneak into Tibet from here, so – unsurprisingly – the local PSB is a little suspicious of foreigners.

Roadwork between Litang and Batang (begun in 2004 and continuing indefinitely) is wreaking havoc with transportation and Batang's infrastructure; hot water and electricity are frequently cut for hours at a time. A torch (flashlight) is essential.

Sights

The Gelugpa-sect **Chöde Gaden Pendeling Monastery** in the southwest of town is well worth a visit. The monks (over 500) are friendly and active (they had just finished building a sand mandala during our visit). There are three chapels behind the main hall; up some stairs via a separate entrance is a room for the Panchen Lama, lined with photos of exiled local lamas. An old, Chinese-style hospital is now used as monk accommodation. Stop in the kitchen for some yak-butter tea before leaving. A kora of prayer wheels surrounds the monastery. To get here, follow Wenhua Jie downhill and keep your nose alert for the smell of yak butter.

There are some fine walks around town. Head north to a lovely Tibetan hillside village and then west to a riverside chörten that attracts a few pilgrims. Alternatively, head south from the town centre over a bridge and then east to a hilltop covered in prayer flags and offering views of the town.

Sleeping

Jinhui Hotel (金汇宾馆; Jinhui Binguan; ☎ 562 2700; dm Y10-15, 3-bed dm Y30, d without bathroom Y100, with bathroom Y160-180) Rooms here are in pretty good shape, for the most part very clean and well maintained. Get a room away from the street to escape the karaoke. The communal hot-water showers are pretty good and there's lots of space for washing clothes. Take the first right after the huge, hard-to-miss golden eagle statue in the little park area; the hotel's a block down on the left.

W Binguan (W宾馆; ☎ 562 3132; 1 Jinxianzi Dadao; d Y68-86) Run by a cool young Tibetan couple, this is a plain but very clean and bright hotel with decent bathrooms. Just a couple of minutes' walk from the bus station, it's also a good bet for early departures or late arrivals. The only downside is its proximity to some thunderously loud karaoke. Walk left coming out of the bus station. The hotel is on your left.

Snowlands Tashi Hotel (雪域扎西宾馆; Xueyuzhaxi Binguan; ☎ 562 3222; Shangmao Jie; r from Y288;) People may try to steer you to this place, supposedly the best in town, but the décor is enough to make you ill (green-, yellow- and burgundy-striped carpets?) and the bathrooms have some serious plumbing problems.

Cui Zhao Mian (脆诏面; 8am-8pm) This sparkling-clean place is the best of an uninspiring lot of restaurants. Its dumplings in broth, *chaoshou* (抄手; Y5), are outstanding. Turn left coming out of the bus station and follow the main road to the first major intersection. This small eatery will be on your left near the corner before you cross the street.

Local supermarkets stock everything from chocolate to French red wine.

Getting There & Away

The **bus station** (6.30am-10pm) has daily buses to Kangding (Y139) and Chengdu (Y239), both leaving at 6am and overnighting in Yajiang. The road to Litang is under major construction work so expect serious delays. Buses normally leave at 7am to Litang (Y59, six hours).

If you have to spend the night at Yajiang, the **Yalongwan Dajiudian** (雅龙湾大酒店; d Y80) at the bus station has electric blankets and is your best lodging option.

Headed west into Tibet, there are buses at 2pm (Y44, four hours) and afternoon microbuses (Y50) to Markham, 138km away inside the TAR. Foreigners may have problems buying bus tickets to Markham but should be able to get on the microbuses.

The bus station is a 10-minute walk from the town centre.

AROUND BATANG

One excellent detour from the Litang–Batang road is to **Tsopu Gou**, a scenic valley, lake and monastery 78km from Batang, then 38km off the main road. From Litang or Batang get off the bus at Cuola, where there is basic accommodation, and arrange a ride up the valley. The route passes the village of Chaluo, a monastery and some hot springs before entering a wide valley and village at the base of the lake.

A beautiful kora leads clockwise around the lake to the Nyingma-sect **Tsopu Monastery**, whose guesthouse offers mattresses on the floor for Y20. Bring your own food and purify the stream water. You can hike for a couple of hours up the valley behind the monastery to a glacial lake, or just get the views from the retreat chapels above the monastery.

BATANG TO POMDA

The road west from Batang crosses the Dri-chu (Jinsha Jiang or Yangzi River) into Tibet at Zhubalong and continues to Markham, where it joins the road from Yunnan.

Markham (芒康; Mangkang; 3900m), traditionally known as Garthok Dzong, is where permitless hitchhikers from Sichuan and Yunnan commonly get caught by the vigilant PSB. Try to avoid the town's main road. Coming from the east, head for the road to the north of town that connects with the main highway. Markham has a county guesthouse. The bus station won't sell tickets to foreigners. There's a checkpost about 3km west of town.

It's 158km on to **Dzogang** (左贡; Zuogong; 3800m), also known as Wamda in Tibetan, over a 4380m pass, dropping to cross the Dza-chu (Mekong River) at Druka, rising again to the 3900m Joba-la, dropping to stunning scenery around Denpa, then rising again to the 5008m Dongdo-la (phew!). There is a basic guesthouse in Dzogang. Transport along this stretch of the road is particularly infrequent.

The road continues along the Yu-chu, a tributary of the Salween River, for 107km to the main Lhasa–Chamdo road at Pomda (see p256).

Trekking

The high mountains, deep valleys and endless plains of Tibet offer incredible opportunities for trekking. The remoteness of Tibet combined with climatic extremes poses special challenges for walkers – and unique rewards. In the higher reaches of the plateau snow storms and blistering heat are both possible on a single day. The wonders of Tibet's natural environment are enhanced by the people met along the trail, heirs to an ancient and fascinating way of life. Blessedly, it is still possible to trek for days in Tibet without having the experience marred by the hubbub of modern civilisation.

Most trekking is done in the centre of Tibet, not far from the major towns and highways. Cities such as Lhasa and Shigatse provide bases from which to equip and launch treks. Mastering the six great treks covered here will serve you well should you decide to venture further afield. There are certainly many new frontiers beckoning the experienced, well-equipped trekker. For the most adventurous and carefree, it is even possible to cross large sections of Tibet's mountain ranges on foot.

The first people trekked over the mountains to Tibet during the Old Stone Age, 40,000 years ago. Over the ensuing millennia invaders, pilgrims and traders covering huge distances made it to the mountain-ringed 'Land of Snows'. In the late 19th and early 20th centuries a slew of spies, explorers and scholars walked great lengths in their attempts to reach the Holy City, Lhasa. For those who survived their Tibetan adventure it was standard practice to regale their fellow countrymen with an adventure book or two. The greatest Tibetan explorer of all time was the Swede Sven Hedin, who made more than a dozen epic trips to Tibet in the early part of the 20th century. One of the most memorable treks was mounted by George Roerich's Central Asiatic expedition in the 1920s. By traversing a great swathe of Tibet's northern plains, Roerich made a series of pioneering archaeological discoveries.

HIGHLIGHTS

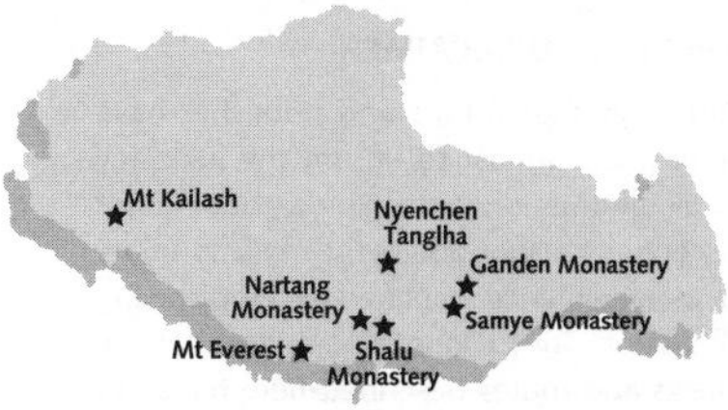

- Walk the old pilgrims' trail from **Ganden to Samye** (p288), a test of one's physical ability and spiritual aptitude
- Follow the Buddhist trade route from **Shalu to Nartang** (p296), a fine introduction to trekking in Tibet and a window on the ancient art of pilgrimage
- Circumambulate **Mt Kailash** (p302) – not merely a walk around a mountain but a journey towards a deeper understanding of the inner self
- Traverse the **Nyenchen Tanglha range** (p308) to the turquoise healing waters of lake Namtso, extending one's reach and endurance
- Trek with **Mt Everest** (p299) as an ever-present beacon, for spectacular scenery, rigorous exercise and the opportunity for fellowship with Tibetans

PLANNING

For all its attractions, Tibet is a formidable place where even day walks involve survival skills and generous portions of determination. As it's situated on the highest plateau on earth and crisscrossed by the world's loftiest mountains, nothing comes easily and careful preparation is all important. Even on the most popular treks, which can involve several days of travel without any outside help, high passes up to 5600m are crossed.

WHEN TO TREK

The best time to plan a trek in Tibet is during the warmer half of the year. May and June are excellent months without much rain or snowfall but some high alpine passes in eastern Tibet may still be closed (although in this chapter we don't cover treks in eastern Tibet). July and August are the hottest months of the year but they tend to be rainy and this can make walking messy and trails harder to find. September and October are excellent months for trekking but in high areas the nights are cold and early snow is always a possibility.

It's a good idea to budget in a few extra days for your trek, especially if much road travel is needed to get to the trailhead, as roads can be blocked, especially in the wet summer months. You might also need additional time hiring local guides and beasts of burden.

Trekkers must be prepared for extremes in climate, even in the middle of summer. A hot, sunny day can turn cold and miserable in a matter of minutes, especially at higher elevations. Night temperatures at 4500m and above routinely fall below freezing even in July and August! At other times of the year it gets even colder. In midwinter in northwestern Tibet, minimum temperatures reach minus 40°C. Yet Tibet is a study in contrasts, and in summer a scorching sun and hot, blustery winds can make even the hardiest walker scurry for any available shade. Between the two extremes, the Tibetan climate – cool and dry – is ideal for walking but always be prepared for the worst.

Before embarking on a trek, make sure you're up to the challenge of high-altitude walking through rugged country. Test your capabilities by going on day walks in the hills around Lhasa and Shigatse. Attempt a hike to the top of a small mountain such as Bumpa Ri (p116), the prayer-flag-draped peak on the far side of the Kyi-chu from Lhasa.

TREKKING DISCLAIMER

Although the authors and publisher have done their utmost to ensure the accuracy of all information in this guide, they cannot accept any responsibility for any loss, injury or inconvenience sustained by people using this book. They cannot guarantee that the tracks and routes described here have not become impassable for any reason in the interval between research and publication.

The fact that a trip or area is described in this guidebook does not mean that it is safe for you and your trekking party. You are ultimately responsible for judging your own capabilities in the conditions you encounter.

WHAT TO BRING

There is a great deal to see while trekking and you will be revitalised by the natural surroundings, but you must be prepared for extremes in weather and terrain. The time of year and the places in which you choose to walk will dictate the equipment you need.

Clothing & Footwear

As a minimum, you will need basic warm clothing, including a hat, scarf, gloves, down jacket, long underwear, warm, absorbent socks, all-weather shell and sun hat, as well as comfortable, well-made pants and shirts. Women may want to add a long skirt to their clothing list. Wear loose-fitting clothes that cover your arms, legs and neck and choose a wide-brimmed hat like the ones Tibetans wear. For information on culturally appropriate dress, see Responsible Tourism (p47).

If you attempt winter trekking, you will certainly need more substantial mountaineering clothing. Many people opt for synthetic-pile clothing, but also consider wool or sheep fleece, which have proven themselves in the mountains of Tibet for centuries. One of your most important assets will be a pair of strong, well-fitting hiking boots. And remember to break them in before starting the trek!

Equipment

Three essential items are a tent, sleeping bag and backpacking stove. There are no restaurants in the remote areas of Tibet and provisions are hard to come by, so you will probably end up cooking all of your own food. Count on camping because, except in certain villages that are on the main trekking routes, it can be difficult to find places to sleep. Invest in a good tent that can handle big storms and heavy winds. A warm sleeping bag is a must. Manufacturers tend to overrate the effectiveness of their bags, so always buy a warmer one than you think you'll need.

You will also need a strong, comfortable backpack large enough to carry all of your gear and supplies. To save a lot of misery, test the backpack on day hikes to be certain it fits and is properly adjusted.

Other basic items include water containers with at least 2L capacity, a system for water purification, a torch (flashlight), compass, pocketknife, first-aid kit, waterproof matches, sewing kit, shrill whistle and walking stick or ski pole. This last item not only acts as a walking aid but, even more importantly, for defence against dog attacks. Tibetan dogs can be particularly large and brutal and they roam at will in nearly every village and herders' camp. Bring your walking stick or pole from home, or purchase Chinese-made trekking poles in Lhasa.

Petrol for camping stoves is widely available in towns and cities but is of fairly poor quality. To prevent your stove from getting gummed up you will have to clean it regularly. Kerosene (煤油, *meiyou* in Chinese, *sanum* in Tibetan) can also be obtained in cities. In Lhasa you will find kerosene vendors on Dekyi Shar Lam, opposite the road to Ramoche.

For details on buying and hiring trekking gear in Tibet, see p126. Nowadays, there are scores of shops in Lhasa selling such equipment.

MAPS

There are numerous commercially available maps covering Tibet, but very few of these maps are detailed enough to be more than a general guide for trekkers. The best overview map currently available is called Tibet, a 1:1,500,000 scale chart by **Reise Know-How** (www.reise-know-how.de) of Germany. The Chinese government produces small-scale topographic and administrative maps, but these are not for sale to the general public. The US-based Defense Mapping Agency Aerospace Center produces a series of charts covering Tibet at scales of 1:1,000,000, 1:500,000 and 1:250,000 (though the last can be hard to find). The most useful of the American 1:500,000 references for trekking in Tibet are H-10A (Lhasa region, Ganden to Samye, Tsurphu to Yangpachen), H-9A (Kailash and Manasarovar) and H-9B (Shigatse region, Shalu to Nartang, Everest region).

Soviet 1:200,000 topographic maps can now be consulted in many large university library map rooms. However, most libraries will not permit you to photocopy them because of international copyright laws. Buying them has become easier with commercial outlets in the West stocking them. Punch 'Tibet maps' into your computer search engine to see who carries them in your area.

The Swiss company **Gecko Maps** (www.geckomaps.com) produces a 1:50,000-scale Mt Kailash trekking map.

For details of places to buy maps of Tibet and Lhasa, see p321.

TREKKING AGENCIES

The kind of trek you take will depend on your experience and the amount of time you have. Unless you have already hiked extensively in the Andes or Himalayas, it may be better to consider organising your walk through a travel agency. This can save much time and worry.

The main advantage of going with an agency is that it takes care of all the red tape and dealings with officials. Most agencies offer a full-package trek, including transport to and from the trailhead, guide, cook, yaks or burros to carry the equipment, mess tent and cooking gear. The package may even include sleeping bags and tents if these are required.

There is now a plethora of private agencies in Lhasa, some of which can arrange treks. Let the buyer beware, for the standard of service fluctuates wildly and may bear no correlation to the amount you pay. In general, standards of service and reliability are much lower than in Kathmandu or other popular trekking hubs. Shop around carefully and compare the services and attitudes of at least several agencies. Shady dealings are part of everyday business in China but they need not scuttle your trip. The good news is that competition between agencies offering trekking services is fierce, impelling the smarter ones to up the quality of their product. If cost is a big issue and you and your party are seasoned trekkers, consider the FIT agencies (see p100). They are cheaper than other agencies, but are known to cut corners on service.

Make sure the agency spells out exactly what is included in the price it is quoting you, and be prepared to provide all your own personal equipment. The quality of equipment and logistics varies widely, and it's a good idea to closely inspect the vehicles and camping gear before leaving Lhasa. It's essential to sign a written contract with the tourist agency arranging your travel. However, as none of the Lhasa companies seem to have standard trekking contracts you may find yourself drafting one up. If so, be certain to include full details of the service you're paying for and money-back guarantees should your operator fail to deliver what has been agreed. For the standard contents of tour contracts, have a look at the brochures of adventure-travel companies in your home country. The best way to insure a good outcome is to pay one-third to a half of the total cost of a trip up front and the balance after the trek is completed. This is now standard operating procedure, so if an operator baulks at this arrangement simply take your business somewhere else.

None of the Lhasa-based agencies that are listed (see below) can be unconditionally recommended, but all have run many successful treks. Trekkers are particularly at the mercy of those driving them to and from the trailheads. To avoid problems, it is prudent to test the driver and guide on a day trip before heading off into the wilds with them. Always have the phone number of your agency so that you can contact them should something go awry. Mobile (cell) phone coverage has now been extended to all the trailheads.

Prices vary according to group size and location but none are cheap. Costs per person tend to be lower in bigger groups. For treks in remote and border areas, expect to wait at least four days for the permits to be sorted. If you feel you have been cheated by your agent, you may find help with the department of marketing and promotion of the **Tibet Tourism Bureau** (Map p96; ☎ 0891-683 4315; fax 683 4632) in Lhasa. This government organisation is in charge of training tour guides and monitoring the performance of all trekking and tour companies.

Tibetan Agencies

On the Tourist's Way (Xizang Rikaze Zhongguo Guoji Lüxingshe; Map p100; ☎ 0891-634 5429; migmatse@hotmail.com; Flora Hotel Office Bldg, Room No 4; per day US$100) Located in the Muslim quarter, this innovative company is run by the popular Migma Tsering and can arrange treks just about anywhere.

Tibet Chamdo International Travel (Xizang Changdu Guoji Lüxingshe; Map p100; ☎ 0891-633 3871; tntc@public.ls.xz.cn; Mandala Hotel, 31 Barkhor South; per day US$100) Managed by a veteran operator named David Migmar. He and his staff have substantial trekking experience and are willing to please.

Tibet International Sports Travel (Xizang Shengdi Guoji Lüxingshe; Map p96; ☎ 0891-633 4082; peldon@tist.com; 6 Lingkhor Shar Lam; per day US$130) The oldest agency specialising in trekking. Located next to the Himalaya Hotel, this is now managed by Peldon.

Tibet Wind Horse Adventure (Longda Guoji Lüxingshe; Map p96; ☎ 0891-683 3009; jampa_w@hotmail.com; www.tibetwindhorse.com; 3fl annexe, Gyadrokling Hotel/Zhazhulin Binguan, 26 Linkuo Xilu; walk-in rafting office (near Shangbala Hotel entrance, Zangyi Lu/Mentsikhang Lam; per day US$120) One of the best managed agencies in town and partnered with several international travel companies. The running of treks is handled by Jampa, the deputy general manager, while Chris Jones is project manager for the white-water rafting trips.

Tibet Yungdru Adventure (Xizang Yunzhu Tanxian; Map p96; ☎ 0891-683 5813; info@tnya.com.cn; No 5 Bldg, New Shol Village; per day US$120-140) A main focus of the managing director Thupten is trekking in the more remote regions of Tibet. The office is impossible to find; call and staff will come pick you up.

Kathmandu Agencies

If you want to organise your Tibet trek from Kathmandu, here are some of the most qualified agencies:

Arniko Travels (☎ 01-443 9906; www.arnikotravel.com; PO 4695, Baluwatar)

Dharma Adventures (☎ 01-443 0499; www.dharmaadventures.com; GPO Box 5385, 205 Tangal Marg)

Great Escapes (☎ 01-441 8951; escape@mail.com.np; PO 9523, Baluwatar)

Malla Treks (☎ 01-441 0089; www.mallatreks.com; PO Box 5227, Lekhnath Marg)

Western Agencies

A few Western companies organise fixed-departure treks in Tibet. These tours can be joined in your home country or abroad, usually in Kathmandu. Prices are higher than treks organised in Tibet or Kathmandu, but they save you a lot of effort and are useful if you have the money but only a couple of weeks.

A trek organised at home includes a Western leader, a local leader, porters, a cook and so on. All your practical needs will be taken care of and you'll be free to enjoy the trekking.

PERMITS

Officially, individuals are not permitted to trek independently in Tibet and are required to join an organised group. Trekking, as with all travel in Tibet apart from that in Lhasa prefecture and Tsetang and Shigatse towns, requires a travel permit (see p324). Note, however, that the Tsurphu to Yangpachen trek covered on p292 doesn't require any permits.

The official requirements hardly stop the independent traveller, but should you opt to go it alone you must be willing to face the consequences. The good news is that the few people who do get caught are usually let off with a talking down and a light fine. Still, in some extreme cases, trekkers have been held by the police for several days and large sums of money demanded; some have even been deported.

That said, a number of trekkers set out alone, in the true spirit of independent travel, and many succeed. If you are caught by the security police without the right documents, be friendly and repentant. You will probably be let off lightly unless you (or the police) lose your cool. It's unusual to be asked for any documentation while on a trek. The most likely time to be apprehended by the police is when hitchhiking, so be particularly careful in towns and at truck stops.

ON THE TREK

Bear in mind that the trekking trails in Tibet are not marked and in many places there are no people from whom to ask directions. Paths regularly merge, divide and peter out, making route finding inherently difficult. If you're not good at trailblazing, your only alternatives are to employ a local guide or to go through a travel agency.

GUIDES & PACK ANIMALS

The rugged terrain, long distances and high elevations of Tibet make most people think twice about carrying their own gear. In villages and nomad camps along the main trekking routes it's often possible to hire yaks or horses to do the dirty work for you.

It's helpful to know some Tibetan to negotiate what you want and how much you are willing to pay. Otherwise write out the figures involved and make sure the owners of the pack animals understand them. Be prepared for a good session of bargaining and don't set out until you and the Tibetans working for you are perfectly clear about what's been agreed. To avoid any misunderstandings, be sure to spell out the amount of time you expect from your helpers and the exact amount you intend to pay. Your mule skinner or yak driver will also serve as your guide, an important asset on the unmarked trails of Tibet. Consider just hiring a guide if you don't want or can't get pack animals – this could save you a lot of frustrating hours looking for the route.

Guides can also share their knowledge of the natural history and culture of the place, greatly adding to your experience. No less than the large trekking companies depend on local guides to make their trips work. Even without language skills much can be gleaned by being a good listener and observer. One technique is just to point at a landmark or plant and have your guide repeat its name. A whole catalogue can be put together in this fashion. You might also request your helpers to write down place names and other information and have

SOCIAL TREKKING

In most out-of-the-way places trekkers can quickly become the centre of attention, and sometimes just a smile may lead to dinner invitations and offers of a place to stay. If you really detest being the star of the show, don't camp in villages; if you do, don't expect Western notions of privacy to prevail.

If you ask directions, be prepared to be sent in the direction you are walking, no matter where you're trying to go. To avoid this age-old travellers' trap, be prepared to patiently and repeatedly explain what your travel goals are and, if in doubt, ask someone else.

If you have any religious sentiments, your trek probably qualifies as a pilgrimage, in which case you will generally receive better treatment than if you are 'just going someplace'. Another helpful hint: if all else fails try a song and dance. Even the most amateur of efforts is met with great approval.

For other cultural considerations related to trekking, see p47.

RESPONSIBLE TREKKING

The environment of Tibet is under tremendous pressure. It is therefore imperative that trekkers make their way lightly and leave nothing behind but their proverbial footprints. Tibet's beautiful but vulnerable alpine tracts deserve the utmost respect. A fire, for instance, can scar the landscape for centuries. Stay off fragile slopes and do not tread on delicate plants or sensitive breeding grounds. Follow the Tibetan ethos, killing not even the smallest of insects. In the long term, this approach will buy trekkers great respect and will help guarantee that later visitors get to enjoy the same pristine environment as you.

Rubbish

Carry out all your rubbish. Don't overlook easily forgotten items, such as silver paper, orange peel, cigarette butts and plastic wrappers. Make sure to have a dedicated rubbish bag. Gain good karma by carrying out rubbish left by others.

Never bury your rubbish: digging disturbs soil and encourages erosion. Buried rubbish will more than likely be dug up by animals. Moreover, it may take years to decompose, especially at Tibet's high altitudes.

Minimise the waste you must carry, bringing in no more packaging than you will need. Take reusable containers, zip-lock bags or stuff sacks from home.

Do not burn plastic and other garbage as this is believed to irritate mountain spirits and affronts the sensibilities of more traditional Tibetans.

Sanitary napkins, tampons and condoms must be carried out. They burn and decompose poorly.

Human Waste Disposal

Contamination of water sources by human faeces leads to the transmission of all sorts of nasties. Where there is a toilet, please use it. Where there is none, human waste should be left on the surface of the ground away from trails, water and habitations to decompose. Aridity, cold and high ultraviolet exposure renders wastes into innocuous compounds relatively quickly.

If you are in a large trekking group, dig a privy pit. Be sure to build it far from any water source or marshy ground and carefully rehabilitate the area when you leave camp. Also, be certain that the latrine is not near mani (prayer) walls, shrines or any other sacred structures.

Washing

In the arid climate of much of Tibet, water is highly regarded. Don't use detergents or toothpaste in or near watercourses, even if they are biodegradable. For personal washing and cleaning cooking utensils, use biodegradable soap and a container (such as a lightweight, portable basin) at

it translated by an English-speaking Tibetan friend in Lhasa.

The rates for pack animals vary widely according to the time of the year and location. Horses and yaks are pricey at Mt Kailash, costing upwards of Y150 per animal. In most other places burros and horses can be had for Y50 to Y100 per head. Local guides and livestock handlers usually command Y50 to Y90 per day. Remember that your hired help will want to be paid for the time it takes them to return home. Sometimes a discount on the daily rate can be negotiated for their homeward travel.

FOOD

You should be self-sufficient wit food since there isn't much to eat along the trail. In most of the villages there is little or no food surplus thus probably nothing to buy. But there is no need to worry about supplies; in Lhasa there are now thousands of stalls and stores selling a huge variety of foodstuffs, making well-balanced, tasty meals possible on the trail. Even in Shigatse and the smaller cities there are many foods suitable for trekking.

Vacuum-packed red meat and poultry, and packaged dried meat, fish and tofu are readily found in Lhasa. Plenty of varieties of packaged and bulk dried fruits are sold throughout the city. The newest and tastiest offerings are peaches and kiwi fruit, which make a great and tasty trail mix when combined with peanuts, cashews, sunflower seeds and walnuts.

least 50m away from the water source. Try using a scourer, sand or snow instead of detergent. Widely disperse the waste water to allow the soil to filter it.

Erosion

Hillsides and mountain slopes, especially at high altitude, are prone to erosion. Stick to existing tracks and avoid short cuts.

If a well-used track passes through a mud patch, walk through the mud to avoid increasing the size of the patch.

Never remove the plant life that keeps topsoil in place.

Fires & Low-Impact Cooking

Building fires is not an option. Wood is nonexistent in much of Tibet and where there are trees and bushes they are desperately needed by locals. Cook on a lightweight kerosene, petrol, alcohol or multifuel stove and avoid those powered by disposable butane gas canisters.

Make sure you supply your guide and porters with stoves. In alpine areas, ensure that all members are outfitted with enough clothing so that fires are not needed for warmth.

Good Trekking Partnership

To insure an ecologically sound trek monitor all your staff members closely. Stress to your agency that you will not tolerate rubbish being thrown along the trail or at the trailheads. During transit explain to your drivers that rubbish should not be thrown out the windows, a common practice in Tibet. Let your helpers select camp sites where it's not necessary to trench around their tents. Make it clear that any gratuities will hinge upon good stewardship of the environment.

Wildlife Conservation

- Do not engage in or encourage illegal hunting.
- Don't buy items or medicines made from endangered wild species.
- Discourage the presence of wildlife by cleaning up your food scraps.
- Do not feed the wildlife as this can lead to animals becoming dependent on hand-outs, to unbalanced populations and to diseases.

Camping

Seek permission to camp from the local villagers or shepherds. They will usually be happy to grant permission if asked.

You can even find almonds and pistachios imported from the USA.

Soybean- and dairy-milk powders can be used with several kinds of prepackaged cereals. Oatmeal and instant barley porridge are now available in the supermarkets. Pickled and dried vegetables are good for dressing up soups and stir-fries. On the Barkhor are stalls selling Indian pickles and curry powders for an added touch. Lightweight vegetables such as seaweed and dried mushrooms can do wonders for macaroni and instant noodles. Wholemeal Chinese noodles and imported Korean spaghetti made of various whole grains are now on the supermarket shelves as well.

Cooking mediums include butter, margarine, vegetable oil and sesame oil. Butter can be preserved for long treks or old butter made more palatable by turning it into ghee (boil for about 20 minutes and then strain). For those with a sweet tooth, all kinds of biscuits and sweets are sold in Lhasa and the larger regional towns. Decent-quality Chinese and Western chocolate is available in Lhasa. Check out p126 for details of good supermarkets in the capital.

DRINK

As wonderfully cold and clear as much of the water in Tibet is, do not assume that it's safe to drink. Livestock contaminate many of the water sources and Tibetans do not always live up to their cultural ideals. Follow Tibetan tradition and eliminate the monotony of drinking plain water by downing as much tea as you can. You can buy Chinese green tea in all its varieties in every city and town in Tibet. If you're offered Tibetan yak-butter tea, have it served in your own cup as per tradition – this eliminates the risk associated with drinking from used cups. More like a soup than a tea, it helps fortify you against the cold and replenishes the body's salts. For information on water purification and traditional beverages consult the Health chapter (p355).

HEALTHY TREKKING

To maintain your health in such a difficult high-elevation environment you will need to take some special precautions. With a little preparation and good sense your trekking experience will be one of the highlights of your trip to Tibet. Bring a first-aid kit (see p347) with all the basics and perhaps some extras as well. Never trek alone and buy health and evacuation insurance. Read the Health chapter (p346) for health considerations that affect visitors to Tibet. Trekkers are particularly vulnerable to sunburn (p354), hypothermia (p354) and acute mountain sickness (AMS; p351): make sure you're prepared. For detailed medical information, see *Medicine for Mountaineering* published by Mountaineers Books.

TREKKING ROUTES

Detailed descriptions of six popular treks are given here. They offer fantastic walking, superb scenery and, with the exception of Lake Manasarovar and Mt Kailash, are close to Lhasa or the main highways. Walking times given are just that; they don't include breaks, nature stops or any other off-your-feet activities. On average, plan to walk five or seven hours at most in a day, interspersed with frequent short rests. You will also need time to set up camp, cook and just plain enjoy yourself.

The trek stages can be used as a daily itinerary, but plan ahead to avoid spending the night at the highest point reached in the day.

GANDEN TO SAMYE

This trek has much to offer: lakes, beautiful alpine landscapes, herders' camps and sacred sites, as well as two of Tibet's greatest centres of religious culture. With so much to offer, its popularity is understandable, but you should not underestimate the trek. Only those with experience hiking and camping in higher-elevation wildernesses should attempt this trek unsupported.

The best time for the trek is from mid-May to mid-October. Summer can be wet but the mountains are at their greenest and wildflowers spangle the alpine meadows. Barring heavy snow, it's also possible for those with a lot of trekking experience and the right gear to do this trek in the colder months. If you're coming straight from Lhasa, you should spend at least one night at Ganden Monastery (4190m) to acclimatise.

SAFETY GUIDELINES FOR WALKING

Before embarking on a walking trip, consider the following points to ensure a safe and enjoyable experience:

- Be sure you are healthy and feel comfortable walking for a sustained period.
- Obtain reliable information about physical and environmental conditions along your intended route (eg from local inhabitants).
- Be aware of local laws, regulations and customs about wildlife and the environment.
- Walk only in regions and on trails within your realm of experience.
- Be aware that weather conditions and terrain vary significantly from one region, or even from one trail to another. Seasonal changes can significantly alter any track. These differences influence the way walkers dress and the equipment they carry.
- Ask before you set out about the environmental conditions that can affect your trek and how local, experienced walkers deal with these considerations.

If you're fit, acclimatised and have a pack animal to carry your bags, it's not difficult to do the trek in 3½ days, overnighting in Hepu/Yama Do, Tsotup-chu and Yamalung, though some groups take the full five days. You'll experience at least three seasons on this trek, probably in the same day! From the wintry feel of the Chitu-la you rapidly descend to the spring-time rhododendron blooms of the middle valley until the summer heat hits you on the final approach to Samye. Pack accordingly.

Public buses run between Lhasa and Ganden (see p127 and p140), and between Lhasa and the Samye ferry crossing (see p172).

Stage 1: Ganden to Yama Do

5-6 hours / 17km / 300m ascent / 450m descent

The trek begins from the parking lot at the base of Ganden Monastery. It's often possible to find a pack animal or porter here to help carry your bags to Hepu or beyond; ask among the incense and prayer-flag sellers near the car park.

Leave the parking lot and look for the well-trodden trail heading south along the side of Angkor Ri, the highest point on the Ganden kora. After 20 minutes the Ganden kora branches off to the right; keep ascending straight for another 30 minutes. You quickly lose sight of Ganden but gain views of Samadro village below you, before reaching a **saddle**, marked by a *lapse* (cairn) 2m tall and 3m in diameter.

From the saddle, look south to see the approach to the Shuga-la in the distance. Traversing the west side of the ridge from the saddle, you briefly get views of Trubshi village below and the Kyi-chu Valley to the west. The trail dips briefly into a gully and reaches a spur surmounted by a cairn after 45 minutes. The trail now descends towards Hepu village. Twenty minutes from the spur is a spring. From here it's a further 30 minutes to the village, 2½ hours or so from Ganden.

There are around 30 houses in the village of **Hepu** (4284m; N 29°42.387′, E 091°31.442′) and it's possible for trekkers to camp or find accommodation among the friendly locals. There's good camping to the south and west of the village. Look for a red-and-yellow masonry structure and white incense hearths at the southeastern edge of the village. This is the **shrine** of Hepu's *yul lha* (local protecting deity), the Divine White Yak.

If carrying your gear up the pass beyond Hepu is not a pleasant thought, you should be able to rent yaks to do the work for you. Villagers charge around Y35 to Y40 per yak per day, plus the same again for the salary of the yak herder. Usually, herders feed themselves and provide their own camping gear,

GANDEN TO SAMYE AT A GLANCE

Duration 4-5 days
Distance 80km
Difficulty medium to difficult
Start Ganden Monastery
Finish Samye Monastery
Highest Point Shuga-la (5250m)
Nearest Large Towns Lhasa and Tsetang
Accommodation camping
Public Transport bus
Summary This demanding trek crosses two passes over 5000m, connects two of Tibet's most important monasteries and begins less than 50km from Lhasa. It has emerged as the most popular trek in the Ü region.

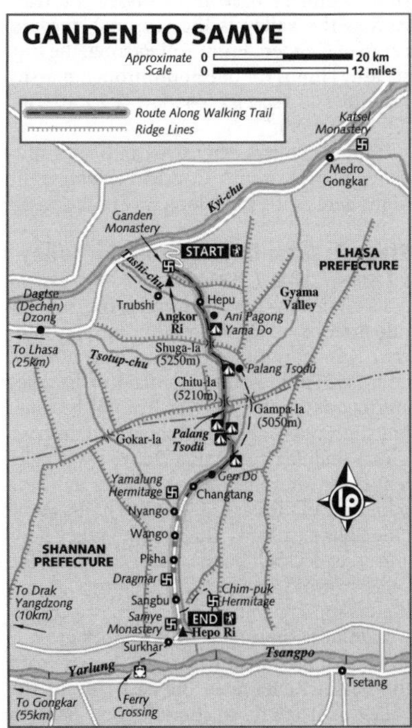

but make this clear before you set out. A yak can carry two or three backpacks, depending on their weight. Small groups of two or three people are more likely to end up with a horse than a yak, as single yaks are notoriously difficult to manage. Pack animals generally only go as far as Nyango, the start of the dirt road, 3½ hours' walk from Samye.

Finding a guide and fetching the pack animals can take several hours, so if you haven't arranged things in advance you may have to spend the night in Hepu. If you have no luck finding pack animals in Hepu, try down the valley in the nearby village of Trubshi, about 45 minutes' walk away.

From Hepu, the trail climbs towards the Shuga-la, 3½ hours away. Walk west downhill from the village towards a bridge crossing the Tashi-chu, near the confluence with another stream. Round the inner side of the confluence and head south upstream along the east bank. You are now following the watercourse originating from the Shuga-la. Near the confluence are good camp sites.

One hour from Hepu you reach **Ani Pagong**, a narrow, craggy bottleneck in the valley. A small nunnery used to be above the trail. Across the valley is the seasonal herders' camp of Choden. From Ani Pagong, the trail steadily climbs for one hour through marshy meadows to **Yama Do** (4456m; N 29°40.650', E 091°30.858').

Yama Do offers extensive camp sites suitable for larger groups. Consider spending the night here as it's still a long way to the pass.

Stage 2: Yama Do to Tsotup-chu Valley

5-7 hours / 10km / 1000m ascent / 450m descent

Above Yama Do the valley's watercourse splits into three branches. Follow the central (southern) branch, not the southeast or southwest branches. The route leaves the flank of the valley and follows the valley bottom. The trail becomes indistinct but it's a straight shot up to the pass. Thirty minutes from Yama Do are two single-tent camp sites, the last good ones until the other side of the pass, at least five hours away. One hour past Yama Do leave the valley floor and ascend a shelf on the east (left) side of the valley to avoid a steep gully that forms around the stream. In another 45 minutes you enter a wet alpine basin studded with tussock grass.

The Shuga-la is at least 1¼ hours from the basin. Remain on the east side of the valley as it bends to the left. You have to negotiate boulders and lumpy ground along the final steep climb to the pass. The **Shuga-la** (5250m; N 29°38.499', E 091°32.016') cannot be seen until you're virtually on top of it. It's marked by a large cairn covered in prayer flags and yak horns. Some maps refer to the pass as the Zhukar-la or Jockar-la. Either way, you've made it to the highest point of the trek.

The route continues over the Shuga-la and to start with descends sharply through a boulder field. Be on the lookout for a clear trail marked by cairns on the left side of the boulder field. This trail traverses the ridge in a southeasterly direction, paralleling the valley below. Do not head directly down to the valley floor from the pass unless you have good reason. It's a long, steep descent and once at the bottom you would have to go back up the valley to complete the trek. In case of emergency, retreat down the valley for a bolt hole back to the Lhasa–Ganden Hwy, a long day of walking away.

The trail gradually descends to the valley floor, 1½ hours from and 200m below the pass. The views of the valley and the lake at its head are one of the highlights of the trek. Cross the large **Tsotup-chu** (4907m; N 29°37.364', E 091°33.307'), which flows through the valley and keep an eye out for the herders' dogs. During heavy summer rains, take special care to find a safe ford. The pastures in the area support large herds of yaks, goats and sheep, and during the trekking season herders are normally camped here. This is an ideal place to camp and meet the *drokpas* (nomads).

An alternative route to Samye via the **Gampa-la** (5050m) follows the main branch of the Tsotup-chu past a couple of lakes to the pass. South of the Gampa-la the trail plunges into a gorge, crisscrossing the stream that flows down from it. These fords may pose problems during summer rains or when completely frozen. See Gary McCue's *Trekking in Tibet – A Traveler's Guide* for details of this route.

Stage 3: Tsotup-chu Valley to Herders' Camps

5 hours / 14km / 300m ascent / 400m descent

From the Tsotup-chu ford, the main watercourse flows from the southeast and a minor tributary enters from the southwest. Follow this tributary (which quickly disappears underground) steeply up for about 30 minutes

TREKKING

until you reach a large basin and a cairn that offers fine views down onto Palang Tsodü lake. Stay on the west (right) side of the basin and turn into the first side valley opening on the right. A couple of minutes into the valley you'll pass a large group **camp site** (5079m; N 29°36.604′, E 091°33.544′), sadly covered in litter. This is a good alternative camp site to the Tsotup-chu but only if you're acclimatised, as it's 100m higher.

Follow this broad valley, which soon arcs south to the Chitu-la. The pass can be seen in the distance, a rocky rampart at the head of the valley. At first, stay on the west (right) side of the valley; there is a small trail. As you approach the pass, the trail switches to the east side of the valley. If you miss the trail just look for the easiest route up; the terrain is not particularly difficult.

The **Chitu-la** (5210m; N 29°34.817′, E 091°33.159′) is topped by several cairns and a small glacial tarn. Move to the west side of the pass to find the trail down and to circumvent a sheer rock wall on its south flank. A short descent will bring you into a basin with three small lakes. The trail skirts the west side of the first lake and then crosses to the eastern shores of the second two. It takes 45 minutes to reach the south end of the basin. Drop down from the basin on the west side of the stream and in 15 minutes you'll pass a collection of **cairns** (5077m; N 29°33.924′, E 091°32.790′) to the right. A further 10 minutes brings you the stone walls of a camp where herders have carved out level places for their tents.

Below the herders' highest camp, the valley is squeezed in by vertical rock walls, forcing you to pick your way through the rock-strewn valley floor. Pass a side stream after 10 minutes and then cross over to the west (right) side of the widening valley to recover the trail. In 10 more minutes you will come to a flat and a seasonal **herders' camp** on the east side of the valley, good for camping. At the lower end of the flat, return to the west side of the valley. The trail again disappears as it enters a scrub willow and rosebush forest, but there is only one way to go to get to Samye and that is downstream.

In 15 minutes, when a tributary valley enters from the right, cross to the east side of the valley. Fifteen minutes further, you will reach another seasonal **herders' camp**, inhabited for only a short time each year. Another 15 minutes beyond this camp, hop back to the west bank to avoid a cliff hugging the opposite side of the stream. Pass through a large meadow and ford the stream back to the east bank. From this point the trail remains on the east side of the valley for several hours.

Camp sites are numerous here. Soon you'll pass herders' tents camped near the spot where the side valley coming from the Gampa-la joins the main valley. Descend the finger of land formed by the river junction and then cross the **stream** (4497m; N 29°31.600′, E 091°32.982′). At times of heavy summer rain you might have to wait for the water to subside in order to cross safely.

Stages 4 & 5: Herders' Camps to Samye Monastery

10 hours / 39km / 1200m descent

The trail is now wide and easy to follow as it traces a course down the east side of the valley. Walk through the thickening scrub forest for one hour and you will come to another stream entering from the east side of the main valley. Look for the wood-and-stone **Diwaka Zampa bridge** (4380m; N 29°30.440′, E 091°33.158′) 50m above the confluence. The valley now bends to the right (west) and the trail enters the thickest and tallest part of the scrub forest. The right combination of elevation, moisture and aspect create a verdant environment, while just a few kilometres away desert conditions prevail.

The next three-hour stretch of the trail is among the most delightful of the entire trek. According to local woodcutters, more than 15 types of trees and shrubs are found here, some growing to as high as 6m. Fragrant junipers grow on exposed south-facing slopes, while rhododendrons prefer the shadier slopes. The rhododendrons start to bloom in early May and by the end of the month the forest is ablaze with pink and white blossoms.

The trail winds through a series of meadows. After 30 minutes the stony flood plain of a tributary joins the river from the north. In another 30 minutes look for a mass of prayer flags and an incense burner at a place known as Gen Do. This is a **shrine** (4180m; N 29°29.530′, E 091°31.810′) to the protector of the area, the ancient goddess Dorje Yudronma. Just past the shrine, cross a small tributary stream. In one hour the forest rapidly thins and **Changtang**, the first permanent village since Hepu, pops up. There's good camping just before the village.

Look south to the distant mountains; this is the range on the far side of the Yarlung Tsangpo Valley. Forty-five minutes down the valley at a prominent bend in the valley is the turn-off for the **Yamalung Hermitage**, visible on the cliff face high above the valley. A small shop run by the nuns of Yamalung sells soft drinks, beer and instant noodles. There's fine camping across the bridge; the path to Yamalung also leads up from here. It's a 45-minute steep climb to the hermitage. Yamalung (also called Emalung) is where Guru Rinpoche is said to have meditated and received empowerment from the long-life deity Tsepame (Amitayus).

The hermitage consists of several small temples, and a handful of nuns live here. Below the temple complex is a sacred spring and an old relief carving in stone of Guru Rinpoche, King Trisong Detsen and the Indian scholar Shantarakshita, all of whom lived in the 8th century. The cave Guru Rinpoche meditated in is enshrined by the Drubpuk Mara Titsang Temple. Inside on the roof are the footprint and handprint of the saint, said to have been created when he magically expanded the size of the cave. Other shrines higher up include the cave retreats of the fifth Dalai Lama and the translator Vairocana, as well as chapels dedicated to the Dzogchen protectors and the Guru Tsengye – the eight manifestations of Guru Rinpoche.

From the turn-off to Yamalung the walking trail becomes a motorable road and the valley much wider. In 15 minutes you will reach a bridge; the road now sticks to the west (right) side of the valley all the way to Samye, a 3½-hour walk away. Twenty minutes from the bridge you will come to the village of **Nyango** with its substantially built stone houses. A big tributary stream, entering from the northwest, joins the Samye Valley here. The old trade route from Lhasa to Samye via the Gokar-la follows this valley. In the lower half of Nyango are several small shops. You will probably bid your guide and pack animals a farewell here. You should be able to find a tractor here to take you all the way down to Samye, should you want one.

Thirty minutes' walk past Nyango is the village of Wango and, an hour beyond it, the hamlet of Pisha. From the lower end of Pisha, a hill can be seen in the middle of the mouth of the Samye Valley. This is **Hepo Ri** (p171), one of Tibet's most sacred mountains. The entire lower Samye Valley – a tapestry of fields, woods and villages – can be seen from Pisha. Pisha is the last place where water can be conveniently drawn from the river. From here on, the trail only intersects irrigation ditches.

Fifteen minutes past Pisha a ridge spur called Dragmar meets the trail. On the ridge is the partially rebuilt **palace** where King Trisong Detsen is said to have been born. Formerly a lavish temple, it now stands empty. Below, just off the road, is a small red-and-white **temple** (3687m; N 29°22.802′, E 091°30.399′), often locked, enshrining the stump of an ancient tree. Legend has it that a red-and-white sandalwood tree grew here, nourished by the buried placenta of Trisong Detsen. During the Cultural Revolution the tree was chopped down.

Twenty minutes further down the trail is Sangbu village, from where there are good views of the golden spires of Samye. The route follows the Land Cruiser track direct to Samye along the margin of woods and desert: it takes about one hour. The closer you get to Samye the hotter the valley can become; in May and June it can be fiery hot. You finally enter the perimeter wall of **Samye** (3630m), about three hours from Nyango. See p168 for details of the stunning monastery complex.

TSURPHU TO YANGPACHEN

Beginning at Tsurphu Monastery, this rugged walk crosses several high valleys before emerging into the broad and windswept Yangpachen Valley. Combining alpine tundra and sweeping mountain panoramas with visits to monasteries and a remote nunnery, this trek nicely balances cultural and wilderness activities.

The best time for this walk is from mid-April to mid-October. Summer can be rainy but be prepared for snow at any time. As you will be in nomad country, beware of vicious dogs, some of which take a sadistic pride in chasing hapless foreigners. Fuel and food are not available, so come prepared. There are few permanent settlements along the way and the inhabitants are often away from home. Your only option on this trek is to be fully self-sufficient.

Tsurphu Monastery (4500m) is a good place to spend a night acclimatising. The area around the Karmapa's former *lingka* (garden), 10 minutes' walk upstream from the monastery, is ideal for camping (see p293). Some of the area's herders spend a lot of time at the monastery, so this is a good place to start looking for guides and yaks. Villagers in Tsurphu ask around Y400 for a guide and horse/yak for a five-day return trip to Yangpachen.

If you're well acclimatised, it's possible to do this trek in three days by continuing on to Tajung on day two and finishing at Yangpachen on day three.

Minibuses leave the Barkhor in Lhasa daily around 7am for Tsurphu (Y15, 2½ hours). Minibuses shuttle regularly from Yangpachen back to Lhasa (Y25, three hours). Buses from Nagchu and Damxung pass nearby Yangpachen town en route to Lhasa, so hitching is also possible.

TSURPHU TO YANGPACHEN AT A GLANCE

Duration 3-4 days
Distance 60km
Difficulty medium to difficult
Start Tsurphu Monastery
Finish Yangpachen Monastery
Highest Point Lasar-la (5400m)
Nearest Large Town Lhasa
Accommodation camping
Public Transport pilgrim buses
Summary An excellent choice for those who want to get a close look at the lifestyle of the *drokpas* (herders; see p148). You need to be well acclimatised for this high-elevation trek, which never dips below 4400m.

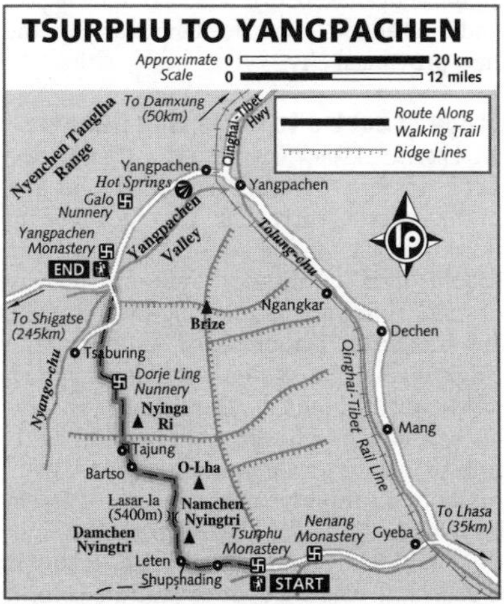

TSURPHU TO YANGPACHEN

Approximate Scale 0 – 20 km; 0 – 12 miles
Route Along Walking Trail
Ridge Lines

Stage 1: Tsurphu Monastery to Leten

3½-4 hours / 11km / 500m ascent

The trek begins by heading west or up the valley. Follow the kora trail 10 minutes west to the **lingka** (4550m; N 29°43.436′, E 090°34.128′), a walled copse of old trees with a brook. This garden-like wood is used by the monks in the summer, so ask permission before you set up camp. The trees here are the last you will see until after finishing the trek. Just above the copse, the valley splits: follow the northwest branch and remain on the north side of the stream.

Forty-five minutes of walking through a rocky gorge along a well-graded trail brings you to **Shupshading** (4700m; N 29°43.574′, E 090°32.876′), a seasonal herders' camp on an easily missed shelf above the trail. After 30 minutes look for a line of ruined chörtens to your right. After a further 10 minutes the valley looks like it splits; follow the main river valley (to the left) and descend to cross the stream on a stick-and-sod **bridge** (4890m; N 29°43.396′, E 090°31.859′). The trail now continues on the south (left) side of the valley. In another 20 minutes you'll pass a popular camping spot. Look out for small herds of *na* (blue sheep) on the slopes to the north.

Twenty-five minutes further on, by a **mani wall** (N 29°43.373′, E 090°30.856′), the trail forks. Both branches lead to Leten, about an hour away, but it's easier to take the right fork that follows the valley floor. This trail passes to the right of a small cliff, past the remains of winter ice, before swinging to the left up into the natural bowl of Leten.

Several families live year-round in the *drokpa* settlement of **Leten** (5090m; N 29°43.557′, E 090°30.094′), braving the severe climate with their livestock. Leten is the last chance to find yaks and a guide, both of which are highly recommended because the route to and from the Lasar-la is not easy to find. Camping spots are limited by the lumpy terrain and over-protective dogs. If you value your peace and quiet, consider camping in the valley below Leten.

Spend at least one night (preferably two) in Leten acclimatising.

Stage 2: Leten to Bartso

5 hours / 15km / 300m ascent / 600m descent

It's about a three-hour walk from Leten to the Lasar-la. Head for the northern half of the settlement (assuming you aren't already there).

The route climbs steeply up a short ridge, reaching the highest house. Bear northwest into a steep side valley. As you ascend, a reddish knob of rock looms up ahead. Angle to the north, or right, of this formation, past a mani wall in the centre of the bowl, and leave the valley by climbing to the top of a spur marked by three **cairns** (5270m; N 29°43.973′, E 090°29.869′). It's a 45-minute walk to here from Leten. The peak attached to this spur is called **Damchen Nyingtri** and is holy to the god ruling the environs.

As per Buddhist tradition, stay to the left of the three cairns and descend sharply into a narrow valley. As you look into the curved valley ahead you'll notice a round, bald, red peak called Tamdrim Dora; the main trail you'll be following for the next hour or so keeps to the right of that.

Once on the valley bottom, cross to the east (right) side of the stream and strike out north (up the valley). In 15 minutes a side-stream enters from the west (left): keep following the main north (right) branch. Cross back to the left side of the stream as the terrain here is easier to traipse over. In another 10 minutes you'll see O-Lha peak, the prominent jagged mountain to the northeast. Walk up the widening valley through arctic-like mounds of tundra for 40 minutes, following a minor trail. Then, as the valley floor veers west, look for a **cairn** (5310m; N 29°45.631′, E 090°29.813′) on the opposite bank of the stream.

Using this cairn as a marker, bear northwestwards over an inclined plain. This plain parallels the valley floor before the two merge. Continue ascending as the plain opens wider in the direction of the pass. The **Lasar-la** (5400m; N 29°46.165′, E 090°29.600′) is a broad gap at the highest point in the plain, beside a small tarn, and is heralded by cairns and prayer flags. (A separate pass to the northwest, the Tigu-la, also descends towards Yangpachen, but this is not the route described here.)

From the Lasar-la descend steeply into the north-running valley. A faint trail can be found on the east (right) side of this valley. Thirty minutes from the pass the trail passes a decent camp site, just before descending into a short gully. A side valley joins from the right, offering fine views of the back side of O-Lha. When this side stream joins the main stream, cross over to the west (left) side of the valley. There are many possible camp sites along this next stretch, as well as views of the snowcapped Nyenchen Tanglha range to the north.

The valley is covered with hummocks, but a trail avoids the ups and downs of these mounds of turf and earth. About an hour from the pass, just past a large corral, you meet a large westward bend in the valley. If water levels are high, you should ford the river here and continue on the north side of the valley. In early summer when water levels are lower you can simply follow the valley as it bends to the west and ford the river further downstream.

As you now head westwards, along the north side of the river, there are superb views of the surrounding mountains. In the north is Brize, which is a heavily glaciated peak enclosing the south side of the Yangpachen Valley, and towards the west is a distinctive pinnacle named Tarze. Brize, meaning 'female-yak herder', and Tarze, 'horse keeper', are just two of many topographical features in a mythical society ruled by the mountain god Nyenchen Tanglha. These two mountains make convenient landmarks for trekkers as you go against the grain by heading north over a series of drainage systems that run from east to west.

Thirty minutes after the big bend the trail hits the settlement of **Bartso** (4950m; N 29°48.962′, E 090°28.091′). This *drokpa* village of five homes with a permanent source of water is a decent place to camp. The hills around the village are still covered in juniper. In the 1960s and '70s huge amounts of this valuable bush were extracted from the region and trucked to Lhasa to feed the hearths of the new provincial city.

Stage 3: Bartso to Dorje Ling Nunnery

3½-4 hours / 15km / 150m ascent / 150m descent

Look northwest from Bartso to the far end of the valley. Clearly visible, a trail winds up from the valley to the top of the ridge. Make for this trail, 25 minutes' walk over marshy ground from Bartso, following the fenceline. It's another half-hour to the summit of the ridge. If you have a guide, a trail leads up to a saddle north of the valley for fine views of Nyenchen Tanglha. However, the more straightforward main path continues down into a gully in about 25 minutes to the village of **Tajung** (4660m; N 29°50.286′, E 090°25.116′), a walk of around 90 minutes from Bartso. Tajung is a decent alternative spot to end the second stage, though the insatiably curious villagers can be demanding of your time and supplies.

Stay to the left of the 14 whitewashed houses and ford the stream below the village. Bear northeastwards into the parting in the ridge and, after a few minutes, cross a low saddle. Continue going northeast in the direction of Brize until a large dip appears in the ridgeline to the west, 40 minutes from Tajung. Leave the trail going towards Brize and head cross-country between the ridgeline and a large hill to the right, using a **cairn** (4630m; N 29°51.353′, E 090°25.740′) on the saddle as your marker. If you have gained enough height, you will be able to see a group of white houses at the base of a hill to the far northwest. The Dorje Ling Nunnery is just downstream of here.

One excellent possible side trip from here is the 20-minute climb to the top of the hill to the right (east), known as **Nyinga Ri** (4800m; N 29°51.688′, E 090°25.990′). Views of the Nyenchen Tanglha mountains, and the distinctive flat-topped 7111m massif that names the entire range, are fantastic from here. Nyenchen Tanglha is the holiest mountain in central Tibet and is said to be inhabited by a god of the same name. Envisioned as a regal white warrior on a white horse, his half-smile, half-grimace symbolises both the benevolent and destructive sides of his personality. The range is part of the trans-Himalaya, which circumscribes the plateau, dividing southern Tibet from the Changtang.

A 25-minute traverse down the valley (or a short, steep descent north from Nyinga Ri) will bring you to a stream at the base of a ridge, aligned east to west. (If you decide to climb Nyinga Ri, you can send your guide ahead to meet you here.) Two trails climb the ridge; one to the right just past a corral, and a gentler path, favoured by herders, 10 minutes downstream. From the top of the ridge, you'll have good views of the village just upstream of Dorje Ling Nunnery. The nunnery, which is out of view, sits at the bottom of a rock outcrop visible from the ridge top.

Strike out directly across the plain for the village, taking in the awesome views of the glaciers tumbling off Brize and the fertile flood plain below. After dipping briefly into a dry gully you crest a small ridge and see **Dorje Ling** (4474m; N 29°53.600′, E 090°24.782′), reaching the nunnery in about one hour (two to three hours from Tajung).

The centrepiece of this friendly nunnery, home to 68 nuns, is the red *dukhang* (assembly hall). Good camping is found in the meadow to the southwest of the nunnery, by a small chapel, or you can stay in a room at the nunnery. A kora path climbs to a hillside meditation chapel before descending around the side of the nunnery.

Stage 4: Dorje Ling Nunnery to Yangpachen Monastery

3½-4½ hours / 14km / mostly level

From Dorje Ling, follow the motorable road west, or downstream. After a couple of minutes fill up your water bottle at a spring, the waters of which power a prayer wheel. After 40 minutes or so, past a fenced area, take the right fork over a ruined concrete **bridge** (4426m; N 29°54.216′, E 090°23.247′) and continue down the east bank of the stream as the valley drains into the huge Yangpachen plain. Below you to the left is Tsaburing village. The track quickly turns into a motorable road and runs north, paralleling the course of the Nyango-chu, which drains the upper Yangpachen Valley. The road stays close to the east bank of the silty river, skirting meadows that afford some fine picnic spots, offering encompassing views of the trans-Himalaya.

Once entering the Nyango drainage area it's a level but draining two-hour walk through the giant landscape to a steel **bridge** (4400m; N 29°59.072′, E 090°24.451′) spanning the river. Cross over the bridge to meet the northern road to Shigatse. Walk northwards (right) on the road for about 10 minutes, suddenly coming to Yangpachen Monastery.

Perched on top of a ridge above the village, the 15th-century **Yangpachen Monastery** overlooks a broad sweep of trans-Himalaya peaks. The monastery was once home to 115 monks, but many of them have fled to Rumtek Monastery in Sikkim and only about half that number remain. Yangpachen is headed by Shamar Rinpoche (also known as the Sharmapa), a leading lama of the Kagyupa order, whose 14th incarnation is based in India. You'll see images here of the important fourth Sharmapa (wearing a red hat), the 16th Karmapa (a black hat) and the 'alternative' rival Karmapa (see p146), who is supported by the Sharmapa in India. If you're interested in seeing what Nyenchen Tanglha looks like, check out the mural by the entryway to the main assembly hall. A glass case in the corner of the main hall displays the stone saddle of Nyenchen Tanglha. *Cham* dances are held at the monastery on the 29th day of the fifth Tibetan month (around July).

From Yangpachen Monastery it's a jarring 18km road journey to Yangpachen town. You might be able to hitch there but there's not a lot of traffic along this road, so consider hiring a minibus in the village (around Y50). Look out for Galo Nunnery, nestled in the hills to the left after about 7km.

For a post-trek treat, the swimming-pool-sized **hot-springs complex** (Yangbajian Wenchuan; admission Y40-60; 7am-9pm), 7km west of Yangpachen town, is great to ease your aching limbs, though it's undergone rapid development in recent years.

From Yangpachen town there are minibuses back to Lhasa (three hours), or continue 2km further to the main Qinghai–Tibet Hwy and hitch from there.

SHALU TO NARTANG

This trek follows the old trade route between the great Buddhist centres of Shalu and Nartang, making a glorious chapter in Tibetan history come alive for walkers. Treading the ancient trail you can almost feel the caravans laden with scriptures and treasures that once passed this way.

The trek begins at the historic Shalu Monastery (p199) and traverses west over a couple of small ranges to Ngor Monastery. From Ngor it's a downhill roll to Nartang Monastery. The route passes through several villages as well as uninhabited dry canyons. It's about a 10-hour walk to Ngor from Shalu, which is best divided into two days, and another five hours from there to Nartang. Finding guides and burros to carry your gear in Shalu is easier than before. Expect to pay Y50 to Y80 for each. Having local support is a good thing because the route is not always easy to discern – the trail tends to vanish in the canyons.

The optimal walking season is from the beginning of April to the end of October. In summer the trail can be sizzling hot, and in other months cold and windy, so be prepared. One advantage of hiking in summer is that this region gets less rainfall than the Ü region.

For information on getting to Shalu, see p200. Lhatse–Shigatse minibuses travel the Friendship Hwy and pass near Nartang.

SHALU TO NARTANG AT A GLANCE

Duration 2-3 days
Distance 45km
Difficulty moderate
Start Shalu Monastery
Finish Nartang Monastery
Highest Point Char-la (4550m)
Nearest Large Town Shigatse
Accommodation camping
Public Transport bus
Summary This walk will give you a feel for trekking in Tibet. The trail and passes are not particularly high or difficult and the trailheads are easily accessible from Shigatse.

Stage 1: Shalu Monastery to Upper Lungsang

5½-6½ hours / 19km / 420m ascent / 240m descent

From **Shalu Monastery** (3980m; N 29°07.625′, E 088°59.590′) walk the motorable road south (up the valley). Thirty minutes from Shalu you will pass by the **Ri-puk Hermitage**, set on a hillside on the west side of the valley. If you wish to visit, cut across the fields and head directly up to the hermitage – the way is not difficult and there are several trails leading up to it.

Forty-five minutes from Shalu the road forks: take the south fork. In the south, a conical-shaped hill and a village at its base can be made out. If you struck out in Shalu, stay on the road to this village, called Phunup, about a one-hour walk away. You may also find a guide and pack animals here. Otherwise, there is a short cut that saves 2km of walking. A few minutes from the fork in the road, look for the base of a long red ridge. Leave the road and skirt the base of this ridge, going in a southerly direction. First cross a flood plain to reach a rectangular red shrine and, beyond it, enter a plain bounded in the south by the red ridge.

Gradually the trail climbs to a small white ridge blocking the route to the south. As you approach you will see a line of white cairns marking its **summit** (4030m; N 29°06.011′, E 088°59.590′). Look for the trail that ascends to the cairns, a one-hour walk from the fork in the road. From the ridge's summit, Phunup village is to the south and the Showa-la is to the west. The pass is the obvi-

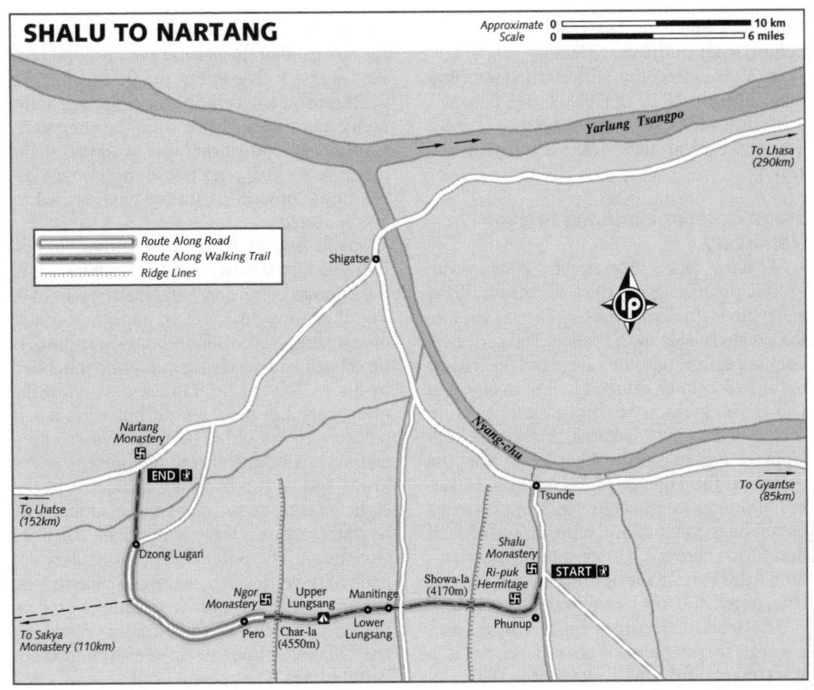

ous low point in the range at least one hour away. The trail descends gradually to enter the stream bed coming from the Showa-la, 30 minutes from the cairns. If you came via Phunup, your route will converge with the main trail here.

The climb up to the pass and the descent on the other side is through some heavily eroded, waterless ravines and slopes. Bring plenty of drinking water from the trailhead. From the stream bed the trail soon climbs back up the right side of the valley only to drop back in and out of the stream bed in quick succession. Don't make the mistake of walking up the stream bed for you would soon encounter ledges and other difficult terrain. After twice briefly dropping into the narrow stream bed, be alert for a trail carving a route up the right slope. It's situated just a few meters before a fork in the stream bed. The trail climbs steeply to a group of ruins and then winds around to the pass in 30 minutes. The top is marked by white cairns.

From the **Showa-la** (4170m; N 29°06.371′, E 088°56.939′), the second pass, the Char-la, can be seen in the range of hills west of an intervening valley. It is the dip in the crest of the range. The easy-to-follow trail descends from the pass along the south (left) side of a ravine. In one hour you will reach the valley floor. Leave the trail just before it crosses a small rise marked with cairns and continue west towards a distant group of trees. Cross over the sandy north–south valley, intersecting a road. Shigatse is about three hours north along this road.

The valley watercourse is dry except during summer flash floods. West of it is a **poplar and willow copse** (3950m; N 29°06.572′, E 088°54.093′), the only bit of shade in the area. Consider stopping here for lunch and a rest. From the copse, you enter a side valley, continuing in a westerly direction towards the Char-la. There are places suitable for camping along the length of this valley and water is available in the villages. In a few minutes you will reach the village of Manitinge, on the southern margin of the valley, and pick up the main cart track going up the valley. The track passes through the village of Siphu and, one hour from the copse, crosses to the south side of the valley. You can glimpse the Char-la from here, which for most of the trek is hidden behind folds in the mountains.

In 30 minutes you will reach **Lower Lungsang** (4060m; N 29°06.265′, E 088°51.824′), a few minutes later **Upper Lungsang**. There is a fine old wood here ideal for camping and resting.

Stage 2: Upper Lungsang to Ngor Monastery

3½-4 hours / 8km / 550m ascent / 240m descent

From Upper Lungsang the trail cuts across the valley floor gradually making its way back to the northern side of the valley. The cart track does not extend past the village and the trail up to the pass may be difficult to find in places. If you are in doubt, try to hire a local person to show you the way. It is at least three hours from Upper Lungsang to the Char-la. At first, the trail skirts the edge of a gravel wash. However, in 15 minutes a series of livestock tracks climbs out of the stream bed and onto an eroded shelf that forms above it. Observe the old agricultural fields here, many of which have been long abandoned due to a lack of water.

The terrain becomes more rugged and a gorge forms below the trail. There is a sidestream and small **reservoir** (4190m; N 29°06.619′, E 088°50.763′) 45 minutes above Upper Lungsang. This is the last convenient place to collect water until over the pass. From the reservoir, the trail descends back to the stream bed but quickly exits the opposite side of the valley.

Look for a series of switchbacks on the southern (left) side of the gorge and then follow them up. A further 15 minutes on, the trail crosses a gully and then another gully in 15 more minutes. The final leg to the pass is pretty much cross-country over a steep slope of raw expanses of rock. From the second gully, the Char-la can be reached in 45 minutes of steep uphill walking. At one time this trail was well maintained and formed a main trade link between Shalu and Sakya Monasteries but it has fallen into disrepair.

Eventually, the white cairns along the summit ridge come into focus. The pass is the obvious notch in the ridge line. From the **Char-la** (4550m; N 29°07.000′, E 088°49.850′), mountain ranges stretch to the west across the horizon and Ngor Monastery is visible directly below. Ngor is a 45-minute steep descent from the pass. The route from the Char-la descends the south (left) side of a ravine that forms below it. Several trails cross the stream that flows from the pass and provide access to Ngor, but the first trail is the quickest route – it climbs the right side of the ravine and traverses directly to the monastery. Consider camping near Ngor or staying in the monastery's little guesthouse and save the last five hours of walking for the next day, when you're rested.

Sakya master Ngorchen Kunga Sangpo founded **Ngor Monastery** in 1429, giving rise to the Ngorpa suborder, a distinctive school of Buddhist thought. Once an important centre of learning, Ngor used to boast four monastic estates and 18 residential units inhabited by about 340 monks. Only a portion of the monastery has been rebuilt but what has is pleasing to behold. The most eye-catching feature is a beautiful row of chörtens at the lower end of the complex dedicated to the eight victorious forms of the Buddha. The largest structure is the assembly hall, called the Gonshung. The outer walls of its gallery are painted in vertical red, white and blue stripes, a characteristic decorative technique used by the Sakya order. The three colours represent the Rigsum Gonpo, the three most important bodhisattvas. The present head of Ngor, Luding Khenpo, resides in northern India.

Stage 3: Ngor Monastery to Nartang Monastery

5-6 hours / 19km / 410m descent

From Ngor, a motorable road runs down the valley that is now suitable for all types of vehicles. Fifteen minutes from the monastery is the sizable village of Pero. Ninety minutes from Ngor the valley and road bend to the north, while the old trade route to Sakya continues west over a saddle. Thirty minutes further, there is a copse at the edge of the flood plain that is good for fair-weather camping.

The road now swings to the west side of the wide alluvial valley and 30 minutes past the copse is the village of **Dzong Lugari** (3910m; N 29°08.171′, E 088°45.741′). The road exits the north side of the village and extends northeast for 10km before joining the Lhatse–Shigatse Hwy 11km from Shigatse, just east of the 4914 road marker. The trail to Nartang Monastery, however, splits from the road on the northern outskirts of Dzong Lugari and heads north. From Dzong Lugari, it's at least a two-hour trek across a broad valley to **Nartang** (N 29°11.490′, E 088°45.927′).

GOOD CITIZENS *John Vincent Bellezza*

Since the 1980s, accounts of unfriendly villagers, petty theft and stone-throwing have come out of the Everest region. Such actions have not helped relations between the local Tibetans and foreigners, but the good news is that in recent years there has been a drop in the number of incidents. While there are no excuses for bad behaviour, there are historical factors that have contributed to antisocial episodes.

Under the Chinese, the entire religious and civic infrastructure of the region was destroyed and never satisfactorily restored, creating many hardships in a particularly high, dry and poor area. The good news is that new economic opportunities spurred on by the burgeoning tourist trade are starting to better the lives of the local people. Add to their optimism by patronising local services and businesses as much as possible and, as always, go that extra mile to make friends and gain insights into the workings of the Everest region.

The trail to Nartang crosses over a small stream and an electric utility line. The track tends to merge with a welter of agricultural trails and if you miss it, simply continue walking north. Soon the massive ramparts that surrounded the Nartang Monastery come into view. Just before arriving, cross the Lhatse–Shigatse Hwy, about 14km west of Shigatse. Donations are expected if you want to visit the chapels and famous printing presses at the **monastery**. There are several shops selling soft drinks and noodle soup on the roadside. It should be pretty easy to catch a ride from here to Shigatse.

EVEREST BASE CAMP TO TINGRI

This thrilling trek in the shadow of iconic Mt Everest provides a heady mix of solitude, wildlife sighting and physical challenge. Onagers (wild asses) and gazelle thrive around the trail, and you might even get lucky and see a Tibetan brown bear rambling in the pastures.

If you drove to Everest Base Camp and are looking for an alternative exit route, this trek to Tingri is an excellent choice. The route passes through an isolated valley on the way up to the Nam-la and then enters a region used by herders and their livestock. Following the Ra-chu Valley, the route swings northwards to the plains of Tingri. It's also possible to do this trek in the opposite direction. If you get tired of trekking along the road, you can always try to get a lift. Vehicles ply the route during summer and there are pony carts along the way if you want a brief respite from carrying your bag.

If you do decide to trek into Everest from Tingri, it is usually possible to hire yaks, guides and even pony carts in Tingri, though if you want to keep a low profile it might be better to organise this in Ra Chu. Animals and helpers can set you back as much as Y100 per head, but try your benevolent powers of persuasion to get the best deal possible.

The trekking season in the Everest region extends from April to late October. This is a difficult high-elevation region with altitudes ranging between 4400m and 5300m, and the high point is at the beginning of the trek! Careful preparation and the right gear are imperative. Subfreezing temperatures can occur even in summer at higher elevations and, conversely, hot gusty winds in May and June can make walking a sweaty experience. For well-equipped and seasoned walkers, winter treks to Everest Base Camp are often possible. Thanks to the rain shadow created by Mt Everest (Qomolangma) and its lofty neighbours, even the monsoon months are relatively dry in the region.

The trek via the Nam-la is the fastest route from Everest Base Camp to Tingri, but if you're short on supplies or not so well equipped, consider one of the alternative passes covered in Gary McCue's *Trekking in Tibet – A Traveler's Guide*. The longer routes may be preferable because they follow more of the main road, reaching villages where supplies might be bought. Once you leave Rongphu Monastery there are no permanent settlements until well in reach of Tingri, three days away. Don't chance this trip unless you are really ready.

Be aware that expeditions beyond Base Camp are only for those very experienced in trekking and mountaineering. It's all too easy, once you have reached Base Camp, to succumb to the temptation to push further up the mountains. Do not do it without adequate preparation. At the very least, spend a couple of days acclimatising in the Rongphu area and doing day hikes to higher altitudes.

For highly fit and prepared groups it's possible to trek beyond Base Camp as far as Camp III. Including time for acclimatising, you would need to allow at least one week for this trek. The route skirts the Rongphu Glacier until Camp I and then meets the East Rongphu Glacier at Camp II. This glacier must be crossed in order to reach Camp III (6340m). For detailed information on reaching the advanced camps, see Gary McCue's book.

There is public transport in the region and it shouldn't be too difficult to get a lift along the Friendship Hwy to either the turn-off to Everest (kilometre marker 5145) or Tingri. Hired Land Cruisers can go all the way to Everest Base Camp, as do some minibuses.

For additional information relating to the Everest region, including the Everest Base Camp, see p206.

EVEREST BASE CAMP TO TINGRI AT A GLANCE

Duration 3-4 days
Distance 70km
Difficulty moderate to demanding
Start Everest Base Camp
Finish Tingri
Highest Point Nam-la (5250m)
Nearest Large Town Shigatse
Accommodation camping
Public Transport bus
Summary This is fine alpine trekking in the shadow of the legendary Mt Everest. See onagers (wild asses) and other wild animals in the valleys and pastures along the way.

Stage 1: Everest Base Camp to Beyond the Nam-la

9½ hours / 27km / 450m ascent / 520m descent

Setting out downstream from Rongphu along the road, the meadows soon recede as the valley narrows between boulder-strewn slopes. A trail angles down a steep embankment from the road to the bridge. Cross the bridge and look for the trail along the west bank of the **river** (N 28°18.164′, E 086°49.988′). Soon the trail starts to ascend the embankment and emerges onto a shelf above the Dza-chu. In a few minutes the trail climbs further and traverses around the base of a slope into the mouth of a side valley. It takes 30 minutes to reach the mouth of this valley from the bridge.

While the majority of the Dzaka Valley is dry and barren, this side valley is relatively luxuriant, hosting a variety of plants and shrubs, and plenty of fresh water. This is a nice place to camp or take a long lunch break. The valley bends to the west as the trail to Nam-la leaves the valley floor and climbs past a corral onto a plain abutting the north (right) side of the valley. The route to the pass now bears west all the way to the summit, paralleling the valley floor. It's at least a 3½-hour hike to reach the pass.

As you begin your ascent towards the pass there is a saddle in the ridge bounding the northern side of the valley – this is the most direct route to the Zombuk Valley. Walk close to the ridge enclosing the northern side of the valley. Past the corral there is no trail. The route clambers over rock-strewn shrubby terrain and then over big plates of tundra that fit together like a giant jigsaw puzzle. About one hour from the corral, a steep slope blocks the view to the west. It takes 10 minutes to climb over this onto another broad tundra-covered pitch. In 10 more minutes you will be able to see the head of the valley; however, the Nam-la is out of sight, tucked behind the folds in the ridge.

The route gradually levels out and in 15 minutes descends into a marshy side valley. There is a small stream in this valley, the last place you can count on for water until well beyond the pass. Look for a small corral on the far side of the side valley and bear to the left of it. Continue walking upward for 10 minutes before gradually descending into the main valley floor in another 15 minutes.

Remain on the north side of the valley, taking the trail that steeply climbs towards the pass. The trail remains clear for 40 minutes until it's absorbed by the tussock grass of the valley floor. The pass is near where the ridge south of the valley bends around to the west. It is still 40 minutes from here to the Nam-la over alpine meadows, but the terrain is now much more open and the gradient less steep.

Proceed west, looking out for the lowest point on the horizon. The **Nam-la** (5250m) is a very broad summit simply delineating the parting of drainage basins over a vast plain. There are a few small cairns on top of the

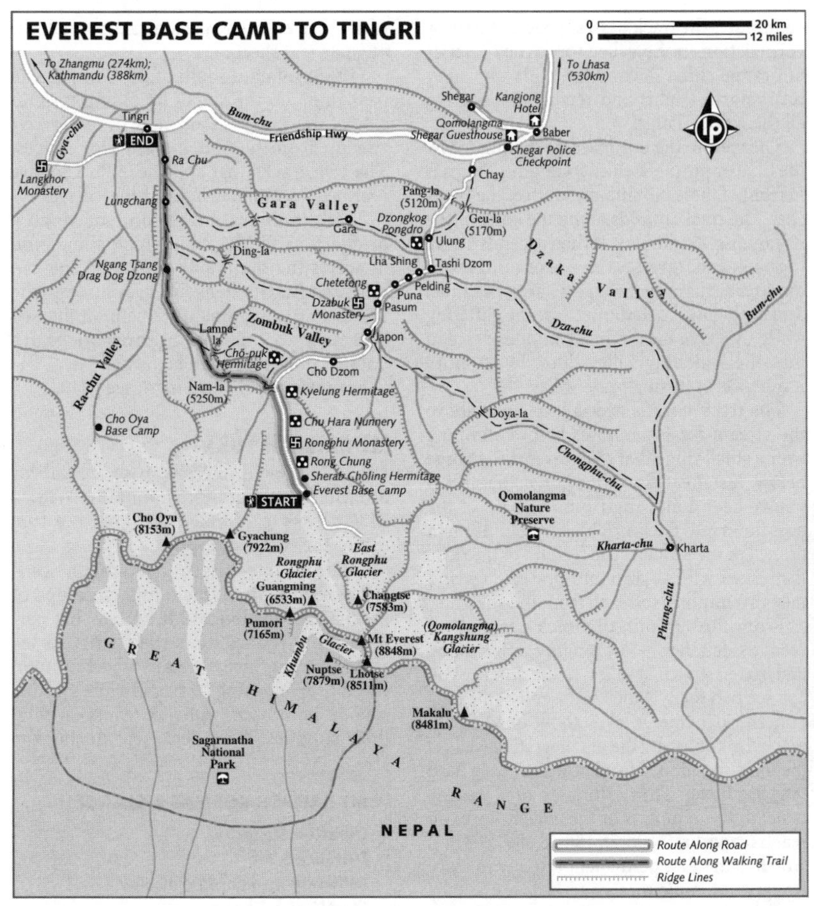

pass, seen only when you are already upon them. Towards the west, and across a wide, wet, downhill slope, is a small valley and the Ra-chu Valley far beyond that. North of the Nam-la, with only a small summit in between, is the Lamna-la coming from the Zombuk Valley.

Descend from the pass in a westerly direction over tussock grasses and tundra for one hour, and cross the cart track coming from the Lamna-la. If the time is right, you may see gazelles during your descent. From the cart track, descend a precipitous slope into the valley floor. There are both springs and a stream in this swampy valley of grasses and wildflowers, a tributary of the Ra-chu. Great camp sites are found on the drier margins of the valley. It's at least a five-hour trek from here to the first village, Lungchang.

Stage 2: Base of Nam-la to Lungchang

5-6 hours / 21km / 200m descent

Do not follow the valley down and northward. It's easier to walk in a westerly direction. You can see the cart track cutting across the ridge from a group of corrals on the west side of the valley. The track goes all the way to Tingri, making route-finding easy.

Follow the cart track for 20 minutes, coming to a junction marked by a cairn. There is a short cut from here that rejoins the main track in 15 minutes. The track angles across the middle of the stony valley and is very wide and straight, like a runway used by bush planes. In

45 minutes the track passes through a narrow constriction in the valley formed by a series of orange cliffs. Beyond the cliffs the valley turns north (right) and retains this bearing all the way to Tingri.

The view to the north is now dominated by the blue or purple Tsebu Mountains. Tingri is in front of these mountains, south of the Bum-chu. The track unfolds along the bank of the stream for 45 minutes. It then ascends above the bank and traverses the side of a ridge with the stream running through a narrow channel directly below. Look south to see the glittering white Cho Oyu massif. In 30 minutes descend into the widening valley floor. In 10 more minutes cross a small side valley.

The track unrolls over a level shelf above the stream for 30 minutes before climbing over a small ridge that circumvents the gorge below. Just upstream of the gorge, the stream you've been following from the base of the pass flows into the much higher-volume main branch of the Ra-chu. The summit of the ridge is marked with a cairn and prayer flags and takes 10 minutes to reach from the shelf.

From the summit, the track descends to cross a side valley before ranging across a long and barren stretch of valley. In the distance you can see two rocky knobs at the end of the long eastern ridge line. It takes about one hour to reach the knobs and the disintegrating walls of the long-abandoned fort known as **Ngang Tsang Drag Dog Dzong**. Thirty minutes after passing beneath the ramparts of the ancient fort you reach **Lungchang** (N 28°28.188′, E 086°39.814′), which is the first permanent settlement since Rongphu. Simple meals and beds are usually available here or with families in the village.

Stage 3: Lungchang to Tingri

3½ hours / 12km / 150m descent

From Lungchang, you can see several low-lying hills in the mouth of the Ra-chu Valley: Tingri is at the foot of the northernmost of these. From Lungchang, the track moves towards the middle of the valley, following a bluff along the edge of the Ra-chu. In 1½ hours it reaches the outskirts of the village Ra Chu. Before the village, at a white shrine, the track splits: the south, or main, branch goes to Tingri via Ra Chu village, while the other jogs west and then north over wide pastures to Tingri. The left fork is the shorter route and is a more pleasant walk. The lower part of the Ra-chu Valley is green during the warmer half of the year; extensive meadows support flocks of goats and sheep.

Fifteen minutes south of Ra Chu you will pass ruins on the slopes bounding the east side of the valley – look back to see Everest rise up from behind the anterior ranges. The two tracks that split near Ra Chu are reunited 45 minutes beyond the village.

Thirty minutes further on, you reach a bridge over the Ra-chu, which allows you to access the south side of Tingri. You can cross the Ra-chu here and pass through the village to the highway or remain on the east bank and cross the new highway bridge. It's only 15 minutes to the highway.

For information on Tingri, see p210.

MT KAILASH KORA

Hike the age-old pilgrims' path around Mt Kailash, Asia's holiest mountain. With a 5630m pass to conquer, this kora is a true test of the mind and spirit.

There's some gorgeous mountain scenery along this trek, including close-ups of the majestic pyramidal Mt Kailash, but perhaps more rewarding is the chance to see and meet pilgrims. Tibetans travel on foot, singing or intoning prayers, while Hindus ride on horseback, with yak teams carrying their supplies. It's a real treat during the

MT KAILASH KORA AT A GLANCE

Duration 3 days

Distance 52km

Difficulty medium to difficult

Start/Finish Darchen

Highest Point Drölma-la (5630m)

Nearest Large Town Ali

Accommodation camping and monastery guesthouses

Public Transport bus, when not restricted to Tibetans only

Summary The circuit, or kora, of Mt Kailash (6714m) is one of the most important pilgrimages in Asia. It's been a religious sanctuary since pre-Buddhist times, and a trek here wonderfully integrates the spiritual, cultural and physical dimensions of any trip to Tibet, which explains its growing attraction. Being able to meet pilgrims from across Tibet and other countries is one of the many alluring factors of this walk.

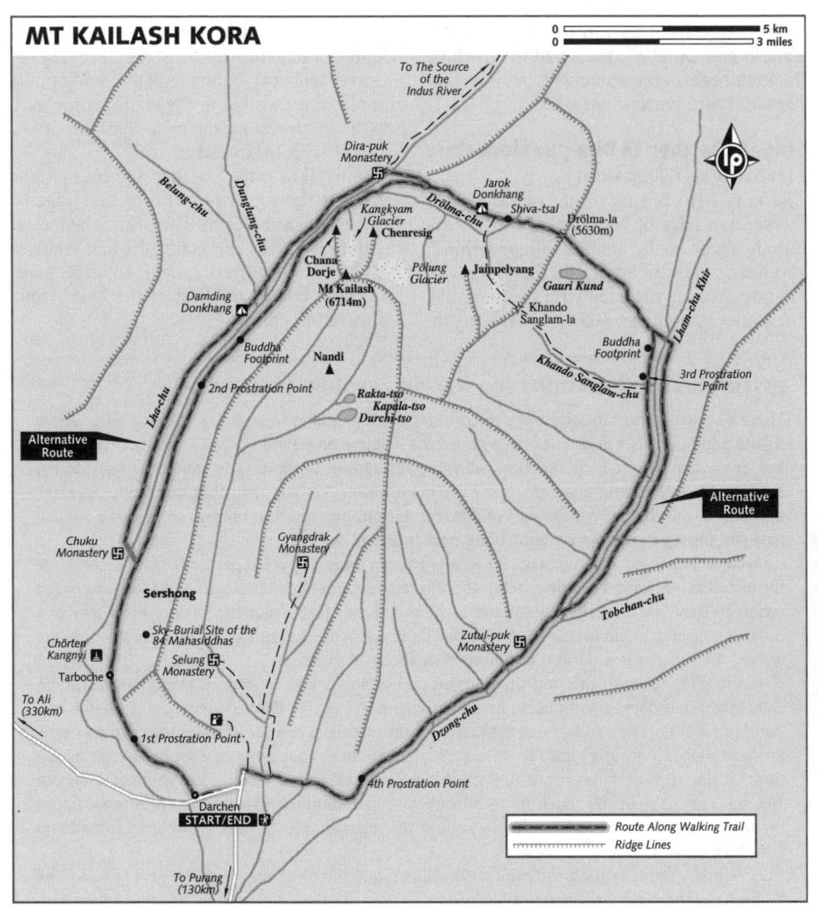

main pilgrim season (June to September) to catch sight of this Asian-styled wild west scene. Both the Tibetan and Indian pilgrims are usually friendly and approachable.

The route around Mt Kailash is a simple one: you start by crossing a plain, then head up a wide river valley, climb up and over the 5630m Drölma-la, head down another river valley, and finally cross the original plain to the starting point. It's so straightforward, and so perfect a natural circuit, it's easy to see how it has been a pilgrim's favourite for thousands of years. Check it out on Google Earth even before you arrive.

The Mt Kailash trekking season runs from mid-May until mid-October but trekkers should always be prepared for changeable weather. Snow may be encountered on the Drölma-la at any time of year and the temperature will often drop well below freezing at night. The pass tends to be snowed in from early November to early April.

The kora is getting more and more popular (and there's the litter everywhere to prove it). A tent and your own food is pretty much necessary no matter when you go as there's no guarantee of getting a bed at one of the primitive guesthouses at the monasteries, or in one of the tents that Indian pilgrims erect near them. Bottled water, instant noodles and snacks are usually available every few hours at nomad tents, especially during the busy Saga Dawa and Indian pilgrim season. Natural water sources abound.

For more information on the kora, Mt Kailash and Darchen, the small town where the kora begins and where you can buy supplies and hire porters, see p226.

Stage 1: Darchen to Dira-puk Monastery

6 hours / 20km / 200m ascent

The kora path begins rather obviously on the western edge of Darchen. Quickly leaving all traces of the grubby village behind, you head westward across the Barkha plain, a sandy expanse speckled with greenery like a massive camouflage jacket. To the north, the east–west ridge blocks your view of Mt Kailash, but to the southeast are clear views of Gurla Mandata (7728m). Api and other peaks in Nepal are visible to the south, while look to the southwest for the twin, sharp humps of Kamet (7756m) in India.

Only 4km from Darchen the trail climbs up over the southwest end of the ridge to reach a cairn at 4730m. The cairn is bedecked with prayer flags and marks the first views of Mt Kailash's southern or lapis lazuli face and a *chaktsal gang*, the first of the kora's four prostration points.

ESSENTIAL CONSIDERATIONS FOR WALKING AROUND MT KAILASH

There a several important questions to consider when planning to walk the 52km circuit – a *kora* if your pilgrimage is a Buddhist one, a *parikrama* if you're on a Hindu circuit – around Asia's most holy mountain. First, which direction will you go? Buddhist or Hindu, you should be walking the mountain in a clockwise direction. But if you meet walkers coming the other way (anticlockwise), don't be surprised; they're followers of Bön, the ancient pre-Buddhist religion of Tibet – a religion that still thrives in remote parts of Tibet, particularly in the east.

Second, how long will you take? If you're a Tibetan Buddhist, you'll probably plan to complete the circuit in one hard day's slog. Achieving this feat requires a predawn start and a late-afternoon return to Darchen. Occasionally, Westerners emulate this feat – modern folklore even tells of a Russian who did 13 circuits in 15 days – but don't expect to be faster than the average Tibetan walker, who makes it around the mountain in about 14 hours.

Hindu pilgrims, with the odd ritual immersion in an icy lake to endure along the way, typically take three days, overnighting in encampments set up for them close to the Dira-puk and Zutul-puk Monasteries. Independent Western visitors usually aim for a three-day circuit as well. Western trekking groups typically do the circuit in three or four days, as a longer circuit allows time for side trips and excursions to such things as the Mt Kailash north-face. Some very devout Tibetans make the round much more difficult by prostrating themselves the entire way. Count on around three weeks to complete a kora in this manner and be sure to wear knee padding and thick gloves.

How many times around the mountain will you go? Once will wipe out the sins of a lifetime if you have the right predeparture attitude and your sin load is not so great (check your current status at the sin-testing stones on the ascent to the Drölma-la). But Tibetans look upon three circuits as a much more satisfactory starting point and 13 as the real minimum. Like gold status for frequent flyers, completing 13 circuits also allows access to high-status detours, such as the short cut over the Khando Sanglam-la, or a visit to an inner kora *(nangkor)* on the south side of the mountain. Real walkers should aim for 108 circuits, which guarantees instant nirvana and a clean sin slate for all your lifetimes. Economisers should note that koras completed during a full moon are better than ordinary ones; ditto for koras during the Tibetan Year of the Horse.

The final question to ask yourself, and this may be the most important, is what you expect from completing this kora. Assuming you're not a Buddhist, Bönpo or Hindu, the promise of liberation may not grab you no matter how caught up in the moment you are. And yet, many foreigners go truly expecting to experience something holy or profound. This is a little like wanting to fall in love. But why not?

It's probably best to approach the kora without too many expectations (which ironically is what a good Buddhist would do anyway). You may experience the divine in nature, or you may just return with a lot of fond memories and some good photos. And any one of these is enough for us to get back on the pilgrim's path.

THE FACES & RIVERS OF MT KAILASH

It's easy to confuse the mystical Mt Kailash, the symbolic Mt Meru of legend reaching from the lowest hell to the highest heaven, with the real one. From the legendary Mt Kailash a river flows into the legendary Lake Manasarovar, from which flow four legendary rivers in the four cardinal directions. In reality, no rivers flow from Manasarovar but four real rivers do issue from the mountain in, more or less, the cardinal directions.

Direction	Face	Mythical River	Real River
south	lapis lazuli	Mabja Kambab (River from the Peacock Mouth)	Karnali
west	ruby	Langchan Kambab (River from the Elephant's Mouth)	Sutlej
north	gold	Seng-ge Kambab (River from the Lion's Mouth)	Indus
east	crystal	Tamchog Kambab (River from the Horse's Mouth)	Yarlung Tsangpo (Brahmaputra)

Very quickly the trail bends round to the north and enters the barren Lha-chu Valley. From here on, the narrow Lha-chu River provides a steady supply of water all the way to Dira-puk Monastery. For the best water, however, look for the occasional side-stream flowing down from the cliffs into the Lha-chu.

The valley is so open at this point you can see ahead to the tall Tarboche flagpole (4750m), which is another hour's walk. The Tarboche area is one of the most significant sites for Tibet's most important festival – Saga Dawa (p229). It's also the point where Indian pilgrims drive to begin their circuit of Mt Kailash. It can be a bit noisy, dusty and dirty here.

Just west of Tarboche is the 'two-legged' **Chörten Kangnyi**. It's an auspicious act for pilgrims to walk through the small chörten's archway. A short climb above Tarboche to the east is the sky-burial site of the 84 *mahasiddhas* (Tantric practitioners who reached a high level of awareness). The site is revered, as it was once reserved for monks and lamas, but is no longer used: too few birds these days and too many wild dogs. The first of the kora's three Buddha footprints is here, but it's hard to find.

Beyond Tarboche, the valley narrows dramatically at an area called Sershong. You can begin to get clear shots of Mt Kailash now, standing to attention above the eastern ridge. After passing a series of ruined chörtens and a number of long mani (prayer) walls the trail reaches a small bridge across the Lha-chu at 4710m. The bridge is less than an hour's walk from Tarboche, about three hours from Darchen, and is directly below Chuku Monastery.

Chuku Monastery (4820m), founded in the 13th century by Götsangpa Gompo Pel, a Kagyupa-order master, is perched high above the valley floor on the hillside to the west. It blends so secretively into its rocky background you may not even notice it's there. All Mt Kailash monasteries were wrecked during the Cultural Revolution and the Chuku (or Nyenri) Monastery was the first to be rebuilt. Inside, look for a glass case over the altar; there's a highly revered marble statue called Chuku Opame (originally from India and reputed to talk!) inside and a conch shell inlaid with silver. Beside the altar there's a copper pot and elephant tusks, offering articles as found in temples in Bhutan.

During the pilgrim season, a few nomad tents may be set up on the other side of the river from the monastery, with food (instant noodles and snacks) and water for sale.

From the Chuku bridge there are alternative trails along the east and west banks of the river. Either way it's about three hours to Dira-puk Monastery. The trail along the eastern bank is the regular pilgrim route, but on the western trail there are some fine grassy camp sites at **Damding Donkhang** (4890m), about an hour before the monastery. The west or ruby face of Mt Kailash makes a dramatic backdrop to this camp site and in the early morning Tibetan pilgrims can be seen striding past on the other side of the river, already well into their one-day circuit.

Be aware, though, that walking on the western side requires crossing the side streams that flow into the Lha-chu. Even in early summer these can be waist high. Wear socks or rubber sandals when you cross; it helps on the slippery rocks.

Take your time between Chuku Monastery and Dira-puk Monastery as this stretch has some of the best scenery of the entire kora.

High sedimentary faces, wonderfully puckered and dented, and chiselled into shapes that seem alive, hem you in on both sides. When the weather is warmer there's even the occasional ribbon of water tumbling down the slopes from hundreds of metres high.

Many of the formations along the way have mythical connections, a number of them related to Tibet's legendary hero Gesar of Ling – but you're unlikely to find them without a guide. You will have no problem, however, finding the **second prostration point** (N 31°04.430′, E 081°16.942′), with its prayer flags and clear view of the east side of Mt Kailash. Thirty minutes later look for the second Buddha footprint, and a **carving** (N 31°05.126′, E 081°17.264′) of the god Tamdrin, a wrathful horse-headed deity, on a black stone smeared with aeons of yak butter. There may be a few nomad tents here selling the usual drinks and snacks.

From the rock, the trail starts to climb and heads northeast toward Dira-puk Monastery. Before reaching the monastery, walkers who have followed the Lha-chu's east-bank trail will find themselves first at an Indian guesthouse and tent camp on the other side of the river. Water and instant noodles are again available for sale. At the time of writing a new, large, stone guesthouse was being built here.

Some groups camp in the vicinity of the Indian guesthouse (or even bed down here for the night, space permitting), but it's a noisy, dirty area. For something more pleasant try the grassy flats below the monastery itself, or even the northern valley (that leads to the source of the Indus River) east of the monastery.

Dira-puk Monastery, which was rebuilt in 1985, sits in a superb location on the hillside north of the Lha-chu across from the Indian tent camp. It directly faces the north face of Mt Kailash, which from this angle appears as a massive, jet-black slab of granite ornamented with alabaster-white stripes of snow. Three lesser mountains are arrayed in front of Mt Kailash: Chana Dorje (Vajrapani) to the west; Jampelyang (Manjushri) to the east ;and Chenresig (Avalokiteshvara) in the centre, but there's no doubting who is the superstar in this band.

Dira-puk Monastery takes its name from the words *dira* (meaning 'female-yak-horn') and *puk* ('cave') – this is where the Bön warrior god king Gekho tossed boulders around with his horns. The great saint Götsangpa, who rediscovered the kora route around Mt Kailash, was led this far by a yak that turned out to be the lion-faced goddess Dakini (Khandroma), who guards the Khando Sanglam-la. The main image in the *dukhang* (assembly hall) is of Chenresig (Avalokiteshvara), flanked by images of the Buddha and a fearsome protector deity.

It's possible to overnight in the monastery's rather basic guesthouse (beds Y40), though be aware that Indian pilgrims often book all the beds here, too. At the time of writing an attractive grey stone guesthouse was being built just below the monastery.

To get to the monastery from the Indian tent camp you must walk downhill to the river and then back up again, a trying ordeal at the end of a long day. There's a bridge to cross but note it's further upstream as you face the monastery.

Stage 2: Dira-puk Monastery to Zutul-puk Monastery

7-8 hours / 18km / 550m ascent / 600m descent

No doubt when you wake in the morning and step outside you'll want to revel in the glory of your surroundings. Mt Kailash's shiny black face dominates the high ground, a rushing river the low, while the middle slopes echo with the moans of yak teams complaining as drivers load them with the day's supplies.

If you have the time, consider walking up to the **Kangkyam Glacier** that descends from the north face of Mt Kailash, between Chenresig and Chana Dorje. It takes about two hours there and back.

Regular kora walkers will head off to the east, crossing the Lha-chu again by bridge. The route then climbs on to a moraine and soon meets the trail on the east bank. The long ascent up the Drölma-chu Valley that will eventually lead to the Drölma-la has begun. Bring water to last a few hours.

Less than an hour along is the meadow at **Jarok Donkhang** (5210m), where some trekking groups set up camp. It's not wise to camp any higher up than here because of the risk of problems with altitude.

Nearby Jarok Donkhang a trail branches off to the southeast, leading over the snow-covered Khando Sanglam-la. This shortcut to the east side of Mt Kailash bypasses the normal route over the Drölma-la, but only those on their auspicious 13th kora may use it. That lion-faced goddess Dakini who led Götsangpa to Dira-puk makes sure of that.

Also nearby, another **glacier** descends from the east ridge off the north face of Mt Kailash, down through the Pölung Valley between Chenresig (Avalokiteshvara) and Jampelyang (Manjushri). This glacier can be reached in a round-trip of a couple of hours from Jarok Donkhang. You can follow the glacial stream that runs down the middle of the valley to merge with the Drölma-chu, or you can avoid losing altitude from Jarok Donkhang by terracing around the side of Jampelyang.

Only a short distance above Jarok Donkhang, about two hours from the day's starting point, is the rocky expanse of **Shiva-tsal** (5330m; N 31°05.795′, E 081°20.856′). Pilgrims are supposed to undergo a symbolic death at this point, entering in the realm of the Lord of the Dead, until they reach the top of the Drölma-la and are reborn again.

It is customary to leave something behind at Shiva-tsal – an item of clothing, a drop of blood or a lock of hair – to represent the act of leaving this life behind. Be aware, though, that to most foreign eyes the result looks more like a garbage dump than holy ground.

After Shiva-tsal the trail mercifully flattens for a time and proceeds along a glacial ridge. There are a number of interesting sights ahead, such as the sin-testing stone of **Bardo Trang** (a flat boulder that pilgrims are supposed to squeeze under to measure their sinfulness), but even your guide may not know where they are.

About 30 minutes from Shiva-tsal the trail turns eastward for the completion of the ascent to the 5630m **Drölma-la**. The saddle is fairly dull looking, just a long slope of boulders and scree, but there are some stark, jagged peaks to the right. Look south for your last glimpse of the north face of Mt Kailash.

Allow around an hour for the 200m climb to the top of the Drölma-la. The trail disappears at times, merging with glacial streams in summer, but the way up, up, up is obvious. Take your time. Let children and old people pass you, and if you can't go more than a few metres at a time, don't.

After a few false summits, the rocky pass is reached. The great cubic **Drölma Do** (Drölma's Rock) that marks the top is barely visible behind an enormous number of prayer flags. Pilgrims perform a circumambulation nonetheless, pasting money onto the rock with yak butter, and stooping to pass under the lines of prayer flags. They also chant the Tibetan pass-crossing mantra, *'ki ki so so, lha gyalo'* (*'ki ki so so'* being the empowerment and happiness invocation, *'lha gyalo'* meaning 'the gods are victorious'). They have now been reborn, and, by the mercy and compassion of Drölma, their sins have been forgiven.

The tale associated with the revered Drölma Do is worth telling. When Götsangpa pioneered the kora and wandered into the valley of Dakini (Khandroma), he was led back to the correct route by 21 wolves that were, of course, merely 21 emanations of Drölma (Tara), the goddess of mercy and protectress of the pass. Reaching the pass, the 21 wolves merged into one and then merged again into the great boulder. To this day Drölma helps worthy pilgrims on the difficult ascent.

Weather permitting, most pilgrims and trekkers pause at the pass for a rest and refreshments before starting the steep descent. Almost immediately, **Gauri Kund** (5608m; one of its Tibetan names translates as 'Lake of Compassion') comes into view below. Hindu pilgrims are supposed to immerse themselves in the lake's green waters, breaking the ice if necessary, but few actually do.

It takes approximately an hour to make the long and very steep 400m descent to the grassy banks of the Lham-chu Khir. You may have to cross snowfields at first, sometimes leaping across streams that have cut through the valley floor, but later the trail turns dry, and rocky. Two walking sticks are useful here.

En route there is a much-revered footprint of Milarepa, though again, spotting it on your own is difficult. When the trail reaches the valley, you may find nomad tents and a teahouse selling drinks and noodles. A huge rock topped by the kora's third Buddha footprint stands nearby.

As with the Lha-chu Valley on the western side of Mt Kailash, there are routes that follow both sides of the river. The eastern-bank trail presents better views and there's less marshy ground but it requires crossing the river by boulder hopping, and later recrossing by wading into the river itself (which may be quite deep during the wetter months).

About 30 minutes south, a valley comes down from the Khando Sanglam-la to join the western trail. This valley provides the only glimpse of Mt Kailash's eastern or crystal face.

MILAREPA VERSUS NARO BÖNCHUNG

All around the Mt Kailash kora there are signs of the contest for supremacy that was fought between Milarepa, the Buddhist poet-saint, and Naro Bönchung, the Bön master. According to the Buddhists, in all encounters it was Milarepa who came out the victor, but despite this he still agreed to a final, winner-takes-all duel, a straightforward race to the top of the mountain. Mounting his magic drum, Naro Bönchung immediately set out to fly to the summit but, despite his acolytes' urging, Milarepa didn't bother getting out of bed. Finally, as the first rays of dawn revealed that Naro Bönchung was at the point of reaching the top, Milarepa rose from his bed and was carried by a ray of light directly to the top. Shocked by this defeat, his opponent tumbled off his drum, which skittered down the south face of the mountain, gouging the long slash marking Mt Kailash to this day. Hindu pilgrims call the slash the 'stairway to heaven'. Gracious in victory, Milarepa decreed that Bön followers could continue to make their customary anticlockwise circuits of Mt Kailash, and awarded nearby Bönri as their own holy mountain.

The kora's third prostration point is at the valley mouth but it's easy to miss this point if you're walking on the eastern bank.

About two hours on, grassy fields appear alongside the river affording those with tents endless spots to set up camp. During the Indian pilgrimage season, you may get to share the site with grazing yaks and horses, an opportunity for some fantastic photographs. Note that by this point, the river has changed name to the Dzong-chu, which translates as 'Fortress River'.

An hour or so from the start of the camping fields is the Zutul-puk Monastery (4790m). The *zutul phuk* (miracle cave) that gives the monastery its name is at the back of the main hall. As the story goes, Milarepa and Naro Bönchung were looking for shelter from the rain. They decided to build a cave together but Milarepa put the roof in place without waiting for Naro Bönchung to make the walls (thus once again showing the supremacy of Buddhism). Milarepa then made a couple adjustments to the cave, which left a footprint and handprint that can still be seen today.

The monastery has a simple guesthouse (beds Y40) but it can only be booked out by Indian pilgrims. The area around the monastery is also littered with rubbish mounting with every pilgrim season.

Stage 3: Zutul-puk Monastery to Darchen

3-4 hours / 14km / 150m descent

If you've camped, it's about 30 minutes to the monastery. From here, the trail follows the river closely for an hour or so then climbs above the river and enters the lovely **Gold & Red Cliffs**, a narrow canyon whose walls are stained purple, cobalt and rust.

When the canyon narrows look for holes gouged into the cliff walls. These are not natural but made by pilgrims looking for holy stones. Also look for prayer flags festooned across the river, and in the far distance the blue waters of the lake Raksas Tal.

Where the trail emerges onto the Barkha plain, close to the fourth prostration point (4610m), Gurla Mandata is again visible in the distance. It's now an easy one-hour walk back to Darchen along a dirt road. While not a very scenic stretch of the kora, the steady ground below does allow you to drift off and reflect on the past three days.

NYENCHEN TANGLHA TRAVERSE

This is a fabulous trek for those who want to see the ecological mosaic of northern Tibet in all its splendour. Close encounters with the *drokpa*, the seminomadic shepherds of the region with their ancient customs and traditions, enliven the trail. Herds of blue sheep live in the crags and in the woodlands the endangered musk deer makes its home.

The trek begins on the main road to the Nam-tso lake, 5km beyond the Damxung–Lhasa Hwy turn-off. The trail cuts across the mighty Nyenchen Tanglha range and heads directly for Tashi Do, the celebrated headland on the southeast shore of Nam-tso. From Tashi Do there is an almost constant stream of Lhasa-bound vehicles, making prospects for a ride back easy. For further information on accessing Damxung and Tashi Do, see p149.

NYENCHEN TANGLHA TRAVERSE AT A GLANCE

Duration 3 days
Distance 60km
Difficulty moderate to demanding
Start Damxung
Finish Tashi Do
Highest Point Kyang-la (5330m)
Nearest Large Town Damxung
Accommodation camping
Public Transport bus
Summary Passing through gorges, forested slopes, alpine meadows and the plains of the Changtang, this is a great walk for those interested in the ecological diversity of northern Tibet.

The route leaves the Damxung valley and wends its way through a rocky defile, the gateway to a high-elevation forest in which dwarf willow and rhododendron are dominant species. A number of stream crossings await you. A tundra-filled upper valley gradually climbs to the Kyang-la (Onager pass), followed by a steep descent onto the Changtang plains. Fantastic views of sparkling Nam-tso and Tashi Do are visible from many vantage points on the trail. And colourful *drokpa* camps dot the way.

The best time to make the Nyenchen Tanglha traverse is from May to October. A winter crossing is also sometimes possible but don't attempt one unless you have the green light from local residents. This is a very high elevation trek with a 5330m pass and minimum elevations of 4310m, so factor in plenty of time for acclimatising. It's prudent to spend two nights in Damxung before setting out (see p149). You will have to be fully equipped with a tent and stove and enough food to reach Tashi Do, three days away. Temperatures even in the summer regularly dip below freezing and gale force winds are common.

Horses and guides should be available in the villages near the trailhead for Y50 to Y90 apiece per day. In June when locals are out collecting caterpillar fungus (see p260) horses may be hard to get. If you're not successful in the nearby villages of Nakya or Baga Ara, try Nya Do, Largen Do or Tren Do, which are a little further afield but larger in size.

Stage 1: Nakya to the Tree-Line

5 hours / 18km / 480m ascent

This trail sets off from villages outside Damxung and makes a beeline directly into the Kyang Valley. From the turn-off for Nam-tso at Damxung proceed along the black-top road 4.5km to the village of **Nakya** or 6km to **Baga Ara**. In both villages there are motorable tracks that head northwest over a plain entering the narrow mouth of the Kyang Valley in just over 2km. Perched 50m above the northeast side of the valley is **Kyang-rag Monastery** (4370; N 30°31.694′, E 091°05.759′).

Kyang-rag Monastery, a glistening white hermitage clinging to the cliff face, was founded by the Panchen Lama Palden Yeshe in the 18th century. It contains just one small chapel featuring various images of the protectress Palden Lhamo, as well as those of the Buddha and Guru Rinpoche.

All the way to the Kyang-la the valley runs in a northwest direction. From Kyang-rag remain on the east side of the valley heading upstream. Along the narrow valley floor are plenty of

KYAN-RAG

It is said that Palden Yeshe and his retinue once camped on the opposite side of the Kyang-chu. One day a *kyang* (onager or wild ass) wandered into camp and entered the tent used by the Panchen Lama for religious practise. The Panchen Lama tossed a sack containing sacrificial cakes on the onager's back. The *kyang* exited the tent, wandered to the other side of the river and disappeared into a cliff. Curious, Palden Yeshe went in pursuit of the *kyang* and reached the cliff where it was last seen. Here he found an old monk who had covered the very spot with his cloak. The Panchen Lama demanded to know what was going on and pulled off the cloak. Immediately his nose began to bleed. Taking this as a mystic sign, he used the blood to paint an image of Palden Lhamo on the rocks. This site became the inner sanctum of Kyang-rag Monastery. As it turned out the *kyang* was no ordinary animal but a local deity and the mount of the great goddess Palden Lhamo. For that reason the place became known as Kyang-rag (Onager Beheld).

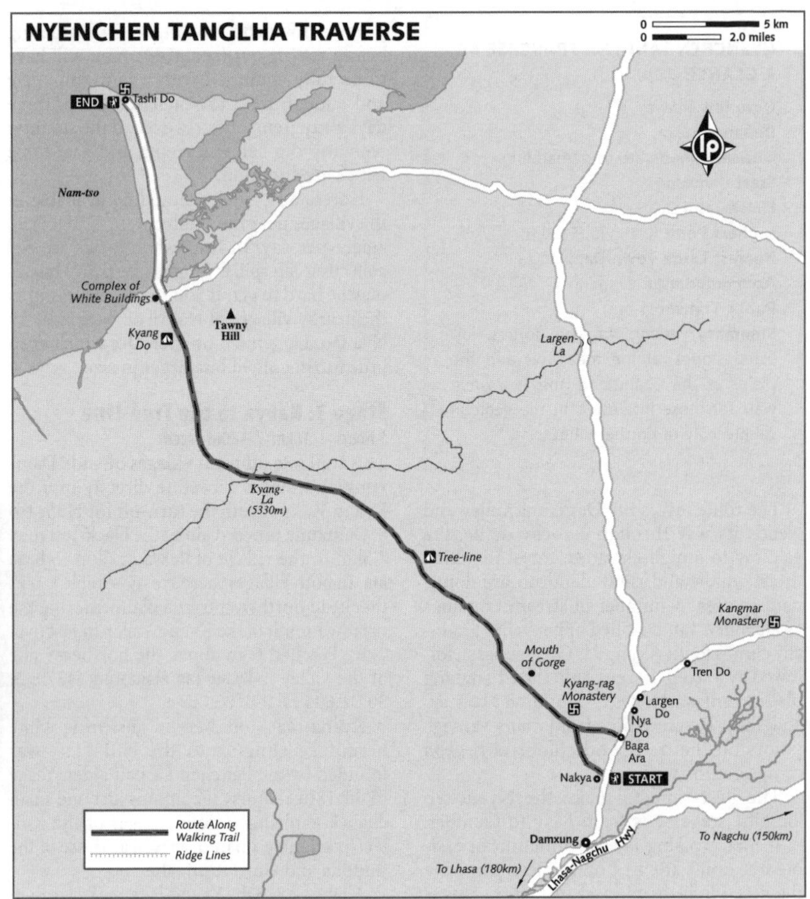

small places to camp. About one hour from Kyang-rag Monastery ford the crystal waters of the Kyang-chu to the west side of the valley and enter a narrow **rocky gorge**. The gorge coincides with the high mountains that close in around the Kyang-chu. Five more fords await, so it's a good idea to bring canvas tennis shoes or rubber sandals especially dedicated to this purpose. A walking stick is also very helpful. The Kyang-chu is a fairly shallow stream but with a swift current, so make sure your walking legs are up to the task.

The trail is clear and easy to follow. In 10 minutes it crosses to the east side of the valley. There are rocks but these may be slippery and it's safer to get your feet wet. Within half an hour the trail crosses the river four more times, breaking out of the gorge at the last ford and landing on the east side of the valley.

The valley is now a little more open and the west slopes quite heavily forested. The trail remains in the valley bottom or along the east edge of the slope. There are a number of places to camp provided they are not already occupied by the *drokpa* shepherds. In two or 2½ hours, reaching the tree- ine, the trail skips over stones to the west side of the valley (4790m; N 30°34.662′, E 91°02.350′). There are a number of excellent camp sites in the vicinity.

Stage 2: Tree-Line to Kyang Do

8-9 hours / 25km / 540m ascent / 490m descent

Twenty minutes up valley **springs** gush out of the base of a cliff. In about 200m the trail returns to the east side of the valley where it remains until the pass crossing. There are good camping sites on both sides of the stream ford. Now the valley becomes more sinuous and somewhat steeper. The trail enters the tundra zone and becomes faint in places. Stay in the valley floor and head upstream. In around 45 minutes enter a long, wide section of the valley gravitating towards its east flank. You will need at least 1½ hours to trek over this stretch of the valley. High peaks of the Nyenchen Tanglha range tower above your line of travel.

Above this point you're not likely to find any more *drokpa* camps until well after the Kyang-la, but there are quite a few places to set up your tent should you decide to tarry in the flower-spangled meadows. Further up the valley narrows a little and becomes steeper. The trail is still near the east edge of the valley but hardly visible in places. In 1½ hours ascend the broad shelf east of the valley. It's only about 10m higher than the valley floor. In the vicinity the Kyang-chu forks: the larger branch flows down from the southwest originating in a group of dark-coloured rocky peaks. The smaller branch cascades down from the pass in the northwest. This is the last place to collect water until after the pass. Paralleling the smaller branch of the stream the trail heads in a northwest and then westerly direction to meet the base of the Kyang-la (5240m; N 30°37.522′, E 090°58.080′) in about 45 minutes.

Climb up to a higher and narrower bench continuing in a westerly direction. The way is moderately steep. Soon a line of brown cairns come into view. These mark the broad saddle rising to the Kyang-la. Continue up walking parallel to these cairns. The high point is **Kyang-la** (5330m; N 30°37.700′, E 090°57.320′), about a 45-minute hike from the base of the pass.

It's only about a 30m descent to the head of the valley on the **Changtang** side of the pass. This valley is also known as **Kyang**. Good drinking water is had here – fill up because water can be scarce down valley. The valley now bends to the north, the direction it takes all the way down to the Nam-tso basin. Soon the great lake in all its glory comes into view. The eastern tip of Tashi Do and a long headland jutting deep into the lake, bright gems on a scintillating cobalt-blue surface, are clearly visible.

Stay on the east side of the valley. In a few minutes the trail leaves the valley and steeply descends through rocky slopes, followed by grassy slopes. In about 45 minutes you reach the **valley floor** (5120m; N 30°38.505′, E 090°56.954′). Note that the **Kyang-chu** on this side of the pass is much smaller and prone to disappear underground in places.

The trail soon crosses to the west side of the valley before returning to the east side in only five minutes. The trail traces the east edge of the valley. In 45 minutes the magnificent Tashi Do comes into full view. In 20 minutes recross to the west side of the stream and point your feet downstream. The terrain is quite gentle and Nam-tso is your constant companion, so going cross-country is easy and fun. The valley is wide open and in 30 minutes there are many excellent camps by the stream at **Kyang Do**.

Stage 3: Kyang Do to Tashi Do

4-5 hours / 17km / 80m descent

A tawny-coloured hill appears in the distance. Leave the valley and skirt its west side by walking across the plain. The base of this hill is reached in approximately one hour. Do not make the mistake of staying in the valley floor, although this may seem the best route. Further down swampy ground would come between you and Tashi Do. After walking around the base of the tawny hill look for a complex of mainly white buildings to the north. Hike directly to it in about one hour. This complex at the base of the Tashi Do headland is part of its management apparatus.

The tourist centre of **Tashi Do** (4730m; N 30°46.652′, E 090°52.243′) is still 8km away on a black-top road. It should be easy should you want to hitch a ride from there. For information on this burgeoning tourist mecca, see p147.

MORE TREKS

LAKE MANASAROVAR KORA

Although there is now a road all the way around Lake Manasarovar (4575m), this is still a very lovely walk. Fortunately, the road can be avoided for much of the 110km mostly level route. Lake Manasarovar reflects the most lucid shades of blue imaginable. She represents the female or wisdom aspect of enlightenment and is a symbol of good fortune and fertility, explaining why

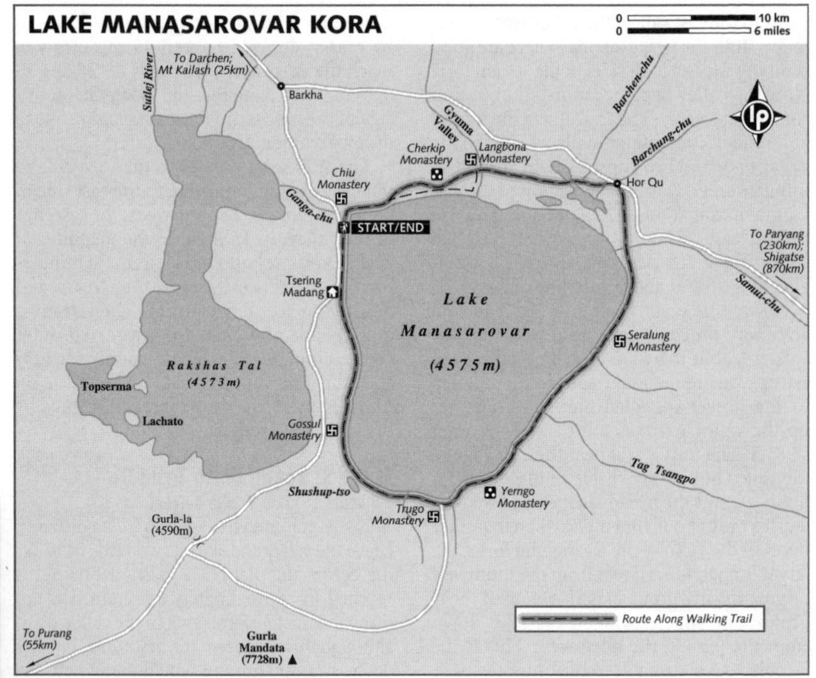

Tibetans are always very eager to circumambulate her. There are five friendly Buddhist monasteries along the way. Public buses now ply the north side of the lake. Horses and guides can be hired in Hor Qu, the town on the northeastern side of the lake. Expect to pay at least Y100 per day for each.

Due to the elevation (averaging 4600m) this is a moderately difficult trek. May, June and September are the best months for the four- or five-day trek; July and August are also good, save for the hordes of gnats that infest the shores. A tent and stove are required and you should be prepared for any kind of weather at any time.

The best place to start the walk is at Chiu Monastery on the northwest corner of the lake. Go in either a clockwise or counterclockwise direction, depending on whether you more closely relate to the Buddhists and Hindus or the Bönpos. If walking in a clockwise direction you will reach Langbona Monastery in about four hours. It's about another four hours to Hor Qu. Seralung Monastery, on the east side of Lake Manasarovar, is approximately three hours from Hor Qu, with four to five more hours bringing you to Trugo Monastery on the southern flank of the lake. You can make it back to Chiu Monastery via Gossul Monastery in nine to 10 hours of walking from Trugo Monastery.

EVEREST EAST FACE

Follow a river conduit breaching the Himalaya to the spectacular forested east flank of Mt Everest. Small lakes and fantastic camping make this a most attractive trek, but route finding is demanding and the terrain difficult so consider a local guide. Drive to Kharta, with its alpine hamlets, some 90km from Shegar on the Friendship Hwy (for getting to Shegar, see p206). Budget at least 10 days for the trek. There are two main passes accessing the east or Kangshung side of Everest: Langma-la (5330m) and Shao-la (5030m). The huge Kangchung glacier reposes on the west end of the Karma Valley. For detailed information, see *Tibet Handbook* by Victor Chan and *Trekking in Tibet* by Gary McCue.

Directory

CONTENTS

ACCOMMODATION

Most towns in Tibet now offer a decent range of hotels, many with hot showers and some three- or four-star options. In smaller towns you may be limited to rooms with a shared bathroom, while in the countryside electricity and running water are luxuries that cannot be expected. Hotels are divided into *binguan* or *dajiudian* (hotels), *zhaodaisuo* (guesthouses) and *lüguan* (simple hostels). The Tibetan terms are *drukhang* (hotel) and *dronkhang* (guesthouse). Midrange hotels generally have rooms with private bathroom and hot-water showers, at least part of the day. Top-end hotels are limited to Lhasa and one or two other towns.

Hot water is provided everywhere in thermoses and even in basic places a basin and drum of cold water is usually provided for washing. Bedding is provided, but in the cheapest places it's often not clean and a sleeping bag is a good idea.

In some towns the local Public Security Bureau (PSB) keeps a pretty tight lid on which places can and cannot accept foreigners. Most tourists will only come up against this problem in Tsetang and Ali, where the budget hotels are not permitted to accept foreigners.

BOOK ACCOMMODATION ONLINE

For more accommodation reviews and recommendations by Lonely Planet authors, check out the online booking service at www.lonelyplanet.com. You'll find the true, insider lowdown on the best places to stay. Reviews are thorough and independent. Best of all, you can book online.

PRACTICALITIES

- Electricity is 220V, 50 cycles AC. Plugs come in at least four designs: three-pronged angled pins (like in Australia); three-pronged round pins (like in Hong Kong); two flat pins (US style but without the ground wire) or two narrow round pins (European style); and three rectangular pins (British style).
- Note that electronics such as laptops and iPods are often affected by altitudes above 4500m and may stop working.
- The metric system is widely used in Tibet. Traders measure fruit and vegetables by the *jin* (500g).
- CCTV 9 is China's only English TV channel (if you are desperate). CCTV 6 occasionally has movies in English.

SLEEPING BAGS

The question of whether you need a sleeping bag or not depends entirely on where you plan to go and how you plan to travel. Those who aim to spend time in Lhasa and then head down to Nepal via the sights of Tsang could do without one, although they are always a nice comfort, especially in budget hotels. Anyone planning on trekking or heading out to remoter areas, such as Nam-tso, Everest or western Tibet, should definitely bring one along. See also p282.

Camping

Camping out is well understood by Tibetans, many of whom still spend their summers herding livestock in mountain valleys. You probably run the risk of an unpleasant run-in with the PSB if you attempt to set up a tent in Lhasa, but get 20km or so out of town and the nearest patch of turf is yours for the picking. Always ask permission if camping near a settlement or encampment, watch out for the dogs (see p317), and expect an audience.

Guesthouses & Hotels

In Lhasa there are several clean, well-run Tibetan-style guesthouses. Similar set-ups can be found in Shigatse, Sakya and Tingri. Tibetan-style guesthouses tend to be much more friendly and homey than Chinese hotels, and they are also much cheaper. Midrange and top-end hotels in Lhasa are 30% more expensive than elsewhere, though standards are 40% higher.

Some monasteries, such as Samye, Ganden, Drigung Til, Dorje Drak, Mindroling, Tidrum and Reting, also have their own guesthouses, normally a bank of carpeted seats that double as beds (bring a sleeping bag). Remoter monasteries often have a spare room, or even a chapel, which they may be willing to let out. Expect to pay around Y20 per person; if no fee is asked, leave a donation in the prayer hall.

Most of the larger hotels are anonymous Chinese-style places that share several traits: the plumbing is often dodgy, the carpets are dotted with a mosaic of cigarette burns, and all offer a ratty pair of flip-flops so you don't have to touch the bathroom floor, but you're better off bringing your own.

Rooms are generally divided into *biaozhun* (标准; standard), which come with an attached bathroom, and *putong* (普通; ordinary). Standard rooms are often divided into *jingji* (经济; economy) and *haohua* (豪华; deluxe) rooms.

Some hotels (generally the cheaper ones) price their accommodation per bed rather than per room, which can work out well for solo travellers. To guarantee that you have the room to yourself you would theoretically have to pay for all beds (and a few hotel owners will try to force you to do so), but usually that's not necessary. If you are alone in a double room or are a couple in a triple room, staff will not normally put others in the room, although they have the right to. They may possibly put other foreigners in the room, but it is rare for a hotel to mix foreigners and Chinese or Tibetans in one room. This depends largely on your negotiations.

ACTIVITIES

Tibet offers the type of topography to delight mountaineers, white-water rafters, horse riders and others, though the problem, as always, is the confusing travel permit system, which many authorities manipulate to their own financial advantage.

Cycling

Tibet offers some of the most extreme and exhilarating mountain biking in the world. If you are fit and well equipped, it's possible to visit most places in this book by bike, although the most popular route is the rollercoaster ride along the Friendship Hwy from Lhasa down to Kathmandu. Shorter excursions could include trips to Ganden and the Gyama Valley, or to the Lhundrub Valley. Mountain bikes can be hired in Lhasa.

Thaizand Bicycle Tours (see p128) in Lhasa offer route information and can provide bikes and logistical support for all kinds of trips. A 10-day ride to Zhangmu for four people,

DISCOUNTS

In many areas of Tibet, and notably in Lhasa, accommodation prices vary seasonally. Throughout this book, we list high-season rates (May to September), followed by the range of discounts you can expect in April and October. Prices will be lower still in winter. In reality some kind of discount is almost always available when the hotel is not full, so always ask.

with jeep support, costs around US$400 per person.

For information on long-distance touring, see p342.

Horse Riding

There's something romantic about travelling across Tibet on horseback. The easiest place to arrange this is in the Kham region of western Sichuan, but even here it's just a matter of coming to an agreement with local herdsmen. A kora of Lake Manasarovar (p229) on horseback is a great idea and a few travellers have managed to arrange this.

Tibet Wind Horse Adventure (www.windhorsetibet.com) offers day trips on horseback in the Tolung-chu and Drigung Valleys and can customise longer adventures (for details, see p117). Contact Chris Jones.

Foreign travel companies, such as **Hidden Trails** (www.hiddentrails.com) and **Boojum Expeditions** (www.boojum.com), offer expensive horse-riding tours in Kham (western Sichuan).

Mountaineering

There are some huge peaks in Tibet, including the 8000m-plus giants of Cho Oyu, Shishapangma and, of course, Everest, which are enough to send a quiver of excitement through vertically inclined explorers. Unfortunately, the Chinese government charges exorbitant fees for mountaineering permits, which puts mountaineering in Tibet out of the range of most individuals or groups devoid of commercial sponsorship.

A few individuals have succeeded in getting to Advanced Everest Base Camp and even beyond but the authorities are clamping down on this (see p209).

Foreign travel companies, such as **Alpine Ascents** (www.alpineascents.com) and **Jagged Globe** (www.jagged-globe.co.uk), arrange for mountaineering trips to Cho Oyu and Shishapangma in Tibet, but these don't come cheap.

Rafting

Tibet Wind Horse Adventure (www.windhorsetibet.com) offers rafting trips in central Tibet, ranging from one to five days, and are absolutely the people to contact if you want to arrange a kayaking trip in Tibet. See p117 for details.

Trekking

One of the remarkable things about Tibet, considering the difficulties placed in the way of those heading up there by Chinese authorities, is that once you are up on the high plateau there is considerable freedom to strike off on foot and explore the Tibetan valleys and ranges. Of course no-one at China International Travel Service (CITS) or any other Chinese organisation will tell you this, but nevertheless it is the case. Experienced and hardy trekkers have the opportunity to visit places that are almost impossible to reach any other way, and are unlikely to find any official obstacles. For detailed information on the most popular trekking routes, see p281.

BATHHOUSES

Cheaper hotels often don't have hot showers but staff can normally direct you a simple bathhouse (淋浴; *linyu; soog-po tru-ya* in Tibetan), where you can get a hot shower for around Y8. These are purely functional places, and sometimes a bit grotty, but after a few days on the road you'll be glad for the wash. Staff normally provide a towel and flip-flops, but bring your own if you have them.

BUSINESS HOURS

Banks, offices, government departments and the PSB are generally open Monday to Friday, with perhaps a half-day on Saturday. Most open from around 9.30am to 1pm and 3pm to 6.30pm. Opening hours listed in this guide are for summer; winter hours generally start half an hour later and finish half an hour earlier.

Most smaller monasteries have no set opening hours and will open up chapels once you've tracked down the right monk. Others, such as Samye, are notorious for only opening certain rooms at certain times. In general it's best to try to tag along with pilgrims or a tour group.

CHILDREN

Be especially careful with children as they won't be on the lookout for signs of altitude sickness. Children don't get on with Tibetan food or toilets any better than grown ups. They also tire more easily from an endless round of visiting monasteries. Bring along a copy of *Tintin in Tibet* for when morale flags. In Kathmandu several bookshops sell Tibetan thangka (religious paintings) and mandala colouring books.

On the upside children can be a great icebreaker and generally generate a lot of interest. Many hotels have family rooms, which normally have three or four beds arranged in two connected rooms.

Tibet is probably not a great place to bring a very small child. You should bring all supplies (including nappies and medicines) with you. Small spoons can be useful as most places have only chopsticks. There's plenty of boiling water to sterilise bottles etc. It's possible to make a cot from the copious numbers of duvets supplied with most hotel rooms.

CLIMATE CHARTS

Tibet has similar seasons to China, though with lower temperatures due to the higher altitudes. Winters (November to March) are cold (the average temperature in January is -2°C) but there isn't all that much snow. Summers (May to September) have warm days with strong sunshine and cool nights. At higher elevations (ie above 4000m) even summer days can be chilly. During spring and autumn you need to be prepared for four seasons in one day, including the possibility of snowfall.

There are some regional variations; northern and western Tibet are generally higher and colder. The monsoon affects parts of Tibet (particularly eastern Tibet) from mid-July to the end of September (July and August bring half of Tibet's annual rainfall).

For suggestions on when to visit Tibet, see p15.

COURSES

It is possible to enrol in a Tibetan-language course at Lhasa's Tibet University. Tuition costs US$1000 per semester; semesters run from March to July and September to January. There are two hours of classes a day and around 70 foreign students currently attend (including some undercover missionaries). For an application form contact the **Foreign Affairs Office** (☎ 0891-634 3254; fsd@utibet.edu.cn; Tibet University, Lhasa 850000, Tibetan Autonomous Region).

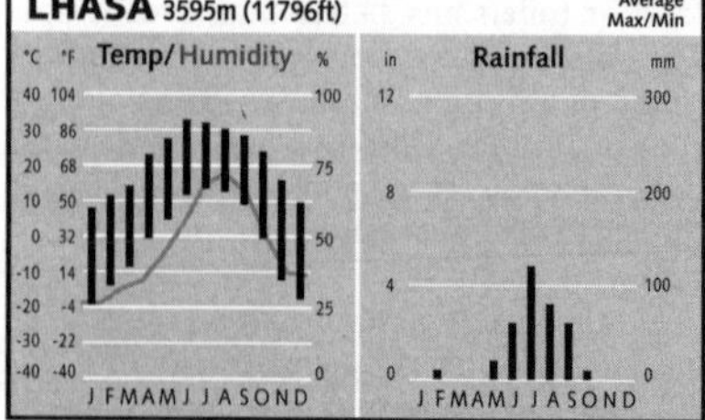

Once you are accepted the university will help arrange a student ('X') visa and, after three months, residency status in Lhasa. Students have to stay in campus accommodation. It should also be possible to hire a private tutor from the university for around Y20 per hour.

Many travellers find it more convenient to study at Dharamsala or Kathmandu, although students say that the mix of dialects and high levels of English make them less effective places to study. Courses offered there include Tibetan Buddhist philosophy, Tibetan language and Tibetan performing arts.

Kopan Monastery (www.kopan-monastery.com) outside Kathmandu, in Nepal, is a particularly popular place to study aspects of Tibetan Buddhism.

The various Tibetan organisations across the world offer courses and meditation retreats. The **Tibet Foundation** (☎ 020-7930 6001; www.tibet-foundation.org) in London, for example, offers a 10-week Tibetan-language course for around UK£130.

CUSTOMS

Chinese border crossings have gone from being severely traumatic to exceedingly easy for travellers. You are unlikely to be even checked when flying in or out of the country.

You can legally bring in or take out only Y6000 in Chinese currency and must declare any cash amount exceeding US$5000 or its equivalent. You are allowed to import a maximum of 72 rolls of film. It's also officially forbidden to bring more than 20 pieces of underwear into the PRC (we kid you not!).

It is illegal to import any printed material, film, tapes etc 'detrimental to China's politics, economy, culture and ethics'. This is a particularly sensitive subject in Tibet, but even here it is highly unusual to have Chinese customs officials grilling travellers about their reading matter. Maps and political books printed in Dharamsala, India, could cause a problem.

It is currently illegal to bring into China pictures, books, videos or speeches of or by the Dalai Lama. Moreover, you may be placing the recipient of these in danger of a fine or jail sentence from the Chinese authorities. Images of the Tibetan national flag are even 'more' illegal.

Be very circumspect if you are asked to take any packages, letters or photos out of Tibet for anyone else, including monks. If caught, you'll most likely be detained, interrogated and then probably expelled.

Anything made in China before 1949 is considered an antique and needs a certificate to take it out of the country. If it was made before 1795, it cannot legally be taken out of the country.

DANGERS & ANNOYANCES

Bookjacking

Tibetans are a curious and devout people and so the slightest glimpse of a photo of a monastery or even a mention of a Dalai Lama picture will result in the temporary confiscation of your Lonely Planet guide. For many Tibetans this is their only chance to see other parts of their country, so try to be patient, even after the 10th request in five minutes. A good deed like this can often open hitherto locked doors (literally) in the monastery you are visiting.

Dogs

Clean-up campaigns in Lhasa and Shigatse have largely done away with packs of rabid-looking dogs that used to make catching a predawn bus a frightening, and even a life-threatening experience. Dogs can still be a problem in smaller towns, though, and you should be especially vigilant when exploring back streets or seeking out an obscure monastery.

The most dangerous dogs belong to remote homesteads or nomad encampments and should be given a very wide berth. Travelling with a walking pole or stick is recommended. Some cyclists and trekkers even carry pepper spray or Chinese fireworks to scare off the brutes. See p350 for information on what to do if you are bitten.

Staring Squads

It is very unusual to be surrounded by staring Tibetans and Chinese in Lhasa, unlike other remote parts of China, but visiting upcountry is another matter. Trekkers will soon discover that it is not a good idea to set up camp beside Tibetan villages. The spectacle of a few foreigners putting up tents is probably the closest some villagers will ever come to TV.

Theft

Tibet is very poor and there is a small risk of theft when travelling here. Trekkers in the Everest region have reported problems with petty theft, and pickpockets work parts of Lhasa. That said, Tibet is much safer than other provinces of China.

Small padlocks are useful for backpacks and some dodgy hotel rooms. Bicycle chain locks come in handy not only for hired bikes but for attaching backpacks to railings or luggage racks.

If something of yours is stolen, you should report it immediately to the nearest foreign affairs branch of the PSB. They will ask you to fill in a loss report, which you will also need to claim the loss on your travel insurance.

EMBASSIES & CONSULATES

Chinese Embassies

For embassies not listed below consult the Chinese Foreign Ministry website at www.fmprc.gov.cn/eng and click on 'Missions Overseas'.

Australia (☎ 02-6273 4783, 6273 7443; http://au.china-embassy.org; 15 Coronation Dr, Yarralumla, Canberra, ACT 2600); Sydney consulate (☎ 02-8595 8000; http://sydney.chineseconsulate.org/eng); Melbourne consulate (☎ 03-9822 0604; http://melbourne.china-consulate.org/eng); Perth consulate (☎ 08-9222 0302)

Canada (☎ 613-789 3434; www.chinaembassycanada.org; 515 St Patrick St, Ottawa, Ontario K1N 5H3); Toronto consulate (☎ 416-964 7260); Vancouver consulate (☎ 604-736 3910); Calgary consulate (☎ 403-264 3322)

France (☎ 01-53 75 89 25; www.amb-chine.fr; 20 rue Washington, 75008 Paris)

Germany (☎ 030-2758 8532; www.china-botschaft.de; Brückenstraße 10, 10179 Berlin)

Japan (☎ 03-3403 3389, 3403 3065; www.china-embassy.or.jp; 3-4-33 Moto-Azabu, Minato-ku, Tokyo) Consulates in Fukuoka, Osaka and Sapporo.

Nepal (☎ 01-4411740; www.chinaembassy.org.np; Baluwatar, Kathmandu; 9.30-11am Mon, Wed & Fri)

Netherlands (☎ 070-355 1515; Adriaan Goekooplaan 7, 2517 JX, The Hague)

New Zealand (☎ 04-472 1382; www.chinaembassy.org.nz; 2-6 Glenmore St, Wellington) Consulate in Auckland.

UK (☎ 020-7299 4049, 24hr visa information 0891-880 808, visa section 020-7631 1430; www.chinese-embassy.org.uk; 31 Portland Pl, London; visa section open Mon-Fri 9am-noon); Manchester consulate (☎ 0161-224 7478); Edinburgh consulate (☎ 0131-337 3220)

USA (☎ 202-338 6688; www.china-embassy.org; Room 110, 2201 Wisconsin Ave NW, Washington DC); Chicago consulate (☎ 312-803 0098; www.chinaconsulatechicago.org/eng); Houston consulate (☎ 713-524 4311; www.houston.china-consulate.org/eng); Los Angeles consulate (☎ 213-380 2508; www.losangeles.china-consulate.org/eng); New York consulate (☎ 212-330 7410; www.nyconsulate.prchina.org/eng); San Francisco consulate (☎ 415-563 9232; www.chinaconsulatesf.org/eng)

Note that Chinese embassies in the USA no longer accept main-in applications, so unless you live in a major city you'll have to use an agent such as the recommended **China Visa Service Center** (☎ 1-800-799 6560; www.my chin avisa.com).

Consulates in Tibet

The only diplomatic representation in Tibet is the **Nepali Consulate-General** (Nipoer Lingshiguan; Map p96; ☎ 0891-683 0609; rncglx@public.ls.x.cn; Luobulinka Beilu; 10am-noon Mon-Fri) in Lhasa. Visas are issued the next day at 4.30pm, though you can sometimes get your passport back the same day. It's located on a side street between the Lhasa Hotel and the Norbulingka.

Visa fees change frequently, but at the time of research a 30- to 60-day visa cost Y255. Bear in mind that if this is your second trip to Nepal in the calendar year and you stayed more than 15 days on your first trip, then your second visa is currently free. All visas are valid for six months from the date of issue. Bring one visa photo. Visits of less than three days are currently visa free.

It is also possible to obtain a Nepali visa for US$30 (in cash US dollars) at Kodari, the Nepali border town, although it would be sensible to check first that this has not changed.

FESTIVALS & EVENTS

Tibetan cultural heritage took such a hammering during the Cultural Revolution that traditional festivals, once important highlights of the Tibetan year, are only now starting to revive.

GOVERNMENT TRAVEL ADVICE

The following government websites offer travel advisories and information on current hot spots.

Australian Department of Foreign Affairs & Trade (☎ 1300 139 281; www.smarttraveller.gov.au)

British Foreign & Commonwealth Office (☎ 0845-850-2829; www.fco.gov.uk/country advice)

Canadian Department of Foreign Affairs & International Trade (☎ 800-267 6788; www.dfait-maeci.gc.ca)

US State Department (☎ 888-407 4747; http://travel.state.gov)

Tibetan festivals are held according to the Tibetan lunar calendar, which usually lags at least a month behind our Gregorian calendar. Ask around for the exact dates of many festivals because these are often only fixed by monasteries a few months in advance. To check Tibetan lunar dates against Western Gregorian dates, try www.kalachakranet.org/ta_tibetan_calendar.html.

The following are just some of the more important festivals:

January

Shigatse New Year Festival Held in the first week of the 12th lunar month.

February/March

Year End Festival Dancing monks can be seen on the 29th day of the 12th lunar month at Tsurphu, Mindroling and Tashilhunpo in this festival, which is held to dispel the evil of the old year and auspiciously usher in the new one. Families clean their houses in preparation for the new year. A huge thangka is unveiled the following day at Tsurphu Monastery.

Losar (New Year Festival) Taking place in the first week of the first lunar month, Losar is a colourful week of activities; Lhasa is probably the best place to be. There are performances of Tibetan drama and pilgrims making incense offerings, and the streets are thronged with Tibetans dressed in their finest. New prayer flags are hung in monasteries and homes.

Chotrül Düchen (Butter Sculpture Festival) Huge yak-butter sculptures are traditionally placed around Lhasa's Barkhor circuit on the 15th day of the first lunar month. The festival is not currently celebrated in Lhasa, though it is in Labrang Monastery in Gansu province.

Mönlam Chenmo (Great Prayer Festival) Held midway through the first lunar month (officially culminating on the 25th). Monks from Lhasa's three main monasteries used to assemble in the Jokhang and an image of Jampa (Maitreya) was borne around the Barkhor circuit. The festival was first instituted by Tsongkhapa in 1409 at Ganden Monastery but was outlawed after political demonstrations ended in violence during the 1988 celebrations.

May/June

Birth of Sakyamuni The seventh day of the fourth lunar month is sees large numbers of pilgrims visiting Lhasa and other sacred areas in Tibet. Festivals are held around this time at Tsurphu (see next entry), Ganden, Reting and Samye Monasteries.

Tsurphu Festival *Cham* dancing (ritual dancing carried out by monks), processions and the unfurling of a great thangka are the highlights of this festival, from the 9th to 11th days of the fourth lunar month.

Saga Dawa (Sakyamuni's Enlightenment) The 15th day of the fourth lunar month (full moon) marks the date of Sakyamuni's conception, enlightenment and entry into nirvana. Huge numbers of pilgrims walk Lhasa's Lingkhor circuit and visit Mt Kailash, where the Tarboche prayer pole is raised each year.

June/July

Gyantse Horse-Racing Festival Currently held from the 15th to 18th of the fifth month (ie around Saga Dawa), though authorities are trying to fix the date in the Gregorian calendar to boost tourism. The fun and games include dances, yak races, archery and equestrian events. A large 480-year old thangka is unfurled at sunrise.

Worship of the Buddha During the second week of the fifth lunar month, the parks of Lhasa, in particular the Norbulingka, are crowded with picnickers.

Dorje Drak Festival Cham dancing is performed on the 10th day of the fifth Tibetan month at this small monastery

Tashilhunpo Festival From the 14th to 16th days of the fifth lunar month, Shigatse's Tashilhunpo Monastery becomes the scene of three days of festivities. A huge thangka is unveiled and cham dances are performed.

Samye Festival Held from the 15th day of the fifth lunar month (full moon) for two or three days. Special ceremonies and *cham* dancing in front of the Ütse are the main attractions. The monastery guesthouse is normally booked out at this time, so bring a tent. Incense is also burnt on this day throughout Tibet.

August/September

Chökor Düchen Festival Held in Lhasa on the fourth day of the sixth lunar month, this festival celebrates Buddha's first sermon at Sarnath near Varanasi in India. Many pilgrims climb Gephel Ri (Gambo Ütse), the peak behind Drepung Monastery, and also the ridge from Pabonka to the Dode Valley, to burn juniper incense. The festival is also called Drukwa Tsezhi.

Guru Rinpoche's Birthday Held on the 10th day of the sixth lunar month, this festival is particularly popular in Nyingmapa monasteries.

Ganden Festival On the 15th day of the sixth lunar month, Ganden Monastery displays its 25 holiest relics, which are normally locked away. A large offering ceremony accompanies the unveiling.

Drepung Festival The 30th day of the sixth lunar month is celebrated with the hanging at dawn of a huge thangka at Drepung Monastery. Lamas and monks perform opera in the main courtyard.

Shötun (Yogurt Festival) Held in the first week of the seventh lunar month, this festival starts at Drepung (see previous entry) and moves down to the Norbulingka. Lhamo (Tibetan opera) and masked dances are held, and locals take the occasion as another excuse for more picnics.

September/October

Bathing Festival The end of the seventh and beginning of the eighth lunar months sees locals washing away the grime of the previous year in an act of purification that coincides with the week-long appearance of the constellation Pleiades in the night sky.

Horse-Racing Festival Held in the first week of the eighth lunar month, this festival featuring horse racing, archery and other traditional nomad sports takes place in Damxung and Nam-tso. A similar and even larger event is held in Nagchu a few weeks earlier, from 10 to 16 August.

Onkor In the first week of the eighth lunar month Tibetans in central Tibet get together and party in celebration of the upcoming harvest.

Tashilhunpo More *cham* dances, from the ninth to 11th days of the eighth month, at Shigatse's Tashilhunpo Monastery.

November/December

Lhabab Düchen Commemorating Buddha's descent from heaven, the 22nd day of the ninth lunar month sees large numbers of pilgrims in Lhasa. Ladders are painted afresh on rocks around many monasteries to symbolise the event.

Palden Lhamo The 15th day of the 10th lunar month sees a procession in Lhasa around the Barkhor bearing Palden Lhamo (Shri Devi), protective deity of the Jokhang.

Tsongkhapa Festival Respect is shown to Tsongkhapa, the founder of Gelugpa order, on the anniversary of his death on the 25th of the 10th lunar month; monasteries light fires and carry images of Tsongkhapa in procession. Check for *cham* dances at the monasteries at Ganden, Sera and Drepung.

GAY & LESBIAN TRAVELLERS

Homosexuality has historical precedents in Tibet, especially in Tibetan monasteries, where male lovers were known as *trap'i kedmen*, or 'monk's wife'. The Dalai Lama has sent mixed signals about homosexuality, describing gay sex as 'sexual misconduct', 'improper' and 'inappropriate', but also by saying 'There are no acts of love between adults that one can or should condemn'.

The official attitude to gays and lesbians in China is also ambiguous, with responses ranging from Draconian penalties to tacit acceptance. Travellers are advised to act with discretion. Chinese men routinely hold hands and drape their arms around each other without anyone inferring any sexual overtones.

Canada-based company **Footprints Travel** (☎ 1-888-962 6211, 416-962 8111; www.footprintstravel.com) and American-based **Hanns Ebensten Travel** (☎ 866-294 8174; www.hetravel.com/gay/travel/tibet_gay.htm) organises gay and lesbian group trips to Tibet, the latter including the train trip to Lhasa.

Utopia (www.utopia-asia.com/tipschin.htm) has a good website and publishes a guide to gay travel in China, though with little specific to Tibet.

HOLIDAYS

The PRC has nine national holidays. These are mainly Chinese holidays and mean little to many Tibetans, but government offices and banks will be closed on many of these dates.

New Year's Day 1 January
Chinese New Year Falls on 7 February in 2008, 26 January in 2009 and 14 February in 2010
International Women's Day 8 March
International Labour Day 1 May, a week-long holiday
Youth Day 4 May
Children's Day 1 June
Anniversary of the founding of the Communist Party of China 1 July
Anniversary of the founding of the People's Liberation Army 1 August
National Day 1 October, a week-long holiday

Chinese New Year, otherwise known as the Spring Festival, officially lasts only three days but many people take a week off from work. Be warned: this is definitely not the time to travel around China, cross borders (especially the Hong Kong one) or to be caught short of money.

You should be aware that 10 March is a politically sensitive date, as it is the anniversary of the 1959 Tibetan uprising and flight of the Dalai Lama. Also, 23 May marks the signing of the *Agreement on Measures for the Peaceful Liberation of Tibet,* while 1 September marks the anniversary of the founding of the Tibetan Autonomous Region (TAR). Other politically sensitive dates marking political protests are 5 March, 27 September, 10 December and 1 October. It may be difficult for travellers to fly into Tibet for a few days before these dates.

Many Tibetan businesses, restaurants, shops and travel agencies are closed on the days of Losar and Saga Dawa (see p318)

INSURANCE

Travel insurance is particularly recommended in a remote and wild region like Tibet. Check particularly that the policy covers ambulances or an emergency flight home, which is essential in the case of altitude sickness. Some policies specifically exclude 'dangerous activities' such as kayaking and even trekking.

You may prefer a policy that pays doctors or hospitals directly rather than you having to pay on the spot and claim later. If you have to claim later, make sure you keep all documentation. Some policies ask you to call to a centre in your home country where an immediate assessment of your problem is made. Note that collect (reverse charge) calls are not possible in Tibet.

See the Health chapter (p346) for further information on health insurance

Worldwide travel insurance is available at www.lonelyplanet.com/travel_services. You can buy, extend and claim online anytime – even if you're already on the road.

INTERNET ACCESS

Internet cafés (网吧; wangba in Chinese) are available in almost every town in Tibet, though locals use them more to play computer games and smoke cigarettes than to surf the web. Most charge around Y3 per hour, though places in western Tibet costs up to Y8. A surprising number operate 24 hours.

Some websites (eg those of the BBC and Dalai Lama) have been blacklisted by the Chinese government and are unavailable inside China.

LEGAL MATTERS

Most crimes are handled administratively by the PSB, which acts as police, judge and executioner.

China takes a particularly dim view of opium and all its derivatives. It's difficult to say what attitude the Chinese police will take towards foreigners caught using marijuana – they often don't care what foreigners do if it's not political and if Chinese or Tibetans aren't involved. Then again the Chinese are fond of making examples of wrongdoings and you don't want to be the example.

Public Security Bureau (PSB)

The Public Security Bureau (PSB; 公安局; Gong'anju) is the name given to China's police, both uniformed and plain clothed. The foreign affairs branch of the PSB deals with foreigners. This branch (also known as the 'entry-exit branch') is responsible for issuing visa extensions and Alien Travel Permits.

In Tibet it is fairly unusual for foreigners to have problems with the PSB, though making an obvious display of pro-Tibetan political sympathies is guaranteed to lead to problems.

Photographing Tibetan protests or military sites will lead to the confiscation of your film and possibly a brief detention.

Attempting to travel into or out of Tibet without a travel permit (mainly through Sichuan or Yunnan) is likely to end in an encounter somewhere en route. If you are caught in a closed area without a permit, you face a fine of Y200 to Y600, which can often be bargained down. Some officers have been known to offer a 'student discount' on fines! See p323 for more on this.

If you do have a serious run-in with the PSB, you may have to write a confession of guilt and pay a fine. In the most serious cases, you can be expelled from China (at your own expense).

MAPS

It shouldn't come as a surprise that good mapping for Tibet is not easy to come by. Stock up on maps before you leave.

Specialist online map retailers include **Stanfords** (www.stanfords.co.uk), the **Map Shop** (www.themapshop.co.uk), **Mapland** (www.mapland.com.au) and **Map Link** (www.maplink.com).

MAPS OF TIBET

Chinese provincial atlases to Tibet are available in bookshops throughout China. They show the most detail, but are of little use if you or the person you are asking doesn't read Chinese characters. Most locals know place names in Tibetan only, not Chinese.

The English-language map *China Tibet Tour Map*, by the Mapping Bureau of the Tibet Autonomous Region, is the best locally produced English-language map and is OK if you are just travelling around Tibet by road.

PASS HEIGHTS

Elevations in Tibet, especially for passes, are notoriously inconsistent, with maps and road signs rarely agreeing over the correct elevation. In this book we have tried to use composite measurements, incorporating the most accurate maps, the most consistently agreed figures and on-the-spot GPS readings (which have their own inconsistencies and inaccuracies). Most figures should be accurate within 100m or so, but use the elevations in this book as a guideline only.

Road maps available in Kathmandu include *Tibet – South-Central* by Nepa Maps; *Latest Map of Kathmandu to Tibet* by Mandala Maps; the *Namaste Trekking Map;* and *Lhasa to Kathmandu,* which is a mountain-biking map by Himalayan Map House. They are marginally better than Chinese-produced maps but still aren't up to scratch.

Gecko Maps (www.geckomaps.com; former Karto Atelier) produce an excellent general *Himalaya-Tibet* map, as well as trekking and panoramic maps of Mt Kailash. The Nelles Verlag *Himalaya* map covers the entire range and has good detail of central Tibet. **ITMB** (www.itmb.com) publish a fairly recent (and, usefully, waterproof) *Tibet* map (1:1,850,000; 2006).

Tibet and Adjacent Areas under Chinese Communist Occupation, published by the **Amnye Machen Institute in Dharamsala** (www.amnyemachen.org) is an unusual map that covers the entire Tibetan world. It uses traditional Tibetan place names, which not everyone in Tibet (certainly not the many Chinese immigrants) will know.

For detailed and downloadable online maps of Tibet, try the **Tibet Map Institute** (www.tibetmap.com).

Google Earth (http://earth.google.com) offers fascinating detail on Tibet, including many monasteries and several treks. Be warned; it's utterly addictive.

MAPS OF LHASA

Gecko Maps produce *The Lhasa Map,* with awesome architectural detail of the old town. More offbeat, and quite dated these days (published in 1995), is the Amnye Machen Institute *Lhasa City* (1:12,500).

On This Spot – Lhasa, published by the **International Campaign for Tibet** (ICT; www.savetibet.org) in 2001, is a unique political map of the Lhasa region, pinpointing the location of prisons, demonstrations, human-rights abuses and more. It's a really fascinating read, but it's too politically subversive to take into Tibet. It can be ordered from ICT.

MONEY

For your trip to Tibet bring a mix of travellers cheques (say 60%), cash in US dollars (40%) and a credit card. Consult the inside front cover for a table of exchange rates and refer to p15 for information on costs.

ATMs

Several ATMs in Lhasa and Shigatse accept foreign cards. The Bank of China accepts Visa, MasterCard, Diners Club, American Express and Plus. The Agricultural Bank accepts Visa, Plus and Electron. Check before trying your card as many ATMs can only be used by domestic account holders.

The maximum amount you can withdraw per transaction is Y2000 with the Bank of China and Y1000 with the Agricultural Bank. Cards are occasionally eaten, so try to make your transaction during bank hours.

For those without an ATM card or credit card, a PIN-activated **Visa TravelMoney card** (☎ US 1-877-394 2247) will give you access to pre-deposited cash through the ATM network.

Credit Cards

You'll get very few opportunities to splurge on the plastic in Tibet, unless you spend a few nights in a top-end hotel. Most local tours (including FIT), train tickets and even flights out of Lhasa still can't be paid for using a credit card. The few shops that do accept credit cards often charge a 4% surcharge.

The Lhasa central branch of the Bank of China is the only place in Tibet that provides credit card advances. A 3% commission is deducted.

Currency

The Chinese currency is known as Renminbi (RMB) or 'people's money'. The basic unit of this currency is the yuan, and is designated in this book by a 'Y'. In spoken Chinese, the word kuai is almost always substituted for the yuan. Ten jiao (commonly known as mao) make up one yuan.

RMB comes in paper notes in denominations of one, two, five, 10, 20, 50 and 100 yuan; and one, two and five jiao. Coins are in denominations of one yuan and five jiao.

China has a problem with counterfeit notes. Very few Tibetans or Chinese will accept a Y100 or Y50 note without first subjecting it to intense scrutiny, and many will not accept old, tattered notes or coins. Check the watermark when receiving any Y100 note.

Exchanging Money

In Tibet, the only place to change foreign currency and travellers cheques is the Bank of China. Top-end hotels in Lhasa have exchange services but only for guests. Outside of Lhasa, the only other locations to change money are in Shigatse, Zhangmu, Purang (cash only) and Ali, and at the airport on arrival. If you are travelling upcountry, try to get your cash in small denominations: Y100 and Y50 bills are sometimes difficult to get rid of in rural Tibet.

The currencies of Australia, Canada, the US, the UK, Hong Kong, Japan, the euro zone and most of the rest of Western Europe are acceptable at the Lhasa Bank of China. The official rate is given at all banks and most hotels, so there is little need to shop around for the best deal. The standard commission is 0.75%.

The only place in Tibet to officially change RMB back into foreign currency is the central Lhasa branch of the Bank of China. You will need your original exchange receipts. You cannot change RMB into dollars at Gongkar airport.

Moneychangers at Zhangmu (by the Nepal border) will change yuan into Nepali rupees and vice versa. Yuan can also easily be reconverted in Hong Kong and, increasingly, in many Southeast Asian countries.

International Transfers

Getting money sent to you in Lhasa is possible but it can be a drag. One option is by using the Bank of China's central office in Lhasa. Money should be wired to the Bank of China, Tibet/Lhasa branch, 28 Linkuo Xilu, bank account No 90600668341, SWIFT code BKCHCNBJ900. Double-check wiring instructions with the bank beforehand.

The second option is via **Western Union** (www.westernunion.com), which can wire money via the Express Mail Service (EMS; see p325) at Lhasa's main post office.

Security

A moneybelt or pockets sewn inside your clothes is the safest way to carry money.

Keeping all your eggs in one basket is not advised – you should keep an emergency cash stash of small-denomination notes in US dollars apart from your main moneybelt, along with a record of your travellers cheque serial numbers, emergency contact numbers and passport number.

Taxes

Although big hotels may add a tax or 'service charge' of 10% to 15%, all other taxes are included in the price tag, including airline departure tax (see p331).

Tipping & Bargaining

Tibet is one of those wonderful places where tipping is not done and almost no-one asks for a tip. If you go on a long organised trip out to eastern or western Tibet, your guide and driver will probably expect a tip at the end of the trip, assuming all went well. Figure on around Y100 per person.

Basic bargaining skills are essential for travel in Tibet. You can bargain in shops, hotels, street stalls and travel agencies, and with pedicab drivers and most people – but not everywhere. In small shops and street stalls, bargaining is expected, but there is one important rule to follow: be polite.

Tibetans are no less adept at driving a hard deal than the Chinese and, like the Chinese, aggressive bargaining will usually only serve to firm their conviction that the original asking price is the one they want. Try to keep smiling and firmly whittle away at the price. If this does not work, try walking away. They might call you back, and if they don't there is always somewhere else.

Travellers Cheques

Besides the advantage of safety, travellers cheques are useful to carry in Tibet because the exchange rate is higher (by about 3%) than it is for cash. The Bank of China charges a 0.75% commission to cash travellers cheques. Cheques from the major companies such as Thomas Cook, Citibank, American Express and Bank of America are accepted.

PERMITS

There are three levels of bureaucracy you need to jump through to travel in Tibet: a visa to enter China, a Tibet Tourism Bureau (TTB) permit to get into Tibet and an Alien Travel Permit to travel to certain regions of Tibet.

Beware that the permit situation is subject to rapid and unpredictable change by the Chinese government, so it's worth checking the current situation with other travellers in Lhasa or Chengdu. Don't trust travel agencies on this one, as they have a vested interest in booking you on one of their tours.

Tibet Tourism Bureau (TTB) Permit

A TTB permit is officially required to get into the Tibet Autonomous Province (TAR). Without one you will not be able to board a flight to Tibet and, *if checked*, you may not be allowed to continue on your bus or train trip.

THE IMPERMENANCE OF TRAVEL

With the arrival of the railway to Tibet, rumours were rife that the illogical and inconsistent permit system would be disbanded. In the event, in 2007 the permit system was actually tightened. Shows what we know!

There's still a good chance that the permit system will be overhauled before too long, perhaps in the wake of the 2008 Beijing Olympics. Don't be surprised if the permit system is radically different from that described in this guide. In fact, expect it. One of the best places for updated information is the Thorn Tree at www.lonelyplanet.com.

How these rules are interpreted depends on the political climate in Tibet. When things are relaxed you can just buy a permit for around Y500 from one of the many budget travel agencies in China, especially Chengdu. The actual permit costs Y50, the rest goes to agency fees and middle men. When restrictions are tighter you will need to book some kind of tour, ranging from a three-day tour of Lhasa to a full tour, depending on the agency.

Whether you need the TTB permit once you get to Lhasa is currently in flux. Up until recently you didn't need it but a tightening of restrictions in 2007 meant that you technically needed it to book a tour to visit other areas of Lhasa.

See p333 for more information on buying air and bus tickets into Tibet from Kathmandu, Chengdu or elsewhere. The amount of time you can stay in Tibet is normally determined by the length of time on your visa, not the TTB permit.

TTB permits are also needed by groups travelling by Land Cruiser, but this will be arranged by the travel agency organising the trip.

Since 2003 Chinese residents of Hong Kong and Macau no longer require a TTB permit to enter Tibet, though foreigners resident in China do. Journalists and embassy staff will find it impossible to get a TTB permit as a tourist. Visitors on a business or resident visa don't seem to have a problem.

TTB permits generally take two or three days to process and are not available during weekends.

Alien Travel Permit

Once you have a visa and have managed to wangle a TTB permit, you'd think you were home dry. Think again. You'll probably need to arrange an alien travel permit for much of your travels outside central Tibet.

At the time of research, travel permits were *not* needed for the towns of Lhasa, Shigatse and Tsetang, or for places in Lhasa prefecture (not just Lhasa city). This includes such places as Ganden, Tsurphu, Nam-tso, Drigung Til and Reting, giving you quite a lot of scope.

All other areas technically require permits, though you are unlikely to be checked in places like the Yarlung Tsangpo Valley (with the possible exception of Samye Monastery) or most places along the Friendship Hwy (with the exception of the Everest region and one checkpoint along the road). You are likely to be checked in the major towns in eastern and western Tibet. See the individual chapter intros for more details on localised requirements.

Lhasa PSB will not issue travel permits to individuals and will direct you to a travel agency. Agencies can arrange a travel permit to most places frequented by tourists but only if you book a Land Cruiser, driver and guide.

Travellers have had mixed experiences with the Ali PSB. Many have written of being given a travel permit to the sights in the Ali prefecture (ie Mt Kailash, Guge Kingdom) on payment of a fine of around Y300. Others have been fined and sent back to Lhasa.

Permits cost Y50 and can list any number of destinations. If you get caught by the PSB without a permit (most likely when you check into a hotel), you theoretically face a fine of between Y200 and Y600, though many travellers have paid lower fines or no fines at all by playing dumb and claiming anything from student poverty to sickness or road closures. The key is to act dumb and obsequious, with lots of time on your hands but no money. Even if you do pay a fine, you've got away with paying less than you would on a tour. Get a receipt to make sure you don't get fined a second time during your return to Lhasa.

You should give your agency an absolute minimum of four working days to arrange your permits, longer if military or other permits are required (see p323). If you are arranging a Land Cruiser trip from abroad, the travel agency may ask for up to one month to arrange permits.

Other Permits

Sensitive border areas, such as Mt Kailash, the road to Kashgar and the Nyingtri region of eastern Tibet, also require a military permit and a foreign-affairs permit.

For Thöling and Tsaparang in western Tibet you may also need a permit from the local Cultural Affairs Bureau. These will be arranged by the tour agency if you book a tour. Dungkar in western Tibet requires a permit from the Ali PSB (see p224).

For remote places such as the Yarlung Tsangpo gorges in southeastern Tibet, or for any border area, you may not be able to get permits even if you book a tour through an ordinary travel agency. For this you will need an agency that has tight military connections.

PHOTOGRAPHY & VIDEO

Film & Equipment

Tibet is one of the most photogenic countries in the world and you should bring twice as much film or memory as you think you'll need.

China has thoroughly embraced digital photography and shops in Lhasa stock a decent range of memory cards and rechargeable batteries. As a guide, a 1GB Sandisk card costs around Y300. Internet cafés or photo shops in Lhasa, Shigatse, Chamdo and Ali can burn your photos onto a CD for around Y20. Opt for brand-name CDs rather than the cheaper Chinese-made versions.

Battery life plummets at Tibet's higher elevations and lower temperatures. Keep your batteries warm and separate from your camera overnight and during cold weather. Just heating up batteries in your pocket or the sun can draw some extra juice from them. Chinese batteries are invariably useless.

Print film is easily available in major towns, though slide film is only available in Lhasa. It is possible to process print film and make digital prints in Lhasa, with fairly good results but there's nowhere to process slide film in Tibet. Even in Kathmandu, with the exception of a couple of professional outfits, it is a risky proposition.

Restrictions

Photographs of airports and military installations are prohibited; bridges are also a touchy subject. Don't take any photos or especially video footage of civil unrest or public demonstrations. The Chinese are paranoid about foreign TV crews filming unauthorised documentaries on Tibet.

Restrictions on photography are also imposed at most monasteries and museums. This is partly an attempt to stop the trade of antiquities out of Tibet (statues are often stolen to order from photos taken by seemingly innocuous 'tourists'). In the case of flash photography, such restrictions protect wall murals from damage. Inside the larger monasteries, a fee of Y20 to Y50 is often imposed in each chapel for taking a photograph. Video fees can be up to Y800 (US$100!) in some monasteries. You are free, however, to take any photos of the exteriors of monasteries.

Technical Tips

Bear in mind, when taking photographs in Tibet, that special conditions prevail. For one, the dust gets into everything – make a point of carefully cleaning your lenses as often as possible. The high altitudes in Tibet mean that the best time to take photographs is when the sun is low in the sky: early in the morning and late in the afternoon. At other times getting a good exposure becomes more difficult – you are likely to end up with a shot full of dark shadows and bright points of light.

One useful accessory to cope with Tibet's harsh light conditions is a polarising filter. When using it, turn the filter until the contrast improves; if there are any clouds in the sky, they will become whiter as the sky itself becomes a deeper shade of blue. Lonely Planet's full-colour *Travel Photography: A Guide to Taking Better Pictures*, written by internationally renowned travel photographer Richard I'Anson, is full of handy hints and is designed to take on the road.

POST

China's post service is pretty efficient and airmail letters take around a week to reach most destinations. Writing the country of destination in Chinese can speed up the delivery.

An airmail letter of up to 20g costs Y6 to any country, plus Y1.8 per additional 10g. Postcards cost Y4.50 and aerograms Y5.20.

Rates for parcels vary depending on the country of destination and seem quite random. As a rough guide, a 1kg airmail package costs around Y144/158.50/162 to Australia/USA/UK. A 1kg packet to the UK costs Y469 by airmail, Y126 by surface mail and Y108 by sea mail. Surface takes around one month, sea mail can take from two to three months; a good compromise is Sea, Air and Land (SAL), which takes about six weeks to the USA. The maximum weight you can send or receive is 30kg. Lhasa is the only place in Tibet from where it is possible to send international parcels.

Post offices are very picky about how you pack things; do not finalise your packing until the parcel has its last customs clearance. If you have a receipt for the goods, then put it in the box when you are mailing it, since it may be opened again by customs further down the line. Lhasa's main post office has a poste restante service, for the time being at least.

Express Mail Service (EMS), a worldwide priority mail service, can courier documents to most foreign countries in around five days. Documents up to 500g cost Y160/220/180 to Australia/Europe/US, with each additional 500g costing from Y55 (Australia) to Y75 (US and Europe). Documents to Hong Kong cost Y90, plus Y30 each additional 500g. Packages cost slightly more. There are charges of Y2.30 for recorded delivery and Y6.50 for registered mail. DHL has an office in Lhasa (see p99). A 500g document couriered to the USA costs Y228 (depending on the fuel surcharge) and a 10kg jumbo box costs Y1126.

SHOPPING

Tibet is not a bad place for souvenir hunting, although much of the stuff you see in markets, particularly the bronzes, has been humped over the high passes from Nepal and can probably be bought cheaper in Kathmandu, where you will have a better selection of quality goods.

For an overview of possible purchases in Tibet, the best place to look is the Barkhor in Lhasa. Prayer flags, shawls, prayer wheels and daggers are all popular buys. Itinerant pilgrims may also come up to you with things to sell – proceeds will often finance their trip home.

Most of the stalls on the Barkhor circuit seem be selling jewellery and most (some would say all) of it is fake. The vast majority of the jewellery on offer is turquoise and coral; Tibetans believe that turquoise is good for the liver and coral for the heart. Locals will tell you that the turquoise comes from the mountains and the coral from the lakes of Tibet – more likely sources are Taiwan and China (if it doesn't come from a factory, that is).

It is easy to tell fake turquoise (or 'new turquoise' as the stall holders call it) from the real thing ('old turquoise'). The fake stuff is bluer and is flawless; beware of a string of identically shaped and rounded beads – nature did not intend them to be this way. The final test is to scratch the surface with a sharp metal object, the fake turquoise will leave a white line, the real stuff won't show a thing. When you've established what you're buying have a closer look at the stone to make sure it's all in one piece. Unscrupulous stall holders glue together tiny bits of turquoise with black glue to make larger pieces of stone.

You'll also see Buddha eye beads, known as *dzi* – black or brown oblong beads with white eye symbols. These are replicas of natural fossils found in rocks in the mountains containing auspicious eye symbols thought to represent the eyes of the Buddha. The real things pass hands for tens of thousands of dollars; copies are more affordable. The more eyes the higher the price.

Be prepared to bargain hard for any purchase, especially in the Barkhor. You can probably reckon on at least halving the price, but there are no hard-and-fast rules. Shop around for a while and get a feel for prices.

Other good buys are Tibetan ceiling drapes and thangkas. Some ceiling drapes and door curtains are very tasteful and can be bought in Lhasa and Shigatse. Most thangkas for sale are gaudy – good ones do not come cheap. There are several workshops in Lhasa's old quarter where you can see thangkas being painted.

SOLO TRAVELLERS

Solo travellers shouldn't be too put off by the seeming official insistence on 'group travel'. For the purposes of getting permits and a group visa, a group can be as small as one person. It's common for travellers to band together in Lhasa to share transport costs and you'll see lots of notices from people looking to find temporary travel or trekking companions.

Single rooms in a hotel are normally the same price (or even more expensive!) than a double room, though you can often pay per bed in a triple or quad – see p314.

TELEPHONE

China's phone system has been rapidly modernised, and long-distance and international direct dialling is available almost everywhere.

International rates have fallen in recent years. China Unicom and private telephone booths offer the cheapest rates: around Y2.40 per minute to the US and Y3.60 or Y4.20 to most other countries. 'Domestic' long-distance calls cost Y1.50 per minute to Hong Kong, Macau and Taiwan and Y0.30 elsewhere in China. Local city calls cost Y0.2 per minute.

Lines are amazingly clear considering where you are. (The biggest problem will probably be the guy yelling in the booth next door on a local call to Shigatse.) Mobile phone coverage is generally excellent, even in Everest Base Camp!

Most hotels in Lhasa have International-Direct-Dial (IDD) telephones but levy a hefty 30% surcharge on calls.

It is still impossible to make collect calls (reverse-charge calls) or to use foreign telephone debit cards. The best you can do is give someone your number and get them to call you back.

Local area codes are given at the start of each town's entry within this guidebook.

TIME

Time throughout China – including Tibet – is set to Beijing time, which is eight hours ahead of GMT/UTC. When it is noon in Beijing it is also noon in far-off Lhasa, even if the sun only indicates around 9am or 10am. See also the World Time map (pp390–1).

TOILETS

Chinese toilets might be fairly dismal, but Tibetan toilets make them look like little bowers of heaven. The standard model is a deep hole in the ground, often without partitions, that bubbles and gives off noxious vapours. Many Tibetans (including women with long skirts) prefer to urinate in the street.

On the plus side there are some fabulous 'toilets with a view'. Honours go to the Samye Monastery Guesthouse, the Sakya Guesthouse, the public toilets in the Potala and the small village of Pasum on the way to Everest Base Camp.

With the exception of midrange and top-end hotels, hotel toilets in Tibet are of the squat variety – as the clichés go, good for the digestion and character building, too. Always carry a small stash of toilet paper or tissues with you.

TOURIST INFORMATION

Tibet is officially a province of China and does not have tourist offices as such. Similarly, the

FINDING OUT MORE

The following organisations do excellent work to help the people of the Tibetan plateau and foster greater awareness of all aspects of Tibetan culture.

- Braille Without Borders – www.braillewithoutborders.org
- Jinpa – www.jinpa.org
- Kham Aid Foundation – www.khamaid.org
- Tendol Gyalzur Orphanage – www.tendol-gyalzur-tibet.ch
- Tibet Foundation – www.tibet-foundation.org
- The Tibet Fund – www.tibetfund.org
- Tibet Poverty Alleviation Fund – www.tpaf.org
- Tibetan Village Project – www.tibetanvillageproject.org

Pro-Tibetan organisations abroad have good news services and often cultural coverage. The **Tibet Support Group** (www.tibet.org) offers online links to most pro-Tibet organisations.

- Australia Tibet Council – www.atc.org.au
- Canada Tibet Committee – www.tibet.ca
- Free Tibet Campaign (UK) – www.freetibet.org
- International Campaign for Tibet – www.savetibet.org
- Students for a Free Tibet – www.studentsforafreetibet.org
- Tibet Foundation (UK) – www.tibet-foundation.org
- Tibet House – www.tibethouse.org
- Tibet Information Network – www.tibetinfo.net
- Tibet Society – www.tibetsociety.com
- Tibetan Centre for Human Rights and Democracy – www.tchrd.org

Tibetan government-in-exile does not provide information specifically relating to travel in Tibet. Several of the pro-Tibetan organisations abroad offer travel advice (see above).

Tibet Tourism Bureau

The main function of the state-sponsored **Tibet Tourism Bureau** (TTB; Luobulinka Lu, Lhasa; 8.30am-1.30pm & 3-5.30pm) is to direct travellers into group tours in Tibet. It issues the permits necessary to enter Tibet (see p323), although very few travellers deal with it directly.

In Chengdu there is a **TTB branch office** (028-8555 1719; 3 Wuhou Hengjie). The TTB branches in Shanghai (www.tibet-tour.com) and Beijing (www.tibettour.net.cn/en) operate like normal travel agencies.

TRAVELLERS WITH DISABILITIES

Tibet can be a hard place for disabled travellers. The high altitudes, rough roads and lack of access make travelling difficult. Monasteries in particular often involve a hike up a hillside or steep, very narrow steps. Few of the hotels offer any facilities for the disabled.

Braille Without Borders (0891-633 1763; www.braillewithoutborders.org) Blind visitors can contact this excellent organisation based in Lhasa. It developed the first Tibetan Braille system and runs a school for blind Tibetan kids. The founder, Sabriye Tenberken, is the author of the book *My Path Leads to Tibet: The Inspiring Story of How One Young Blind Woman Brought Hope to the Blind Children of Tibet* and stars alongside blind climber Erik Weihenmayer in the documentary film *Blindsight* (www.blindsightthemovie.com).

Navyo Nepal (01-428 0056; www.navyonepal.com; Kathmandu, Nepal) This Nepal-based company has some experience in running tours for the disabled to Tibet and Nepal.

VISAS

Visas for individual travel in China are easy to get from most Chinese embassies, though it's important not to mention Tibet on your visa application. The Chinese government has been known to stop issuing individual visas in summer or the run-up to sensitive political events, as a control of tourist numbers.

Most Chinese embassies and consulates will issue a standard 30- or 60-day, single-entry tourist (an 'L' category) visa in three to five working days. The 'L' means *lüxing* (travel). Fees vary according to how much your country charges Chinese citizens for a visa. At the time of writing, a standard 30-day visa cost A$30 in Australia, €30.50 in France, UK£25 in the UK and US$50 in the USA. Fees must be paid in cash at the time of application and you'll need two passport-sized photos. It's possible to download an application form at embassy or visa agency websites. Express services cost double the normal fee. Your application must be written in English, and you must have one entire blank page in your passport for the visa.

Some Chinese embassies (not the US) offer a postal service for a fee, but this takes around three weeks. If you live in the US but not near an embassy, you'll have to use a visa agent, such as the recommended **China Visa Service Center** (☎ 1-800-799 6560; www.mychinavisa.com; 10700 Richmond Ave, Ste 211, Houston, TX 77042).

The visa application form asks you a lot of questions (your entry and exit points, travel itinerary, means of transport etc), but once in China you can deviate from this as much as you like. When listing your itinerary, pick the obvious contenders: Beijing, Shanghai and so on. Don't mention Tibet, don't list your occupation as journalist and don't mention bicycles (otherwise you may be told erroneously that you have to take a tour to travel by bike).

Visas valid for more than 30 days can be difficult to obtain anywhere other than Hong Kong, although some embassies abroad (in the US and UK, for example) often give you 60 or even 90 days if you ask nicely. This saves you the considerable difficulty of getting a visa extension in Tibet. Most agencies in Hong Kong can arrange a 90-day visa.

It's now possible to travel in Tibet with a resident or business visa. This means you could get a six-month business visa (easily obtained in Hong Kong) and stay in Tibet for most of that time!

A standard single-entry visa is activated on the date you enter China, and must be used within three months from the date of issue. There is some confusion over the validity of Chinese visas. Most Chinese officials look at the 'valid until' date, but on most 30-day visas this is actually the date by which you must have *entered* the country, not the visa's expiry date. Longer-stay visas are often activated on the day of issue, not the day you enter the country, so there's no point in getting one too far in advance of your planned entry date. Check with the embassy if you are unsure.

If you want more flexibility to enter and leave China several times, most Chinese embassies will issue a double-entry visa.

Hong Kong

In Hong Kong, the cheapest 30-day visas can be obtained from the **visa office** (☎ 3413 2300; 7th fl, Lower Block, China Resources Centre, 26 Harbour Rd, Wan Chai; 🕑 9am-noon & 2-5pm Mon-Fri). Visas processed here in one/two/three days cost HK$400/300/150. Double/six-month multiple/one-year multiple visas are HK$220/400/600 (plus HK$150/250 for express/urgent service). US citizens face an additional surcharge. You'll have to queue but you'll save a few dollars. You must supply two passport photos. From Tsim Sha Tsui on the Kowloon side, the cheapest and easiest way to get there is to take the Star Ferry to Wanchai Pier (not to Central), one block away from the China Resources Building.

China Travel Service (CTS; ☎ 2315 7188; 1st fl, Alpha House, 27-33 Nathan Rd, Tsim Sha Tsui, enter from Peking Rd) is a more convenient and very popular place to get a visa, as is **Forever Bright Trading Limited** (☎ 852-2369 3188; www.fbt-chinavisa.com.hk; Room 916-917, Tower B, New Mandarin Plaza, 14 Science Museum Rd, Tsim Sha Tsui East, Kowloon).

Kathmandu

Regulations at the Chinese embassy in Kathmandu change frequently. At the time of writing the embassy was not issuing visas to individual travellers, only to those travellers booked on a tour (see p335) and even then only group visas. If you turn up with a Chinese visa already in your passport, it will be cancelled (and, no, you won't get a refund).

A group visa is a separate sheet of paper with all the names and passport numbers of the group members. It's important to get your own individual 'group' visa (a 'group' can be as small as one person!), as otherwise, come the end of your tour in Lhasa, you will either have to exit China with your fellow group members or split from this group visa, at considerable cost and hassle. Splitting from a group visa can only officially be done by the Chinese partner of the Nepali travel agency that arranged your travel into Tibet. It is a *real* pain to be avoided at all costs.

Group visas are generally issued for between 21 and 28 days. Note that it is very difficult to extend the duration of a group visa, regardless of what agents in Kathmandu may tell you. It's easier to split from a group visa (ie convert this into a normal tourist visa) and then extend that.

In the past the Chinese embassy in Kathmandu has allowed travellers to travel on their existing individual visas, so there's always the possibility that the situation will change.

Note that if you are flying from Kathmandu directly to Chinese cities outside Tibet (ie Chengdu or Shanghai), you can enter China on an individual tourist visa issued from abroad.

Visa Extensions

The *waishike* (foreign affairs) section of the local PSB handles visa extensions. Extensions of one week are generally obtainable in Lhasa (see p100) but are only processed the day or so before your visa expires, so it's a bit of a gamble. It is far easier to extend your visa in Chengdu, Leshan, Zhongdian, Xining or Xi'an, where a 30-day extension is commonplace.

Travel agencies in Lhasa can arrange a visa extension for the number of days you are on one of their tours. Extensions are also theoretically possible in Ali or Chamdo, as long as you are on a legitimate tour.

Fees vary according to your nationality but generally cost around Y160, except for American citizens who pay around Y400.

VOLUNTEER

There are limited opportunities for volunteer work in the TAR. There are considerable more opportunities outside the TAR, in Tibetan areas of Sichuan and Qinghai, and especially in Dharamsala (see www.volunteertibet.org), and you can always volunteer at any of pro-Tibet organisations (see the boxed text, p327).

The following organisations offer volunteer placements:

Global Crossroad (USA ☎ 1-800-413-2008, UK ☎ 0800-310-1821; www.globalcrossroad.com) Teaching English and work in an orphanage in Lhasa.

Rokpa (www.rokpauk.org/volunteering.html) Teaching in Tibetan areas of Sichuan and Qinghai.

United Planet (www.unitedplanet.org/quest/tibet.html) Teaching in Yushu in Qinghai.

WOMEN TRAVELLERS

Sexual harassment is extremely rare in Tibet and foreign women seem to be able to travel here with few problems. Naturally, it's worth noticing what local women are wearing and how they are behaving, and making a bit of an effort to fit in, as you would in any other foreign country. Probably because of the harsh climate, Tibetan women dress in bulky layers of clothing that mask their femininity. It would be wise to follow their example and dress modestly, especially when visiting a monastery. Several women have written of the favourable reactions they have received from Tibetan women when wearing Tibetan dress; you can get one made in Lhasa (see p125).

Women are generally not permitted to enter the *gönkhang* (protector chapel) in a monastery, ostensibly for fear of upsetting the powerful protector deities inside.

Transport

CONTENTS

Tibet has never been all that accessible, which has always been part of the thrill of finally getting here. For better or worse, huge improvements in Tibet's transport infrastructure over the last few years have removed much of the discomfort of getting onto the high plateau.

For most international travellers, getting to Tibet will involve at least two legs: the first to the gateways of Kathmandu (Nepal) or Chengdu (China) and the second from these cities into Tibet. The first section of this chapter details long-haul options to/from China and Nepal, while the second section details the practicalities of actually getting into and around Tibet. The Gateway Cities chapter (p87) offers basic information for travellers transiting through Kathmandu or Chengdu.

Once you are within the region, the most popular options into Tibet are flights from Kathmandu, Chengdu, Zhongdian or Beijing; the new train link from Qinghai to Lhasa; or the overland drive from Kathmandu to Lhasa along the Friendship Hwy.

> **THINGS CHANGE...**
>
> The information in this chapter is particularly vulnerable to change. The current pace of change in Tibet means that travel options are changing monthly. Tibet's permit requirements in particular change like the wind and there is always the hope that they'll be removed completely. The details given in this chapter should be regarded as pointers and are not a substitute for your own careful, up-to-date research.

At the time of writing, bureaucratic obstacles to entering Tibet (a potentially more insurmountable barrier than even the Himalaya) were in flux. Whichever way you enter Tibet from China you will likely have to join some kind of nominal 'tour' in order to get to Lhasa, though after that you can break off on your own. The situation from Nepal is trickier because of ever-changing visa requirements.

Political events, both domestic and international, can change overnight the regulations for entry into Tibet. It would be wise to check on the latest developments in Tibet before setting out. Note also that it can be very hard to get hold of air and train tickets to Lhasa around the Chinese New Year and the week-long holidays around 1 May and 1 October.

Flights, hotels and tours can be booked online at www.lonelyplanet.com/travel_services.

GETTING THERE & AWAY – GATEWAY CITIES

ENTERING THE COUNTRY

Arriving in China is pretty painless these days. All travellers fill in a health declaration form on arrival in China. You can expect closer scrutiny of your group documents and luggage when crossing into Tibet/China from Nepal at Zhangmu, where some travellers have on occasion had Tibetan-related books and images confiscated.

Passports

Chinese embassies will not issue a visa if your passport has less than six months of validity remaining.

AIR

There are no direct long-haul flights to Tibet. You will probably have to stop over in Kathmandu, Chengdu, Beijing or Hong Kong, even if you are making a beeline for Lhasa.

Airports & Airlines

To China, you generally have the choice of flying first to Beijing, Shanghai or Hong Kong, although there are a small but growing number of flights direct to Chengdu or Kunming (see below). The new terminal at **Beijing Capital Airport** (www.bcia.com.cn) is the world's largest. Hong Kong's **Chek Lap Kok Airport** (www.hkairport.com) is also new. There's little difference in fares to these airports, though a stopover in Hong Kong allows you to get a longer-stay visa for China/Tibet (see p328).

Full-fare flights to Chengdu from other Chinese cities include Beijing (Y1570), Shanghai (Y1660), Guangzhou (Y1300), Kunming (Y700) and Hong Kong (Y2200), though discounts of up to 40% are common on Chinese domestic airfares. Chengdu–Beijing flights can be discounted to as low as Y600.

If you are heading straight to Chengdu (www.cdairport.com), you can fly direct from Amsterdam, Bangkok, Singapore, Tokyo, Fukuoka, Osaka and Seoul (flights from Vienna and Macau are planned). **KLM** (www.klm.com) flies direct from Amsterdam to Chengdu three times a week and offers connections from many cities.

Generally speaking, fares to/from Kathmandu are not all that cheap as there is a limited number of carriers operating out of the Nepali capital. The main carriers into Kathmandu are Gulf Air, Indian Airlines, Qatar Airways and THAI. The national carrier, Royal Nepal Air, is to be avoided if possible. Depending on where you are coming from, it may be cheaper to fly to Delhi and make your way overland from there.

Tickets

If you want to get to Tibet as quickly as possible (perhaps to get the maximum use from your visa), consider buying a domestic Air China ticket to Chengdu as part of your international ticket. Some Air China offices will give you a discount on the domestic leg if you buy the long-haul leg through them. Airfares to China peak between June and September.

Another ticket worth looking into is an open-jaw ticket. This option might involve, for example, flying into Hong Kong and then flying out of Kathmandu, allowing you to travel overland across Tibet.

Buying domestic Chinese tickets abroad is possible but at relatively high fares. Better value online Chinese ticket agencies such as **Elong** (www.elong.net) and **CITS Anhui** (www.chinaticketmaster.com) sell discounted domestic flights in the form of e-tickets, meaning you can transfer directly onto a domestic flight once you enter China.

Online travel agents can save you money if you have the time to invest in them, though in general you'll always get the best fares from travel agencies that cater to expat Chinese travellers (often based in Chinatowns in larger cities). The following online ticket agencies book flights originating in the USA but have links to specific country websites across the world:

Cheapflights.com (www.cheapflights.com)
Expedia (www.expedia.com)
Last Minute.com (www.lastminute.com)
Lonely Planet (www.lonelyplanet.com) Click on Booking and Services to book flight tickets.
Priceline (www.priceline.com) Aims to match the ticket price to your budget.
STA Travel (www.statravel.com)
Travelocity (www.travelocity.com)

DEPARTURE TAX

Departure tax in China is worked into the price of both domestic and international tickets, so there's nothing additional to pay at the airport.

Australia & New Zealand

The cheapest flights from Australia to China generally route via one of the Southeast Asian capitals, such as Kuala Lumpur, Bangkok or Manila. **Singapore Airlines** (www.singaporeair.com) in particular offers good connections to Chengdu five times a week from major Australian cities.

Low-season return fares to Shanghai or Beijing from the east coast of Australia start at around A$1000, with fares to Hong Kong starting from A$910. Flights from New Zealand cost from around NZ$1380 during the low season.

Return fares to Kathmandu from the east coast of Australia range from around A$1300 to A$1500, depending on the season. A one-way ticket costs around A$1000 with Thai Airways (this requires an overnight in Bangkok). Return flights from New Zealand cost from around NZ$1800 to NZ$2200.

Flight Centre (www.flightcentre.com; Australia ☎ 133 133; New Zealand ☎ 0800 24 35 44)

STA Travel (www.statravel.com; Australia ☎ 1300 733 035; New Zealand ☎ 0508 782 872)
Trailfinders (☎ 1300 780 212; www.trailfinders.com.au) In Australia only.
Travel.com.au (www.travel.com.au) Online website.

Continental Europe

Air fares to the Indian subcontinent and China are generally cheaper in the UK than they are in the rest of Europe. Return fares to Beijing from major Western European cities start at around €900 with Lufthansa, Air France and KLM.

STA Travel (www.statravel.com; Paris ☎ 01 43 59 23 69; Frankfurt ☎ 69-430 1910) has dozens of offices across Europe, as does **Nouvelles Frontières** (www.nouvelles-frontieres.fr).

In Germany try **Just Travel** (☎ 089-747 3330; www.justtravel.de); in Italy try **CTS Viaggi** (☎ 06-462 0431; www.cts.it); in the Netherlands try **Airfair** (☎ 0900-7717 717; www.airfair.nl); in Spain try **Barcelo Viajes** (☎ 902 200 400; www.barcelo viajes.com).

In France try **Voyages Wasteels** (☎ 01 42 61 69 87; www.wasteels.fr) and **Voyageurs du Monde** (☎ 01 40 15 11 15; www.vdm.com).

Hong Kong

Hong Kong is part of the People's Republic of China, though most nationalities don't need a visa for the city. Many travellers make their way from Hong Kong into China by train or ferry, but there are also daily direct flights from Hong Kong to Chengdu for around HK$2000.

Note that it is considerably cheaper to fly to Chengdu from neighbouring Shenzhen or Guangzhou. From Shenzhen it costs around Y1420, often discounted to Y900; fares from Guangzhou are sometimes even cheaper.

The Shenzhen airport is just an hour-long TurboJet hydrofoil ride (HK$200) from Hong Kong's Tsim Sha Tsui district (see www.turbojet.com.hk for schedules), or a 40-minute ride from Hong Kong airport (www.turbojetseaexpress.com.hk; HK$230).

Buses operated by CTS Express Coach (http://ctsbus.hkcts.com) and other companies run from Hong Kong International Airport to Guangzhou (HK$250).

A flight from Hong Kong to Kathmandu costs around US$400 one way.

China Travel Service (CTS; ☎ 2315 7188; www.ctshk.com; 1F, Alpha House, 27-33 Nathan Rd, Tsim Sha Tsui) Can book domestic air tickets and offers a discount deal on hydrofoil tickets booked in conjunction with a flight out of Shenzhen.
Phoenix Services Agency (☎ 2722 7378; info@phoenixtrvl.com; Rm 1404-5, 14th fl, Austin Tower, 22-26a Austin Ave, Tsim Sha Tsui) A recommended travel agency.

Southeast Asia

There are direct flights from Bangkok and Singapore to Chengdu and from Bangkok, Chiang Mai, Yangon (Rangoon), Vientiane and Singapore to Kunming.

Bangkok is a popular place to pick up air tickets, and prices are generally very competitive. The best place to shop around is the Bangkok backpacker ghetto of Khao San Rd. Flights from Bangkok to Chengdu/Kunming cost around US$230/190 one way. From Singapore it's slightly more expensive. It's also possible to fly direct twice weekly from Chiang Mai to Kunming for around US$150 (Y1345 in Kunming). Flights to Kathmandu can be picked up for around US$400.

STA Travel (☎ 02-236 0262; www.statravel.co.th; Room 1406, 14th fl, Wall Street Tower, 33/70 Surawong Rd, Bangkok) Also operates branches in Singapore and Kuala Lumpur.

UK

Those looking at travelling via the Indian subcontinent and shaving costs wherever possible may find it cheapest to fly to Delhi and then travel overland to Nepal. Fares to India generally start from UK£400 return. The cheapest high-season return fares to Kathmandu are around UK£600 with Qatar or Gulf Air. The cheapest one-way fares from Kathmandu to London cost around US$400, also with Gulf Air.

Summer peak-season fares to Beijing cost around UK£300 one way and UK£500 return, although low-season return flights can be as little as UK£350. Cheap flights (often with Middle Eastern Airlines) to Hong Kong cost around the same price.

Several specialist agencies in London can book both international and Chinese domestic tickets, including **China Travel Service and Information Centre** (☎ 020-7388 8838; www.chinatravel.co.uk; 124 Euston Rd, London NW1 2AL).

Travel agents in London's Chinatown that deal with flights to China include **Jade Travel** (☎ 0870-898 8928; www.jadetravel.co.uk; 5 Newport Place, London) and **Sagitta Travel Agency** (☎ 0870-077 8888; www.sagitta-tvl.com; 9 Little Newport St, London).

Flightbookers (☎ 0870-814 4001; www.ebookers.com)
Flight Centre (☎ 0870-499 0040; www.flightcentre.co.uk)

CLIMATE CHANGE & TRAVEL

Climate change is a serious threat to the ecosystems that humans rely upon, and air travel is the fastest-growing contributor to the problem. Lonely Planet regards travel, overall, as a global benefit, but believes we all have a responsibility to limit our personal impact on global warming.

FLYING & CLIMATE CHANGE

Pretty much every form of motorised travel generates CO_2 (the main cause of human-induced climate change) but planes are far and away the worst offenders, not just because of the sheer distances they allow us to travel, but because they release greenhouse gases high into the atmosphere. The statistics are frightening: two people taking a return flight between Europe and the US will contribute as much to climate change as an average household's gas and electricity consumption over a whole year.

CARBON OFFSET SCHEMES

Climatecare.org and other websites use 'carbon calculators' that allow travellers to offset the level of greenhouse gases they are responsible for with financial contributions to sustainable travel schemes that reduce global warming – including projects in India, Honduras, Kazakhstan and Uganda.

Lonely Planet, together with Rough Guides and other concerned partners in the travel industry, support the carbon offset scheme run by climatecare.org. Lonely Planet offsets all of its staff and author travel.

For more information check out our website: www.lonelyplanet.com.

North-South Travel (☎ 01245-608 291; www.northsouthtravel.co.uk) Donates part of its profit to projects in the developing world.
STA Travel (☎ 0870-163 0026; www.statravel.co.uk)
Trailfinders (☎ 0845-058 5858; www.trailfinders.co.uk)

USA & Canada

It is far cheaper to fly to Hong Kong or Beijing from the USA or Canada than it is to fly to India. This might work out quite well if your ultimate destination is India. Overland travel from Hong Kong to Nepal and India through Tibet is reasonably time-consuming – but what a trip!

From the US west coast, low-season return fares to Hong Kong or Beijing start at around US$850, rising to around US$1000 in summer. Fares from New York are around 15% more expensive.

A useful website with information about international flights and domestic airfares in China is www.flychina.com.

Tickets from the US west coast cost around US$1700 return to Kathmandu. From the east coast you are looking at around US$1000 return to Delhi. From Kathmandu, a one-way ticket with Northwest or THAI to the west coast costs US$700.

The cheapest tickets to Hong Kong are offered by bucket shops run by ethnic Chinese in San Francisco, Los Angeles and New York. Online agencies include www.cheaptickets.com and www.orb itz.com.

Reliable, long-running agencies:

Gateway Travel (☎ 800-441 1183, 214-960 2000)
STA Travel (☎ 24hrs 800-781 4040; www.statravel.com)
China Travel Service (☎ 1-800-899 8618; www.chinatravelservice.com) Flights and independent tours.

Canadian prices are similar to those available in the USA. Try **Travel Cuts** (☎ 1-866-246 9762; www.travelcuts.com) for excellent deals on tickets to Asia. The new budget airline **Oasis Hong Kong** (www.oasishongkong.com) flies six times a week from Vancouver to Hong Kong for as low as C$300 one way.

GETTING THERE & AWAY – TIBET

This section details how to get into Tibet from Nepal or China.

AIR

Flights into Lhasa are shared by **Air China** (CA; www.airchina.com.cn), **China Southern** (CZ; www.csair.com), **Sichuan Airlines** (3U; www.scal.com.cn), **Hainan Airlines** (HU; www.hnair.com) and **China Eastern** (MU; www.ce-a ir.com).

There are flight connections to Lhasa from half a dozen Chinese cities but most travellers fly from Chengdu because arranging a permit is generally easier from there. Flights from Lhasa to Shenzhen and Hong Kong (around Y4200 one way) are expected to start before long, as is a Kunming–Nyingtri flight. Airport tax (Y50) and a fuel surcharge (around Y80) are figured into the cost of domestic airfares.

In 2006 Tibet's third airport opened south of Nyingtri, though it's of very limited use to tourists. The Ngari Kunsha airport in Ali is scheduled to open in 2010.

The Bank of China beside Lhasa's Gongkar airport changes US dollars into yuan but will not change Chinese currency back into US dollars – see p164.

Permits are very rarely checked on arrival at or departure from Lhasa's Gongkar airport, though they are checked when checking in for your flight to Lhasa.

While it can be difficult to get a ticket into Tibet, once there you face no restrictions on buying air tickets out of the province.

Note that flights to and from Lhasa are sometimes cancelled or delayed in the winter months, so if you are flying at this time give yourself a couple of days' leeway if you have a connecting flight.

Baggage allowance on domestic flights to Lhasa is 20kg in economy class and 30kg in 1st class, so you'll have to limit your gear to that to avoid penalties, regardless of what you are allowed to bring on your international flight into China.

Nepal

Flights between Kathmandu and Lhasa run four times a week in the high summer season and twice a week in the low winter season.

Individual travellers can't buy air tickets from the Air China office in Kathmandu without a Tibet Tourism Bureau (TTB) permit. To get a ticket you'll have to purchase a three- to eight-day package tour through a travel agency.

At the time of research, the cheapest air package was a three-day tour for around US$510. This includes the flight ticket (around US$330), airport transfers, TTB permit and accommodation for three nights in Lhasa. With this package you'll probably only get a 15-day group visa. For a list of travel companies in Kathmandu, see p87.

The Chinese embassy in Kathmandu does not give Chinese visas to individual travellers and will even cancel any existing Chinese visa you have. See p328 for more on visa headaches in Kathmandu.

It is possible to buy air tickets from Kathmandu to destinations in China such as Chengdu, Shanghai and Hong Kong. You don't need a TTB permit to take these flights.

Chengdu

Flights between Chengdu and Lhasa cost around Y1600, but you'll be very lucky if this is all you end up paying for the flight. In Chengdu, as in other cities, Air China will not sell you a ticket to Lhasa unless you already have a TTB permit.

To get around this, many travel agencies will sell you a 'tour' that allows them to arrange a ticket for you. What the tour consists of depends largely upon the political climate in Lhasa. Out of the high tourist season (July to September) you can normally get away with booking only a ticket and a TTB permit. At the height of summer, agencies may have to book airport transfers, three nights' dormitory accommodation and a simple tour in Lhasa in order to get the TTB permit.

In 2007 the cheapest Tibet package, consisting of one airport transfer and a one-way flight, cost around Y2000. In other years three-day packages have reached Y2400. Packages are generally cheaper in March and April and start rising by May, reaching a peak in August. Agencies normally need at least two days to procure the TTB permit.

In past years travellers never even saw their TTB permit but at the time of research you needed a physical copy of the permit to show at check-in and customs in Chengdu.

On a clear day the views from the plane are stupendous so try to get a window seat. In general the best views are from the left side of the plane from Chengdu to Lhasa and on the right side from Lhasa to Chengdu.

Zhongdian & Kunming

China Eastern operates a useful daily flight from Kunming to Lhasa via Zhongdian in northwest Yunnan (also rather ridiculously called Diqing Shangri-La, or Xi'anggelila, by the Chinese). China Southern also flies from Lhasa to Zhongdian en route to Guangzhou. As with other flights to Lhasa, foreigners need to sign up on a 'tour' to get a ticket.

REGIONAL AIR ROUTES

All of the following flights operate in both directions. Fares given are one way.

From	To	Flights per week	Fare (Yuan)
Lhasa	Beijing (via Chengdu)	7	2560
Lhasa	Chamdo (Bamda/Bangda)	1	930
Lhasa	Chengdu	60-70	1630
Lhasa	Chongqing	7	1760
Lhasa	Guangzhou (via Zhongdian)	2	2630
Lhasa	Kathmandu	3-4	2920
Lhasa	Kunming (via Zhongdian)	7	2090
Lhasa	Lanzhou	7	1600
Lhasa	Shanghai Pudong (via Xi'an)	2	2890
Lhasa	Xi'an	4	1780
Lhasa	Xining (sometimes via Chengdu)	4	1740
Lhasa	Zhongdian	7	1510
Chamdo (Bamda/Bangda)	Chengdu	3	930
Nyingtri	Chengdu	3	1510

The cheapest tour package from Zhongdian costs around Y2610 (including the air ticket and TTB permit), though they can go as low as Y1800 if flights are discounted. Flight packages from Kunming start at about Y2700.

LAND

Many individual travellers make their way to Tibet as part of a grand overland trip through China, Nepal, India and onwards. In many ways, land travel to Tibet is the best way to go, not only for the scenery en route but also because it can help spread the altitude gain over a few days.

Road

In theory there are several land routes into Tibet. The bulk of overland travellers take the Friendship Hwy between Kathmandu to Lhasa. Other possible routes (officially closed to permitless travellers) are the Sichuan–Tibet Hwy, the Yunnan–Tibet Hwy and the Xinjiang–Tibet Hwy.

If you decide to try these latter routes on your own (ie not in a Land Cruiser tour), you'll stand a better chance of getting through if you keep a low profile in towns, avoid hotels and bus stations in towns such as Chamdo and Bayi, and cross checkposts into Tibet during the evening. Know that you have a fairly good chance of being caught, fined and sent back in the direction you came. If you do get stopped by the Public Security Bureau (PSB), always claim to be heading in the opposite direction. Then you'll be sent 'back' in the direction in which you actually want to travel!

Even if you don't make it to Lhasa you can still get to see something of the region. If you are caught in Chamdo, for example, the PSB will fine you between Y200 and Y500 and then put you on bus back to Derge or Zhongdian. If you've come from Derge but tell them you came from Zhongdian then you'll at least get to travel along the Chamdo–Markham road. Be patient whenever dealing with the PSB; try not to be belligerent and always get a receipt for fines paid so that you don't have to pay again later.

See p344 for advice on hitching through Tibet.

FRIENDSHIP HIGHWAY (NEPAL TO TIBET)

The 865km stretch of road between Kathmandu and Lhasa is known as the Friendship Hwy. The journey is without a doubt one of the most spectacular in the world.

From Kathmandu (elevation 1300m) the road travels gently up to Kodari (1873m), before leaving Nepal to make a steep switchback ascent to Zhangmu (2250m), the Tibetan border town, and then Nyalam (3750m), where most people spend their first night. The road then climbs to the top of the Tong-la (4950m), continuing to Tingri (4250m) for the second night. Most of the road is now paved.

It is essential to watch out for the effects of altitude sickness during the early stages of

CONTACTS FOR PERMITS AND AIR/TRAIN TICKETS

The following companies can arrange air and train tickets to Lhasa alongside a TTB permit. All update prices and services frequently according to the changing regulations. A TTB permit generally costs around Y500 in Chengdu but can cost twice this elsewhere (for example in Zhongdian).

If you want to limit the time you spend waiting for permits you can normally get the bureaucratic ball rolling by emailing a scan of your passport and Chinese visa and wiring a deposit.

Beijing

- **Far East International Youth Hostel** (☎ 10-5195 8811; www.fareastyh.com; 90 Tieshu Xiejie, Xuanwu District)
- **Leo Hostel** (☎ 10-8660 8923; www.leohostel.com; Guangjuyuan Binguan, 52 Dazhalan Xijie, Qianmen) Can arrange tickets and permits only but you may need to pay a Y500 deposit, refundable in Lhasa.

Chengdu

- See p91.

Kunming

- **Mr Chen's Travel** (☎ 0871-318 8114; www.kmcamelliahotel.com; qijia_chen@yahoo.com.cn; Room 3116, No 3 Bldg Camellia Hotel, 154 Dongfeng Lu) Better for air tickets than overland trips.

Xining

- **Tibetan Connections** (☎ 0971-820 3271; www.tibetanconnections.com; Guoji Cun Gongyu Bldg 5, 15th flr, Lete Youth Hostel) Train tickets to Lhasa and overland trips, especially good in Amdo.
- **Qinghai Tibet Adventures Company** (☎ 0971-824 7377; www.cqta.com; 13 Beida Jie, Xining) Permit alone Y200 to Y400.

Zhongdian

- **Khampa Caravan** (☎ 0887-828 8648; www.khampacaravan.com; Heping Lu)
- **Tibet Café** (☎ 0887-823 0019; www.tibetcafeinn.com; Changzheng Lu)
- **Tibet Tourism Bureau** (☎ 0887-822 9028; yunnantibettour@yahoo.com.cn; Room 2206, Shangbala Hotel, 36 Changzheng Lu)

this trip (see p351). If you intend to head up to Everest Base Camp (5150m) you really need to slip in a rest day at Tingri or Nyalam. See the Tsang chapter (p180) for details of sights and landmarks en route.

This highway is very well travelled nowadays and is a pleasant journey, except for one major problem – the Chinese authorities will not let individual travellers enter Tibet from Nepal without a TTB permit and tour.

Because of this, several of Kathmandu's travel agencies (p87) offer 'budget' tours of Tibet to get you into Lhasa. At the time of research the cheapest of these tours cost from around US$400 to US$450 per person for a basic eight-day trip to Lhasa, stopping in Zhangmu/Nyalam, Lhatse, Shigatse, Gyantse and then Lhasa for three days. These trips generally run every Tuesday and Saturday. A nine-day trip that adds on a visit to Everest Base Camp costs US$650 per person but these are harder to find. Prices include transport, permits, a Chinese group visa, dormitory accommodation for the first two nights and then shared twins, a fairly useless guide and admission fees.

Bear in mind that most agencies are just subcontractors and normally pool clients, so you could find yourself travelling in a larger group than expected and perhaps on a bus instead of the promised Land Cruiser. Other potential inconsistencies may include having to share a room when you were told you would be given a single, or paying a double room supplement and ending up in a dorm. We do get a fair number of complaints about the service of some of these tours; it's best just to view it as the cheapest way to get to Tibet.

For more information about the visa snags involved in a trip from Kathmandu, see p328.

Headed in the other direction, a private Land Cruiser tour from Lhasa to the Nepali border costs around Y6000 for a four- or five-day trip, which works out around US$200 per person. This includes a guide, permits and transport only.

A direct bus runs twice a week from Lhasa's Northern Bus Station to Kathmandu and back but foreigners are currently not allowed on this.

If you are going direct to Nepal you might be able to find a Land Cruiser heading down to the border to pick up groups arriving from Kathmandu. Check out the notice boards in Lhasa and ask at the various FIT agencies (see p100). These Land Cruisers generally drive nonstop through the night.

See p214 for details of the border crossing to Nepal. China is 2¼ hours ahead of Nepali time.

QINGHAI–TIBET HIGHWAY

The 1115km road journey between Golmud and Lhasa is the subject of an ancient Chinese curse: 'May you travel by Chinese bus from Golmud to Lhasa.' Actually, we made that one up – but it deserves to be. Now that you can make the journey by train, it's hard to see why anyone would want to make the 20-hour journey in a cramped, smoky sleeper bus, especially as you are forced to buy bus tickets from the local **CITS** (☎ 0979-413 003; 2nd fl, Golmud Hotel) at a massive mark-up.

A few hardy souls make the trip by bike, crossing into Tibet over the 5180m Tangu-la pass. A checkpoint 30km south of Golmud checks for permits.

An unusual, way-off-the-beaten-track route into Tibet is the back-door route from Yushu (Jyekundo) in southeastern Qinghai to Chamdo in eastern Tibet, via the towns of Nangchen and Riwoche. Yushu itself is a 20-hour sleeper-bus ride from Xining, though an airport is scheduled to open here in 2009. From Yushu you can get a seat in a Land Cruiser (Y40, three hours) along the paved road to Nangchen, a former Tibetan kingdom. From Nangchen it's a remote and rough 245km trip to Riwoche. The first 100km is on a dirt road that can be impassable during heavy rains. You may find a Land Cruiser making the trip if there are enough passengers (Y100 per seat), otherwise you'll have to hitch (see p344) and lay low as you cross the border. You'll face difficulties travelling independently through the rest of Eastern Tibet – see p242.

SICHUAN–TIBET HIGHWAY

The road between Chengdu and Lhasa is an epic 2400km or 2100km, depending on whether you take the northern or southern route.

The Sichuan section of the Sichuan–Tibet Hwy is open to foreigners as far as the Tibetan border. Beyond this, the road is closed to individual travellers, although the occasional tour group and renegade explorer passes along it. Hitchers should budget from 10 days to two weeks for the trip.

For coverage of the sights along the route, see the Overland Routes from Sichuan (p267) and Eastern Tibet (p241) chapters. For an overview of routes, see p23. Long-distance public buses run along the main highways but permitless foreigners are more likely to get on the private minibuses that run between most towns in Eastern Tibet.

The 780km stretch of road between Markham and Bayi is likely to be the biggest hurdle for travellers making their way to Lhasa. Markham is where the Yunnan–Tibet Hwy joins the Sichuan–Tibet Hwy and so the local PSB is pretty vigilant about making sure that no travellers continue on to Lhasa. Nyingtri, Bayi and Chamdo also have pretty strict PSB offices.

A Land Cruiser tour from Lhasa to Chengdu costs from Y16,000 to Y20,000.

YUNNAN–TIBET HIGHWAY

The Yunnan–Tibet Hwy is a wonderful way to approach Tibet, though once again the route is officially limited to organised groups. From loved-to-death Lijiang a road heads up to the Tibetan towns and monasteries of Zhongdian (Gyeltang), Benzalin and Deqin (Jol), from where there are public buses north across the Tibetan border (and checkpost) 112km to Yanjing. From here it's 111km to Markham, where the road joins the Sichuan southern route (see p279). For details on the Tibetan areas of northwest Yunnan, see Lonely Planet's *China* or *China's Southwest* guides.

OVERLAND TRAVEL AGENCIES IN CHINA

A few Chinese adventure travel agencies specialise in travel in western Sichuan and northwest Yunnan, including organised overland trips to Lhasa through remote Kham.

- **China Minority Travel** (0872-267 7824; www.china-travel.nl) Dutch-Chinese operation based at Jim's Tibetan Guesthouse in Dali; runs a nine-day overland trip from Zhongdian to Lhasa for US$680 per person.
- **Forbidden Frontier** (☎ 021-6445 9937; www.forbiddenfrontier.com; Suite 504, Bldg 2, 298 Anfu Rd, Shanghai) Trips throughout Kham.
- **Haiwei Trails** (☎ 0887-828-9239; www.haiweitrails.com; 19 Beimen Jie, Zhongdian) US-British company that runs 4WD trips and charters into central and eastern Tibet.
- **Khampa Caravan** (☎ 0887-828 8648; www.khampacaravan.com; 117 Beimen Jie, Zhongdian) Overland trips from Zhongdian to Lhasa, with an emphasis on sustainable tourism and local communities. Contact Dakpa or Yeshi.
- **Tibetan Connections** (☎ 0971-820 3271; www.tibetanconnections.com; Guoji Cun Gongyu Bldg 5, 15th fl, Lete Youth Hostel, Xining) Excellent for tours to Amdo and Kham, specialising in Qinghai province. Contact Lobsang.
- **Tibetan Trekking** (☎ 028-8675 1783; www.tibetantrekking.com; Room 1614, Zhufeng Hotel, 288 Shuncheng Lu, Chengdu) Contact Gao Liqiang for treks and 4WD trips in western Sichuan.
- **Wild China** (☎ 010-6465 6602; www.wildchina.com; Room 801, Oriental Place, 9 Dongfang Donglu, North Dongsanhuan Rd, Chaoyang District, Beijing) Professionally run trips in Yunnan and Sichuan regions of Kham.

The Yunnan route is officially closed to independent (ie permitless) travellers but increasing numbers of people are getting through. Markham (see p279) is the place where most permitless travellers get caught and sent back. A few travel companies are starting to organise nine- or 10-day overland tours on this route, including the excellent Khampa Caravan in Zhongdian (see the boxed text above). TTB permits take around five days to arrange so contact these agencies in advance.

The Zhongdian **TTB office** (☎ 887-822 9028; yunnantibettour@yahoo.com.cn; Room 2206, Shangbala Hotel, Chengzheng Lu) can organise eight- to 10-day overland trips to Lhasa for about US$625 per person in a group of four and can also arrange budget packages.

Travellers can get the permit process rolling in advance through the **MCA Guesthouse** (☎ 0872-267 3666; mcahouse@hotmail.com; Wen Xi'an Lu) in Dali, before travelling on to Zhongdian.

FIT in Lhasa (see p100) charges from Y12,000 to Y15,000 for an eight-day Lhasa–Bayi–Pomi–Pomda–Markham–Deqin Land Cruiser trip, which works out at about US$500 per person. Prices can be as low as Y8000 when they have a Land Cruiser returning empty to Zhongdian. From Zhongdian figure on between Y15,000 to Y20,000 to Lhasa.

Surprisingly, the Zhongdian bus station will sell foreigners bus tickets to Lhasa (Y580, three days), though you face a good chance of being fined and sent back once you get into the Tibet Autonomous Region (TAR).

XINJIANG–TIBET HIGHWAY

The Xinjiang–Tibet Hwy is officially off limits without travel permits, but interestingly, at the time of research, there were quite a number of travellers who were managing to get through, even on bicycles. Approximately 1350km of road separates Kashgar from Ali in western Tibet and for the adventurous this can form a wild extension to a trip along the Karakoram Hwy.

With at least two passes more than 5400m, the Xinjiang–Tibet Hwy is the highest road in the world. It can be bitterly cold and closes down for the winter months from December to February. The whole trip takes at least four days of travel, depending on how lucky you are with lifts. There are truck stops along the way, about a day's travel apart, but it's wise to bring food and a sleeping bag. A tent can be useful in emergencies. Coming from Kashgar, you have to be particularly careful about altitude sickness as the initial rate of altitude gain is dramatic.

There are buses every half-hour from Kashgar to Karghilik (Yecheng; Y29, four hours), and a sleeper bus run by the Tibetan Antelope Travel and Transportation Co (藏羚羊旅运有限公司; see p226) makes the journey between Yecheng and Ali (Y500, 50 hours) twice a week. The Tibetan Antelope bus station is hard to find but bus 2 runs there.

If you're hitching from Yecheng to Ali, the truck stop 4km southeast of Yecheng is the best place to sniff out a lift. Accommodation is available here and trucks depart in the early morning. Expect to pay Y150 to Y500 for a lift, depending on the road conditions.

FIT in Lhasa (see p100) offers a three-week Mt Everest–Kailash–Guge-Kingdom–Yecheng–Kashgar Land Cruiser trip for about Y25,000, which works out at around US$800 per person for four sharing.

Caravan Café (☎ 0998-298 1864; www.caravancafe.com; 120 Seman Lu) in Kashgar can arrange transport from Kashgar to Lhasa.

John's Café (www.johncafe.net), with branches in Lhasa and Kashgar, can arrange 15- to 18-day vehicle hire along this route from €3000.

The Route

Leaving Yecheng, the road climbs past Akmeqit village to Kudi Pass (kilometre marker 113; 3240m) then follows a narrow gorge to the truck stop and checkpost at **Kudi** (kilometre 161, 2960m). From Kudi it's 80km over the Chiragsaldi Pass (kilometre marker 217; 4960m) to the village of **Mazar** (kilometre marker 241; 3700m), which has some shops and restaurants. The road turns east and climbs over the Kirgizjangal Pass (kilometre marker 09; 4930m) to the large village of **Xaidulla** (kilometre marker 363; 3700m), the largest town en route, with shops and restaurants. The road climbs again over the 4250m Koshbel Pass to the truck stop of **Dahongliutan** (kilometre marker 488; 4200m), which offers basic food and lodging.

From here the road turns south, and climbs to the Khitai Pass (kilometre marker 535; 5150m), past the military base of Tianshuihai. About 100km from the pass you cross another 5180m pass (kilometre marker 670) to enter the remote region of Aksai Chin. For the next 170km road conditions are bad and progress is slow. The construction of the road here, through a triangle of territory that India claimed as part of Ladakh, was a principal cause of the border war between India and China in 1962. The fact that the Chinese managed to build this road without India even realising that it was under construction is an indication of the utter isolation of the region!

The road passes Lungma-tso, shortly afterwards entering the Changtang Nature Preserve, and 15km later reaches the small village of **Sumzhi (Songxi)** (kilometre marker 720; 5200m), which has basic accommodation and a restaurant. Finally at kilometre marker 740 you come to the edge of the Aksai Chin region and climb up to the **Jieshan Daban pass** (5200m). From here, Ali is around 420km away via the village of Domar (kilometre marker 828; 4440m), the eastern end of **Pangong-tso** (Palgon-tso; 4270m) and **Rutok Xian** (kilometre marker 930; p237). From here it is 130km south to Ali.

OTHER ROUTES INTO TIBET

Since 1994 another route into Tibet has been open, to trekking groups only, passing through Purang (Nepali: Taklakot). Special visas are required for this trip. Trekkers start by travelling by road or flying from Kathmandu to Nepalganj, then flying from there to Simikot in the far west of Nepal. From Simikot it's a five- or six-day walk to the Tibetan border, crossing the Humla Karnali. You can then drive the 28km to Purang and 107km on to the Mt Kailash area via Lake Manasarovar. See Lonely Planet's *Trekking in the Nepal Himalaya* for details of the trek. For details on the route from the Nepali border to Mt Kailash, see p238.

Indian travellers can cross into Tibet's Yadong region from Gangtok in Sikkim via the 4310m Nathu-la, tracing the former trading routes between Lhasa, Kalimpong and Calcutta, and the path taken by Younghusband's invasion of Tibet in 1903. The route opened to locals in 2006 but is not scheduled to open to third-party nationals until 2011.

There is talk of opening the Kyirong-la (Kerong-la) to organised tour groups headed to/from the Langtang region of Nepal but there are no definite plans as yet. Roads are in place on both sides of the border.

Indian pilgrims on a quota system travel to Purang via the Lipu Lekh pass from Pithoragarh.

Train

For years an impossible dream, the new 1956km train line from Golmud to Lhasa was finally inaugurated in July 2006 and at least four passenger trains trundle up onto

THE WORLD'S HIGHEST TRAIN RIDE

There's no doubt the Qinghai-Tibet train line is an engineering marvel. Topping out at 5072m, it is the world's highest railway, snatching the title from a Peruvian line. The statistics speak for themselves: 86% of the line is above 4000m, and half the track lies on permafrost, requiring a cooling system of pipes driven into the ground to keep it frozen year-round and avoid a rail-buckling summer thaw. Construction of the line involved building 160km of bridges and elevated track, seven tunnels (including the world's highest) and 24 hyperbaric chambers, the latter to treat altitude-sick workers.

Aside from the environmental concerns (see p85), Tibetans are most deeply concerned about the cultural impact of the train. While the highly subsidised line will doubtless boost the Tibetan economy, decreasing transport costs for imports by up to 75%, the trains also unload 2500 Chinese tourists and immigrants into Lhasa every day. Trains to Lhasa habitually arrive full and depart half-empty.

The authorities like to stress the economic benefits of the line but Tibetans remain economically marginalised. More than 90% of the 100,000 workers employed to build the line came from other provinces and few, if any, Tibetan staff actually work on the trains. The US$4.1 billion cost of building the line is greater than the amount Beijing has spent on hospitals and schools in Tibet over the last 50 years combined.

As with most of Beijing's epic engineering projects, the results are as much symbolic as real, connecting China's rail network to the only province in China lacking a rail link and forging Tibet and China together in an iron grip. It did a similar thing with the 1999 railway line to Kashgar in Xinjiang; now it's the turn of its other troublesome border province.

the high plateau every day. The engineering marvel is not without controversy (see the boxed text, above) but there's no doubt that the line has quickly become one of the world's classic train trips.

Trains run daily from Beijing, Chengdu and Xining, and every other day from Guangzhou and Shanghai. Trains also run every other day from Chongqing (via Xi'an) and Lanzhou, which link up with the Chengdu and Xining trains respectively. See p341 for schedules and fares. Train services alternate between daily and every other day, according to the month. A 250km extension line to Shigatse is due to open by 2009.

All trains cross the Tibetan plateau during daylight, guaranteeing you great views (the scenery is impressive in scale rather than beautiful). From Golmud the train climbs through desert into the jagged caramel-coloured mountains of Nanshankou (Southern Pass), passing what feels like a stone's throw from the impressive glaciers beside Yuzhu Feng (Jade Pearl Peak; 6178m). Other highlights include the nearby tunnel through the 4776m Kunlun Pass, where you can see the prayer flags at the top of the pass, and Tsonak Lake, 9½ hours from Golmud near Amdo, claimed to be the highest freshwater lake in the world at 4608m. Keep your eyes peeled throughout the journey for antelope, fox and wild asses, plus the occasional impressed-looking nomad. The train crosses into Tibet over the 5072m Tangu-la (Tanggula Shankou) Pass, the line's high point.

For more details on the train, services and schedules see the following:

China Highlights (www.chinahighlights.com/china-trains/index.htm) Searchable timetables.

China Tibet Train (www.chinatibettrain.com) Good background info.

Lulutong (www.railway.com.cn) Chinese-language website.

Seat 61 (www.seat61.com) General info on trains in China.

Travel China Guide (www.travelchinaguide.com/china-trains/) Searchable timetables.

Tibet Train Travel (www.tibettraintravel.com) Background info and mini-tours.

A luxury joint-venture train, the Tangula Express (www.tangula.com.cn) is due to start operation in 2008 from Beijing to Lhasa, with glass observation cars, fine dining and luxury cabins provided by the Kempinski hotel group. The US$1000 per day (!) tariff gets you butler service, showers, fine dining and on-board internet access.

PRACTICALITIES

At the time of writing, foreigners needed a TTB permit (see p323) to buy a ticket and board the train, though some travellers have managed to take the train without one. Golmud and Xi'an seem to be the most difficult places to buy tickets without a TTB permit. Several agencies such as Leo's Hostel in Beijing and Sim's Cozy Guesthouse in Chengdu (see the boxed text, p336) sell tickets and TTB permits, though sleeper berths can be hard to secure from Beijing, Chengdu and Xi'an. You can buy tickets up to 10 days in advance.

The online agency www.china-train-ticket.com sells train tickets and will deliver them to your hotel in China, for a fairly hefty 40% mark-up on the ticket price. Chinese sites such as www.piao.com/train are cheaper, if you read Chinese. Either way you face complications getting a TTB permit this way.

Once aboard the train you have to fill out a health card. The carriages are much better than your average Chinese train and are more like the express trains that link Beijing with Shanghai. All passengers have access to piped-in oxygen through a special socket beside each seat or berth and all carriages are nonsmoking after Golmud. There are power sockets by the window seats, though beware that laptops and MP3 players often stop working at points during the trip, due to the altitude. Each train has a small but decent dining car (mains Y15 to Y25).

Hard-sleeper (硬卧; *ying wo*) carriages are made up of doorless six-berth compartments with bunks in three tiers, and sheets, pillows and blankets are provided. There is a small price difference between berths, with the lowest bunk the most expensive and the top-most bunk the cheapest. Four-bed soft-sleeper (软卧; *ruan wo*) berths come with individual TVs and doors that close and lock. Hard seats (硬座; *ying zuo*) are just that.

GETTING AROUND

Tibet's transport infrastructure is poorly developed and, with the exception of the Friendship Hwy and the Qinghai–Tibet Hwy, most of the roads are in rough condition. Work is being undertaken to improve this situation – a vital aspect of Chinese plans to develop Tibet – but it is unlikely that travel in large parts of Tibet will become comfortable or easy in the near future.

The main problem for travellers short on time is the scarcity of public transport. There are no internal flights (except to Chamdo, a closed area) and only a handful of buses and minibuses plying the roads between Lhasa and other major Tibetan towns such as Shigatse and Tsetang.

Most travellers band together to hire a Land Cruiser to get around Tibet but this isn't absolutely necessary. Minibuses run to most monasteries around Lhasa, and to Shigatse, Gyantse, Sakya and Lhatse. Hitching is another possibility; you will still have to pay, but only a fraction of the amount for a Land Cruiser. You'll need to be more self-sufficient and prepared to wait perhaps for

TRAIN SCHEDULES TO LHASA

Train No	To/From	Departure	Distance	Duration	Hard seat/hard sleeper/ soft sleeper
T27/8	Beijing	daily 9.30pm	4064km	48 hr	Y389/813/1262
T22/3	Chengdu	daily 6.18pm	3360km	48 hr	Y331/712/1104
T223/4	Chongqing	7.20pm	3654km	48 hr	Y355/754/1168
T264/5	Guangzhou	1.07pm	4980km	58 hr	Y451/923/1434
T164/5	Shanghai	4.11pm	4373km	52 hr	Y406/845/1314
K917/8	Xining	daily 4.45pm	1972km	27 hr	Y226/523/810
K917/8	Lanzhou	4.45pm	2188km	30 hr	Y242/552/854
**	Xi'an	-	2864km	27 hr	Y296/650/1008*
**	Golmud	-	1135km	14 hr	Y143/377/583

NB Sleeper fares are for lower berth. Unless noted, services run every other day.

* Fares slightly more expensive on the Chongqing train

** Multiple train options

TRANSPORT

hours for a ride. Hitching in Tibet can be the best way to get around but it can also be very frustrating, and there are risks (see p344).

Those with more time can, of course, trek or cycle their way around the high plateau. A combination of hiking and hitching is the best way to get to many off-the-beaten-track destinations.

By 2009 you may even be able to take the train from Lhasa to Shigatse.

BICYCLE

Long-distance cyclists are an increasingly frequent sight on the roads of Tibet, especially along the Friendship Hwy, though also increasingly through eastern Tibet. In theory cyclists face the same travel and permit restrictions as other travellers, though local authorities often turn a blind eye to travellers on bikes, unsure of what to do with them.

You can rent Taiwanese-made mountain bikes in Lhasa for around Y30 per day, which are fine for getting around town. Test the brakes and tyres before taking the bike out onto the streets. An extra padlock is a good idea, as there is a problem with bicycle theft in the capital.

Most long distance cyclists bring their own bikes to Tibet, though a few buy mountain bikes in China or Lhasa. Nowadays it is possible to buy a Chinese-made or (better) Taiwanese-made mountain bike in Lhasa for about Y500 or, if you are lucky, a good quality Thai bike for around Y2000. Standards aren't all that bad, although you should check the gears in particular. Do not expect the quality of such bikes to be equal to those you might buy at home – bring plenty of spare parts. Bikes have a relatively high resale value in Kathmandu and you might even make a profit if the bike is in good shape (which is unlikely after a trip across Tibet!).

Touring

Tibet poses unique challenges to individual cyclists. The good news is that the main roads are in surprisingly good condition (the Friendship Hwy was recently upgraded and roads everywhere are under improvement) and the traffic is fairly light. The main physical challenges come from the climate, terrain and altitude: wind squalls and dust storms can make your work particularly arduous; the warm summer months can bring flash flooding; and then there is the question of your fitness in the face of Tibet's high-altitude mountainous terrain.

A full bicycle-repair kit, several spare inner tubes, and a spare tyre and chain are essential. Preferably bring an extra rim and some spare spokes. Extra brake wire and brake pads are useful (you'll be descending 3000m from Lhasa to Kathmandu!). Other useful equipment includes reflective clothing, a helmet, a dust mask, goggles, gloves and padded trousers.

You will also need to be prepared with supplies such as food, water-purifying tablets and camping equipment, just as if you were trekking. Most long-distance cyclists will probably find formal accommodation and restaurants only available at two- or three-day intervals. It may be possible to stay with road repair camps (known as *daoban* in Chinese) in remote places.

The Trailblazer guidebook *Tibet Overland: A Route and Planning Guide for Mountain Bikers and Other Overlanders,* by Kym McConnell, has useful route plans and gradient charts aimed at mountain bikers, with a notice board at www.tibetoverland.com.

There are several good accounts of cycling in Tibet in the 'Travelogues' section of the website www.bikechina.com.

Obviously you need to be in good physical condition to undertake road touring in Tibet. Spend some time acclimatising to the altitude and taking leisurely rides around Lhasa (for example) before setting off on a long trip.

On the plus side, while Tibet has some of the highest-altitude roads in the world, gradients are usually quite manageable. The Tibetan roads are designed for low-powered Chinese trucks, and tackle the many high passes of the region with its low-gradient switchback roads.

Touring Routes

The most popular touring route at present is Lhasa to Kathmandu, along the Friendship Hwy. It is an ideal route in that it takes in most of Tibet's main sights, offers superb scenery and (for those leaving from Lhasa) features a spectacular roller-coaster ride down from the heights of the La Lung-la into the Kathmandu Valley. The trip will take a minimum of two weeks, although to do it justice and include stopovers at Gyantse, Shigatse and Sakya, budget for 20 days. The entire trip is just over 940km, although most people start from Shigatse. The roadside kilometre markers are a useful way of knowing exactly how far you have gone and how far you still have to go. For a rundown of the route and its markers, see p198.

If you are travelling via Kathmandu, Nepali mountain bike agencies such as **Massif Mountain Bikes** (www.massifmountainbike.com), **Himalayan Mountain Bikes** (www.bikeasia.info) and **Dawn Til Dusk** (www.nepalbiking.com) can offer tips, equipment and also organised biking tours in Tibet. It's currently not possible to cycle independently from Kathmandu to Lhasa due to the fact that you have to enter Tibet on an organised tour; you'll have to take your bike to Lhasa and cycle back.

Keen cyclists with good mountain bikes might want to consider the detour to Everest Base Camp as a side trip on the Lhasa-Kathmandu route. The 108km one-way trip starts from the Shegar turn-off, and it takes around two days to Rongphu Monastery – less once the road is paved in 2008.

Other possibilities are endless. Tsurphu, Ganden and Drigung Til Monasteries are relatively easy trips and good for acclimatisation (though the road to Tsurphu is rough and Ganden has a fierce final 10km uphill section). The Gyama Valley is an easy detour on a bike if you are headed to Ganden. Cycling in the Yarlung Valley region would be a wonderful option if it were not for permit hassles. Some cyclists even tackle the paved road to Nam-tso, although the nomads' dogs can be a problem here.

Hazards

Cycling in Tibet is not to be taken lightly. Dogs are a major problem, especially in more remote areas. You may have to pedal like mad to outpace them. Children have been known to throw stones at cyclists. Erratic driving is another serious concern.

Wear a cycling helmet and lightweight leather gloves and, weather permitting, try to keep as much of your body covered with protective clothing as possible. It goes without saying that cyclists should also be prepared with a comprehensive medical kit (see p347).

BUS

Bus travel in Tibet is limited but with some time and a little effort you can get to most places in this book by bus or minibus,. Most services originate in Lhasa or Shigatse and run to any town that has a sizeable Chinese presence. Smaller towns may have just one daily bus that runs to Lhasa in the morning and returns in the afternoon.

Many bus stations in Tibet will not sell bus tickets to foreigners, which leaves you in the hands of private or pilgrim bus services. Even the larger private buses may be reluctant to take foreigners (notably between Lhasa and Shigatse) because they don't have government permission and/or insurance to take foreigners. Accidents do sometimes happen: in 2007, 13 tourists were killed when their tourist bus crashed between Lhasa and Shigatse.

On a long-distance bus you will probably be required to stow your baggage on the roof if you have a bulky backpack. If possible, check that it is tied down properly (bus drivers normally do a good job of checking such details), lock your pack as a precaution against theft and make sure you have all you might need for the trip (food, water, warm clothes etc). Try to see what everyone else is paying for the fare before you hand over your cash. You can expect to spend a lot of time sitting around waiting for minibuses to fill up.

CAR

Renting a Land Cruiser (plus driver) and splitting the cost among a band of travellers has become the most popular way of getting around in Tibet. Tourists are not permitted to drive rental vehicles in Tibet.

Prices depend largely on the kilometres driven (roughly Y3.50 per km) not the time taken, meaning that you can often add an extra day to your itinerary for minimal extra cost. Prices are higher on trips where a permit and both guide and driver are needed. Guide fees are normally calculated at around Y150 per day and permits generally cost around Y150 per person.

Land Cruisers have room for four passengers (plus a guide) and their luggage. Even then, someone will have to sit on a fold-up seat in the back. The guides provided on budget tours are normally useless. The best learned their English in Dharamsala but don't have a formal guide licence (the government won't give licences to Tibetans who have travelled to Dharamsala).

The best place to hire vehicles is Lhasa. Before organising a vehicle, check the notice boards at the main budget hotels. The most popular destinations are the Nepali border,

Nam-tso and Mt Kailash, but there will probably be a few notices about more-obscure destinations. The availability of vehicles has improved recently, but in the peak months of May, August and September there can still be a squeeze and prices can rise. For an idea of prices, see p127.

Hiring a vehicle is subject to a few pitfalls (see Organising a Land Cruiser Trip, opposite, for some guidelines) and we get many complaints from travellers over the quality of the car, the guide and problems relating to reimbursements after an unsuccessful trip. If possible, it is a good idea to reach an agreement that payment be delivered in two instalments: one before setting off and one on successful completion of the trip. This gives you more leverage in negotiating a refund if your trip was unsuccessful (one reason why agencies are loathe to do this).

Drawing up a contract in English as well as Tibetan or Chinese can be a good idea and your agent may already have one. List your exact itinerary, the price and method of payment and pin down in writing any detours or monasteries you want to visit. Once you are on the road your driver will be reluctant to detour even a few kilometres off the listed itinerary.

Above all, get together with the driver before the trip and go through the main points of the agreement verbally. You are likely to have far fewer problems if you can reach friendly terms with your driver by treating him with respect – giving him some cigarettes or some kind of small gift – rather than waving a contract in his face.

Remember, it may be worth spending a few hundred yuan extra (it's not much spread between four people) to hire a vehicle from a bigger and more reliable agency. Note that most higher-end agencies can only arrange your trip if you book it from outside Tibet, so that they provide the original TTB permit to get you into Tibet.

HITCHING

Hitching is never entirely safe in any country in the world, and we don't necessarily recommend it. Travellers who decide to hitch should understand that they are taking a small but potentially serious risk. That said, in Tibet hitching is often the only alternative to hiring an expensive Land Cruiser and so has become a fairly established practice.

Few foreigners travel long distances by truck these days. The authorities impose heavy fines on truck drivers caught transporting foreign travellers and may even confiscate their licence. Sometimes you can get a lift on a pilgrim truck or an organised passenger truck.

If you are headed out to fairly remote destinations you should be equipped to camp out for the night if you don't get a ride. One guy we heard of waited so long for a lift to Mt Kailash that he built a chörten from stones out of boredom. By the time he got a ride it was more than 1m tall!

There are also plenty of half-empty Land Cruisers heading down the Friendship Hwy to pick up a group, or returning after having dropped one off. It's a wonderful feeling to finally get a lift in an empty Land Cruiser after being rejected all day by a stream of dilapidated trucks travelling at 30km/h!

Normally you will be expected to pay for your lift, especially in a Land Cruiser. The amount is entirely negotiable, but in areas where traffic is minimal, drivers will often demand quite large sums.

It's a good idea to start hitching a few kilometres out of town because then you know that traffic is going in your direction and is not about to turn off after 400m. This is especially important if there is a checkpost nearby. It's best to walk through the checkpost yourself and wait for a lift out of sight on the other side.

The most common hitching gesture is to stick out one or two fingers towards the ground and wave them up or down.

If you are hitching long distances without a permit you'll have to lay low at checkposts. Perhaps your best chance is to hook up with a truck that is itself slightly illegal and therefore inclined to drive through the checkposts at night. Apart from the checkposts, the likeliest place to be caught is at a hotel.

LOCAL TRANSPORT

Local city transport only really operates in Lhasa and Shigatse. Minibuses run on set routes around Lhasa and Shigatse and they charge a fixed fare of Y2.

Pedicabs (pedal-operated tricycles transporting passengers) are available in Lhasa, Gyantse, Shigatse and Bayi, but require some extensive haggling.

A couple of towns in eastern Tibet have motorised three-wheeler rickshaws that take passengers around town or to destinations (eg monasteries) just outside of town. Negotiate the fare before you set off.

ORGANISING A LAND CRUISER TRIP *Andre Ticheler*

When dealing with an agency to rent a vehicle, you need to establish a few ground rules. First, work out a detailed itinerary for your trip. This will allow the agency to give you a firm quote based on distance covered and number of days on the road.

You'll need to fix the rate for any extra days that may need to be tacked onto an itinerary. For delays caused by bad weather, blocked passes, swollen river crossings and so on, there should be no extra charge for jeep hire. At the very least the cost for extra days should be split 50% between your group and the agency. For delays caused by vehicle breakdowns, driver illness etc, the agency should cover 100% of the costs and provide a backup vehicle if necessary.

Second, ask the agency about its policy on refunds for an uncompleted trip. Some agencies refuse any kind of refund, others are more open to negotiation.

Third, clarify whether the price you agree on covers all permit costs, and establish which costs are not covered in the price (for example, the Y405 vehicle fee to drive to Everest Base Camp and Y40 vehicle fee at Peiku-tso).

Finally, be aware that the vehicle you receive has probably been subcontracted from outside the agency; you should verify that the agency will take responsibility in the event of a vehicle breakdown. Some reputable agencies will calmly refuse to take any role in disputes between you and the owner of the vehicle. Find out where you stand in advance.

Once you are sorted with the agency, it's a good idea to organise a meeting between your group and the driver(s) and guide a day or two before departure. Make sure the drivers are aware of your itinerary (it may be the first time they have seen it!). Ensure that the guide speaks fluent Tibetan, good Chinese and useable English. Strong personality clashes would suggest a change of personnel.

Unless you are a qualified mechanic, inspecting the soundness of the vehicle may prove to be difficult, but you should carry out the following basic checks. First make sure that the 4WD can at least be engaged (not just that the stick moves!) and that the 'diff lock' can be locked and unlocked (this is usually done via tabs on the front wheel hubs). For longer trips, make sure that at least one shovel and a long steel tow cable (rope cables are useless) are supplied. Tyres and spares should be in reasonable condition (by Tibetan standards). Check that fuel cans don't leak and that there's rope to tie baggage to the roof rack.

The only other predeparture issues to consider for long trips are warm clothing, a good sleeping bag, plenty of food and perhaps a small stove. A tent is an excellent backup. A few plastic barrels or sacks (available in most markets) are useful to protect your gear and food from the dust and general thrashing it will get in the back of the truck. Some travellers invest in a decent piece of foam mattress to save their backside from the worst punishments of the road (a square big enough to sit on costs Y10). Jerry cans to carry water (and even *chang*, or Tibetan barley beer!) are always a good idea.

One result of China's economic infusion into Tibet is the large number of taxis now available in most towns, even Ali in western Tibet (you have to wonder how they got there!). Taxis in Lhasa, Shigatse and Ali charge a standard Y10 to anywhere in the city; for longer trips negotiate a fare. Fixed-route passenger taxis (which you can pay for by the seat) run between several cities, including Lhasa and Tsetang.

Tractors can be an option for short trips in rural areas, especially in the Yarlung Valley. For a few yuan, drivers are normally quite happy to have some passengers in the back. Rides of anything over 10 minutes quickly become seriously uncomfortable unless on a tarmac road.

TOURS

Most travellers to Tibet hire a Land Cruiser, with a driver and often a guide, to effectively arrange their own do-it-yourself tour within Tibet. For detailed information on 'do-it-yourself' tours, see p343 and above.

If you want a fully organised tour into and around Tibet, an internet search will trawl up hundreds of companies offering upper-end package tours. Travellers have recommended **Shangrila Tours** (www.shangrilatours.com), **Shigatse Travels** (www.shigatsetravels.com), **Visit Tibet Travel and Tours** (www.visittibet.com) and Nepali-based **Roger Pfister** (www.snowjewel.com), the latter for trips to Mt Kailash.

Health

CONTENTS

Tibet poses particular risks to your health, although for the large part these are associated with the high average altitude of the plateau.

There is no need to be overly worried; very few travellers are adversely affected by the altitude for very long, and greater risks are present in the form of road accidents and dog bites. Insect-borne and infectious diseases are quite rare because of the high altitude.

Sensible travellers will rely on their own medical knowledge and supplies when travelling throughout Tibet. It is a very isolated place, and outside the city of Lhasa there is not much in the way of expert medical care available.

BEFORE YOU GO

Make sure you're healthy before you start travelling. If you are going on a long trip, make sure your teeth are OK. If you wear glasses, take a spare pair and your prescription.

If you require a particular medication take a good supply, as it may not be available in Tibet. Take along part of the packaging showing the generic name rather than the brand to make getting replacements easier. To avoid problems, it's a good idea to have a legible prescription or letter from your doctor to show that you legally use the medication.

INSURANCE

Keep in mind that Tibet is a remote location, and if you become seriously injured or very sick, you may need to be evacuated by air. Under these circumstances, you don't want to be without adequate health insurance. Be sure your policy covers evacuation.

RECOMMENDED VACCINATIONS

China doesn't officially require any immunisations for entry into the country; however, the further off the beaten track you go, the more necessary it is to take all precautions. The World Health Organization (WHO) requires travellers who have come from an area infected with yellow fever to be vaccinated before entering the country. Record all vaccinations on an International Health Certificate, available from a doctor or government health department.

Plan well ahead and schedule your vaccinations because some require more than one injection, while others should not be given together. Note that some vaccinations should not be given during pregnancy or to people with allergies.

It is recommended that you seek medical advice at least eight weeks before travel. Note that there is a greater risk of all kinds of disease with children and during pregnancy.

Discuss your requirements with your doctor, but vaccinations you should consider for this trip include the following:

Diphtheria & Tetanus Vaccinations for these two diseases are usually combined and are recommended for everyone. After an initial course of three injections (usually given in childhood), boosters are necessary every 10 years.

Hepatitis A The vaccine for Hepatitis A (eg Avaxim, Havrix 1440 or VAQTA) provides long-term immunity (at least 20 years) after an initial injection and a booster at six to 12 months. Hepatitis A vaccine is also available in a combined form, Twinrix, with hepatitis B vaccine. Three injections over a six-month period are required, the first two providing substantial protection against hepatitis A.

Hepatitis B China (although not so much Tibet) is one of the world's great reservoirs of hepatitis B infection, a disease spread by contact with blood or by sexual activity. Vaccination involves three injections, the quickest course being over three weeks with a booster at 12 months.

Polio This serious, easily transmitted disease is still prevalent in many developing countries, including Tibet's neighbouring countries, India, Pakistan and Nepal. Everyone should keep up-to-date with this vaccination, which is normally given in childhood. One adult booster is then needed (as long as the full childhood course was completed), particularly if travelling to a country with recent polio activity. This should be discussed with your doctor.

Rabies China has a significant problem with rabies, which is worsening. Rabies is now the most common infectious disease cause of death in China. Only India reports more human cases annually. The vaccination is strongly recommended for those spending more than a month in Tibet, especially if you are cycling, handling animals, caving or travelling in remote areas, and for children. Pretravel vaccination means you do not need to receive Rabies Immuno Globulin (RIG) after a bite. RIG is very unlikely to be available in Tibet, and there is such a worldwide shortage that for the first time the CIWEC Clinic in Kathmandu reports that it cannot source any (at the time of writing). If you are prevaccinated and then bitten, you need only get two further shots of vaccine, as soon as possible, three days apart. If not prevaccinated, you require RIG plus five shots of vaccine over the course of 28 days. Thus the management of any bite or scratch is greatly simplified if you have been vaccinated. Current expert opinion is that the full series of vaccination does not require any boosters *unless* a bite occurs.

Tuberculosis The risk of tuberculosis (TB) to travellers is usually very low, unless you'll be living with or closely associated with local people in high-risk areas. As most healthy adults don't develop symptoms, a skin test before and after travel to determine whether exposure has occurred may be considered. Recommendations for BCG vaccination vary considerably around the world. Discuss with your doctor if you feel you may be at risk. It is strongly recommended for children under five who are spending more than three months in a high-risk area.

Typhoid This is an important vaccination to have for Tibet, where hygiene standards are low. It is available either as an injection or oral capsules. A combined hepatitis A-typhoid vaccine was launched recently but its availability is still limited. Check with your doctor to find out its status in your country.

Yellow Fever This disease is not endemic in China or Tibet and a vaccine is only required if you are coming from an infected area. These areas are limited to parts of South America and Africa.

Measles-mumps-rubella (MMR) All travellers should ensure they are immune to these diseases, either through infection or vaccination. Most people born before 1966 will be immune, those born after this date should have received two MMR vaccines in their lifetime.

Chickenpox (Varicella) Discuss this vaccine with your doctor if you have not had chickenpox.

Influenza The flu vaccine is recommended for anyone with chronic diseases, such as diabetes, lung or heart disease. Tibet has a high rate of respiratory illness, so all travellers should consider vaccination.

Pneumonia A vaccine is recommended for anyone over 65 or those over 55 with certain medical conditions.

MEDICAL CHECKLIST

Following is a list of items you should consider including in your medical kit for travelling – consult your pharmacist for brands available in your country.

- Antibiotics – useful for everyone travelling to Tibet to avoid risks of receiving poorly stored local medications; see your doctor, as antibiotics must be prescribed, and carry the prescription with you
- Antifungal cream or powder – for fungal skin infections and thrush
- Antihistamine – for allergies, eg hay fever; to ease the itch from insect bites or stings; and to prevent motion sickness
- Antiseptic (such as povidone-iodine) – for cuts and grazes
- Bandages, Band-Aids (plasters) and other wound dressings
- Calamine lotion, sting-relief spray or aloe vera – to ease irritation from sunburn and insect bites or stings
- Cold and flu tablets, throat lozenges and nasal decongestant
- Homeopathic medicines – useful homeopathic medicines include gentiana for altitude sickness, echinacea for warding off infections, and tea-tree oil for cuts and scrapes
- Insect repellent, sunscreen, lip balm and eye drops
- Loperamide or diphenoxylate – 'blockers' for diarrhoea
- Multivitamins – for long trips, when dietary vitamin intake may be inadequate
- Paracetamol (acetaminophen in the USA) – for pain or fever
- Prochlorperazine or metaclopramide – for nausea and vomiting
- Rehydration mixture – to prevent dehydration, which may occur, for example, during bouts of diarrhoea; particularly important when travelling with children
- Scissors, tweezers and a thermometer – note that mercury thermometers are prohibited by airlines
- Sterile kit – in case you need injections in a country with medical hygiene problems; discuss with your doctor
- Water purification tablets or iodine

INTERNET RESOURCES

There are a number of excellent travel-health sites on the internet. From the Lonely Planet website (www.lonelyplanet.com) there are links to the WHO and the US Centers for Disease Control & Prevention.

FURTHER READING

Lonely Planet's *Healthy Travel – Asia & India* is a handy pocket size and packed with useful information, including pretrip planning, emergency first aid, immunisation and disease information, and what to do if you get sick on the road. *Travel with Children* from Lonely Planet also includes advice on travel health for younger children.

Other detailed health guides that you may find useful:

Complete Guide to Healthy Travel provides recommendations for international travel from the US Centers for Disease Control & Prevention.

Medicine For Mountaineering by James Wilkerson is still the classic text for trekking first aid and medical advice.

Pocket First Aid and Wilderness Medicine by Jim Duff and Peter Gormly is a great pocket-sized guide that's easily carried on a trek or climb.

Staying Healthy in Asia, Africa & Latin America by Dirk Schroeder is a detailed and well-organised guide.

The High Altitude Medicine Handbook by Andrew J Pollard and David R Murdoch is a small-format guide full of valuable information on prevention and emergency care.

Travellers' Health by Dr Richard Dawood is comprehensive, easy to read, authoritative and highly recommended, although it's rather large to lug around.

Where There Is No Doctor by David Werner is a very detailed guide intended for people going to work in a developing country.

IN TRANSIT

DEEP VEIN THROMBOSIS (DVT)

Deep vein thrombosis (DVT) occurs when blood clots form in the legs during plane flights, chiefly because of prolonged immobility. Although most of these blood clots are reabsorbed uneventfully, some of them may break off and travel through the blood vessels to the lungs, where they may cause life-threatening complications.

The chief symptom of DVT is swelling or pain of the foot, ankle or calf, usually but not always on just one side. When a blood clot travels to the lungs, it may cause chest pain and difficulty in breathing. Travellers with any of these symptoms should immediately seek medical attention.

To prevent the development of DVT on long flights you should walk about the cabin, perform isometric compressions of the leg muscles (ie contract the leg muscles while sitting), drink plenty of fluids, and avoid alcohol and tobacco.

MOTION SICKNESS

Eating lightly before and during a trip will reduce the chances of motion sickness. If you are prone to motion sickness, try to find a place that minimises movement – near the wing on aircraft, near the centre on buses. Fresh air usually helps; reading and cigarette smoke don't.

Commercial preparations for motion sickness, which can cause drowsiness, have to be taken before the trip commences. Ginger (available in capsule form) and peppermint (including mint-flavoured sweets) are natural preventatives.

IN TIBET

AVAILABILITY & COST OF HEALTH CARE

Self-diagnosis and treatment can be risky, so you should always seek medical help where possible. Although we do give drug dosages in this section, they are for emergency use only. Correct diagnosis is vital.

Top-end hotels can usually recommend a good place to go for advice. Standards of medical attention are so low in most places in Tibet that for some ailments the best advice is to go straight to Lhasa, and in extreme cases get on a plane to Chengdu or Kathmandu.

Global Doctor Chengdu Clinic (☎ 8522 6058, 24hr emergency number 139-8225 6966; www.globaldoctor.com.au; Ground fl, Kelan Bldg, Bangkok Garden Apts, Section 4, 21 Renmin Nanlu) offers pre-Tibet medical examinations and a Tibet Travellers Assist Package that can be useful if you are worried about an existing medical condition. See the website for details. In Kathmandu, the **CIWEC Clinic Travel Medicine Center** (www.ciwec-clinic.com; Lazimpath) near the British embassy, has a lot of experience with altitude-related illnesses and is a good resource if on the way to or coming from Tibet. The website also offers useful medical advice.

Antibiotics should ideally only be administered under medical supervision; however, this may not always be possible. Ensure you have been given clear instructions by your prescribing doctor. Take only the recommended dose at the prescribed intervals and use the whole course, even if the illness seems to be cured before the medication is finished. Stop immediately if there are any serious reactions and don't use the antibiotic at all if you are unsure that you have the correct one. Some people are allergic to commonly prescribed antibiotics such as penicillin; carry this information (eg on a bracelet) when travelling.

INFECTIOUS DISEASES

Avian Influenza (Bird Flu)

Influenza A (H5N1) or 'Bird flu' is a subtype of the type A influenza virus. This virus typically infects birds and not humans. There have been some cases of bird-to-human transmission, although this does not easily occur. Very close contact with dead or sick birds is the currently principal source of infection.

Symptoms include high fever and typical influenza-like indicators, with rapid deterioration leading to respiratory failure and, in many cases, death. The early administration of antiviral drugs such as Tamiflu is recommended to improve the chances of survival. Immediate medical care should be sought if bird flu is suspected.

There is currently no vaccine available to prevent bird flu. For up-to-date information check these two websites:

- www.who.int/en/
- www.avianinfluenza.com.au

Hepatitis

A general term for inflammation of the liver, hepatitis is a common disease worldwide. There are several different viruses that cause hepatitis, and they differ in the way that they are transmitted. The symptoms are similar in all forms of the illness and include fever, chills, headache, fatigue, feelings of weakness and aches and pains, followed by loss of appetite, nausea, vomiting, abdominal pain, dark urine, light-coloured faeces, jaundiced (yellow) skin and yellowing of the whites of the eyes. People who have had hepatitis should avoid alcohol for some time after the illness, as the liver needs quite a while to recover.

Hepatitis A is transmitted by contaminated food and drinking water. You should seek medical advice if symptoms present, but there is not much you can do apart from resting, drinking lots of fluids, eating lightly and avoiding fatty foods.

Hepatitis A is most often spread in China and Tibet as a result of the custom of sharing food from a single dish rather than using separate plates and a serving spoon. It is wise to use the disposable chopsticks now freely available in most restaurants in Tibet, or else buy your own chopsticks and spoon. Hepatitis E is transmitted in the same way as hepatitis A; it can be particularly serious for pregnant women.

There are almost 300 million chronic carriers of hepatitis B in the world, and China has more cases than any other country; almost 20% of the population are believed to be carriers. It is spread through contact with infected blood, blood products or body fluids, for example through sexual contact, unsterilised needles and blood transfusions, or contact with blood via small breaks in the skin. Other risk situations include contaminated medical equipment or having a shave, tattoo or body piercing with contaminated tools. The symptoms of hepatitis B may be more severe than those for type A, and the disease can lead to long-term problems such as chronic liver damage, liver cancer or a long-term carrier state. Hepatitis C and D are spread in the same way as hepatitis B and can also lead to long-term complications.

There are vaccines against hepatitis A and B, but there are currently no vaccines against the other types. Following the basic rules about food and water (hepatitis A and E) and avoiding risk situations (hepatitis B, C and D) are important preventative measures.

HIV & AIDS

Infection with human immunodeficiency virus (HIV) may lead to acquired immune deficiency syndrome (AIDS), which is a fatal disease if untreated. Any exposure to blood, blood products or body fluids may put the individual at risk. The disease is often transmitted by sexual contact or dirty needles. Vaccination, acupuncture, tattooing and body piercing can be potentially as dangerous as intravenous drug use. HIV/AIDS can also be spread through infected blood transfusions; some developing countries cannot afford to screen blood used for transfusions.

HIV cases in Tibet are on the rise, and anyone who intends to work or study in Tibet for longer than 12 months is required by the Chinese authorities to undergo an AIDS test.

If you do need an injection, ask to see the syringe unwrapped in front of you, or take a needle and syringe pack with you when travelling. Fear of HIV infection should never preclude treatment for serious medical conditions.

Rabies

This fatal viral infection is found in many countries. Many animals (such as dogs, cats, bats and monkeys) can be infected and it is their saliva that is infectious. Any bite, scratch or even lick from an animal should be cleaned immediately and thoroughly. Scrub gently with soap and running water, and then apply alcohol or iodine solution. Prompt medical help should be sought to receive a course of injections to prevent the onset of symptoms and save the patient from death.

At the time of writing, no treatment for rabies was available anywhere in Tibet. If you have any potential exposure to rabies, seek medical advice in Lhasa (or ideally Kathmandu or Chengdu) as soon as possible in order to receive post-exposure treatment. Even in these centres full treatment may not be available and you may need to travel to Bangkok or Hong Kong.

Respiratory Infections

Upper respiratory tract infections (like the common cold) are frequent ailments all over China, including Tibet. Why are they such a serious problem in China? Respiratory infections are aggravated by the high altitude, the cold weather, air pollution, chain smoking and overcrowded conditions, all of which increase the opportunity for infection. Another reason is that Chinese people tend to spit a lot, thereby spreading the disease.

Some of the symptoms of influenza include a sore throat, fever and weakness. Any upper-respiratory-tract infection, including influenza, can lead to complications such as bronchitis and pneumonia, which may need to be treated with antibiotics. Seek medical help in this situation.

The Chinese treat bronchitis, which can be a complication of flu, with a powder made from the gall bladder of snakes – a treatment of questionable value, but there is no harm in trying it.

No vaccine offers complete protection, but there are vaccines against influenza and pneumococcal pneumonia that might help. The influenza vaccine is highly recommended for travellers to China and Tibet, and is good for up to one year.

Sexually Transmitted Infections

While HIV/AIDS and hepatitis B can be transmitted through sexual contact, other sexually transmitted infections (STIs) include gonorrhoea, herpes and syphilis. Sores, blisters or rashes around the genitals and discharges or pain when urinating are common symptoms. In some STIs, such as wart virus or chlamydia, symptoms may be less prominent or go completely unobserved, especially in women. Syphilis symptoms eventually disappear but the disease continues and can cause severe problems in later years. Although abstinence from sexual contact is the only 100% effective prevention, using condoms is also effective in the prevention of some infections. Gonorrhoea and syphilis are treated with antibiotics. Different STIs each require specific antibiotics. There is no cure for herpes or AIDS.

Condoms are available in China – the word is *baotao* (保套), which translates literally as 'insurance glove'.

TRAVELLER'S DIARRHOEA

Simple things like a change of water, food or climate can all cause a mild bout of diarrhoea (*la duzi* – spicy stomach – in Chinese), but a few rushed toilet trips with no other symptoms are not indicative of a major problem. Even Marco Polo got the runs.

Dehydration is the main danger with any diarrhoea, particularly in children or the elderly as it can occur quite quickly. Under all circumstances, fluid replacement (at least equal to the volume being lost) is the most important thing to remember. Weak black tea with a little sugar, soda water, or soft drinks allowed to go flat and diluted 50% with clean water are all good. With moderate to severe diarrhoea a rehydrating solution is preferable to replace lost minerals and salts. Commercially available oral rehydration salts (ORS) are very useful; add them to boiled or bottled water. In an emergency you can make up a solution of six teaspoons of sugar and half a teaspoon of salt to a litre of boiled or bottled water. You need to drink at least the same volume of fluid that you are losing in bowel movements and vomiting. Urine is the best guide to the adequacy of replacement –

if you have small amounts of concentrated urine, you need to drink more. Keep drinking small amounts often. Stick to a bland diet as you recover.

Loperamide or diphenoxylate can be used to bring relief from the symptoms, although they do not actually cure the problem. However, neither is available in China. A good Chinese alternative treatment is berberine hydrochloride *(huang lian su;* 黄连素*)*. Only use these drugs if you do not have access to toilets, eg if you *must* travel. These drugs are not recommended for children under 12 years. Do not use these drugs if you have a high fever, are severely dehydrated or have blood in the bowel motions.

In certain situations antibiotics may be required: diarrhoea with blood or mucus (dysentery), any diarrhoea with fever, profuse watery diarrhoea, persistent diarrhoea not improving after 24 hours and severe diarrhoea. These suggest a more serious cause, in which case gut-paralysing drugs should be avoided without seeking medical advice.

In these situations, a stool test may be necessary to diagnose what bug is causing your diarrhoea, so you should seek medical help urgently. Where this is not possible the recommended drugs for bacterial diarrhoea (the most likely cause of severe diarrhoea in travellers) are norfloxacin 400mg twice daily for three days or ciprofloxacin 500mg twice daily for three days. These are not recommended for children or pregnant women. There can be resistance to these medications for some of the bacterial causes of diarrhoea; in those cases, azithromycin, 500mg once a day, is recommended. This is also the drug of choice for children with dosage dependent on weight. A three-day course is given. Azithromycin may be considered under medical supervision in pregnancy. There is a new oral cholera vaccine that offers some protection against travellers diarrhoea, but only about 20% for three months. It may be suggested if you are at high risk of complications from diarrhoea.

Two other causes of persistent diarrhoea in travellers are giardiasis and amoebic dysentery.

Amoebic Dysentery

Caused by the protozoan *Entamoeba histolytica*, amoebic dysentery is characterised by a gradual onset of low-grade diarrhoea, often with blood and mucus. Cramping abdominal pain and vomiting are less likely than in other types of diarrhoea, and fever may not be present. It will persist until treated and can recur and cause other health problems.

You should seek medical advice if you think you have giardiasis or amoebic dysentery, but where this is not possible, tinidazole or metronidazole are the recommended drugs. The better option of the two is tinidazole, which is not easily obtained in Tibet. If you are going to be travelling in high mountain areas, it might be a good idea to keep your own stock with you.

Cholera

This is the worst of the watery diarrhoeas. Outbreaks of cholera are generally widely reported, so you can avoid problem areas. Fluid replacement is the most vital treatment: the risk of dehydration is severe, as you may lose up to 20L a day. If there is a delay in getting to hospital, begin taking Doxycycline. This may help shorten the illness, but adequate fluids are required to save lives. Seek medical advice if you think you may have this disease.

Giardiasis

Known as giardia, giardiasis is a type of diarrhoea that is relatively common in Tibet and is caused by a parasite, *Giardia lamblia*. Mountaineers often suffer from this problem. The parasite causing this intestinal disorder is present in contaminated water. Many kinds of mammals harbour the parasite, so you can easily get it from drinking 'pure mountain water' unless the area is devoid of animals. Simply brushing your teeth using contaminated water is sufficient to get giardiasis, or any other gut bug. Symptoms include stomach cramps, nausea, a bloated stomach, watery, foul-smelling diarrhoea and frequent gas. Giardiasis can appear several weeks after you have been exposed to the parasite. The symptoms may disappear for a few days and then return; this can go on for several weeks. Treatment is with tinidazole, 2g in a single dose for one to two days.

ENVIRONMENTAL HAZARDS

Acute Mountain Sickness

Acute mountain sickness (AMS, also known as altitude sickness) is common at high elevations; relevant factors are the rate of ascent and individual susceptibility. The former is the major risk factor. On average, one tourist

is bleeding. An insect repellent may help keep them away.

Food

There is an old colonial adage: 'If you can cook it, boil it or peel it you can eat it…otherwise forget it.' Vegetables and fruit should be washed with purified or bottled water or peeled where possible. Beware of ice cream that is sold in the street or anywhere it might have been melted and refrozen; if there's any doubt (eg a power cut in the last day or two) steer well clear. Undercooked meat should be avoided.

If a place looks clean and well run, and the vendor also looks clean and healthy, then the food is probably safe. In general, places that are packed with travellers or locals will be fine, while empty restaurants are questionable. Chinese food in particular is cooked over a high heat, which kills most germs.

Frostbite

This is the freezing of extremities, including fingers, toes and nose. Signs and symptoms of frostbite include a whitish or waxy cast to the skin, or even crystals on the surface, plus itching, numbness and pain. Warm the affected areas by immersing them in warm (not hot) water or with blankets or clothes, only until the skin becomes flushed. Note: frostbitten areas should only be rewarmed if there is not a likelihood they can be frostbitten again prior to reaching medical care. Frostbitten parts should not be rubbed. Pain and swelling are inevitable. Blisters should not be broken. Get medical attention right away.

Heat Exhaustion

Dehydration and salt deficiency can cause heat exhaustion. Take time to acclimatise to high temperatures, be sure to drink sufficient liquids and do not do anything too physically demanding.

Salt deficiency is characterised by fatigue, lethargy, headaches, giddiness and muscle cramps; salt tablets may help, but adding extra salt to your food is better.

Hypothermia

Tibet's cold climate must be treated with respect. Subfreezing temperatures mean there is a risk of hypothermia, even during the summer season. Even in midsummer, passes and high areas around northern Tibet and the Changtang can be hit without warning by sudden snow storms. Exposed plains and ridges are prone to extremely high winds and this significantly adds to the cold. For example, on a 5000m pass in central Tibet in July, the absolute minimum temperature is roughly -4°C, but regularly occurring 70km/h winds plunge the wind-chill factor or apparent temperature to -20°C.

The message is that you should always be prepared for cold, wet or windy conditions, especially if you're out walking, hitching or trekking at high altitudes or even taking a long bus trip over mountains (particularly at night).

Hypothermia occurs when the body loses heat faster than it can produce it and the core temperature of the body falls. It is surprisingly easy to progress from very cold to dangerously cold through a combination of wind, wet clothing, fatigue and hunger, even if the air temperature is above freezing.

It is best to dress in layers. Silk, wool and some of the new artificial fibres are all good insulating materials. A hat is important, as a lot of heat is lost through the head. A strong, waterproof outer layer and a 'space' blanket for emergencies are essential. Carry basic supplies, including food that contains simple sugars to generate heat quickly and fluid to drink.

Symptoms of hypothermia are exhaustion, numb skin (particularly toes and fingers), shivering, slurred speech, irrational or violent behaviour, lethargy, stumbling, dizzy spells, muscle cramps and violent bursts of energy. Irrationality may take the form of sufferers claiming they are warm and trying to take off their clothes.

To treat mild hypothermia, first get the person out of the wind and rain, remove their clothing if it's wet and replace it with dry, warm clothing. Give them hot liquids (not alcohol) and some high-energy, easily digestible food. Do not rub victims; instead, allow them to slowly warm themselves. This should be enough to treat the early stages of hypothermia. The early recognition and treatment of mild hypothermia is the only way to prevent severe hypothermia, which is a critical condition.

Sunburn

It's very easy to get sunburnt in Tibet's high altitudes, especially if you're trekking. Sunburn is more than just being uncomfortable. Among the undesirable effects (apart from the immediate pain and agony) are premature skin ageing and possible skin cancer in later years. Wear sunglasses, loose-fitting clothes that cover your arms, legs and neck, and a wide-brimmed hat like the ones Tibetans wear. Calamine lotion is good for treating mild sunburn.

Choose sunscreen with a high sun protection factor (SPF). Those with fair complexions should bring reflective sunscreen (containing zinc oxide or titanium oxide) with them. Apply the sunscreen to your nose and lips (and especially the tops of your ears if you are not wearing a hat).

Water

The number-one rule is be careful of the water, especially ice. If you don't know for certain that the water is safe, assume the worst. In urban centres Tibetans, like the Chinese, boil their drinking water making it safe to drink hot or cooled. In the country and while trekking you should boil your own water or treat it with water-purification tablets, as livestock contaminate many of the water sources. Milk should be treated with suspicion as it will be unpasteurised in the countryside, although boiled milk is fine if it is kept hygienically. Soft drinks and beer are always available wherever there is a shop, and these are always safe to drink, as is tea. Locally brewed beer, *chang*, is another matter. It is often made with contaminated well water and there is always some risk in drinking it.

WATER PURIFICATION

The simplest way to purify water is to boil it thoroughly. At Tibet's high altitude water boils at a lower temperature and germs are less likely to be killed, so make sure you boil water for at least 10 minutes.

Consider purchasing a water filter for a long trip. There are two main kinds of filters. Total filters take out all parasites, bacteria and viruses, and make water safe to drink. They are often expensive, but can be more cost-effective than buying bottled water. Simple filters (which can even be a nylon mesh bag) take out dirt and larger foreign bodies from the water so that chemical solutions work much more effectively; if water is dirty, chemical solutions may not work at all. It's very important when buying a filter to read the specifications, so that you know exactly what it removes from the water and what it doesn't. Simple filtering will not remove all dangerous organisms, so if you cannot boil water it should be treated chemically.

Chlorine tablets (eg Puritabs or Steritabs) will kill many pathogens, but not giardia and amoebic cysts. Iodine is more effective for purifying water and is available in tablet form (eg Potable Aqua). Follow the directions carefully and remember that too much iodine can be harmful.

WOMEN'S HEALTH

Pregnancy

It is not advisable to travel to some places while pregnant as some vaccinations normally used to prevent serious diseases (eg yellow fever) are not advisable during pregnancy. In addition, some diseases are much more serious for the mother (and may increase the risk of a stillborn child) in pregnancy.

Most miscarriages occur during the first three months of pregnancy. Miscarriage is not uncommon and can occasionally lead to severe bleeding. The last three months should also be spent within reasonable distance of good medical care. A baby born as early as 24 weeks stands a chance of survival, but only in a good modern hospital. Pregnant women should avoid all unnecessary medication, although vaccinations should still be taken where needed. Additional care should be taken to prevent illness and particular attention should be paid to diet and nutrition. Alcohol and nicotine, for example, should be avoided.

TIBETAN MEDICINE

The basic teachings of Tibetan medicine share much with those of other Asian medical traditions, which, according to some scholars, made their way to the East via India from ancient Greece. While the Western medical tradition treats symptoms that indicate a known medical condition (measles or mumps, for example), the Eastern medical tradition looks at symptoms as indications of an imbalance in the body and seeks to restore that balance.

It is not correct to assume, however, that Tibetan medicine was practised by trained doctors in clinics scattered across the land. The Tibetan medical tradition is largely textual. It derives from Indian sources and was studied in some monasteries in much the same way that Buddhist scriptures were studied. When Tibetans needed medical help they usually went to a local 'apothecary' who sold concoctions of herbs; equally, help was sought in prayers and good-luck charms.

The theory of Tibetan medicine is based on an extremely complex system of checks and balances between what can be broadly described as three 'humours' (related to state of mind), seven 'bodily sustainers' (related to the digestive tract) and three 'eliminators' (related to the elimination of bodily wastes). And if the relationship between bodily functions and the three humours of desire, egoism and ignorance were not complex enough, there is the influence of harmful spirits to consider. There are 360 harmful female influences, 360 harmful male influences, 360 malevolent *naga* (water spirits) influences and finally 360 influences stemming from past karma. All these combine to produce 404 basic disorders and 84,000 illnesses!

How does a Tibetan doctor assess the condition of a patient? The most important skill is pulse diagnosis. A Tibetan doctor is attuned to 360 'subtle channels' of energy that run through the body's skin and muscle, internal organs and bone and marrow. The condition of these channels can be ascertained through six of the doctor's fingers (the first three fingers of each hand). Tibetan medicine also relies on urine analysis as an important diagnostic tool.

If Tibetan diagnostic theory is mainly Indian in influence, the treatment owes as much to Chinese medicine as to Indian practices. Herbal concoctions, moxibustion and acupuncture are all used to restore balance to the body. Surgery was practised in the early days of Tibetan medicine, but was outlawed in the 9th century when a king's mother died during an operation.

Yuthok Yongten Gonpo (1182-1251), the physician of King Trisong Detsen, who was born near Ralung Monastery, is credited as the founder of the Tibetan medical system. For more on Tibetan medicine see the website www.tibetan-medicine.org.

If you get sick, you can get a diagnosis from Lhasa's **Mentsikhang** (Traditional Tibetan Hospital; Map p100; 9.30am-12.30pm & 3.30-6pm) opposite the Barkhor. Two English-speaking doctors attend to foreigners on the 3rd floor.

Language

CONTENTS

The two principal languages of Tibet are Tibetan and (Mandarin) Chinese. The importance of Chinese is an unfortunate reality in Tibet, and all Tibetans undertaking higher studies do so in Chinese. In urban Tibet (the countryside is another matter) almost all Tibetans speak Chinese. Nevertheless, even if you have studied or picked up some Chinese in China, it's worth trying to get a few phrases of Tibetan together. It will be much appreciated by the Tibetans you encounter on your travels.

Linguistically, Chinese and Tibetan have very little in common. They use different sentence structures, and the tonal element is far less crucial in Tibetan than in Chinese. Also, unlike the dialects of China, Tibetan has never used Chinese characters for its written language.

TIBETAN

Tibetan is a member of the Tibeto-Burman family of languages, and is spoken in Tibet and within exiled communities of Tibetans. Lhasa dialect, the standard form of Tibetan, employs a system of rising and falling tones, but the differences are subtle and meaning is made clear by context. Beginners need not worry about them.

Like Chinese, Tibetan has no articles (a, the) and doesn't use plurals. Here the similarity ends, however. Tibetan differs from European and Chinese languages, as it has a subject-object-verb sentence structure. Thus, where in English we would say 'I see John' (subject-verb-object), in Tibetan the sentence is *nga John thong gi duk*, ('I John see', subject-object-verb). In another marked difference from Chinese, Tibetan has tenses and conjugates its verbs with particles. There's also a fairly complicated system of prepositions (words like 'in' and 'on').

If all this makes Tibetan sound extremely difficult to pick up on the road, don't fret; providing you relax a little, it's fairly easy to get together a basic repertoire of phrases that will win you friends and help to get things done. For information on language courses, see p316. Lonely Planet's *Tibetan Phrasebook*, which includes sections on trekking, visiting temples and handicrafts, is also recommended.

THE WRITTEN LANGUAGE

The Tibetan script was developed during the reign of Songtsen Gampo in the 7th century. It was founded on Indian models and comprises 30 basic letters including the vowel 'a', and four extra vowel signs for 'e', 'i', 'o' and 'u'. Each letter can be written in three different styles, depending on the context in which a text is to be used. This 7th-century Tibetan script was based on the language spoken in Tibet at the time, and spellings have never been revised since. As a result of significant changes in spoken Tibetan over the last 12 centuries, written

TIBETAN TREKKING ESSENTIALS

How many hours to ...?
... བར་དུ་ ཆུ་ཚོད་ ག་ཚོད་འགོར་གི་རེད།
... bahtu chutsö kâtsay gogiray

I want to rent a (yak/horse).
ང་ གཡག་/རྟ་གཅིག་གླ་དགོས་ཡོད།
nga (yâk/ta)-chig lagöyö

I need a porter.
ང་དོ་པོ་ཁུར་མཁན་གཅིག་དགོས།
nga dohbo khukhen-chig gö

I need a guide.
ང་ ལམ་རྒྱུས་བྱེད་མཁན་གཅིག་དགོས།
nga lâmgyü chaykhen-chig gö

How much does it cost per day?
ཉིན་མ་ རེ་རེ་ལ་གླ་ཆ་ ག་ཚོད་རེད།
nyima rayrayla laja kâtsay ray?

Which way to ...?
... འགྲོ་ཡག་གི་ལམ་ག་ག་གི་རེད།
... dohyagi lâmga kagiray?

Is this the trail to ...?
འདི་ ... འགྲོ་ཡག་གི་ལམ་ག་རེད་པས།
di ... dohyagi lâmga rebay?

What is the next village on the trail?
ལམ་ཀ་དེ་ནས་ཕྱིན་ན་དང་པོ་ལུང་པ་ག་རེ་སླེབས་ཀྱི་རེད།
lâmga tenay chin-na dângpo loongpa karay lebkiray?

I have altitude sickness.
ང་ལ་དུག་ན་གིས།
nga lâdu nagi

I must get to low ground as quickly as possible.
ང་ས་དམའ་སར་གང་མགྱོགས་མགྱོགས་འགྲོར་དགོས་ཀྱི་འདུག
nga sa mahsa gâng gyokgyok joh gokidu

Slowly, slowly!	ཀ་ལེ་ཀ་ལེ།	*kalee kalee*
Let's go!	ད་འགྲོ།	*ta doh*
sleeping bag	ཉལ་ཁུག	*nye-koog*
tent	གུར་	*gur*
road/trail	ལམ་	*lam*
mountain	རི་	*ri*
cave	བྲག་ཕུག་	*dâgphuk*
pass	ལ	*la*
river	གཙང་པོ་	*tsângpo*
valley	ལུང་གཤོང་	*loong shong*
lake	མཚོ་	*tso*
hot spring	ཆུ་ཚན་	*chu-tsen*
north	བྱང་	*châng*
south	ལྷོ་	*lho*
east	ཤར་	*shâr*
west	ནུབ་	*noob*

Tibetan and spoken Tibetan are very different, and the development of a transliteration system for use by speakers of European languages is a formidable task.

In this book we've generally chosen the most commonly used spelling of each term. In cases where there is wide disagreement, we have chosen the spelling that's easiest to pronounce.

PRONUNCIATION

Tibetan has some tricky sounds for English speakers – there are quite a few consonant clusters, and, like Korean and Thai, Tibetan makes an important distinction between aspirated and non-aspirated consonants.

Vowels

The following pronunciation guide is based on standard British pronunciation.

a	as in 'father'
ay	as in 'play'
e	as in 'met'
ee	as in 'meet'
i	as in 'begin'
o	as in 'go'
oo	as in 'soon'
ö	similar to the 'u' in 'put'
u	as in 'rude'
ü	similar to the 'u' in 'flute'

Consonants

With the exception of the examples listed below, Tibetan consonants should be pronounced as in English. Where a consonant is followed by an **h**, it means that the consonant is aspirated (accompanied by a puff of air). An English example of this might be 'kettle', where the 'k' is aspirated and the 'tt' is non-aspirated. The distinction is fairly important, but in simple Tibetan the context should make it clear what you are talking about.

ky	as the 'kie' in 'Kiev'
ng	as the 'ng' in 'sing'
r	like a slightly trilled 'r'
ts	as the 'ts' in 'bits'

ACCOMMODATION

Where's a ...?	... ག་པར་ཡོད་རེད།	*... kabâh yöray?*
guesthouse	མགྲོན་ཁང་	*dhön khâng*
hotel	འགྲུལ་ཁང་	*drü-khâng*

HEALTH & EMERGENCIES

Help!
རོགས་གནང་དང་། *rog nângda!*
Fire!
མེ་འབར་གྱིས། *may bahgi!*
Thief!
རྐུ་མ་འདུག *kuma du!*
Go away!
ཕར་རྒྱུགས། *phah gyuk!*
I'm ill.
ང་ན་གི་འདུག *nga nagidu*
It's an emergency.
ཛ་དྲག་པོ་རེད། *za dâgpo ray!*
Call a doctor!
ཨེམ་ཆི་སྐད་གཏོང་དང་། *âmchi kay tongda!*
Call the police!
སྐོར་སྲུང་བ་སྐད་གཏོང་དང་། *korsoong-wa kay tongda!*
I'm lost.
ང་ལམ་ཀ་བརླགས་ཤག *nga lâmga lasha*
Where are the toilets?
གསང་སྤྱོད་ག་པར་ཡོད་རེད། *sângchö kabâh yöray?*

hospital	སྨན་ཁང་	*menkhâng*
diarrhoea	གྲོད་ཁོག་བཤལ་བ	*dröko shewa*
fever	ཚ་བ་	*tsawa*

Do you have a room available?
khâng mi yöbay?
ཁང་མིག་ཡོད་པས།
How much is it for one night?
tsen chik la katsö ray?
མཚན་གཅིག་ལ་ག་ཚོད་རེད།
I'd like to stay with a Tibetan family.
nga böpay mi-tsâng nyâmdo dendö yö
ང་བོད་པའི་མི་ཚང་མཉམ་དུ་བསྡད་འདོད་ཡོད།
I need some hot water.
ngala chu tsapo gö
ང་ལ་ཆུ་ཚ་པོ་དགོས།

CONVERSATION & ESSENTIALS

Hello.	བཀྲ་ཤིས་བདེ་ལེགས།	*tashi dele*
Goodbye. (when staying)	ག་ལེ་ཕེབས།	*kalee pay*
Goodbye. (when leaving)	ག་ལེ་བཞུགས།	*kalee shu*
Thank you.	ཐུགས་རྗེ་ཆེ།	*tujay chay*
Sorry.	དགོངས་དག	*gonda*
I want ...	ང་ལ་ ... དགོས།	*nga la ... gö*
good	ཡག་པོ	*yâg-po*

What's your name?
kerâng gi tsenla kare ray?
ཁྱེད་རང་གི་མཚན་ལ་ག་རེ་རེད།
My name is ... – and yours?
ngai ming-la ... sa, a- ni kerâng-gi tsenla kare ray?
ངའི་མིང་ལ ... ཟ། ཨ་ནི། ཁྱེད་རང་གི་མཚན་ལ་ག་རེ་རེད།
Is it OK to take a photo?
par gyâbna digiy-rebay?
པར་བརྒྱབ་ན་འགྲིག་གི་རེད་པས།
Where are you from?
kerâng loong-pa ka-ne yin?
ཁྱེད་རང་ལུང་པ་ག་ནས་ཡིན།

I'm from ...	*nga ... ne yin*	ང་ ... ནས་ཡིན།
Australia	*autaliya*	ཨོ་ཊ་ལི་ཡ་
Canada	*canada*	ཁེ་ན་ཊ་
New Zealand	*shinshilen*	ནིའུ་ཛི་ལནཊ་
UK	*injee loongpa*	དབྱིན་ཇི་ལུང་པ་
USA	*amerika*	ཨ་མེ་རི་ཀ་

Yes & No

There are no words in Tibetan that are the direct equivalents of English 'yes' and 'no'. Although it won't always be correct, you'll be understood if you use *la ong* for 'yes' and *la men* for 'no'.

DIRECTIONS

Where is the ...?
... ག་པར་ཡོད་རེད།
... kabâh yö ray?
I'm looking for ...
... ག་བར་ཡོད་མེད་མིག་བལྟ་གི་ཡོད།
... ka-bâh yö-may mik tagiyö

right	གཡས་པ་	*yeba*
left	གཡོན་པ་	*yönba*
straight ahead	ཤར་རྒྱུག་	*shar gya*

LANGUAGE DIFFICULTIES

Do you speak English?
དབྱིན་ཇི་སྐད་ཤེས་ཀྱི་ཡོད་པས།
injeeke shing gi yö pe?
Do you speak English?
ཁྱེད་རང་དབྱིན་ཇི་སྐད་ཤེས་ཀྱི་ཡོད་པས།
kayrâng injikay shing-gi yöbay
I don't understand.
ཧ་གོ་མ་སོང་།
ha ko masong
I understand.
ཧ་གོ་སོང་།
ha kosong

NUMBERS

1	གཅིག་	*chik*
2	གཉིས་	*nyi*
3	གསུམ་	*soom*

4	བཞི་	*shi*
5	ལྔ་	*nga*
6	དྲུག་	*doog*
7	བདུན་	*dün*
8	བརྒྱད་	*gye*
9	དགུ་	*gu*
10	བཅུ་	*chu*
11	བཅུ་གཅིག་	*chu chik*
12	བཅུ་གཉིས་	*chu nyi*
13	བཅུ་གསུམ་	*chok sum*
14	བཅུ་བཞི་	*chu shi*
15	བཅོ་ལྔ་	*chö nga*
16	བཅུ་དྲུག་	*chu dug*
17	བཅུ་བདུན་	*chu dun*
18	བཅོ་བརྒྱད་	*chob gye*
19	བཅུ་དགུ་	*chu gu*
20	ཉི་ཤུ་	*nyi shu*
21	ཉི་ཤུ་རྩ་གཅིག་	*nyi shu tsa chik*
30	སུམ་བཅུ་	*soom chu*
40	བཞི་བཅུ་	*shib chu*
50	ལྔ་བཅུ་	*nga chu*
60	དྲུག་བཅུ་	*doog chu*
70	བདུན་བཅུ་	*dün chu*
80	བརྒྱད་བཅུ་	*gye chu*
90	དགུ་བཅུ་	*goob chu*
100	བརྒྱ་	*gya*
1000	ཆིག་སྟོང་	*chik tong*

SHOPPING & SERVICES

I'd like to buy ...
ང་ ... ཉོ་འདོད་ཡོད། *nga ... nyondo yö*

How much is it?
གོང་ག་ཚོད་རེད། *gong katsö ray?*

It's expensive.
གོང་ཆེན་པོ་རེད་ཤག *gong chenpo resha*

I don't like it.
བློར་འགྲོ་མ་སོང་། *loh doh masong*

I'll take it.
དེ་ཉོ་གྱི་ཡིན། *te nyogi yin*

TIME & DATES

What's the time?
ཆུ་ཚོད་ག་ཚད་རེད། *chutsö katsö ray?*

... hour ... minute
ཆུ་ཚོད་ ... སྐར་མ་ ... *chutsö ... karma ...*

When?	ག་དུས་	*kadü?*
now	ད་ལྟ་	*tânda*
today	དེ་རིང་	*tering*
tomorrow	སང་ཉིན་	*sângnyi*
yesterday	ཁ་སང་	*kaysa*
morning	ཞོགས་སྐད་	*shogay*
afternoon	ཉིན་དགུང་རྒྱབ་ལ་	*nyin goong gyab la*
evening/night	དགོང་དག་	*gongta*

SIGNS – TIBETAN

ཉེན་ཀ་	*nyen-ga*	Danger
འཛུལ་ས་	*zü-sa*	Entrance
ཐོན་ས་	*dönsa*	Exit
ཁ་བཀག་	*kah kag*	Stop
སྒོ་ཕྱེ་	*go-chay*	Open
སྒོ་བརྒྱབ་	*go-gyâb*	Closed
པར་བརྒྱབ་མི་ཆོག་	*pah gyâb michok*	No Photographs
ཐ་མག་འཐེན་མི་ཆོག་	*thama ten michok*	No Smoking
གསང་སྤྱོད་	*sâng chö*	Toilets

TRANSPORT

I want to go to ...
ང་ ... ལ་འགྲོ་འདོད་ཡོད།
nga ... la drondö yö

Can I get there on foot?
ཕ་གིར་གོམ་པ་བརྒྱབ་ནས་སླེབས་ཐུབ་ཀྱི་རེད་པས།
phagay gompa gyâbnay leb thoobki rebay?

Where is the bus going?
མོ་ཊ་འདི་ག་པར་འགྲོ་གི་རེད།
mota-di kabâh dohgi ray

Is this bus going to (Ganden Monastery)?
མོ་ཊ་འདི་(དགའ་ལྡན་དགོན་པ་)འགྲོ་གི་རེད་པས།
mota di (ganden gompa) dohgi rebay?

What time do we leave?
ང་ཚོ་ཆུ་ཚོད་ག་ཚོད་ལ་འགྲོ་གྱི་ཡིན།
ngatso chutsö katsö dohgi yin?

What time do we arrive?
ང་ཚོ་ཆུ་ཚོད་ག་ཚོད་ལ་སླེབ་ཀྱི་རེད།
ngatso chutsö katsö lepgi ray?

Where can I hire a bicycle?
ཀང་སྒ་རིལ་གླ་ས་ག་པར་ཡོད་རེད།
kanggari lahsa kabah yo ray?

How much per day?
ཉིན་མ་གཅིག་ལ་གོང་ག་ཚོད་རེད།
nyima chik-la gong katsö ray?

What time is the ... bus?
མོ་ཊ་ ... ཆུ་ཚོད་ག་ཚད་ལ་འགྲོ་གི་རེད།
mota ... chutsö katsay dohgi ray?

next	རྗེས་མ་དེ་	*jema-te*
first	དང་པོ་དེ་	*tângpo-te*
last	མཐའ་མ་དེ་	*thama-te*

airport	གནམ་ཐང་	*nam-tâng*
bicycle	ཀང་སྒ་རིལ་	*kâng gari*
bus	སྤྱི་སྤྱོད་རླངས་འཁོར་/ མོ་ཊ་	*chichö lângkho/ mota*
pack animals	ཁལ་སེམས་ཅན་/ ཁལ་མ་	*kel semchen/ kelma*
porter	དོ་པོ་ཁུར་མཁན་	*dohpo khukhen*
yak	གཡག་	*yak*

MANDARIN

Travellers going from China into Tibet or from Tibet onwards into China are well advised to pick up a Chinese phrasebook such as Lonely Planet's *Mandarin Phrasebook*. It should help you through most of your travel needs, in both Tibet and China.

PRONUNCIATION

The dialects of China are tonal, which means that variations in vocal pitch within words are used to determine their meaning. When learning Mandarin Chinese, the standard example given to demonstrate the principle of its four tones is *ma*:

high tone: *mā* – 'mother'
rising tone: *má* – 'hemp' or 'numb'
falling-rising tone: *mǎ* – 'horse'
falling tone: *mà* – 'scold' or 'swear'

Pinyin

The standard form of Romanisation for Mandarin adopted by China is known as Pinyin. It means literally 'spell the sounds', and once you get used to the idiosyncrasies of its spellings it is an accurate way of representing the sounds of Mandarin. The pronunciation of Pinyin spellings are by no means obvious to speakers of European languages, however, and need to be memorised. There's no way of knowing, for example, that a Pinyin **x** is pronounced like an English 's' or that **zh** is pronounced like a 'j'.

Vowels

Pronunciation of Mandarin vowels can be fairly tricky for English speakers. In some instances they change depending on the consonant that precedes them, and in others they're sounds that aren't used in English.

The following examples of vowel sounds follow standard British pronunciation.

a as in 'father'
ai as in 'aisle'
ao as the 'ow' in 'cow'
e as in 'her'
ei as in 'rein'
i as in 'police' when preceded by **j**, **q**, **x** or **y**
i as in 'fir' when preceded by other consonants
ian as in 'yen'
iao as in the exclamation 'yow!'
ie as in 'pier'
o as in 'or'
ou as the 'oa' in 'boat'
u as in 'flute' after **j**, **q**, **x** or **y**
u as in 'rude' when preceded by other consonants
ü as the 'u' in 'flute'
ui as the word 'way'
uo as the word 'war'

Consonants

Many Mandarin consonants are pronounced differently from their English equivalents. Some pairs of consonants have the same pronunciation as each other (eg **q** and **c** sound the same), but the sound of the following vowel changes depending on which is used. Thus **ci** is pronounced 'tser', while **qi** is pronounced 'tsee'. There are three such pairs of consonants in Pinyin: **c/q**, **j/z**, and **s/x**.

c as the 'ts' in 'bits'
ch as the 'ch' in 'church'
j as the 'ds' in 'suds'
h as the guttural 'ch' in Scottish *loch*
q as the 'ts' in 'bits'
r between an English 'r' and the 's' in 'pleasure'
s as in 'sock'
sh as in 'shack'
x as the 's' in 'sock'
z as the 'ds' in 'suds'
zh as the 'j' in 'judge'

ACCOMMODATION

I'm looking for a ...
Wǒyào zhǎo ... 我要找. . .
guesthouse
bīnguǎn 宾馆
hotel
lǚguǎn 旅馆

Do you have a room available?
Nǐmen yǒu fángjiān ma
你们有房间吗?
May I see the room?
Wǒ néng kànkan fángjiān ma
我能看看房间吗?
Where's the bathroom?
Yùshì zài nǎr?
浴室在哪儿?

Where's the toilet?
Cèsuǒ zài nǎr?
厕所在哪儿?

How much is it ...?
... duōshǎo qián? . . . 多少钱?
per night
měitiān wǎnshàng 每天晚上
per person
měigerén 每个人

CONVERSATION & ESSENTIALS

Hello.	*Nín hǎo.*	您好
Goodbye.	*Zàijiàn.*	再见
Please.	*Qǐng.*	请
Thank you.	*Xièxie.*	谢谢
Many thanks.	*Duōxiè.*	多谢
You're welcome.	*Búkèqi.*	不客气
Excuse me, ...	*Qǐng wèn, ...*	请问, . . .

Yes & No

There are no words in Mandarin that specifically mean 'yes' and 'no' when used in isolation. When asked a question the verb is repeated to indicate the affirmative. A response in the negative is formed by using the word 不 *bù* (meaning 'no') before the verb. When *bù* (falling tone) occurs before another word with a falling tone, it becomes *bú* (ie with a rising tone).

Are you going to Shanghai?
Nǐ qù shànghǎi ma? 你去上海吗?
Yes.
Qù. (go) 去
No.
Bú qù. (no go) 不去

No.
Méi yǒu. (don't have) 没有
No.
Búshì. (not so) 不是

DIRECTIONS

Where is (the) ...?
... zài nǎr? . . . 在哪儿?
Go straight ahead.
Yìzhí zǒu. 一直走
Turn left.
Zuǒ zhuǎn. 左转
Turn right.
Yòu zhuǎn. 右转
at the next corner
zài xià yíge guǎijiǎo 在下一个拐角

EMERGENCIES

Help!
Jiùmìng a! 救命啊!
There's been an accident!
Chūshìle! 出事了!
I'm lost.
Wǒ mílùle. 我迷路了
Go away!
Zǒu kāi! 走开!
Leave me alone!
Bié fán wǒ! 别烦我!
Could you help me please?
Nǐ néng bunéng bāng wǒ ge máng?
你能不能帮我个忙?

Call ...!
Qǐng jiào ...! 请叫. . . !
a doctor
yīshēng 医生
the police
jǐngchá 警察

at the traffic lights
zài hónglǜdēng 在红绿灯
Could you show me (on the map)?
Nǐ néng bunéng (zài dìtú shang) zhǐ gěi wǒ kàn?
你能不能（在地图上）指给我看?

behind	*hòubianr*	后边儿
in front of	*qiánbianr*	前边儿
near	*jìn*	近
far	*yuǎn*	远
opposite	*duìmiànr*	对面儿

HEALTH

I'm sick.
Wǒ bìngle.
我病了
It hurts here.
Zhèr téng.
这儿疼
Is there a doctor here who speaks English?
Zhèr yǒu huì jiǎng yīngyǔ de dàifu ma?
这儿有会讲英语的大夫吗?

I'm ...
Wǒ yǒu ... 我有. . .
asthmatic
xiàochuǎnbìng 哮喘病
diabetic
tángniàobìng 糖尿病
epileptic
diānxiánbìng 癫痫病

I'm allergic to ...
Wǒ duì ... guòmǐn. 我对...过敏
antibiotics
kàngjūnsù 抗菌素
aspirin
āsīpīlín 阿司匹林
bee stings
mìfēng zhēcì 蜜蜂蜇刺
nuts.
guǒrén 果仁
penicillin
qīngméisù 青霉素

LANGUAGE DIFFICULTIES

Do you speak English?
Nǐ huì shuō yīngyǔ ma?
你会说英语吗?
Does anyone here speak English?
Zhèr yǒu rén huì shuō yīngyǔ ma?
这儿有人会说英语吗?
I understand.
Wǒ tīngdedǒng.
我听得懂
I don't understand.
Wǒ tīngbudǒng.
我听不懂

NUMBERS

0	*líng*	零
1	*yī, yāo*	一, 幺
2	*èr, liǎng*	二, 两
3	*sān*	三
4	*sì*	四
5	*wǔ*	五
6	*liù*	六
7	*qī*	七
8	*bā*	八
9	*jiǔ*	九
10	*shí*	十
11	*shíyī*	十一
12	*shí'èr*	十二
20	*èrshí*	二十
21	*èrshíyī*	二十一
22	*èrshíèr*	二十二
30	*sānshí*	三十
40	*sìshí*	四十
50	*wǔshí*	五十
60	*liùshí*	六十
70	*qīshí*	七十
80	*bāshí*	八十
90	*jiǔshí*	九十
100	*yìbǎi*	一百
1000	*yìqiān*	一千

SIGNS – MANDARIN

入口	*Rùkǒu*	Entrance
出口	*Chūkǒu*	Exit
问讯处	*Wènxùnchù*	Information
开	*Kāi*	Open
关	*Guān*	Closed
禁止	*Jìnzhǐ*	Prohibited
有空房	*Yǒu Kòngfáng*	Rooms Available
客满	*Kèmǎn*	No Vacancies
警察局	*Jǐngchájú*	Police Station
厕所	*Cèsuǒ*	Toilets
男	*Nán*	Men
女	*Nǚ*	Women

PAPERWORK

name	*xìngmíng*	姓名
nationality	*guójí*	国籍
date of birth	*chūshēng rìqī*	出生日期
place of birth	*chūshēng dìdiǎn*	出生地点
sex (gender)	*xìngbié*	性别
passport	*hùzhào*	护照
visa	*qiānzhèng*	签证
visa extension	*yáncháng qiānzhèng*	延长签证
Public Security Bureau (PSB)	*gōng'ānjú*	公安局
Foreign Affairs Branch	*wàishìkē*	外事科

SHOPPING & SERVICES

I'd like to buy ...
Wǒ xiǎng mǎi ... 我想买...
How much is it?
Duōshǎo qián? 多少钱?
I don't like it.
Wǒ bù xǐhuan. 我不喜欢
That's too expensive.
Tài guìle. 太贵了
I'll take it.
Wǒ jiù mǎi zhèige. 我就买这个

TIME & DATES

What's the time?
Jǐ diǎn? 几点?
... hour ... minute(s)
... diǎn ... fēn ...点...分

When?	*Shénme shíhòu?*	什么时候?
now	*xiànzài*	现在
today	*jīntiān*	今天
tomorrow	*míngtiān*	明天
yesterday	*zuótiān*	昨天

TRANSPORT

I want to go to ...
Wǒ yào qù ...
我要去...

I'd like to hire a bicycle.
Wǒ yào zū yíliàng zìxíngchē.
我要租一辆自行车

What time does ... leave/arrive?
... jǐdiǎn kāi/dào?
...几点开/到?

intercity bus/coach	
chángtú qìchē	长途汽车
microbus taxi	
miànbāochē, miàndī	面包车, 面的
the plane	
fēijī	飞机

When's the ... bus?
... bānchē shénme shíhou lái?
...班车什么时候来?

first	
tóu	头
last	
mò	末
next	
xià	下

I'd like a ...
Wǒ yào yíge ...
我要一个...

one way ticket	
dānchéng piào	单程票
return ticket	
láihuí piào	来回票

LANGUAGE

Glossary

For ease of reference, this glossary is divided into two sections. The first section, 'Who's Who', provides succinct descriptions of some of the deities, historical figures and other people mentioned in this book. The second section covers general terms used. Non-English terms are always given in Tibetan, unless otherwise indicated. (S) denotes Sanskrit, (M) denotes Mandarin.

WHO'S WHO

Many of the terms in this section are of Sanskrit origin. Generally, the main entries are the Tibetan terms. An exception is Sakyamuni (Sakya Thukpa), in which case the Sanskrit 'Sakyamuni' is commonly used in Tibet. For more information on who's who in Tibet, see the Tibetan Buddhism chapter.

Akshobhya – see *Mikyöba*
Amitabha – see *Öpagme*
Amitayus – see *Tsepame*
Atisha – see *Jowo-je*
Avalokiteshvara – see *Chenresig*

Bhrikuti – the Nepali consort of King Songtsen Gampo
Büton Rinchen Drup – compiler of the Tibetan Buddhist canon; established a sub-school of Tibetan Buddhism, based in Shalu Monastery

Chana Dorje (*Sanskrit:* Vajrapani) – the wrathful Bodhisattva of Energy whose name means 'thunderbolt in hand'
Chenresig (*Sanskrit:* Avalokiteshvara) – an embodiment of compassionate bodhisattvahood and the patron saint of Tibet; the Dalai Lamas are considered to be manifestations of this deity
Chögyel (*Sanskrit:* Dharmaraja) – Gelugpa protector deity; blue, with the head of a bull
Chökyong (*Sanskrit:* Lokapalas) – the Four Guardian Kings
Citipati – dancing skeletons, often seen in protector chapels

Dalai Lama – spiritual heads of the Gelugpa order, ruled over Tibet from 1642 until 1959; the term is an honorific title that means 'ocean of wisdom' and was bestowed by the Mongolian Altyn Khan; believed to be the manifestation of Chenresig (Avalokiteshvara); the present (14th) Dalai Lama resides in Dharamsala, India
Dharmaraja – see *Chögyel*
Dorje Chang (*Sanskrit:* Vajradhara) – one of the five Dhyani buddhas, recognisable by his crossed arms holding a bell and thunderbolt
Dorje Drolo – wrathful form of Guru Rinpoche, seated on a tiger
Dorje Jigje (*Sanskrit:* Yamantaka) – a meditational deity who comes in various aspects; the Red and Black aspects are probably the most common
Dorje Lekpa – Dzogchen deity, recognisable by his round green hat and goat mount
Dorje Semba (*Sanskrit:* Vajrasattva) – Buddha of purification
Dorje Shugden – controversial protector deity outlawed by the Dalai Lama
Drölma (*Sanskrit:* Tara) – a female meditational deity who is a manifestation of the enlightened mind of all buddhas; she is sometimes referred to as the mother of all buddhas, and has many aspects, but is most often seen as Green Tara or as Drölkar (White Tara)
Dromtönpa – 11th-century disciple of Jowo-je (*Atisha*) who founded the Kadampa order and Reting Monastery
Dusum Sangye – Trinity of the Past, Present and Future Buddhas

Ekajati – see *Tsechigma*

Gesar – a legendary king and also the name of an epic concerning his fabulous exploits; the king's empire is known as Ling, and thus the stories, which are usually sung and told by professional bards, are known as the *Stories of Ling*
Gompo Gur – a form of Nagpo Chenpo (Mahakala) and protector of the Sakyapa school
Guru Rinpoche – credited with having suppressed demons and other malevolent forces in order to introduce Buddhism into Tibet during the 8th century; in the Nyingmapa order he is revered as the Second Buddha

Hayagriva – see *Tamdrin*

Jamchen Chöde – disciple of Tsongkhapa and founder of Sera Monastery; also known as Sakya Yeshe
Jampa (*Sanskrit:* Maitreya) – the Buddha of Loving Kindness; also the Future Buddha, the fifth of the 1000 buddhas who will descend to earth (Sakyamuni or Sakya Thukpa was the fourth)
Jampelyang (*Sanskrit:* Manjushri) – the Bodhisattva of Insight; usually depicted holding a sword, which symbolises discriminative awareness, in one hand, and a

book, which symbolises his mastery of all knowledge, in the other
Jamyang Chöje – founder of Drepung Monastery
Je Rinpoche – see *Tsongkhapa*
Jowo-je (*Sanskrit:* Atisha) – 11th-century Buddhist scholar from contemporary Bengal whose arrival in Tibet at the invitation of the king of Guge was a catalyst for the revival of Buddhism on the high plateau
Jowo Sakyamuni – the most revered image of Sakyamuni (Sakya Thukpa) in Tibet, it depicts the Historical Buddha at the age of 12 and is kept in the Jokhang in Lhasa

Karmapa – a lineage (17 so far) of spiritual leaders of the Karma Kagyupa; also known as the Black Hats
Khenlop Chösum – Trinity of Guru Rinpoche, Trisong Detsen and Shantarakshita, found at Samye Monastery
Kunga Gyaltsen – see *Sakya Pandita*

Langdharma – the 9th-century Tibetan king accused of having persecuted Buddhists
Lokapalas – see *Chökyong*
Longchen Rabjampa – (1308–63) *Nyingmapa* and *Dzogchen* teacher and writer, revered as a manifestation of Jampelyang; also known as Longchenpa

Machik Labdronma – (1031–1129) female yogini connected to Shugsheb Nunnery
Maitreya – see *Jampa*
Mahakala – Sanskrit name for Nagpo Chenpo
Manjushri – see *Jampelyang*
Marpa – 11th-century ascetic whose disciple, Milarepa, founded the Kagyupa order
Mikyöba (*Sanskrit:* Akshobhya) – the Buddha of the State of Perfected Consciousness, or Perfect Cognition; literally 'unchanging', 'the immutable one'
Milarepa – (1040–1123) disciple of Marpa and founder of the Kagyupa order; renowned for his songs

Nagpo Chenpo – The Great Black One, wrathful manifestation of Chenresig that carries echoes of the Indian god Shiva; see *Mahakala*
Namgyelma – three-faced, eight-armed female deity and one of the three deities of longevity
Namse (*Sanskrit:* Vairocana) – Buddha of Enlightened Consciousness, generally white; also a renowned Tibetan translator
Namtöse (*Sanskrit:* Vaishravana) – the Guardian of the North, one of the Lokapalas or Four Guardian Kings
Nechung – protector deity of Tibet and the Dalai Lamas; manifested in the State Oracle, who is traditionally installed at Nechung Monastery
Nyenchen Tanglha – mountain spirit and protector deity that has its roots in Bön
Nyentri Tsenpo – legendary first king of Tibet

Öpagme (*Sanskrit:* Amitabha) – the Buddha of Perfected Perception; literally 'infinite light'

Palden Lhamo (*Sanskrit:* Shri Devi) – special protector of Lhasa, the Dalai Lama and the Gelugpa order; the female counterpart of Nagpo Chenpo (Mahakala)
Panchen Lama – literally 'guru and great teacher'; the lineage is associated with Tashilhunpo Monastery, Shigatse, and goes back to the 17th century; the Panchen Lama is a manifestation of Öpagme (Amitabha)
Pehar – oracle and protector of the Buddhist state, depicted with six arms, wearing a round hat and riding a snow lion

Rahulla – Dzogchen deity with nine heads, eyes all over his body, a mouth in his belly and the lower half of a serpent (coiled on the dead body of ego)
Ralpachen – 9th-century king whose assassination marked the end of the Yarlung Valley dynasty
Rigsum Gonpo – trinity of bodhisattvas consisting of Chenresig (Avalokiteshvara), Jampelyang (Manjushri) and Chana Dorje (Vajrapani)
Rinchen Zangpo – (958–1055) The Great Translator, who travelled to India for 17 years and established monasteries across Ladakh, Spiti and Western Tibet

Sakya Pandita (S) – literally 'scholar from Sakya'; former abbot of Sakya Monastery who established the priest-patron system with the Mongols; also known as Kunga Gyaltsen
Sakyamuni (S) – literally the 'sage of Sakya'; the founder of Buddhism, the Historical Buddha; known in Tibetan as Sakya Thukpa; see also *Siddhartha Gautama* and *buddha*
Sakya Thukpa – see *Sakyamuni*
Samvara – a wrathful multi-armed deity and manifestation of Sakyamuni (Demchok in Tibetan)
Shantarakshita – Indian scholar of the 8th century and first abbot of Samye Monastery; Kende Shewa in Tibetan
Shenrab – founder of the Bön faith
Shiromo – Bönpo deity, the equivalent of Sakyamuni
Shri Devi – see *Palden Lhamo*
Siddhartha Gautama (S) – the personal name of the Historical Buddha; see also *Sakyamuni* (Sakya Thukpa)
Songtsen Gampo – the 7th-century king associated with the introduction of Buddhism to Tibet

Tamdrin (*Sanskrit:* Hayagriva) – literally 'horse necked'; a wrathful meditational deity and manifestation of Chenresig, usually associated with the Nyingmapa order
Tangtong Gyelpo – (1385–1464) Tibetan yogi, treasure finder (*terton*), bridge builder, medic and developer of Tibetan opera; often depicted holding a chain link in his hands
Tara – see *Drölma*
Tenzin Gyatso – the 14th and current Dalai Lama
Terdak Lingpa – founder of Mindroling Monastery

Trisong Detsen – 8th-century Tibetan king; founder of Samye Monastery
Tsechigma (*Sanskrit:* Ekajati) – protectress with one eye, one tooth and one breast, associated with the Dzogchen movement
Tsepame (*Sanskrit:* Amitayus) – a meditational deity associated with longevity; literally 'limitless life'; often featured in a trinity with Drölma (Tara) and Namgyelma (Vijaya)
Tseringma – protector goddess of Mt Everest, depicted riding a snow lion
Tsongkhapa – 14th-century founder of the Gelugpa order and Ganden Monastery, also known as 'Je Rinpoche'

Vairocana – see *Namse*
Vaishravana – see *Namtöse*
Vajradhara – see *Dorje Chang*
Vajrapani – see *Chana Dorje*
Vajrasattva – see *Dorje Semba*
Vijaya – Sanskrit name for Namgyelma

Wencheng – Chinese wife of King Songtsen Gampo; called Wencheng Konjo in Tibetan

Yama (S) – Lord of Death, who resides in sky burial sites
Yamantaka – see *Dorje Jigje*
Yeshe Tsogyel – female consort of Guru Rinpoche and one-time wife of King Trisong Detsen

GENERAL TERMS

Amdo – a traditional province of Tibet, now Qinghai province
AMS – acute mountain sickness; often referred to as altitude sickness
ani – Tibetan for 'nun', as in *'ani gompa'* (nunnery)
arhat (S) – literally 'worthy one'; a person who has achieved nirvana; the Tibetan term is *'neten'*
Bardo – as detailed in 'The Tibetan Book of the Dead', this term refers to the intermediate stages between death and rebirth
Barkhor – an intermediate circumambulation circuit, or *kora,* but most often specifically the intermediate circuit around the Jokhang temple of Lhasa
binguan (M) – guesthouse or hotel
Black Hat – strictly speaking, this refers to the black hat embellished with gold that was presented to the second Karmapa of the Karma Kagyupa order of Tsurphu Monastery by a Mongol prince, and worn ceremoniously by all subsequent incarnations of the Karmapa; by extension the black hat represents the Karma Kagyupa order
Bö – Tibetans' name for their own land, sometimes written 'Bod' or 'Po'
Bodhgaya – the place in contemporary Bihar, India, where Sakyamuni, the Historical Buddha, attained enlightenment
bodhisattva (S) – literally 'enlightenment hero'; the bodhisattva chooses not to take the step to nirvana, being motivated to stay within the Wheel of Life by compassion for all sentient beings
Bön – the indigenous religion of Tibet and the Himalayan borderlands; in its ancient form its main components were royal burial rites, the cult of indigenous deities and magical practices; in the 11th century, Bön was systematised along Buddhist lines and it is this form that survives today
Bönpo – a practitioner of Bön
buddha (S) – literally 'awakened one'; a being who through spiritual training has broken free of all illusion and karmic consequences and is 'enlightened'; most often specifically the Historical Buddha, Sakyamuni
Büton – suborder of Tibetan Buddhism based on the teachings of Büton Rinchen Drup, the 14th-century compiler of the major Buddhist texts; associated with Shalu Monastery, near Shigatse

CAAC – Civil Aviation Authority of China
chakje – handprint of a deity or a religious figure made in rock
chaktsal – ritual prostration
chaktsal gang – prostration point
cham – a ritual dance carried out by monks and lamas, usually at festivals; all participants except the central lama are masked
chang – Tibetan barley beer
Changtang – vast plains of north Tibet extending into Xinjiang and Qinghai; the world's largest and highest plateau
chö – see *dharma*
chömay – butter lamp
chörten – Tibetan for stupa; usually used as reliquary for the cremated remains of important lamas
chu – river, stream, brook etc
chuba – long-sleeved sheepskin cloak
CITS – China International Travel Service
CTS – China Travel Service
cun (M) – village; *'tson'* in Tibetan

dakini – see *khandroma*
dharma (S) – *'chö'* in Tibetan, and sometimes translated as 'law', this very broad term covers the truths expounded by Sakyamuni, the Buddhist teachings, the Buddhist path, and the Buddhist goal of nirvana; in effect it is the 'law' that must be understood, followed and achieved in order for one to be a Buddhist
doring – stele; carved obelisk commemorating a historic event or edict
dorje – literally 'diamond' or 'thunderbolt'; a metaphor for the indestructible, indivisible nature of buddhahood; also a Tantric hand-held sceptre symbolising 'skilful means'
drokpa – nomad
drubkhang – meditation chamber

dukhang – assembly hall
dukkha (S) – suffering, the essential condition of all life
dungkhar – conch shell
dürtro – sky-burial site
dzo – domesticated cross between a bull and a female yak
Dzogchen – the Great Perfection teachings associated with the Nyingmapa order
dzong – fort

Eightfold Path – one of the Four Noble Truths taught by Sakyamuni; the path that must be taken to achieve enlightenment and liberation from the Wheel of Life

FIT office – Family (or Foreign) and Independent Traveller office
Four Noble Truths – as stated in the first speech given by Sakyamuni after he achieved enlightenment, the Four Noble Truths are: the truth that all life is suffering; the truth that suffering originates in desire; the truth that desire may be extinguished; and the truth that there is a path to this end

Ganden (S) – the pure land of Jampa (Maitreya), and the seat of the Gelugpa order; '*Tushita*' in Tibetan
garuda – mythological bird associated with Hinduism; in Tibetan Tantric Buddhism it is seen as a wrathful force that transforms malevolent influences; '*khyung*' in Sanskrit
gau – an amulet or 'portable shrine' worn around the neck, containing the image of an important spiritual figure, usually the Dalai Lama
Gelugpa – major order of Tibetan Buddhism, associated with the Dalai Lamas, the Panchen Lamas and Drepung, Sera, Ganden and Tashilhunpo Monasteries; founded by Tsongkhapa in the 14th century and sometimes known as the Yellow Hats
geshe – title awarded on completion of the highest level of study (something like a doctorate) that monks may undertake after completing their full indoctrinal vows; usually associated with the Gelugpa order
gompa – monastery
gönkhang – protector chapel
Guge – a 9th-century kingdom of western Tibet
guru (S) – spiritual teacher; literally 'heavy'; the Tibetan equivalent is lama

Hinayana (S) – also called Theravada, this is a major school of Buddhism that follows the original teachings of the Historical Buddha, Sakyamuni, and places less importance on the compassionate bodhisattva ideal and more on individual enlightenment; see also *Mahayana*

Jokhang – situated in Lhasa, this is the most sacred and one of the most ancient of Tibet's temples; also known as the Tsuglhakhang

Kadampa – order of Tibetan Buddhism based on the teachings of the Indian scholar Atisha (Jowo-je); the school was a major influence on the Gelugpa order
Kagyupa – order of Tibetan Buddhism that traces its lineage back through Milarepa and Marpa and eventually to the Indian mahasiddhas; divided into numerous suborders, the most famous of which is the Karma Kagyupa, or the Karmapa; also known as Kagyud
kangtsang – monastic residential quarters
Kangyur – the Tibetan Buddhist canon; its complement is the Tengyur
karma (S) – action and its consequences, the psychic 'imprint' that action leaves on the mind and that continues into further rebirths; the term is found in both Hinduism and Buddhism, and may be likened to the law of cause and effect
Karma Kagyupa – suborder of the Kagyupa order, established by Gampopa and Dusum Khyenpa in the 12th century; represented by the Black Hat
Kashag – the cabinet of the Gelugpa lamaist government
kathak – prayer scarf; used as a ritual offering or as a gift
Kham – traditional eastern Tibetan province; much of it is now part of western Sichuan and northwestern Yunnan
Khampa – a person from Kham
khandroma (*Sanskrit:* dakini) – literally 'sky dancer' or 'sky walker'; a flying angel-like astral being that communicates between the worlds of Buddhas, man and demons
Khangjung – Land of Snows
khenpo – abbot
kora – ritual circumambulation circuit; pilgrimage circuit
kumbum – literally '100,000 images', this is a chörten that contains statuary and paintings; the most famous in Tibet is the Gyantse Kumbum in Tsang

la – mountain pass
lama – literally 'unsurpassed'; Tibetan equivalent of guru; a title bestowed on monks of particularly high spiritual attainment
lamaism – term used by early Western writers on the subject of Tibet to describe Tibetan Buddhism; also used by the Chinese in the term '*lamajiao*', literally 'lama religion'
lamrim – the stages on the path to enlightenment; a graduated approach to enlightenment as expounded by Tsongkhapa; associated with the Gelugpa order
lapse – a cairn
lha – life spirit; it may also be present in inanimate objects such as lakes, mountains and trees
lhakhang – chapel
ling – Tibetan term meaning 'royal', usually associated with lesser, outlying temples
lingkhor – an outer pilgrimage circuit; famously, the outer pilgrimage of Lhasa
Losar – Tibetan New Year
lu (M) – road; see also *naga*

mahasiddha – literally 'of great spiritual accomplishment'; a Tantric practitioner who has reached a high level of awareness; there are 84 famous mahasiddhas; the Tibetan term is *'drubchen'*
Mahayana (S) – the other major school of Buddhism along with Hinayana; this school emphasises compassion and the altruism of the bodhisattva who remains on the Wheel of Life for the sake of all sentient beings
mandala – a circular representation of the three-dimensional world of a meditational deity; used as a meditation device; the Tibetan term is *'kyilkhor'*
mani – prayer
mani lhakhang – small chapel housing a single large prayer wheel
mani stone – a stone with the mantra *'om mani padme hum'* ('hail to the jewel in the lotus') carved on it
mani wall – a wall made with mani stones
mantra (S) – literally 'protection of the mind'; one of the Tantric devices used to achieve identity with a meditational deity and break through the world of illusion; a series of syllables recited as the pure sound made by an enlightened being
meditational deity – a deified manifestation of the enlightened mind with which, according to Tantric ritual, the adept seeks union and thus experience of enlightenment
momo – Tibetan dumpling
Mönlam – a major Lhasa festival established by Tsongkhapa
Mt Meru – the sacred mountain at the centre of the universe; also known as Sumeru

naga (S) – water spirits that may take the form of serpents or semi-humans; the latter can be seen in images of the *naga* kings; the Tibetan term is *'lu'*
nangkhor – inner circumambulation circuit, usually within the interior of a temple or monastic assembly hall, and taking in various chapels en route
neten – see *arhat*
Newari – the people of the Nepali Buddhist kingdoms in the Kathmandu Valley
Ngorpa – subschool of the Sakya school of Tibetan Buddhism founded by Ngorchen Kunga Sangpo and based at Ngor Monastery in Tsang
Ngari – ancient name for the province of western Tibet; later incorporated into Ütsang
nirvana (S) – literally 'beyond sorrow'; an end to desire and suffering, and an end to the cycle of rebirth
Norbulingka – the summer palace of the Dalai Lamas in Lhasa
Nyingmapa – the earliest order of Tibetan Buddhism, based largely on the Buddhism brought to Tibet by Guru Rinpoche

'om mani padme hum' – this mantra means 'hail to the jewel in the lotus' and is associated with Chenresig, patron deity of Tibet

oracle – in Tibetan Buddhism an oracle serves as a medium for protective deities, as in the State Oracle of Nechung Monastery near Drepung, Lhasa; the State Oracle was consulted on all important matters of state

Pandita – a title conferred on great scholars of Buddhism, as in Sakya Pandita
parikrama – the Hindu equivalent of a kora
PLA – People's Liberation Army (Chinese army)
PRC – People's Republic of China
protector deities – deities who can manifest themselves in either male or female forms and serve to protect Buddhist teachings and followers; they may be either wrathful aspects of enlightened beings or worldly powers who have been tamed by *Tantric* masters; the Tibetan term is *'chojung'*
PSB – Public Security Bureau; the Chinese term is *'gong'anju'*
puk – cave
pure lands – otherworldly realms that are the domains of buddhas; realms completely free of suffering, and in the popular Buddhist imagination are probably something like the Christian heaven

Qiang – proto-Tibetan tribes that troubled the borders of the Chinese empire
Qomolangma – Tibetan name for Mt Everest as transliterated by the Chinese; also spelt 'Chomolangma'
Qu (M) – administrative district

rangjung – self-manifesting or self-arising; for example, a rock spire could be a *rangjung* chörten
rebirth – a condition of the Wheel of Life; all beings experience limitless rebirths until they achieve enlightenment
regent – a representative of an incarnate lama who presides over a monastic community during the lama's minority; regents came to play an important political role in the Gelugpa lamaist government
ri – mountain
Rinpoche – literally 'high in esteem', a title bestowed on highly revered lamas; such lamas are usually incarnate but this is not a requirement
ritrö – hermitage
RMB – acronym for Renminbi or 'people's money', the currency of China
rogyapas – the 'body breakers' who prepare bodies for sky burial

sadhu – an Indian ascetic who has renounced all attachments
Saga Dawa – festival held at the full moon of the fourth lunar month to celebrate the enlightenment of Sakyamuni
Sakyapa – Tibetan Buddhist order associated with Sakya Monastery and founded in the 11th century; also known as the Red Hats

samsara (S) – *'kyor dumi'* in Tibetan; the cycle of birth, death and rebirth
Samye – the first Buddhist monastery in Tibet, founded by King Trisong Detsen in the 8th century
sang – incense
sangha (S) – community of Buddhist monks or nuns
sangkang – pot-bellied incense burners
Sanskrit – ancient language of India, a classical mode of expression with the status that Latin had in earlier Western society
self-arising – thought to have been created naturally (ie not by humans); often applied to rock carvings; see also *rangjung*
serdung – golden funeral stupa
shabje – footprint of a deity or a religious figure made in rock that has become a sacred icon
Shambhala – the mythical great northern paradise, believed to be near the Kunlun mountains
Shangshung – ancient kingdom of western Tibet and place of origin of the Bön faith
shedra – Buddhist college
sky burial – funerary practice of chopping up the corpses of the dead in designated high places *(dürtro)* and leaving them for the birds
spirit trap – collection of coloured threads wrapped around a wooden frame, used to trap evil spirits
stupa – see *chörten*
sutra (S) – Buddhist scriptures that record the teachings of the Historical Buddha, Sakyamuni

Tantra – scriptures and oral lineages associated with Tantric Buddhism
Tantric – of Tantric Buddhism, a movement combining mysticism with Buddhist scripture
TAR – Tibetan Autonomous Region
tarchok – string of prayer flags
Tengyur – a Tibetan Buddhist canonical text of collected commentaries on the teachings of Sakyamuni
terma – 'discovered' or 'revealed' teachings; teachings that have been hidden until the world is ready to receive them; one of the most famous *termas* is *'The Tibetan Book of the Dead'*
terton – discoverer of *terma*, sometimes referred to as a 'treasure finder'
thamzing (M) – 'struggle sessions', a misconceived Chinese tool for changing the ideological orientation of individuals; ultimately a coercive tool that encouraged deceit under the threat of torture
thangka – a Tibetan religious painting usually framed by a silk brocade
Theravada – see *Hinayana*
thugpa – traditional Tibetan noodle dish

torana – halo-like garland that surrounds Buddhist statues
torma – offerings of sculptured *tsampa*
trapa – Tibetan for 'monk'
tratsang – monastic college
Tripa – the post of abbot at Ganden Monastery; head of the Gelugpa order
trulku – incarnate lama, sometimes inaccurately called a 'Living Buddha' by the Chinese
tsampa – roasted-barley flour, traditional staple of the Tibetan people
tsangkhang – inner chapel
tsangpo – large river
tsatsa – stamped clay religious icons
tsenyi lhakhang – debating hall
tso – 'lake'
tsogchen – cathedral or great chapel, also an assembly hall
tsuglhakhang – literally 'grand temple', but often specifically the Jokhang of Lhasa
TTB – Tibetan Tourism Bureau

Ütsang – the area comprising the provinces of Ü and Tsang, also incorporating Ngari, or western Tibet; effectively central Tibet, the political, historical and agricultural heartland of Tibet
Vajrayana (S) – literally the 'diamond vehicle', a branch of Mahayana Buddhism that finds a more direct route to bodhisattvahood through identification with meditational deities; vajrayana is the Sanskrit term for the form of Buddhism found in Tibet, known in the West as tantrism

Wheel of Life – this term refers to the cyclical nature of existence and the six realms where rebirth take place; often depicted in monasteries

xian (M) – country town
xiang (M) – village

yabyum – Tantric sexual union, symbolising the mental union of female insight and male compassion; fierce deities are often depicted in yabyum with their consorts
yidam – see *meditational deity;* may also have the function of being a personal protector deity that looks over an individual or family
yogin – an adept of Tibetan Buddhist techniques for achieving a union with the fundamental nature of reality ('yoga' in Sanskrit); the techniques include meditation and identification with a meditational deity
yuan (M) – unit of Chinese currency

zhaodaisuo (M) – guesthouse, usually a basic hostel

The Authors

BRADLEY MAYHEW **Coordinating Author**

Bradley first made it to Tibet when he raced two Oxford classmates to Lhasa on a summer break, finally winning a crate of Lhasa Beer for his endeavours. That trip, followed by a reading of Peter Matthiessen's *The Snow Leopard*, cemented an enduring affinity with the Tibetan world.

Bradley has been back to Tibet half a dozen times, covering the breadth of the region from Mt Kailash in the west to Kham in the east for the last four editions of Lonely Planet's *Tibet* and *China* guides, along with extended visits to the Tibetan areas of Ladakh and Spiti in northern India, and Sichuan, Gansu and Qinghai in China. A graduate of Oriental Studies from Oxford University, he speaks Chinese but would always rather try out his stumbling Tibetan.

ROBERT KELLY **Tsang & Western Tibet (Ngari)**

Ever since he learned that his dad's airline job meant he could fly for peanuts, Robert has been travelling. His interest in Tibet can probably be traced to early readings of *Tintin in Tibet* and, later, to a love of trekking. Robert, a Canadian, lives in Taiwan and speaks Mandarin, but was happy to research remote western Tibet, if only for the pressure of having to learn some Tibetan. (Sonam, his teacher, should be proud that at least one shopkeeper understood Robert's request for tea.) Robert's most gratifying memory of Tibet is the three seconds in which he witnessed a timeless local ceremony at Phuntsoling Monastery before being pulled away by the Public Security Bureau (PSB). *Tibet* is Robert's third title for Lonely Planet.

LONELY PLANET AUTHORS

Why is our travel information the best in the world? It's simple: our authors are independent, dedicated travellers. They don't research using just the internet or phone, and they don't take freebies in exchange for positive coverage. They travel widely, to all the popular spots and off the beaten track. They personally visit thousands of hotels, restaurants, cafés, bars, galleries, palaces, museums and more – and they take pride in getting all the details right, and telling it how it is. Think you can do it? Find out how at lonelyplanet.com.

CONTRIBUTING AUTHORS

John Vincent Bellezza

Trekking

Born in New York City, John escaped the concrete jungles of the northeastern United States and landed in India a quarter of a century ago. For over a decade he wandered alone around the most remote regions of the Himalaya, Hindu Kush, Karakoram and Tibetan Plateau, clocking many thousands of miles on foot and learning Hindu, Pahari, Urdu, Nepali, Tibetan and a smattering of other Oriental languages along the way. John has become a recognised expert in the pre-Buddhist civilisation of upper Tibet. In addition to numerous scholarly papers and articles, he has published five major academic books. His latest work is *Zhang Zhung: Foundations of Civilization in Tibet.*

Tsering Shakya

Tsering Shakya wrote the timeline for the History chapter. Tsering is the author of *The Dragon in the Land of Snow*, widely acclaimed as the definitive guide to the history of modern Tibet. He was born in Lhasa in 1959 before fleeing with his family to India after the Chinese invasion. Since then he has established himself as a noted Tibetan scholar, graduating from London University's School of Oriental and African Studies with a BA Honours in Social Anthropology and South Asian History. He received his MPhil in Tibetan Studies in 2000 and PhD in June 2004. He is the author of numerous books that explore a range of contemporary and historic issues facing Tibet, and has written for international journals and magazines, including *Time* and *New Left Review*.

Behind the Scenes

THIS BOOK

For this 7th edition of *Tibet* Robert Kelly updated the Tsang and Western Tibet (Ngari) chapters, as well as the Mt Kailash kora trek and Kathmandu for the Gateway Cities chapter. The Trekking chapter was coordinated and researched by John Bellezza. The History timeline was written by Tsering Shakya. Dr Trish Batchelor checked the Health chapter. Bradley Mayhew, who has worked on the last four editions of *Tibet*, coordinated this edition. Bradley researched the Lhasa, Ü, Eastern Tibet (Kham), Overland Routes from Sichuan and Gateway Cities chapters, as well as the Ganden to Samye and Tsurphu to Yangpachen treks, and updated the rest of the book.

This guidebook was commissioned in Lonely Planet's Melbourne office, and produced by the following:

Commissioning Editors Holly Alexander, Emma Gilmour, Marg Toohey, Tashi Wheeler
Coordinating Editor Jeanette Wall
Coordinating Cartographer Jacqueline Nguyen
Coordinating Layout Designer Carol Jackson
Managing Editors Melanie Dankel, Martin Heng, Katie Lynch
Managing Cartographers Shahara Ahmed, David Connolly
Managing Layout Designer Celia Wood
Assisting Editors Carolyn Bain, Daniel Corbett, Kristin Odijk, Susan Paterson, Kirsten Rawlings
Assisting Cartographers James Bird, Anna Clarkson, Joshua Geoghegan, Joanne Luke, Amanda Sierp
Cover Designer Rebecca Dandens
Language Content Coordinator Quentin Frayne
Project Managers Eoin Dunlevy, Chris Love
Thanks to Yvonne Bischofberger, David Burnett, Sin Choo, Hunor Csutoros, Jennifer Garrett, Mark Germanchis, James Hardy, Geoff Howard, Lauren Hunt, Laura Jane, Stacey Kersting, Margot Kilgour, Yvonne Kirk, Lisa Knights, Rebecca Lalor, John Mazzocchi, Adrian Persoglia, Suzannah Shwer, Sandup Tsering, Ji Yuanfang

THANKS

BRADLEY MAYHEW

Cheers to wingman Sjoerd Sanders for joining me on the Tsurphu–Yangpachen trek and the crazy pilgrimage to Drak Yangdzong. The trip out to Eastern Tibet was made much easier by mellow fellow travellers Jae, Jin Gi and Hon Foong. Cheers guys. Thanks to Jae and Jingi for the photos, and to our guide Dorje for his help and insights along the trip. Thanks to Wangdu in Hebu for guiding me on the Ganden trek. Best wishes to Jamin in Amdo. Cheers to coauthors John and Robert for their fine work. Thanks to Lhamo Dondrup for his help generating the Tibetan script.

THE LONELY PLANET STORY

Fresh from an epic journey across Europe, Asia and Australia in 1972, Tony and Maureen Wheeler sat at their kitchen table stapling together notes. The first Lonely Planet guidebook, Across Asia on the Cheap, was born.

Travellers snapped up the guides. Inspired by their success, the Wheelers began publishing books to Southeast Asia, India and beyond. Demand was prodigious, and the Wheelers expanded the business rapidly to keep up. Over the years, Lonely Planet extended its coverage to every country and into the virtual world via lonelyplanet.com and the Thorn Tree message board.

As Lonely Planet became a globally loved brand, Tony and Maureen received several offers for the company. But it wasn't until 2007 that they found a partner whom they trusted to remain true to the company's principles of travelling widely, treading lightly and giving sustainably. In October of that year, BBC Worldwide acquired a 75% share in the company, pledging to uphold Lonely Planet's commitment to independent travel, trustworthy advice and editorial independence.

Today, Lonely Planet has offices in Melbourne, London and Oakland, with over 500 staff members and 300 authors. Tony and Maureen are still actively involved with Lonely Planet. They're travelling more often than ever, and they're devoting their spare time to charitable projects. And the company is still driven by the philosophy of Across Asia on the Cheap: 'All you've got to do is decide to go and the hardest part is over. So go!'

Back at LP, thanks to Marg for her help throughout the project and to the perfectly named Tashi for guiding the project through its middle courses. Thanks as ever to Kelli, who hardly saw me during the crazy busy summer. Thanks, honey.

ROBERT KELLY

Big thanks to Marg Toohey at Lonely Planet for her support when it looked like I'd never get into Tibet, and to Bradley Mayhew for seeking me out in Lhasa (good detective work) and giving up his time for questions. Norbu and Tenzin, you guys were great companions on the road to Mt Kailash. Thanks for all the tsampa. Steve Wilson, your hilarious stories about heading out to Mt Kailash with completely unsuitable companions and a lying guide deserve a whole chapter of thanks. Finally, best wishes to Sonan, my Tibetan teacher, Udeni, Paljor, Chris Nelson and Huei-ming.

JOHN VINCENT BELLEZZA

Once again I salute the people of Tibet for their help and kindness over the years. Without their assistance every turn of the way I would not have gotten very far.

SEND US YOUR FEEDBACK

We love to hear from travellers – your comments keep us on our toes and help make our books better. Our well-travelled team reads every word on what you loved or loathed about this book. Although we cannot reply individually to postal submissions, we always guarantee that your feedback goes straight to the appropriate authors, in time for the next edition. Each person who sends us information is thanked in the next edition – and the most useful submissions are rewarded with a free book.

To send us your updates – and find out about Lonely Planet events, newsletters and travel news – visit our award-winning website: **www.lonelyplanet.com/contact**.

Note: we may edit, reproduce and incorporate your comments in Lonely Planet products such as guidebooks, websites and digital products, so let us know if you don't want your comments reproduced or your name acknowledged. For a copy of our privacy policy visit www.lonelyplanet.com/privacy.

OUR READERS

Many thanks to the travellers who used the last edition and wrote to us with helpful hints, useful advice and interesting anecdotes:

A Juan Antonio Alegre **B** James Bains, Amanda Banks, Shantel Beckers, Michael Berman, Liz Bissett, Mike Bissett, Roelof Bosscher, Sigrid Bub, Rolf Bueschi **C** Lorenzo Campins, Anita Conz, Stephen Cooper, Hernan Corizzo **D** Talvard Damien, Anne Dickson, Sabine Dorfer, Oyuna Dougarova, Neil Duggan **E** Peter Edworthy, Esther Ehren, Tess Evasdotter, Derek Eyre **F** Christopher Feierabend, Four Paths One Mountain Project (Students & Faculty) **G** Tali & Omer Gottlieb, Chris Grabe, Christl & Rainer Graenzer, Fredrik Graffner, Tenzing Gyatotsang **H** Caroline Hall, Ron Hamilton, Jean Hanus, Halle Henderson, Volker Hetzer, Gernott Hoffmann, BJ Hoogland, Bauke Hoogland, Rose Hull, Aaron Hurvitz **I** Yuki Inoue **J** Tom Jerrom, Rowan Jones, Rowan & Anna Jones **K** David Kerkhoff **L** Fredrik Larsen, Madeline Lasko, Duncan Lau, Jean-Claude Legrand, Pavel Luksha **M** Kate Majzoub, Steve Mcfarlane, Alick Mighall, Anze Mihelic, Joyce Mulleners, Clive Munday **N** Sandra Noel **O** Lorraine O'Gorman, Karin Ohlin, Marco De Oliveira, Sarah Orr **P** Lars Pardo, Terence Parker, Inge Peters, Guillaume Pétriat, Fabrice Ponti, Martijn Prins **R** Madeline Ravesloot, Monica Raymond, Jeanette Renk-Mulder, Uli Renk-Mulder, Nicky Rivett, Caroline Rouse, Bruce Rubin **S** Kathrin Samwer, Ed Sander, Sebastian Schrott, Robert Schönfeld, Leo Shapiro, Sara Shneiderman, Chris Stolz, Daniel Sunaryo **T** Noreen Tai, Sandro Todeschini **V** Michel J van Dam, Liselot van Delden, Arie van Oosterwijk, Luc De van Velde, Filip Vandamme, Sabine Verhest, Albert Verleg, Metten Vincent **W** James Webb, Brian Worsley

ACKNOWLEDGMENTS

Many thanks to the following for the use of their content:

Globe on title page ©Mountain High Maps 1993 Digital Wisdom, Inc.

Index

000 Map pages
000 Photograph pages

INDEX

INDEX

000 Map pages
000 Photograph pages